A History of the Conservative Party

Editorial Board

John Barnes
Lord Blake
Lord Boyle of Handsworth
Chris Cook

Volume One

The Foundation of the Conservative Party
1830–1867
Robert Stewart

Volume Two

The Rise of the Tory Democracy 1867–1902
Paul Addison

Volume Three

The Age of Balfour and Baldwin 1902–1940
John Ramsden

Volume Four

From Affluence to Disillusion 1940–1974
John Barnes

A History of the Conservative Party

The Age of Balfour and Baldwin 1902–1940

John Ramsden

Longman
London and New York

Longman Group Limited London

Associated companies, branches and representatives throughout the world

Published in the United States of America by Longman Inc., New York

© John Ramsden 1978

First published 1978

ISBN 0582 50714 6

British Library Cataloguing in Publication Data

A history of the Conservative party.
  Vol.3: The Age of Balfour and Baldwin,
  1902–1940
  1. Conservative and Unionist Party – History
  I. Ramsden, John, b.1947
  329.9'41   JN1129.C72   77-30745
  ISBN 0-582-50714-6

Printed in Great Britain by Richard Clay (The Chaucer Press) Ltd, Bungay, Suffolk

Contents

List of illustrations

Acknowledgements

The preliminary research for this book was undertaken for an Oxford doctoral thesis, and I am conscious of a special debt of gratitude to the Warden and Fellows of Nuffield College, who provided me with a home and with much other assistance at that time. For the advice and encouragement of my supervisors, Robert Blake, David Butler and Cameron Hazlehurst, I owe more than I can adequately express. Other friends who have generously given of their time and trouble during the past seven years have been John Barnes, Alan Beattie, Geoffrey Block, Martin Ceadel, David Cuthbert, Martin Gilbert, Iain MacLean, Gillian Peele, Michael Pinto-Duschinsky, John Stubbs and Ken Young. All historians of modern Britain are indebted to Chris Cook and his team on the SSRC Political Archives Project, and I am no exception, but Chris has given far more assistance than this alone would suggest.

A contemporary historian must pursue the survivors of the period about which he is writing and the current custodians of the institution which he is investigating. In this sense I have gained much from the help of Lord Butler of Saffron Walden, the Hon. Mrs Vera Butler, Mr Percy Cohen, Mr Sidney Cooke, Lord Fraser of Kilmorack, Mr Keeble Hawson, Lord Hailsham of St Marylebone, Lord Home of the Hirsel, Sir Harold Jackson, Sir Peter Roberts Bt, and Captain Matt Sheppard. I have learned a great deal from the hundred or so Conservative agents to whom I have talked, many of whom have spent a great deal of time in helping to trace local party records from pre-war days. Finally, I owe much to my friends in Wanstead and Woodford who have given me a greater understanding of the Conservative Party than I could ever have acquired in any other way.

As in every book that ranges so widely, I have drawn heavily on the work of other historians. The judgements are my responsibility alone, but many of them would be impossible without the work of others. For permission to quote from

We are grateful to the following for permission to include copyright material:
Conservative and Unionist Central Office and The National Union of Conservative and Unionist Associations for extracts from past *Minutes,*

Documents and Publications; Oxford University Press for extracts from *Whitehall Diary* by Thomas Jones, ed. K. Middlemas Vol. 1. 1916–1925 and *A Diary With Letters 1931–1950* by Thomas Jones (1954); George Weidenfeld & Nicolson Ltd for extract from *Diaries of Sir Henry Channon* by Henry Channon; Paul Addison for extract from his unpublished D. Phil. Thesis *Political Charge in Britain 1930–1940* (Oxford 1970); J. M. McEwen for extracts from his unpublished Ph.D. Thesis *Conservative and Unionist M.P.s 1914–1939* (Univ. of London 1959); Alan Harding for extracts from his unpublished M.A. Thesis *The Conservative Party and the General Election of 1935* (Queen Mary College 1976) Lord Bledisloe for excerpts from the *Bledisloe Papers*; Bodleian Library for excerpts from *Selborne Papers* and *Worthington-Evans Papers*; The British Library for excerpts from *Balfour Papers* and *Cecil of Chelwood Papers*; University of Birmingham (Special Collection) for excerpts from *Austen and Neville Chamberlain Papers*; Clerk of the Records, House of Lords for excerpts from *J. C. C. Davidson Papers, Bonar Law Papers* and *Willoughby de Broke Papers*; Sir Peter Roberts for excerpt from the *Roberts Papers*; Sauchie Estate Office for excerpt from the *Steel-Maitland Papers*; Syndics of Cambridge University Library for excerpts from the *Baldwin Papers*; The Warden and Fellows of New College, Oxford for excerpts from the *Milner Papers*; We regret that we have been unable to trace Grace Jones for permission to include extract from her unpublished Ph.D. Thesis *National and Local Issues in Politics* (Univ. of Sussex 1965).

Introduction

This book is an account of the actions and expressed opinions of British Conservatives between the accession of Arthur Balfour to the leadership in 1902 and the retirement of Neville Chamberlain in 1940. It may be as well to begin with an explanation of the ground that it covers and the areas that it does not even aim to cover. The book does not delve into the philosophy of conservatism as such, although the ideas of party Conservatives are examined; it makes few international comparisons; it does on the other hand take an unfashionable interest in the role of the party organization and the actions of ordinary party members. The reason for this shading is not to be found solely in the interests of the author, but is to a large extent dictated by the title of the series of which this volume forms a part.

A *History of the Conservative Party* does not in truth owe much to the work of philosophers, for they were at most tangential in their impact on the party. It would be possible to devote chapters to W. H. Mallock and T. S. Eliot, but it would add little to our understanding of the subject. Such theorists no doubt convinced a few that conservatism was a course of political action that could be held by respectable and responsible men, but they had no discernible influence on either the party leaders or the rank and file. Arthur Balfour was certainly the most philosophical leader of his generation, a man whose speeches were often criticized because their intellectual content was said to go over the heads of his party audience. His philosophy was thought as idiosyncratic as everything else in his make-up, and the mainspring of his politics was negative pessimism rather than any objective or positive 'conservative' ideology. Stanley Baldwin did more than anyone of his age to deepen the creed of Conservatives by underlying its elements of positive belief, but his views too were highly personal; it is unlikely that Baldwin was much affected by any political theorist, as Frank Pakenham found when he asked the great man who had influenced him most:*

> He reflected for a moment and then spoke quietly and emphatically to this effect: 'There was one political thinker who has had more influence on me than all the others – Sir Henry Maine. When I was at Cambridge, his authority was complete and I never ceased to be grateful for all I learned from him.

---

*References and Notes at the end of this introduction and the end of each chapter.

Armed with this exciting news, Pakenham pressed on and asked Baldwin what in his view had been Maine's great contribution:

> Mr. Baldwin paused perhaps a shade longer and then said with conviction: 'Rousseau argued that all human progress was from contract to status, but Maine made it clear once and for all that the real movement was from status to contract.' He paused again and this time for quite a while, and suddenly a look of dawning horror, but at the same time of immense humanity and confederacy stole across his face. 'Or was it,' he said leaning just a little towards me, 'or was it the other way round?'[1]

Baldwin generally spoke of Conservative principles, prejudices or instincts rather than of philosophers or theorists or thinkers, and he saw even these as guides to a political style rather than a direct recipe for policy. His successor, Neville Chamberlain, was a far more systematic thinker than Baldwin, but a pragmatist through and through, and a man whose whole political instinct was for the means of solving obvious problems rather than the steady contemplation of distant ends. It may be doubted indeed whether any of the party leaders of this period were actually themselves 'conservatives' in the philosophical sense of that word; Bonar Law would perhaps come closest and (as Keynes pointed out) Law was very choosy about the things that he thought worth conserving, and was prepared to abandon the Church, the land and the aristocracy if it would help to save the rest.[2] A recent survey of MPs in *New Society* has demonstrated that few Conservative MPs in 1976 had been much influenced by what they had read, and that for those influenced by books, history and biography had been of far greater importance than theory or philosophy. There is no reason to doubt that a similar survey in the 1920s would have found a similar pattern, except that it would have been even more marked. The reputation of Disraeli and the speeches of Joseph Chamberlain or Stanley Baldwin influenced men in their thousands, but the philosophy of Mallock had no such effect. The Conservative party rarely appealed to the electorate on a matter of belief, much more often on its past record, its general fitness to be trusted in government, its immediate programme and (most important) the proposals of the other side. It was on these grounds that the electorate judged it, and it is on these grounds that historians must assess it too.

It is exactly this point that makes comparison with parties of the right in other countries so difficult. A recent work on 'Conservatism' has found little in the party conservatism of Britain in this century that could be related to trends of thought abroad.[3] The conscious rejection of ideology by British Conservatives has indeed been one of their most distinctive features, and arguably one of the reasons for their long-term success. The parties of the right in the Empire seemed to provide a partial exception to this general rule; British Conservatives certainly identified with the Conservatives of Canada in 1911 although they felt no such affinity with parties in Europe or the United States. And even this affinity was rather bogus; as Max Aitken discovered in and after 1910, the word 'conservative' had a very different political meaning in Canada and Britain.

The concentration of the book on Tapers and Tadpoles is justified by the importance that they had assumed in the affairs of the party by the early part of this century. By the 1920s, finance and fêtes were as much a part of the Conservative party as foreign policy, while electioneering was developing so far as to add to the weight and importance of party organs that dealt with it. This was in itself a major transformation. The party structures developed in the aftermath of the second Reform Act had been artificial growths, fostered by the few to involve and socialize the many into the disciplines of party. Party organization had been a deliberately low-key affair, in which the leaders asked for only a limited commitment from their followers and were in return left free to run the machine in any way they liked. Such a half-hearted commitment could not long survive the arrival of the Labour party at Westminster or in the town halls of the land. When the party really began to take off as a social and political organism after the First World War, the level of commitment increased and the internal balance in the party shifted too; those who were now asked to pay the piper also began to pay more attention to the music. For all that, most Conservatives took no direct interest in matters of policy as long as their party was in power; and many of the policy disputes of the years of opposition were more concerned with means of getting back to power than with doing things afterwards. This negative pragmatism was another basic feature of the party; it was this readiness to subordinate policy and ideology to the drive for power that enabled the party leaders to draw their followers steadily to the left, never quite losing touch with the currents of popular opinion, for this was the means to power – and even a 'liberal' or 'semi-socialist' conservatism was better than the full programme of the other side. It was this openness to the ideas of the left that made the party an attractive haven for those antagonized by the parties of the left itself; Liberal Unionists after 1886, Lloyd George Liberals after 1916, Liberal Nationals after 1931, were all valuable recruits who helped to top up the forces of reaction and at the same time make them less reactionary. The present post-war generation of Conservatives is the only one in a century that has not been able to recruit from the left, but then it is also the first generation that has had to face a party that is as pragmatic in government and as conscious of the need for party unity as the Conservatives themselves have always been.

Finally, it may be felt that the author's own political opinions have led him to take too lenient a view of the Conservatives of a previous generation. It is certainly true that this book is markedly less choleric than has been fashionable when it considers Bonar Law's attitude to Ulster or Baldwin's attitude to the miners in 1926. In general, Balfour receives less praise in these pages than has been usual, and Bonar Law and Baldwin receive rather more. The problem is largely one of selection. Much research on the early history of the Labour party has been done by socialists and much of the work on Edwardian Liberalism by Liberals, and in neither case has sympathy diminished the value of their work. Nor do many people write biographies of men whom they do not like or sympathize with. In its very nature, party history is partisan history, for it seeks to explain the actions of those who grouped together precisely because they were partisans. In this field as in all others, the task of the historian is to explain how and why people acted as they did, rather than to praise or blame them, but in the nature of party history, the heroes must be those for whom the dictates of party were paramount, the villains those for whom personal or national considerations assumed a greater weight. The guideline laid down for this series was 'objective sympathy'; the author can attest to the latter, but only the reader can decide on the former.

Notes and references

1 Frank Pakenham [Lord Longford], *Born to Believe*, London 1953, 71–2.
2 J. M. Keynes, *Essays in Biography*, London 1933, 42–3.
3 M. O'Sullivan, *Conservatism*, London 1976, Ch. 5.

THE TARIFF QUESTION THIRTY YEARS AGO — MR. JOSEPH CHAMBERLAIN'S HISTORIC OBJECT-LESSON : THE APOSTLE OF PROTECTION EXHIBITING PROTECTION AND FREE TRADE LOAVES AT BINGLEY HALL, BIRMINGHAM, ON NOVEMBER 4, 1903.

The introduction by the Chancellor of the Exchequer of a Government Tariff Bill recalls the Protectionist fight which his father was waging some thirty years ago. It is interesting, therefore, to reproduce this drawing by S. Begg, then the Special Artist of "The Illustrated London News" in Birmingham, which was published in our issue of November 14, 1903. There appeared beneath it the legend : "Displaying two loaves which he had had made to illustrate the difference in size which his tax would make in the loaf,. Mr. Chamberlain said : ' I know there is a difference, because I know that the smaller loaf contains a few ounces less flour to correspond with the amount of the tax. But it is still, I think, a sporting question which is the big one and which is the little one.' "

Frontispiece. From the Illustrated London News *November 1932.*

Part I

Unionism in retreat and recovery

The combination of the Liberal and Labour Parties is much stronger than the Liberal Party would be if there were no third party in existence. Many men who would in that case have voted for us voted on this occasion as the Labour Party told them – for the Liberals. The Labour Party has 'come to stay'. . . . The existence of the third party deprives us of the . . . 'swing of the pendulum', introduces a new element into politics, and confronts us with a new difficulty.
(Austen Chamberlain to Arthur Balfour, 29 January 1910.)

Chapter 1

Heading for disaster, 1902–1906

The change of Unionist party leader in July 1902 was a remarkably uncomplicated affair in view of what was to follow. It had been widely known that Salisbury would retire when the new King was firmly established, and so in the previous February Joseph Chamberlain had been urged by supporters to press for the vacancy that must soon arise. His reaction was to let it be known to Arthur Balfour, through Balfour's ubiquitous secretary Jack Sandars, that he would serve under Balfour with perfect satisfaction. Balfour had finally won Chamberlain over with his firmness in the Boer War and by the confidence that he exhibited in him as Colonial Secretary. So, when Salisbury finally tendered his resignation to the King on 11 July 1902, Balfour was accepted as the only possible successor and Chamberlain had signified his approval in advance. Nevertheless, Salisbury informed Chamberlain the day before he told the King, and Balfour did not accept the King's commission until he too had had a chance to consult Chamberlain. The court that was paid to Chamberlain by the Cecils reveals his importance to their Cabinets; he might realistically stand aside and disclaim the premiership, but it was impossible to imagine a Unionist Cabinet without his approval or a Prime Minister who did not take Joe into his confidence.[1]

Balfour's succession to his uncle received a mixed reception in the party; his success in Ireland, his central position in Salisbury's governments and his strong attitude to the Boers had not eradicated the earlier feeling that 'Prince Arthur' was too clever by half, a man of great wit but little character or judgement. This is shown up by the stance taken by the *Morning Post* and the *Spectator*, at opposite ends of the spectrum of Unionist attitudes and shortly to be locked in combat over tariffs. The *Morning Post* noted that:

> Mr. Balfour is Prime Minister by the acclamation of his friends, because among them he has no rival. . . . When the Duke of Devonshire and Mr. Chamberlain are both of them entirely satisfied the unanimity of the party is complete. Accordingly at the Foreign Office meeting, Mr. Balfour received assurances of support, strong and authentic assurances, from persons representing all branches of the Unionist party. It appears to be the simple truth that no man ever took up the position of Prime Minister and leader of a party with the unanimous support of politicians representing so large a body of public opinion.[2]

Despite this there were doubts. Balfour would be given a fair trial because it was in the nature of the British people to do so, but

> as time passes, he will be judged on his merits. . . . Mr. Balfour's future rests with himself. So long as he is able to lead on, his countrymen will be ready to follow him.

Further defects were noted when the paper reported the reactions of others; there would be general approval in the party and from the electors of Balfour's constituency in South Manchester,

> but it is not quite so certain that the businessmen of Manchester are thoroughly enamoured of the new Premier. Of course they admire him as a personality. It might even be said that they are proud and fond of him. But from the business point of view they are not absolute devotees of his.[3]

St Loe Strachey in the *Spectator* gave a more generous welcome to Balfour, noting his outstanding ability, his popularity, and the 'serenity' which enabled him to accept many of the buffets of political life. He was not blind though to Balfour's defects, which he identified as a reluctance either to delegate or to superintend properly, and a reluctance to blame others for their own mistakes:

> A Prime Minister who does not show a certain hardness of temperament, who strives too much to save men from the results of their own mistakes, is sure to encounter grave difficulties. Administrators, civil and military, must take the consequences of their failures, and cannot be allowed to distribute the loss amongst their colleagues.[4]

These criticisms were to recur over the next nine years, but it was left to the German press to identify the likely short-term consequences of Salisbury's departure and Balfour's promotion. The *National Zeitung* feared that Salisbury's departure would be followed by the departure of his generation; the *Vossische Zeitung* felt that the resignation of Sir Michael Hicks Beach from the Exchequer

> signifies the loss of a mighty bulwark against Protection. It is only too probable . . . that there may be summoned to preside over the British Treasury a politician who will not hesitate to interfere with the system of Free Trade in the hope of establishing closer relations between the Mother Country and the colonies.[5]

Balfour duly accepted office, was elected leader of the party at a meeting of MPs and peers at the Foreign Office on 14 July, and set about the continuation of Salisbury's government with as little change as possible. He tried to persuade Hicks Beach to stay on, both because of his personal standing and because of the effect that losing the Chancellor might have on business confidence, but Hicks Beach was quite determined to retire.[6] Balfour did not suggest the transfer of Chamberlain from the Colonial Office and Chamberlain himself brushed aside suggestions that he should demand the Exchequer as the price of his support; neither appreciated the importance of the position, for neither foresaw that fiscal policy would be the storm-centre of the government – indeed of the entire party for the next thirty years. In

1902 Chamberlain must have had the Exchequer if he had demanded it, and Balfour might have been well advised to suggest it himself, but instead he promoted the Home Secretary, C. T. Ritchie.

Other changes were minimal: Lords James and Cadogan were dropped and George Wyndham and Austen Chamberlain were promoted in their places. Balfour protested that the greater changes which Chamberlain had asked for were rendered impossible by the lack of able younger men.[7] One appointment of no significance at the time was that of Andrew Bonar Law to be Secretary of the Board of Trade. Law owed his promotion to his strong defence of the decision to impose a corn duty a few months earlier; any suggestion that he would be Balfour's successor would have been greeted with derision. The new government was not well received, for it was felt that Balfour had missed the opportunity to use the change of leader to mark a new departure, and so to halt the government's declining popularity:

> For all practical purposes it is the old Government, even if the old Government with a difference. . . . We regard Mr. Balfour as a great asset in our public life . . . and we should feel a sense of national loss and injury if he suffered political eclipse through the failure of his first Administration to obtain a hold on the nation. We do not, of course, assert that it will not, but we cannot deny that we see a real danger in the half-hearted and perfunctory patching which has taken place in lieu of remaking.[8]

Nor did Balfour ever enjoy the honeymoon of popularity as a new leader which had been promised. His early performance as Prime Minister served only to reinforce fears that he was not entirely suited for the job. So, within a few days, the *Morning Post* was commenting scornfully on his flippant reply to a parliamentary question about naval efficiency:

> When reminded that he was asked what steps he proposed to take, he added 'I shall be glad to avail myself of such talent as may be available'. These answers raised a ripple of laughter, and indeed they would have made the fortune of a contributor to *Punch* . . . The net result must be to confirm the belief, already not uncommon, that the element of dilettantism is stronger than it should be in the traditions and practice of a British Government.[9]

The *Morning Post* was a hard taskmaster, but it was also a dangerous opponent; it was not a good start for a Unionist leader that he was from the start distrusted by the newspaper most read by Unionists.

The ease with which Balfour slipped into the premiership is clear testament to the continuing strength of the great 'cousinhood' and to the continuing vitality of the strategy that Salisbury and Balfour had built around the 'Hotel Cecil' regime in the 1890s. In truth, the retirement of Salisbury and the easy succession of his nephew seemed as natural a phenomenon as the succession of Edward VII in the previous year. It seemed appropriate too that the solidly Victorian figure of Salisbury should be succeeded by the urbane and quintessential Edwardian Balfour, evidence of the viability of the old ruling class in the new century; Salisbury retired but the regime went on.[10] Balfour's government gave much evidence for such a view. He had in his cabinet his brother Gerald and his brother-in-law Selborne; Salisbury's heir Lord Cranborne had been a junior minister since 1900 and would be promoted in due course, as would his brothers Lords Hugh and Robert Cecil, both men of conspicuous talent. A wider group in the parliamentary party was linked by marriage, by business connection or by tradition with the Cecils; Salisbury, and later Balfour, presided with feudal authority over the Primrose League; party organization was run almost as a family concern and much of the money required came from Hatfield; large party meetings in London were often held in the Hotel Cecil itself.[11] All in all the family connection that underpinned Balfour's succession seemed still to be firmly in control; when a discontented backbencher had dared to criticize the situation in 1900 he had been put down by Balfour himself in a speech of biting sarcasm.[12] The great cousinhood also went further than the direct connections of the Cecils. Selborne was related not only to the Cecils but also to another Cabinet Minister, St John Brodrick; and the Lord President of the Council was the massively somnolent Duke of Devonshire, a pillar of feudal conservatism and relative of half of the aristocracy. The political system of the regime was best summed up many years later in Balfour's description to Blanche Dugdale of Lord Lansdowne, Foreign Secretary from 1900 and leader in the House of Lords after Salisbury retired:

> I shouldn't call him very clever. He was – I don't quite know how to put it – better than competent.
> *Myself*: Sort of typical 'governing classes' kind of ability do you mean?
> *A.J.B.*: Yes, that's what I do mean I think. Lansdowne had the mentality of the great Whigs – remember he was descended from a great line of them . . . I was always very fond of him. I was his fag at Eton you know.[13]

The strategy followed since 1886 had been to cement the social and political ties, so consolidating the traditional ruling class into one homogeneous group.[14] The second aim, at first less prominent because less probable of success, was to keep Chamberlain and his radical friends in the Unionist fold by concession on social issues and by accentuating the external policies that held Unionists together rather than divided them. By 1902 both strategies had more or less succeeded; Whigs and Tories had been fused into one social elite that was almost indistinguishable, but the result was greater difficulty in relating that elite to the rest of the party. From 1886 there was a Unionist majority in the House of Lords that was embarrassingly large and which made it difficult to use the House of Lords at all. So many peers and their relatives, all looking for preferment, gave the party an oddly top-heavy look. On the other hand, the radicals were an asset that declined in value. Chamberlain was such a good catch in 1886 because he had so recently been the spokesman for democratic Liberalism and because he continued to parade his radical credentials. By 1895 the Liberals had moved into a new phase of more advanced radicalism, and by then Chamberlain was using the word 'radical' with a sneer on his lips.[15] In some places, Liberal Unionism was still a significant force, mainly in Scotland and the West Midlands, but it survived by dint of becoming increasingly conservative, not by revivifying its radicalism.[16]

The imperial connection was vital because it emphasized all that the Unionists agreed on, in Ireland, in the Empire itself, and at home; it also provided a stick with which to beat a divided Liberal party. However, imperialism remained an appearance rather than a policy, and an appearance that would prove much less attractive after the South African War than it had done before or during the conflict. Chamberlain's biographer notes that 'though the world might think him the master of the Government, he was more nearly its prisoner'.[17] He was imprisoned in an alliance that had cut him off from his past career, steadily devalued him as an asset to his allies, and tied him to a political stance that urgently needed reconsideration. Undeniably, Unionists needed some more positive article of belief around which to hang their policies and, equally undeniably, Britain's imperial role would have to be the means of that definition.

The influence that brought this strategical weakness to a head was the Boer War. Once the outcome of the war was assured, there was an almost universal bout of national introspection. Within the government this spurred the creation of the Committee of Imperial Defence and the passing of the 1902 Education Act. At the Foreign Office it helped to hasten 'the end of isolation' with the negotiation of an alliance with Japan, also in 1902. For the Fabians and the Coefficients, the situation highlighted by the war demanded reactions that were more basic to the national character. Lord Rosebery had already launched the campaign for National Efficiency that was to wreck his career and divide his party.[18] It is hardly surprising that the party of imperialism, and the Colonial Secretary in particular, should have joined in this debate about the whole future of the race. For the lessons of the Boer War came as the climax of twenty years of *kulturpessimismus* amongst thoughtful men of all parties. Britain's industrial strength was slipping back and Britain's naval supremacy was under challenge for the first time in memory. In a whole range of activities, Britain seemed incapable of meeting the challenges of the modern world, unable to produce competitively, unable to master science and technology, unwilling to make resources available to defend herself, and unsure about her very existence as an imperial power. For all of this the Boer War came as unwelcome confirmation, for it seemed to prove that Britain was unfit, disorganized and weak, in every way unable to fulfil a world role. The opponents of imperialism found the confidence to voice doubts that had been cloaked in hesitation. J. A. Hobson gave the anti-imperialists a logical and consistent rationale for their case and Lloyd George – and eventually Cambell-Bannerman too – showed that it could be brought into the mainstream of British politics.

The advocates of empire responded with desperation, but for the first time there were within the parties and the administration men who were prepared to put Britain's imperial role ahead of domestic interests. To them the Boer War showed precisely the opposite of what the radicals claimed. Rather than showing that Britain had inadequate resources for an imperial role, they argued that the war showed that Britain would need to be more committed in order to carry out her responsibilities. Near defeat might therefore bring the British people to face their moral and political decline while it could still be halted; in Kipling's graphic line, 'We have had an imperial lesson; it may make us an Empire yet'.[19] Such was the argument presented to Chamberlain by the exponents of empire, echoed at the Colonial Conference of 1902, and greatly amplified by those he met in Milner's entourage in South Africa in the following winter. It is this conviction of the scale of the issues at stake – the whole future of the race – that alone explains the virulence with which tariffs were discussed when they came back on to the political agenda in 1902.

Although free trade had been the orthodoxy in both parties by the 1860s, there had always remained an undercurrent of opposition in the Conservative party. Agricultural depression in the 1870s brought demands for 'fair trade' and retaliatory tariffs; in 1887 this policy was backed by the National Union Conference.[20] But up to that point, the protectionists in the party had remained what they had been in the 1840s, the spokesmen of a single depressed industry. The consequence of this was that the party was as reluctant as ever after 1846 to accede to demands which would raise the price of food. By 1902 though, this undercurrent found an echo among some industrialists too, attributing Britain's relative industrial decline to her rivals' secure domestic markets behind tariff walls. The confidence about Britain's industry that had characterized the transition to free trade now worked in reverse. So the spokesmen for tariffs in the early twentieth century were not only the spokesmen of agriculture like Henry Chaplin, Walter Long and Charles Bathurst, but also the spokesmen of industry like Bonar Law, and most of all the Birmingham screw manufacturer who articulated their fears.

Industry was by no means united in demanding protection, not least because each trade had its own problems. Coal was enjoying a boom that would go on until 1914, and so there was little support for tariffs from the powerful industrialists of coal and its associated trades. Cotton was already unable to compete effectively with low-cost producers abroad, but cotton was the mainstay of the great citadel of free trade, Lancashire, and the beliefs of three generations could not be discarded overnight. The metal and engineering trades, equally threatened by competition and less committed to free trade by sentiment and history, were much more ready to rally to a call for protection.[21] The pull of traditional belief was at least as important as the pull of economic interest, and even in the community of the land there were many who would resist any attempt to reverse 1846. Farmers who had survived the bleak 1880s, when industry had turned a deaf ear to their pleas, could see little point in changing now to satisfy the demands of industrialists.

So when the leaders of industry began to come over to a traditionally agricultural cause, they found that neither industry nor agriculture could be rallied wholeheartedly to challenge fiscal orthodoxy.

The occasion of the dispute, in 1902 as after 1815, was the need to decide whether wartime expedients were to be carried over into peacetime. Hicks Beach had introduced a corn duty in his 1902 budget, in order to raise revenue for the war, and he had secured the overwhelming support of the party. By the autumn, however, the war was over and Hicks Beach had been replaced by Ritchie; in the 1880s, Ritchie had been a supporter of tariffs and had crossed swords with Joseph Chamberlain when Chamberlain had been the defender of free trade. Chamberlain now argued that the corn duty should be retained, but that it should be payable only on foreign produce and not on imports from the Empire. This would enhance the prospects of imperial economic integration by providing a carrot to entice the Dominions towards greater integration in other spheres. Chamberlain had hoped for a greater achievement from the recent Colonial Conference, even for payments towards the costs of imperial defence, and was now convinced that Britain must make the first move.[22] As the Cabinet debated the issue in October and November of 1902, Chamberlain prepared to leave for South Africa on the first of a series of tours that were designed to drum up support for the new departure. His visit to South Africa confirmed him in his most extravagant hopes for the future, but his absence from London did as much as anything to vitiate his purpose.

The cabinet ended its discussions on 19 November; as reported to the King by Balfour, it was decided 'as to present advised' to continue the corn duty and 'to remit the tax in favour of the Empire'. Chamberlain certainly believed, and was encouraged in this by Balfour, that the real decision had been taken, and that he could therefore go to South Africa to pursue his forward policy. Unfortunately the decision of 19 November was interpreted very differently by other ministers. Devonshire and Ritchie had both spoken against the corn duty and had been supported by Hamilton and Balfour of Burleigh. These four argued that only a temporary decision had been taken and that the issue would be taken up again in the preparations for the 1903 budget.[23] Balfour was exasperated when the free trade ministers insisted on reopening the question, but it is difficult to exclude him from some responsibility. His byzantine subtlety and his determination to draw harmony from a cabinet that patently did not agree led him into the imbroglio that followed. Rather than force the free traders to acknowledge that their views had been rejected, he allowed them to believe that the issue was still open. They for their part were perhaps willing to be misled, and the fact that no minutes of the cabinet's meetings were kept added to the confusion. Balfour thus unveiled the policy of delay that was to be the cornerstone of his own position for the next four years. But while Balfour delayed, the groups on both sides of him mobilized for action. November 1902 was the last time that a decision might have been taken cleanly and without a party split from top to bottom.

While Chamberlain was drinking in the intoxicatingly imperial air of the veld, the free-trade ministers were confirming their beliefs and Ritchie was establishing his support from the orthodox financiers of the Treasury; Balfour was later to place much blame on advice given to Ritchie by his civil servants.[24] The issue surfaced again in March 1903 with the discussion of Ritchie's budget plans and the imminent return of Chamberlain. Hearing what was now proposed, Balfour immediately warned Chamberlain (who was already at sea) and consulted Austen Chamberlain, who was his father's spokesman. No Cabinet was held on the subject in Chamberlain's absence but one was called for the day after his return on 14 March. Again Balfour played for time and kept the issue open; he could not allow the Chancellor of the Exchequer to resign on the eve of his first budget and Chamberlain had no desire to force Ritchie's resignation either. The Cabinet therefore accepted the proposal to end the corn duty but agreed also to go through the entire argument again in the summer. This time it was Chamberlain who failed to see that the issue had really been decided.[25] By accepting the discontinuation of the corn duty without either resigning or calling for Ritchie's resignation, he lost the initiative and was never to regain it. As long as the duty still existed, it might have been possible for a strong lead to pull the party together round a policy of imperial preference, but once the duty had gone it would be far more difficult to justify. Arguments against food taxes carried more weight with the waverers in the cabinet and party when the issue was the imposition of a tax rather than merely its continuation; henceforth inertia was on the side of free trade. Balfour had succeeded in his short-term objective, since none of his cabinet had resigned, but the party now fell into three factions.

The free-traders, conscious of their success, were the first to widen the area of dispute. In introducing his budget on 23 April, Ritchie defended the decision to abandon the corn duty in trenchant terms, disclaiming not only the particular duty but also the entire principle of taxes on food. The free-trade press celebrated the 'final and, we believe, except in time of war, irrevocable relief of the bread of the people from taxation'.[26] The reaction of the protectionists was to accuse the government of running away from their beliefs and even the *Spectator* agreed that 'the agitation against the repeal of the corn duty grows in volume'.[27] A deputation led by Henry Chaplin was received by Balfour on 15 May but was given no satisfaction. Both Balfour and Chamberlain were coming under pressure from supporters and every word that each uttered was scrutinized for hidden meanings. Hence, Chamberlain's speech at Birmingham, also on 15 May, was intended to say much what was being said by Balfour in London, but instead burst on the political world like a bombshell. Whereas Balfour accepted the possibility that the corn duty might be revived as part of a general change in the fiscal system – by which he meant but did not *say* imperial preference – Joseph Chamberlain focused his attention on the imperial aspects of the policy and his view on the far horizons.

The response to this was immediate, giving a political lead both to old-fashioned protectionists and to the younger idealists of empire. Leo Amery saw it as 'a challenge to Free Thought as direct and provocative as the theses which Luther nailed to the church door at Wittenberg', and with Leo Maxse he set about creating a Tariff Reform League to provide support for Chamberlain's policies.[28] Spurred on by the enthusiastic response, Chamberlain became less guarded; although he had agreed to remain in the cabinet to await its further discussions, his language became increasingly intemperate, and among those who regarded themselves as imperialists he was regarded as a new prophet. The *Morning Post* reminded its readers that in the past he had 'lifted British politics to a high level of national action' and that he had now revealed 'a breadth of view and magnanimity of spirit that had not been visible in our public life for perhaps a whole generation'. Such tributes were the most significant when they came from Conservatives who had not always admired Chamberlain and when they were linked with a derogatory attitude to Balfour. The *Morning Post* was not impressed by Balfour's reply to Chaplin's deputation:

> No one would desire to impugn the credit and honour of the Government in the ordinary sense of those terms, but a policy of vacillating shilly-shally is not very creditable or honourable in a political sense. To throw a back somersault may be an accomplishment of a kind, but it is not very dignified.[29]

This groundswell of enthusiasm, mobilized by the embryonic Tariff Reform League, made it difficult for Chamberlain to accept Balfour's position, and on the other side Hicks Beach came out in support of Ritchie with all the authority of the man who had imposed the corn duty in the first place. Against the Tariff Reform League the free-traders set up a Free Food League and by the summer of 1903 the party in parliament had two embattled factions, with each organization forming local branches. Faced with the disintegration of his party, Balfour called for loyalty to cabinet responsibility and tried to engineer a compromise that both sides could accept without loss of face. He held Chamberlain to his promise to hold his hand until the cabinet reached a decision and rebuked the free-traders for acting as a dissident group in his government, almost a 'cabinet in a cabinet'.[30] His suggested compromise accepted most of Chamberlain's plans for the future of the Empire but had none of their ardour or conviction. 'Philosophic doubt' was after all Balfour's stock-in-trade and he certainly manifested it in relation to tariff reform and free trade. In Austen Chamberlain's description of his views, 'protection was not a dogma, but an expedient, and its expediency was to be judged according to the need of the particular cases'.[31] So by August 1903 the party was split three ways, along lines that were to remain into the 1920s. At one extreme were the convinced protectionists, led by the Chamberlains and drawing them further and further away from the party leadership, and on the other were equally convinced defenders of free trade. Between the two was a substantial centre group, loyal to the leadership, distrustful of the dogmas of both sides and worried as to the future of the party if unity were not somehow maintained.

A cabinet smash was now inevitable, but Balfour was still working to avoid one by keeping the issue open. His compromise policy stood a good chance of acceptance by the party as a whole, but it could hardly be accepted by either group of convinced believers. Hence Balfour was faced with the probability of losing ministers from both sides, with the further consequence that the resigned ministers would use their freedom to spread the conflict throughout the party. This was exactly what Chamberlain determined to do; with Balfour's apparent approval he decided to resign before the critical cabinet on 14 September in order to devote himself to educating public opinion for his policies. Balfour now embarked on a complex intrigue in order to rid himself of Ritchie, Hamilton and Balfour of Burleigh, without losing Devonshire, by not telling them that Chamberlain had resigned. Professor Gollin had praised the surgical skill with which this delicate operation was performed, but a little butchery at an earlier date would have been far more effective, for his plans failed anyway.[32] Devonshire felt that his months of working as a group with the other free-traders had tied him to them; pulled one way by loyalty to Balfour and the other way by his sense of honour, he eventually resigned too. The complexity of the intrigue is underlined by the fact that Balfour's correspondence with at least one colleague at this time was conducted in code.[33] Balfour thus lost five cabinet ministers at once, a much more damaging outcome in September 1903 than need have occurred if the issue had been allowed to come to a decision in either the previous November or March.

Tied now to a compromise that few in the party wanted and hardly anyone actually believed in, Balfour was obliged to continue the split in his new cabinet as in the old one. Strenuous attempts were made to find a heavyweight replacement for Chamberlain at the Colonial Office, but Milner could not be persuaded to come in and Balfour had to make do with Alfred Lyttleton. Joseph Chamberlain was compensated for his resignation by the appointment of Austen to the Exchequer – a clear indication that free-traders would not have it all their own way – and by the promotion of H. O. Arnold-Forster to the War Office (at Chamberlain's request and much against the wishes of the King).[34] At the same time however, one of the vacancies in the cabinet was filled by the promotion of Lord Derby (a convinced free-trader and a guarantee to Lancashire that tariff reform would be held in check), and another by the appointment of the new Lord Salisbury, another strong opponent of tariffs. The new cabinet therefore accepted the principle of the Balfour compromise, for the sake of party unity, but most of its members were openly committed to one of the groups now fighting for control of the party outside. In seeking above all to avoid a split, Balfour institutionalized it and made it permanent.

Once the conflict came into the open, the expectation was that a short public debate would confirm or refute Chamberlain's plans and settle the matter once and for all. There was certainly a good deal of political activity in the next two years, but all contestants stopped short of a final breach and none of the issues was ever really settled. Chamberlain's campaign got off to a tremendous start and seemed poised to sweep the party away with its enthusiasm and the response that it evoked. He outlined his full policy for the first time at Glasgow on 6 October, calling for a general tariff and food taxes and for full remission on colonial produce. In the following three months he devoted his considerable energy to building up organizational and press support, and he undertook a lengthy series of public meetings in provincial centres, culminating with a London rally on 19 January 1904. By that time, the campaign seemed to have captured the party almost intact.

The Unionist press had come out almost unanimously for Chamberlain, with the exception only of the *Standard* of the London dailies and the *Spectator* of the weeklies (and even the *Standard* was bought over to the cause in 1904.)[35] The Liberal Unionist party contained a significant minority of free-traders in its parliamentary ranks, but the party at large was strongly for Chamberlain and he managed to link its organization with that of the Tariff Reform League. In his 'Grand Duchy' of Birmingham, he was almost unopposed and it was indeed the solidity of support there that guaranteed his ultimate control over the Liberal Unionist Council. Argument went on into the early months of 1904, and a new constitution had to be forced through to guarantee Chamberlain's control, but the outcome was never in doubt. In June 1904 Devonshire finally seceded and left tariff reform indisputably in control of the party that he had helped to found. The TRL itself generated a powerful organization and spent over £50,000 in the first three months of the campaign. Chamberlain had built up an annual income of £140,000 by the end of 1904 and expected to raise it to £200,000.[36] The position in the Conservative party was less clearly expressed but on balance much the same. Balfour's compromise policy was warmly supported at the National Union Conference of September 1903 in Sheffield, but thereafter county and constituency associations affirmed their support for tariff reform in a more positive manner. Resolutions achieved overwhelming majorities for the full tariff programme and, although the party remained loyal to Balfour for its immediate policy, it is clear that sentiment went much further. There was, though, a reluctance by Conservative party managers to link their party machine with the TRL, lest this should show a partiality between the two extremes and undermine Balfour's middle position. With no connection or collaboration between bodies that were allies, they drifted into a situation of overlapping, duplication and rivalry.[37]

The truce imposed on his new cabinet by Balfour in October 1903 kept most of the party leaders silent on the one issue that most concerned their followers. This further concentrated attention on the personal role of

Chamberlain and made his campaign even more like a one-man crusade. Against him at first were only a few demoralized free-traders on the Unionist side, unsure of their positions for, once Balfour had opted for a tariff even in hypothetical conditions in the future, their position became very difficult. They were also divided in their own ranks on the question of loyalty. At one extreme were the young idealists like Winston Churchill, who quickly drifted into total opposition, opened up relations with the Liberals and castigated their recent friends with all the heat occasioned by a sense of betrayal.[38] On the other hand were Hicks Beach and Devonshire, still trying to find some way of reconciling their views with those of Balfour. Dividing the party now might bring defeat and a radical government that would do at least as much harm as would tariffs.

In the end it was the free-traders who fired the first shot in turning the battle into one of personality as well as policy. Unable to raise either the funds or the enthusiasm to counter the TRL and feeling the political ground to be slipping from beneath their feet, they took the battle to the electorate. The Balfour government had been losing by-elections regularly in 1902 and 1903, so that the effect of the tariff campaign was eagerly awaited in two contests due in December 1903. Devonshire, goaded beyond endurance by tariff reform activity in his party, urged Unionist voters at Lewisham not to vote for the Unionist candidate because he was a 'whole-hogger'. Henceforth tariff reformers could argue that they were merely retaliating when they carried the war into the free-traders' own constituencies. In the event, Unionists held both Lewisham and Dulwich on 15 December and held Ludlow a week later. This perhaps constituted the last of the lost opportunities, a chance for Balfour to dissolve parliament and secure either a narrow victory or such a narrow defeat that the party could come together in resolute opposition to a Liberal government forced into Home Rule by the Irish MPs. It was thus a chance to bypass all the difficulties of the next seven years and to rally the party on the fighting lines of 1912. Chamberlain urged dissolution on Balfour but, having already resigned in September, he had nothing left with which to enforce his views. One reason for Balfour's refusal to dissolve may have been the fear that a tariff reform victory would deliver him to Chamberlain bound hand and foot, but it is more likely that he was swayed by considerations other than those of party. The session of 1904 would see the completion of the new agreement with France and would allow Balfour to complete one of his pet schemes, the provision of an eighteen-pounder gun for the army. A dissolution in December 1903 with at least an even chance of defeat would risk both of these objectives which Balfour felt to be paramount. So Balfour's resolve to put the national interest before the party brought several years of despair for the party and ultimately brought his own leadership to a degrading end.[39]

With the opening of the new session in February 1904 the tide turned again and the common features of the next seven years were established.

Chamberlain retired to Egypt after his exhausting campaign and without his drive and his vision the steam went out of the movement. At the same time, free-traders shook themselves out of their torpor and began a counter-attack.[40] Party bickering intensified, by-elections reverted to their previous disastrous trend, and no further opportunity occurred for Balfour to dissolve with even a theoretical chance of success. From now on Balfour and his lieutenants, mainly his brother Gerald, Akers-Douglas, Acland-Hood and Sandars tried desperately to escape from a tightening tariff reform grip on the party and a worsening electoral situation. Liberals exploited Unionist divisions with a sequence of motions on the fiscal question and whenever Balfour tried to placate the Unionist free-traders – who were after all still keeping him in power – he was met with accusations and recriminations from the other side. He finally devised yet another scheme of delay, specifically designed to cut the ground from under Chamberlain's feet before he began another autumn campaign. At Edinburgh on 3 October 1904 Balfour announced that he would not introduce imperial preference until after a second general election, leaving Chamberlain no alternative but a grudging acceptance, for by this time he saw no chance of winning the next election anyway.[41] For Balfour the motivation of all this skirmishing was not just the need to keep his majority together but also to avoid committing the party to an unpopular cause from which it would never be able to break free. As he told Chamberlain on 18 February 1905.

> The local leaders, the squires, the middle class members of the Associations and so forth are as a rule highly sympathetic to Tariff Reform, and, indeed, often hold protectionist views which I am quite unable to share. . . . The obstacle with which the candidate is confronted is not the opinion of the local leader but the absolute impossibility of inducing the mass of voters to do anything . . . [to] increase the price of bread.[42]

Chamberlain believed though that there could and would be a widespread popular support for tariffs if only the leader would come off the fence and campaign for them with the full weight of prime ministerial power and authority. In the nature of the argument neither could prove their case; defeats in elections could be explained as due either to local opposition to food taxes or to the lack of a clear lead on the issue. With hindsight we may incline more to Balfour's view, but without the evidence from a general election after a united tariff campaign we cannot be sure. Balfour's strategy was therefore a hopeless one, for he was trying to convince the electorate that tariffs were virtually impossible while convincing his party that he was broadly in favour of them. In both cases he achieved the opposite of his aim, for electors clearly expected a Unionist victory to increase prices while the tariff reformers did not believe Balfour's commitment to be genuine and hence moved increasingly into opposition. And in the short run it produced a terrible prospect for the party, as Austen Chamberlain told Balfour on 12 September 1904:

Looked at from the standpoint of party, I fear that the policy you sketch means
further disunion, a prolongation of the present uncertainty, a controversy over
and therefore a hardening of our views, wherever we disagree among ourselves.
The struggle in the Party will continue, and each section will try, and will be
bound to try, to make itself as strong as possible, by enforcing pledges and
capturing associations and seats. As to the ultimate result of such a struggle I have
no doubt. But meanwhile it involves the Party in serious divisions, in perpetual
controversy, and parliamentary impotence.[43]

The Unionist free-traders had been a minority from the start, but they
were certainly in decline from early 1904. In the House of Commons they
numbered at most eighty-three out of the 392 Unionists, the number who
signed the resolution against fiscal change in July 1903. Sixty-five of these
joined the Free Food League, the supporters of Balfour already leaving, and
forty-seven voted with the Liberals on one or more occasion in 1904–05. By its
dissolution the Free Food League had forty-three MPs, but its successor, the
Unionist Free Trade Club founded in April 1905, had only twenty-nine. The
wilder spirits had gone over to the Liberals (eleven by the general election of
1906, six more later) and the least steadfast had been forced to abandon the
fight by the struggle in their constituencies. Finally the approach of a radical
government rallied men like Hugh Cecil back to the cause and the leadership,
even though he was being harried by tariff reformers in his constituency at
Greenwich.

In contrast the tariff reformers went from strength to strength, with a
strong press, an active organization and overwhelming party support. In
Chamberlain's absence, 112 MPs were mustered to threaten the defeat of the
government in February 1904 if it did not withdraw a compromise designed to
save the face of the free-traders. In July 1904 177 MPs gathered to celebrate
Chamberlain's birthday, a deliberate demonstration of strength. In April 1905
a deputation to Balfour claimed the support of 245 MPs out of the 374
Unionists still in the House and assessed their opponents' numbers at twenty-
seven; on this reckoning more than twice as many backed Chamberlain as
Balfour.[44] By 1905 then the heavy majority of the party had come over to tariff
reform and the free-trade wing was no longer sufficient to be used as a
counterweight.

From the autumn of 1905 the end of the government could not be long
delayed. Chamberlain's frustration and the discontent of the other tariff
reformers would soon bring an irrevocable split, but the continuing failure of
Unionists in by-elections made dissolution a suicidal course. Balfour had now
secured the eighteen-pounder gun and the French alliance and so was no
longer so reluctant to leave office. In the end it was Chamberlain who
effectively took the decision and an apparent tactical opportunity that
persuaded Balfour to accede. In November 1905 Chamberlain began a series
of speeches that were aimed directly at Balfour's leadership and individual
tariff reformers like Sir Joseph Lawrence formally repudiated Balfour,

perhaps sensing that they were now strong enough to risk a direct confrontation. Rather than see his government collapse, Balfour resigned on 4 December 1905 and thus became the last Prime Minister to instal his opponents in office while retaining a majority. Rumours of Liberal divisions had reached him and it seemed possible that the fragile unity of the Liberal party might be destroyed by the difficulty of forming a government; Liberal divisions might at least cancel out Unionist divisions. Balfour had incurred much odium over the past three years in order to defend the Unionist free-traders, so it may be appropriate to quote the verdict on his premiership in the *Spectator*, the only Unionist free-trade paper:

> We wish, now that Mr. Balfour has fallen, to deal as leniently as we can with his past conduct. As Unionists however, it is impossible for us to refrain from drawing attention to the position in which he leaves the party, and from declaring that Unionists in the country will demand an account of his stewardship. When Mr. Balfour became Prime Minister the Unionist Party was powerful, united, respected, and worthy of respect. It had a definite policy and definite aims, and no one was in doubt as to what views were held by its chiefs. Look at it now. As we have said before, if Lord Salisbury could revisit the earth, would he not address his nephew as the Emperor Augustus addressed his General: 'Varus, Varus, what have you done with my legions?' Mr. Balfour's tactics may be very clever, but they have ruined the party. It is idle for his defenders to say that it is all the fault of Mr. Chamberlain. If when Mr. Chamberlain first launched his scheme Mr. Balfour had refused to sanction it in any shape or form, he might, no doubt, have met with many difficulties and troubles; but such difficulties and troubles, when honestly met, brace rather than demoralise a party. As it was, Mr. Balfour instead of withstanding Mr. Chamberlain, wished him all success, and with that wish sealed the doom of himself and his party. Not till the party is purged of Balfourism as well as Chamberlainism can it be re-established on a firm basis.[45]

The tariff reform press naturally argued the case against Balfour in an exactly opposite direction, but they reached an equally damning verdict.

Other problems from the past four years had added to Balfour's general discomfiture and were now to contribute to his defeat: South Africa, education, licensing, labour relations, India and Ireland had all caused trouble, Unionist satisfaction with the victory over the Boers had been matched by a Liberal determination not to allow the public to forget the means by which victory had been achieved, and Cambell-Bannerman had used the issue as a means to party unity. The controversial issue of using indentured Chinese labourers in the South African mines was badly handled in the extreme by the government. Balfour saw well enough how the corporal punishment of Chinese coolies by white employers would appear to the British public and had originally opposed the policy, but he eventually allowed it to go ahead. He described this policy of his own government as 'this amazing blunder which seems to violate every canon of international law'.[46] Hardly surprising then that Unionists found themselves faced with heckling about 'Chinese Slavery', and with posters that showed Chinese coolies being flogged; they had no answer to either, and it was a charge that tarnished the whole imperial stance of the party.

The educational question had been settled, so far as the government were concerned, by the Act of 1902, handled by Balfour himself, but again there were unforeseen consequences. During 1904 and 1905, as the Act was implemented, there was civil disobedience in Wales where nonconformist hostility was strongest, and there were denunciations of the Act by members of the school boards that were being abolished. Chinese Slavery and the education controversy put the Unionists on the defensive against strong nonconformist feeling, and the Licensing Act of 1904 completed the trilogy of nonconformist popular causes. There was in any case a considerable nonconformist revival in the early years of the century and Liberals were able to use these issues to guide it into political channels.[47] There was therefore an unusually active nonconformist campaign against the Unionist government, especially embarrassing to the Liberal Unionists who frequently depended on nonconformist votes.

Labour relations attracted great attention as a cause of defeat *after* the election but it was little discussed in advance. Chamberlain had warned Balfour against antagonizing the trade unions and so driving them into alliance with the Liberals, but he had evoked no response.[48] So the government did nothing to restrain the employers' attack on the trade unions that was really enabling a Labour party to get going at last. For though the effectiveness of Liberal–Labour cooperation on by-elections could be detected, the scale of the threat could not be gauged. In the more general field of social issues, Chamberlain had been urging the adoption of a positive social policy by the party for many years but again with little result. He had been told in 1902 that a social policy was now rendered impossible by the cost of 'his war' in South Africa; he therefore made the need for income from tariffs to pay for such things as old age pensions a central point of his campaign.[49]

Other wounds were also self-inflicted and added to the general tide of woe. Over a period of years, Balfour engaged in a running battle on the question of civil-military relations in India, a battle of epic proportions since Curzon was Viceroy and Kitchener was Commander-in-Chief. Again Balfour allowed matters to drag on and on, characteristically remarking when Curzon decided not to resign in February 1905, 'manifestly, acquiescence is the only course'.[50] Over Ireland, George Wyndham had pursued the classic Unionist policy of 'killing Home Rule with kindness' through the Land Act of 1904, but he had been forced to resign when it was discovered that his civil servants had been preparing a scheme for the devolution of power to Ireland. Wyndham was at best a part-time politician who had probably not fully understood what was going on. Taking his stand correctly on the protection of civil servants, Balfour refused to publish the correspondence and so failed to quieten either Unionist fears of what had been intended or Liberal hints that all had not been revealed. The Indian and Irish disputes were both characteristics of a government divided and lacking in leadership. Only foreign affairs and defence were left as Unionist strong cards and Balfour hoped to use these as issues on which to fight the coming election.

When Balfour resigned office, defeat was inevitable. By-elections had been going badly for years and many hitherto safe seats had been lost. The effect of these losses, together with the series of policy failures and the tariff split, was to destroy Unionist morale and the belief even in the possibility of Unionist victory. Chamberlain, as a relative optimist, saw the coming defeat as a springboard for subsequent victory; Hicks Beach as a pessimist foresaw 'the very greatest smash that any party has had in my time'. The *Morning Post* reviewed 'all recent signs and portents' on the day of Balfour's resignation and predicted from them a Liberal and Labour majority of about 140 seats.[51] The recipe for such a catastrophe was completed by the futility of Balfour's tactical resignation of office. He was misinformed of the likely effect of cabinet making on the Liberal party (although so too were many others), but in the event Campbell-Bannerman outmanoeuvred his colleagues with dexterity and plunged the country straight into a general election that would now be fought entirely on the Unionists' record in office.

When the campaign began, Balfour's tactics were exposed in two other ways. Liberals reacted strongly to Unionist charges that a Liberal government would bring Home Rule, the end of the Empire and a policy of Little England; if Unionists believed all this, why had they run away from office and put the Liberals into power? Balfour's resignation therefore invalidated the claim that Unionists were the only party capable of looking to the country's defence – the only policy stance that Balfour had had left. Finally, Campbell-Bannerman himself mounted a direct attack on Balfour's leadership; in parliament the Liberal leader had already shown his contempt for Balfour's methods and after the election he was to do so with even greater effect in his 'Enough of this foolery' speech. At the Albert Hall on 21 December he critized the Unionists for using too much tactics and for picking and choosing issues and attitudes 'somewhat as a holiday tripper . . . might exercise a choice between Ramsgate and Margate'.[52] It was an effective line of attack for it did no more than echo what many Unionists had already said themselves.

The election campaign of December 1905–January 1906 revealed the weakness of the Unionists and the bouyancy of their opponents. The party organization had not kept up with the advances made by the Liberals under Herbert Gladstone and Sir Robert Hudson, and had suffered greatly from the consequences of party divisions. Late in 1905 Sandars reported to Balfour that the agents were pleading for more time to prepare for an election, when it had been clear for months that an election must come soon. The disorganization was shown up by the lateness of the nominations on the Unionist side, by the fact that thirty-two Liberal or Labour candidates were unopposed (as were only five Unionists), and by the generally feeble and misdirected campaign.[53]

Unionists placed the fiscal issue at the centre of the campaign, with 98 per cent mentioning it in their election addresses and 97 per cent espousing some form of tariff reform. But here agreement ended; about half approved of Balfour's compromise policy and the rest went for Chamberlain's 'whole-hogging' policy. No other issue except the negative defence of past policy characterized the Unionist campaign.[54] Balfour's speech at Leeds on 18 December did a little to improve morale, and Chamberlain produced some fine oratory later, but the rest of the front bench reflected exactly the lack of talent that Balfour had lamented in 1902. Most candidates found the response hostile, the heckling unusually fierce, and passions unusually high. The traditional Unionist response would be to hit back on the issue of Home Rule but this had been made difficult by Wyndham's resignation less than a year earlier. It became impossible when Campbell-Bannerman made it as clear as he dare that he would not bring in a Home Rule Bill in the next parliament; the *Spectator* had indeed seen this at the outset, telling its readers that 'the Home Rule scare is entirely factitious, and . . . the cause of the Union is not in the slightest danger'.[55] All doubt on this issue was removed when the first results made it clear that the Liberal government would not need Irish support, and in the last days the attack shifted from the Irish to the Labour bogey. But the old cries and the new fears were equally irrelevant in a campaign fought on the defensive by a party that never expected to win.

The first results confirmed the worst fears. Winston Churchill was elected as a Liberal and Balfour lost his seat, both at Manchester on the first full day of polling. The Northern towns showed an earthquake sweeping the Unionists out of power and hopes that the rest of the country would stem the tide were shortlived. The scale of the disaster was indeed unprecedented, for 245 seats were lost; the new House of Commons would include only 157 Unionists out of 670 and only three of Balfour's outgoing cabinet. Every part of the country shared in the rout: there were no Unionists at all elected for Welsh seats, there were thirty-one losses in London, twenty-seven in the south-east, twenty-five in the south-west and twenty-two in Lancashire. Chamberlain's citadel of support in Birmingham had survived, but it had been cut back 'from a continent to an island'.[56] One factor of interpretation actually made the results worse than they appeared: in many constituencies the Unionist candidate had polled more votes than in 1900 but had been borne down by huge increases in the Liberal vote. Some at least of the Liberal–Labour victory was made up by their ability to bring to the poll electors who had seldom or never voted before; the outrage of nonconformists, the defence of low bread prices, and active cooperation of trades unions with Liberal candidates is a sufficient explanation, but the high level of turnout was a particularly dangerous portent for the Unionists. They might win back some Unionists who had defected over free trade but it would need more than an ordinary recovery to match the Liberal inroads into the ranks of the uncommitted and apathetic.

In the longest term there were consequences of the 1906 debacle that were beneficial to the party. The scale of the defeat cleared out a whole generation of backbenchers from seats that were usually safe; a new generation of recruits were elected for these seats in 1910 and this new generation provided the party's leadership in depth for the inter-war years. As in 1945, only a massive defeat could open the way for the new men to come in. In the meantime, with so few ex-ministers in the House of Commons, the party was forced into two expedients, one good and one bad. The lack of experience meant that more reliance had to be placed on untried men; this enabled Bonar Law and F. E. Smith to make their names in a way that would have been impossible in any other House than that of 1906. On the bad side the lack of experience in the Commons meant that the party would be weighted to the Lords. In the longer term defeat gave a spur to party organization and prompted a modernization of institutions and attitudes; reorganization did not come at once after 1906 but it was then that the demands began and the ultimate course was set. Finally, and most distantly, 1906 tied the Liberals to the Labour party and *vice versa*; there would soon be openings for Unionism as a refuge for those frightened by the radicalism of 'New Liberalism' and by the aspirations of Labour. More than anything, Unionism had lost its way in its twenty years of dominance since 1886 because it had nothing positive to propose and nothing that was sufficiently frightening to oppose. One at least of these omissions would now be made good.

Unionists embarked on opposition with the memory of 1892–95 to cheer them, preparing to use Liberal divisions and the powers of the House of Lords to continue their influence on events. The new government would be 'a majority of groups held together by the slenderest of threads' but its Liberal and Nationist supporters would be able to enforce Home Rule and the Labour programme by threatening the government 'with the hostility of a hundred and twenty members whose presence may be always relied on'.[57] This very weakness of Liberalism was delayed by the size of Campbell-Bannerman's majority in 1906, but it was to re-emerge after 1910 as the greatest source of Unionist displeasure.

Notes and References

1 J. E. Amery, *Joseph Chamberlain*, iv, 452–66; Dugdale, *Balfour*, i, 337; The *Spectator*, which was no admirer of either Chamberlain or his policies, commented on his indispensability in its editorial of 12 July 1902.
2 *Morning Post*, 15 July 1902.
3 *Morning Post*, 14 July 1902.
4 *Spectator*, 19 July 1902.
5 Quoted in the foreign news section of the *Morning Post*, 16 July 1902.
6 Dugdale, *Balfour*, i, 333–4.
7 Balfour to Chamberlain, 25 July 1902, quoted in Amery, *Joseph Chamberlain*, iv, 469–70.
8 *Spectator*, 16 Aug. 1902.
9 *Morning Post*, 23 July 1902.
10 *Spectator*, 19 July 1902.
11 Information from Mr Percy Cohen, employed at Central Office before the First World War; Cornford, 'Parliamentary foundations'; Ben Jones, 'Balfour's reform of party organisation', 94.
12 Dugdale, *Balfour*, i, 315–16.
13 *Ibid.*, i, 335–6.
14 Cornford, 'Parliamentary foundations', 306–7.
15 Quoted in Jay, *Joseph Chamberlain*, (forthcoming.)
16 Pelling, *Social geography*, 182
17 Amery, *Joseph Chamberlain*, iv, 472.
18 Searle, *National Efficiency*, 107–41.
19 'The lesson 1899–1902 (Boer War)' in *Rudyard Kipling's Verse*, 299.
20 Shannon, *The Crisis of Imperialism*, 211.
21 Rempel, *Unionists Divided*, 97–104.
22 Amery, *Joseph Chamberlain*, iv, 448.
23 Holland, *Devonshire*, ii, 28.
24 Balfour to Devonshire, 29 Aug. 1903: quoted in Dugdale, *Balfour*, i, 346.
25 Rempel, *Unionists Divided*, 26–7.
26 *Spectator*, 23 May 1903; Dugdale, *Balfour*, i, 345.
27 *Spectator*, 16 May 1903.
28 L. S. Amery, *My Political Life*, i, 236.
29 *Morning Post*, 16 May 1903.
30 Balfour to Ritchie, 29 Aug. 1903: quoted in Holland, *Devonshire*, ii, 347.
31 Austen Chamberlain to Blanche Dugdale, 11 Nov. 1929: quoted in Dugdale, *Balfour*, i, 343.
32 Gollin, *Balfour's Burden*, 116.

33 See for example Balfour's letters to Selborne on 23 and 25 Sept. 1903, both from Balmoral, in cipher, and with copies numbered: Selborne MSS.
34 Sandars to Selborne, 21 Sept. 1903: Selborne MSS.
35 Rempel, *Unionists Divided*, 149.
36 *Ibid.*, 76.
37 Russell, *Liberal Landslide*, 54.
38 Churchill, *Winston S. Churchill*, ii, 99.
39 Rempel, *Unionists Divided*, 73–4.
40 *Ibid.*, 83.
41 Fraser, *Joseph Chamberlain*, 256.
42 Amery, *Joseph Chamberlain*, vi, 657.
43 Quoted in Austen Chamberlain, *Politics from the Inside*, 32–3.
44 Figures derived in the main from Rempel, *Unionists Divided*; the last figure quoted by Balfour in his letter to Selborne, 18 Apr. 1905: Selborne MSS.
45 *Spectator*, 9 Dec. 1905.
46 Balfour to Selborne, 21 Sept. 1905: Selborne MSS.
47 Stephen Koss, 'Revival and revivalism' in A. J. Morris, *Edwardian Radicalism*, 75–93.
48 Amery, *Joseph Chamberlain*, v, 5–7.
49 *Ibid.*, v, 227.
50 Balfour to Selborne, 1 Feb. 1905: Selborne MSS.
51 *Morning Post*, 4 Dec. 1905.
52 Russell, *Liberal Landslide*, 101.
53 *Ibid.*, 56.
54 *Ibid.*, 83.
55 *Spectator*, 2 Dec. 1905.
56 Russell, *Liberal Landslide*, 154.
57 *Morning Post*, 4 Dec. 1905.

Chapter 2

Drifting, 1906–1911

The first priority for a party defeated as heavily as the Unionists had been in 1906 is to construct an explanation of the disaster that is consistent both with the facts and with collective self-respect. The Conservatives were able to achieve this after 1832 and after 1945; Unionists in 1906, like Labour in 1931 and Liberals after 1918, were not able to agree on the causes of their difficulties and so their recovery was correspondingly delayed.

Balfour's explanation was that the influence of Labour had been decisive, a theory that he developed only after the results were known and outlined to Lady Salisbury:

> If I read the signs aright, what has occurred has nothing whatever to do with any of the things we have been squabbling over the last few years. C.–B. is a mere cork, dancing on a torrent which he cannot control, and what is going on here is a faint echo of the same movement which has produced massacres in St Petersburg, riots in Vienna, and Socialist processions in Berlin.[1]

The same view was reported by Salisbury to Selborne in South Africa, in a more sceptical form:

> The catastrophe is so amazing in its completeness that no doubt you will be anxious to know anything we have to say in explanation of it. But I don't think we can help you much. Arthur professes to think that none of the burning questions which we were struggling over before the Election had anything to do with it. He looks upon the disaster as a mild attack of the revolutionary malady in Russia and the Socialist complaint in Germany and Austria. I dare say this is true to some extent – that is to say that the Labour Movement and Organisation (of the magnitude of which our clever wire-pullers never seem to have had a glimmering although it must have been going on under their very noses for months or even years) has been of incomparably greater importance than anything else. But no doubt the other issues contributed. . . . [Chinese Labour] was merely an expression of the Labour Movement and as I say the Labour Movement has left the fiscal question a long way behind in importance. . . . To the workingman a food tax is probably only another example of the indifference of capital to the struggles of the poor; but it is only an element and by no means the largest in their attitude.[2]

These letters illustrate the range of Unionist scapegoats – the Labour movement, their own party organizers, the food tax, and Chinese Slavery, but few put them all together to make as convincing an overall view as that of Salisbury. The letters also illustrate a difference of approach that explains

Balfour's continuing failure in the next five years. To Balfour, tariff reform was 'things we have been squabbling over' while to Salisbury it was 'the burning questions which we were struggling over'. Nothing better illustrates Balfour's detachment from party passions and his indifference to what Graham Wallas was calling 'human nature in politics'. However, Balfour and Salisbury agreed on one central point, that the defeat could not be regarded simply as a vote against tariffs. Chamberlain and his supporters put the same view with greater force and drew different conclusions. Whereas Balfour accepted that tariffs had not actually lost the election for the party, Chamberlain continued to argue that the full tariff policy could have won the election if it had been properly advocated: 'The division in our Party and the uncertainty as to Balfour's views has handicapped us seriously and has prevented our new policy from being put forward with the conviction and earnestness which alone could have made it a strong steadying influence.'[3] The debate over future strategy therefore continued after the election in much the same way as before, but with tariff reform in the ascendant.

Some of the Unionist free-fooders had left to join the Liberals or had retired; many more had been defeated and the new parliament contained only a remnant of their old strength. The old leaders were fading out, with Ritchie dying in 1906 and Devonshire in 1908, and with St Aldwyn (Hicks Beach), George Hamilton and Balfour of Burleigh abandoning the struggle. The few survivors were concerned only to continue surviving rather than to exert influence over party policy.[4] The election had also decimated the moderates who had followed Balfour's halfway policy and had left tariff reform with a clear majority in the parliamentary party. The new balance which had been emerging in 1905 and had prompted Balfour's resignation of office was completed by the election. Now Chamberlain was urged to seize the leadership itself while Balfour was out of the House of Commons. He was determined, though, not to enter into a contest for the leadership, but instead to use his influence to tie Balfour to a more positive policy. Hence he sent Balfour a letter which demanded a party meeting to make temporary arrangements for Balfour's absence and to give the new leader 'a clear mandate'.[5] Balfour again prevaricated but found Chamberlain inexorable in his demands. When the two men met for discussions, Balfour had found a safe seat in the City of London and so the question of the leadership was only a short-term one. Balfour had been deluged with letters from all sides, with Salisbury and Lansdowne urging him against a party meeting and a closer commitment to tariffs as strongly as Chamberlain had urged the opposite course. The mediation of Chaplin, Long and Austen Chamberlain brought the two together on 2 February 1906 but they could not reach agreement, mainly because Balfour resisted any commitment that would risk driving free-traders out of the party – especially his Cecil relatives. Joe Chamberlain concluded sourly that Balfour 'believes in the Balfourian policy of delay and mystification, and perhaps at the bottom of his heart hopes to tire out his opponents and get rid of the subject altogether'.[6]

However, further pressure produced a more conciliatory attitude from Balfour on 6 February, when he wrote to Chamberlain to accept the idea of a party meeting. Dispute followed on the policy resolution that would be put to the meeting and also on Chamberlain's proposal for a new democratically controlled party organization which would include both Conservatives and Liberal Unionists. Chamberlain thus wanted to keep Balfour as leader while taking away his effective freedom of action in both policy and organization. The organizational dispute could not be resolved but the question of policy was settled in two days of direct negotiation on 13 and 14 February, culminating in an exchange of letters that were drafted jointly by Austen Chamberlain, Acland-Hood and Akers-Douglas. By these 'Valentine Letters', published on 15 February, Arthur Balfour accepted in principle Chamberlain's case for imperial preference and agreed that fiscal reform 'is, and must remain, the first constructive work of the Unionist Party'. For his part, Chamberlain accepted Balfour's definition of party policy and gave an unqualified commitment of his loyalty. Agreement had come in the nick of time, for the party meeting was to be held on 15 February and Chamberlain had already begun his preparations for all-out war on the assumption that the negotiations would fail.[7]

The party meeting on 15 February was therefore a tame affair with a hesitant speech from Balfour, general agreement on policy from all but the extreme free-traders, and a vote of confidence in Balfour that was not opposed. Balfour had in fact said little in his letter and speech that he had not accepted on many occasions before and he had kept the authority of his leadership intact without driving anyone out of the party. Yet he had been seen to be pushed back from the position that he wished to occupy and he had, as Austen Chamberlain noted, finally and in short space set down his views in unmistakable form. There would now be no room for him to cloud the issue with further explanations. The Valentine Compact, as an agreement between two entrenched groups, assumed the character of a contract and so bound the leader to a policy that he fundamentally distrusted.[8]

Meanwhile, the battle for control of the party went on. By refusing to accept the Valentine Compact, the free-traders opened themselves to unrestrained attack by tariff reformers. Henceforth, Central Office was unable to protect the free-traders and Balfour made little attempt to do so, so that after January 1910 only Hugh Cecil of the whole group remained in Parliament.[9] Conflict also continued in the party organization, where the Liberal Unionist machine had been captured for tariffs in 1904 and the Conservative National Union in 1905. At their 1905 Conference, Conservatives had not only voted for the full tariff policy but had also supported demands for a more democratic party. This seemed to be a throwback to the claims of Randolph Churchill but was actually more serious than his campaign had ever been, as Robert Blake has noted: 'Joseph Chamberlain had a clear cut policy which everyone could understand; Churchill had not. Moreover, Chamberlain, from long experience of the Liberal Caucus, was a past master at the art of mass organisation – a real professional; whereas Churchill for all his genius was a mere amateur at the game.'[10] On 15 February Balfour accepted the need for new departures and suggested the appointment of a committee. Matters were then delayed by Balfour's contest in the City of London and by the demands of parliamentary business; they were also delayed by the determination of Balfour's organizational lieutenants to protect his position and their own from the insolent democrats. Chamberlain had no doubt that he could control a democratically constituted organization and Balfour had no doubt that *he* could not. Long negotiations between teams nominated by Balfour and by the National Union went on through the spring and summer of 1906; the end product was a new supervising body of six, to be nominated equally by the leader and the National Union and charged with control over the party. The new committee never did any effective work and seems to have ceased to exist soon after its formation.[11]

Baulked of their demand for control over Central Office, the National Union turned instead to the removal of Central Office control over their own affairs and to the devolution of power within the National Union itself. Lionel Wells, Principal Agent since the retirement of 'Captain' Middleton in 1903, had not been Honorary Secretary of the National Union as well (as both Gorst and Middleton had been) and so coordination of the two bodies had been less effective. This separation was now carried out at every level. By the National Union constitution of July 1906, Provincial Divisions were abolished and each county was made entirely independent for organizational purposes, each new county association appointing its own secretary instead of using the Central Office District Agents as before. At the centre, literature services were to be run by the National Union's own staff under the control of an elected committee. Similarly, an Organization Committee took over from Central Office the supervision of agents and local parties. Instead of Chamberlain's proposed strong and professional system, the reforms led to even less centralization and more amateurism. Balfour kept personal control over Central Office but found that it had lost its influence over the party; the tariff reformers completed their control over the National Union, but found it to be quite unsuited for the task that they had set it. The party funds remained under the Chief Whip, a nominee of Balfour, while most of the spending departments were now run by the National Union.[12]

However, by the time the reorganization of 1906 had been effected the mainspring of the tariff reform attempt to take over the party had gone. Chamberlain had taken a large share of front-bench duties in the spring of 1906 as he had so few experienced colleagues with whom to share the task. When Balfour returned to the Commons he continued to rely on Chamberlain's advice and support. Chamberlain was at the pinnacle of his influence, but he was approaching his seventieth birthday and had been working under a severe strain for many years. In July 1906, following a long and exhausting series of celebrations in Birmingham to mark his birthday and his thirtieth anniversary as an MP for the city, he suffered a severe stroke. The seriousness of his illness was kept secret for several weeks and hopes of his ultimate recovery were entertained well into 1907, but he never returned either to parliament or to the platform. At the very height of his influence he was struck down, leaving his followers leaderless.[13] He lingered on until 1914, still exercising an influence over the party from his seclusion at Highbury and acting through Austen, but he was never able to fulfil the hopes of 1906. Balfour was now the only possible party leader, incomparably more able and more experienced than any alternative, and Chamberlain's enforced retirement guaranteed his survival for a further term. For the tariff reformers Chamberlain's stroke was a blow from which the campaign never recovered for it lost them at once their focus of loyalty and their only effective control over Balfour. Henceforth the extreme tariff reformers moved towards opposition to Balfour, supported by a section of the Unionist press. The Valentine Compact remained the policy of the party but the political base on which it was built had gone.

The early years of the new parliament were taken up with business from the last. The agitation against Chinese slavery was followed by the reversal of the policy by the new government and then by the public censure of Milner's High Commissionership by the Commons. The Unionists reacted in a fury, but the debates did provide a chance to refute the half-truths that had been spread during the election. Ministers were forced to admit that some of their recent supporters might have overstepped the mark. Churchill was the chief target because of his slighting references to Milner. Milner was regarded by Unionists as a great imperial hero, Churchill as a renegade who deserved no quarter.[14] The government also moved quickly to satisfy its supporters on the labour, education and licensing issues. The Trades Disputes Act was rushed into law in the first session and scarcely opposed by Unionists, conscious now of the dangers of antagonising the trade unions. It was passed more through fear than conviction by both Liberals and Unionists, as Lansdowne made clear when he advised the Lords to give their approval.[15] Education was however an old issue between Unionists and Liberals rather than between the Unionists and the whole of the government majority. There was the usual embarrassment over sectarian education, but as in 1902 the Conservatives insisted on a strong line and the Liberal Unionists acquiesced. Balfour led a strong attack in the Commons, indignant at the attempt to amend his Act of 1902, and the Lords used their powers without compunction to wreck the Bill.[16] Licensing followed a similar course in 1908, with Unionists again defending their recent legislation and again using the House of Lords to destroy the Liberals' proposals. This established the pattern that was followed

in other less contentious matters: legislation that was of prime interest to
Labour was passed with little opposition while Bills that appealed only to
Liberals and Irish Nationalists were remorselessly opposed in the Commons
and mutilated in the Lords.

Balfour was not a good leader of opposition. His leadership had already
come in for criticism before the election but his position as Prime Minister
had silenced much discontent. After 1906 dissatisfaction grew and soon
included many who counted themselves as his supporters. Their demand was
not for a different leader but for a more effective lead from Balfour himself.
But in temperament he was unsuited for the rough and tumble of opposition,
and especially for an opposition so weak in numbers that particular emphasis
was thrown on to the leader. He could rouse himself to take great stands on
subjects that interested him, defence or education, but neither of these could
carry an entire opposition strategy in 1907–08. For a short time, after the
sinking of the Russian fleet in 1905 and the launching of the *Dreadnought* in
1906, there was a pause in the naval race, and only in 1908 did it again provide
the Unionists with a winning suit. But Balfour's ineffectiveness went much
deeper than the short-term tactical situation, to his character and his
philosophy of party.

Balfour held an elevated view of the Unionist party and of his own position
as leader. The party was to him one of the great institutions of State and must
be kept intact so that opponents would not be able to damage the other great
institutions. Thus he placed the maintenance of party unity as the first of the
leader's responsibilities, even in situations where unity did not actually exist.
Robert Cecil was one sympathetic observer who noted this failing:

> For four years Balfour has devoted a vast amount of the highest intellectual effort
> to discovering a fiscal policy which should be acceptable to protectionists and not
> objectionable to Free Traders. What has been the result? Sometimes both wings
> have claimed him as an adherent. At others both have rejected him. Meanwhile the
> body of electors regard his utterances as either intentionally ambiguous or else
> marked by culpable levity. . . . If anyone could reconcile the irreconcilable it
> would be he. But it cannot be done. And the attempt to do it merely taints the
> party with a suspicion of dishonesty, the most fatal of all accusations in English
> politics.[17]

In opposition a leader must give a clear statement of his views, acting as a
standard around which his party can group, and he must give his time and his
enthusiasm to the task. In power, the works of government can be a substitute
for the faith of party; not so in opposition. Balfour did not fit these
requirements, but he was further handicapped by a philosophy of opposition
that was constitutionally impeccable but practically damaging. In his view,
opposition ought not to be irresponsible and should certainly stop short of
anything that would hinder the proper business of the government:

> I doubt if you would find it written in any book on the British Constitution that the
> whole essence of British Parliamentary Government lies in the *intention to make the*

thing work. We take that for granted. . . . Indians, Egyptians and so on . . . learn about our Parliamentary methods of obstruction, but nobody explains to them that when it comes to the point all our Parliamentary parties are determined that the machinery shan't stop. 'The King's Government must go on', as the Duke of Wellington said. But their idea is that the function of opposition is to stop the machine. Nothing easier of course, but hopeless.[18]

Years later he repeated this view as a groundrule of British democracy in his introduction to Bagehot's *The English Constitution*.[19] From Wellington he drew the lesson that in the end government must be allowed to go on; from Peel he drew the lesson that a party leader must avoid a split in his party. In his years as opposition leader he struggled vainly to reconcile the two views.

Temperamentally Balfour had little time for the impassioned public pronouncements that can be vital to the work of opposition. He was too responsible to make capital from government failings where the national interest was involved and too responsible as party leader to give hostages to fortune by extreme reactions to government measures. His style of life contributed further to the impression that he was too detached to be effective; he was never physically strong and he found that opposition was only to be borne with frequent excursions to Bad Gastein and Scotland, where he could be unavailable to colleagues. He rarely read newspapers and delegated much of the routine of organizing the opposition to his confidential aide Jack Sandars. There is little truth in the view that Sandars exercized undue influence over Balfour, but he made little attempt to correct this impression – if he was ever aware of it.[20] Colleagues who wished to hear Balfour's views found it easier to converse with Sandars, and when Balfour was out of London Sandars was the focal point of the opposition; on one occasion Sandars called a meeting of the shadow cabinet and reported its views to Balfour in Germany.[21] Finally, Balfour was reluctant to engage in the detailed organization of the party machine and reluctant to stump the country in the search for party support. He acted as leader in parliament, but the leadership in the country went by default, as George Wyndham noted:

> It is very desirable that A.J.B. should . . . lead an attack. He ought to speak in Edinburgh . . . and I wish he would speak in the Free Trade Hall, Manchester, and the Albert Hall before the session. He is our leader and the only person, besides Rosebery and C.B. who is reported. Anything we say is without authority to our audience and rarely goes beyond that audience except in fragments selected by our opponents' Press.[22]

Demands for a lead by Balfour were heard especially from tariff reformers and younger Unionists, despairing of effective action to repair the damage of 1902–06. In the absence of a lead, these younger men resolved to take the lead themselves, all pulling in different directions. Leo Maxse spoke for many when he denounced Balfour's style in the *National Review*:

> The old game between the ins and the outs may be very amusing – like lawn tennis – but after all it is only a game. It is not business. A new and more serious spirit is

spreading among the Unionist rank and file, especially among those who have not yet had the heart taken out of them by the enervating atmosphere of the House of Commons. . . . People ask themselves what is the use of all this marvellous sword-play, and these unrivalled dialectics. It is quite beyond the intelligence of the man in the street, who wants to have plain issues forcibly and clearly put before him in language understanded of the people.[23]

The same point was made, and just as sharply, by Councillor Howell of Manchester, writing to the *Morning Post*:

I have said that Lancashire can be won. I would say it will be won if I were sure the Unionist leaders realized the importance of organization and inspiration. Let them find their Kitchener and tell him that Lancashire must be won. If they have the right man he will take the responsibility of the actual organization upon his shoulders. But the inspiration is a responsibility that cannot devolve upon anybody.[24]

The vacuum at the top could in some part be made up from below, and so the party made some recovery. In parliament the front bench soon accommodated themselves to defeat and made the most of the available talent. F. E. Smith won good opinions for his maiden speech, in which he twitted Churchill with the way in which he had fought the recent election, and Smith's speeches were thereafter the highlight of the Unionist team in the lower House. Austen Chamberlain assumed the lead of the tariff reform wing of the party, reporting back to Highbury but never quite antagonizing Conservatives as his father had done. Walter Long, Bonar Law and Carson all proved worthy of the greater responsibilities thrust on them. Curzon strengthened the shadow cabinet and the team in the House of Lords on his return from India. The younger men in the party were also trying their hand at policy-making to give their party the modern look that it had conspicuously lacked in 1906; the results of their work were published as *The New Order* in 1908, showing the real possibilities for a coherent party stance based on tariff reform and with moderate social policies.[25] None of this was official, for Balfour eschewed anything that would commit a future government.

These efforts no doubt helped the Unionists to recover some ground in the constituencies in 1907–08, but other factors helped too. A dip in the trade cycle and unemployment helped the process, as did disillusion in Liberal ranks with a government that seemed unable to govern.[26] In local government elections, Unionists made steady advances and in 1908 took control of several provincial boroughs, including Sheffield, Nottingham and Leicester. In 1907 they mounted for the first time a coordinated attack on the London County Council and won a spectacular victory. Fighting as Municipal Reform and attacking the Lib–Lab alliance as both dangerously radical and profligately spendthrift, Unionists won 89 of the 137 seats, took control and then held it until 1933. It was the fear of municipal socialism that brought in votes for the Unionists, a fear that was decidedly premature in most places but which existed for all that. Since 1899 the non-socialist parties in Glasgow had cooperated to keep Labour off the Council; a Labour victory in one ward in Sheffield in 1908 produced Liberal–Conservative talks aimed at a similar pact. Cooperation against Labour at the local level and the fears of the more prosperous voters were to be rich seams for Unionists to mine in the years to come.[27] In parliamentary by-elections too Unionists were making gains, assisted by their calls for a faster naval building programme. Elections in 1906 showed a swing-back from the general election, one seat was gained in 1907, and seven of the fifteen Liberal seats defended in 1908 went to Unionists. Peckham was a particular triumph, but the sweetest victory was the defeat of Churchill in Manchester. All in all, the political tide seemed to be moving to the right by 1908.

The end of 1908 seemed indeed to mark a new departure for government and opposition alike, as both ceased to mull over the last election and began to prepare for the next. The government had settled down to a long period of power and had shed under Asquith some of the weaker members of Campbell-Bannerman's team. Ministers were concerned by their apparent impotence in the face of the House of Lords and by the weakening of ties between Liberals and Labour. In 1907, as well as losing ground to the Unionists, Liberals had lost two seats to the left.[28] There seemed to be some danger to the electoral coalition that had put the Liberals in power in 1906 unless the Liberals could find some way of breaking the parliamentary deadlock in order to make a social bid that would rival that of Labour. The situation was saved in 1908 by the government's scheme for old age pensions, but their tactical problem remained and was complicated by the demands of the Navy: German naval building now meant that the two-power standard of parity for the Royal Navy would only be maintained by a considerable increase in spending. This was generally agreed, but there was disagreement as to how the increased expenditure should be financed. Liberals were therefore committed simultaneously to increased social expenditure (to head off Labour) and to increased naval expenditure (to head off Unionists and the Navy League). To do both at once would require massive increases in taxation and this would in turn strike at the economics of tariff reform: for six years, Unionists had been proclaiming that free-trade finance would be incapable of providing adequately for national defence and for a positive social policy. If Lloyd George were to find ways of financing the increased expenditure without a tariff, he would also destroy much of the case for tariff reform.[29] The budget of 1909 might therefore settle the financial debates of the past few years, that is if the House of Lords were to allow the government to decide.

Since 1906 the House of Lords had been Balfour's sole means of influencing government policy, much as Unionist oppositions had done in 1884–85 and in 1892–95. For all his elevated view of the responsibilities of opposition, Balfour was not prepared merely to sit back and allow the government to govern. In an unguarded moment after his defeat in 1906 he had spelt out his views: it would be his duty to see that 'the great Unionist party should still control, whether in power or whether in opposition, the destinies of this great Empire'. In a letter to Lord Lansdowne, he explained the tactical use that he intended to make of the House of Lords to secure this end:

> I conjecture that the Government methods of carrying on their legislative work will be this: they will bring in Bills in a much more extreme form than the moderate members of the Cabinet probably approve: the moderate members will trust to the House of Lords cutting out or modifying the most outrageous provisions: the left wing of the Cabinet, on the other hand . . . will be consoled for the anticipated mutilation of their measures by the reflection that they will be gradually accumulating a case against the Upper House, and that they will be able to appeal at the next election for a mandate to modify its constitutions. The scheme is an ingenious one, and it will be our business to defeat it as far as we can. I do not think the House of Lords will be able to escape the duty of making serious modifications in important Government measures, but, if this is done with caution and tact, I do not believe that they will do themselves any harm.[30]

Balfour was thus aware of the risks but his acute analysis was not followed by appropriate action. The House of Lords mutilated Liberal measures in every session and did not use either caution or tact in doing so. Balfour also used his authority against the one procedure that might have allowed the House of Lords to counter the Liberal strategy of 'filling the cup'. In 1907 Unionist peers introduced proposals to reform the composition of their House so as to allow its powers to be used less contentiously. It is unlikely that the scheme would have succeeded, any more than all the other schemes that were proposed over the next half century, but it is certain that it could have succeeded only if it had the backing of the party leader. Balfour opposed it on the disingenuous grounds that any strengthening of the Lords would be at the expense of the Commons, which he as a good House of Commons man could not support. This argument hardly carried much weight when advanced by a man who was regularly advising the Lords to reject measures over-whelmingly approved by the Commons.[31] So the Unionists drifted into a policy of Commons propose, Lords dispose; Balfour might stop short of opposition that would halt the government machine, but he intended to decide exactly what the government should be allowed to do. Liberals thus built up their case against the peers for the next election while Unionists failed to use the time to find an effective answer.

It has been much debated how far the 'People's Budget' of 1909 was a deliberate attempt to exploit this weakness in the Unionist position. Only a considerable increase in taxation could meet government expenses in 1909 and only a bold stroke would revive flagging Liberal morale. It is not necessary though to impute machiavellian motives to the new Chancellor Lloyd George, nor necessary to assume that he was hoping for rejection of his budget by the peers in order to justify an attack on them, for no such tactical decision had to be made. If the Lords were to pass the budget, then the government's triumph would retrieve their financial position and provide a great boost to free trade; if the Lords were to reject the budget, then they would prove beyond doubt the case for a reduction of their powers. There was thus no dilemma for the government, for they would win in either case.[32] In so far as they needed to make a decision at all, they plumped for the moderate course; the budget was introduced in moderate tones, Lloyd George was kept firmly under Asquith's control and it was only in response to Unionist attacks that Liberals raised the temperature.[33] On the other hand, the budget itself, however moderately it was described, was certain to provoke the opposition to rage. The provisions for a land tax seemed to be a way of tacking a policy of social redistribution on to a financial measure (so directly provoking the Lords), the licensing duties were a direct attack on the trade most loyal to Unionism, and the increased death duties smacked again of egalitarian redistribution.[34]

The immediate Unionist response was a guarded one, not least because it took them several days to absorb the full enormity of what was being proposed, but when the real reaction came it was unanimous. The battle began in parliament at the beginning of May and went on until the end of September with fifty MPs in four fighting groups resisting it line by line. In June a Budget Protest League was set up under Walter Long to carry the fight to the country. It seems clear though that until the summer the Unionist leaders had decided to resist the Bill as much as possible but not to defeat it in the Lords. On 16 July Lansdowne told Unionists that the House of Lords would 'do its duty' but not 'without wincing'.[35] However, while the battle went on in the Commons, the campaign in the country moved into another phase that took away the Unionist leaders' freedom of manoeuvre.

Lloyd George's speech at Limehouse on 30 July 1909 brought a torrent of hostile reaction from the Unionist press and the campaign of the Budget Protest League raised Unionist expectations. Lloyd George seemed to have declared war not on poverty but on the rich, on landowners, and on 'the trade'. The Unionists, invigorated by the campaign as they had rarely been invigorated by Balfour's leadership, expected the Lords to treat the budget as they had treated other pieces of Liberal legislation.[36] Unionists argued that the budget was unconstitutional because it was a tacking measure and that it was a divisive attack on groups of people who had deserved better treatment. So by the end of the summer the Unionist leaders had little choice but to have the Bill defeated in the Lords, and Balfour went so far as to make it known that he would resign if the peers did not reject the Bill.[37] The peers themselves, equally incensed by the budget and by Lloyd George's invective, were only too happy to accede to their instructions. The Bill was finally passed by the Commons on 4 November and defeated by 350 votes to 75 in the Lords on 30 November; in moving the rejection, Lansdowne based his case on the need to refer the budget to the people for a decision. Both parties had thus manoeuvred themselves into a deadlock that could only be broken by a general election and parliament was duly dissolved with polling to take place during January 1910.

The general election certainly presented the Unionists with an opportunity better than 1906. The party had now had an agreed tariff policy for almost four years and, although the tariff reformers had sometimes despaired of the lack of enthusiasm with which Balfour expounded it, there had been much less damaging disagreement than in the run-up to 1906. Party unity had been forged in opposition to the budget and the enthusiastic response to the Budget Protest League seemed to show that the party in the country was ready for a fight. Memories of Unionist government had faded from memory and the budget debates had raised new issues to eradicate those fought over in 1906. And the probability of at least some Unionist gains meant that Asquith would be forced back into reliance on the Irish Nationalists for a majority; weak points in the government coalition and public hostility to Home Rule could then be exploited.[38] On the issue of 'Peers v. People', Unionists could put forward the reasonable case that it was only the peers who had given the people a chance to decide on a budget that was undeniably important; and they could point to a lack of Liberal agreement as to what should actually be done to the House of Lords. The results represented as great a gain as could be realistically expected; 116 seats were gained, almost all in England, and the last Liberal majority in parliament was destroyed. The Asquith government would now be forced back to dependence on its allies, and especially on Redmond, who controlled eighty-two seats and held the balance of power. Balfour had probably not wished to take office at this juncture and was apparently satisfied with the dilemma that the results created for Asquith.[39]

After the election Asquith plunged into bargaining with Redmond while Balfour waited on the sidelines for the outcome, offering to support the government, so removing the Irish stranglehold, but only if Asquith would abandon the budget and the reform of the House of Lords. But it was really Balfour rather than Asquith who faced the dilemma; Unionists in the country had been elated by the events of 1909 and by the fact that the election had apparently given them increased influence in a divided House of Commons. They were now in no mood to accept a compromise and were especially hostile to anything that might emerge from a deal between Asquith and Redmond, which would constitute 'log-rolling' such as the Unionists had professed to see in the last parliament. Asquith's deal with Redmond to pass the budget, to abolish the veto powers of the Lords and then to press straight on with Home Rule thus cut the ground from under Balfour's feet. The logic of the Unionist appeal to the people now demanded that they should accept the people's verdict and let the budget pass, and Balfour's determination to stop short of anything that might actually break the government would now come into play. The death of the King on 7 May provided a breathing space, but the tactical dilemma remained into 1911.

The death of the King seemed to open up a chance of settlement by negotiation between the parties; a 'truce of God' was declared, though not without difficulty, for some Unionists were so hostile to the Asquith government by this time that they were prepared to believe that the death of Edward VII had been hastened by harassment by his ministers.[40] A conference was held behind closed doors in the autumn and political debate was put on ice for several months. The occasion of all the trouble, the Lloyd George budget, meanwhile passed into law, so that the debate now centred on the powers of the House of Lords. Unionist peers had reacted to the election results by reviving the reform plans debated in 1907 and pressed on with proposals to alter the composition of the Upper House as an alternative to reducing its powers. Balfour, Austen Chamberlain, Lansdowne and Cawdor represented the Unionists in the conference, sitting with four Liberals. Following their acceptance of the budget, these four now agreed to the removal of the Lords' powers over money Bills but pressed the need for a change of composition. Negotiations failed though on the Unionist insistence that there should be some form of excepted legislation that would remain subject to the Lords' veto in any future system, a corpus of 'organic' or constitutional measures that clearly enough included Home Rule. The disagreement was funda-mental: to Unionists, a reform of the House of Lords would be justified only if it strengthened the peers in relation to a Commons majority that did not represent popular feeling or a majority held together by log-rolling; to Liberals, any scheme must allow them to pass Home Rule without impedance, for otherwise Redmond would vote them out of office. The chances of success were therefore never good and talks only dragged on for so long because neither side wished to incur the odium of ending the truce. Lloyd George's secret plan to bypass the debate by the creation of a Liberal–Unionist Coalition was a desperate attempt to reconcile the irreconcilable; F. E. Smith supported the idea but neither Balfour nor Austen Chamberlain ever believed it to be practicable.[41] A great agitation in favour of agreement was mounted in the Unionist press, but Balfour was well aware of the reaction that he would have to face if he made an agreement that included Home Rule as one of its basic ingredients.[42] So Balfour rejected the coalition scheme on 1 November 1910, by which time the ordinary business of the conference had already failed; although Balfour and his colleagues agreed to make one more attempt to avoid another election there was no chance of success. The conference broke up on 10 November, to the apparent relief of the Unionists involved, who had been unhappy with the prospect of having to sell any compromise agreement to their followers. Debate therefore went back to the original Liberal proposals to abolish the veto powers of the Lords and, with the Lords about to reject these proposals and with the Palace now bludgeoned into giving guarantees to enforce an election result by the creation of peers if necessary, parliament was again dissolved.

The December 1910 general election opened the last chapter of the party leadership of Arthur Balfour because it reopened the internal party feud on tariffs. The narrowness of their defeat in January quite naturally led Unionists to scrutinize their programme closely to see if some unpopular policy could be jettisoned to give them the crucial edge over their opponents. The negative attitude to the House of Lords that had existed since 1906 was replaced by an apparent eagerness for reform, provided as always that this centred on changes of composition rather than powers. This brought a heavily sarcastic response from Liberals but it went some way towards providing a response to the attacks on the peers.[43] The question of Ireland could again be brought to the forefront for Redmond had returned to Ireland on 28 November with large sums of money subscribed by Irish Americans; Redmond was thus denounced as 'the dollar dictator' who would destroy the British Constitution for the sake of Ireland.[44] Reform of the House of Lords would be the prelude to the passing of Home Rule in the same parliament and so Unionists would be cheated of their desire to put Home Rule to the electoral test. In this sense the December 1910 election was as much about Home Rule as about the House of Lords, however much Liberals might strive to ignore the fact, and it became even more important to shed electoral burdens that might cost votes.

At heart the party still divided into two camps on the taxation of food, not so much on its desirability as on the practicality of getting the electors to vote for it. To the moderate tariff reformers, food taxes were an incubus that would have to be cast off if ever a Unionist government were to be elected. A meeting of Unionists on 14 November decided to stick to the existing policy but, once the candidates dispersed to their constituences, the pressure to reduce the effects of tariffs as a vote-loser became irresistible. Letters flooded in to Balfour from candidates in hard contests, almost all urging him to declare against food taxes. The culminating influence came from Lancashire, an area with a disproportionate number of marginal seats as always, an area that polled on the first full day and so set an example to the country, and an area that was in any case seen as a political trend-setter. F. E. Smith in Liverpool and Bonar Law in Manchester, both staunch tariff reformers, agreed with the proposal for a change of policy.

The pressure was orchestrated by the impresario of tariff-reform Unionism, J. L. Garvin of the *Observer*, in an editorial calling for a referendum on tariffs.[45] The referendum had been one of the ideas floated at the recent conference as a means of settling disputes between Lords and Commons; Unionists had wanted a referendum so that a vote could be taken on tariffs without involving the whole fortunes of the party, but Liberals did not accept a device that could be used to stop Home Rule. This argument was now to be put before the electorate; at the Albert Hall on 29 November Balfour announced that a Unionist government would submit its tariff proposals to a referendum if the Liberals would do the same with Home Rule.

The referendum pledge, designed to pull the party together, to embarrass the Liberals and to win over floating voters, failed on all counts. Instead of unity the party exploded into discord: as soon as Balfour's intentions were made known to him, Austen Chamberlain tried to get him to change his mind, and when the announcement was made the extreme tariff reformers made it abundantly clear that they did not agree with the decision. Distrust of the Chamberlains was revived with a vengeance: Derby exclaimed, 'Damn these Chamberlains! They are the curse of our party and of the country.'[46] This open division vitiated any good effects that Balfour's pledge might have had on the electorate; as soon as the early results made it clear that the Unionists were not going to win the election, smouldering dispute burst into open warfare. Nor did the pledge embarrass the Liberals, who saw it for exactly what it was, a mere tactical ploy designed to win votes in Lancashire, treated it with contempt and refused to make any reciprocal pledge on Home Rule.[47]

The results, declared between 2 and 20 December, were a great blow to the Unionists. Although they lost only one seat overall and now had exactly the same number as the Liberal government, they had made no inroad into the Labour and Nationalist control of the balance in the House of Commons; there would now be no chance of defeating either House of Lords Reform or Home Rule in the new parliament. Worst of all, although there was little overall change, many seats had changed hands in each direction; there was thus evidence to justify the claims of both factions in the Unionist camp. Balfourites pointed to the gain of four seats in Lancashire to show the success of the referendum policy and hinted that the lack of further gains was due to disloyalty during the campaign. Tariff reformers pointed to losses elsewhere and claimed that these would not have occurred had the tariff policy been preached with enthusiasm. *The Times* and the *Observer* put the blame for defeat on the party organization, perhaps to divert attention away from their own part in foisting the referendum policy on to Balfour.[48]

In parliament the two elections of 1910 had produced a new balance. The Unionists recovered their losses of 1906 in the south and east of England but had made only a modified recovery in the north and had made almost no progress in Scotland and Wales. Frustration was increased by the feeling that the Liberal–Labour alliance that worked so well at the polls and kept the Liberals in power was an unnatural deal between two groups that did not fundamentally agree. So Unionists referred to the government as a 'coalition' (not strictly true since only Liberals held office), rather than a minority government which is what it was. Irrevocable changes in the constitutional structure of the United Kingdom, coming from such an unnatural combination through log-rolling, would be in themselves equally unnatural. In the frustration of defeat, Unionists managed to convince themselves that the government had not won fairly and that they would therefore be justified in using extreme measures to resist it.[49] It was a conviction fraught with danger for the party, and in the first instance for the leader.

The Unionist performance in parliament in the session of 1911 seemed to presage the disintegration of the party. Recriminations after the election were reinforced by arguments over tactics, disputes over future policy, and ultimately by debates on the leadership question. The long accumulation of grievances against Balfour now accelerated and came out into the open; men who had looked for a strong lead in years past now looked for a new leader. Tariff reform enthusiasts followed Austen Chamberlain into opposition and the peers were antagonized by Balfour's handling of the issue of Lords reform. The initiative drifted out of Balfour's hands in the House of Lords crisis in July and August 1911 and the party made one of its worst ever showings in parliament.

It was clear after the election that the government would press on with its Bill to reduce the powers of the Lords, that it would have a substantial majority in the Commons for its plans, and that it would have the support of the King if necessary. Despite this the Unionists fought even harder in 1911 than in 1909 and 1910, a fight made more bitter by the certainty of ultimate failure rather than by the chances of success. The Lords' amendments to the Parliament Bill made a great constitutional clash inevitable, and on grounds that the Unionists could not – and *should not* – hope to win. On 24 July there was uproar in the House of Commons, with so much personal abuse hurled at Asquith that the session had to be suspended.[50] By this time though, with party passions raised to fever pitch in the midst of an unusually hot summer, the leaders already knew that they would have to give way in the end. Balfour had deluded himself that the King could be brought over and had intrigued with the Palace to give him unconstitutional advice, but there was never any realistic hope of success.[51] The shadow cabinet had thus to make an unpalatable choice between continuing the resistance of the Lords, which would result in the creation of a permanent Liberal majority (and hence in Home Rule, Welsh disestablishment, a Plural Voting Bill, licensing reform, and every other Liberal cause being passed at once), or surrendering to the Parliament Bill and so salvaging the Unionist majority in the House of Lords and the right to delay Bills for two years. On 21 July the shadow cabinet voted narrowly to 'hedge' rather than to 'ditch' – to save what they could from an impossible situation. It needed all of Balfour's remaining pull on his colleagues to ensure a majority for this decision and the minority would give no promise to accept the decision.[52] Balfour announced on 25 July that the Lords would be advised to pass the Bill, but on the following day a dinner was given for Lord Halsbury by several hundred peers and MPs who were determined to carry on the fight. Halsbury was accepted leader of the ditchers in the House of Lords, but he was supported by Milner, Selborne, Carson, Smith, Austen Chamberlain and others in the shadow cabinet. The dinner was a deliberate slight to Balfour and the formation of a Halsbury Club afterwards was a sign that the split would outlast the current debate.[53] Balfour, having given the party his advice and seen it widely rejected, left for Germany before the critical vote was taken. On 10 August the peers decided their fate; the bulk of the Unionist peers accepted Lansdowne's advice, sullenly abstained and challenged the government to find its own majority.

However even this did not save the party from further embarrassment for 114 diehards kept up their opposition to the last; the Bill was saved only by the votes of thirty-seven Unionists under Curzon who voted *for* the Bill with the bishops and the Liberals. The outcome was thus that the Unionist peers split three ways and that the Bill passed – despite all the sound and fury – by Unionist votes.[54]

The hostility aroused by the Lords crisis could not be contained within normal channels. After the debate Curzon and his followers were not invited to several fashionable drawing-rooms and the bishops were singled out for special abuse: the word 'Judas' was hurled at the bishops by some, and others wondered if they had traded their votes for a reprieve for the Welsh Church establishment.[55] Balfour was spoken of with contempt and the vitality that had been generated by the diehards was contrasted with the lethargy that characterized the party's official efforts. So Maurice Woods, secretary of the Unionist Social Reform Committee and no diehard himself, wrote to tell Lord Willoughby de Broke that 'the House of Lords hasn't saved itself by its exertions but you people have saved the party by your example'.[56] The Halsbury Club was thus to remain in existence to carry over this enthusiasm into other areas of the party. Two other similar bodies already existed: the Confederacy had been set up in 1905 to press for tariff reform and was by 1911 a powerful, semi-secret society that was supported by at least fifty MPs and peers; the Reveille had wider aims but contained many of the same people. By 1911 the overlapping membership of these organizations gave evidence of the declining support for Balfour among even members of the shadow cabinet and among Unionist editors (especially Gwynne of the *Morning Post* and Maxse of the *National Review*). For Balfour the party was becoming unleadable.[57]

The same divisions were to be found in the party in the country, a legacy of eight years of strife. The clearest example was the poor relations that still existed between Conservatives and Liberal Unionists. Conservative suspicion was enhanced by the apparent overlap between Liberal Unionists and the Tariff Reform League, as Sandars told Balfour in 1907:

> Percival Hughes comes to me with the complaint that everywhere the Liberal Unionists – posing as Liberal Unionists but in reality Tariff Reform Leaguers – are, with the encouragement of Austen and Co., trying to squeeze out or capture our local Conservative Associations. It is only the same movement below as that which is going on above, and which only indicates the Party fissure – alas! widening and not closing up.[58]

Suspicion was also enhanced by the fact that it was always the Liberal Unionists who were pressing for closer relations and always the Conservatives who were resisting, fearful that their party would be taken over in the process, as Sandars again related to Balfour, this time in 1908:

> Joe's scheme of reorganization of *our* Party while himself retaining control of Birmingham and Co. is frank and amusing. He little knows the prejudices opposed

to him. . . . What people like Bob [Akers-Douglas], Walter [Long], and Alick [Acland–Hood] will say to the organizer of Birmingham attempting to secure both central and local control of the party organizations I can well imagine.[58]

So the suspicion went on. When looking for the chairman of a committee on party organization in 1911, Sandars was surprised by Milner's suggestion of Selborne for 'there comes the Liberal Unionist difficulty, which had not occurred to him'. Also in 1911, Conservatives were doubtful of Austen Chamberlain's candidature for the party leadership because he was a Liberal Unionist – the party was already led in the Lords by a Liberal Unionist, Lansdowne. For their part, the Liberal Unionists wanted no more than to be treated as equals and for their allies to take politics and organization more seriously. Lord Selborne believed that the problems would disappear if the two groups were united and if the Liberal Unionists were to join the Carlton Club.[60]

Cutting across these barriers were others caused by the needs of propaganda and organization. The Union Defence League, under Walter Long, was the main agency opposing Home Rule; the Budget Protest League, also under Long, was the agency opposing Liberal financial management; the Tariff Reform League and the Tariff Commission were putting the case for tariffs. As well as these, the party was paralleled by the Primrose League, the Victoria League, the Middle Class Defence League, the Anti-Socialist Union, the Constitutional Speakers' League, the Junior Imperial League, the National Conservative League, and at least five organizations aimed specifically at working men.

There was of course much criticism of such unnecessary duplication. In January 1910 the *Conservative Agents' Journal* called for a committee of businessmen who would sweep away all of the existing organizations and set up 'an efficient and unitary organization'. In October a letter to the *Morning Post* called for an end to the 'legion of leagues'. Evidence to the Unionist Organization Committee in 1911 agreed that the multiplicity of bodies was 'a perfect curse to the party', that the Leagues 'spend money but do little work', and they 'should be under some sort of control'.[61] Only in the summer of 1911 though did the position of the party and the mood of the diehards allow these organizations to reach the peak of their popularity and their maximum capacity for disruption. In October 1911 Arthur Steel-Maitland wrote to Halsbury to urge him not to sanction the formation of a permanent Halsbury Club, for 'in the first place, such separate organizations mean friction, overlapping, waste of money (which is much needed), waste of effort. . . . Secondly, the object of the Association, stripped of all verbal trimmings, can be nothing else than hostility to Mr. Balfour and Lord Lansdowne.'[62] Making only feeble attempts to rebut the charges of disloyalty, the Halsbury Club went ahead. Lord Graham summed up the position three weeks later in a letter to *The Times*:

There is a Tariff Reform League to push for a tariff, the Land Union to advocate the same. The Union Defence League to oppose Home Rule for Ireland. The Income Tax League to reduce income tax. The Junior Conservatives to advance Conservative policy. The Confederates to do ditto. The Imperialist League, the 1900 Club, the Primrose and a number of others for much the same purpose. Now what policy is there in all these societies and leagues which cannot be advocated equally well from the platform of the Party proper?[63]

The answer to his question was that no policy matter as such separated these bodies from the party proper but that they all shared a lack of faith in the party leadership. Specialist organizations believed that they needed to work outside the party to get across their point of view, and by 1911 the diehards did not believe that the party was strong enough on any issue. All the splinter groups included at least one member of the shadow cabinet; when loyal men like Bonar Law, Walter Long and Austen Chamberlain all found the need to work outside normal channels, it is little surprise that others did so too.

In the autumn of 1911 the party had thus passed the point where it could be rallied without a new focus of loyalty. The *National Review* under Leo Maxse had been running a campaign with the simple message 'Balfour must go', and the letters BMG were in widespread use. In October, Maxse's editorial concluded starkly that 'the Unionist Party, in fact, is condemned to impotence as long as it is led by Mr. Balfour'.[64] Behind the scenes the diehards prepared for a showdown at the National Union Conference in November, preparing to mount such a show of their opposition as to force Balfour out. Selborne, a close supporter of Balfour at an earlier stage, was now prepared to conspire to force his retirement but was trying to contain the conspiracy within moderate bounds. In August he wrote to George Wyndham to resist 'the suggestions made for the formation of a new party. My reply to that is, and I have had some experience in the formation of a new party, that the task is impossible to carry out successfully, and that the attempt to do it would be a disastrous blunder.'[65] Instead he urged united action by the diehards 'to make our views prevail within the Party, which is the same thing as capturing the Party and the Party machine'. At the conference the diehard peers would show their responsibility by disowning Maxse's personal attacks on Balfour but they would at the same time secure the election of their own nominees as officers of the National Union and pass resolutions that would make Balfour's position impossible.

Balfour was informed of this activity on his return from Germany but it probably came too late to affect him, for he seems to have decided to resign the party leadership while in Germany. If any doubt remained then it must have been set aside by reports from the Chief Whip and Party Chairman that greeted his return.[66] He announced his resignation to these two in September, made his preparations and then informed his leading colleagues early in November. The King was told on 7 November and a public announcement was made to Balfour's constituency association on the following day.[67]

Balfour was thus driven from office by his party, a fact that was hardly disguised by his pleas of illness or by the fulsome resolutions of regret that were now passed by Unionists up and down the country; but neither can it be doubted that his discomfiture was a consequence of his own performance as leader. The verdict on Balfour's leadership must be a harsh one; to lose three successive elections, to leave the party in the state that he left it in, and to leave no clear successor, are all facts that cannot be easily explained away. He had been a disastrous leader in opposition and – at least from the party viewpoint – he had been no more successful as Prime Minister. In his defence it can certainly be urged that circumstances would have made the task wellnigh impossible for any man at the time and that Balfour tried hard to carry out his duties responsibly. As he told Sandars, 'some people do not like the qualifications in my speeches. They are not expressed to save myself, but to protect my Party in the future when the statements of leaders are recalled to injure the Party.'[68] All this can be adduced in defence, but the verdict remains harsh, for Balfour lacked an essential quality of political leadership that ruined his good intentions and turned their effect to nothing. He equivocated too much and never grasped the effect of his equivocation on his party supporters. He lacked above all a sense of what could be achieved by a sense of momentum and what could be covered by the existence of something in which to believe. For all its technical skill, Balfour's leadership did not give his party enough to hold on to; in government, and especially in opposition, philosophic doubt was not enough. He postponed issue after issue and so kept divisions open: it is doubtful whether any of the possible outcomes of the tariff controversy in 1903 would have been more damaging than allowing it to drag on and on. And in 1909–11 Balfour encouraged his followers to die in the last ditch while he scrambled nimbly over the hedge on the far side. Concerned above all with the unity of his party, determined not to be 'another Sir Robert Peel', Balfour ended by leaving his party much as Peel had done: weak, divided and leaderless.[69]

Notes and References

1   Balfour expressed the same view to several others too: see Dugdale, *Balfour*, ii, 20–1.
2   Salisbury to Selborne, 19 Jan. 1906; Selborne MSS.
3   Chamberlain to Parker Smith, 27 Jan. 1906: quoted in Amery, *Joseph Chamberlain*, vi, 793.
4   Rempel, *Unionists Divided*, 171–86.
5   Chamberlain to Balfour, 6 Feb. 1906: quoted in Dugdale, *Balfour*, ii, 22.
6   Chamberlain to Garvin, 5 Feb. 1906: quoted in Amery, *Joseph Chamberlain*, vi, 815.
7   *Ibid*, vi, 832–3.
8   *Ibid*, vi, 848.
9   Rempel, *Unionists Divided*, 199.
10 Blake, *Conservative Party*, 188.
11 R. B. Jones, 'Balfour's reform of party organisation', 92.
12 Ramsden, 'Organisation', (Thesis), 134–5.
13 Fraser, *Joseph Chamberlain*, 278–9.
14 See for example Chamberlain's remark, quoted in Churchill, *Winston S. Churchill*, ii, 181.
15 Rowland, *Last Liberal Governments*, i, 86.
16 Balfour did not even pretend to any reluctance to use the House of Lords, as his comments in the House of Commons on the Education Bill demonstrated: quoted in *ibid*, i, 78.
17 Cecil of Chelwood, *All the Way*, 109.
18 Quoted from a conversation with Blanche Dugdale in Dugdale, *Balfour*, ii, 363–4.
19 Bagehot, *The English Constitution*, intro. by Balfour, 262.
20 An exaggerated account of the role of Sandars is given by Petrie in *The Powers behind the Prime Minister*. As late as 1911 Balfour was still writing to 'Mr Sandars'. Blanche Dugdale was convinced that Sandars kept Balfour fully informed at all times, but she recognized that this was not always seen to be the case: Dugdale, *Balfour*, i, 42.
21 Sandars to Balfour, 22 Mar. 1907: Balfour MSS, Add. MSS 49766.
22 Wyndham to Akers-Douglas, 2 Nov. 1907: quoted in Rowland, *Last Liberal Governments*, i, 128.
23 *National Review*, Sept. 1910.
24 *Morning Post*, 24 Aug. 1910.
25 Malmesbury, *The New Order*.
26 Rowland, *Last Liberal Governments*, i, 166–8, 213.
27 Cook, 'Labour and the downfall of the Liberal party', in Cook and Sked, *Crisis and Controversy*, 55.

28   Pelling, *Popular Politics*, 146.
29   Fraser, *Joseph Chamberlain*, 290–1.
30   Balfour to Lansdowne, 13 Apr. 1906: quoted in Newton, *Lansdowne*, 354.
31   Dugdale, *Balfour*, ii, 34.
32   Murray, 'The politics of the people's budget'.
33   Rowland, *Last Liberal Governments*, i, 223–5.
34   See for example Garvin's view, quoted in Fraser, *Joseph Chamberlain*, 291.
35   Rowland, *Last Liberal Governments*, i, 222.
36   *Ibid*, 228–9.
37   Dugdale, *Balfour*, ii, 57–8.
38   Rowland, *Last Liberal Governments*, i, 230.
39   *Ibid*, 246.
40   Sanders Diary, 6 May 1910.
41   Searle, *Quest for National Efficiency*, 192–5.
42   Dugdale, *Balfour*, ii, 76–7.
43   Blewett, *Peers, Parties and People*, 173–5.
44   The *Conservative and Unionist* carried a full-page cartoon on this theme in its special election issue of Dec. 1910.
45   Gollin, *Observer and J. L. Garvin*, 259.
46   Derby to Sandars, 15 Dec. 1910: Balfour MSS, Add. MSS 49743.
47   Blewett, *Peers, Parties and People*, 177.
48   Gollin, *Observer and J. L. Garvin*, 318–9.
49   Blake, *Conservative Party*, 191.
50   Rowland, *Last Liberal Governments*, ii, 50–1.
51   Nicolson, *King George V*, 208.
52   Dugdale, *Balfour*, ii, 68.
53   R. B. Jones, 'Conservative Party' (Thesis), Ch. 5.
54   Jenkins, *Mr Balfour's Poodle*, 265–6.
55   See for example the letters to Lord Willoughby from Henry Page Croft, Lord Northumberland and Lady Halsbury, all 11 Aug. 1911: Willoughby de Broke MSS.
56   Maurice Woods to Willoughby de Broke, 16 Aug. 1911: Willoughby de Broke MSS.
57   Ramsden, 'Organisation', (Thesis), 79.
58   Sandars to Balfour, April 1907: Balfour MSS, Add. MSS 49766.
59   Sandars to Balfour, 21 Jan. 1908: Balfour MSS, Add. MSS 49766.
60   Selborne to Balfour, 24 Dec. 1910: Selborne MSS.
61   Ramsden, 'Organisation', 15.
62   Steel-Maitland to Halsbury, 2 Oct. 1911: quoted from the Halsbury MSS by Jones, 'Conservative Party', Ch. 5.
63   *The Times*, 20 Oct. 1911.
64   *National Review*, Oct. 1911.
65   Selborne to Wyndham, 22 Aug. 1911: Selborne MSS.
66   Ramsden, 'Organisation', 80.
67   Dugdale, *Balfour*, ii, 89–90.
68   Quoted in Young, *Balfour*, 316.
69   For Balfour's view of Peel see for example Dugdale, *Balfour*, ii, 75.

Chapter 3

Party reorganization, 1911

In the aftermath of defeat in 1910 there were demands for drastic reforms and for scapegoats. This time the pressure was too great to be resisted and so a committee was appointed to review the entire organization of the party. This Unionist Organization Committee created the broad pattern of party organization that lasted until the Maxwell–Fyfe reforms of 1948. This chapter begins though with a review of the state of the organization in the early years of the century and before reform had been implemented.

At the head of the organization from 1902 was Sir Alexander Acland-Hood, Chief Whip and hence controller of the Whip's office, the Central Office, the regional offices and the party funds. This task would have been an insuperable burden in modern conditions for the most able of organizers, but Acland-Hood was not especially good at the job anyway. He was a country gentleman of the old style, known as 'the pink un' because of his passion for hunting, and alleged to have neither knowledge nor interest in organization outside his own constituency of West Somerset.[1] He was capable enough in the narrow role of Chief Whip in parliament but he did not have either the drive or the knowledge that were needed to ginger up the party in the country, as Leo Amery told Bonar Law:

> The key of the position is Acland-Hood, and till he gets poisoned or pensioned we shall not get a step forward. At present there are I believe combined in him three different function which no one man, however able, could fulfil effectively, and none of which he is capable of fulfilling at all. These are –
> (a) The Chief Whip of the Party in the House of Commons.
> (b) The chief organiser of the party in the country, responsible for the campaign as a whole, for the selection of candidates, and for the general efficiency of all local organisations.
> (c) The man who collects an adequate party war chest.[2]

With Acland-Hood exercising only a general oversight, these tasks were either delegated to others or not done at all. The party machine was effectively run by the Principal Agents, Wells (1903–06) and Percival Hughes (1906–12), neither of whom was a professional organizer. The most common criticism of Central Office was indeed of the general competence of its staff. Staff could be recruited either from the ranks of the constituency agents or from the amorphous group of lawyers, political secretaries, journalists and civil servants who gathered around the parties in Westminster. Agents had the appropriate knowledge of local organization but had a low social status and could have gained little experience of the running of a large organization. Non-agents might have the right social graces but could not have a detailed grasp of the law and practice of elections. Acland-Hood and Hughes opted exclusively for the promotion of agents to Central Office jobs and Acland-Hood even promised as much when he addressed Conservative agents in 1907.[3] This practice was not very successful, as Jack Sandars reported to Balfour on Christmas Day 1910:

> There is in fact . . . almost an agents' ring which is ultra-conservative in ideas, looks to and gets support from the C.C.O., is very loyal to that institution because it recognises and protects their interests. Those interests in the main are concerned with rigid promotion in the agents' class. So much is this the rule that even the Heads of Department in Hughes' Office are all promoted agents. They are excellent men of their type, skilled in the technique of agents' election work, but they have no sympathy with new ideas, no imagination, no elasticity of method: in a word they are old-fashioned.[4]

In the following year, Arthur Steel-Maitland was even harder in his verdict on the staff at Central Office: 'I fear that the senior men I found at the Central Office are all useless, except Vesey. . . . Gales is useful at calculations and possesses much knowledge, but is idle and has no administrative capacity. Zobel is very honest but really unequal to the work as I conceive it.'[5] Central Office needed then a ruthless new broom, not only to deal with the incapacity of the staff but also to deal with the problems of accommodation and structure. Amery was certain that much stemmed from the Office's inadequate premises:

> The whole housing arrangements of the Central Office make any real efficiency and decency impossible. Fifteen or twenty men at a time, candidates, deputations wishing to interview Percival Hughes etc. are shoved into a little coal hole which is also a main thoroughfare for clerks, and kept waiting by the hour. The officials themselves are packed into little dens with no room to spread their papers, with the incessant noise of half a dozen telephones, and with clerks running in and out all the time. All this, though trivial in itself, seriously impairs efficiency. The whole thing wants clearing out and putting into a decent building, well lit, and reasonably spacious, and candidates, deputations, members of parliament, and others should have at least two or three tolerable waiting rooms not inferior to those of the average dentist.[6]

From the inside, Steel-Maitland was able to recall the state of things when he arrived in 1911:

> Of management there was absolutely none, save that letters were filed and a note made of promises of election expenses. I was prepared for a lack of system but not for what I found. No attempt was made at departmentalising work. There was no control of ordinary office matters such as office expenditure, telephones etc.; no proper system of reports from the district agents; no control of expenditure. . . . Vague verbal assurances were the rule, not satisfactory at the moment and

productive of trouble later. Engagements which were practically never kept. And in general work was done which could not be put off, but all problems and responsibilities were shelved if possible. This sounds extravagant. It is literally true.[7]

Perhaps the most serious complaints centred on the handling of the party funds. Amery again:

It seems to me quite absurd that our Party with the enormous reserve of wealth behind it should actually have less money than its opponents. As far as I can make out no attempt is really made to get at the people who have money. I have been told that the whole of Cadogan Square does not subscribe more than £5 a year to the Unionist Party.[8]

In this judgement, Amery was certainly unfair, for others paid tribute to the success of Acland-Hood in raising money.[9] His other commitments no doubt made it necessary for Acland-Hood to base his fund-raising on a few wealthy individuals; more would be available if more time were available for collection. However, the administration of the funds when once collected was another occasion for complaint. Steel-Maitland recalled that

there was . . . no control of their expenditure. What is more there was no annual balance sheet. They could not tell you within £10,000 what the year's expenditure had been; probably not within £20,000. There was no proper classification of expenditure, no recovery of loans; no following up of lapsed subscriptions.[10]

Finance thus followed the rest of the organizational pattern.

The chaos at Central Office was mirrored at the National Union, responsible since 1906 for the organization of literature and speakers. Steel-Maitland was not impressed with the way in which Thomas Cox ran the Speaker's Department:

His system is wooden and rigid; he sacrifices the work to it, and its effectiveness is halved. Thus, if a constituency will not take the individual speaker he sends, it can go without altogether. Thus complaints are fairly numerous. His wares are to be taken or left. They ought to be adapted and pushed.[11]

The National Union's system of control by committee was also defective:

There is no real selection of the best and most suitable men for the various committees. Worthington-Evans, for example, for a busy man is very good. So are other individuals. But for the most part the Committees are a chance collection, and the theory that they contribute the best brains of the Party in each subject goes utterly by the board.[12]

All these charges were borne out by the witnesses interviewed by the Unionist Organization Committee in 1911. In all then, the party's institutions were in urgent need of reform, and the same could be said of the local associations too.

In January 1911 *The Times* ran a series of articles by its Political Correspondent, A. P. Nicholson, which let the central institutions of the party off rather lightly and concentrated its fire on the local parties.[13]

Liverpool was cited as the example of how local parties should be run; here the party was said to rely on the shillings of the working men and, because a sophisticated voluntary machine was needed to collect so many small subscriptions, support could be mobilized quickly for elections. Nicholson's account of Liverpool (based on information from Archibald Salvidge of the Liverpool Workingmen's Conservative Association) did not mention how far the party in Liverpool depended on income from the wealthier members in the Liverpool Constitutional Association.[14] But there was some substance in what was claimed and these articles transformed Salvidge from a local party boss into a party figure of national significance. *The Times* went on to paint a lurid picture of the more typical constituency.

> The local agent, generally a solicitor, looks out for a rich candidate who will pay expenses, however undesirable he may be in other directions. The rich candidate, when found, thinks he will save money by holding off to the last moment. Meanwhile, in the period between elections when the real work should be done, the organisation lapses and nothing takes place except a few perfunctory committee meetings. . . . The battle is lost, the local agent gets his salary and perquisites, and the Unionist Association in the division settles down to another period of quiescence.[15]

This was a caricature that ignored advances that had been made since 1906, but it was an accurate enough picture of the most backward constituencies. The main weakness of the local parties though was not the chaotic state of the worst but the apathetic state of the majority. They had been designed for a different political world and were ill equipped to meet the pressure put on them by the advent of Labour and the 'New Liberalism'.

The traditional style of local party, described in Ostrogorski's *Democracy and the Organisation of Political Parties* in 1902, was an artificial creation set up by a few local luminaries. These few then continued to dominate through the structure of the institutions and by encouraging a deferential attitude amongst the rank and file. The caucus system described by Ostrogorski 'eventually ends by being a hierarchy of wirepullers'.[16] This control was preserved by the simple expedient of making subscriptions optional; if the ordinary member did not share the financial burden then he could not call the tune: 'Sometimes the paying members of the Council is one half, sometimes less; in certain Associations, for one member who contributes there are nineteen who do not pay, and there are organisations in which nobody pays.'[17] Of course, somebody did always pay, and received in return an enhanced influence. It was easy to acquire a Vice-Presidency for a few guineas in most local parties and this carried a seat on the Central Council. So in West Derbyshire in 1911 a tariff of charges was agreed for different levels of influence; five shillings bought membership of a branch committee, half a guinea membership of the polling district committee, one guinea membership of the divisional association and five guineas membership of the Central Council. In the same way, all subscribers of over five pounds in Newbury in

1906 were made Vice-Presidents. Huddersfield had fifty-four, and Newark set out in 1907 to recruit 150 Vice-Presidents by lowering the qualification to one guinea. Nor was the position purely honorific: in Kincardine in 1909 the Executive Committee – the supreme body in the Association – had an elected chairman together with twenty Vice-presidents (by virtue of their five pound subscriptions) and only twelve other representatives from the branches and clubs in the constituency.[18]

Local parties were able to recruit large numbers of members because there was neither entrance fee nor compulsory subscription, but the meaning of membership was correspondingly low. In 1907 the West Birmingham Liberal Unionists had 3,862 members but subscriptions from them totalled only twenty pounds; in 1913 Bewdley had a membership of several thousands, but only 125 subscribers. So, in Joseph Chamberlain's constituency and in Stanley Baldwin's, members clearly did not join to exert influence: neither association allowed its members any real say in the election of officers, framing of resolutions or choice of candidates. At this stage, though, members joined local parties for reasons that had little or nothing to do with political influence.[19] Where else, asked the Primrose League, could a working man join a social institution that included a duchess or his employer? Where else could a middle-class professional man show off his newly acquired distinction for as little as five guineas a year?[20] The Primrose League raised this attitude to a basic creed, but it was typical of the rest of the party too. Ostrogorski described the Primrose League as

> amongst other things, the great, the greatest promoter of the "socialisation of politics". . . . Great, immense as is the success of the League, it has nevertheless to be always making fresh efforts in the same direction; for the voter is a frivolous being, he soon gets tired. "Our greatest difficulty," the representative of a Tory Organisation confided to me, "is to keep them amused".[21]

This institutionalization of social inequality was basically two-sided: the few provided bread and circuses 'to keep them amused', and the many were supposed accept the habits of social deference that the institutions themselves reflected. This 'social consideration', Ostrogorski concluded, was merely 'a safe means of electoral bribery'.[22] It was not only safe but also effective. Deference has been reckoned to be one of the most effective strings that tied working-class voters to the Conservative Party and socialization through party institutions must have been one of the most powerful methods.[23]

In a well-organized division, each polling district was like a small constituency, each with its paid part-time agent, each with its local elite and its committee, and each conscious of its independence. The West Derbyshire Unionist League had thirty-two such polling districts and a similar pattern existed in South Monmouthshire, Harborough and South Oxfordshire. This decentralization inevitably led to difficulty, not least where geographical remoteness was added to differing attitudes: in the High Peak Division of Derbyshire the businessmen of Glossop found it difficult to work with the

hoteliers and retired officers of Buxton or with the farmers in the rest of the
constituency. But High Peak was entirely independent and unknown to the
County Association at Derby, to the regional office at Leicester or to the
Central Office in London. In such backwoods bribery still flourished, with
sides of beef and cash still changing hands at elections.[24]

All types of local party shared a similar limitation of aims. Outings and
concerts were favourite activities and these social events were often treats for
supporters paid for by the candidate, often in conjunction with the local
political clubs. As the Yorkshire Report for 1909 noted, 'political clubs are all
too often used for social purposes alone', and a constant effort had to be made
to maintain the clubs as rival centres of socio-political loyalty to the
nonconformist chapels. So Colonel Rutherford, MP for Darwen, was urged
to visit the clubs more often to keep them loyal to the party, and Conservative
agents were advised to slip in at least one political speech at every smoking
concert, if only to remind the revellers that they were on political premises.
Much could be achieved by using the clubs against Liberal licensing plans: in
1908 the Hitchin clubs raised £800 to resist the Licensing Bill and the Welsh
Clubs were agitated for the same cause in 1921.[25] Clubs thus continued to play
an important role in the local structure of the party; in some areas of
Lancashire and Wales they were the only local party structures that existed.
They were kept under control by the Association of Conservative Clubs, a
body founded in the 1890s; the ACC worked because it made itself useful to
the clubs with advice on audit stock-taking and management, but it had a
typically undemocratic structure.[26] The party organization was thus social
rather than truly political; a limited commitment was asked for from
members and only limited concessions to effectiveness or democracy were
made in return.

This limited approach to politics could not long survive the arrival of the
Labour Party, and some advances were made after 1900. The most pressing
demands for change were for more professional agents and for a more
democratic structure for the local parties themselves. The Vice-Chairman of
the Brighton Unionists made the second point emphatically in 1907:

> These are democratic days. If the Conservative Party is to be in power, it must be a
> democratic party. It must trust the people and have the confidence of the people.
> Forty or fifty years ago it was all very well to manage things with a party of a few
> gentlemen, but those days are gone for ever.[27]

The same view was expressed in an anonymous *Memorandum on Electoral
Organization* which circulated in the party in 1906:

> The National Union . . . represents in its delegates not the mass of the constituents
> but that small body of Conservatives who are zealous and rich enough to give £10
> or £20 a year to the party funds of their division. If this is to be remedied it must be
> done by producing in each division a large representative body of keen
> Conservatives who shall be both in fact and theory the local Association.[28]

Evidence given to the Unionist Organization Committee in 1911 suggested much the same: Leigh Maclachlan of Central Office stated that local organizations were 'democratic on paper only, officers usually nominated'; Pike Pease of the Whip's Office demanded that local organizations 'should be democratic – everyone should be asked to subscribe'.[29] *The Times* had said much the same in its eulogy of Liverpool and reformed associations held themselves up as examples just as Liverpool had done. The Unionists of Hastings described their system to Percival Hughes in 1910:

> Our Association work is based on Democratic Principles and this fact has a great deal to do with our success. The working-men regularly attend the Monthly Committee Meetings for the purpose of Registration and other work. We invite and encourage them to do this by placing them on our Executive Committee, our Central Governing Committee and other Committees.[30]

Democracy was thus perceived as the spirit of the age, but it was also a net with which to catch working-class conservatives; pure socialization might not now be enough, but the direct involvement of working men in party institutions might be as effective. So some parties did reform themselves before 1911, but without a strong lead from Central Office and constant pressure from the professional agents any change would be patchy and slow.

The agents at the beginning of the century were as old-fashioned as the rest of the organization. The atmosphere in the agents' magazines had more in common with the Tapers and Tadpoles of *Coningsby* than with the professional agents of the 1920s. Appointments showed traditional features: many were solicitors taking on registration as part of their ordinary practice and so looking on it from a purely legal point of view; others were the land agents for MPs and others were political secretaries. Most were described in their own magazines as being 'Mr Wild's election agent' or 'General Harrison's agent' rather than as 'agent for North Devon'; employment was still personal rather than territorial because the agent's salary was more likely to come from the candidate than from the local association.[31] It was quite normal for a different man to run election campaigns from the one who ran registration canvassing; a third might administer the local association and a fourth appear in the revision courts for the party. This was the position in West Derbyshire, where the 'Chief Agent' never ran an election campaign in forty years service. The first decade of the century was in fact the watershed, with all types of party agent existing side by side; the final product was an amalgam of the lawyers, land agents, political secretaries and electioneering specialists who had called themselves agents before. The vital influence was the shift to full-time employment, especially after the defeat in 1906, for once the agency was a full-time job, and costing £150 a year or more, the logic of the situation demanded that he should take over all of the subsidiary tasks connected with registration, elections and running the local association.

Regional professional associations of agents had sprung up in the 1890s, the lead being taken by professionals like T. H. Packer (Cheltenham), J. H.

Bottomley (Clapham) and C. G. Briggs (Plymouth). These were finally brought together into a National Society of Conservative Agents in 1904, with Packer as its first chairman. The *Conservative Agents' Journal* was successfully and permanently revived in 1907 and became a propagandist for more professional practices among the agents themselves, edited by Packer until 1920.[32]

The 1906 defeat was the shock that prompted many local associations to make the change: in the parts of Sussex and Lancashire studied by Grace Jones, solicitors were election agents in nine out of seventeen constituencies in 1906 but in only four by December 1910.[33] This differed from the rest of the country only in the extent to which Sussex had begun to make the change (following local by-election defeats) before 1906. Overall then, at least two-thirds of agents were still lawyers in 1906 but less than a quarter were lawyers by 1911, a change reported by the *Daily Telegraph*:

> Some solicitors still act in the capacity of agents, but they are the best of the class. The gentlemen who have since 1906 given up the office are solicitors with big professional connections, and they could afford only a little spare time to carry out their duties as agents. There has been an attempt to train a number of young men of good education to become agents.[34]

Lawyers had always wielded strong influence in the party because of the extreme complication of the system of registration. In the more politically backward areas they continued to do so, but these were exactly the places where small electorates and stable voting patterns made it possible to continue as before. In the more populous areas the day of the lawyer was over.[35] The method of training adopted by Hughes to find replacements for the lawyers was to use promoted agents to overhaul the machinery at the grass roots. Thus, when the new County Associations were set up in 1906, he ensured that the new county secretaries were all experienced constituency agents.

However, in July 1909 the *National Review* could still conclude that 'the majority of Party agents in this country are about as well fitted for their duties as is a sergeant of marines to navigate a ship'. Not only were the agents still disparaged, but they were still seen only as NCOs. For much of this Hughes was to blame, for he could hardly know as an amateur who would be the best professionals to promote, but the process would inevitably have been a slow one. Promotion by seniority might work when the basic system was working well, but it would not be sufficient when great changes were needed. Promotion though was still a reward for the last job rather than a preparation for the new one, as Steel-Maitland noted: 'As regards agents, Hughes has gained great popularity with them, partly by real sympathy, partly by lack of discipline, and by being ready, if a man is dismissed for gross incompetence, to recommend him elsewhere.'[36] In the management of the agents, much that Hughes attempted was the basis of later success, but it was carried out by his successors with two differences. At the top there was a more ruthless attitude to individuals and at the top also were men experienced in the field, men able to pick the right man from a sure sense of what the job was really about. Among the professional agents, as in the local parties there was thus a trend of improvement but one that could not be properly harnessed by existing personnel at the centre.

The need for change was underlined by long-term influences in the early part of the century, the most important of which were the increased size of the electorate and changes in political behaviour. The old style of organization depended on small electorates that could be manipulated by teams of lawyers and on voters who would remain loyal to a party. Organization was not intended to convert opponents but to retain known supporters, and there was no doubt of the effectiveness of this approach. Real gains could be made by organization in a division where it was much better organized than its opponents. Claims were made by party agents for net gains made at the annual revision courts and over a period of years these could be impressive; net gains were calculated by subtracting the successful Liberal claims from the successful Unionist claims, so giving a measurement of how much more favourable the new register would be when compared to the old one. Some such claims are listed in Table 3.1.[37]

Table 3.1   Net Unionist gains claimed in selected constituencies, 1909–1914

	1909	1910	1911	1912	1913	1914
Abingdon		+179				
Barkston Ash		+376	+314	+265	+214	
Bewdley		+350	+258	+307	+371	+402
Derbyshire West			+103	+61	+159	+112
Hampstead	+687					
Handsworth					+484	
Lincoln						−148
Monmouth		+498	+572	+508	+365	+48
Newbury	+429		+436			
Rushcliffe		+200	+294	+337	+397	+360

At a time when the average constituency had only a little over ten thousand electors and when most majorities were numbered in hundreds, a run of successful registration campaigns could change the probable result of an election. Successful registration was certainly one reason for the Liberal triumph of 1906, coming at the end of several years when local Unionism had been in a state of disarray; recovery for Unionists was partly based on the same foundations.[38] However, the system was very expensive, which is why few local parties could afford a full campaign each year; registration canvassers were paid and lawyers had then to be briefed to fight out claims before the Revising Barrister. It was lack of money that caused the poor result in Lincoln in 1914, and it was the running out of money that led to the slackening of the Monmouth Unionists' efforts. When operating well, though, a strong local party could keep tight control of its electorate: in

December 1910 the Abingdon Unionists did no canvassing for the election and yet were able to predict the results within sixteen votes through their knowledge of the register.[39] Notwithstanding the cost, a small and stable electorate could still be controlled with great efficiency.

But the old system was breaking down precisely because the electorate was becoming neither small nor stable. The registered electorate increased from 6:7 million in 1900 to 7:7 million in 1910; the proportion of the population registered increased from 15 per cent to 17½ per cent, and all this without any change in the legal basis of the franchise.[40] The change was due to the continuing increase in the population, to the ageing of the population after the falling-off of the birth rate, and to the effects of inflation on a franchise based partly on annual rentals: the effect of all these influences was to add over a million electors (more than the number added in 1832 and as many as 1867). This problem was compounded by the increasing propensity of the electorate to vote. The actual number of votes cast in a contested seat rose by a quarter between 1900 and December 1910. Organization thus became even more expensive and control of the increased electorate became more difficult, not least because the increase was concentrated in urban areas where Unionism was least well organized anyway. In the counties much of the old system remained until the First World War and was as effective in 1910 as it had been in 1890, but in the towns the old system was dead.

Difficulties in the towns were accentuated by the rise of the Labour Party and the success of its alliance with the Liberals. The support of the Labour Movement produced Liberal votes from electors who had usually abstained or voted against Liberals in deference to employers and landowners. This appeal therefore threatened the whole basis of the Unionists' electoral strategy. Before 1900 most leaders of organized labour had supported the Liberals, but there had been important regional variations and little uniformity in the voting even of trade unionists. There was a greater tradition of working-class Conservatism in the north-west than in the rural south – a divergence that predated the existence of the Conservative Party itself, for Tory Radicals like Oastler had found Lancashire responsive in the 1820s and 1830s.[41] Grace Jones has described this tradition through James Mawdsley, leader of the United Textile Factory Workers' Association and Winston Churchill's colleague as candidate for Oldham in 1899:

> He belonged to the old school of Lancashire working man who supported the Conservative and Unionist Party and did so for two main reasons. Disraeli's brand of Conservative Social Reforms appealed more strongly to him and to many Lancashire working men than the financial and administrative reforms of Gladstone; and this was reinforced by a strong dislike of capitalistic Liberalism, for almost all of the Lancashire millowners were staunch supporters of the Liberal Party.[42]

This pillar of Conservatism in a critical area was undercut by the increasing tendency of millowners to be Unionists themselves, so alienating their employees, and by the Liberals' drive for working-class votes to offset their loss of middle-class votes to the right. By 1900 Mawdsley was one of the last of his kind; when he died, his union in 1902 affiliated to the Labour Party with an affirmative vote of 76 per cent.[43] Labour thus had an appeal that cut right across old party lines and was for the present using that appeal in the service of the Liberals. It was for that reason that Bonar Law went to fight North-West Manchester in 1910, to focus attention again on the old issues; it was for the same reason that Balfour gave his referendum pledge. Lancashire was in fact the only region where the Progressive Alliance worked so smoothly; in London, where Liberals and Labour were at each others' throats, Unionist fortunes prospered, and all over the country the alliance broke down in 1912–13. However, even a limited success for a Progressive Alliance in the north-west greatly reduce the chances of a Unionist victory, for the party's success in England would have to be overwhelming if it was to offset the rest of the United Kingdom. The party needed to win over 300 of the 465 English seats to secure an overall majority, and this would be unlikely without a clean sweep of the Lancashire towns such as had been achieved in 1895 and 1900. Until parliamentary seats were redistributed this strategic weakness would remain; the 'New Liberalism' might not secure much of a majority for itself, but it was still able to deny victory to the Unionists.

Within the Unionist party, the main demand in reaction to Liberal and Labour success was for a more positive appeal to working men. It was seen that Labour could offer something that went beyond any matter of mere policy:

> The Labour Party has a ready made organization of an almost perfect character in the Trades Unions. It deals very largely (apart from its Socialist theories) with everyday facts relevant to the lives of its supporters and easily understood by them. Its real work is done, as the work of political conversion must be done, not on the platform but in the workshop and the home.[44]

Socialization, for so long a principal weapon in the Unionist armoury, was now being turned against the party. Efforts would therefore have to be made to make the Unionist party more responsive to the interests of working men. This explains the demands that Balfour should speak in 'language understanded of the people', and perhaps also the reaction that followed when Bonar Law did so; it also explains the urgency with which the local parties tried to make themselves more representative. Labour's clearest success, the actual election of working men to parliament, would be countered by the promotion of Unionist working-men candidates, and party meetings voted in favour of such schemes without dissent. In December 1910 there were six working men in the ranks of the Unionist candidates, financed from a fund collected by the *Standard*, but none was successful.[45] The Unionists were in fact meeting exactly the problem that had faced the Liberals in the 1890s; the party as a whole wished to promote working-class candidates, but no winnable constituency could ever be found to accept one for itself. Only in hopeless constituencies, where the local party was used to accepting any candidate who could pay his expenses (or have them paid for him in this case), were working men ever selected. Much was made of the mere fact of having working men as Unionist candidates, but far more could have been made if even one or two had been elected.

The long-term position therefore looked bleak. Unionists could not hit back at Labour organizations as they had hit back at Liberals for they had no effective social institutions through which to propagate their case. Political clubs were less effective in resisting Labour candidates because the clubs were themselves units of class solidarity when other sorts of focus were needed. Nor could middle-class bodies be used as rallying points: Chambers of Commerce and Employers' Associations still contained too many Liberals to allow them to be used politically. The answer – short of a collapse of the Liberal–Labour alliance – was a whole new approach to organization. The party would have to abandon the narrow legal approach and the assumption that the electorate was stable in its views. Instead there would be a campaign of propaganda and political education, a drive to convert voters who were on the register anyway rather than a determination to allow only known supporters to register.

The Unionist party was actually well suited for this transformation – far better than the Liberals, who had moral scruples about uninhibited electioneering and who preferred to see the electorate as a great national jury who would weigh the issues dispassionately. When the London Unionists went over wholeheartedly to propagandist methods in 1907 they were surprised by the ease with which they triumphed.[46] But it would be a long process before the whole party could be schooled to forget the methods of half a century, and this too would be achieved only by strong and determined leadership from the centre. So in 1911 all of the problems of organization came down to the machinery and personalities at the centre.

Attempts to reform the central administration of the party before 1911 had foundered on Balfour's determination to maintain the prerogatives of the leader. Central Office, the Whip's Office and the funds were all under his personal control and so any attack on them must be taken as an attack on the leader. So in 1906 Balfour himself beat off the attempt of the National Union to place the Chief Whip under the authority of a committee. In the years following, Acland-Hood, Sandars and Hughes fought off all attempts to enforce changes of personnel or method. At the end of 1909 the Northcliffe newspapers, generally inclined to back the party but frustrated by its amateurishness, mounted a campaign for changes; Hughes panicked and believed that Northcliffe was trying to take over Central Office itself. The result was that Northcliffe's help was refused and instead Hughes set up a press bureau at Central Office, yet another task for which he had neither time nor experience.[47] By 1910, critics spoke of 'the old gang' and of 'the small *coterie* who imagine that the Party exists for their benefit'.

After defeat in January 1910 Acland-Hood wished to step down, feeling personal responsibility for the second successive defeat over which he had presided and resenting the attacks of the diehard press, but his resignation was not accepted. Sandars's letters to Balfour show that the leader was made aware of Acland-Hood's failings, but both Balfour and Sandars were determined that the Chief Whip could not resign when he was under attack. (The comparison may be made with the acceptance by Baldwin of Davidson's resignation in 1930; a colleague thrown to the wolves could buy time for the leader and assist party unity.[48]) In the absence of a new Chief Whip in 1910, all reform was stymied for another year, a delay for which Balfour must take full responsibility. The system was not changed to reduce Acland-Hood's over-large duties lest that should imply criticism of his past work, and he was not allowed to resign for the same reason.

The failure to secure an effective organization was indeed becoming one of the diehards' main planks in the attack on Balfour, as the *National Review* made clear:

> If the Central Office were manned by archangels, it would remain inefficient as long as it is centralised in the Whip's Room of the House of Commons. Sir Alexander Acland-Hood is attempting to do what no man, however able, could do successfully. . . . Unfortunately the Unionist Leader takes no interest in Party management and seems indisposed to delegate this distasteful task to any of his colleagues, just as he is reluctant to appoint a deputy leader during his absence from the House of Commons. Mr. Balfour is probably more ignorant of his party than any of his predecessors.[49]

However, criticism among the diehards became far more strident after another defeat was incurred in December 1910:

> Organisation is regarded as being beneath the dignity of our Leader. It is as though commissariat were beneath the dignity of a General. Everyone learnt from the last election that Manchester Conservatism was in an unspeakable condition. What has been done to put things right in a city which would inevitably be the pivot of the next plot? Nothing. . . . Take the state of Bradford, where a single individual is allowed to block the way; of Leeds, where no candidates were selected until the eleventh hour. The state of affairs in London is an open and notorious scandal, but no practical steps are taken to abate it. Why is thusness? Simply because our Leader is not a practical man and takes no interest in practical affairs, which accordingly drift into inferior hands.[50]

In December 1910 the pressure could be resisted no longer. All the Unionist papers carried editorials that spoke of the party organization with contempt, and all printed letters calling for sackings. At last the other leaders of the party moved to bring Balfour into line. On 17 December Lansdowne warned Balfour that 'I hear bitter complaints of the Central Office, and I anticipate a demand for further changes.' The final spur was a meeting at Hatfield attended by Salisbury, Derby, Curzon, Hugh Cecil and others. Derby wrote to Balfour on 19 December and Curzon delivered an ultimatum from the meeting in the form of a demand for a high-powered committee to investigate and reform the whole organization. With the Hotel Cecil itself in revolt, Balfour could only give way.[51]

Negotiations continued over Christmas and the New Year, with the 'old gang' trying to defuse the attack and the reformers pressing their case. So Sandars told Balfour on 25 December that

> I should be sorry if any well-intentioned actions were construed by Alick and Hughes as tantamount to putting them on trial for inefficiency or incapacity. For this reason I think we should persuade rather than coerce our present organizers at headquarters, and if possible associate them directly with the investigation.[52]

Acland-Hood tried to head off the enquiry by putting the blame on the National Union and by changing some of his junior Whips but the pressure could not be diverted. The original plan was for Curzon himself to head the enquiry but he was too much involved in drawing up plans to reform the House of Lords, and he was replaced by Akers-Douglas, Acland-Hoods predecessor as Chief Whip. The *Morning Post* broke the news of the enquiry on 14 January 1911 and Acland-Hood then claimed that he had himself suggested the idea. The appointment of the Unionist Organization Committee was finally announced on 1 February, with nine members chosen to represent all branches of the party:[53]

1. Aretas Akers-Douglas (ex-Chief Whip), Chairman.
2. Edward Goulding (Tariff Reform League).
3. Walter Long (Union Defence League; Budget Protest League).
4. Sutton Nelthorpe (National Union Lincolnshire Area Chairman).
5. Archibald Salvidge (Liverpool).
6. Lord Selborne (diehard Peer, ex-Liberal Unionist Chief Whip).
7. Arthur Steel-Maitland (Birmingham).
8. Lord Willoughby de Broke (Reveille; Confederacy; Halsbury Club).
9. George Younger (Scottish Whip).
10. Ralph Glyn MP, Secretary.

The committee was generally welcomed and criticism centred only on the time that had been taken in setting it up and on the choice of Akers-Douglas, who might be too soft on his ex-colleagues. The *National Review* regarded it as a mere charade, intended to buy time, and the *Morning Post* warned the committee to remember the urgency of their task: 'There seems to be some danger of the Committee developing into a sort of Royal Commission and mapping out for itself a plan of operation which must involve the expenditure of more time than any of the nine members would deem necessary.'[54]

The UOC met for the first time on 14 February and proceeded to act exactly like a Royal Commission. It met in formal sessions, occupied an office with paid staff, printed its evidence and reports, and finally sent its findings to Balfour in a style reminiscent of royal protocol. But it was not at all like a Royal Commission in the urgency with which it tackled its work. Most of its witnesses were seen before the end of March and an Interim Report which dealt with urgent problems and the central structures was in Balfour's hands early in April. Thereafter, the UOC was split into smaller groups which travelled the country to take evidence on the local parties. The *Morning Post* noted the existence of the Interim Report early in May and wondered 'whether anything will result from it'. By early June, the press had a good idea what was being suggested, but the diehards had almost given up hope:

> The Interim Report – the "real part of our work" as a member of Committee described it – has, so far, produced no result. The fact of the inquiry, still more the presentation of the Interim Report, has naturally tended to a suspension of activity at headquarters – at the best it could not conduce to an expansion of zeal. Party organisers in London are anxiously waiting for some indication that the Interim Report is either to be permanently pigeon-holed or acted upon. The present state of suspense is in every way bad; and it is hoped that Mr. Balfour will soon make up his mind, and when he has made it up will act without delay.[55]

Balfour was heavily occupied in May and June of 1911 with the future of the House of Lords, but the UOC reports presented him with some difficult decisions.

The UOC had concentrated on structures rather than personnel, but they had prefaced each section of their reports with trenchant criticism of existing systems. Publication or implementation of the reports would thus endorse these criticisms, which is exactly what Balfour had hoped to avoid. This difficulty was exacerbated by their actual recommendations, the chief of which were as follows:

1. Two new posts should be created so that the direction of the party organization would become tripartite. The Chief Whip would continue to look after the House of Commons; a 'Party Treasurer' would raise money; a 'Chairman of the Party' would take over Central Office and the party outside parliament. This last would need to be 'of Cabinet rank' so that he could deal with National Union leaders on equal terms.
2. Central Office and the National Union office should be merged and the close relations of the two organizations, interrupted in 1906, should be resumed. Central Office should use the National Union as sounding board, but only Central Office would have executive authority.
3. The accommodation of Central Office should be improved and the new Chairman should have a free hand as to its staffing.
4. There should be co-ordination between the Whips and Central Office. Each Whip should supervise an area corresponding to a Central Office Area and a National Union Provincial Division. Scotland should remain separate, with a Scottish Whip occupying a position much like that of the Party Chairman.
5. There would need to be a wholesale improvement of the methods of the local parties, a transition to permanent organization and a more active concern with propaganda. Agents should be trained and should be

encouraged to regard themselves as a profession.
6. The amalgamation of Conservative and Liberal Unionists would not yet be possible.[56]

Taken as a whole, these recommendations undoubtedly strengthened the position of the party leader, for they confirmed his control over the organization through directly nominated subordinates, increased the flow of information to him on opinion in the party at large, and removed once and for all the encroachments of the National Union.[57] But in the short term they would involve another source of friction when tempers were high and would necessitate the removal of Balfour's most loyal supporters from their posts. Acland-Hood could not stay on; Percival Hughes did not have the status for the proposed office of chairman, and it would be difficult to appoint a shadow cabinet colleague to the post in the conditions of 1911 without creating a rival for the leadership itself. Balfour was thus forced to do exactly what he had wished to avoid: he would have to sack Acland-Hood, he would have at least to demote Hughes, and he would have to rely on the new chairman rather than on Sandars as his channel of communication with the party. The delay was no doubt at least partly due to Balfour's wish to evade or soften this outcome. By mid June, he had found his means of escape: Acland-Hood would be made a peer in the Coronation Honours List – a rare chance for the opposition leader to join in recommending for honours – and so he would have to resign his seat in the Commons and his post as Chief Whip. At last the reorganization of the party could go ahead.

The internal workings of the UOC are not easy to trace, for little internal correspondence has survived. However, an index of evidence has survived in print, listing all the witnesses and summarizing their evidence. This is enough to refute the charges later made by Jack Sandars, himself one of the men whose influence was most severely curtailed by the committee's work. Writing much later, he claimed that there had been an 'envenomed intrigue' against the Chief Whip' by his enemies.

> There was no mistaking the temper and complexion of the Committee. Steel-Maitland had done his lobbying, and Goulding had perfected his subterranean plot, with the result that the distracted Chairman had to present a Report that sealed the fate of Hood and the Chief Agent.[58]

Goulding and Steel-Maitland certainly took an active part in the work of the UOC,[59] but the main recommendations of the committee were not suggested by either of them. Akers-Douglas told Balfour on 8 June that they had decided to accept 'Selborne's plan'; he gave no hint that he was 'distracted' by the outcome, but it is in any case unlikely that the two most junior members of the committee could have carried it along against its will.[60] In any case, the evidence presented to the UOC more than justified their criticisms of existing methods. Sandars himself had been providing Balfour with highly unflattering pictures of Acland-Hood and Hughes at work; the only dispute was whether men who were admitted to be unsuitable for their posts should be removed from them, and on this point the committee made no direct comment.

Acland-Hood's peerage was announced on 19 June 1911 and he was replaced as Chief Whip by Lord Balcarres – a choice that was popular with the parliamentary party.[61] There was less obvious agreement though on the choice of a Party Chairman, for at least three members of the UOC may well have been thinking of themselves as appropriate for the post. Balfour had to resort to a transparent ruse to deflect the opposition of Walter Long when he finally decided to appoint another member, Steel-Maitland. Steel-Maitland was very young for such responsibility and appointing him would involve promoting him to the shadow cabinet rather than appointing as Chairman an existing member. He was only thirty-five in 1911, had been Milner's secretary in South Africa and was now a Birmingham MP; this made him acceptable enough to Liberal Unionists, tariff reformers and imperialists, but it also meant that his appointment was bound to antagonize the English country gentlemen for whom Long spoke. After long consultations, Balfour informed Long just as he was leaving for his constituency and the furious response was written at Paddington while Long awaited his train: '5 minutes to answer such a tremendous question! Can you wait for a letter I will write on train and send? I like the man, can however say little of his qualifications for such great promotion. It will of course be said that you are handing the party over to Birmingham! This is really serious.'[62] On the following day, when Balfour wrote in full to justify his choice, the news was in the press, so Long's objections were too late to be effective. Balfour had a very different view of the appointment from that of Long. The post of 'Chairman of the Party' had now become 'Chairman of the Party Organization', the fact that he was of cabinet rank could not be made known, and Balfour regarded Steel-Maitland's inexperience as a positive advantage:

> He must be able, energetic, with a capacity for organization and a love of it; he must be in Parliament; he must not be in the House of Lords; he must be independent as regards money; he must be able to devote his whole time to the work and he must have a great ambition to carry things through. S.M. has all these qualifications. I have been hunting for a year or more to find *anybody else* who has, and have quite failed in the attempt. I do not think you need be at all afraid of any attempt on the part of S.M. to exercise undue authority in the way you fear. His junior position in the Party will make this impossible.[63]

So Steel-Maitland became Party Chairman and took over Central Office on 26 June, but Balfour had certainly underestimated him. By the autumn Steel-Maitland had successfully pressed Balfour to make it known that he was of cabinet rank, since this addition to his status would help in overcoming resistance to his reforms; he was in any case attending meetings of the shadow cabinet from his appointment. The changes were completed by the appointment of Lord Farquhar as party treasurer; Balcarres, Steel-Maitland and Farquhar now set about putting the work of the UOC into practice.

Implementation of the UOC proposals required careful handling of the National Union, whose role was to be reduced and which might therefore be expected to resist. Curzon was used to announce what was intended at a National Union dinner in July, when he explained that 'nothing would be done to impair the credit of the National Union'.[64] Balfour also used Sandars as an intermediary and a great deal of lobbying had to be done to square influential people before the matter was settled.[65] Balfour recommended the changed system to the Central Council of the National Union on 21 July and they voted to accept it in principle. The proposals were finally accepted in detail and new rules adopted in October and November, only a few days before Balfour's own resignation. The only occasion of real dispute was the suggestion that the county associations should be re-merged into provincial divisions to correspond with Central Office and Whips' areas. This sensible scheme was deemed to be an unwarrantable intrusion into local autonomy and had to be abandoned; instead the shape, and indeed the existence, of the provincial divisions was left for local decision. In some areas the amalgamations took place as suggested, in some they were delayed, and in some they did not take place at all; it was not until the next great shake-up took place in 1930 that a uniform system of area organization could be re-established. Local autonomy once granted could not be revoked. With this single exception though, the National Union surrendered all its gains of 1906. It had been obvious enough that the division of responsibilities had been disastrous, and it was clear even to the National Union that executive action could not be adequately supervised by committee. Henceforth literature was discussed in detail by the Literature Committee, but the actual publication was done by Central Office. The reunion was no doubt assisted by the fact that Central Office was now under a tariff reformer from Birmingham rather than a Balfourite. As Party Chairman, Steel-Maitland became *ex-officio* chairman of the National Union Executive Committee and the Principal Agent was again appointed honorary secretary, so restoring the close collaboration that had proved its worth between 1870 and 1903.[66]

The reorganization of 1911, coming in unpromising circumstances and at the nadir of the party's fortunes, may be taken as the beginning of the climb back to power, but it also marked important long-term advances. Henceforth the new approach to organization was given free rein and the local parties were given every encouragement to modernize themselves. In the Party Chairmanship, the UOC created a vital pivot in the party and Steel-Maitland proceeded to make the post into the one that the committee had envisaged rather than the one to which Balfour had appointed him. He summed up the new approach when he told a meeting of agents, soon after his appointment, that the party now had three priorities: 'In the first place we must organize, in the second place we must organize, and in the third place we must organize.'[67]

Notes and References

1 Sandars to Balfour, 18 Mar. 1910: Balfour MSS, Add. MSS 49766.
2 Amery to Law, 16 Dec. 1910: Law MSS 18/6/146.
3 National Society of Conservative Agents, Minutes of A.G.M., 14 Feb. 1907.
4 Sandars to Balfour, 25 Dec. 1910: Balfour MSS, Add. MSS 49767.
5 Steel-Maitland to Balfour, 5 Nov. 1911: Steel-Maitland MSS GD 193/108/3.
6 Amery to Law, 16 Dec. 1910: Law MSS 18/6/146.
7 Steel-Maitland to Balfour, 5 Nov. 1911: Steel-Maitland MSS GD 193/108/3.
8 Amery to Law, 16 Dec. 1910: Law MSS 18/6/146.
9 Memorandum by Steel-Maitland for Law, Dec. 1911: Steel-Maitland MSS, GD 193/108/3.
10 *Ibid.*
11 *Ibid.*
12 *Ibid.*
13 *The Times*, 16, 23 and 30 Jan. 1911.
14 Salvidge, *Salvidge of Liverpool*, 106; Clarke, *Lancashire and the New Liberalism*, 48–9.
15 *The Times*, 30 Jan. 1911.
16 Ostrogorski, *Democracy*, i, 352.
17 *Ibid.*, i, 336.
18 Ramsden, 'Organisation' (Thesis), 161.
19 *Ibid*, 162.
20 See Curzon's introduction to *The Primrose League Election Guide*, 1914, 3–6.
21 Ostrogorski, *Democracy*, i, 440.
22 *Ibid*, i, 546.
23 McKenzie and Silver, *Angels in marble*, 241.
24 A. H. Birch, *Small Town Politics*, 1959, 45–8; Autobiographical memorandum of Samuel Roberts M.P. (Roberts's father was Unionist candidate for High Peak.)
25 Ramsden, 'Organisation' 166–7; *Hitchin Conservative Gazette*, Sept. 1909.
26 Lord Bayford found in 1933 that the ACC still had over 1,500 affiliated clubs and a total membership of over half a million; Sanders Diary, 31 July 1933.
27 *Brighton Herald*, 9 Feb. 1907, quoted in Grace Jones, 'National and local issues' (thesis), Ch. 4.
28 This document circulated in the party after the defeat of 1906. Judging from the style and the fact that it was typed and duplicated in an agency in Oxford, it was probably written by W. J. Joel. Joel was the agent for Oxford and one of the most advanced of the agents, a regular contributor to the *Conservative Agents' Journal*.
29 *Unionist Organisation Committee*, Index of Evidence, 24, 30, 36.
30 Quoted in Grace Jones, 'National and local issues', Ch. 4.
31 *The Tory* (intermittent in the 1890s) and the *Conservative Agents' Journal* (founded in 1902 but ceased publication in 1904.)

32   Ramsden, 'Organisation', 315.
33   Jones, 'National and local issues', Ch. 5.
34   Quoted in the *Conservative Agents' Journal*, Oct. 1909.
35   In Sheffield, the proportion of lawyers among all office-holders in Unionist organizations in the city fell from 35 per cent in 1900–08 to 25 per cent in 1909–18 and to 8 per cent in 1919–31. In Scotland, especially in Edinburgh and the eastern area, lawyers continued to predominate; Urwin, 'Politics and the development of the Unionist Party in Scotland' (thesis), Ch. 6.
36   Memorandum by Steel-Maitland for Law, Dec. 1911: Steel-Maitland MSS GD 193/108/3.
37   As these claims were usually published in the local press after being presented to AGMs of the respective associations, they cannot be unduly optimistic; Ramsden, 'Organisation', 21.
38   A. K. Russell, 'Laying the charges for the landslide' in Morris, *Edwardian Radicalism*, 62–73.
39   Abingdon Conservative Association, Minutes 27 Apr. 1911.
40   Butler and Freeman, *British Political Facts*, 155.
41   Robert Stewart, *History of the Conservative Party*, i., 166.
42   Jones, 'National and local issues', Ch. 2.
43   *Ibid*.
44   *Memorandum on Electoral Organisation*, 1906 (see note 28 above.)
45   Blewett, *Peers, parties and People*, 272.
46   McKibbin, Matthew and Kay, 'The franchise factor', 747–8; Young, *Local Politics*, 93–5.
47   Ramsden, 'Organisation', 231–2.
48   See page 303 below.
49   *National Review*, Oct. 1910.
50   *Ibid*, Jan. 1911.
51   Ramsden, 'Organisation', 25.
52   Sandars to Balfour, 25 Dec. 1910: Balfour MSS, Add. MSS 49767.
53   Ramsden, 'Organisation', 26–7. The comments on the qualifications of members of the committee are drawn from the reports of *The Times* and *Morning Post*, which coincide so closely as to suggest a common source in a press briefing, and from the *Conservative Agents' Journal*.
54   *Morning Post*, 14 Feb. 1911.
55   *Morning Post*, 3 and 25 May 1911; *The Times*, 18 May and 1 June 1911.
56   *Unionist Organisation Committee*, Interim and Final Reports, April and June 1911.
57   R. B. Jones, 'Balfour's reform of party organisation', 101.
58   J. S. Sandars, *Studies of Yesterday*, 167–8, quoted in Chilston, *Chief Whip*, 350.
59   See for example Sutton Nelthorpe to Steel-Maitland, 6 June 1911: Steel-Maitland MSS GD 193/151/1.
60   Akers-Douglas to Balfour, 8 June 1911: Balfour MSS, Add. MSS, 49772.
61   Sanders Diary, 20 June 1911.
62   Long to Balfour, 1 June 1911: Balfour MSS, Add. MSS 49777.
63   Balfour to Long, 2 June 1911: Balfour MSS, Add. MSS 49777.
64   *The Times*, 6 July 1911.
65   Sandars to Balfour, 30 June 1911: Balfour MSS, Add. MSS 49767.
66   Ramsden, 'Organisation', 112; National Union Executive Committee, Minutes 15 March and 14 June 1912.
67   *The Times*, 8 July 1911.

Chapter 4

Revival under Law, 1911–1914

Few contemporaries would have expected Balfour's retirement to lead to a Unionist recovery. The party was in a mutinous condition in November 1911 and there was no apparent successor who would have even half of Balfour's political gifts. Nor was it clear that Balfour's departure was universally desired: at the National Union Conference a few days later, Leo Maxse was booed off the platform, and constituency parties everywhere passed resolutions regretting Balfour's decision. A great many crocodile tears were shed, for, since Unionists had such an elevated view of the principle of leadership, they were unable to accept that they had just driven their own leader from office. The shock caused by Balfour's going thus did something to steady the party and it certainly produced a real determination to settle the affairs of the party with less friction than had been fashionable of late.

The main contenders for the leadership were Austen Chamberlain and Walter Long, representing the two different establishments of the Edwardian Unionist party – the opposite worlds of Birmingham and Wiltshire – but the situation was complicated by the intervention of two outsiders, Edward Carson and Andrew Bonar Law. Two strong groups emerged behind Long and Chamberlain, about equal in numbers, but there were few backers for Carson or Law. Carson thereupon fell out of the contest – or rather announced that he was not standing, for no official nominations had been made. The party officers and Whips were solidly behind Chamberlain, but Law drew off some of his support among tariff reformers and, urged on by Edward Goulding and Max Aitken, he refused to withdraw unless his continued candidature would allow Long to win. Against Chamberlain it was remembered that he was a Liberal Unionist (as was Lansdowne, who led the Unionists in the Lords) and that he had not been entirely loyal to Balfour since the referendum pledge. Long was supported by the bulk of the English county members but by few of the party's men of talent. By the morning of Friday 10 November it was clear that neither Chamberlain nor Long would secure a majority and that some supporters of each of them would not contentedly follow the other.[1] A party meeting was to be held on the following Monday and the Whips were making preparation for a vote to be taken. Chamberlain provided the way out by suggesting to Balcarres that both he and Long should withdraw and so allow Law to be elected unanimously; he also turned down

Balcarres's remarkable advice that he should allow Long to be elected since Long would make such a mess of things that Chamberlain would be bound to succeed within the year. Faced with Chamberlain's proposition, and without a majority of his own, Long had no option but to agree. Bonar Law, backed by fewer MPs than any of the other three contenders at the beginning of the week was now to be the unanimous choice.[2] Robert Sanders reported the 'election' meeting on 13 November with evident satisfaction:

> The Carlton meeting on Monday went off quite admirably. Harry Chaplin in the chair a very great success. A good many men came into the room by no means inclined to acquiesce in the proposed arrangement. Walter Long proposed Bonar Law. His speech was one of the best things I have heard. Manly and rather touching. The country gentleman at his best. He spoke and evidently felt strongly of the degradation that it would have been to the party to have elected a leader by secret ballot. Austen followed. . . . When Austen sat down Chaplin suggested that he had better put the question at once and on getting an affirmative shout did so. A clever way of stifling discussion and few could have done it so well. Motion carried unanimously. Bonar Law then sent for. . . . His speech struck me as the feeblest of the day. He was evidently moved and nervous. The meeting separated in great content with the Conservative Party all round. It was certainly creditable.[3]

The urgency of the events following Balfour's resignation was due to the need to find a new leader before the National Union Conference. So within a few days of his grudging acceptance by his parliamentary colleagues, Law's leadership was ratified by the throng of party notables at Leeds; here he received a reception more typical of what was to come in the future.

In 1911 Law was known – in so far as he was known at all in the parliamentary party – as a spirited debater. A. J. P. Taylor has noted that Law was trained, if he was trained for anything in his early career, to be a debater. In Glasgow he had picked up many of the skills that a more highly-born politician might have acquired in the Oxford Union or at the Bar, but skills that were very different in appearance.[4] His concern was solely with effectiveness rather than style; he rarely spoke with more than brief notes and left it to the occasion to furnish the words. (When he became Chancellor of the Exchequer this practice caused consternation at the Treasury, when he used only a page of notes to assist him in moving complicated resolutions on wartime finance; he relied successfully on his memory to provide details and figures.) As an extempore speaker he was able to tailor his words to his audience's reactions and so convey the impression of personal conversation even when addressing thousands. In parliament he was wont to abandon an argument half-completed if he sensed that his point had been made; the speeches that appear in *Hansard* were touched up by his staff, and his speeches in the country were given to the press in advance.[5] In debate he was a formidable opponent, and one that Asquith was never able to master, for all his forensic skills. Again Law succeeded by unorthodoxy; he was quick to grasp the essentials of an opponent's argument and quite prepared to be rude or direct if the situation demanded it. In the long debates over Marconi in 1913 and over the Curragh 'mutiny' in 1914 Law was able to nail Asquith's evasions where a more polished stylist might have been foiled. Occasionally, in the onrush of pursuit, he gave commitments that were later regretted, but these were a small price to pay.[6]

The Unionist recovery was built around Law's leadership, but what Asquith called the 'new style' of obstruction, threats and offensive behaviour did not originate with Law. The beginnings are to be found in the diehard campaign against the Parliament Bill. It was in June 1911 that the first scenes of disorder were mounted in the House of Commons, led by Lord Hugh Cecil. In August 1911 the diehard peers used language as violent as any that Law was to use later, and in the crucial decision on the House of Lords Law sided with the hedgers rather than the ditchers. Ulster's opposition to Home Rule long pre-dated Law's leadership and he had rarely even spoken on Irish affairs in parliament before becoming leader.[7] Before he succeeded Balfour then, Law was not associated with any of the features that were to characterize his party leadership; his contribution was to use the leadership in the service of all of these causes, to make himself the spokesman for the most spirited sections of the party.

Law conceived of the role of the leader in an exactly opposite sense from Balfour: he sought to foster unity by placing himself at the head of the discordant elements where Balfour had thrown the leadership on the side of restraint. Their respective positions explain this in part: as ex-Prime Minister and a considerable figure in his own right, Balfour had the confidence to believe in his own judgement even when isolated from the bulk of the party; as the *tertium quid* in the recent contest, Law had neither the weight nor the confidence to take such a detached view. His strategy was rather to canalize the enthusiasm of the diehards into party channels, to articulate their views, and to create unity from the sense of movement. In his characteristic phrase, 'I am their leader, I must follow them' – but he determined to follow them from the front. As a result of this he was labelled as a diehard and a bigot, when he actually distrusted the diehards and was himself distrusted by the bigots. Much of his leadership was thus a form of pragmatic extremism, extreme action and the threat of more extreme action to come, but used in the cause of more limited objectives. He certainly held deep convictions as to the absolute wrongness of the Liberal policies that he opposed, but at least a part of his apparent hostility was assumed for the occasion, a hard line that might secure a better compromise in the end. So in his first major speech as leader in parliament he wasted little time on the customary compliments and warned the government that he intended to play hard. In private conversation he told Asquith 'I am afraid that I shall have to show myself very vicious Mr Asquith this session. I hope you will understand.' In later conversations about Ulster, Law was frank enough to point out that bloodshed in Ulster would be the best way of ensuring an electoral landslide for the Unionists.[8] There was then an open toughness about party tactics; before the Buckingham Palace Conference in 1914 he had Central Office work out the electoral effects of excluding nine, six or four counties of Ulster from an independent Ireland – the concern of a calculating pragmatist not of a bigot.[9] From the party viewpoint Law's methods were successful but dangerous; expectations raised when the party was in full cry were not easily set aside for an eventual compromise, and the only outcome that would fully vindicate the methods was the recovery of power.

The basis of recovery was then Law's fighting capacities as leader. In parliament there would be a carefully organized campaign of resistance that would at least slow the government down and raise Unionist morale. Improved morale would also make possible organizational advances outside parliament, all linked to the issue of Ulster, and with the sights fixed firmly on the next election, an election that would make or break the Union, the Empire, and Law's leadership of the party. All was linked to the sense of a new departure, a 'new style', a 'new regime in politics' and a new team at the helm: as well as a new leader, the party had by the middle of 1912 a new Chief Whip, Party Chairman, party treasurer, principal agent, press adviser, and an almost entirely new team of Whips and organizers.

Party organization provided the easiest advances because it was the only area entirely under the party's control. No general election was fought by the organization set up after 1911, but there is little doubt that there was a massive improvement; criticisms that were commonplace in 1910 were not to be heard by 1913. The space available to Central Office was increased by the acquisition of St Stephen's House as well as St Stephen's Chambers, which had been occupied since 1874; the new office cost £3,000 a year in rent alone. The quality of the senior staff was improved by the appointment of three specialists. John Boraston took over as Principal Agent in 1912, having been a professional organizer all his career and latterly chief agent to the Liberal Unionist Council. He joined William Jenkins, appointed chief organizing agent in 1911 and previously district agent for the Midlands Liberal Unionists. The party was indeed handed over to Birmingham. Finally, Malcolm Fraser, ex-editor of the *Standard* and of the *Daily Express* became first honorary press adviser and subsequently was employed to run the press bureau at the colossal salary of £1,200. Steel-Maitland, Boraston, Jenkins and Fraser made up a team of experts, all of sufficient status to deal with politicians who might call into the office; the work of the office was departmentalized for the first time and the heads of department brought together into a supervising board.[10] The influence of Central Office toned up the rest of the organization. A new canvass system was introduced in 1911 so that all county constituencies would operate the same system and so that duplicate records could be kept at area level. This was important at a time when outvoters were a larger group in many constituencies than the size of the majority and when the outvoters were overwhelmingly Unionist. In 1914 a register of car owners was compiled, also important when some voters could cast several votes in an election when polling went several days. By November 1912 only fifty-one constituencies in Great Britain were without candidates, a much better position than the position at dissolution in either 1909 or 1910; few of these fifty-one constituencies were winnable, but in any case most of them had candidates by the end of 1913. A programme of speakers for a general election was also ready by 1913, with both constituencies and politicians told in advance what they might expect. The financial mismanagement that had reigned before 1911 was ended with the employment of professional accountants.[11]

Expenditure on Central Office, district offices and the London office doubled from £32,466 in 1909–10 to £68,957 in 1913–14; the total expenditure of the party organization from central funds also doubled from £73,000 to over £150,000. To pay for this outpouring, a great drive was mounted for additional income by Farquhar and Steel-Maitland. In 1912 ordinary subscriptions still brought in only £12,000 a year and it proved difficult to raise them to anything like what was needed. The method adopted was to canvass for capital donations that could then be invested to bring in a regular income, and both Balfour and Law were used to raise the wind. Steel-Maitland told Balfour that 'Farquhar and I are endeavouring to raise more money. I think we are likely to succeed – thanks in part to the *very* generous example set by Lord Rothschild. But I would be very glad if I might see you on your return to ask you to help me in two cases.' Systematic collections were made from peers and from the City; by the outbreak of war the invested funds amounted to £671,000 – twice the sum in 1911 and worth four years' expenditure – and there was a special cash deposit of £120,000 for the coming election.[12]

In three other areas, as much political as organizational, advances were made towards the management of the press, the coordination of the heterogeneous collection that made up the party, and the fostering of modern attitudes in the local parties. Under Malcolm Fraser the party began to make effective use of its support in Fleet Street. It had been recognized that Liberals had been more adept at handling the press because they were more ready to stoop to newspaper practices, as Sandars had reported in 1909:

> I told Northcliffe that if his people would make enquiries at our Central Office, he would find that our nightly regiment of speakers was at least as well worth reporting as the Radical contingent, but that I realized that from the Press point of view, no doubt, our speakers did not play up to the reporters by handing them their speeches in advance, and by other tricks of the kind to which the Radical orators have recourse.[13]

This was the essence of the problem: the press could only be managed by someone who knew their methods and who would not expect them to come round to Central Office to search for news. The UOC found that 'it is patent that some feeling exists among the Unionist Press that, while in the past they have done much for the Party, the Party has not assisted in their work. In many quarters it is asserted that the Unionist Press are treated with greater courtesy by the Radicals than by their own side.'[14] Fraser dealt with this problem without difficulty and explained to Law in 1913 that 'the importance of getting important speeches in advance is shown in concrete manner by your Wallsend speech on October 29th. The verbatim reports reached most of the newspapers in places such as Aberdeen at one o'clock in the morning of the 30th.' He went on to quote the response that had been received from editors:

> *Manchester Dispatch:* I hope you will continue this form of enterprise. You fully know as an old pressman the difficulty of dealing with a big speech late at night . . .

> *Daily Express:* I am much obliged to you for the precis of Mr Bonar Law's speech last night. It was a great help to us. The speech came over the wires so late and the sheets were so confused by the Post Office – which is usual in these cases – that without the precis we could not possibly have got the leader through in time for the first edition.[15]

So in the supply of information to newspapers predisposed to support the party, much was achieved merely by employing a specialist. The other side of press management, depending on informal contacts, is less easy to assess. In 1911 Steel-Maitland invited Blumenfeld of the *Daily Express* to Central Office for a two-way exchange of ideas and advice. He also used Law himself to impress editors who were on less familiar terms with Fraser, as with Marlowe of the *Daily Mail*, and Law took a direct interest in negotiations with the most difficult of all the Unionist editors, J. L. Garvin of the *Observer*. Law personally conducted the negotiations with Gardner Sinclair over the sale of the *Observer* and the *Pall Mall Gazette* in 1914; this negotiation also demonstrates that, as well as producing information and nursing editors, the party had to work hard to keep some of the newspapers in business. Sinclair did buy the *Observer* and the *Pall Mall* in the end, but not before he had been given a £45,000 guarantee from party funds. Such investments had a double purpose, for they could bring in income and provide a political bonus. One such scheme involved the purchase of the *Daily Express* by Max Aitken with party funds, but the party was also propping up the *Globe*, the *Standard*, and a wide range of provincial dailies. All these transactions were secret, for there would be little use in keeping a paper alive if it were known to be owned by a political party. The papers were therefore bought through nominees or bank loans backed with party capital.

It was usual to extract some form of guarantee in exchange for party support but the secrecy prevented such undertakings from being enforced. Sinclair thus gave an undertaking that his papers would always remain Unionist, but Steel-Maitland doubted if such a promise had any value. The later history of the *Daily Express* suggests not: when the *Express* became hostile in the 1920s, Younger raged 'when I think of the large sum of money this office has put into that gutter print it makes my blood boil'. The justification for pouring out large sums without a certain return was the even greater cost of any real alternative. The support for the *Express* in 1912 'provides for the introduction of £50,000 or £60,000 to retain the only half-penny paper the Party possesses in London, and no less a sum than £700,000 to £1,000,000 would be necessary to start a similar paper if the *Daily Express* were allowed to go.' The struggle therefore went on to keep the Unionist press alive, and in 1912 and 1913 both Aitken and Northcliffe stood by the party and gave valuable support in their papers.[16]

The coordination of competing party bodies was carried out with surprising ease. The National Union was merged with Central Office in 1911 and fusion with the Liberal Unionists followed in 1912. Joseph Chamberlain retained his preference for independence but allowed himself to be overruled by Austen and by the overwhelming wishes of the Liberal Unionist Council to merge.[17] To cater for all susceptibilities, the party became the 'National Unionist Association of Conservative and Unionist Associations' – a decision that allowed some local parties to go on calling themselves Conservative, but the name 'Liberal' was at last dropped. The Liberal Unionists were admitted to the Carlton Club and a longstanding source of tension was eradicated. This was in itself a striking commentary on what had already been done: Liberal Unionists who had resisted amalgamation under Balfour and Acland-Hood in 1911 acquiesced meekly under Law and Steel-Maitland in 1912.

Other organizations could not be absorbed but could still be brought within the Central Office orbit. So in 1911 Steel-Maitland offered to join the Halsbury Club in order to guide it on to safer lines – and was immediately accused of disloyalty by Walter Long. Long helped though by placing both Steel-Maitland and Boraston on the Executive Committee of the Union Defence League for the same purpose.[18] Steel-Maitland also explained to Lord Robert Cecil that 'it has been arranged that the National Conservative Union should send out leaflets produced by several of the ancillary organizations, such as the Tariff Reform League, the Anti-Socialist Union, the Primrose League, the London Municipal Society etc.'[19] The Central Office attitude was flexible, for outside bodies would always exist and could even be made use of:

> They represent a time when either their objects were not the same as those of the official organization, or the CCO was not enterprising enough to suit them. But some caution should be observed. It may be wise, while retaining or regaining control, to trade under different names. In some cases additional subscriptions may be obtained, in others full responsibility may be avoided.[20]

With open allies like the Primrose League, the case for collaboration was strong; for the first time in thirty years of existence the Primrose League formally linked itself with the party in 1914.[21] On the other hand, the independence of the Tariff Reform League was a positive advantage: after January 1913 the party supported the tariff policy but was not including them in its immediate programme, so that Central Office could continue to distribute tariff propaganda from the TRL without compromising party policy. In general, efforts to ensure better coordination were a matter of the patient building up of contacts, although the improved party morale and the greater efficiency of Central Office had removed their justification for existence. It was the First World War that finally killed off the 'legion of Leagues', but it had ceased to be a problem before 1914.

Modernization at the local level was also a matter of patience:

> The difficulty of all this work is trebled through the fact that the Office cannot say 'go and he goes, and come and he comes' as in a factory. It is always 'by your leave and if you please', and the influence in controlling, which might be very great . . . is only exerted through position, knowledge and willingness to help.'[22]

Steel-Maitland's method was the systematic collection of information by the Central Office district agents in constituency books that recorded all income, expenditure and political activity. The National Union and the Whips were used when necessary to exert pressure for reform, but the main influence was the Central Office agents:

> I propose to make proper local centres of the Central Office Agents. If they are to get full influence for the purpose of bringing constituencies up to the mark, they can only get it by being the channels for help. I propose therefore that speakers in a locality should be supplied by the Agent in charge of it; and that grants of literature and money to organizations be made through them.[23]

By 1913–14, over £25,000 was being given away in this manner and in return the Central Office agents were able to ensure the appointment of suitable constituency agents and the choice of good candidates. The outlay constituted only about a tenth of the whole of the local parties' expenditure, but a much higher proportion of the expenditure of the backward parties most in need of reform. The First World War interrupted the process, but it is clear that much had been done by 1914.

In the political world there were issues that Unionists could always exploit against a Liberal government such as defence policy and the administration of the Empire. The threatening international situation gave new impetus to demands for a larger navy and a conscript army, both taken up by Unionists. The National Service League ran the campaign for conscription and the Navy League the campaign for faster naval building, but both were led by known Unionists. In 1912 the Conference gave its support and condemned 'the criminal failure of H.M. Ministers to maintain the British Navy and the British Army at a standard of strength adequate to National and Imperial needs'. In the following year an even stronger resolution on the navy was passed unanimously, but a resolution calling for national service was conveniently not reached at the end of the order paper;[24] there was an undoubted commitment to a stronger army and navy but some doubt about the widsom of a party commitment to conscription in peacetime. In any case, all this helped to prepare for the militarist attitude that the party was to take when war came, when it could advocate conscription without any fear of the electoral consequences. Individual Unionists pursued the defence issues even more strongly than the leaders. Lord Charles Beresford continued his campaign against the Admiralty that had originated in his personal feud with Admiral Fisher, and he made the most of Churchill's unhappy relations with his admirals. The *Morning Post* joined in when the First Sea Lord, Sir Francis Bridgeman, resigned in 1912 and Bonar Law took up the issue too, suggesting that Bridgeman had been 'brutally ill-used' by Churchill.[25] The Secretary of State for War, John Seely, was also a favourite target, for he too was a renegade Unionist. In 1913 he came under pressure in the Commons for his failure to promote an air force; Samuel Hoare demonstrated the ineffectiveness of the government's policy by visiting the air bases to see them for himself.[26] Unionists had easy openings on defence issues, for many Unionist MPs were ex-officers, but the experience of the country in the first two years of War suggests that their criticisms were not exaggerated.

Defence was linked in the Unionist mind with imperial consolidation through tariffs: the new policy of 1901–2 had followed directly from the military weakness revealed by the Boer War and the approach of probable European conflict reinforced the same cause. The tariff reform camp had a bonus in 1911 from events in Canada: Laurier's Liberal government had negotiated a Reciprocity Agreement with the United States that cut across all of the arguments for imperial preference. Liberals saw this as evidence that the dominions were more interested in going their own way, but Unionists retorted that Canada like Britain had been led astray by a radical government and that Canada's decision was the result of Britain's failure to offer preference. Unionists were therefore beside themselves with joy when the Canadian electorate removed Laurier from office in September 1911 and replaced him with a Conservative, Sir Robert Borden, who now repudiated reciprocity. Unionist associations passed resolutions of support and the Unionist press hailed Borden as the hero who had saved the empire.[27] This boost did much to wipe out the effect of Balfour's referendum pledge, which had been made a month before the Reciprocity Agreement and was erroneously believed to be its cause.

It was now of the utmost importance for the Unionists to clarify their own position; Balfour's pledge had been a conditional one and was not in any case binding on his successor, but the unpopularity of food taxes remained. The shadow cabinet decided in April 1912 that it would abandon the referendum idea and return to the full tariff policy.[28] The decision was not an easy one and was criticized by many who feared the consequences, as Salisbury told Law: 'If it may be said to have finally made possible the destruction of the constitution, the prostitution of the Prerogative, the Repeal of the Union and the Disendowment of the Welsh Church, it will probably rank as the most costly policy in history.'[29] Salisbury was supported in his attitude by his brothers, by Curzon and by Selborne; he would certainly be supported by Derby and by the weight of opinion on Lancashire. The shadow cabinet therefore took its decision in the clear knowledge that it would have a fight on its hands, but it did so with the support of Lansdowne and Law. Replying to Salisbury, Law urged the positive side of the tariff policy for the economy and the danger of a party split if the referendum were *not* repudiated; there was a minority of free-traders, but there was also a vociferous majority of tariff reformers. The real reason though went deeper than tactical manoeuvring:

> I really believe, and it is here I think that I differ from you, that there is a great deal in Tariff Reform; and I believe also that there is a great deal even in the food part of it. I do not now allude to preference though of course that comes first. . . . In fact my real belief is that in the troubles ahead of us connected with labour we are moving very fast in the direction of revolution; and though you will consider my hope a baseless one I still entertain it – that it is by Tariff Reform that we might, so to speak, get the train at least shifted on to other lines.[30]

These two motivations are worth considering on their merits, for they reveal Bonar Law as a thinker of some insight.

The imperial preference aspect was important because it might arrest the trends pulling the Empire apart; reciprocity had shown the danger and there was little time left to halt the slide. In retrospect it may seem that the trend was already irresistible – the First World War certainly made it so – but who is to say that a positive imperial policy pursued energetically in 1902 or 1912 was inevitably doomed to failure? This was the pure gospel of Joseph Chamberlain, especially real to Law because of his Canadian connections, but the real significance of the decision was felt by few in Britain, even on the Unionist side. We can at least now see how important a policy it might have been, how great a shift in the tides of history that it was attempting. In the domestic sphere the policy was equally fundamental, for tariff reform was seen as the antithesis of socialism. The Bismarckian social policy implied by tariffs, the success of the policy in places like Birmingham where it was properly advocated, and its attraction to social engineers like the early Fabians, all lend a certain plausibility to the idea. If something drastic were not done, then British politics would drift into class antagonism such as could be observed in France.

The elections of 1906 and 1910 had shown the danger to the Unionist party from a Liberal–Labour alliance on class lines; the budget of 1909 had shown how far that alliance might threaten the social base on which Unionism itself rested; and the encroachments of the syndicalists suggested that there might be dangerous forces yet to be released. The only hope for a pessimist like Law was to 'get the train . . . on to other lines' – to focus the attention on the national unity of Britain rather than on internal divisions; in other words to emulate Germany rather than France. Again this hope seems set against the tides of history, but again we cannot be certain that a positive policy of Empire and tariffs could not have turned back the tide in 1902 or 1912. The infant Labour Party was just building its strength, but it was not yet capable of winning seats on its own, and it might have been checkmated for a generation by a positive social policy financed from tariffs. The tariff policy therefore carried with it the last hope of consolidating the Empire and the last hope of reversing the drift into class politics; as a pessimist, Law saw further ahead than most of his contemporaries, and events proved him to be more nearly right than they were.

In deference to the opposition within the party, the abandonment of the referendum was kept secret until Law had been able to consult with Borden, who of course insisted that tariffs without food taxes would be no value to Canada, but who also refused to make a public intervention in British politics.[31] Fortified by assurances that confirmed his own views, Law pressed ahead, and the Tariff Reform League was mobilized for another great campaign. Lansdowne announced the changed policy at an Albert Hall rally on 14 November 1912, and Law gave his support at Ashton-under-Lyne on 16 December. The only modification offered by Law in response to the outcry from Unionist free-traders was that food taxes would be imposed only if requested by the Dominions; after his talks with Borden, there was no doubt about this anyway.

By Christmas the party was in a furore, with the Cecils and Stanleys agitating against the new policy. Derby found a means of holding his leader to ransome: a meeting of Lancashire Unionists which threatened to disown the new policy was adjourned for three weeks at his suggestion. He protested to Law that he was doing everything possible to hold Lancashire steady, but he was actually doing all he could to keep the issue alive, including the sending of a questionnaire to all the Lancashire constituencies.[32] Law was thus besieged with demands that he should retreat to a compromise position as Balfour had done in 1910, and again these demands came from tariff reformers as well as free-traders. The leaders would now have to resign, to change their policy, or to see their policy rejected by Lancashire Unionists early in the new year. Both Lansdowne and Law opted to announce their resignation at a party meeting, which would revive the open warfare over tariffs that had existed before 1906, and this would ensure the defeat of all the other party causes too.

Long was now unwell and Austen Chamberlain could hardly become leader if Law had resigned over food taxes, so that there was no credible successor to Law. Law had indeed already done enough as leader to make his departure unthinkable and so a memorial was drawn up by Carson and signed by almost all the party's backbenchers, stating full confidence in Law and begging him to stay on with a revised tariff policy.[33] Lansdowne and Law could only accede with as good a grace as they could muster; the party was therefore committed to a full policy of imperial preference, but food taxes would be excluded unless approved by a second general election. Law was bound to give way but in doing so he sacrificed the only positive policy he had. Without food taxes, he would have nothing to offer the Dominions to induce concessions in return and it would be impossible to advocate the policy with the fervour that would alone enable it to challenge the distribution of wealth as the central political issue of the future. In the urge to protect itself for the negative battles of the present, the party thus pulled back from its only truly positive policy for the future. This dispute was the only major internal wrangle between Law's election and the war, but it illustrated the fragility of his achievement as a flash of lightning illuminates a landscape. Relations with Austen Chamberlain were never quite the same and although only a handful of MPs refused to sign the memorial they included personal friends of Law like Amery and Aitken.[34] The unity of the party survived and was even strengthened by the clearing of the air, but the crisis left a bitter taste.

Behind the scenes efforts were being made to broaden the party's appeal by strengthening its policies for social reform, the essential counterpoint to the theme of tariffs. This had been the intention of *The New Order* in 1908 and many of its contributors were enthusiastic backers of the Unionist Social Reform Committee when it was set up in 1911. This was always an unofficial research body, but it employed full-time staff, was housed at Central Office, and used the full machinery of party publicity to make itself known. This may have been due to the support of Steel-Maitland who was a founder member before he became Party Chairman and who later served on its committee on mental health. The purpose of the USRC was explained by its secretary to Lord Willoughby de Broke in August 1911: 'I still remain convinced as I have always been that unless you put yourself straight with the people on Social questions all your Tariff Reform, Home Rule or Constitutional thunderbolts will be discharged in vain. You have to establish your bona fides before you can be listened to.'[35] F. E. Smith was chairman of the new organization and announced its formation in a party magazine in the previous month; the range of subjects being investigated then included such diverse topics as police, aliens, asylums and railway clerks' compensation. The committee 'had secured the services of some of the best experts available' and had sent observers to examine social legislation abroad. 'By this means we hope to place at the disposal of our party in Parliament and in the country a trained body of fully formed critics, able not only to expose and correct the usual crudities of Radical–Socialist legislation, but to give form to a comprehensive policy of social reform.'[36] The USRC was therefore set up to play a role like that of the Conservative Research Department after 1929, but more unofficially.

The committee's main concerns reflected the interests of its keenest members: the law of aliens covered by Edward Goulding, the poor law covered by Jack Hills, and rural housing covered by Arthur Griffith-Boscawen. By 1914, Maurice Woods was able to announce that the committee had completed its immediate programme in every field but one and had therefore embarked on several secondary projects.[37] The most successful project was on housing, which was exploited by the USRC in parliament and by Central Office in its propaganda. Griffith-Boscawen introduced in 1912 a Bill to make improvement grants for rural housing, a proposal that provided a Unionist response to Lloyd George's Land

Campaign. Unionist MPs made much capital from the embarrassment of Liberals who had to vote the Bill down and from the ineffectiveness of John Burns, one of the weakest of the Liberal ministers. *Our Flag* covered the debates in detail and three leaflets were published, the last with the pithy legend 'The Housing Problem – Radicals block Unionist *Action*.[38] The aim of the USRC was to create just such an impression as Disraeli had done – that Unionist action would be worth more than Liberal words – and they often quoted him with pride.

The greatest difficulty for the USRC was within the party, for any commitment to a positive social policy would be resisted by those whose vested interests were threatened, as Robert Sanders noted over labourers' wages:

> George Kidner came to me in a great state of mind because he has been asked to appear before a committee consisting of C. Bathurst, Peto & C. Mills & sitting at Central Office. This committee suggested to him a policy that included a tribunal to fix the labourers' wages. Kidner much perturbed at such a suggestion. St. Audries actually wrote Bonar Law on the subject & got a reply saying the policy was quite unauthorised.[39]

The USRC therefore made only a limited impact; most of its members sat for industrial seats and its propaganda was concentrated there for their benefit. Bonar Law was prepared to make the right noises – in 1913 at Manchester he called for a positive social policy in Disraelian lines for 'the swing of the pendulum is not enough', but he would give no more active support.[40] The value of the USRC was thus of an indirect kind; by involving more than seventy MPs and peers in social research the Unionist belief that the party was a party of reform was re-established; it began the trend towards research for political action that was to accelerate after the war; and it affected much later policy by influencing those who were to make it. Baldwin, Steel-Maitland, Hills, Griffith-Boscawen, Ashley, Ormsby-Gore and Baird were all members of the USRC, and all ministers after 1922. When in 1918 the party needed a social programme for negotiations with Lloyd George, it was to the work of the USRC that they turned; in 1922 Griffith-Boscawen was able as Minister of Health to do some of the things he had attempted in 1912; much of Neville Chamberlain's work as a reformer of the Poor Law was presaged by a USRC report of 1913 written by Hills. (Neville Chamberlain was not himself a member of the USRC because he was not an MP but worked with it.) The value of the USRC lies in its long-term contribution to Conservative policy and in its re-creation of the tradition of Conservative reform that perished with Randolph Churchill.[41] Paul Smith has argued that Disraeli was no great reformer but was of enormous value to the party because he was believed to have been one; in rediscovering Disraeli, the USRC rediscovered the myth too.[42]

Little of this positive side of Unionism was visible in 1912 and 1913 for it was submerged in the negative task of weakening the Liberal government and resisting Home Rule. More typically, the Unionist belief in the Empire was set against the Liberal plans to break up the United Kingdom, as in the leaflet *Under which flag?* of July 1914: this made the comparison between Unionists who had fought in South Africa and Liberals who had been pro-Boer and who would now shoot loyal Ulstermen. This stark contrast provided the basis for Unionism's last great campaign.[43]

The parliamentary battle had an air of shadow-boxing about it, for the ultimate outcome was certain from the start and the timetable could be predicted almost as easily. Under the Parliament Act the Lords could hold up legislation for two years, so Home Rule and Welsh Disestablishment would both become law in 1914, at least a year before an election need be held. There was no doubt that the Liberals would press on with this timetable, and little doubt that the Labour and Irish MPs would support them; Unionists could not therefore stop Home Rule becoming law. Their tirades in parliament were designed for consumption outside, to be read in the constituencies, in Ulster, and at the Palace. The anger of the Unionists was based partly on the old political frustration of government by log-rolling, and partly on a new constitutional point. In 1910 few Liberals had argued for Home Rule in their election addresses or speeches, so they could not be said to have a clear mandate for it.[44] Nor had the Liberals said clearly what sort of reform they would impose on the House of Lords, and the reform that was passed in 1911 left a serious constitutional problem. Asquith's reform had been presented as an interim measure and the preamble to his Bill stated that the Lords' powers were being curtailed pending the introduction of a reform of their composition.[45] The government made no effort to redeem this promise but Unionists believed that they were in a temporary phase pending the reconstruction of the upper house, and that it was therefore no business of the government to bring in other constitutional Bills before they had settled the constitution itself. For the time being the constitution was as Bonar Law argued 'in suspense', and so unconstitutional opposition would be justified.

The Unionists also had two other arguments in their case. In the first place it could be argued that a democratic government would not impose unreasonably on minorities; this exposed the party to Liberal charges that they were indifferent to the Irish Nationalists, but it also exposed the weakness of the government's position, as Law explained to the Commons in January 1913:

> If you say that the Nationalists of Ireland have a right to claim to go out of the United Kingdom as a community, if you say that five or six per cent of the whole of the United Kingdom have that right because they wish to have separate rule for themselves, how can you say that a body in Ireland, not five or six per cent, but twenty-five per cent of the whole population, has not an equal right to separate treatment? That argument has been put by many of us, and by myself many times, and it has never been answered.[46]

The second argument had a more practical flavour and consisted simply of a demand that the issue should be put to the test of an election. Since there had been no clear mandate in 1910 and since the Lords could not now force another election, Unionists would have to resist until the government called one themselves. Asquith replied that the question of mandates was not so simple, but he was opposed to an election for the same reason as Unionists wanted one: – both knew that Home Rule was not a winning policy outside Ireland. Law taunted Asquith with this in March 1914:

> I said to the Prime Minister: Make certain – and surely, in face of all this trouble it is worthwhile making certain – that you have the will of the country behind you, and, so far as the Unionist party are concerned, we will absolutely cease all unconstitutional opposition to the carrying of your measure.[47]

Note Law's own use of the word 'unconstitutional' to describe his actions and the extent to which all was pinned on an election. At bottom then there was some democratic basis for the Unionist case, for the government was pressing on with a reform that they knew was not backed by the electorate. It may be alleged that such Unionist arguments were specious, that their concern was solely to exploit a winning issue at any cost to the nation, but this would be to misunderstand the Unionists themselves. Many believed that the Liberal–Labour alliance was a threat to a system of government built up over centuries and they were not prepared to see this done without at least a clear decision by the electorate. And it is vital to see that there was a real Unionist case against the government, for this alone explains the popular support that was mobilized and the impression that was made on the army and the King – the only forces left to stop the government.

There is no doubt that Unionists believed in what they were doing or that they saw the government's actions as justifying their responses. In 1912 Walter Long accepted the phrase 'the new style' and flung it back at the government: 'The New Style consists in the cynical violation of the honourable traditions of public life. Government in the New Style consists in gambling with the interests of the nation to propitiate the various mutinous factions which hold the balance in the House of Commons.'[48] Law also charged the government with being under the control of Redmond:

> I am not going to say anything about the subserviency of the Government. There is no need to tell the country about that. Everybody has seen it. It is impossible to look at any of their actions during the past three years without seeing that they are carrying Home Rule at the dictation of the Nationalist party, but that in order that Home Rule may be carried they are turning up everything in the country.[49]

These statements spoke for the whole Unionist party in their vigorous tone, in the denial that Unionists were responsible for the state of things, and in the laying of blame on the Nationalists.

In Parliament there was non-cooperation that became almost a guerrilla war between the parties. Exchanges between Bonar Law and the government became ever more abrupt, as the following example from March 1914 shows:[50]

> *Mr Churchill:* . . . It is admitted that a misunderstanding on the point arose.
> *Mr Bonar Law:* Rubbish!
> *Mr Churchill:* Do I understand the Right Honourable Gentleman to say 'Rubbish'?
> *Mr Bonar Law:* Yes.

Meanwhile, the Whips pursued the government in the hope of catching them out in a snap vote; at the least this would disrupt their progress and there seemed an outside chance that the government would tire of the interminable pressure and throw in the sponge. It might not succeed in stopping Home Rule, but it could certainly take up enough time to stop a Plural Voting Bill from getting through. The government's full majority of over a hundred was difficult to muster because of the absence of Irish MPs, and the effective majority was gradually reduced by constant harassment. In February 1912 the majority was down to fifty or sixty; in June the Unionists made their first real attempt to 'snap' the government and got the majority down to twenty-two. At the same time Unionist speakers philibustered all other Bills and pairing was stopped. In July the government majority fell to three on one vote but this narrow margin produced better attendances on the government side; Unionists therefore sent their MPs off to speak around the country 'with an occasional rush to London to keep the Rads. there'. These wearing tactics led to the government's defeat in November 1912. All was carefully organized, not only for the debate and the vote, but also for the disorder that would follow when Asquith moved to rescind the vote: Ministers were shouted down, a copy of Standing Orders was thrown at Churchill, and the Speaker had to suspend the House until the following week because of the danger of actual fighting in the House.[51] After the weekend, the Unionist Whips decided that they had taken things far enough, having wasted an entire week of parliamentary time and given their supporters a sign of the vigour with which the fight was being waged. For the rest of the session and in the spring of 1913, the Liberals took no risk of further defeat, but this required constant attendance at the House by Liberal MPs; the result was that there was no autumn session in 1913 and no Plural Voting Bill was passed. It would now be too late to force the abolition of plural voting on the House of Lords before the next general election; something at least had been achieved.[52]

In 1913 the Unionists found a new line of attack through the Marconi Scandal. This has to be seen against the Unionist belief that Asquith's government was corrupt as well as irresponsible and radical. At the Albert Hall in January 1912 Law had made this point with characteristic bluntness: Liberals were expert only 'in electioneering, in the small trickery of politics'. They had given rewards and favours to their supporters, especially in Wales, and 'have succeeded in six years in creating a political spoils system which already rivals that of the United States. . . . If we have a few more years of Georgian finance, the only attractive, the only lucrative profession left in this country will be that of a Radical Welsh politician.'[53] Steel-Maitland wrote to *The Times* in 1913 to accuse the Liberals of corrupt practices at the Wick

Burghs by-election, and Sanders noted that at Taunton they had given away half-crowns wrapped in Liberal leaflets; both contests went against the trend, so there may be some truth in the allegations. In April 1914, George Younger wrote in *Our Flag* about 'Radical "Buy" Election promises' and cited ten cases from the past six years when Liberal by-election candidates had made promises to local groups of voters on behalf of the government – promises of a change in policy to benefit local crafts or industry or employment. Such actions did not infringe the Corrupt Practice Acts but they did make them virtually inoperative. Unionist publications also devoted much attention to Asquith's Honours Lists, and in October 1912 *Our Flag* listed thirty-nine 'Radical Plutocrats', of which twenty-three had been ennobled by the Liberals – 'so far'. The allegation that the Liberals were selling honours in return for political contributions was brutally clear.[54] It was in this general context that the Unionist attitude to Marconi was set.

In October 1912 both Rufus Isaacs and Lloyd George denied that they had engaged in dealings in Marconi shares, but a Select Committee was set up to investigate the allegations of sensationalist newspapers. Only when it became clear, through a libel action against *Le Matin* early in 1913, that the government had misled the Commons did the Unionists move into action. The Liberals secured the majority report of the Select Committee but the Unionist members under Lord Robert Cecil extracted ever more damaging evidence from the witnesses interviewed. Debates followed in parliament with the Unionists in full cry, for the Liberals seemed to have been caught out in a case of open corruption. In the end of course the government's majority triumphed and the whole affair died away, but Marconi remained a favourite cry of Unionist hecklers in 1914.[55]

It must be noted first that the Liberals really did have something to hide over Marconi, but it must be noted also that Unionists were not being very honest in their more general allegations. The misleading of the Commons by ministers, the deliberate absence from Britain of the Master of Elibank (so that he could not be questioned), and the evasions of the Prime Minister all created the suspicion that something was wrong and Unionists were perfectly justified in their attempts to find out what it was. On the more general point, charges of corruption were disingenuous. The practice of selling honours had been increasing under all governments and it was becoming more marked in both parties.[56] Lord Hugh Cecil doubted if his father had dealt in such things but suspected 'that both Asquith and A. J. B. know quite well that honours are sold'. In 1913 Lord Selborne tried to mount a campaign against the sale of honours but he had a lukewarm response: Salisbury thought it would not achieve anything useful, Lansdowne urged that the views of the party organizers should be sought, and Law urged him 'not to obscure the Marconi issue'. Law knew that 'a year's peerages have been hypothecated' even before he became leader, and he probably knew that the party could not do without this source of income. It was also useless to pretend that corruption at elections was one-sided; the scale was far smaller than thirty years earlier, but it went on just the same in both parties.[57] Marconi thus had a special importance because it provided an issue of corruption that could not be turned back by Liberals against the Unionists, and for this the Liberals had only themselves to blame. Asquith's appointment of Isaacs as Lord Chief Justice just a few months after he had narrowly escaped (and actually deserved) parliamentary censure, was a brave example of loyalty to a colleague, but it also demonstrated exactly the insensitivity that Unionists had denounced.[58] This ambivalence towards public morality was crucial when set alongside the Unionists' extra-legal activities over Ireland.

It was the campaign out of doors over Ulster that was the centre piece of the whole Unionist campaign. For all the noise and fury, the Home Rule Bill was passed by the Commons in January 1913 and again in July, and would become law in the autumn of 1914. If it were to be stopped at all, then it could only be by means that fell entirely outside the constitution. The first such means involved the King and the second the army, but both rested on the assertion that Ulster would not accept Home Rule. It was argued that the King might intervene either to persuade Asquith to call an election or to refuse his assent to Home Rule until there had been one; this was certainly within the theoretical Royal Prerogative, for the King had an undoubted right to advise his ministers and – by the Unionist argument at least – his power of veto had been necessarily restored by the removal of the powers of the Lords. Only the King could now give his people the right to vote on a divisive issue, a situation that naturally appalled the Palace. Law pessimistically told the King that he would in any case alienate half of his subjects, Unionists if he gave his assent to Home Rule and Liberals if he did not.[59] Such warnings succeeded in bringing the King into the negotiations; by 1914 the King was trying to secure a compromise settlement, in itself a major advance for an opposition.

It was the second Unionist lever against Home Rule that helped to involve the King, for it assumed that Home Rule would become law, would be repudiated in Ulster, and that then the army would refuse to enforce it. The resistance of Ulster had not been created by British Unionists and could hardly be said to depend on them, but the knowledge of support was certainly useful to Carson and Craig in giving their plans for rebellion an official look. At Blenheim in July 1912 Law spoke to a mass rally of English Unionists, including over a hundred MPs, and made his commitment to Ulster absolutely specific.[60] Categorically, he argued that force in Ulster would overthrow parliamentary majorities if necessary and he assured the party's support in advance with no limitations. In a similar rally in Belfast in April he had taken the salute from over 100,000 Protestants in military formation. He went on to commit the party in support of the creation of the Ulster volunteers, of the formation of a Provisional government, and of the gun-running at Larne in April 1914. Again and again he spelled out his commitment – almost always linked to the question of the mandate, as in the Commons in January 1913:

> Suppose we submit it to the electors? . . . I say that, so far as I am concerned . . . if that is done we shall not in any way, shape or form encourage the resistance of Ulster. I say that without hesitation. [MR WINSTON CHURCHILL: Are you encouraging it now?] I rather differ from the Rt Hon. Gentleman. I am never ashamed to say exactly what I am doing. I have said before, and if it be any satisfaction to him I repeat it now, that if you attempt to enforce this Bill, and the people of Ulster believe, and have a right to believe, that you are doing it against the will of the people of this country, then I shall assist them in resisting it.[61]

Not only would Ulster be right to resist, but so would army officers who refused to enforce the decision of parliament:

> Put yourselves in the position of an officer. He believes in his heart and conscience, as I do, that the Government are doing this thing without the consent of the country, that in pressing it forward without the approval of the country they are as much a revolutionary committee as President Huerta who governs Mexico. That is really my position and, unless I believed in it I would not feel justified in the course I have taken.[62]

Unlimited support was promised, and unlimited support was given; that was indeed the only way in which the strategy of stopping Home Rule 'out of doors' might succeed.

Behind the scenes though, neither Law nor his party was so sure of the grounds and there was certainly some fear of the consequences. Austen Chamberlain represented such fears when he told Willoughby de Broke of what might be yet to come in November 1913:

> Civil War is an awful thing, not to be lightly encountered, but it is not the greatest evil which confronts us if the coercion of Ulster is tried. For if that is done, the House of Commons v. *the Army* will break in the process. . . . If officers throw up their commissions and troops refuse to fire, Home Rule is dead, but a great deal else is dead too. I won't dwell on the dangers of foreign complications, real though they be, but how will you meet another general strike on the railways or in the mines? It is not civil war that is the greatest peril but anarchy.[63]

And despite his public utterances Law too was ready to take up a more pragmatic attitude when negotiating; if Ulster could be excluded, he was quite prepared to abandon the rest of Ireland to Home Rule; Carson shared Law's view and was kept in touch with the negotiations throughout.[64]

Two problems intervened though to prevent a compromise, both in the secret negotiations of 1913 and the Buckingham Palace talks of July 1914. On the Unionist side men who had been fed with the heady talk of absolute resistance mobilized to resist what they now saw as the sell-out of the Southern Irish Unionists. The diehard peers began to organize another revolt, and the threat of a split like 1911 loomed. This gravely restricted Law's room for manoeuvre and made it impossible for him to accept the only compromise that Asquith could offer.[65] On the Liberal side, anger at the illegal campaign against Home Rule had made it equally difficult for Asquith to compromise, and he too could see no other way forward. By 1914 the terms of a possible compromise were emerging, by which Unionists would accept Home Rule and Liberals would agree to exclude Ulster; argument continued over the exact size of an excluded Ulster and the length of time involved in exclusion, but the logic of the negotiations pointed to this settlement in 1914 just as it was to do in 1921–22. The tragedy of 1914 was that neither side could accept this obvious compromise because neither could sell it to their own followers. Law had indeed brought Asquith to the point of conceding all that could be hoped for from Ulster's resistance, but he was unable to seize the fruits. He believed that Asquith 'is in a funk about the resistance of Ulster, and I am convinced that he will not face it when it comes to the point'.[66] Compromise having failed, there was left only force.

The final Unionist weapon would then be the army and the last political tactic was the scheme to amend the annual Army Bill in the House of Lords. As this was a Bill that was passed for one year only, the refusal to pass it would effectively restore the Lords' power over the government by taking away its legal control over the army. In the early months of 1914 the Unionist leaders prepared for this desperate throw, and the plan was only abandoned when the 'mutiny' at the Curragh showed that it was unnecessary, for the officers would not in any case agree to coerce Ulster. The Curragh incident was a sad case of panic, bungling and hesitation by the Liberals, for which the Unionists bear only an indirect responsibility,[67] but once the crisis broke the Unionists were quite convinced that it was the result of a plot against loyal Ulster – an 'Ulster Pogrom'. Movements of the fleet, secret meetings at the War Office, and the equivocations of the Prime Minister all lent some credence to this view, but there is no doubt that the Unionists themselves believed it.[68]

Unable to accept concessions in negotiation, Law now saw much the same deal offered in public by the Liberals themselves, when Asquith announced an Amending Bill to satisfy Ulster's fears of Home Rule with a period of exclusion. There remained doubt about the length of the exclusion, but it would certainly go past the next election and so allow a Unionist government to make it permanent.[69] The campaign of resistance had then succeeded, but few Unionists were celebrating; Lord Winterton in Sussex and Willoughby de Broke in Warwickshire were among the Unionists who were preparing to spread an Irish civil war to England by setting up 'commandos' of diehards among the yeomanry – but it was not clear whom they would fight if the army refused to support the government.[70] With the failure of the Buckingham Palace Conference in July 1914 the party prepared to redeem the pledges to Ulster of the past three years. From this grim situation the party was saved by the First World War.

The verdict on Bonar Law's first three years as leader must be a two-sided one. From the national viewpoint there are some credits and one massive debit. It was Law's achievement to keep the extreme right within the mainstream of the political system when it might have felt the need to abandon party politics altogether. It is the particular genius of British politics that the major parties have always managed to hold on to their respective extremists and so to draw their teeth. This was never more threatened from the right than in the years before 1914 and a leader who had respected constitutional niceties at that time would have driven them out of the system where they could have been far more dangerous. Law's campaign against Home Rule also brought the Liberal government face to face with power politics and showed up the hollowness of the reasoned optimism that underlay Edwardian Liberalism. The First World War provided a similar test and again only the Labour and Unionist parties were able to meet it squarely, but the battles of 1912 and 1913 had given advance warning of what was to come.[71] The imperial and defence campaigns perhaps did something to prepare the nation for war and they certainly prepared the party to take the lead when war did come in 1914. Against these points must be set the fatalism with which Law watched his country drift into civil war; the patriotic party became begetters of rebellion, the party of order suborned crime and mutiny, and the leader of the opposition in parliament approved and supported the destruction of both the practice and the authority of parliament. It should not be thought that Unionists enjoyed such a situation, for they certainly did not, but nor can it be suggested that they saw any real alternative, for in truth the basis of agreement on which parliamentary government rested had all but broken down. So Law said of the Liberals in 1914: 'They have become revolutionaries, and becoming revolutionaries they have lost the right to that implicit obedience that can be claimed by a Constitutional Government.'[72] In this Law shared the view of his party, but it would have been substantially the same without him. It is indeed hard to see how any Unionist leader in these years could have acted against such firm convictions to put the national interest first.

From the party point of view, Law's leadership had been a considerable success. He inherited a party that was weak and unsure of itself, he raised its morale, gave it purpose and pulled it together. Without this revival before 1914 it is difficult to see how the party could have survived the ten turbulent years that followed. By 1914 Unionists again really believed in their cause, as few had done in 1911.

By 1914 the Liberal party was on the ropes and the Unionists could look forward confidently to the election that could not be long delayed. Debate has been fierce between Liberal and Labour historians as to what can be proved from the by-elections of 1911–14 about the relative strength of the two Progressive parties; it is an indecisive argument in its very nature because of the confused pattern of results and the lack of any truly comparable figures for 1910 or 1906.[73] What cannot be doubted is that Unionists, who had drawn level with the Liberals in 1910, had made up more ground on them since. By the outbreak of war, the party had 287 MPs, thirty more than the Liberals and almost as many as the combined Liberal–Labour vote. Of these by-election gains, more than half had been in straight fights, the implications of which were unmistakable. An article in *Our Flag* in November 1912 pointed out that the average turnover of votes in by-elections had been about 1,300 votes per contest and that only 250 votes per contest was needed for an overall Unionist majority.[74] So in straight fights the Unionists were apparently on their way to a big win and the Labour–Liberal battles in three-cornered contests were merely an added bonus. Local elections confirmed the trend and their historian has interpreted them as showing that 'by 1913, the Conservatives had rarely been stronger in the Councils of the land, or indeed more poised for success in the forthcoming general election'.[75] Much would depend on the exact state of affairs in Ireland and something would depend on the success of the Progressive parties in patching up a new electoral pact (although after the events of 1912 and 1913 it could not be expected to work as well as in 1910), but all of these factors would operate in the broad context of a probable Unionist victory. So in saving the party from a desperate situation in Ireland, the First World War also robbed the Unionist party of a return to power.

Notes and References

1 Sanders Diary, 12 Nov. 1911.
2 Petrie, *Austen Chamberlain*: i. 300–6.
3 Sanders Diary, 15 Nov. 1911.
4 Taylor, *Beaverbrook*, 46; Blake, *Unknown Prime Minister*, 37.
5 Rhodes James, *Memoirs of a Conservative*, 51.
6 One such error was Law's hasty promise that he would repeal the 1911 National Insurance Act; Blake, *Unknown Prime Minister*, 139–140.
7 Law made this point in the House of Commons in January 1913, when he claimed that he had only spoken in parliament on Irish affairs on one occasion before becoming leader.
8 Blake, *Unknown Prime Minister*, 96, 162.
9 Steel-Maitland to Law, 20 July 1914: Law MSS 33/1/37a.
10 Ramsden, 'Organisation', 272–5.
11 *Ibid*, 278.
12 *Ibid*, 328–331.
13 Sandars to Balfour, 16 Dec. 1909: Balfour MSS, Add. MSS 49766.
14 *Unionist Organisation Committee*, Interim Report, April 1911, 19.
15 Fraser to Law, 17 Nov. 1913: Law MSS, 30/4/39.
16 Locker-Lampson to Steel-Maitland, 24 June 1912: Steel-Maitland MSS GD 193/80/2; Ramsden, 'Organisation', 233–5.
17 J. E. Amery, *Joseph Chamberlain*: vi, 976–7.
18 Long to Balfour, 19 Oct. 1911: Balfour MSS, Add. MSS 49777; Long, *Memories*, 198.
19 Steel-Maitland to Lord Robert Cecil, 17 Apr. 1912: Cecil of Chelwood MSS, Add. MSS 51071.
20 Memorandum by Steel-Maitland for Law, Dec. 1911: Steel-Maitland MSS GD 193/108/3.
21 *The Primrose League Election Guide*, 1914, included an article (pp. 7–12) by G. A. Arbuthnot, Vice-Chancellor of the League, explaining that the revolutionary tendencies of the radicals had forced the League to make public its commitment to the Unionist party. The same proposal had been indignantly rejected only three years earlier; Primrose League, Grand Council Minutes, 16 Mar. 1911.
22 Memorandum by Steel-Maitland for Law, Dec. 1911: Steel-Maitland MSS GD 193/108/3.
23 *Ibid*.
24 National Union Conference Minutes, London Conference of Nov. 1912 and Norwich Conference of Nov. 1913.
25 Churchill gave a spirited and on the whole convincing defence of his actions;

Churchill, *Winston S. Churchill*, ii, 636–41.

26 *Gleanings and Memoranda*, May and June 1913; *Our Flag*, Oct. 1913; National Union pamphlet no. 1670, May 1913.

27 The *Conservative and Unionist* celebrated it with a front-page spread and the caption 'One in the eye for free trade' in Nov. 1911.

28 Blake, *Unknown Prime Minister*, 108.

29 Salisbury to Law, 1 May 1912: quoted in Blake, *Unknown Prime Minister*, 108–9.

30 Law to Salisbury, 3 May 1912: quoted in Blake, *Unknown Prime Minister*, 109.

31 Taylor, *Beaverbrook*, 75–6.

32 Churchill, *Lord Derby*, 170–82.

33 Gollin, *Observer and J. L. Garvin*, 384–5.

34 Taylor doubts whether Aitken really played the role in this affair that he afterwards claimed (*Beaverbrook*, 77). Robert Sanders did not list him among the eight backbenchers known to the Whips as having refused to sign the Memorial by 12 January: Sanders Diary, 12 Jan. 1913.

35 Maurice Woods to Willoughby de Broke, 16 Aug. 1911: Willoughby de Broke MSS.

36 *Conservative and Unionist*, May 1911.

37 *Our Flag*, June 1914.

38 National Union pamphlets nos 1665, 1669 and 1685, May and June 1913.

39 Sanders Diary, 13 Oct. 1912.

40 *Gleanings and Memoranda*, Apr. 1913; Blake, *Uknown Prime Minister*, 140.

41 Ramsden, 'Organisation', 254.

42 Smith, *Disraelian Conservatism and Social Reform*, 325.

43 National Union pamphlet no. 1726, July 1914.

44 Only 41 per cent of Liberal candidates in December 1910 had mentioned Home Rule, compared to 88 per cent of Unionists. Only 3 per cent of Liberals had mentioned Disestablishment (Blewett, *Peers, Parties and People*, 326). Similar figures were quoted by The *Conservative and Unionist* in its own survey, printed in the edition of Dec. 1911.

45 Hanham, *The Nineteenth Century Constitution*, 197.

46 *Hansard*, 5th series, xlvi, 467, 1 Jan. 1913.

47 *Ibid*, xlix, 429, 25 Mar. 1914.

48 *Our Flag*, June 1912.

49 *Hansard*, 5th series, xxxix, 1802, 19 June 1912.

50 Blake, *Unknown Prime Minister*, 192; see also p. 96 for a similar exchange with Asquith.

51 Sanders diary, 17 Nov. 1912.

52 *Gleanings and Memoranda*, March 1913.

53 Quoted in Blake, *Unknown Prime Minister*, 94–5.

54 *Our Flag* also alleged that Liberal ministers and MPs stood to profit by the government's Indian currency policy (Feb. 1913) and that half of the Liberal peers who voted for Home Rule in 1913 had been ennobled by Campbell-Bannerman or Asquith since 1906 (Aug. 1913).

55 Donaldson, *The Marconi Scandal*, 231–9.

56 Selborne MSS (correspondence on 'Honours', 1912–14); Hanham, 'The sale of honours in late Victorian England', Pumphrey, 'The introduction of industrialists into the British peerage', *American Historical Review*, 1959.

57 Helmore documents a good example from a close contest at Exeter in 1910 in his *Corrupt and Illegal Practices*, C. O'Leary, *Elimination of Corrupt Practices*, 209–28;

Blake, *Unknown Prime Minister*, 100.

58   Blake. *Unknown Prime Minister*, 148.

59   *Ibid*, 133.

60   *Ibid*, 130–1.

61   *Hansard*, 5th series, xlvi, 468, 1 Jan. 1913.

62   *Ibid*, xlix, 432, 25 Mar. 1914.

63   Austen Chamberlain to Willoughby de Broke, 23 Nov. 1913: Willoughby de Broke MSS.

64   Blake, *Unknown Prime Minister*, 135–6.

65   *Ibid*, 166; see for example Lord Saltoun to Willoughby de Broke, 16 Jan. 1914: Willoughby de Broke MSS.

66   This was also the view of the diehards of course. See for example the opinion of Lord Peel, who believed that 'the government have no intention of using force, but they will bluff till the very last minute, or I know them not', Peel to Willoughby de Broke, 15 Jan. 1914: Willoughby de Broke MSS.

67   A. T. Q. Stewart, *The Ulster Crisis*, 171–2.

68   *Ibid*, 175; this also enabled Law to make one of his most telling remarks when it was explained that Seely had resigned but that Asquith had refused to accept his resignation: 'We have heard of people being thrown to the wolves but never before have we heard of a man being thrown to the wolves with a bargain on the part of the wolves that they would not eat him', Blake, *Unknown Prime Minister*, 201.

69   Rowland, *Last Liberal Governments*, ii, 337.

70   Willoughby de Broke to General Richardson, 21 Jan. 1914: Willoughby de Broke MSS; Winterton, *Orders of the Day*, 38; Gollin, *Proconsul in Politics*, 175–6.

71   Dangerfield, *The Strange Death of Liberal England*, 280. In dismissing the fancies and extravagances of Dangerfield, historians have all too often forgotten that his book has a core of sound argument.

72   *Gleanings and Memoranda*, Jan. 1914, quoting a speech by Law at Caernarvon on 11 Dec. 1913. The same view was expressed by Lord Milner: 'There are a great many people who still fail to realise what the strength of our feeling is on this subject. They think it is just an ordinary case of opposition to a political measure, a move in the party game. And so it may be to a great many Unionists, but there is certainly a very large *body* who feel that the crisis altogether transcends anything in their previous experience, & calls for action which is different, *not only in degree but in kind* from what is appropriate to ordinary political controversies': Milner to Selborne, 18 Feb. 1914: Selborne MSS.

73   Roy Douglas, 'Labour in decline' in Brown, ed., *Essays in Anti-Labour History*, 105–25, gives the Liberal view; McKibbin, Matthew and Kay, 'The franchise factor' gives the Labour view, although some of their points were met in advance by Peter Clarke in his review of McKibbin's *The Evolution of the Labour Party*, *English Historical Review*, 1976, 157–63.

74   With the small and uneven sizes of electorates before 1918 this method of calculation may be no more inaccurate than the 'swings' which have been rather anachronistically calculated for these contests.

75   Chris Cook, 'Labour and the downfall of Liberalism', in Cook and Shed, *Crisis and Controversy*, 63.

Chapter 5

Bonar Law's party

Bonar Law was a startling choice for the party of the 'Hotel Cecil', for he was a self-made and almost self-educated businessman from the outlying parts of the Empire (Scotland, Ulster and Canada provided his roots). He was inexperienced and little known before he was propelled into the highest office by his friends' ambition for him and by the deadlock between Long and Chamberlain in 1911. He had entered parliament in 1900, twenty-six years after Balfour, he had held no Cabinet post, he had taken no active role in party institutions, and he had not involved himself much in the social world of Westminster. However, his candidature in 1911 had been aided by three factors: he was a Conservative rather than a Liberal Unionist, but he was the sort of Conservative who would be acceptable to Liberal Unionists as well; he was a diehard in opinion, but he had remained loyal to Balfour's policy throughout the recent twists and turns; and he had staked a claim by his abandonment of his safe London seat to fight North-West Manchester in December 1910 (at no real risk, for an alternative safe seat was always available to him if and when he lost).[1]

Law's claims were therefore substantial, but they were known to few outside parliament, Glasgow and Manchester. In welcoming him, the party thus welcomed him as a stereotype. One thing about him that was widely known was the fact that he was a businessman, and so it was as such that he was welcomed; the party could even claim some credit for being the first to elect a businessman as its leader – much as it claimed credit in 1975 for electing a woman, although Margaret Thatcher had certainly not been chosen for that reason. At the National Union rally at Leeds the week after Law's election, a local delegate called John Gordon remarked that Law was 'a man of enormous business capacity (Hear, hear)', and suggested that there should be more such men in parliament. On the previous day, Alfred Hobson of Sheffield had told a party lunch that

> they had been fortunate in securing a businessman, whose qualifications in that respect would certainly appeal to men in the North of England. (Hear, hear). At present, we did not pay the same attention to the commercial development of our country that other nations paid to their development on those lines. We wanted more businessmen at the head of affairs.[2]

Others who were less impressed by what they knew about Law were surprised by what they discovered of his actual abilities, perhaps because his anonymity had prepared them for the worst. Lady Dawkins, who had never heard him speak before, surprised herself by her reaction when she heard him speak at the Albert Hall in January 1912:

> It was a splendid meeting yesterday and they gave Bonar Law a magnificent reception. His delivery was extraordinarily good and, though he spoke for an hour and a half I should think, his voice never failed him and every word was clear – and bold. It wasn't brilliant oratory, no flowers of rhetoric à la Curzon, or subtle 'nuances' à la Balfour, but it was *good hard sound commonsense* and the way he showed up the government was admirable. What I liked about it was that though it was biting sarcasm, the way he spoke it gave you the impression not of a man who was bitter in any way, but of a man who pitied the members of the government for being so rotten and pitied us for being governed by such scum. He held his audience *all through* his speech, you felt he was in touch and in sympathy with them and they with him. He was so extraordinarily quiet and self-possessed, it was almost as if he were chatting to us confidentially about it all instead of making an elaborate speech.
>
> I am bound to say that his personality and his voice with his Glasgow accent were a little disconcerting at first (I felt rather as if I were being addressed by my highly educated carpenter), but he inspired me with such confidence as he went on that I forgot that, and of course one has to recognise that a new era in political life has dawned for England, the old aristocratic school is practically swept out of it, it is the dawn of the new 'regime'. As long as we are in safe hands, while we are with a sincere man like B.L. we are safe, but I am not sure that it is a good thing on the whole. Still, I suppose we must move with the times.[3]

This account sums up much of Law's appeal and explains his quick success as leader. He combined a cold approach with references to emotive issues like the Boer War, he spoke in a matter-of-fact way, he made clever use of sarcasm at the expense of opponents, and he recognized the value of a decisive attitude that would be firmly grasped by a party audience. His unconventionality, his unorthodoxy and his accent all helped the party to feel that it had made a step forward: 'the dawn of the new regime'. As Lloyd George perceptively remarked in 1911, 'the fools have stumbled on the right man by accident'.[4]

Bonar Law has usually received a bad press from historians, who have portrayed him as a hard, dour, humourless fanatic.[5] The balance was righted by Robert Blake's biography, a book of great judgement and insight but still without great sympathy for the man. For it is the personality of Law that has remained as elusive to historians as it was to his own contemporaries. He remained a very private individual during his twelve years at the top, rarely venturing into society and always preferring a quiet dinner alone or with chosen friends to an elaborate occasion. After the death of his wife in 1909 he took no interest in the society of women, he had little interest in food and he was a teetotaller. As leader of the party he gave the usual dinner for colleagues at the start of the session but he was happy to leave the rest of the social management of the party to Lady Londonderry. He was obliged to attend some party functions and to receive the chief guests along with the hostess, but he received little pleasure from such occasions and rarely attended them outside London.[6] His lack of social graces could be an embarrassment, for he had no polite small-talk and did not pretend to any; his visits to Windsor were an ordeal for guest and hosts alike, to him because he disliked formality and to his hosts because he was so difficult to entertain and because he did not mince words with the King.[7] He thus remained an enigma, a man who could not be known as most politicians were known and who seemed to shun such contacts. The outward appearance of gloomy taciturnity was therefore taken for the whole man.

To friends, though, Law appeared very differently, and the people who became his friends provide testament to the fact; he was very close with both Max Aitken and David Lloyd George, neither of whom was very likely to enjoy the company of a gloomy boor. Indeed, when Law left the government in 1921, Frances Stevenson noted in her diary that Lloyd George had 'lost an ideal companion with whom he could laugh and joke and enjoy himself'.[8] Both Aitken and Stanley Baldwin had an admiration for Law that bordered on veneration. Others never managed to penetrate his reserve, for he had a deep suspicion of others who could turn out a compliment at will or turn a barbed shaft with a sally of their own, and above all he hated pomposity and egotism; this goes far to explain his view of Churchill and of F. E. Smith. When offered the leadership for which he had fought so hard, Law almost lost it by his apparent doubt; in his speech of acceptance he spoke at length of his unfitness for the job; when told that he was now a great man and must learn to behave like one, he replied 'If I am a great man, then a good many great men must have been frauds.'[9] Indeed Law determined not to try to look like a great man and therein lay the secret of his success. He put himself forward as a self-consciously ordinary man, a politician who asked to be identified with as an equal rather than deferred to as a leader. Even Lloyd George, whose origins were as lowly as Law's had been, could not stoop to so humble a style, and only Stanley Baldwin (who drew much of his inspiration from Law) was able to do so successfully. If Law had a political model, then it must have been Sir Henry Campbell-Bannerman, a fellow Scot who had shown that an ordinary man could hold the highest office without discredit and that he could beat the clever and the politically sophisticated at their own game.

Commentators on Bonar Law's election to the leadership all agreed that the party had taken a decisive turn. For Walter Long, proposing Law as leader, the decision marked the end of an era, the swansong of the country gentleman.[10] For H. G. Wells, the change to Bonar Law marked a distasteful new attitude by the Unionists; when Balfour's 'essential liberalism came face to face with this new baseness of commercialized imperialism, with all its push and energy, he made a very poor fight for it. He allowed himself to be hustled into the background of affairs by men with narrower views and nearer objectives.'[11] As far back as 1904 Winston Churchill had foreseen the same change when he predicted the tariff reformers' coming takeover of the party.[12] Lord Robert Cecil detected the same change when he deplored the tariff reformers' 'whole way of looking at things. It appears to me utterly sordid and materialistic, not yet corrupt but on the high road to corruption.'[13] Tory aristocrats, Liberals and Fabians all saw in Law's election the triumph of this 'new mercantile Conservatism' and the final triumph of tariff reform; the party was now in the hands of hard-faced businessmen, and all sorts of undesirable results would inevitably follow.

Law gave credence to such fears by his unashamed espousal of the image created round him; in May 1912 he told the National Union that 'nobody knows better than I do that political work cannot be done on strictly business lines, but the nearer you can approach to business lines the better for the political work'.[14] Steel-Maitland was running Central Office like a business enterprise, not in order to make a political point, but because it was as natural to him as it had been foreign to Percival Hughes. The party magazine *Conservative and Unionist* quite specifically welcomed Law's election, because 'as a great captain of industry, his knowledge of the conditions of the workers will be an invaluable guide in the development of the Unionist policy of Social Reform'.[15] The resistance of Ulster was also linked to its business roots with such slogans as 'Industrial Ulster is united' or 'They mean business', and Law made the same point when he described in Norwich a recent meeting that he had addressed in the Ulster Hall:[16]

> That meeting consisted of practically the whole business community of Belfast. They are the very class which hate disorder, which know that disorder injures their business, perhaps ruins their business, yet this class showed an enthusiasm which equalled, if not surpassed, the enthusiasm of the workers in the shipyards.

The merging of Conservatives and Liberal Unionists was described by John Boraston on similar lines:

> The promoters of the amalgamation are a body of keen businessmen, well knowing the difference between an investment and a speculation. They regard the fusion as a sound investment and, although Unionist stock has appreciated greatly since the new issue, there is not a man of us who has the slightest intention of selling out.[17]

So under Law the language of the boardroom became commonplace on the platforms and in the propaganda of the party. There has rarely been a clearer example of the extent to which a Conservative leader sets the keynote for the party, the extent to which it is moulded round its leader.

In all this, it was easy to forget the fortuitous circumstances in which Law had actually become leader in 1911. Walter Long was a country gentleman who played up to that image for all he was worth, using Henry Chaplin – 'the squire' – as his political model.[18] Austen Chamberlain had been trained to be a conventional statesman; Rugby, Cambridge and a determination to live down his father's reputation had all combined to make him the most conformist of politicians. Neither Long not Chamberlain would have made great changes in the party, and the election of either would not have seemed to signify a great change. Moreover they and their supporters were still present in Bonar Law's party, so that the scale of the real change would be heavily circumscribed. Law could give his party a new image, but the reality would remain much as before. The leadership was actually a collective one rather than a personal domination, and Law recognized his obligation to take the advice of those who were seen to be worthy of consultation by the party as a whole. He called the shadow cabinet together rarely and restricted its membership, but this did not remove the obligation to take advice.[19] We must turn to Law's leading supporters as well as to himself in order to assess the real character of the party.

Our Flag printed New Year messages in 1914 from Lansdowne, Bonar Law, Selborne, Austen Chamberlain, Long, Carson, Smith, Steel-Maitland, Lord Edmund Talbot, and George Younger, in that order; the last three were presumably included as Party Chairman, Chief Whip and Scottish Whip, but the rest of the list may be taken as indicative of a rough order of precedence at that time. Lansdowne came first because he had been leader in the House of Lords since 1902; he was too old to be a rival to Law and he cooperated with him fully, though not without some condescension. He played a vital role because the Lords were central to Unionist tactics and because the only alternative leaders there – Selborne or Curzon – had each alienated some Unionist peers by their actions in 1911. Law consulted Lansdowne on all matters of importance, kept him informed of the progress of negotiations over Ulster, but found him difficult to convince of the merits of compromise. Lansdowne was more exposed to the views of the real diehards and was thus a restraining influence on Law. With Lansdowne should be linked Balfour who, though he occupied no official position after 1911, was still close to the centre of the party. Relations with Law were cool but courteous and his tactical advice was always available on difficult issues, such as the question of the Army Act in 1914.[20] Selborne was of significance because he was a man who had a foot in every camp; related to the Cecils, he was also a Liberal Unionist, a tariff reformer, a diehard, and a Liberal Unionist. He had been Liberal Unionist Chief Whip, with Joseph Chamberlain at the Colonial Office, First Lord of the Admiralty, Milner's successor in South Africa, and a ditcher over the House of Lords. In 1914 he was still only fifty-five and could look forward to a major job in the next Unionist government. He had not wished to leave the Commons when he inherited his title in 1895 and thereafter he became an unceasing advocate of the House of Lords, defending its powers, resisting the sale of peerages, and demanding its reconstruction so that its powers could be restored.

Austen Chamberlain and Walter Long were both treated with respect by Law, tribute to their withdrawal in his favour in 1911, but they reacted very differently. Long was a choleric, short-tempered man who was a constant trial to colleagues in opposition or in power. He had a good platform manner and a great capacity for work but he was an inveterate intriguer. He had constantly worked against Balfour, criticizing him freely in letters to colleagues and using his party positions as independent bases against the leader.[21] From 1912 though, his health was not good and he was no real threat to Law, but he retained the backing of a large section of the rank and file in the House of Commons. Austen Chamberlain on the other hand was always reserved and never seems to have fully understood Law's belief in his party nor his readiness to sacrifice even profound beliefs for the sake of unity. He was hurt by his failure to win the leadership in 1911 and by the hostility to his family manifested during the contest. He made it clear to Law that he did not think that Law was well qualified to be leader and that he reserved the right to contest any future vacancy, but Austen was too loyal a man to conspire; relations were not very friendly, but there was total cooperation.[22]

Sir Edward Carson occupied an independent position as the spokesman of Ulster. Although not an Ulsterman himself, he gave to Ulster the charismatic lead that transformed resistance into armed rebellion, and he was a popular platform speaker with Unionists on both sides of the Irish Sea. Although the leader of the Union Defence League in succession to Walter Long, he shared Law's belief in the inevitability of ultimate compromise, and this made him, like Law, an object of suspicion to the diehard Irish Unionists.[23] F. E. Smith worked closely with Carson in the Ulster campaign. He was the rising man in the party, only thirty-nine in 1911 when he joined the front bench, as brilliant an advocate as Carson and a man of devastating wit. He was by far the most popular Unionist speaker after Law in 1912 and 1913, the man that every local association wanted to open their bazaars and fêtes. His speeches in parliament were separately published, as were those of no other Unionist of the time except Balfour,[24] and he received the signal honour of a Privy Councillorship on the recommendation of the Liberal Prime Minister in June 1911.[25]

These then were Law's senior colleagues in the work of opposition and would have presumably occupied the senior posts in a Law government; they scarcely add up to the image of a party of ruthless businessmen and, if other probable ministers are added to the list – Lords Derby, Curzon, Salisbury and Crawford, together with Finlay and Cave, both lawyers – then it seems even less so. The only Unionists who conformed to the picture of what the party was supposed to be like were either men outside the mainstream like Milner, or men too junior to have much real influence like Steel-Maitland, Aitken, Amery and Goulding. Bonar Law himself was the only one of the shadow cabinet who fitted the image of his party, and for him part at least was assumed for the occasion. Most of the party leaders were in any case inherited from Balfour and it would take time to find men of the new stamp, even if this were possible. The Balfourites did gradually fade from the scene; Acland-Hood, Wyndham and Lyttleton all died, Halsbury and Akers-Douglas became too old, and Midleton was dropped. But in their place, Law did not fill his shadow cabinet with assertive businessmen. Far from it, for even after the influx into parliament of the 'hard-faced men' of 1918 the Law government of 1922 included as many old-established peers as any of the time. Salisbury had remarked in 1911 that 'whatever your own opinions, the Conservative party can only assimilate change gradually',[26] and this was certainly so in the case of personnel at the top. A Law government in 1915 would have included hardly any more MPs from a business background than Disraeli's 1874 Ministry or Salisbury's of 1895. Not all members would have been aristocratic or from the gentry, but the fastest route to the top was still through the law rather than through commerce.

Unionist MPs in 1910–14 have been exhaustively studied by J. M. McEwen and J. A. Thomas, and the following analysis is based on their work.[27] The clearest characteristic of the parliamentary party was its strongly regional base. Unionists held 54 per cent of the English seats, but only 18 per cent of the rest, and this severely limited the recovery from 1906. Ireland outside Ulster was intractable, but the lack of a Unionist revival in Scotland and Wales cost the party about thirty seats when compared to 1895 or 1900. Within England too there was a heavy concentration: the party held most of the seats in the Home Counties, Wessex, the West and the West Midlands; just over half in London, the East and the North-west; well under half in the East Midlands and North. Strength was still predominantly in the counties; the English counties returned almost half of the parliamentary party, the squires who made Walter Long such a force, and of these 128 MPs over a hundred owned land or lived in the division that they represented, a strong territorial base. This was further reflected by the fact that a third of the MPs did not keep up a house in London, confirmation of roots outside Westminster; sessions lasted for only about thirty weeks a year and even during session the attendance of backbenchers was sometimes spasmodic.

Unionists had a slight majority of the English borough seats, but this was based on the small towns of the West and South rather than the heavy industrial centres of the North. The Unionist preponderance in London rested on the western residential suburbs, eighteen constituencies that elected Unionists at all elections from 1885 to 1910. Of the major cities only Birmingham, Liverpool and Sheffield elected more Unionists than Liberals in 1910, but Unionism was also strong in Plymouth, Brighton, Preston, and Bath. Where old cries could still be made to work, old strongholds in the seaside resorts, cathedral towns, market towns and suburbs returned to their previous loyalty. Where the joint appeal of Liberals and Labour had bitten more deeply into the Unionist vote there was no visible recovery of ground; so in 1914 there were no Unionist MPs at all from Leeds or Bradford, Leicester or Derby or Stoke, Newcastle upon Tyne, Sunderland, Southampton, Stockport, Bolton, Blackburn or Northampton.[28] Every one of these towns had returned Unionists in 1895 or 1900 and no Unionist government would be elected without some victories in such places. The by-election gains in Manchester in 1912 and in Ipswich on the eve of the war perhaps showed that this recovery was at hand. The borough MPs were very different from their county colleagues, and only thirty-seven of the eighty-six from English boroughs even lived in the same towns; many were carpet-bagging lawyers, induced to stand at the last moment and at the expense of Central Office. This distribution was much like that of the 1880s: the reliance on the counties, the growth of suburban strength, and the lack of strong local roots in the industrial areas were all traditional features.

In background, the party was less exclusive than might be expected. Only nineteen MPs were heirs to peerages and of these seven were from families that had been Liberal before 1886 and another five were new creations since then; thirty-eight MPs were related to peers by blood and another forty by marriage. Only sixteen Unionist MPs were baronets (less than the number of Liberals, a testament to the eight years of Liberal government), and these were the owners of new wealth rather than old titles.[29] There were twenty-one knights, but these too were more often lawyers, merchants and colonial administrators rather than landed gentry. Eighty-one MPs had some connection with a landed family (on Burke's celebrated definition) and fifty-five of these sat for seats that were adjacent to their family holdings; conversely there were only two whose fathers had been working-class (Jessie Collings and Henry Duke) but a host whose fathers had been lawyers, clergymen or doctors (including Law, Smith and Aitken). Fifty-three were the sons of MPs (18 per cent, much like the 17 per cent of Liberals) and twelve of these sat for the same seat, although few like Stanley Baldwin succeeded directly; fifteen of these fifty-three were sons of Liberals, further evidence of the value of recruits brought over in 1886.

Unionists were most distinct from Liberals and from other generations of Conservatives in their age; the average age was only fifty in 1914, there were four Unionist MPs under thirty and sixty-two under forty, and half of the party had been under forty when first elected. This reflected the extent to which politics was a career that followed quite naturally from station and the clearing out that had taken place after 1906. Few Unionist MPs had any need to earn their livings, and it was usually the lawyers and businessmen who were the older members. The parliamentary party was thus a relatively young group of men, with the most privileged also the youngest.[30]

In education the party conformed more to what would be expected: 196 MPs had been to public schools (68 per cent of the party, twice the proportion of Liberals) and eighty-six of these had been at Eton, almost a third of the party. Only thirty-four had been to other secondary schools, scarcely more than the number from the second most popular public school, Harrow. The same pattern can be seen in higher education, with 144 Unionists going to Oxford or Cambridge (88–53 to the dark blues), again twice the proportion of Liberals.[31] A few had been to other universities, to Sandhurst, Dartmouth or an agricultural college, making 190 in all who had had some form of higher education. The educational background of the party thus suggests a single integrated elite still drawing heavily on the most exclusive sources. The difficulty of interpreting such information is highlighted though by the fact that this educated elite, two-thirds of whom had been to public schools and universities, chose as their leader a man who had been to neither.

The problem of interpretation is compounded in considering MPs' occupation and interests; it was not unusual for a young man from a landed family to be called to the Bar (but not to practice), to serve in the armed forces (but not to become a professional soldier), and then to settle down to a political career with several directorships. It would be misleading to classify such a man as 'lawyer', 'officer' or 'businessman'. So 156 MPs had some identifiable business interest, a little over half of the party, but for most of them some other interest seemed to predominate. Occupations are therefore given, subject to these limitations of interpretation, in Table 5.1, with the figures for Liberals as a comparison.[32]

Table 5.1   Occupations of Unionist MPs and Liberals, 1914

	Unionist	Liberal
Land		
Large landowners	32	9
Small landowners	19	3
Heirs to estates	16	4
	67 (23%)	16 (6%)
Official services		
Army	53	15
Navy	2	1
Diplomatic	5	4
Civil Service	3	4
	63 (22%)	24 (9%)
Professions		
Barristers	79	59
Solicitors	12	12
Authors/Journalists	7	13
Printers/Publishers	2	10
Lecturers/Teachers	3	10
Others	–	7
	103 (36%)	111 (43%)
Commerce		
Merchants	14	24
Stockbrokers	6	3
Bankers	7	4
Insurance	1	3
Accountants	3	1
Others	9	6
	40 (14%)	41 (16%)

Industry

Manufacture	7	18
Shipowners	2	8
Textiles	2	14
Iron	6	8
Coal	1	8
Engineering	3	5
Building	–	2
Brewing	9	1
Working men	–	8
	30 (10%)	72 (27%)

Land no longer dominated the party, the bulk of which was now made up of officers and lawyers, with army officers and lawyers between them making up almost half the total. In the less prestigious occupations, Unionists were still more likely to have investments in railways, banking or insurance than in coal, textiles or engineering, more likely engage in commerce than in industry. The parliamentary party on the outbreak of the First World War can therefore be seen to be in a rough state of balance, with the interests of land, services, professions and business in a near equality. Any change would of course be a small one and would only be seen in candidates adopted after the 'new regime' of 1911 and fighting for the marginal industrial seats of the North. The MPs elected in 1918 came near to meeting the expectations of 1911 and many of these had indeed been selected as candidates before the war: in 1918 the average age rose sharply (over half were over fifty), the proportion with interests in the land fell, and the proportion with interests in business rose from 24 to 41 per cent.[33] This generation of new men might not have been elected but for the war but they would certainly have been *trying* to get elected in a general election in 1915.

The final characteristic of the MPs that can be traced is religion, which shows as traditional a pattern as any. Very few Unionists were Nonconformists and most of these had come into the party from the Liberal Unionist side. There were rather more Presbyterians, a few Roman Catholics and Jews, and an overwhelmingly Anglican majority, at least 90 per cent of the party. In an age when all Unionists professed some form of religious belief and when Anglicanism was the assumption of those who professed no other form of Christianity in England, some of this may be taken to be assumption rather than conviction. But to exaggerate this would be to misjudge the tone of the party in religious affairs, for if the Church of England was the 'Tory party at prayer' then the party was also the Church of England in politics. Many Unionist politicians were prominent laymen in their own right, as were Selborne, Joynson-Hicks, Samuel Hoare and Edward Wood. The Cecils regarded the protection of the Church as a special family responsibility and Lord Hugh was as moved to indignation by the disendowment of the Church in Wales as by the People's Budget or the attack on the House of Lords. To Selborne it was no more nor less than 'robbing the church' and many

Unionists saw it in such simple terms.[34] The party's Anglican commitment was as firm as ever before 1914, even though it was being led for the first time by a man who was not an Anglican himself.

Holding the elements of the party together were two factors of a very different kind: the social world of clubland and society cemented the ties between leaders and followers, and the organizational web of the National Union extended the same ties through the country. Bonar Law might dislike the social round and might rarely visit the Carlton Club, but he did not try to change its role. Party meetings continued to be held at the Carlton and it played a greater part in holding the party together when the Liberal Unionists joined. Other clubs did much the same things for provincial leaders; it was to the Constitutional Club that Salvidge went when in London and it was there that he stayed.[35] It was to the Carlton as well as the Whip's Office that Robert Sanders went to hear the news and discuss political events, and it was to the Carlton too that he went for recreation when the business of the House was too tedious to be borne any longer. Social forces could be used even for directly political purposes, as Sanders himself found when he needed speakers for the South Somerset by-election in 1911; F. E. Smith could in fact be prised away from the West End only by social pressure:

> A comic little episode about the South Somerset election. I asked F. E. to go down, so did Talbot. But he declined on ground of being too busy. Doughty the same. I then suggested putting the Carnarvons on F.E. This was quite effective – a countess on the doorstep brought F.E. in at once. He is to go down Monday next. Doughty on getting a letter from Carnarvon, actually came and asked to go.[36]

Curzon was more difficult to drive down to the provinces, as Steel-Maitland reported to Law in 1914: '*Sunderland*: He says he cannot manage these distant meetings. They are beyond his strength. . . . If we come in, you ought to be kind to him and not ask him to sacrifice his health by taking office.'[37] In general though the social world played a more nebulous role, oiling the wheels, providing opportunities for informal meetings and leisurely discussions, as Lord Midleton recalled in 1929 when bewailing Baldwin's neglect of such methods:

> We all know how the week runs away with official interviews and calls, and how difficult it is to remember all the people with whom you ought to keep in touch, but when I think of the number of things which people of different types, like Lady Londonderry and Lady St Helier and others, have got settled by letting people meet at the dinner table, I despair of a man who never sees even those who have been longest in office on any occasion. Your statement that he never once consulted you on a church appointment is conclusive. After all, if you happened to be next him after dinner for ten minutes, he would get invaluable hints.[38]

A hostess like Lady St Helier, an open-handed host like the Duke of Marlborough at Blenheim, or a fixer like Aitken with a house near to London, could all be useful in keeping the wheels of party turning.

The structure of the National Union was a recognition of the reality of local powers and in this respect the party resembled less a unitary structure than a collection of private franchises. The authority of the Earl of Derby in the North-west, celebrated in the soubriquet 'King of Lancashire', was only the best known of the independent fiefs where the writ of the party leader did not run. In 1912–13 Derby demonstrated his power by mobilizing Lancashire to wreck Law's policy on food taxes. Derby used the machinery of the Lancashire Provincial Division to gather his forces, but it would be a mistake to see his institutional position as a source of strength; the President of the Lancashire Unionists was a man of influence because he was Earl of Derby and not vice versa. He gave authority to the party rather than drawing from it, for the local standing of the Stanleys was altogether independent of party.[39] They had consolidated their position since the fifteenth century and had latterly built up an impregnable position in the social infrastructure of the region. A brother of the Earl was MP for Bootle until 1910, when he gave up his seat to Bonar Law after Law's defeat in Manchester. Ormskirk and Chorley were both county seats under the family influence and Stanleys had sat for both seats in the recent past. Local parties, local clubs, churches and voluntary organizations were all patronized by Stanleys and proud to have a Stanley as patron. It was inevitable that the Earl should be Lord Lieutenant of the County, and that he should be President of the Lancashire Unionists. Part of the basis of this local standing was financial – the generosity with which the family backed local institutions and the land held directly from them – but part was also due to more intangible influences. The Stanleys were careful to place themselves at the head of local opinion rather than ride the county roughshod and their identity of opinion with local Unionists on political and religious matters made them even more powerful.[40]

Something of the same territorial influence can be detected in other counties too; in the East Midlands, the spheres of the Dukes of Rutland and Devonshire were rarely challenged. Nor were such examples confined to feudal counties, for family influence could also be seen in boroughs and on occasion even in big cities. Folkstone was a pocket borough of the Rothschilds, Southend was falling under the control of the Guinness family, Plymouth was learning to love the Astors, and Samuel Roberts was building up the influence in Sheffield that was to provide a seat for his family until 1966. A combination of public philanthropy and attention to local interests could yield quick results, even for an outsider like Max Aitken in Ashton-under-Lyne.[41]

Others were content to wield power in the party machines rather than in the public eye. Salvidge of Liverpool was the best-known example, becoming chairman of the National Union in 1913 and often cited as the only party boss on the American model in English politics, but his authority in Liverpool was no greater than that of Sir James Oddy in Bradford or Sir Percy Woodhouse in Manchester. Such men owed their positions to the constant manipulation of the party machinery – and so confirmed the worst of Ostrogorski's fears; they sat on every local committee, raised money for the local party, decided the selection of candidates and kept their fingers firmly on the local pulse.

The true pinnacle of success in this field was the Chamberlains in Birmingham, who combined an attention to organizational detail with a liking for the limelight. When Neville Chamberlain became Mayor of Birmingham in 1915, he was the eighth member of the family to hold the office in half a century, and he was never to forget the influence of his local roots. Even when a cabinet minister he found time to write round for subscriptions for the Birmingham Unionists and to attend their routine meetings. When facing a critical party conference in 1921, Austen Chamberlain had urged Neville to see that suitable people were selected to represent all twelve Birmingham divisions and to pay their expenses to make sure that they got to Liverpool. Birmingham was quite independent of the party and as late as 1929 was not afraid to show its independence: in that year Neville Chamberlain complained bitterly when he discovered that the Party Chairman had written to businesses in Birmingham for contributions to party funds, for this was regarded as poaching from local preserves. In the previous year, Central Office wished to promote Captain Edwards, the chief agent for Birmingham, to be a Central Office district agent, but they were thwarted by the Chamberlains, who wished to keep him to look after Birmingham; Neville Chamberlain arranged to have Edwards paid enough in Birmingham to keep him there and the interests of Birmingham thus prevailed over those of the party as a whole.[42]

In organizational terms, the question of local independence was mainly one of finance. Central party funds could not pay more than a tiny proportion of the total cost of running a local association in every constituency; not paying the piper they were unable to call the tune. The dangers of dependence on rich men would be and were regularly pointed out: if the local parties were not themselves independent, then they would have to turn to rich outsiders to fight their elections for them, as *The Times* pointed out in 1911:

> If the local organization after an election remained active, on a permanent basis of annual subscription, with a permanent organizing secretary who would attend to the registration work and become the agent at the next election, a candidate could, and probably would, be selected on his merits, and the constituency would be independent of men whose only merit was their wealth.[43]

Independence was thus a two-way phenomenon; local parties should be independent not only of central direction but also of individuals. This explains the popularity of Liverpool as a model for local associations after it was publicized in 1911, for Liverpool was popularly believed to exemplify such local independence. So when a new agent was appointed in Ecclesall in 1912 he was recommended as having come from 'the great school of Liverpool, where he worked for Mr James Thompson'. When the structure of organization in the whole city was reviewed in Sheffield in 1911, it was to Salvidge that local Unionists turned for advice, as did the Manchester

Unionists at the same time. When Harold Smith, the brother of F.E., was asked for advice in organization by Huddersfield Unionists, he delivered them a lecture on Liverpool methods, and in the following year they elected F.E. Smith as their President to carry through reforms that would make Huddersfield like Liverpool. When Darwen needed a new agent in 1911, it was to Salvidge rather than Central Office that they turned for help in finding one.[44] Even if Liverpool methods had been universally adopted – and very few areas had the same religious background as Liverpool, the real basis of Salvidge's success – then change would be slow and limited. The most that could yet be achieved was independence from rich outsiders; independence from rich local men was as far away as ever, even in Liverpool.

Nor is this surprising when the actual cost of politics is remembered; about £400 a year was needed to finance an effective local party, and this excluded registration or special campaigns. It also excluded the cost of elections, for these were a financial problem for the candidate, not for the local association; in a large county division an election could cost as much as £2,000, and even an unopposed return in a borough would cost a few hundred pounds to the lucky winner.[45] Over a long period then, the cost of elections was still more than the cost of the permanent organization, and this cost was so great as to rule out all but a tiny minority. The cost was indeed so great that there were not even enough rich and unsuitable candidates to buy up the nominations. Many seats went uncontested in 1910 because of the lack of moneyed candidates, and in December Central Office paid out over £100,000 in subsidies. Most of this largesse went to the most hopeless seats, to constituencies where no real preparations had been made, to places where nobody would risk his own money. The effect of this was that Central Office, for all its generosity, did not have much control over the selection of candidates in places where the man selected might actually win, and this did not change much before 1914. Balfour explained this in 1908 over his inability to protect Robert Cecil, ingeniously making a virtue out of necessity:[46]

> Top talks as if it rested with *me* to settle who were to be the Unionist candidates for the constituencies. This has never been the Conservative system. . . . Both in theory and in practice we endeavour to have a representative Association in each Division, and on them – and them only – lies the responsibility of selecting their candidate. With that choice the Headquarters of the Party never interfere.

In 1912 the same principle was reaffirmed to W. A. S. Hewins by Bonar Law, in a letter that was actually drafted for him by Steel-Maitland: 'If a constituency definitely refuses to accept a candidate, even if the Central Office wish them to do so, they cannot be forced to take action against their will. In the ultimate resort also, the association of a constituency must be held to be the proper exponent of its wishes.'[47] This was not just a polite brush-off, for Steel-Maitland was anxious to find a seat for Hewins (who was a tariff reform professor of economics who would be a great asset in parliament) and finally managed to do so. But Central Office could exert only informal pressure, since it could neither bully nor bribe its local supporters, and this is exactly what Steel-Maitland set out to do through his district agents. Any change would be gradual and for the time local parties were left with a free choice.

Nothing better illustrates the social balance in the party and the fierce independence of the local parties than the argument about the selection of working-class candidates. Resolutions were passed by the National Union in favour of the principle, but as before no local party would put the good intentions into practice. A resolution proposed at the 1912 National Union Conference tells the whole story; originally the resolution approved, 'the candidature of Unionist working men and earnestly recommends the allocation to one of them of a safe and suitable seat at some by-election in the near future, as evidence of the reality of the movement'. This got to the heart of the matter, the need to make reality out of pious hopes, and it recognized the propaganda value of a contest between a Labour candidate and a Unionist working man in a critical by-election. One such seat would not seem to be an excessive demand in pursuit of an accepted objective, but it was more than the Conference would accept. Steel-Maitland explained that a working man was being selected at Bolton as the choice of the local party, on that very evening, but he did not approve of such specific commitment as the resolution suggested. The recent reorganization of the party had been carried out because 'they wanted to get a real popular element in the direction of the party, but no attempt should be made to interfere autocratically from the H.Q. to the constituencies. . . . Time after time he had pressed the claims of a workingman candidate on a constituency', but they had properly chosen the man who was considered to be most suitable for the constituency. Other delegates supported his view and the motion was amended to read:

> That this Conference, while recording its desire to see working men in Parliament on the Unionist side, thinks it undesirable that any distinction should be made between them and other members, and therefore expresses the opinion that all Unionist organizations should select and support with all their power the best candidate they can find to represent their constituency, irrespective of his social and financial status.[48]

This was little help: giving a working man equality of opportunity was tantamount to rejecting his claims outright, for the scales of wealth and influence would remain weighted against him. Labour's success was based not on equality of opportunity but on the assertion that a working man was more equal than others in his claim to represent the working-class electorate. As long as a Unionist MP had to pay his election expenses, or an association chairman to 'treat' the party workers, or a constituency delegate to pay his own expenses to a midweek conference, then few working men would ever be selected for any of these posts. The party's real attitude was shown clearly enough in the Conference of 1913, when it reaffirmed its opposition to the payment of MPs (another form of scarcely disguised class discrimination) by an almost unanimous vote.[49]

Funds were organized as before to pay election expenses for working-class candidates, based on Liverpool and Birmingham, and publicised by the *Standard* and the *Morning Post*. Hampstead Unionists agreed to support one such fund by levying a guinea subscription from all members of their Executive Committee – a decision that says much about the composition of the Executive Committee itself. Monmouth Unionists backed another fund, but for their own candidate they chose the nephew of their president, Lord Tredegar. Bosworth Unionists agreed to accept 'an assisted candidate', but only if no 'man of means' could be found.[50] And in Bolton, where an assisted candidate was selected by an association with a large working-class element, he found himself facing a Liberal rather than a Labour opponent and went down to defeat.

In its social character and its local structures, the Unionist party of 1914 was caught in a dilemma. Old antagonisms had been revived by the tariff dispute, but time would heal these wounds and continue the long-term trend towards one homogeneous propertied elite. This would solve many of the party's difficulties inherited from the past, but it would do little to settle the pressing problems of the present and future. The gradual consolidation of wealth in the party was making it more difficult to preserve the classless, 'one nation' appeal to working-class supporters. It was increasingly difficult to appeal to the working man whose vote might put the party back into power without antagonizing the wealthy man whose financial assistance was crucial. Robert Sanders noted exactly this problem when the party had to formulate and answer to Lloyd George's land campaign of 1913: 'A certain number of our party go openly for wage boards. Men like St. Audries and Banbury scout the idea and say "stick to the farmer who is on our side and never mind the labourers whose votes you won't get anyhow".'[51]

A crushing Unionist victory in 1915, bringing with it disaster for the Labour party and a major setback for the 'New Liberalism' might have ended the difficulty, but when the First World War intervened the problem remained.

Notes and References

1   Blake, *Unknown Prime Minister*, 66.
2   National Union Conference Minutes, Leeds Conference of Nov. 1911.
3   Lady Dawkins to Milner, 27 Jan. 1912: Milner MSS.
4   Lloyd George expressed much the same view to Lord Riddell: quoted in Rowland, *Last Liberal Governments*, ii, 79.
5   See for example Dangerfield, *The Strange Death of Liberal England*, 76–7.
6   Blake, *Unknown Prime Minister*, 88–9.
7   *Ibid*, 133.
8   Quoted in Taylor, *Beaverbrook*, 47.
9   Blake, *Unknown Prime Minister*, 85.
10 Sanders Diary, 12 Nov. 1911.
11 Wells, *An Experiment in Autobiography*, 773–5.
12 Churchill, *Winston S. Churchill*, ii, 89–90.
13 Quoted in Blake, *Conservative Party*, 182.
14 National Union Conference Minutes, Special London Conference, May 1912.
15 *Conservative and Unionist*, Dec. 1911.
16 *Our Flag*, Dec. 1913.
17 *Our Flag*, Aug. 1913.
18 See Long's introduction to his autobiography, *Memories* and the frontispiece to the book which shows him in full hunting pink. Despite this most of his income was derived from investments rather than from land. For most of his political career he represented urban seats in Liverpool, Dublin, Bristol and Westminster.
19 Blake, *Unknown Prime Minister*, 103.
20 *Ibid*, 176–7.
21 See for example Long to Selborne, 25 Nov. 1907: Selborne MSS, and Long to Charles Bathurst, 10 Aug. 1911: Bledisloe MSS.
22 J. E. Amery, *Joseph Chamberlain*, vi, 982.
23 See for example G. F. Stewart to Carson, 8 Oct. 1913: Carson MSS, D 1507/1/1913/5, and F. S. Wrench to Carson, 14 Nov. 1913: Carson MSS, D 1507/1/1913/9.
24 F. E. Smith, *Speeches, 1906–9*, Balfour, *Opinions and Arguments*.
25 Birkenhead, *Frederick Edwin, Earl of Birkenhead*, i, 213–15.
26 Salisbury to Selborne, 12 Sept. 1911: Selborne MSS.
27 Thomas, *The House of Commons, 1906–1910*, McEwen, 'Conservative and Unionist M.P.s' (thesis).
28 Pelling, *Social Geography*.
29 McEwen, 'Conservative and Unionist M.P.s', Ch. 3.

30 *Ibid.*

31 *Ibid.* The most popular colleges were Trinity College Cambridge with 29 and Christ Church with 27.

32 *Ibid.* The equivalent percentages for 'interests' cited by J. A. Thomas were: land 45 per cent, services 21 per cent, professions 37 per cent, commerce 53 per cent, industry 41 per cent. Thomas did not try to differentiate where an MP had more than one 'interest'.

33 *Ibid*, Ch. 5.

34 *Ibid*, Ch. 3; *Our Flag*, June 1912.

35 Salvidge, *Salvidge of Liverpool*, 105–11; Petrie, *The Carlton Club*, 173.

36 Sanders Diary, 15 Nov. 1911.

37 Steel-Maitland to Law, 18 Mar. 1918, Law MSS 83/1/15.

38 Midleton to Selborne, 19 Jan. 1929: Selborne MSS.

39 Ramsden, 'Organisation', 63.

40 R. Stewart, *History of the Conservative Party*, i. 204, 207–8.

41 Taylor, *Beaverbrook*, 50–1.

42 J. C. C. Davidson to Lord Stanley, 25 Jan. 1928: Davidson MSS.

43 *The Times*, 30 Jan. 1911.

44 Ramsden, 'Organisation', 184–5.

45 The average cost per candidate in January 1910 was £985, in December 1910 it was £821, but Unionists tended to spend more than Liberal and Labour candidates. Butler and Freeman, *British Political Facts*, 156.

46 Balfour to Selborne, 6 Mar. 1908: Selborne MSS.

47 Law to W. A. S. Hewins (draft enclosed in letter from Steel-Maitland to Law), 20 Jan. 1912: Law MSS, 25/1/41.

48 National Union Conference Minutes, London Conference of Nov. 1912.

49 National Union Conference Minutes, Norwich Conference of Nov. 1913.

50 Ramsden, 'Organisation', 183.

51 Sanders Diary, 13 Nov. 1913.

Part II

War and Coalition

'Lloyd George . . . would secure a greater hold on the rank and file of our party and he would also be so dependent on that party after the election that he would permanently be driven into the same attitude towards our Party which Chamberlain was placed in before, with this difference – that he would be the leader of it. That would, however, I am inclined to think not be a bad thing for our Party and a good thing for the Nation. I am perfectly certain, indeed I do not think any one can doubt this, that our Party on the old lines will never have any future again in this country.'
(Bonar Law to Balfour, 5 October 1918).

Chapter 6

The First World War

It is often asserted that the First World War rescued the Unionist Party from an impossible position and left it poised to become the dominating force; the war broke up Liberalism and destroyed the Liberal–Labour alliance, so opening the way for Unionism; Lloyd George carried the party to victory in 1918, incurred the odium for the post-war slump and was cast aside ungratefully in 1922. John Stubbs has identified other effects of the war in the growth of backbench activity, the ending of old issues like Ireland and the strengthening of the Unionist case in others, especially tariffs.[1] Such objective judgements have some validity, but they do not distinguish between the positive effects of war and the damaging effects of coalition. In assessing the decline of Liberalism, it is usual to separate the effects of war and coalition, and it is equally necessary in assessing the survival of Unionism. The prospering of Unionism had less to do with the war than is generally assumed, and it was more healthy in 1914 and less certain of prosperity in 1922. Unionists of the time would scarcely have recognized the terms of the debate, for in 1922 the party was still embroiled with Ireland and the House of Lords, held a smaller share of the popular vote than ever before, and was still split as it had been since 1902; few Unionists would have seen the war as a turning-point for the better in the party fortunes. Only after 1922, with the war at last receding from memory and coalition over, did the party take the decisions that led to its successes of the next twenty years. The good effects of war can be detected only in the long term, and there were bad effects too, while the consequences of coalition for the party were immediate and almost wholly negative. It is necessary then to consider in turn the war, the effects of coalitionism, and the years between the end of coalition and the party recovery in 1924. Conservative recovery after war and coalition does not demonstrate recovery *because* of war and coalition, and indeed the opposite might well have been the case.

The effect of the war can be seen under five heads, all following from the actual European conflict: the running of the war effort; the advance of Labour; the advent of democracy in 1918; the effect of war on the party structure and organization; and the effect of war on popular attitudes. The advent of war was not seen by Unionists as a need to turn back to a conventional patriotism, for Unionists had never doubted the patriotism of their previous stance. In resisting Home Rule and arguing for tariffs, Unionists had seen themselves as acting in the interests of nation and empire against a government that had the interests of neither at heart. The war vindicated the anti-German tone of the tariff campaign, the calls for a stronger navy, the demands for national service, and the defence of the army. If Unionists were vindicated by the war, not just in its taking place but in its nature, then by the same token Liberals were exposed. The war took away the unfortunate necessity, as Unionists saw it, to play with fire in the national interest, but it did not materially alter their view of themselves. If the war brought them more into line with popular feeling, then it was not because they had changed, but because popular opinion (or at least the Liberal–Labour part of it) had at last seen the light.

This was demonstrated in the first political crisis of wartime, a carry over from peacetime. Home Rule and Welsh Disestablishment would become law in the autumn of 1914 and there could now be no election to stop this from taking place. Negotiations centred on the need for national unity in the face of an agreed threat, and provided a test of the genuineness of the parties' commitment to the national cause. A political truce was called within a few days of the outbreak of war; a pact to end contested by-elections was first signed on 6 August, and a joint recruiting drive began before the end of the month. But the Irish and Welsh issues remained; the National Union agreed to approve the truce only on a strict understanding that both issues would be satisfactorily settled. Unionists demanded that both Bills should be frozen in their present position, as passed but not to become law for the duration, but Asquith would not accept this for fear of criticism on his own side. The government thus decided that both Bills would become law, but would then be suspended for the duration. A few Unionists wished to use the Lords to block this procedure, so prompting a constitutional crisis in wartime, but Law and Lansdowne persuaded the shadow cabinet to swallow their feelings. Party opinions were partially assuaged by a protest meeting at the Carlton Club and a demonstration walkout of the Commons by the entire party, but the outcome was not affected, and so Home Rule became law. The success of the party's resistance to Home Rule had been founded on absolute faith that it was the most important issue, but by 1914 this was no longer the case. Nevertheless, the party made only a limited concession; Home Rule's suspension was real, and every attempt to implement it in wartime provoked sufficient Unionist outrage to stop it. Opposition to Home Rule was put on ice for the duration with the Bill, but opposition was as genuine in 1918 as it had been in 1914.[2]

In the meantime, the war gave chances to show the responsible nature of the party through its collective action in parliament, through the restraint of its leaders and through the patriotic actions of its individual members. Winston Churchill had welcomed Bonar Law as party leader in 1911 with the reflection that 'if ever a national emergency makes party interests fade, we shall find in the Leader of the Opposition one who in no fictitious sense places the country and the Empire first', a tribute that was certainly justified by Law's role between 1914 and 1918. More than a hundred Unionist MPs were usually away from the House on military service, and 125 Unionist agents served in the trenches; the party organization was used in the war effort at no cost to the country; every local party was decimated by volunteers who joined up in the first rush; and at every level, the number who joined up was more than matched by those indirectly involved through recruiting, raising money, running war charities or breeding remounts.[3] The party as a whole proved the reality of its patriotism from the first days of the war, and the logic of this continuation from peacetime was underlined by the speed with which Ulster Unionists rallied to the flag in 1914, and the gallantry with which they died on the Somme in 1916. The war underlined the Unionist belief in the patriotism of the British people and their belief in the failings of the Liberals, but for themselves it merely confirmed what they knew already.

At first all criticism of the running of the war was muted and was aimed at measures rather than men. In parliament it was difficult to adjust to the new situation, whereby the party was supposed to abstain from all criticism of the government but had no say in its decisions. Such an open-ended commitment to a government that most Unionists regarded with contempt could hardly last for long: Law found it convenient to make use of the Unionist Business Committee, constituted in January 1915 as an official opposition group, and he suggested Walter Long as its chairman, so harnessing Long's vindictive powers and giving the party some means of influencing the government without breaking the party truce. It was only the first of many devices that articulated party opinion against governments that the party theoretically supported. Unionist concerns were still as much with traditional areas of disagreement with the Liberals as with the War; the UBC made the running with its concern to shield British industry from the war, much as it had previously been intended to protect it through tariffs, and Stanley Baldwin first made his name through its committees.[4] As John Stubbs has written, 'that backbench activism was centred in such an essentially non-landed element of the Conservative Party tends to confirm the view that the party's centre of gravity was increasingly urbanised, commercialised and industrialised'.[5] It also reflects the fact that many of the younger, landowning county MPs were simply absent from Westminster; as Yeomanry officers they were liable for service in wartime and, although the Yeomanry could not be compelled to serve abroad, few did not volunteer. The UBC was never more than a small minority of the parliamentary party, with a general attendance of about forty, and its influence was more a result of its being first in the field of opposition, than of its numbers or its members' economic power. It is clear though that the economic tide was running very much in the party's direction in 1915–16; in 1915 the first industrial tariffs for half a century were imposed, and by a Liberal Chancellor; in 1916 even the Manchester Chamber of

Commerce joined in the demand for industrial protection, causing the resignation of its chairman in protest at the abandonment of a century of belief in free trade.[6] In parliament, the bitterest domestic dispute concerned one of the oldest issues of all, drink; Lloyd George proposed restrictions on the drink trade to help the war effort, and suggested that the trade should be nationalized. A pilot scheme was introduced but Unionist indignation was fierce, led by Sir George Younger for the brewers. Bonar Law first welcomed the idea as a means of reducing his party's dependence on 'the trade', but opposed it when he recognized the scale of party feeling.[7]

Throughout 1915–16 though the issue of increasing importance was the running of the war. A party that had thrown itself so uncompromisingly into the campaign against Home Rule, and which had long ago accepted the need for 'organization' in domestic affairs, could hardly accept for long the leadership by ineffective compromise which was what Asquith offered. Nor could Unionists, who had flocked to the colours in 1914, accept for long inequality of sacrifice when the nation's greatest need was manpower. Unionists had less compunction than Liberals in employing compulsion for desirable ends, and the Milnerite wing of the party had been preaching the gospel of 'national efficiency' through organization, making a positive virtue of compulsion.[8] Once the war came, and especially after the flow of recruits proved insufficient in 1915, Unionists called for conscription and for a nationally organized war effort. At first the party leaders resisted such demands as being likely to destroy the party truce and so tried to avoid the public discussion of such subjects. In February 1915 the National Union Executive refused to sanction a scheme to use the party agents to find recruits, since it 'might savour of compulsion' and in April the Committee refused to debate a motion on compulsory service because of the party truce. In September, the Executive asked to meet Bonar Law to discuss the subject, now that Unionists were in government, but Law refused any outside discussion until the cabinet had made up its mind.[9] Throughout the winter of 1915–16, Law played for time and stalled demands for a meeting of the Central Council, while Unionist ministers pressed the party case in cabinet. Party opinion was mollified by the Derby Scheme of November 1915, whereby the agents and activists of both parties were used to canvass for recruits; the party organization was turned over entirely to recruiting and the scheme cost the party £29,000.[10] By February 1916 pressure was mounting again, and resolutions calling for compulsory national service were flowing in; the Executive refused to debate them, but passed them on to Law nevertheless. In cabinet Unionists pressed the Liberals steadily towards a full policy of conscription, which was finally introduced in May. Criticism of the running of the war went on though, and in June the Executive passed a resolution calling for a more active prosecution of the War.

The Easter Rising in Dublin and the government's abortive plan to rush through a Home Rule settlement caused an even greater furore; this time

Bonar Law had to agree to a meeting of the Central Council, but only after the cabinet had dropped the Home Rule idea, and with a stipulation in advance that questions would be allowed but not resolutions.[11] Throughout the autumn, the barrage of criticism went on in parliament and in the party. After Carson resigned from the government in November 1915 he became the acknowledged leader of the hardliners, organized in the Unionist War Committee.

The UWC was a far more serious threat than the UBC had been: it was entirely outside the control of the party leaders and backed by over a hundred MPs; it was aimed at a government that included Unionists as well as Liberals; and it seemed likely to be a vehicle for the overthrow of Bonar Law by Carson. Its importance was based on two temporary factors, the great Unionist support for its ideas rather than its leaders, and the loyalty of Law to Asquith, which left an opening for Carson. Once Law resolved, after the Nigeria debate of November 1916, that he would work with Carson and Lloyd George to enforce on Asquith the policy that the Unionist MPs wanted, his position was safe. Law's feeling for the sense of the party was less sure than usual in 1916 but, once certain of the party feeling and the national interest, he did not waver in his demand for a different sort of government. Once the political crisis of December 1916 had been weathered and a government had been formed to pursue the Unionist war policy, and with Law himself entrenched at its centre, Unionist support for both Law and for the government remained until the war's end.

Agreement on the prosecution of the war remained through 1917 and 1918, and effective opposition to the government passed from the Unionist back benches to the Asquithian Liberals and the House of Lords. From his position as Chancellor, Law could exercise sufficient influence on the domestic management of the war to avoid further problems, and as Leader of the House of Commons and *de facto* deputy Prime Minister he could also deal with most of the political problems as they arose. So he headed off demands for a capital levy, knowing it to be unacceptable to his party, but Britain nevertheless paid for a higher proportion of the costs of the war from taxation than the other combatants; he was also able to launch the Victory Loan of 1917 at an interest rate of only 5 per cent, having a surer sense of the patriotism of potential subscribers than did the Treasury.[12] There was thus a community of interest in the war between party and government in 1917–18 as there had not been before, and the party was hardly shaken by the secession of a few diehards to form Henry Page Croft's National party. There was no danger that the party would be outflanked on the right as long as the war remained the most pressing national and party interest, and the National party was a complete fiasco.[13] Commitment to the war could have become a problem in itself as the chances of victory became remote. Just as Unionists had rejected an Irish compromise in 1914 after years of commitment to Ulster, so they could not envisage anything short of total victory after the national sacrifices since

1914. When Lansdowne communicated his despair about the war to the press in 1917 and called for negotiations, there was a storm of protest. He had been fading from importance for some time, had been replaced as Unionist leader in the Lords by Curzon and was not a minister under Lloyd George. He was now reviled by the party that he had helped to lead for fifteen years; in his own word he was 'excommunicated'.[14]

Commitment to the war also determined the Unionist response to Lloyd George's disputes with the generals in the winter of 1917–18. Sympathy was with the generals rather than the Prime Minister, hardly surprisingly in view of past events, but sympathy never went far enough to weaken Lloyd George's position greatly. Haig was saved from dismissal by defenders on the Unionist side, but Robertson's removal caused a small stir, and Unionists voted in force to save Lloyd George's face in the Maurice debate. It was doubly difficult for Unionists to resist the substitution of Sir Henry Wilson for Robertson, for Wilson was the most Unionist of all the General Staff and Robertson had not enjoyed good relations with Unionists; Derby's weakness at the War Office and Law's loyalty to Lloyd George were sufficient to defuse the situation. The dismissal of Haig would have been much more serious, but with Law's advice Lloyd George did not take the risk. Over Maurice's allegations, Unionists voted under no illusions; Maurice had indicted Law as well as Lloyd George, and a packed meeting of the UWC under Carson resolved to back the government, not because they believed its explanations but because of their belief in the war. The only alternative to Lloyd George's lies were Asquith's half measures.[15]

There was a continuity then in Unionist attitudes to the war, going on into the post-war years in demands for a harsh treatment of Germany after defeat. Lloyd George discovered in 1919, as Law had done in 1914, that a Unionist party that had given its total commitment to a cause would not be fobbed off with a compromise. In the years before 1914 the iron of partisan politics had entered into the Tory soul, and in the battle for Ulster every weapon had been deemed acceptable. After 1914 there was the same certainty about the war, and it was indeed the inflexible determination of the Unionist party, sure about ends and pragmatic as to means, that was the bedrock on which Britain's war effort rested. Opposition to Home Rule had been canalized into a patriotic war and so the party ended the war in a confident mood, as it had begun it. In the shared community of sacrifice the party had undoubtedly widened its community of interest with the British people, and was able to speak for all of the people in 1917–18 as it had spoken for only an embattled half in 1913. The party therefore reaped the benefit of its national identity in the election of 1918, capturing the mood of the moment as surely as Lloyd George did. In the strident campaign of December 1918 the Unionists were in their element, sure of what must be done as no other party was sure. In its external elements then, the war widened the Unionists' confidence and appeal rather than created it, lining up the nation with the party rather than the reverse. In its domestic aspects though, things had gone very differently.

Unionist fears about the growth of Labour extremism had been widespread before the war and had stemmed from two different factors. There had been good reason to know that Labour could damage Unionist electoral prospects and the dangerous prospect of a class-based party system had been present in the Liberal–Labour alliance. Underlying this had been a deeper fear of more extreme socialists, especially the syndicalists, who might threaten violence and revolution. The War threatened to sweep away such fears in the uninhibited jingoism that greeted the outbreak of hostilities. The train was at last 'on different rails' and Unionists could not fail to rejoice at the disarray on the left, but the different rails might prove more suitable for Trotsky's 'locomotive of History' than for Unionist imperialism.

By 1917 Unionists had more cause to fear than to rejoice, for the Labour movement had been greatly strengthened by the war in both its aspects; increasing membership and growing militancy in the trades unions, growing confidence in the Labour party, the arrival of organized revolutionary extremism in the shop-stewards' movement all pointed to a grim future. The troubles in Sheffield and South Wales, the example of 'Red Clydeside' and the inspiration of revolutionary Russia might all be signs of a new and terrible future. Unionist fears were based overwhelmingly on ignorance, in isolation from working-class attitudes at home and in the trenches, and on the certainty that things could not be the same again. By 1918 these fears had reached fever pitch; one Conservative MP recalled that his family had expected that the end of the war would be followed by atrocities like those in Russia, that 'families like ours would be strung up from the nearest lamp post'; Robert Sanders was surprised to see on Armistice Day that the crowds were actually cheering the King, so unlike the fate of the Russian royal family a few months earlier.[16] Such fears were vastly exaggerated, for if Britain ever did reach a stage of possible revolution, then it was certainly after rather than during the war, but in isolation from working-class opinions, they seemed real enough to Unionist MPs and their supporters in 1918.

Unionist reactions were twofold, first to play up the war itself as a unifier of classes, and second to exploit divisions in the Labour movement in the hope of carrying them over into peacetime. The party's first object was the prosecution of the war, and this could be linked convincingly enough with attacks on malingerers and deserters; long after 1902 Unionists had continued to revile radical Liberals (including Lloyd George) as pro-Boers, and this view was easily adaptable to the Labour party in the new war. The campaign for conscription was at least in part intended to force opponents of the war out into the open, so that their lack of patriotism could be exposed when it would be unpopular. When conscription came into force, Unionists pressed for the disfranchisement of conscientious objectors, more because it would be a sign of civic excommunication than because their numbers were significant. The reverse of this policy was a Unionist proposal that all men in the armed forces should qualify for the franchise as of right. A clear division was to be made then, with all who served their country being enfranchised and all who refused being disfranchised, in both cases irrespective of age or other considerations; the war was to be the test and the policy was to be 'What did you do in the war, Daddy?' Neither policy was implemented, although gestures were made in each direction. As President of the Local Government Board, Walter Long surprised opponents and supporters alike by the fairness with which he treated conscientious objectors, but local Unionists on the appeals tribunals were far less tolerant. The franchise was eventually widened as a result of the Unionist demand, but not as they had expected. Unionists did though make war service a main plank of their electioneering whenever they had the chance. In 1918 Sanders noted that 'I had a contest with Plummer, the Bridgwater Trades Union Secretary. His supporters said he had got wages raised and would get the agricultural labourer 40/- a week. My supporters said "Sanders went to fight and Plummer did not." On such issues are the fates of Empire divided.'[17] After the war, Unionist candidates with commissions, good war records and decorations made the most of their advantages, especially when they could be set against opponents who had opposed the war or stayed at home. Ramsay MacDonald was beaten by such a campaign in 1921 with language that made the general election of 1918 seem tame. As late as 1931, the war records of Labour candidates were still held against them, although by then Ramsay MacDonald, like Lloyd George before him, had been forgiven his sins.

Exploitation of divisions in the Labour movement was the concern of only a small number of Unionists, linked mainly with Lord Milner and with Central Office. The British Workers' League was founded under Milner's wing as a front organization that was linked in principle with the coalition as a whole but was run from the Unionist side. Its leader was Victor Fisher and it was dedicated to providing a point around which 'patriotic labour' could rally. It asserted the need for social reform within a broad imperial policy and attacked the official leaders of the Labour movement for their failure to dissociate themselves from pacifists and militants. In the Labour movement it never made much impact, for it always remained an alien force, financed and directed from outside, but it achieved something in taking the battle on to the streets in order to break up the meetings of the left. Even here more was achieved by the 'patriotic labour' men who had originated in the Labour movement and stayed in it, such as Jack Jones in West Ham. Central Office had great difficulty finding seats for the candidates of the National Democratic Party (NDP), as the BWL had become by 1918, and it took some time even to find a place for Victor Fisher himself before he was finally installed for Stourbridge. Unionists did not wish to stand down where they had a candidate of their own ready to fight; in these circumstances, the NDP did remarkably well in 1918, winning eleven seats, all in Labour strongholds where neither Unionists nor Coalition Liberals had much desire to stand, and they beat both MacDonald and Henderson. After the election, though, the NDP faded into the ranks of the coalition majority, having neither roots nor party organization of their own, and Unionist efforts were carried on instead through a Labour wing in their own party. The Labour vote was badly hit by the NDP even in working-class strongholds, but no impression was made on the Labour movement.[18]

The general question of Unionist attitudes to Labour was highlighted at the Special Party Conference in 1917 where Law came under a strong attack. He gave his followers an analysis of the situation straight from the shoulder, with no false optimism about the immediate prospects and considerable perception about future events:

> There is another thing which I know you were thinking about a great deal, which all of us must think about. That is, the future of our Party after the War is over. You would like, I daresay, if I could give you a clear and definite policy. Well, I cannot. We are looking into a fog. It is absolutely futile to try to make plans for conditions which you cannot foresee, (Hear, hear). But this I would say to you. I am not sure that you will agree with me, but I have no doubt about it; our Party on the old lines will have no future in the life of this Country (Hear, hear). What is the future likely to be? It is all guesswork, but we cannot help thinking about it, and I have thought a great deal about it. There seems to be two possible ways in which our Party can keep its old force. One would be if – I will not say the Labour Party but the extreme Labour Party – were to get so powerful that it would be a menace and we should have thrown on the other scale all that was moderate in the Liberal Party as well as our own Party. That is not going to happen in my judgement without some leader who commands the support of a large section of the country, and I do not see where that leader is going to come from. But the other way in which our Party has a future is the way in which I would like to see it have a future. In the past we have suffered tremendously, because we have always had the whole of organised Labour against us. It is that that defeated our Tariff Reform proposal – that and that alone.
>
> Well, gentlemen, there is splitting in all parties, and when you feel that our Party is suffering a great deal, look at the others and ask which of them is worse? There is splitting in all parties, and nowhere is it more marked than in the Labour Party (Hear, hear). Now, gentlemen, this war has shown that among the leaders of Labour there is a body which is national and patriotic (Hear, hear and applause,) and feels these sentiments as strongly as we do. I feel it is our duty to try to get – I will not say on our side but to work with us – the section of Labour which is national and imperialistic (Applause) . . . We have got to get on our side if we can, the section of Labour which recognises that for all classes, employers and employed, production is the one thing to be aimed at (Applause), and that anything which is detrimental to that is detrimental to anybody.
>
> Well, gentlemen, you have cheered this. Everybody in our Party welcomes that with their lips, but I will tell you what I think about it, and I am going to speak quite frankly. There are a great many who imagine that we can get Labour to take the shilling for us as it were and to fight simply for our old aims as an adjunct to our Party. That is not going to happen (Hear, hear). If we are going to become part of that larger Party we will have to pay the price. I am not going to attempt today to foresee what that price will be. It may be that it is a price which none of us will

pay. It may be that when the time comes our Party will be divided in regard to this matter. But, gentlemen, of this I am certain, the Conservative Party has been a good thing for this country and it is our business today, and as long as we can, to keep that Party solid; and if splits must come, to delay them as long as we possibly can (Applause).[19]

In this single speech, Law foreshadowed the development of the party for the next fifteen years; the strategic dilemma over relations with the other parties after the war, the need to make real concessions to make a coalition workable, the openings that could be created by a national leader of independent reputation (Baldwin as it turned out), and the outcome when the moderate men of all parties came together in 1931.

At the same conference, Law warned the Unionists that they must accept the government's plans to extend the franchise, whatever their personal opinions:

It is very difficult to see . . . how you could stop much short of the Bill which is now before the House of Commons. And, gentlemen, I should like to say this also; our Party if it is properly conducted has no reason to fear that the mass of the people in this country will not support it (Hear, hear). If we cannot win that support, we may as well go out of business, and it is our duty now at all events to make the best of the situation which has arisen and to see that everything is done to make our Party what Disraeli called it – and what, if it is to have any existence, it must be – a really national party.

It is ironical that one of the most beneficial developments of the war years, the Representation of the People Act of 1918, should have occasioned so much party opposition. Consideration of the franchise had followed Unionist demands for votes for servicemen, and a Speaker's Conference was set up in 1916, with the Unionist members led by Sir William Bull and Sir Harry Samuel.[20] It seems that a deal was hatched behind the closed doors of the Conference, by which Unionists accepted a widening of the franchise to include all men and some women, in return for a Liberal agreement to accept some plural votes and a complete redistribution of seats. Liberals had argued for a wider franchise for years and Unionists had demanded a redistribution, so both sides got something of what they wanted and proportional representation was thrown in with the present mood of Labour in mind, so that the anti-socialist parties would be able to consolidate their position if necessary.

Unionist reactions to these proposals, published and embodied in the Representation of the People Bill early in 1917, were very hostile indeed; it seemed a reckless step to give the biggest ever increase in the franchise in the midst of a major war, to throw away some of the plural votes on which the party had relied, and to receive in return a redistribution that could bring almost anything. A bitter debate in the Executive of the National Union on 8 February 1917 resulted in the setting up of a special sub-committee to consider the Bill; a suggestion that MPs should be ineligible for the sub-committee because they had let down the party so badly in the Speaker's Conference was only narrowly lost. At the next meeting, the proposals were considered one by one, along with the views of the sub-committee; every proposal was criticized and a highly critical sub-committee report was adopted *nem. con.*, with Sir Harry Samuel finally abstaining after failing to convince his colleagues of the rightness of the proposals. The party view, expressed well by the *Conservative Agents' Journal*, was that the Unionists in the Speaker's Conference had been taken in by the Liberal members, that they had not sought or received any professional advice, and that they had blundered accordingly.[21] However, the Central Council recognized in April that a franchise change could not now be avoided, but resolved to support it only if the government would agree to restore the House of Lords at the same time.

Reports from the constituencies in May showed 259 local parties against the Bill and only thirty-two in favour; eighty-three suggested no change in wartime; twice as many local parties supported votes for women as opposed the idea, by ninety-eight to forty-four, and there was little or no support for proportional representation.[22] By May the principle of change had been accepted as inevitable, for once an extension of the franchise had been proposed, it would be suicidal for the party to oppose it, and there was thus a need to concentrate on pressing detailed amendments, for example to protect the interests and representation of agriculture. But the partisan warfare went on: Walter Long and his PPS, Sir William Bull (who had been on the Conference himself), reacted angrily to complaints from the agents and suggested that the professional organizers wanted to keep the system as complicated as possible so that they could keep their pay and privileges. The agents took this as a slander on their profession and replied in kind. Bull also continued the fight with greater subtlety through the *Daily Telegraph*: he wrote for the *Telegraph* regularly in 1917, either directly as 'our political correspondent', or indirectly by feeding information on the Bill to the paper, and this helped to keep at least one part of the Unionist press briefed with the official party line.[23]

It was increasingly difficult to see what the party line was: the Chief Whip, Lord Edmund Talbot, had summoned Robert Sanders back from war service and after his return in May 1917 he was pressed into the party's service. Sanders had been a Whip and a specialist in franchise matters before the war, so his return to Westminster gave an added impetus to the party campaign against the Bill; he became a sort of unofficial party Whip against a government that the party supported, cooperated closely with George Younger, by this time Party Chairman, and eventually became deputy chairman of the party himself in 1918.[24]

The battle now shifted to parliament, where the second reading was carried by a huge majority on 22 May; many Unionists spoke against the Bill, but few could bring themselves to oppose it in principle, and so Sanders could mobilize only forty MPs to go with him into the No lobby. But this signalized the beginning of the open fight. In June the National Union finally decided its attitude: it was duly recorded that:

the Unionist party . . . has always been in favour of:
1. An extension of the franchise.
2. [votes for servicemen]
3. Simplification of Registration.
4. An Equitable scheme of Redistribution.
5. *All* of these proposals to be applicable to the *whole* of the U.K.
6. Concurrently, a scheme for the reconstitution of the Second Chamber with adequate powers to be introduced.
It will thus be seen that the Party is in favour of Electoral Reform being dealt with on a sound basis, but at the proper time.[25]

Since reform was now unavoidable it must be made certain that Ireland would be included under the redistribution clauses and that the House of Lords should be restored to entrench resistance to Labour. The details of amendments to the Bill needed to press these points were sent to each Unionist MP, from Central Office not from the official Whips, and a special committee of agents and National Union leaders was set up to give MPs professional advice. By mid July Unionists in the Commons had tabled and spoken to over 160 amendments, with the heaviest burden falling on Younger and Sanders. Pressure was such that the government, in the person of George Cave the Unionist Home Secretary, was frequently forced to allow free votes, so several useful amendments were carried. Instructions to the boundary commissioners were revoked and amended so that they would be able to consider economic interest as well as population and community in the drawing up of the new constituencies; this was regarded as vital by the Unionists, for it seemed likely that the merging of the small boroughs into the county constituencies would take away the last of the agricultural seats. Similarly, an amendment carried in November 1917 did much to nullify the reduction of plural voting rights for town dwellers. Before 1918 electors could have more than one vote, provided that they could quality in different towns or counties; it was now proposed by Unionists that the qualifying area in boroughs should become the constituency rather than the borough itself. A shopkeeper with a shop in Bristol Central and a home in Bristol West would now qualify for a vote in both constituencies; under the new system, there were few ways to qualify for plural votes, but it was much easier actually to qualify, and so tens of thousands of new plural votes were created, overwhelmingly Unionist.[26]

At the end of 1917 there was much parliamentary manoeuvring over proportional representation. The original proposal had been for PR in the cities but this was opposed by Unionists who were concerned to protect the efficacy of the business vote; Central Office also opposed the alternative vote when it was put forward in the debates, and the majority of Unionist MPs and the National Union never backed either system. The Commons could not agree on a scheme and several were inserted in the Bill by a temporary majority of one day and then removed by another majority later. The Lords entered the fray in December with a strong preference for PR as a means of keeping both the Labour party and the Commons in check, so that in January 1918 there were disputes between the two houses as well as between and within the parties. The outcome, perhaps inevitably, was that no new voting system at all was introduced, except for the university constituencies (for it was deemed that graduates would be able to follow the mysteries of PR even if the rest of the electors could not). The Representation of the People Act thus became law in February 1918, ushering in an era of near democracy, increasing the electorate from the 7.7 million of 1910 to 21.4 million in 1918, over three-quarters of whom had never voted before.

The Act of 1918 set the scene of the entire political world between the wars, often through consequences that were not seen for a generation. Unionists proved quite able to handle the new mass electorate, and their efforts to gear up to meet new challenges in and after 1911 had set them on the right road. The party took more easily to modern electioneering than did the Liberals, and gained an unexpected bonus in the votes of women, who have been a force for conservatism since their enfranchisement in 1918. What could be anticipated with confidence was the beneficial results of redistribution, for Unionists had expected them for some time. Before the war, Unionists had pointed to the huge disparity between the smallest and largest seats (in 1910 Kilkenny had an electorate of a few hundred and Romford an electorate of over 50,000), and had noted that Unionist constituencies were on average larger than Liberal constituencies, far larger than those of Nationalists in Ireland. Increasing population in England and migration of middle-class voters from the towns to the suburbs had led to these disparities and to a situation where any redistribution would help Unionism. In 1911–12 Major Morrison-Bell MP constructed a model to demonstrate these disparities of distribution and had toured the country with it for propaganda purposes; the obvious over-representation of Ireland was especially useful to a Unionist party that wished to claim that Redmond was holding the Empire to ransom. The changes in population in the decade 1901–10, revealed in the 1911 census, demonstrated the rapid increase of population in Unionist areas and the static position in Liberal and Nationalist areas. The LCC area had declined in population by 0.2 per cent overall, but within that Lewisham had increased by 26 per cent and Wandsworth by 34 per cent; the population of Middlesex was up by 42 per cent in ten years, Essex and Surrey both by 30 per cent, while the population of Ireland had fallen by another 2 per cent. Time was clearly on the Unionist side. [27]

In the event, the actual redistribution of 1918 came as something of a disappointment, for although there was redistribution *within* Ireland, the overall number of Irish seats remained the same, and there was only a small increase in the number of English seats. But there was a net gain of some thirty seats to the Unionists in direct comparison with the last elections in 1910, a strong position for a party that was already the largest in parliament. This position was further improved by the effective withdrawal of Sinn Fein from Westminster after the election of 1918 and the second redistribution in Ireland in 1921 after the Government of Ireland Act, which gave another bonus to the Unionists by removing about seventy opponents from the House of Commons. The net effect of the Acts of 1918 and 1921 was thus to improve the Unionist position by a hundred seats, not just in that parliament but in every succeeding one too. In other words, quite apart from the franchise changes that did the party no net harm, the changes of 1918–21 transformed the Unionists from the natural minority that they had been in 1914 to a natural majority party until the Second World War. Under the electoral system of 1918, the Unionists had a minimum vote of at least 38 per cent of the electorate, and this would bring at least 250 seats in a parliament of 615; in a political world of three parties this almost guaranteed that no other party would govern alone and that the Unionists would usually have a majority.

Within this there was an equally important change, for not only did the number of Unionist seats increase, but so did the number of safe seats. Neal Blewett found just forty-eight 'predominantly middle-class' constituencies in 1910, while Michael Kinnear found seventy-five in 1921 (and Kinnear's figure is certainly an understatement, for he could not get figures for divided boroughs outside London, many of which certainly would come into his category, so the real figure may be more like ninety). The already safe seat at Wandsworth was divided in 1918 into five safe seats; Lewisham, Hammersmith and Fulham were each divided into two seats; the number of seats in the outer London suburbs of Kent, Surrey, Essex and Middlesex went up from fifteen to forty, of which thirty-five were held by Unionists at every election before 1945. The value of such an expansion of political suburbia has been demonstrated by Michael Kinnear. There were 200 seats with a substantial middle-class element, and these were overwhelmingly Unionist at each election between the wars.[28] If the agricultural seats are added to the middle-class strongholds, it can be seen why Conservatism was so strong between the wars, for the party could count well over 200 seats as unshakably safe and on 300 as reliable enough to be won except in a very bad year. At a time when many middle-class voters would be looking for the party that would best defend them from Labour, this Conservative strength would be of vital importance. The Conservatives would not always win under the electoral system of 1918, but they would rarely do so badly as to allow anyone else to win.

The revival of activity occasioned by the 1918 Act and its redistribution may have helped to revive local Unionist parties, but in fact the war had a less serious effect than might be expected. In the first months, when hostilities were expected to last for only a few months, party activity was hardly affected at all. A registration campaign was conducted in the autumn of 1914 and Central Office encouraged the continuation of normal activities. Continuation of the war in 1915, together with the absence of key figures at every level, led to a suspension of all but routine party business. The typical pattern was for the local parties to meet only once a year in 1915 and 1916, to re-elect their officers for another year; agents who had enlisted were kept on the books by retaining half their normal pay, to compensate them for loss of earnings in the national interest and to keep them available for a resumption of partisanship. Central Office tried to keep the local parties alive, for the party truce was only renewed for a few months at a time and parliament was prolonged beyond its five-year term only for a few months at a time too. Subscriptions fell steadily and expenditure fell even more sharply with the reduction of salaries and the suspension of propaganda, so that most local parties ended the war with a substantial profit; but this concealed a real weakness, for expenditure could be revived by a single decision, while income could only be revived by many years of patient work. In 1917 the state of readiness slipped further, with most local parties holding no meeting at all, some sacking their agents, and closing their offices. The agents who remained operated a skeleton service for several constituencies, with the salary shared out too; they visited each office once a week to answer letters and transact routine business; the Annual Report for the Yorkshire Area for 1916–17 claimed 'we still say no offices entirely closed' but this was no longer a realistic picture of party activity. Things had got even worse on the voluntary side, for without subscriptions to collect or canvassing to do, the whole basis of the voluntary party had gone. The Yorkshire Annual Report for 1920 recalled that 'November 1918 found all Party organizations the worse – not for War but for inactivity'. The party structure was probably saved by two features, the recruiting of 1915–16 and the need to cope with the Representation of the People Act in 1918.[29]

The Parliamentary Recruiting Committee ran the national campaign for recruits in the first eighteen months of the war, through party rather than national channels. The Committee was convened by the Chief Whips of the parties, and the chief professional organizers became joint secretaries. Boraston was thus directly involved in administration, and Central Office looked after the organization of recruiting meetings; the Liberal offices dealt with literature for recruitment and Malcolm Fraser was transferred to Abingdon Street to help with the management of the press. The entire effort was run like a political campaign, with the canvassers, speakers, stewards and publicity all run on tried and familiar lines.[30] District and constituency offices were similarly involved and in many areas the national example was followed, with the agents of both parties working under a mayor or lord lieutenant. The Derby Scheme of 1915 allowed the local parties to mount a full-scale exercise in canvassing and knocking-up. When the state took over recruitment under the Military Service Acts, the party continued to be involved: many agents were transferred to the army, where they continued to do the same job, and many party offices were lent to the government as recruitment centres. In 1917 party organization was used for the War Savings and War Aims movements. This all reflects the important part that political organizations played in the Edwardian era, for when politicians needed means of communication and organization in a time of crisis it was to the parties rather than to the state that they turned for the machinery and the expertise; it was not to be the same in 1939, with consequent effects on the state of the local parties by 1945. Through recruiting and War Aims publicity, even tapers and tadpoles could play their part in the national cause.

Central Office was able to keep going at full capacity through 1915 and 1916, but here again there was a falling off in 1917. Boraston was so much involved in war work that his assistant, William Jenkins, had to be promoted to Joint Principal Agent to look after the party, and he was also given a promise of the reversion of Boraston's job. By this time too there were economies in staff and publications because of the war: *Gleanings and Memoranda*, the *Constitutional Year Book* and other semi-partisan pieces of literature were suspended in 1917 for the duration.[31]

The middle of 1917 saw the party at its lowest ebb, but the demands of an approaching general election produced a recovery. Professional advice was important to the MPs fighting the Representation of the People Bill and National Union committees began to meet again at every level to discuss the Bill's consequences for the party. There was a conference in late 1917, the Executive met regularly, and the Central Council met a record four times in 1917. The rules of the national Union were changed to allow a special appeal to working-class and women voters. Constituency parties had to be wound up and re-formed to conform to the new boundaries, and all this at the worst point of the war. Local campaigns to resist unsatisfactory new boundaries were run and in some cases were very successful. In Cheshire the plans put forward by the boundary commissioners were opposed by local Unionists and counter-proposals put forward by their chairman, Sir Alan Sykes, were adopted instead: this produced a new constituency called Eddisbury, which would be a most peculiar shape, but which would be almost wholly agricultural – and strongly Unionist.[32] Finally, the passage of the Act into law made a general election a certainty in the near future. For the local parties this increased the urgency of changing the local structures and settling candidates; for Central Office it meant the negotiation of a pact with the Coalition Liberals and the NDP, the arrangements of a joint platform, and the production of anti-Labour party literature, all of which were under discussion from the spring of 1918. In every way, then, the party organization emerged from the war years in reasonably good shape; it had played its part in the war and its local and national structures were attenuated but intact (a major and significant contrast with the effect of war on the Liberals), and a large reform had been carried out with little trouble. Great efforts would be needed to restore the party to its strong position of 1914 and to carry on with the fundamental changes that had been under way then, but the war years had done no lasting damage.[33]

The final effect of the First World War was less tangible, the impact of war on the attitudes of Unionists themselves, but there is no doubt that the holocaust did leave lasting effects. The effect of war on religion was among the most profound of these influences. For the party that had leaned heavily on the established Church and derived satisfaction from its role as defender of the Church, the decline of religion was a serious blow. After the war clouds rolled away old arguments about Home Rule were quickly resumed, but the issue of the Welsh Church was easily settled: Lloyd George offered compensation and the Welsh Church was duly disestablished in 1920 with little Unionist complaint. The House of Lords, trade unions, and licensing continued to raise as much heat as before in Unionist minds, but the issue of the Church was drowned in the mud of Flanders. Fisher's Education Act of 1918 raised far less sectarian strife than Balfour's had done in 1902, less even than Butler's was to do in 1944. In part, the death of the old politics of Church and Chapel was a consequence of the catastrophic effect of the war on militant Nonconformity, and especially on Nonconformist Liberalism, but in part it was also due to a new doubt on the Unionist side. The Prayer Book debates of 1928 and the arguments over tithes in the 1930s showed that many Unionists still counted the interests of the Church high in their priorities, but the battles were no longer party ones. The party was as sure as ever about Christian principles, and the advent of women into the organization may even have strengthened the connection, but there was no longer certainty about forms and institutions.

Baldwin was one party man who remained a convinced Christian but without certainty about forms, and he was also characteristic of one sort of party response to the suffering caused by the war itself. Bonar Law became ever more pessimistic after the death of his sons in action in 1917, but the reaction of Baldwin and Neville Chamberlain was more positive. To both of them, the human sacrifice of 1914–18 created not just a deep loathing of war but also a determination that such sacrifice should not be in vain. Baldwin had a profound distaste for those who had made money out of the war and in 1919 he made an anonymous donation of part of his wealth to the nation as his personal sacrifice; Neville Chamberlain was greatly affected by the death of his cousin Norman and determined that such sacrifice should not be wasted.[34] For many there was a conviction that the post-war world must be made a better place, a view that recurred regularly over the next twenty years. In 1925 Winston Churchill, no empty idealist, introduced his pension scheme with the hope

> that the sufferings, the sacrifices, the sorrow of the war have sown a seed from which a strong tree will grow. . . . This is the finest war memorial you could set up to the men who gave their lives, their limbs, or their health, and those who lost their dear ones in the country's cause.[35]

For the older men, who had sent their sons to slaughter, there remained a determination to make conditions better; for the younger men there was an almost obsessive guilt at having survived the holocaust when so many friends had died. In their different ways, Harold Macmillan and Anthony Eden shared the same reaction; the young Robert Boothby was one of the few who were disappointed by the Armistice, because he had been too young to fight.[36] Not everyone was affected by the war in this way, but a large group in the party were scarred by the First World War for the rest of their lives, and as a result the party acquired a moral calibre that it had not had before.

The Unionist party thus emerged from the war reassured in its identity as the national party, more closely in touch with the national mood than in 1914, with its electoral prospects much improved, but, like the rest of the nation, affected deeply by the war. The only cloud, and in 1918 a threatening thunderstorm to all appearances, was the challenge from Labour. The struggle to determine the party's attitude to the aspirations of Labour was to be its chief battleground for the next six years.

Notes and References

1 Cook and Peele, *Politics of Reappraisal*, 14–39.
2 Blake, *Unknown Prime Minister*, 227–30.
3 Churchill, *Winston S. Churchill*, comp. vol. ii, 1337; Ramsden, 'Organisation', (thesis) 41–5; Fawcett, *Conservative Agent*, 20.
4 Minutes of the Unionist Business Committee, W. A. S. Hewins MSS.
5 Cook and Peele, *Politics of Reappraisal*, 24.
6 *Gleanings and Memoranda*, April 1916.
7 Blake, *Unknown Prime Minister*, 239–40.
8 Scally, *The Origins of the Lloyd George Coalition*, 1975, 105–8.
9 National Union minutes, Executive Committee, 18 Feb., 24 Apr. and 16 Sept. 1915.
10 *Ibid*, Executive Committee, 11 Nov. 1915.
11 *Ibid*, Executive Committee, 8 June and 9 Aug. 1916.
12 Davidson, *Memoirs of a Conservative*, 57–9.
13 Rubinstein, 'Henry Page Croft and the National Party'.
14 Blake, *Unknown Prime Minister*, 363–4.
15 John Stubbs, in Cook and Peele, *Politics of Reappraisal*, 30.
16 National Union minutes, transcript of Special London Conference, 30 Nov. 1917; Sanders Diary, 16 Nov. 1918.
17 National Union minutes, Executive Committee, 22 Apr. 1915; Rae, *Conscience and Politics*, 41; Sanders Diary 5 Jan. 1919.
18 Stubbs, 'Lord Milner and patriotic labour', Douglas, 'The N.D.P. and the B.W.L.'
19 National Union minutes, transcript of Special London Conference, 30 Nov. 1917.
20 *Conservative Agents' Journal*, Oct. 1916.
21 *Ibid*, Apr. 1917; National Union minutes, Executive Committee, 13 Jan. 1917.
22 National Union minutes, Central Council, 8 June 1917.
23 Annotated press cuttings in the Bull MSS; *Conservative Agents' Journal*, July 1917.
24 Sanders Diary, 27 May 1917.
25 National Union minutes, Executive Committee, 7 June 1917.
26 Sanders Diary, 22 Nov. 1917.
27 *Morning Post*, 26 May and 1 July 1911.
28 Ramsden, 'Organisation', 51–2; Kinnear, *The British Voter*, 122–4.
29 Ramsden, 'Organisation', 45.
30 Minutes of Joint Parliamentary Recruiting Committee, Add.MSS 54192.
31 Ramsden, 'Organisation', 223; The volumes of *Gleanings and Memoranda* for 1917 and 1918 were published retrospectively in 1919.
32 *Stockport Advertiser*, 3 Aug. 1917.

33 Ramsden, 'Organisation', 45.
34 Middlemas and Barnes, *Baldwin*, 72–3; Gilbert, *The Roots of Appeasement*, 21.
35 Gilbert, *Winston S. Churchill*, v, 115.
36 Macmillan, *Winds of Change*, 101; Colin Coote, 'Pre-1914 and all that' in *The Times*, 5 June 1976.

Chapter 7

Coalition troubles, 1915–1921

For ten years after 1914 the theme of party was accompanied by a strong counterpoint: the idea of coalition. For Rosebery, for Milner, even for Lloyd George, there had been temptation in coalition ever since the Boer War, but such dreams had never come into the political daylight. But when war came the persistent pedal-point of coalitionism sounded all the louder for the sudden silence of the party truce. A coalition government was formed in May 1915, continued under Lloyd George in December 1916, and carried over into peacetime in 1918. Once established, coalition proved difficult to shift and coalitionists developed an ideology of their own. During Lloyd George's premiership, the counterpoint of coalition almost drowned the theme of party, and many Unionists feared for the survival of politics as they knew it. The coalition facilitated a realignment from the two-party Liberal–Unionist contest in 1914 to the Labour–Conservative battles of the late 1920s; only with the triumph of coalition in 1916 did the old politics die, and only with the destruction of coalitionism in 1924 could the new politics be born. It is necessary to examine the idea of coalitionism and the political forces that made it a powerful alternative before considering its direct impact on the Unionist party.

The most positive argument for coalition, and the one that tipped the balance in its favour, was the experience of war. The Boer War brought the first murmurs of coalitionism, a sense of national crisis brought the first attempt to form a coalition, and the advent of the First World War made it a practical possibility. In each case the argument was much the same: in crisis, it was the duty of politicians to come together so that the best men could be used to the greatest advantage, and so that shibboleths of party could be discarded. Without a combination the nation could not be properly mobilized, for any party government would be opposed by half the nation, and would be forced to consider its own extremists as more important than moderates on the other side. Coalition was the negation of the party system, for as party assumed a grouping from the centre to one of the extremes, coalition assumed a grouping at the centre to the exclusion of extremists. A coalition in 1910 would have excluded Ulster, Irish Nationalists, and Labour; coalition in 1915 excluded anti-war MPs and diehards. The very existence of coalition meant a struggle for the survival of party, a struggle that the Liberals lost, that Labour won by keeping clear, and that Unionism almost lost too.

By May 1915 Unionist leaders were convinced that they must give up some independence if they were to influence the war; the liquor issue seemed to show the danger of staying aloof, and the shell scandal seemed to show that they were needed inside. National and party interest thus combined to make Bonar Law promote a coalition, but it was the national interest that was cited as the reason for joining Asquith.[1] It was also the national cause that prompted Law to accept a junior position; he took the Colonial Office himself, a backwater in wartime, and Liberals retained most of the major posts. In a negative way, Unionists had an important influence on the new government, securing the removal of Haldane, the demotion of Churchill and the placing of munitions under Lloyd George. Unionist ministers were also able to move the Liberal majority closer to the Unionist view of how the war should be run, notably on conscription and compulsion.

Asquith's 1915 government was only halfway to coalition; it was in fact a coalition of parties rather than a coalition of men, and it was run so as to maximize continuity. Unionists were therefore soon frustrated by what seemed the weakness of their leaders in swallowing Asquith and getting nothing in return. In parliament the position seemed worse now that the Unionist leaders sat on the government front bench while their followers continued to sit as the opposition. But it was the continuing failure in the war and Asquith's inability to take important decisions in time that really fuelled Unionist discontent in 1916. By the summer of 1916 the Unionist backbenchers were used to voting against the government, and were close to acting as a full opposition again under Carson.[2] In the crucial Nigeria debate in November Law actually did quite well, for he persuaded a narrow majority of Unionists to back the government. At the height of the criticism, Law met constituency chairmen and agents at the Queen's Hall and told them that

> the question whether or not this government was wise must be judged on very broad grounds. This is the question which everyone ought to ask himself, and the only question – are we as a nation in a better position to prosecute the war as a consequence of it than we would have been by any other arrangement? I have no doubt of it.

A year later he recalled that he had supported Asquith because 'rightly or wrongly, I was afraid of any alternative *at the time*'. In 1916 he cited conscription and the suspension of trades union restrictions as things that coalition had done for the nation; *Gleanings and Memoranda* headlined the speech 'The Coalition Form of Government almost indispensable.'[3] The argument for coalition was pragmatic, that no other government was fitted to the war effort, but it had significant undertones: coalition was especially useful in providing the party with allies more able to secure the cooperation of the working class.

Although the Nigeria debate was a relative success after a year of criticism, its significance was not lost on Law: it was held on the subject central to

Unionist economic attitudes; Law and Steel-Maitland were singled out for censure, a pointer to the level of party discontent. Party feeling had built up much as Law's own had done; having fought off the direct attack, he took the party along with him in the effort to reconstruct the government on more businesslike lines. There is no question of Carson, Law and Lloyd George conducting a conspiracy to unseat Asquith in December 1916; Law and Lloyd George at least wished to retain Asquith in government and they kept him informed about their plans. Asquith's fall was the result of his own miscalculation, especially of his reluctance to believe that the Unionists would prefer Lloyd George to himself in a contest. When the real crisis broke the Unionist ministers acted to strengthen Lloyd George's hand, from a conviction that only greater power for Lloyd George could put enough drive into the war effort. Unanimity was less marked in the scramble for office after Asquith's departure; 'the three Cs', Curzon, Chamberlain and Cecil, managed to keep official party interests to the fore by ensuring that Curzon rather than Carson should join the war cabinet – disloyalty might be useful but it should not be seen to pay. For the rest of the war, the party's loyalty to Lloyd George was strengthened when he became not only the organizer of victory but the inspiration of the country. National service remained the prime reason for coalition.[4]

With the approaching end of war in 1918 coalition became more positive because the coalition now had to deal with the issues that had been put aside for the duration, and more controversial because this pushed some Unionists into outright opposition. The government had prepared ambitious reconstruction plans, partly devised to put a moral basis into the war effort and partly produced by progressive ministers and their advisers. It could now be argued that the unity of wartime should be carried on to deal with peacemaking, demobilization and economic reconstruction. The government that had won the war would smooth the transition to peace and would redeem its promise of a land fit for heroes. Such was the argument adopted by most Unionist candidates in the 1918 election, a positive programme of the sort put forward by Lloyd George in 1910. A deal on the government's actual policies was done, again like that proposed in 1910, except that the Unionists now held rather more of the cards. The basis of the argument was still the national interest, but the emphasis was now on positive domestic possibilities rather than on negative foreign problems.

Underlying the Unionist acceptance of coalition in 1918 was a darker attitude to the future than appeared in the coalition programme. It was important to retain Lloyd George, not just as the man who had won the war but also as a man who could talk to the working class; and if a revolutionary situation were to arise, then it would be far better if Unionists could call on Liberals to help resist it. The post-war coalition thus had two distinct justifications, a positive sense of what could be done and a negative dread of the alternative. In 1920 Birkenhead put forward both lines of argument when he argued for greater coalition cooperation in the press. Gradually, though, the failure of coalition policies, failure to deliver the goods in almost every sphere, reduced the positive side of the argument to nothing. By 1922 coalition was based on fear, though by that time on fear of parliamentary Labour rather than revolution as such. It was still possible to argue, as Younger did in January 1922, that a coalition could best carry through the policies that Unionists wanted, but by then the main Unionist demands were directed against Labour anyway, the reform of trade union law and restoration of the House of Lords. By the autumn, the arguments for coalition were entirely negative.[5]

Coalitionism, though, was a matter of men as well as measures. The change to a real coalition in 1916 had been occasioned by the need to give Lloyd George a freer hand as much as by concern for structures. The government then developed a momentum of its own as a focus of loyalty that ran against the party system. There had always been more in common between the front benches than either had in common with their followers in the country. By 1920 several Unionists actually thought of themselves as coalitionists. Austen Chamberlain made no secret of his belief that coalition produced better government than party, and he reached a stage of heavy dependence on Lloyd George; Birkenhead found it more congenial to work with men of ideas like Churchill than with the squires who would fill out a Unionist ministry; Balfour had always striven to practise government by agreement, and Curzon was attracted by the glamour of the 'first eleven'. By 1922 the team of brilliant men who had governed for the past six years could not but see themselves as irreplaceable. They could not easily accept a return to old party cries or the need to oppose men who had become close friends.

Nor were such responses confined to the cabinet, for many Unionist MPs could not bring themselves to oppose Lloyd George in 1922 after six years of backing him, and one at least never broke the habit: 'He had become fascinated by Lloyd George, and until the end of his life he would not allow a word of criticism to be heard in his house. If anything went wrong in any part of the world he always said "That's because you got rid of the little man".'[6] In the organization too there were exponents of continued cooperation; although Younger worked to defeat coalition in 1922 he did not rule it out as a future possibility. Locally, electoral pacts between Liberals and Unionists to resist municipal Labour created the same direct contacts and in some places the pacts remained for the rest of the inter-war years. Coalitionism was not then only a political creed, but also a web of friendships and habits that underpinned political cooperation. By 1922 it was for some such a strong attitude as almost to obliterate the normal responses of party.

Coalitionists saw well enough the contradiction between politicians who were elected through parties and a government that was the negation of party, and party men saw it too; hence the contentiousness of the various schemes to square the circle by fusing the two coalition partners into one organization. Coalition had become a political habit that would be quite difficult to break and had sapped the party's confidence in itself. Most MPs who voted against Lloyd George in 1922 did not envisage a Unionist government as the final outcome, and the defeated ministers did not expect their discomfiture to be permanent. When coalition died in 1924, not all recognized that coalitionism must die with it.

In the coalition years the party encountered severe difficulties, some endemic to coalition as such, some related to the times, but together they created a general frustration from which the party was lucky to emerge so well. The first source was frustrated ambition: for seven years from 1915 the party had a share of government, but not a full or fair share. In the Asquith coalition Unionists had eight cabinet posts and Liberals thirteen, although there were far more Unionists in the Commons. Unionists had a majority in Lloyd George's war cabinet, but were little better placed in his government as a whole. From 1916 Unionist MPs were the only reliable support for the government, and from 1918 they had a parliamentary majority of their own, with three times as many seats as the rest of the coalition, but they never held as many as half of the government posts, as table 7.1 demonstrates.[7] At the highest level, Unionists could be satisfied, for they held the most prestigious offices, but the number of jobs was never sufficient to reward the deserving aspirants. Throughout the coalition, there were never more than fourteen offices of cabinet or departmental rank to satisfy the combined ambition of 300–359 MPs and a large number of peers. Normally, the ratio was roughly equivalent to one post for every seven MPs; in coalition, Liberals were appointed on a ratio close to that norm, but Unionists had a proportion of jobs to MPs more like one to twelve or fifteen.

Table 7.1   *Unionist share of coalition governments, 1915–1922*

	Cabinet Ministers	Unionists in cabinet	Total no. of ministers	Total no. of Unionists
May 1915	22	8	24	9
December 1916	23	13	32	14
January 1919	21	10	30	14
January 1921	21	12	29	14
October 1922	22	11	29	13

The discontent caused by lack of opportunity can be clearly seen in a number of cases, but was a general phenomenon that affected all but the top dozen in the party's collective leadership. At its simplest, about a dozen men were not ministers who would have held office in a Unionist government, and about thirty junior men did not hold a post at all as a result of coalition. (And this at a time when the Unionists could install their own government whenever they wished through their control of both Houses.) Selborne had resigned from Asquith's government in 1916 and was not offered a post by Lloyd George. From the House of Lords and the National Union he became a thorn in the flesh of the party leaders, where in a party government it would have been inconceivable that such a man, at the height of his powers and with powerful connections, should be left out.[8] Steel-Maitland had been appointed Party Chairman in 1911 to a post 'of cabinet rank', and had served loyally for four years without pay or reward. When the Asquith government was formed there was of course no post for such a recent recruit to the front bench. He wrote to Law to protest when he was offered only an under-secretaryship, pointing out that he had only accepted the Chairmanship because of the offer of a cabinet post. Law consulted Balfour and replied that Balfour had not promised in such a way as to bind his successor, that 'of cabinet rank' did not imply a seat in the cabinet (if not, it is hard to see what it did imply!), and that all must make sacrifices. For eighteen months Steel-Maitland worked with Law at the Colonial Office, a useful liaison that kept the leader and Chairman in close touch. When Lloyd George formed his government, there was a bitter exchange of letters, for Steel-Maitland was now expected to serve under Walter Long, an old enemy. In disgust Steel-Maitland resigned as Party Chairman and in 1919 he despaired of ever getting a senior post and resigned from the government too.[9] He was a man of strong ambition and had a doubtful reputation as an intriguer, but he was an able man who had deserved better of his party. After six years as Chairman, he knew all the important party figures and he became a dangerous foe; in the National Union he combined with Selborne to mount a campaign against coalition and as a Birmingham MP he threatened even Austen Chamberlain's home base.[10]

In normal times, Selborne and Steel-Maitland would have been tolerated and both would have been at least partially silenced by the restraint of office. The same can be said of the junior ministers who finally wrecked the government in 1922; many of these would have been cabinet ministers in a party government, as indeed they were in 1922–23, but they had few prospects under coalition. The careers of Bridgeman, Wood, Amery, Sanders and Lloyd-Greame would at the least be held up for years by coalition, for there was no room for their promotion. This is not to say that they opposed coalition in 1922 merely from personal motives; they had a legitimate ambition to serve their country and resented what they saw as the promotion of less able Liberals. They could only blame the coalition system, for only a change of system would give them their chance. In 1918 Sanders thought he had a chance to become Chief Secretary for Ireland, but was soon reduced to considering himself as a possible Speaker; in 1921 he was passed over for Chief Whip because it did not suit the coalition to have such a partisan in so sensitive a post, and he was fobbed off with an under-secretaryship; in 1922 he worked actively to bring the coalition down.[11]

The cases of Lord Robert Cecil and Lord Derby illustrate a different truth about coalition. Both held high office under Lloyd George, but both chose eventually to leave the government. Derby was a weak man whose subservience could usually be taken for granted (in Haig's words he was like 'the feather pillow [who] bears the marks of the last person who has sat on him'), but he was very conscious of his position in the party. Lloyd George dominated him but could never prise him away from his party roots; when Lancashire opinion moved away from coalitionism in 1922 Derby moved with it, and provided the opposition with added credibility. Cecil was more concerned with policy than with party or personal ambition; he parted company with Lloyd George over the League of Nations and post-war diplomacy; once outside the government he manoeuvred with other discontented 'outs', with Steel-Maitland to project Grey as a possible national leader, and with Salisbury to provide principled leadership for discontented Unionists.[12] Thus the existence of coalition served to divide the collective leadership by separating those who had power and influence from those who did not, by separating the senior men from their junior colleagues and by cutting off those under the Prime Minister's influence from the rest.

Difficulties were accentuated by personal prejudices that had not been broken down. The senior ministers fell easily into the habit of cooperation, but many in the party refused even to attempt the transition. Lloyd George had been the Liberal most hated before 1914 and, after a brief honeymoon with Unionists in 1917–18, he regained his old standing by 1920. Early in 1918, a meeting of Unionist leaders considered future relations with Lloyd George and 'Bob Cecil and Curzon [were] against touching him on the ground that he is such a dirty little rogue'. To diehards, Lloyd George was 'the "Welsh Walpole" and friend of MacDonald who would peddle any opinion and give in to any Labour leader if it would help him to stay in office'. Neville Chamberlain referred to him as 'this dirty little Welsh attorney' and Stanley Baldwin called him, somewhat ambiguously, 'the goat'. There was then a deep distrust throughout the party, as Law discovered in 1920:

> Bonar addressed a mass meeting. He spoke on excess profits, negotiations with Russia and Ireland. His audience was against him on all these questions and there was no enthusiasm. After the meeting he said to one of the local people that it was very unlike the Last Conference in 1913 when he attacked L.G. for 45 minutes amid great applause. The local man replied 'There would have been as much enthusiasm if you had done the same tonight.'[13]

The honours scandals, the employment of the press lords, incessant changes of policy, and a profligate waste of money were all taken as signs of the degradation of office by Lloyd George.

Other Coalition Liberals were disliked as warmly as Lloyd George, more for their present policies than for their past. Edwin Montagu was accused of anti-British motives for his Indian policy; with Reading as Viceroy there were openings for the diehards' latent anti-semitism. Christopher Addison was unpopular because of his advanced social policy and he was eventually driven out by the Unionists. But the *bête noire* second to Lloyd George was Churchill, whose war record seemed to prove all that Unionists had alleged about his excitability and his unfitness for office. Law was very angry when

Churchill was put in office by Lloyd George in 1917, and the National Union resolved that it was 'an insult to the Army and Navy and an injury to the Country'.[14] The men at the head of Coalition Liberalism were therefore execrated as dangerous, corrupt, or irresponsible enemies, and the same gulf separated Unionists from the rest of the party, especially when the 'coalies' tried to keep open their avenue of escape by parading their Liberalism. At Leamington, in May 1920, the coalitionists were finally driven out of the Liberal party, but Walter Long only noticed what they had said before they were excommunicated:

> We have been patient, loyal, self-sacrificing and what do we find? Our Liberal colleagues go down to Leamington and ask the audience to believe that they are just as Liberal as ever they were. In other words that there has been no Coalition, no mutual concessions, but that they have swallowed us.[15]

To frustrated ambition was added frustrated partisanship, as Unionists were denied the opportunity to criticize men who were still regarded as enemies, just because they were colleagues. Some refused to accept the restriction but many more nursed resentment in their hearts.

Throughout the coalition Ireland, the Empire and the House of Lords continued to divide Liberals and Unionists as always. Over India the Unionists resented the Montagu–Chelmsford reforms in general, but nothing stirred their animosity more than the treatment of General Dyer after the massacre at Amritsar. Dyer was applauded by the diehard press to make up for his censure by the government, and a collection for his benefit soon raised £15,000. Any post-war government would have met Unionist critics in its reconsideration of Britain's imperial role, but the existence of a bipartisan policy did not help to secure acceptance. Criticism ran along similar lines over Lloyd George's middle eastern policy, and over his preference for Greece over Turkey.

Ireland provided a clearer division. Unionists were critical of Ulster obscurantism when voiced by Carson in 1918 and in no mood to fight another war in Ireland, but neither would they tolerate the coercion of Ulster.[16] While Asquithians were attacking the Black and Tan policy as immoral, the Unionists were accusing the government of irresolution. The truce of 1921 was attacked as a typical piece of Lloyd George chicanery, and it needed all the efforts of the party leaders to stop the party from breaking up the government there and then. Finally, the House of Lords was a prime domestic reason for Unionist acceptance of coalition, but a constant source of friction. No agreed reform plan had been forthcoming in 1917–18 but it remained an agreed priority of the government to the end, and pledge after pledge was given. Each year it was put off because of the impossibility of devising an acceptable scheme. It was exactly the issue that could be best settled by a bipartisan government, for that would avoid charges of the gerrymandering of the constitution; time would show whether the coalition would deliver the goods, and coalition would be judged accordingly.

In all these policy questions, and in the others that still separated the parties, the party reacted as an independent group and not as a partner, for the Lloyd George government was never a focus of loyalty for Unionists. Complaints about government appointments or policies could only be met by Law with the barren reply that the party could not expect total control and that in coalition such things must happen – which is just what the critics were saying too. Individual Unionists played important parts in the government and many Unionist policies were implemented in full, but the party as a whole never took the government to heart as its own. The party never indeed accepted coalition as an idea; a majority of MPs accepted the advice of its leaders to keep the actual government in being, but it was always a decision for now, never one for always.

Coalition thus involved inevitable difficulties which could only be kept in check as long as the sense of crisis lasted. The decision to continue collaboration after 1918 can only be understood through the actual events of that year. Active consideration of the future began early in the year, for a general election could not be long delayed after the new franchise came into effect and the war was at a particularly gloomy stage. No advice to the government expected victory before 1919 at the earliest, and after the rout of the Fifth Army in March 1918 defeat stared the government in the face. So in the winter of 1917–18 murmurs of opposition began to grow louder than at any time since Lloyd George became Prime Minister, the Asquithians revived their interest as they scented a chance to bring Lloyd George down, and the press became more hostile – *The Times* and the *Morning Post* as well as the Liberal papers. The idea of a general election was therefore a tempting one for the government, for a khaki election like that of 1900 would present the government as the war party and leave Asquith and the Labour party no way to avert destruction.

In March 1918 the Unionist leaders agreed to open up negotiations with Lloyd George's supporters and set up a sub-committee of Law, Long, Younger and Clyde to investigate. Behind the scenes talks about a coalition programme were initiated and the party managers met to share out the candidatures for the projected election. By July an outline agreement had been presented to Law and Lloyd George, by which 150 seats were allocated to Coalition Liberals, but no decision of principle was taken.[17] Throughout this time, the assumption was that the government was seeking a mandate to continue the war, and as late as October Bonar Law could still see 'almost no chance of any joint action of this kind unless it is begun as the result of an election which takes place during the war and under the pressure of war conditions'.[18] But by that time a renewed coalition and a coalition election would not be arranged to get a mandate for war so much as to reap the benefits of victory. A few months later Sanders recalled that Lloyd George had 'prophesied great unpopularity for the government during the period of demobilisation and said if we had an election in the Spring we might get a

Bolshevik Government. I always held that view and did all I could to press for an election before Christmas in order that we might get a majority large enough to stand the racket.'[19]

In the course of negotiation, the Unionist leaders realized how much of their own programme could be extracted from Lloyd George, and they recognized too the enormous boost to his prestige that had come with victory. For Law, the issue was that many Unionists would in any case feel compelled to support Lloyd George and that he might command a large personal following in the constituencies; it would be useful to capture him as Joseph Chamberlain had been captured in 1886. There was then little belief in the value of the Coalition Liberals, but a strong belief in the value of Lloyd George; he would be a good advocate with the new electorate and he would in due course be disarmed as Chamberlain had been. As Law told Balfour, 'that would . . . be not a bad thing for our Party, and a good thing for the nation'.

The final decision was taken at the end of October, with victory only a few days away, and was announced with the publication of a letter from Lloyd George to Bonar Law, a letter actually drafted by Law as a summary of their agreement. By the time that the deal was presented to Unionist MPs on 12 November, two important developments had taken place. The war had come to an end, so an election would now be very soon indeed, and Asquith had turned down Lloyd George's suggestion that he rejoin the government. Law supported the offer to Asquith, and it was logical for him to do so; a government bent on post-war reconstruction and resistance to Labour would be strengthened by Asquith's presence. But Asquith's refusal greatly strengthened the Unionist position, as it left Lloyd George wholly dependent on his allies. The deal done between the Whips was in any case a good one for the Unionists: Coalition Liberals would have a free run in 150 constituencies (a figure suggested by Guest, but then rigidly adhered to by Younger), but Unionists would have at least twice as many, and they would now be free to attack sitting Asquithians too, and with Lloyd George as an ally. The joint manifesto proclaimed that imperialism would be the coalition's chief objective, and on specific issues that interested the Unionists Lloyd George promised an open mind on tariffs and no coercion of Ulster. Commending this agreement to his followers, Law was anxious that they recognise the advantage of Lloyd George as an ally, for 'at this moment, Mr Lloyd George commands an amount of influence in every constituency as great as has ever been exercised by any Prime Minister'.

Law was equally keen to point out that little was being risked, and to set at rest the fears of his supporters:

> What I propose does not mean that our Party is going to cease to exist. We go into this election – at least if I have my way – as a Unionist Party forming a portion of a coalition. I should be sorry if it were otherwise. From the time that my colleagues in the House of Commons did me the honour of electing me to be their leader I

have felt that I was in the position of a trustee; and even throughout the war the one thing that I have aimed at constantly has been to preserve, if it could be done, the unity of our Party.[20]

What was proposed was not the submersion of party in a wider unit, but a parliament of collaboration between independent groups; no more was discussed in 1918 and, despite the strength of the arguments for further collaboration, they would scarcely have carried the party to a greater commitment.

The scale of what had been achieved in capturing Lloyd George was underlined by incidents surrounding the letter of agreement between Law and Lloyd George. At the meeting of Unionists of 12 November, Law read the letter and impressed his audience with the concessions that Lloyd George seemed ready to make. At the meeting of Coalition Liberals though, Lloyd George gave only a summary of the letter and stressed its Liberal contents. When MPs returned to the Commons, it soon became clear that all was not well, as Robert Sanders noted:

> Our people became suspicious at once. I spoke to Guest and urged the publication of the letter. On Wednesday afternoon [13 Nov.] Bonar sent me word to come to Downing Street where I found L.G., Balfour, Bonar, and Auckland Geddes. Meanwhile there had appeared in The Times a fairly full report of L.G.'s speech to his own followers. L.G. said it must have been sent by someone in the audience who could write shorthand. He said he spoke impromptu, that he had a difficult job and that he was anxious to make things easy for his Liberal supporters. It was agreed that a joint meeting should be held, at which he, Bonar and Barnes should speak. I pressed for the publication of the letter. L.G. rather deprecated that saying he was not in love with it.[21]

Further pressure was applied by the Unionists and the joint meeting on the 16th went off well, with 'the famous letter' duly printed and handed out. Unionists were only interested in a deal that would make Lloyd George's capture public, both to give them maximum advantage at the coming election and to spread the maximum disaffection in the Liberal party. The election was announced, parliament was dissolved, and polling arranged for 14 December.

One problem remained to be settled, which was the working out of the electoral pact. No details were given to the National Union or to the constituencies involved, so much hard work had to be done and much recrimination endured before the party could settle down to the campaign. Overall the party had done very well, getting 362 of the 531 'coupons' that were offered by Lloyd George and Law to approved candidates,[22] but locally the position could look very different. In Wales the Unionists had only two coupons out of twenty-two, because most of the sitting Liberals backed Lloyd George, but this did not much impress Welsh Unionists. In Brightside the Unionist candidate had been specially demobilised for the election; the Central Office agent for Yorkshire persuaded him to stand down, but it took a visit to Central Office before his supporters could be persuaded to support a Coalition Liberal that they had opposed at the last three elections.[23] It was only the fear of Labour and strong pressure from Central Office, including the withdrawal of financial aid, that kept the local parties in line, and some rash promises had to be made. So in Banbury and in Newport local Unionists were assured that the deal was for one election only, and that acceptance would not preclude them from running a Unionist next time, promises that caused trouble later. Leigh Maclachlan of Central Office later recalled the anguish that such talks caused there:

> Deputation after deputation came pouring in from constituencies whose candidatures had been assigned to Lloyd George Liberals. At last, after one particularly painful interview, Sir Robert Sanders, looking thoroughly upset, turned to the writer and said 'You must see any further deputations there may be. I won't be a party to turning down any more of these good fellows.'[24]

Financial control may have been a vital weapon, for the local parties that defied the pact were mostly from strong and independent city parties used to financial independence. Overall, though, only nineteen Unionists stood against couponed opponents; in only one constituency, Morpeth, did such Unionist defiance cost the coalition the seat. On the other hand, five of the nineteen rebels won comfortably on their own, against Coalition Liberals, Labour, the coupon, and their own leaders.

A case can be made out for the 1918 election as a Unionist victory rather than a coalition victory. Unionists had some success against the coupon and even more in places where no coupons were allocated, as in Cardiff and in Manchester. The issues of the election were certainly more likely to benefit Unionists than anyone else: an outspoken patriotism, a pursuit of the fallen foe, and a call to restore the conditions of 1914.[25] Lloyd George received a hero's welcome wherever he went, but then so did Churchill in 1945, and it is impossible to tell now whether Lloyd George would have fared so well if he had had Liberals rather than Unionists at his back. Unionist candidates used his letter to Law as an election leaflet to reassure their supporters and to parade his capture to the nation. There is little doubt that the coalition was returned to power mainly on Unionist votes, although this was not widely recognized at the time; the Unionists had never won so many votes before, and it was perhaps natural to attribute their success to their new asset. In the general pattern of inter-war elections though, 1918 fits in easily enough: in 1922 the party won the same share of the vote with a similar number of candidates, but without Lloyd George. The scale of the triumph of 1918 no doubt owed something to Lloyd George, but the fact of Unionist victory did not, for without the pact the party would certainly have won some of the Coalition Liberal seats that it prevented them from attacking, and these would have made up for some of the others perhaps won for them by Lloyd George. It may even be that the coupon helped to limit the size of the Unionist victory and to prolong the life of the Liberal Party.

In parliament there was no mistaking the size of the victory: there were 382 Unionist MPs out of 707: without Sinn Fein the Unionist preponderance became overwhelming. Not all Unionist MPs ever supported the coalition, but almost all of them took the Whip at some time; the Unionists made up three-quarters of the government side of the House. Unionists therefore looked forward to domination of the government: but this never happened, and the party as a whole played only a junior role for the next four years. Their majority gave Unionist MPs a virtual veto over policies and appointments in the long run, but their junior position in government prevented any more positive control. This tension led on to attempts to fuse the government parties in 1920, to the failure of almost every government policy, and to complete deadlock by 1921.

Fusion became possible in 1920 because of the difficulties already met by the government. Lloyd George's absence in Paris had accentuated the arguments about policy; peacemaking had produced a major Unionist rebellion in a telegram to Lloyd George from 233 Unionist MPs in April 1919, urging stronger action on reparations; the appointments of F. E. Smith as Lord Chancellor (as Lord Birkenhead), and of Churchill and Addison, had been much criticised. The attack on Birkenhead was especially revealing; it centred on his lack of gravity in the highest legal office, but it was occasioned too by his lack of concern for party in the excitement of office. Unionists also resisted Lloyd George's attempt to go on running things as in wartime, insisting that the war cabinet should be wound up after peacemaking was completed.[26] Nor did they like Addison's reconstruction plans: his Ministry of Ways and Communications Bill was eventually passed, setting up a Ministry of Transport, but only after Unionist MPs had shorn it of railway and electricity nationalization. Similar action forced the abandonment of coal nationalization after the Sankey Report, and of parts of the Excess Profits Tax.[27] Bonar Law was now Leader of the House of Commons without a department, and it was indeed a full-time job to keep the governmental process going there.

Outside Westminster the government was losing support : eight seats were lost at by-elections in the first eighteen months of peace. Turnout rose as the opposition parties recovered from their disarray of 1918 and there was a large turnover of votes. When local elections were resumed in 1919 there was a large Labour advance, and only local pacts stemmed the tide in 1920.[28] The weakness of the government at its roots was demonstrated by the events at Stockport in March 1920, when a vacancy occurred there; weeks of argument were solved only by the resignation of the other sitting member, so that there could be a double by-election with one Unionist and one Liberal candidate as in 1918.[29]

By the time Stockport had been settled Lloyd George was moving to prevent such situations from recurring. He proposed the fusion of the two coalition parties into a new party, which would be launched on an inspiring programme of strong government and social betterment. The serious economic situation and the delicate state of Labour relations demanded a stronger government to hold the ring, for the attempt at fusion took place just a month before the post-war boom began to collapse, a development that punctured the inflationary crisis and took the heat out of the Labour militancy. So, for various different reasons, most of the Unionist leaders approved of Lloyd George's intentions; the party managers agreed because they feared that continuing disorganization on the Coalition Liberal side might eventually wreck the government. Birkenhead put the case for a new party in articles in the *Weekly Dispatch*, a round robin from ninety-five MPs supported fusion, and Balfour formally proposed fusion in a letter to Bonar Law on 10 March 1920. Other Unionists, including Law himself, were less sure, even though they shared their colleagues' concern about the political and economic situation; nevertheless it was agreed to go ahead, but that Lloyd George should make the first move. Lloyd George would propose fusion to his Liberal supporters, and Bonar Law would follow suit on the next day. In the event the reactions of Coalition Liberal ministers were so uniformly hostile that Lloyd George moved quickly into reverse; when he met Coalition Liberal MPs, he merely suggested greater cooperation with Unionists and did not mention fusion as such. Bonar Law promptly gave up the whole idea, with obvious relief, as he told Balfour:

> The result of this will probably be not to attempt any real fusion of the Parties but to get cooperation, something on the lines of the Liberal Unionists and Conservatives in the early days. This will be difficult to arrange and will certainly not be efficient, but personally I am not sorry at the turn events have taken. I do not like the idea of complete fusion if it can be avoided, but I had come to think, as you had also, that it was really inevitable if the Coalition were to continue. But it always seemed to me more important from L.G.'s point of view than from ours. As a Party we were losing nothing and, since the necessity of going slowly in the matter has come from L.G.'s own friends, I do not regret it.[30]

In March 1920, as in November 1918, Lloyd George's open dependence on the Unionists had been openly demonstrated. When the Coalitionists were driven out of the Liberal fold at Leamington in the following May dependence became even greater, for it removed the only theoretical alternative that Lloyd George and his friends had left.

It remains to decide whether the Unionists would have accepted fusion if Lloyd George could have made it a real option in 1920. The party in the Commons would probably have done so, though not without a severing of all connections by a determined minority; there is little doubt though that the party outside parliament would *not* have accepted fusion, or that they could have prevented its implementation. The parliamentary party could determine the shape of governments and election campaigns, but they could not change the structure of the party itself without a positive vote from the National Union and overwhelming approval in the constituencies. At the Party

Conference of 1920, which coalitionists had hoped would approve fusion, it was estimated that about five-eighths of the delegates were in favour of the existence of the coalition, and the rest against it on principle, but that hardly any of them approved its current policies. The Executive elected at that Conference was packed with diehards, and a debate on cooperation against Labour revealed the depth of division: a motion calling for closer collaboration met strong opposition, but so did one calling simply for a Unionist government: 'They must turn out the man who was the greatest danger to the Conservative Party', (a voice – 'Lloyd George'). 'Yes, if you allow conditions to continue as at present you will find a deliberate attempt is being made to assassinate the Conservative Party.'

In the end a meaningless compromise was made, and the Conference called on all good men to come together to resist socialism, but also insisted that the Unionist party should not sacrifice any of its independence in the process. It is difficult to see how this Conference could possibly have approved fusion; even if it had done, half the constituencies would probably have refused to implement the decision. A motion which would have specifically committed the party against fusion was not put on the chairman's decision; the diehards accepted this ruling without demur, no doubt because they felt that they had already made their point.[31] Bonar Law's position remains enigmatic, for he promoted fusion and yet was glad to see it fail. He was never an ideological coalitionist and never fell under L.G.'s spell, for all their good personal relations. Had his colleagues backed fusion in 1920 Law would have accepted it, but he would hardly have stuck to that position in the party crisis that must have followed. His relief in avoiding such a parting of the ways is understandable.

With the failure of fusion, and with the subsequent failure of Liberal reunion in May 1920, the coalition settled into a stage of continuous crisis. The deepening economic recession defused the worst industrial problems, but the failure of fusion had deprived the government of the only way of bringing coalition and party into line. From now on time was on the side of the anti-coalitionists, for the approach of another election would eventually reopen the argument to their advantage. By the time of the next possible resolution of the problem at the end of 1921, coalition had signally failed to provide Unionists with what they had hoped for, and Lloyd George had become an electoral albatross rather than an asset.

The failure of the programme of 1918 stemmed above all from the lack of real agreement at the time; despite the negotiations, the coalition's electoral manifesto and campaign of 1918 went little further than Lloyd George's letter to Bonar Law. When coalition ministers began to bring forward legislation in 1919 they met a hail of criticism, from Liberals hostile to decontrol and Unionists lukewarm on social reconstruction. To keep all his supporters in balance, Lloyd George had to offer something to all of them, but this meant that every coalition scheme was also hotly opposed by a part of the coalition.

Lloyd George disarmed his opponents on Ireland with his Russian policy, and his opponents on Russia with his Irish policy, and they did not combine to oppose him. Another example of this division of opponents was the Amritsar Debate of July 1920. Conservative MPs . . . voted 122 to 93 against the government. Lloyd George was upheld in this division by the votes of Labour and Asquithian Liberal M.P.s who at the time vigorously opposed his repression of Ireland.[32]

Such a balancing act could keep his government in being only by increasing his own reputation for lack of principle.

Instead of a systematic policy of imperialism, Unionists had Montagu's Indian policy and Milner's policy in Egypt; instead of settlement in Ireland there were outrages; instead of a broad social policy there was first a reckless waste of money and then an abandonment of almost all that had been proposed. In only one area did the coalition succeed totally, but this argument was a double-edged sword: Lloyd George had weathered the storm of labour unrest, and after 'Black Friday' this was clearly abating. What was now needed was a means of countering Labour's electoral appeal, and for this a Prime Minister with a cleaner political reputation would be needed. The more the revolutionary threat receded, and the more Lloyd George appeared as a loser of votes, the more the Unionists would be tempted to cast him adrift.

In most of this Lloyd George was desperately unlucky, both in the failures and reconsiderations of policy and in the development of his own reputation. Many coalition schemes were wrecked by Unionist hostility, yet Unionists also complained when the government then changed course. The following scenario was typical: government introduces social scheme balanced to meet Liberal and Unionist influence in government, but tilted slightly to Liberalism by the minister in charge; Unionists in the House of Commons wreck the plan and denounce the waste of public money; government withdraws the scheme and is then accused of unprincipled change of front by Unionists. Such was the logic of coalition when the balance of the government did not correspond to the balance of parliament. Successes of the government would always be claimed by all its members, but failures would be left to the Prime Minister.

Rapid changes of policy were in any case dictated by circumstances. The uncertain foreign situation was typified in Eastern Europe where in 1920 the Poles seemed likely to extinguish the Bolshevik regime, and a year later the Bolsheviks almost took Warsaw. At home the sudden switch from inflation and boom to stagnation and slump in a few months made changes in policy inevitable. Ireland was a nightmare for all parties; the fifty-year respite gained by Lloyd George in 1921 was certainly based on pragmatism rather than principle, but no other policy could have worked. In field after field the government was forced to change course, earning a reputation for dishonesty and lack of principle that, when allied to Lloyd George's prior reputation, could only do him great damage. Nothing exemplified this more than the campaign for public economy which shook the government in 1921. A public that had seen income tax rise fivefold in five years were only too ready to believe that their money was being wasted. During the war the national crisis kept discontent within bounds, but when income tax actually went up again in 1919 (to pay amongst other things for homes for heroes) the reaction of taxpayers was very hostile indeed, especially when in 1920 inflation reached unprecedented levels too. The first to sense the new mood was the press, and an Anti-Waste League was founded by Lord Rothermere. Two by-elections at the Wrekin and one at Dover showed the threat that independents could pose on the anti-spending tack, and Lord Salisbury tried to guide the agitation into respectable channels through a People's Union for Economy. Two further Anti-Waste victories in June 1921, on Salisbury's doorstep in Hertford and in the ultra-safe Unionist seat of St George's Westminster, were too threatening to be ignored.[33]

Government spending had already been reviewed and cut substantially, but the time had now come for a great public gesture; this was supplied by the appointment of the Geddes Committee, a typical Lloyd George manoeuvre using businessmen instead of MPs or ministers. When the 'Geddes Axe' fell in February 1922, it proposed cuts in the social services which alienated once and for all the Prime Minister's last admirers on the left; moderate Unionists like Stanley Baldwin disliked the Geddes Axe as being too arbitrary and too indiscriminate, but the rest of the party criticized it as too little, too late, and unlikely to be implemented anyway. Resolutions continued to call for further economies and lower taxation, so the government got no credit for what it had done. After the summer of 1921 the Anti-Waste threat receded, but this was largely because Unionist candidates were now on the bandwagon with them, demanding cuts as loudly as anyone. After St George's, almost all Unionist candidates ran without making promises to support the coalition; this did not mean that all of them joined the diehard group when elected, but it showed that coalition was no longer seen to be a winning ticket.

By 1921 indeed frustration with coalition was building up such a head of steam as seriously to threaten its future. The party managers continued to bewail the organizational weakness of Coalition Liberalism, but there had been little opportunity for organizational collaboration; one of the few joint ventures, a magazine called *Popular View*, was abandoned in 1921 because of the impossibility of producing a lively magazine out of continuous compromise.[34] Money was short in the party by 1921 because there had been no proper revival since the war; members were constantly described as apathetic, and were in no mood to give their time or their money to a party that did not know where it was going. The state of the organization was causing concern to the party managers, for it would deteriorate further unless some definite decision about the future were taken. At the end of 1921 Younger still favoured coalition, but the balance had become a fine one.

The National Union had much less doubt, and by 1921 it was committed firmly against coalition. Younger was in a very exposed position, for he was

Chairman of the National Union Executive responsible for carrying out its decisions, as well as Party Chairman and so committed to the leader and the coalition. He tried to escape the cross-fire by getting the two offices separated but could not get the new rules approved.[35] The actual administration of the National Union was separated from Central Office in 1921, and it appointed its own secretary thereafter; it was a change of no great importance, for the National Union continued to work from Central Office and the Principal Agent continued to be Honorary Secretary, but it was a minor declaration of independence. The question that exercised the National Union most of all was the House of Lords, and regular deputations were sent to Law to press for action. By early 1922 tempers were short and the Chairman of the Central Council publicized the dispute in March with an open letter to Austen Chamberlain. This brought a reply from Salvidge, still a convinced coalitionist:

> I read with amazement Sir Alexander Leith's letter to you in this morning's press. The inference in his letter is that he speaks for the Council of the National Union of which he is chairman. As a member of that Council I emphatically deny that he has had any mandate, or that he is justified in assuming that the Council as a whole takes his view.[36]

Despite Austen's soothing reply, Salvidge took the matter up at the next meeting of the Executive, when he demanded whether or not Leith had been satisfied with Austen's reply. Salvidge was right to claim that Leith had overstepped the mark and that he had no mandate for his action, but it is clear that he rather than Salvidge really represented the views of the National Union. In March he explained that he had acted in a personal capacity only and that Chamberlain had suggested that their correspondence be published. At the May Executive the government was rapped over the knuckles for its failure to reform the House of Lords, 'a breach of the understanding upon which the allegiance of the Unionist Party to its leaders depends'. Salvidge proposed to delete these insulting words but could not even find a seconder; nine MPs were present, including Younger, Sanders and Neville Chamberlain, all of whom must have approved of the resolution or seen the futility of attempting to amend it. The National Union also reacted fiercely to the attacks on Younger by coalitionist ministers, most of all Birkenhead's description of him as 'the cabin boy' and Lloyd George's of 'a second-class brewer'. There were fears that it was intended to remove him and substitute someone more acquiescent. In March 1922 Steel-Maitland proposed a strong motion of confidence in Younger that was a clear rebuke to his critics; Younger lowered the temperature by asking Steel-Maitland to withdraw the motion, but the Executive accepted this only 'on the understanding that Sir Laming Worthington-Evans would make known to his colleagues in the Government that the Committee would bring the matter up again unless the attacks by Ministers on Sir George Younger ceased'.[37] The National Union was then hostile to coalition and quite determined to use its independence if necessary to protect the interests of the party.

The views of the local parties were less clearcut – although the National Union itself was no more than the sum of the local party leaders. There was support for coalition in the North and in Scotland, where local cooperation was pushing back municipal socialism in 1920–21, and also in Birmingham, where Austen Chamberlain traded on the family name and Neville brooded uneasily on the course of events. In southern England, there was forthright opposition, for here the benefit of cooperation was negligible and the Labour threat more remote. Sanders found that Somerset was almost wholly hostile to coalition, and Middlesex and London were both equally critical. It was now that the assurances of 1918 that the pact would be for one election only came home to roost; wanting to be ready in plenty of time, many local parties were by 1921 selecting candidates who would oppose sitting Coalition Liberals. In Newport it was the Licensing Act of 1921 that brought about this decision, but in other places it was India, or Ireland, or public spending. Local parties also pressed sitting MPs to declare that they would fight next time without the coalition label and many gave way to these suggestions. Local parties were not very representative of Unionist voters, but this did not affect their independence or their control over their candidates. There was little to be done to prevent this inexorable build up of pressure from the roots.[38]

Taking the lead against the coalition was a small but implacable group of diehards; they were never more than a few dozen in the Commons and, although they attracted shifting support on particular issues, they never threatened the coalition majority. The Lords were more diehard, as they had been ever since 1911, but unless their powers were restored they would denounce the government in vain. Diehard opinions ranged from the virulent obscurantism of Northumberland, Page Croft and Cooper, who saw politics as a black-and-white struggle between good British imperial-minded Christians and Jewish-dominated marxist wreckers, to the high-minded Association of Independent Peers, who were primarily concerned with the effect of coalition on the standards of public life and its failure to halt the drift towards class politics. The strongest weapon in the diehard armoury was the press, for it had the reliable support of the *Morning Post*, *National Review* and *Spectator*, and intermittent backing from the papers of Beaverbrook, Rothermere and Northcliffe. Of the Unionist press, only the *Daily Telegraph* supported the coalition, and it could make little head against such a tide.[39]

This motley bunch of adventurers, undesirables and patriots had by 1921 accepted the general lead of Lord Salisbury. As the son of a Unionist Prime Minister, Salisbury used his name and connections to weld the diehard opposition together and awaited his opportunity. He was desperately worried that coalition, as a cynical combination to keep Labour down, would produce a reaction among working-class electors that would eventually put Labour in power. This was the most respectable strain of Unionist opposition to the coalition. When the Unionist won the by-election at Newport in 1922, on working-class votes and on an anti-coalition platform, his agent explained that 'the working classes had never understood the Coalition. They had regarded it rightly or wrongly as a wangle and as an attempt to ally capitalist forces against the worker.' It was such fears that Salisbury set out to quieten, using his People's Union for Economy to widen the diehards' appeal, and calling for a return to the classless tradition of Conservatism. His own group called itself the Free Conservatives, set up an office to rival that of the official party, and supplied money and professional assistance to rebels at by-elections. Salisbury did not share half the views held by those who accepted his lead, but he was a focus for the increasing Unionist discontent, a respectable public figure acting from the highest motives; by 1921 he had made the diehard opposition a formidable force.[40]

In any calculation of the party's future prospects Bonar Law would be a key figure. Throughout the coalition, Law was prepared to support its continuation, but he was rarely prepared to argue for concession that would weaken his own party. In private he got on very well with Lloyd George, but he never hid his doubts; in 1917 he told Unionists that Lloyd George was 'a man who has the defects of his qualities', and told his audience that he was saying no more than he had told the Prime Minister to his face; when in 1920 he was told that Unionists would rather hear him attack Lloyd George than defend him, he told this story to the Prime Minister too.[41] For ten years Law had been at the heart of the party's reactions to political events, largely because his own views mirrored those of his followers almost exactly. The extreme diehards had written off Law as the dupe of Lloyd George because he did not come out fighting against coalition policies, hence the witticism that the coalition was an alliance between a flock of sheep led by a crook and a flock of crooks led by a sheep. But to the bulk of the party, Law's presence in government was a guarantee of the party's independence; with Law in charge the party would extract from coalition whatever there was to be gained, but at no risk, and when stripped of all complications this was more or less what Bonar Law intended all along. He was therefore as vital a figure as Salisbury, and in something of the same way: Salisbury was the link between the anti-coalition forces outside the government, and Law was the link between anti-coalitionists outside and critical Unionists within. Successive crises were dealt with by Law without resolving the fundamental disequilibrium of the situation, for the conflict between coalition and party was as real in Law's own mind as in the minds of a host of Unionists who continued to give general support to the government.

It was therefore an event of major significance when Law's retirement was announced in March 1921. He had been unwell for some time and had now gone into a state of collapse. Lloyd George announced his resignation to the Commons on 17 March in a speech that was close to tears, and the reaction of Unionist MPs was equally emotional, testament to Law's great standing in his party. The effect of the resignation was increased by its suddenness: within two days Law had laid down all his offices and gone abroad. Maurice Cowling has suggested that Law's resignation was tactical, that he could not face reconciling his party to the coming Irish negotiations, and that he was giving up office so as to be available as an alternative to coalition in the future; in Gaullist terms he was becoming a Prime Minister 'in the reserve of the republic'. Lloyd George perhaps entertained similar doubts, for his first reactions were to suggest that he should resign too, and to ask if he might speak to Bonar Law's doctor. But there can be no real doubt that it was on medical advice that Law resigned, for he was advised that only a complete break would save him from total breakdown, and he was actually suffering from the disease that was to kill him in less than three years. For six months in 1921 Law was in France, cut off from most political information and from all political action. His position after his return in September should not affect the assessment of his resignation in March.[42]

The effect of Law's abrupt departure was magnified by the departure at about the same time of Walter Long, the only other Unionist of weight who combined an acceptance of coalition (as a defence against Labour) with a determination that the integrity of the party should not be compromised in any way. Long's health had been deteriorating for years, but he had kept open his channels of communication; like Law his influence was based on years of devotion to the interests of the party, and like Law's that influence had been used to argue the case for coalition. In February 1921 he gave up office and soon afterwards he accepted a peerage and retired from active politics. With the passing of Law and Long there were no Unionists in the cabinet who had both authority and detachment; the link had been broken, but its importance was demonstrated with devastating effect when both intervened to influence the events of October 1922.

By this time Long would not have been a possible leader, and so the third contender of 1911 alone remained: Austen Chamberlain. There was some speculation about alternatives, with some canvassing the claims of Derby and Salisbury and others imploring Lloyd George to take over the leadership and unite the parties in a shotgun wedding, but Austen's claims were undeniable. He was elected leader of the party at the Carlton Club on 21 March 1921, proposed by Captain Pretyman who coined in his speech the idea that Conservative leaders 'emerged' rather than being elected. Austen had certainly emerged as leader, for nobody could have stood against him with any prospect of success, and it was appropriate that his succession should be marked by Pretyman, who was a respected backbencher of long service and represented the inarticulate centre of the party.

At the time of his election, Austen was seen as a party man who would be even more attentive to Unionist interests than Law had been. This was a natural enough view for those who remembered his tariff opinions before the war, his stout defence of Ulster and his diehard opinions in 1911. But by 1921

Austen was an ideological coalitionist for both personal and tactical reasons: he had fallen under the personal sway of Lloyd George, he was influenced by Birkenhead and Horne, and he had no doubt that a coalition alone would be able to contain Labour. The intolerance he had shown for free-traders before 1914 was now turned on rebel Unionists who rocked the coalition boat. He had perhaps been too long in high office, too isolated from discordant views by the well-oiled Birmingham machine to take full account of the volume of dissent. Any doubt about his attitude should have been set aside by the speech with which he accepted the leadership:

> There are moments when the insistence upon party is as unforgiveable as insistence upon personal things, when the difficulties which the nation has to confront call for a wider outlook and a broader union than can be found even within the limits of a single party, and when the traditions of more than one party, the ideas of more than one party need to be put into the common stock.[43]

For the next eighteen months, Austen Chamberlain worked behind the scenes to maintain the interests of his party, just as Law had done, but he had no personal sympathy for the diehards or their views, and he made no gestures of conciliation to them. His public speeches were all aimed at converting the party to a positive belief in coalition, leading it from the front – and in a direction where many Unionists did not wish to follow. In losing Law the party had lost a conciliator; in electing Austen it had gained an inflexible leader who would not always put party first. There was reason to think, as the *Financial News* suggested, that 'Mr. Bonar Law's resignation is more than a nine-days wonder. It is probably the beginning of the end of Coalition Government.'[44] The advent of a convinced coalitionist to the leadership of the largest coalition party was indeed the beginning of the end for coalition.

Notes and References

1 Blake, *Unknown Prime Minister*, 238–47.
2 John Stubbs, in Cook and Peele, *Politics of Reappraisal*, 28–9.
3 *Gleanings and Memoranda*, Sept. 1916; National Union Conference minutes, transcript of Special London Conference, 30 Nov. 1917.
4 Cameron Hazlehurst, 'The conspiracy myth', in Gilbert, *Lloyd George*, 148–57.
5 Morgan, *Age of Lloyd George*, 196–7; Younger's letter to constituency chairman, 9 Jan. 1921, Sanders MSS.
6 Samuel Roberts's Autobiographical Memorandum.
7 Compiled from Butler and Freeman, *British Political Facts*, 8–13.
8 See for example, Selborne to Younger, 6 Feb. 1919: Selborne MSS.
9 See for example, Steel-Maitland to Law, 19 July 1917, Law MSS: 82/2/10.
10 Austen Chamberlain to Steel-Maitland, 23 Mar. 1922: Steel-Maitland MSS, GD 193/95/4.
11 Sanders Diary, 5 May 1918 and 24 Mar. 1921.
12 Cowling, *Impact of Labour*, 103–6.
13 *Ibid*, 83: Sanders Diary, 23 June 1920.
14 National Union Minutes, Central Council, 8 June 1917.
15 Long to Law, 8 May 1920: Law MSS, 102/5/16.
16 Blake, *Unknown Prime Minister*, 378.
17 Gest to Lloyd George, 20 July 1918: quoted in Morgan, *Age of Lloyd George*, 188–9.
18 Law to Balfour, 5 Oct. 1918: Balfour MSS, Add.MSS 49693.
19 Sanders Diary, 20 Oct. 1918 and 8 May 1919.
20 Blake, *Unknown Prime Minister*, 388.
21 Sanders Diary, 16 Nov. 1918.
22 Craig, *British Parliamentary Election Statistics, 1918–1970*, 2.
23 Interview with Captain Matt Sheppard, Unionist candidate.
24 *The Times*, 14 Feb. 1940
25 Sanders Diary, 5 Jan. 1919.
26 Blake, *Unknown Prime Minister*, 396–9.
27 Abrams, 'The failure of Social Reform, 1918–20'.
28 Cook and Ramsden, *By-elections*, 17–19.
29 D. Cuthbert, 'Lloyd George and the Conservative Central Office', in Taylor, ed. *Lloyd George*, 167–89.
30 Law to Balfour, 24 Mar. 1920: Law MSS, 95/4.
31 National Union Conference minutes, Birmingham Conference, 10 June 1920.
32 Kinnear, *Fall of Lloyd George*, 3.
33 Cowling, *Impact of Labour*, 56–7.
34 Younger to Sanders, 23 Sept. 1921: Sanders MSS.

35 National Union minutes, Executive Committee, 20 Oct. 1921.
36 Salvidge to Chamberlain, 9 Mar. 1921: Austen Chamberlain MSS, 33/1/27.
37 National Union minutes, Executive Committee, 14 Mar. and 9 May 1922.
38 Kinnear, *Fall of Lloyd George*, 63–74; Sanders Diary, 3 Oct. 1921; P. E. Pilditch to Younger, 13 Sept. 1921: Austen Chamberlain MSS, 24/3/83.
39 Cowling, *Impact of Labour*, 76–87.
40 *Ibid*, 90.
41 National Union Conference minutes, transcript of Special London Conference, 30 Nov. 1917; Sanders Diary, 23 June 1920.
42 Cowling, *Impact of Labour*, 117–8; Blake, *Unknown Prime Minister*, 423–4.
43 *The Times*, 23 Mar. 1921.
44 Blake, *Unknown Prime Minister*, 424.

Chapter 8

The turning point, 1921–1924

The turnaround in Unionist fortunes from Chamberlain's election in March 1921 to Baldwin's triumph in 1924 was remarkable. At the outset, the party faced an uncertain future, divided and unsure, still fearing Labour but unwilling to make the only concessions to coalition that seemed to give it a chance to deal with Labour. By 1924 the party was united and in government on its own, under a man who had not even been in cabinet before Chamberlain became leader; with Unionist connivance, the Liberal party had been destroyed and Labour installed as the second party in the state. These developments centred on a basic tactical decision that the party had struggled to make, a decision that shaped the whole future of British politics.

Following 1906, and especially since 1917, the issue was the 'impact of Labour', but by 1921 the urgency had begun to go out of it. Black Friday and the end of the Russo-Polish War seemed to mark the end of the domestic and international threat from revolutionary socialism; strikes at home and revolutions abroad no longer filled the daily press, and Lloyd George had even been able to conclude a trade agreement with the Bolsheviks without prompting the overthrow of his government. Discussion of future relations with Labour could thus proceed on more rational lines than in the past four years. In by-elections, Labour had made eight net gains by mid 1921 and at least as threatening was the level of Labour's poll in such places as St Albans or Bromley, which the coalition had managed to hold. As 1921 wore on it seemed that the Labour tide might have ebbed, but a further spate of Labour gains occurred in the winter of 1921–22; by that time a general election was no more than two years away and nothing appeared to have been done to reduce the electoral threat. Local election results showed the same pattern, with Labour at first falling back from the great surge forward of 1919 but then making steady progress. The local elections also showed two ways of resisting Labour, either through the union of the Conservatives and Liberals under a new name (as in Bristol and Leicester) or for the Liberals to be pushed out altogether and so leave the field clear for Unionists (as in London.)[1]

The difficulty was that these two strategies were mutually contradictory. Although Labour presented the real threat, the tactical dilemma was not about relations with Labour but about relations with the Liberals: the first strategy would require close collaboration while the second would require hostility to the Liberals at every level. That these two approaches were seen to be contradictory is shown by the changing position of Austen Chamberlain. Right to the end of 1923 Austen remained an advocate of cooperation with Liberals, but when the last chance of this vanished in the winter of 1923–24, he switched to the other strategy, writing to Hoare that 'our business now is to smash the Liberal Party – two-thirds of it is already Labour in all but name. We ought to give a new meaning to Unionism by drawing over and eventually absorbing the other third.'[2] At root the two strategies both envisaged the full voting strength of the Unionists being added to part of the Liberal vote; the rest of the Liberals could stay aloof or vote Labour, but it would not matter much, for the anti-socialist combination would be enough without them. The question was how such a coalition at the polls could be put together, and here it was a question of parties rather than voters. The Liberal party could be discredited and 'smashed', so that Liberals would have to vote Unionist to keep Labour out, or the Liberal Party could be cultivated, so that it would actually advise Liberals to vote Unionist. Again a contradiction, and both tactics had drawbacks attached to them, the pro-Liberal strategy because there was no way of being nice enough to the Liberals to ensure their help without alienating some Unionists, the anti-Liberal strategy because there was no way of knowing if it would work.

There was also a sub-plot to the debate, more directly concerned with Labour. Although the revolutionary threat had in fact receded by 1921, not all Unionists recognized the fact or drew the same conclusions from it. The need to resist Labour as a political party did not blind Unionists to the continuing presence of extremists in the Labour ranks; diehards saw no meaningful distinction between the socialism of J. H. Thomas and Robert Smillie (a clear example of Hexter's Law), and all Unionists saw a militant industrial threat lurking behind the facade of parliamentarianism.[3] Nor was this entirely fanciful in 1921, for the Labour moderates had not yet gained control after the militancy of 1919–20, the organic link between Labour and Communist parties remained until 1924, and in the trade unions for longer. The memory of *how* the Russian Revolution had taken place was another reason; it may now seem ludicrous to cast MacDonald and Smillie in the roles of Kerensky and Lenin, but the comparison seemed less farfetched to a conservative mind in 1921. Unionists agreed that the Labour threat was more serious than it now appeared to be, but did not agree on how to deal with the threat. Again there were contradictory ways; one tactic was to continue absolute resistance to reduce the effective power of the Labour movement, and the other was to try to conciliate working-class opinion, strengthen the hands of the Labour moderates against their own extremists, and reduce antagonism. The first approach was the policy adopted by the coalition, though never carried to logical extremes, and the second was favoured only by a small group of high-minded Unionists, notably Salisbury and Baldwin, but it was the view that was to win in the end.

The creation of a Unionist labour organization within the party had produced a pressure group for a diehard attitude to Labour. The working-class Unionists who made up these labour committees favoured a legislative programme to break what they called the 'Labour' movement. Such a policy would certainly have weakened the Labour movement for a time, but would have run a grave risk of increasing the Labour hold on the working class. In 1921 the labour committees were still an expanding force in the party, pressing it towards a policy of class war. The final outcome of these two strategic dilemmas, whereby the party helped to smash the Liberal party in alliance with the Labour moderates, was one that few would have cared to predict in 1921. The decision owed something to the debates on strategy, rather more to chance circumstances, and most of all to sheer political prejudice; 'on such issues are the fates of Empires decided'.

The tactical debate had more than a distant significance in March 1921 because of two urgent problems that would indicate which path the party had chosen to take. The settlement of Ireland would show how far Unionists would subordinate party to the need for compromise, and the next general election would show if collaboration with Liberals could ever be put on a more lasting basis than that of 1918.

Until the spring of 1921 the coalition's Irish policy had satisfied nobody: the opposition and a few Unionists had denounced it as irresponsible, while most Unionists had seen it as too weak. It was therefore necessary for the government to cover its tracks carefully as it prepared to turn from reprisals to negotiations, and this made the reversal seem even more abrupt than it was. On 21 June Birkenhead made one of the government's most uncompromising statements of their determination to fight to the end, and three days later Lloyd George invited De Valera and Craig to send delegates to a Conference.[4] Unionists were critical not because they were all against negotiations as such, but because of yet another sudden change of policy, only a month after part of the Agriculture Act had been repealed. For one newly elected MP this was too much to take:

> In my first election campaign . . . I was encouraged . . . to proclaim that the Agriculture Act was the Farmers' Charter and would ensure prosperity to the farmer, good wages to the worker and a happy countryside. With regard to Ireland, we must suppress the rebellion and never shake hands with murderers. Within one year of my election, I was asked to vote for the repeal of the Agriculture Act and a Treaty of Appeasement with the Irish murderers. I could not do this. I voted and spoke against the repeal of the Agriculture Act, and joined the small opposition to fight the surrender of Ireland.[5]

The opposition was keen, but the numbers were still small, for public opinion was strongly in favour of Irish talks after four years of European war. For the time being there was a cessation of bloodshed and the possibility of agreement, a situation that hardly anyone could oppose. By the time the negotiations came to a head in October 1921 though, things were very different. Bonar Law had returned from exile and resumed connections with old friends, which made him a threat to the government whether he meant to be or not; a party conference scheduled for November would play an important part in the negotiations, for a resolution that opposed talks would wreck them, while the absence of such a resolution would be a great asset to the government.

The government resolved to challenge the party with a resolution that specifically welcomed negotiations on the future of Ireland, its strongest card since it did not imply any particular form of settlement. In the week before the Conference Birkenhead made a secret visit to Liverpool to ensure the support of Salvidge, acknowledged leader of protestant Unionism. The Conference was held in Liverpool itself on 17 November, with an amendment moved by Salvidge and Derby, supported for the government by Worthington-Evans, Secretary of State for War but also a National Union man of long experience. The diehards were placed in an exposed position, and much was made of Lloyd George's threat to resign and leave the Unionists saddled with an unpopular war; emotions ran high, but the government's amendment was overwhelmingly approved, after Worthington-Evans had given firm assurances about the limits of concession and against the coercion of Ulster.[6] Party loyalty was thus exploited to the full and the leadership won what was virtually a vote of confidence, but it was a dangerous method of proceeding, for the reserves of loyalty would not be available for use more than once. When the terms of the Irish Treaty were actually announced, the party opposition increased somewhat, but by then it could only be expressed in parliament and was in any case insufficient to disturb a government that could rely on Labour and Asquithian support. Bonar Law was less easily dealt with, for he thought that the government was prepared to 'let Ulster down badly, and in that case was quite prepared to come out against them and thought that 90 per cent of the Unionist party would have backed him'.[7] Law intervened to persuade the Ulster leaders to reject terms that they had already once accepted and, since assurances had been given that Ulster would not be coerced, the government could only try to coerce the Nationalists instead. Within weeks of his return, Law emerged as an alternative leader such as the coalition had never had to face before, not just a man who might get a majority at a future election, but one who might fashion an anti-coalition majority in the present House of Commons. In the bluffing all round that accompanied the settlement of Ireland, Law was able to trump Lloyd George's ace because he was a credible alternative Prime Minister.

The settlement of Ireland had involved regular talk of an election. Lloyd George had threatened dissolution on a war policy to frighten the Nationalists and had then threatened dissolution on a peace policy to bring the Unionists into line. But after parliament approved the Treaty, there was an opportunity to call an election to exploit the government's victory.

The proposal to hold a quick election originated with Birkenhead, partly because he despaired of agreement on the House of Lords question (for which he was responsible as Lord Chancellor) and partly because it was the best opportunity yet to get a fresh mandate for coalition. The failure of fusion had destroyed the only chance of prolonging coalition by full-hearted agreement (if there ever was one); the only way now was to 'bounce' the party into acceptance by dissolving parliament. Faced with an election under a Prime Minister who had just achieved a signal personal triumph, Unionists would have to come into line as in 1918, or see their party decimated at the polls. It took little to persuade Lloyd George of the merits of this idea and Balfour was a willing accomplice in persuading the rest of the cabinet. By mid December, rumours of an election were circulating at Westminster and on 20 December 1921 a meeting of Lloyd George, Churchill, Birkenhead and Chamberlain tried to decide on one. Chamberlain was well aware of the likely party reaction and was not at all keen on a dissolution in January; no decision was taken and so ministers dispersed for Christmas, Austen to consult his colleagues and the rest to whip up support. Chamberlain did not want an election, and was much relieved when it eventually fell through, but he would not use his party position to stop it; in his view the Prime Minister alone had the right to seek a dissolution, an unchallengeable opinion in normal times, but not so certain when another leader had a majority in the House of Commons. He therefore told the party managers what was intended and conducted his soundings into party opinion. Younger reacted with characteristic forthrightness, telling Chamberlain that the party would not stand for such treatment, and also telling Lloyd George that the Unionist party would not fight as a coalition, whatever Chamberlain might say.

Austen's soundings were conducted through private letters to Derby, Salvidge, Sanders, J. C. Williams (Chairman of the National Union Central Council), Malcolm Fraser (Principal Agent), and his brother Neville. Derby gave an indecisive reply and Salvidge provided the unhelpful advice that 'if the Coalition wished to continue, they must bring back Bonar Law'; Sanders, Williams and Neville Chamberlain all pointed to the local difficulties that an election would cause, and Fraser reported that it would 'split our party from top to toe'. Neville Chamberlain argued for many when he suggested that the Geddes cuts should be implemented before the voters would consider their demands for economy to have been met. Unionists who opposed an election did not of course do so for the same reasons, and none of those consulted actually wished to end the coalition. Chamberlain had probably hoped for such a response, since it would strengthen his hand when the final decision was taken, but he certainly did not expect the ferocity with which other Unionists reacted when they heard the news.[8]

Meanwhile the controversy opened up a guerrilla campaign in the press. Lloyd George was out of the country from Boxing Day 1921, but in his absence the convinced coalitionists set about creating the impression that the decision to dissolve had already been effectively taken. Birkenhead and

Beaverbrook on one side and the Lloyd George Whips on the other set about a carefully orchestrated press campaign over the New Year weekend. But as Sanders noted, 'Downing Street has been working the press as usual; now Malcolm Fraser is working it in the opposite direction.' A memorandum for Austen Chamberlain entitled 'A short diary of a press campaign' shows what was done: it began with a leak to *The Times, Daily News* and 'specially favoured provincials', and, after three days of more leaks to all the national papers, interviews with Younger were put out by the Press Association and the *Evening News*. On 8 January Younger contributed a signed article to the *Weekly Dispatch* (which was of course taken up in the rest of the press) and on 11 January a letter from him appeared everywhere. The effect was an avalanche of letters from MPs, agents, local parties and chairmen, almost all against a snap election and many of them denouncing it as a trick to take away the independence of the party. Austen Chamberlain was on the receiving end of this reaction: an abstract of the views of thirty-four MPs, of whom thirty-one were against an election and three were undecided; reports in the local press indicating that provincial party leaders were against the idea in London, Birmingham, Bristol, Cardiff, Leeds, Liverpool, and Manchester; Austen 'heard of only one Unionist who favoured dissolution and he was a man who was not going to stand again'. By 5 January Lloyd George in Paris had agreed to defer the decision, and by the 14th he had decided against an election; Austen announced the decision on the 19th and Lloyd George confirmed it on the 21st. The hostility of the Unionists had taken the decision out of its leader's hands; the party would not be bounced.[9]

The masterstroke was the letter that Younger had sent to constituency chairmen on 9 January, which had then been published on 11 January. This was the first direct notification to the local parties that an election might be on the way (although Younger said that he knew of no plans for an election, the rest of the letter made it clear that he knew exactly that); this helped to generate the hostile reaction, but it also set out terms on which coalition could and should continue. No election should be held before economies had been effected and trade revived; there was no need for one on these grounds, for the present Unionist majority in the Commons would support appropriate policies anyway. The most important point though was Younger's reference to the House of Lords, for this contained both an argument for coalition and a stern warning:

> Only a coalition like the present could successfully deal with that vital question, and the Government has given the most specific pledges to deal with it in the coming session of Parliament. They command a majority which can secure a reasonable settlement of what is admittedly a difficult question, and there would be bitter resentment if they lay down office before a serious attempt had been made to fulfil those pledges.[10]

It was largely on Younger's terms that the Party accepted coalition for a further year ('I believe you will agree that the foregoing views correctly interpret the feelings of our friends as a whole') but it would be on trial. If coalition failed to reform the House of Lords, then it would have proved its uselessness and the unreliability of its leaders; if it succeeded in reconstituting the Lords, then it would have no further reason to exist. The failure of the election kite of January 1922 meant that the coalition could now go neither forwards nor backwards, and that its days were numbered.

In these dire circumstances Lloyd George considered resignation in order to recover his freedom of action. Bonar Law refused his offer of the Foreign Office and so remained an outside focus for discontent. Austen Chamberlain did not react favourably to Lloyd George taking a rest from office, partly from reluctance to reach the premiership over the corpse of a friend and partly because Lloyd George outside would be a far more serious threat than Bonar Law. For a month the entire government was in disarray, until in March Lloyd George pulled it together and determined to have one more try to make it work. The House of Lords would be taken up seriously and he would play what he regarded as the government's strongest card, his personal diplomacy, in a last effort to regain popularity.[11]

Nevertheless, the last six months of Lloyd George's premiership went badly in every sphere, and although not dictating the Unionist withdrawal at the end of that time, it certainly helped them to take a clear decision and make a clean break. First, the policy that was supposed to revive the government went disastrously wrong when the Genoa Conference ended in humiliation for Lloyd George instead of triumph. In fact the Prime Minister did reasonably well and improved his standing in internationalist circles by standing up to French intransigence. This, however, began the series of events that eventually detached Curzon from the government, for Curzon saw the French alliance as the cornerstone of his policy. In any case, it was insufficient that Genoa had not been a setback, for in domestic terms it needed to be an unmistakable triumph. The second main foreign initiative of the year was in the Near East, culminating in the Chanak crisis of September–October. Lloyd George's policy of backing Greece owed something to Liberal memories of Gladstone's anti-Turk crusade and something to promises made to Venizelos during the war, but neither of these made much impression on Unionists. Lloyd George again came into conflict with Curzon, conscious of Britain's standing as a great Muslim power (in India) and of her historic role as defender of the Turks. It also led the government into a more bellicose position when Kemal routed the Greeks and threatened their British supporting units. There were fears, too, that the coalition had hoped to exploit a victory over the Turks to distract attention from its domestic failures, perhaps even with another khaki election. Finally, Chanak gave Bonar Law the chance to mark his return to the political arena by a critical letter to *The Times*.[12] A Lloyd George resignation over Ireland in November 1922 would have left the Unionists stuck with an unpopular war; Law was now able to adopt the popular peace position over Chanak and to accuse the government of irresponsible warmongering. The abandonment of Edwin Montagu and his Indian policy to diehard critics in March 1922 was equally ineffective. Montagu was added to the ranks of the government's critics, and diehards merely believed that it showed Lloyd George's desperation.

Domestic issues went equally badly. Ireland, which might have been the note of triumph in a February election, was not so clearly a plus factor a few months later. There were unseemly wrangles over the arbitration of the Northern Ireland–Free State border, and the outbreak of civil war in the South made the Treaty of the previous year look less like the final settlement of a historic problem. This was brought right home when Sir Henry Wilson was murdered by terrorists in Eaton Square on 22 June. Wilson had been a Unionist hero for some time, a diehard MP, and a strong critic of Lloyd George's Irish policy in the last months of his life. Gunfire in the West End and the assassination of an MP (albeit one whose past career and recent actions might have made the event less than surprising) had a more disquietening effect than years of outrages in Ireland, and the mood of the Commons was very jittery in the next few weeks.[13] In the debate that followed, Law announced that he was dissatisfied with the government's Irish policy and that he thought that he had been mistaken in his support for the Treaty; he stopped just short of accusing the government of deceiving him, but he sat down to an ovation from Unionist MPs and gave private warnings that he would not be able to stand aside for much longer unless things improved.

The Birthday Honours List, also in June 1922, prompted a different sort of attack. For several years some Unionists had been concerned that Lloyd George's Whips were selling honours on the open market, and these fears had come to a head with stories about Maundy Gregory, a middleman who could apparently secure an honour for anyone rich enough to pay for it. It was a situation that men like Baldwin saw as the inevitable result of unprincipled government. The 1922 list was the most blatant example yet of honours going to men whose only qualification was their wealth, especially Sir Joseph Robinson, a shady South African financier whose claims were swiftly refuted by the South African government and stongly resisted by the King. Hostility in parliament was such that Lloyd George had to accept the appointment of a Royal Commission to investigate the whole system whereby honours were awarded on the Prime Minister's advice.[14] In the meantime, he admitted that 'mistakes' had been made, and the worst was generally believed.

More typical government problems also mounted in 1922, with rising unemployment and a low level of trade. Unemployment had reached over two million in the winter of 1921–22 and, though it then fell back somewhat, it was always at or over a million and a half. Imports were falling but exports were still low, and there remained a sizeable deficit on the balance of trade. Economies had been made on the Geddes lines, but these had provoked opposition even from Unionists (to cuts in defence and in education) and income tax was still at its highest ever level of 6s in the pound. The government groped feebly for a response to the poor state of the economy and Unionists cast their minds back to earlier days for solutions. A battle in the cabinet over the protection of fabric gloves showed that the government would not easily use the powers that it had under the Safeguarding of Industry Act of 1921. Baldwin had to threaten resignation to get his way for the Board of Trade, but the issue showed clearly enough the government's inability to use the economic weapon in which most Unionists still believed. This is not to argue that the state of the economy caused the government's disintegration, but merely that the government's failure took away another possible prop of its survival.[15]

One area of economic discontent was of greater political importance to Unionists, and that was the state of agriculture. World over-production in wartime had left British farmers unable to compete in the post-war world, a position that was unfairly blamed on the chopping and changing of government policy, proposing and then abandoning the Agriculture Act of 1919 and then doing almost nothing. By 1922 about three-quarters of a million acres had gone out of cultivation since the war and rural distress had been widespread. Griffith-Boscawen, Minister of Agriculture, had almost resigned when the government would not allow him his way over the importation of Canadian cattle, and over the summer of 1922 he was pressing unavailingly for help for the farmers. The issue had a sharp political impact because of the number of Unionists who sat for rural seats and depended on the votes of farmers. Pressure on these men, who made up much of the solid centre of the party, was an important factor in the politics of 1922, as Griffith-Boscawen told Chamberlain:

> The political difficulties of the Party are great, and we are faced anyhow with an early election; we have in the House a solid block of county members who really are the backbone of our party and without them we can never hope to have a majority. . . . Their leaders are among our best friends, e.g. Fitzroy, Pretyman, Lane Fox, Townley, Courthorpe, Spender-Clay, Murrough Wilson and others, and unless we have something definite to say to them by way of assistance to agriculture at the present moment, their position in the constituencies will be one of great difficulty and I fear we will lose many seats.[16]

These leaders of the Agricultural Members' Committee were the more vital because they tended to act as a group, because of their high standing on the back benches, and because of their generally moderate attitude. They had been solidly behind the coalition and behind Chamberlain, whose leadership Pretyman had proposed. In October 1922 Chamberlain fell after a resolution which Pretyman proposed and Lane Fox seconded, and for which all seven men named by Griffith-Boscawen voted. Failure to offer help to the farmers was probably the coalition's costliest single mistake in 1922, for it helped to swing forty or fifty votes at the Carlton Club and so provided the anti-coalitionists with their majority.

The final policy failure was House of Lords reform. Chamberlain urged Curzon to take the matter up, because he could be expected to treat it more seriously than Birkenhead would do, and because the National Union was proving so 'troublesome' and 'reproaching me with our silence'.[17] Chamberlain hoped to press ahead, so that reform resolutions could be presented in time to head off the July meeting of the National Union Executive. This idea went badly wrong when Curzon's plans were strongly opposed by Churchill, Mond, and Fisher, and no real reform could be agreed in cabinet. On the issue that many Unionists felt had alone justified the continuation of coalition into 1922, and which was its real test, the government could not deliver.

The failure of policy during 1922 added fuel to the diehard demand for an end of coalition, but it also produced the cracks in the government itself that finally brought it about. A substantial body of MPs who had on balance supported the coalition in January were opposed to it by October, and leaders were emerging to guide the discontent into safe channels. Outside the government, Law and Derby were preparing to intervene, and among Unionist ministers a division was appearing. Curzon, Baldwin and Griffith-Boscawen had all found themselves in fundamental disagreement with the Prime Minister over their own areas of policy, and each was apparently looking for the right issue on which to make a break with him. At the same time the junior ministers began to work as a team and to press their views on Chamberlain. They were more impressed than their seniors by the diehards and some at least were concerned about Lord Salisbury's threat to put up Conservative candidates against coalitionists at an election.

An election could not now be delayed for long, because the government was failing fast, and at two meetings the junior ministers demanded an assurance from Chamberlain that a Unionist majority after the election would result in a Unionist Prime Minister. Lloyd George must be told to stand down.[18] It is worth emphasizing that the demand was not for an end to coalition, but for an end to *Lloyd George's* coalition; in resisting it and defending Lloyd George, Chamberlain was actually keeping himself out of Downing Street. He consulted Lloyd George, who seemed willing to accept the ultimatum, perhaps because he did not envisage that there would be a Unionist majority anyway, but the other Unionist coalitionists were very angry when they heard about these mutinous demands from the lower deck. At a third meeting on 3 August, Balfour and Birkenhead told the junior ministers that they must accept the decisions of their betters.[19] Although Chamberlain sympathized with these views, he postponed a decision until after the recess; deadlock would thus go on until October, and the junior ministers had in the meantime to make up their minds without guidance. Many of them told their local associations that they would stand at the next election without a coalition label, hoping no doubt to protect their seats and keep their diehard supporters happy. Most of all, the bulk of Unionist MPs outside the cabinet were determined that no commitments should be given to

Lloyd George that would break up their own party. If the diehards were prepared to split the party to wreck the coalition, then the moderates would have to join them in wrecking the coalition in order to save the party. There was conviction as well as mere trimming in these calculations; few Unionists had any faith in Lloyd George by 1922, or in the strength of Coalition Liberalism, so it had become vital to preserve the effectiveness of the Unionist party as the only force left to resist Labour. In the summer of 1922 then, the argument shifted from the future of the Lloyd George coalition to the possible alternatives.

The coalitionist ministers were well aware of their increasing isolation and so, led by Birkenhead and Churchill, they determined on one last desperate throw to keep coalition alive. An election would be sprung on the party, as intended in January, and all decisions about the future would be left to a party meeting after the election was over. Expecting that no party would get a majority, they therefore expected also that they would be able to continue the coalition once the results were declared. This decision, taken at a cabinet meeting on 17 September, plunged the party into a month of wrangling that eventually produced an entirely new regime, a 'slice off the top'. The attempt to bounce the party into an election was alleged to have failed in January only because it had not been tried with enough determination. The difference this time was that Austen Chamberlain had been captured by the coalitionists: in January he had been a clear if irresolute opponent of an election, but in September he was a clear (if equally irresolute) supporter. Chamberlain had never ceased to preach the virtues of cooperation, as in an important speech at Oxford in March, but he had not committed himself or his party to any specific way in which coalition should be continued. He had changed, though, in his attitude to his position and to his critics: in the autumn of 1922 he was unbending and severe throughout the crisis. As an honourable man, trying to live down his father's reputation, Austen had always set great store on loyalty to properly constituted authority; the criticism that had come his way ever since March 1921 had played on his nerves and made him more than ever conscious of his dignity, more determined not to sacrifice the authority of his leadership; if his advice were to be rejected by his party, then his party must find another leader. [20]

The confused tangle of events in the month that followed the cabinet decision of 17 September has been unravelled by Maurice Cowling and need not be repeated in detail here, but it will be worth recounting the views of the various protagonists. The cabinet coalitionists continued to take a high line, and Birkenhead, Balfour and Horne continued to screw up Chamberlain's courage for him; if the party decided against coalition, then it would lose not just its leader but all its men of talent. The discontented minority in the cabinet were less certain of their actions; Baldwin and Griffith-Boscawen gradually assumed the lead of the junior ministers, but it was only late in the day that Baldwin emerged as its spearhead; Curzon made his position clear to

Bonar Law, but his intended resignation was not widely known. The party managers struggled to win Chamberlain over to their view that an election would be catastrophic, and when they failed in this they tried to bring back Bonar Law to save the unity of the party. Sanders and Younger (Chairman and Deputy Chairman), Wilson (Chief Whip), and Fraser (Principal Agent) acted as a team and eventually threw their considerable weight into the scale against Chamberlain; Sanders provided a link with the junior ministers too.

The National Union responded to the news in great agitation, and a special meeting of the Executive on 18 October decided to escalate the conflict. It was correctly believed that the decision to rush an election had been taken partly to avoid the coming Party Conference, due on 15 November and expected to pass anti-coalition resolutions. The National Union did not intend to let Chamberlain get away with flouting its views so openly; it was decided to hold a special conference *before* the projected election. A conference at such a time would be a bitter affair that would wreck party unity on the eve of an election, and instead of avoiding antagonism (as Chamberlain had hoped) would create it.[21] The moderate MPs were mobilized in the last week by Sir Samuel Hoare and others; their cool reception by Chamberlain and the warm response of Bonar Law helped to push them into opposition. Austen Chamberlain himself was striving to save party unity but also to salvage the dignity of his own position and to remain loyal to Lloyd George. He gradually saw the impossibility of reconciling all these aims, and so he summoned the MPs to a meeting at the Carlton Club on 19 October, to confront his critics and demand obedience. The final division in the party was not taken on the question that he had wanted (to postpone decisions until after the election), but on a resolution formulated by his opponents and hence designed to widen their appeal as far as possible. Bonar Law resisted the pressure to return until the last possible moment, but he eventually accepted the persuasion of Younger, Davidson, Beaverbrook and many others, that 'since neither Lloyd George nor Austen were prepared to make any attempt to liquidate the situation, the time had come when he must either leave politics or take action himself'. As soon as the decision was taken, on the evening of 18 October, Beaverbrook shrewdly made sure that it should appear in the papers, so that Law had no chance of changing his mind.[22]

When they assembled at the Carlton Club on the morning of 19 October, Unionist MPs knew that Chamberlain would offer no guarantee about a future government or future Prime Minister that would avoid a split with the diehards. They also knew that Law, Baldwin, Griffith-Boscawen, and possibly Curzon and Peel of the present cabinet were available to them, and that with Derby, Salisbury and the junior ministers they would make up a cabinet without the coalitionists if necessary. They knew that the decision for a coalition election would produce a contentious party conference, a split in the constituencies, and hence also defeat for at least some of them. The result of the Newport by-election, announced at 2 a.m. that morning, provided the final argument. It was generally expected at Westminster that the independent Unionist would lose, and that Labour would gain the seat on the split of the anti-socialist vote: Austen Chamberlain had believed this and had actually arranged the meeting for the 19th in order to have the result to hand before the vote was taken. This went sadly wrong when the Unionist won Newport with a good majority. *The Times* was the only paper able to print a comment as well as the figures, and this gave much heart to Chamberlain's opponents:

> The country will see in it a most complete condemnation of the Coalition Government as such and a vindication of those Conservatives throughout the country who have been determined to preserve their individuality in previous by-election contests. By these the Newport result will be hailed as the emancipation of their party.

This interpretation was almost wholly belied by what had actually been happening in Newport in the previous three weeks, but this did not matter much, for the figures told the story effectively enough without comment. Newport may have clinched the argument: a coalition election would produce a certain split and a likely catastrophe, but an election as an independent party might avoid a split and produce a victory as well.[23]

The speeches at the meeting confirmed previous intentions; Austen Chamberlain was 'clumsy and ineffectual', demanding that his lead be followed and giving no assurances as to his actions in the future; Baldwin was short and very effective, arguing that further collaboration with Lloyd George would increase division until 'the old Conservative Party were smashed to atoms and lost in ruins'; Pretyman and Lane Fox called for the resumption of the party's independence, but did not rule out cooperation with Liberals either at the election or afterwards; Law made known his availability and reminded the party of what had happened in and after 1846; Balfour was out of touch with the meeting in his high-handed insistence on loyalty to Chamberlain, and Wilson gave his opinion as Chief Whip that many MPs would refuse to accept the terms Chamberlain had offered. It was Wilson's intervention that most upset Austen, who saw it as especially treacherous for a Chief Whip to speak against his leader, but this was rather unfair to Wilson, who had tried to resign in the previous week and had been told to await the outcome of the crisis. Smarting under these accumulated criticisms, Chamberlain pressed on to his doom, ignoring pleas that he should accept the mood of the meeting and so allow it to avoid a vote. He insisted on a vote and Pretyman's motion was passed by 185 votes to 88, a clear rejection of his advice. Lloyd George resigned the same day, and most Unionist cabinet ministers resolved to stand by Chamberlain by staying out of any alternative government.[24]

The breakdown of votes at the Carlton Club was on predictable lines: of the sixty MPs identified by Professor McEwen as regular critics of coalition, forty-five voted for the motion and only two against; of the keenest coalitionists, fifty-three voted for Chamberlain and four against him. MPs with marginal seats were more favourable to coalition than those who were safe, and MPs from Scotland, the North and the Midlands were more likely to stick with Chamberlain than those from Wales, the South and the West. What was most clear was that the real decision had been taken not by the diehards or the convinced coalitionists but by the core of centrist MPs for whom Pretyman and Lane Fox could claim to speak and to whose opinions Bonar Law and Baldwin were so responsive. In the week before the meeting, the opponents of Chamberlain had not dared to hope for success, and the junior ministers had thought, like Baldwin, that they were destroying their careers to save their party. They were vindicated by the party's solid heart, by MPs who set store above all on party unity and who, when faced with the awful choice between unity and loyalty, had to put unity first. A significant pointer to this was the fact that every past or future Party Chairman or Chief Whip who voted was in the majority and against Chamberlain.[25] Bonar Law's emergence as an alternative leader was therefore crucial, for it provided the legitimation for revolt against the elected leader. Earlier in 1922 it had been suggested that only Balfour or Bonar Law could overthrow Chamberlain because only they would possess a leader's authority to set against loyalty to the man in office; Balfour had refused to do so, and Law had only just come round in time, but once he did so he made sure that there was no mistake. In his speech, Law turned Chamberlain's argument about loyalty on its head and argued that 'this is a question in regard to which our system . . . has hitherto gone on this principle: that the party elects a leader, and that the leader chooses the policy, and if the party does not like it, they have to get another leader'. Having taken that responsibility, Law now had to pick up the pieces.

Law was sent for by the King as soon as Lloyd George resigned, but would not accept office until his position in his party had been regularized; he cannot have been sure of the reactions of Curzon, Derby and Salisbury, all of whom might have hoped to become Prime Minister themselves. By the time that Law was formally re-elected leader at the Hotel Cecil on 23 October, the position had been clarified and his government was as good as formed; he became Prime Minister the same day, announced his cabinet on the next, and announced the dissolution of parliament two days later. A government formed on new lines needed a new mandate, but it was a guide to the new situation that there was now no objection to an election in a party that had just fought a last-ditch resistance to avoid one. The National Union Executive met again on 19 October and cancelled the special conference they had arranged on the previous day, and a week later they postponed the ordinary conference too.[26]

The business of forming a government was considerably complicated by the intransigence of the coalitionists; within hours of the Carlton Club Meeting, thirteen ministers (including nine of the outgoing cabinet) signed an agreement marking their continued support for Chamberlain. They did not oppose Law's election to the leadership, but they remained apart; at a dinner in Chamberlain's honour on 30 November there were forty-nine MPs present to hear his defence of his actions and to express their support, a number that comes close to Bridgeman's estimate that half of those who voted with Chamberlain at the Carlton Club were actually glad to see him defeated.[27] Enquiries were made to test the strength of Chamberlain's support, but no offers were taken up. Law was therefore left to make up his government from those who had voted with him on the 19th and from sympathetic peers, but this at least guaranteed that the government was united on the basic principle that had brought it about. The only foray outside the Unionist ranks was the offer of the Exchequer to Reginald McKenna, an ex-Liberal Chancellor and banker whose experience was thought valuable in bringing City support to the government; McKenna preferred to stay with the Midland Bank, but he made known his support for the government, partly through conviction and partly perhaps because of his pleasure at the discomfiture of Lloyd George. Baldwin was then appointed to the Exchequer, a natural enough choice in view of his experience as Financial Secretary under Law himself. The rest of the cabinet was made up of Curzon, Peel and Griffith-Boscawen, together with promoted juniors and outsiders.

Churchill immediately castigated it as 'a government of the second eleven' and Birkenhead spoke caustically of 'second class brains', an analysis that has stuck to it ever since. In fact, Law had as much experience and talent available to him as is customary for incoming governments, and he was able to dispose of some that was available. As well as himself and the four cabinet ministers who continued in office, he appointed Salisbury and Derby (both of whom had been in Balfour's cabinet), Cave (who had been in Lloyd George's cabinet), and several junior ministers who had served a long enough apprenticeship to be worth higher office. Eight of the sixteen cabinet ministers had been in cabinet before, a higher proportion than any of the incoming governments of 1905, 1945, 1951, 1964 or 1970, and it is by such a standard that Law's government must be judged, for it was the first Unionist cabinet formed for twenty years. That he was not concerned by the relative inexperience of his team is shown clearly enough by his failure to appoint Selborne or Cecil (both ex-cabinet ministers) or Steel-Maitland (a man 'of cabinet rank'). Selborne later recalled that he had not wished to join in 1922 because he did not expect Law's ministry to last, but he could certainly have been persuaded if Law had felt the need to do so.[28] The only diehard in the cabinet was therefore Salisbury, but he was both more moderate and more weighty than the bulk of his followers.

Another favourite criticism of the government was the number of peers holding high office (five of the seven Secretaries of State), a point made brilliantly by Peter Wright of the *Evening News*[29] Here again the criticism was hardly justified. If the coalitionist ministers had joined Law's government, then at least two of them would have been in the House of Lords, and it is unlikely that they would have displaced many more than two other peers from the cabinet. When Baldwin formed his second ministry in 1924, with the whole party to choose from, he still chose six peers for his cabinet compared to the seven of 1922. The real point behind these attacks was valid enough; the government did not really lack experience or administrative ability, but it certainly did lack brilliance, communicative skills and men of ideas. Law's was an honest and capable government, but a government without star performers, hence the approach to McKenna. In terms of its legacy for the future it was more successful, for Law gave their first major posts to Edward Wood, Samuel Hoare, Douglas Hogg, Neville Chamberlain and Philip Lloyd-Greame, the group that was to fill Conservative cabinets for the next twenty years. It was, as Sanders noted, 'a real old Tory government', one that reflected the important part that the solid, but far from brilliant, centre of the party had played in bringing it into existence.

Two decisions taken at once gave some indication that Law did not intend a diehard policy. He decided to wind up the 'garden suburb' of advisers to the Prime Minister, but to retain the Cabinet Office itself; the clock would not be turned back indiscriminately. Ireland was also settled by implication, by the decision to call an election at once; this would be needed if parliament was to meet again to pass the legislation needed to implement the Treaty of 1921 before the end of the year (as had been agreed), and a quick election would leave very little time for the Commons to go over the old ground again. Law's government was the first not to include an Irish Secretary and, once the tidying-up legislation could be passed, he did not intend to have an Irish policy either. These two matters having been settled, the party plunged straight into an election.[30]

Few Unionist MPs who voted either way at the Carlton Club believed in the possibility of what almost all of them really wanted, a Unionist government re-elected with a clear majority. As the election approached, this pessimistic view still prevailed, and the confused campaign (in which both Unionists and Liberals operated as two factions) did nothing to assist predictions. Chamberlain's supporters, conscious of their weak position, stood as official Unionist candidates and were backed by their local associations. There were a few rumblings of the party split in the campaign, as when Cecil told Birkenhead that England preferred second class brains to second class characters, but with each Unionist candidate looking to his own survival such bickering was not widespread. Coalition Liberals were even more aware of their exposed position and anxious to make electoral pacts on any terms that Unionists were prepared to offer. In Scotland a pact covered the whole of Clydeside, where Labour was most feared. Law campaigned shrewdly on a platform that had no policy basis whatsoever, except the existence of his government. He dropped anything that was contentious enough to threaten party unity or cost votes, and he renewed his pledge of 1913 not to introduce tariffs without another election first. His manifesto made a positive virtue of the lack of policy and reflected his whole campaign:

> There are many measures of legislative and administrative importance which, in themselves would be desirable, and which, in other circumstances, I should have recommended to the immediate attention of the electorate. But I do not feel that they can, at this moment, claim precedence over the nation's first need, which is, in every walk of life, to get on with its own work with the minimum of interference at home and of disturbance abroad.[31]

The keynote of the campaign was 'tranquillity', a slogan well chosen to contrast with the political atmosphere of the past decade, and many leaflets also carried the legend 'safety first'. The Unionists were put forward as the solid rock on which sensible, moderate and normal political life would be re-established; the comparison with Labour's alleged extremism and with the divisions of the Liberals was obvious enough. There is no doubt too that Law's appeal touched a deep chord in the public mind, a yearning for the world before 1914, a pessimism about the future and a doubt about experiment or innovation; it was much the same mood that had carried Warren Harding to the Presidency of the United States to restore 'normalcy'.

Party organization played little part in the campaign. Virtually no literature was available at the outset, for nobody knew a month before polling day on what basis the election would be fought. A *Campaign Guide* appeared, but was too late to be much use. Everywhere local parties were rushed into a battle for which they were not ready, candidates were only chosen at the last moment, and there were few associations that mounted a good canvass. Money was short at the local level, and even shorter at Central Office because of an embarrassing overhang from the coalition which deprived the party of its own money. The party treasurer was still Lord Farquhar, appointed in 1911 by Balfour; he was seventy-eight in 1922 and had become highly eccentric as well as a strong coalitionist in the past six years. He had kept the party's funds in personal bank accounts, something over a million pounds in all, and he now argued that it was the coalition's money and so was not for party use. Younger argued frustratedly that most of it had been subscribed before the coalition had existed, and that it was party money in any case, but he made no impression on Farquhar's failing mind. The money could not be touched without Farquhar's approval and so the campaign began with an urgent appeal for money.[32] Enough came in to keep Central Office going, but not to mount a large campaign effort. All this mattered less than usual, for two reasons: first, the whole campaign became almost a national referendum on the party's decision to dispose of Lloyd George, and was influenced more by press comment than by conventional organization, and secondly, the confused state of the parties ensured that the result would be determined above all by the pattern of candidates. The party press gained a welcome recruit when *The Times* was bought at the beginning of the campaign by the Walter family, with money from the Astors; henceforth it was a reliable party paper. Law's friendship with Beaverbrook secured the temporary support of the *Daily Express*, and Lord Riddell's break with Lloyd George brought the unexpected assistance of the *News of the World*; despite Law's refusal to accept Rothermere's nomination of his son to a cabinet post, Rothermere gave general support. The press as a whole gave the new government an easy ride.

At the end of 1921, Malcolm Fraser had predicted that the party would win between 306 and 367 seats, depending on circumstances, and it now fell to him to make his prediction come true. He left the work of making local pacts to the local parties (the Clydeside pact was made in Glasgow, not in London), so avoiding the friction that had occurred in 1918, but he was prepared to intervene to encourage contest when he saw a chance to win the seat. Sanders, who had managed the pact in 1918, expected during the campaign that the Unionists would get between 335 and 350; he had made a general agreement with Freddy Guest allowing general cooperation with Coalition Liberals but, after he had departed for his constituency, Fraser decided to strike out on his own. He called the Liberal bluff and put up candidates against all the Liberal ex-ministers where he saw a chance of winning. The result was that the Unionists gained several extra seats, including Guest's own.[33]

The public response to Law's campaign had been recognized, but the result still came as a surprise; Unionists won 344 seats out of 615, an overall majority of seventy-five. Comment centred on the size of the Labour breakthrough and on the flimsy nature of the Unionist victory. Labour had polled four million votes (compared with five and a half million Unionist votes) and had become the strongest party in the cities, the mining areas and South Wales, mainly at the expense of the Liberals. The Unionist performance was not as bad as it seemed, for although the party had got its overall majority from just over 38 per cent of the popular vote, this was misleading. Forty-two safe Unionist seats had not been contested and many candidates had stood down in favour of Liberals; a full slate of Unionist candidates and a contest in every seat would have produced at least another three-quarters of a million votes, pushing the share up to at least 42 per cent. The real weakness of the Unionist position was the way in which votes had been affected by Fraser's activities, for Unionists had been able to draw all the advantages of pacts without giving much in return. At a future election where the party had to meet the Liberals united and unwilling to make deals, the Unionist performance would deteriorate.

None of this mattered much in the euphoria that followed the victory in 1922, for the party had won its first clear triumph in twenty-two years. The Party Conference in December became a victory jamboree, and Law's speech struck the right tone when he observed that 'we may not have, at least I would not like to assert that we have, a monopoly of first class brains (laughter) but we are, I hope, and believe, a government composed of men with good judgement (hear, hear) and what is perhaps not less important, they are a government of first class loyalty'. It was, as Younger wrote, 'the story of a great recovery'.[34]

With its celebrations over, the Law government had to face the problems that had helped to drive Lloyd George from power, and it made an undistinguished attempt to deal with them. Law sought to carry on with tranquillity and the avoidance of commitments by a deliberate Prime Ministerial withdrawal. So he relinquished the control that Asquith and Lloyd George had acquired over their cabinets, leaving more business to departmental ministers. He made his point by refusing to see a delegation from the unemployed, arguing that it was a political manoeuvre and that they should go to the Ministry of Labour. The reaction on the left was one of outrage, but the decision was popular in the Unionist party. Baldwin was given considerable freedom and sent off to settle the question of outstanding war debts to the United States; Curzon had a similar freedom at the Foreign Office. Tranquillity would be shown by the almost complete absence of legislation in 1923, on the view that industrial confidence required time to settle things down. Unfortunately, ignoring problems did not make them go away.

Labour began to act with a new confidence after the 1922 election and, although the Liberals were wasting their opportunity to reunite, Lloyd George was taking a rest and biding his time. Coalition Unionists were still unreconciled and Birkenhead in particular was looking for a chance to get back into power; their main target was Curzon, because of his late desertion of the coalition ship, and intrigues were going on with the press lords to embarrass the government. A chance was offered by the fact that a number of ministers had lost their seats at the general election, including Wilson and Griffith-Boscawen. Wilson was a popular man and was returned within a few weeks, but the inconvenience of a month without Chief Whip was as nothing compared to the difficulty caused for and by Griffith-Boscawen. He could not long remain in the cabinet without a seat, and it was not possible to place another minister in the Lords (not least because he represented the main social department), but it was very difficult to find him a new seat. Central Office searched widely and at least seventeen constituencies turned him down before he was adopted for a by-election at Mitcham in February 1923. He was never a popular MP and had already gained the reputation of a poor candidate when he had lost Dudley at a by-election in 1920, under an onslaught from the Beaverbrook press. This time it was Rothermere who took the lead against him, by putting up an Independent Conservative candidate in collaboration with Oliver Locker-Lampson, a close associate of Austen Chamberlain. Apart from general dissatisfaction with the government's inaction, the main issue that told against Griffith-Boscawen was the decontrol of rents, for which he was personally responsible as Minister of Health; a desperate attempt to change policy in mid campaign did not help, and two years to the day after Dudley he lost Mitcham too, with the Independent getting enough votes to let Labour in and destroying Griffith-Boscawen's career for ever.[35]

The loss of East Willesden to the Liberals on the same day and of Liverpool Edge Hill to Labour three days later made up a black week for the government, largely produced by the hostility of men who still called themselves Unionists. But that week in early March was the government's only time of electoral difficulty, for they never again met such determined hostility or suffered such results; over the parliament as a whole the government lost four seats and gained one, and by the summer its candidates were doing quite well. Even Mitcham produced a silver lining, for it led to the promotion of Neville Chamberlain to the Ministry of Health, where he soon became the government's greatest asset. His Housing Act owed something to the work of the Unionist Social Reform Committee before the war and was one of the government's major achievements; under its auspices, over 300,000 houses were built, far more than under Wheatley's Act of 1924, despite its great reputation.[36]

The Mitcham defeat was greater in its impact because the government had been severely shaken by an internal crisis in January 1923. When the cabinet received news from America about the terms that Baldwin had secured for settlement of the war debts, there was disagreement about whether they should be accepted. Baldwin and his advisers counselled their acceptance, but Law would not have them at any price and curtly told Baldwin to return home. When the cabinet discussed the question in detail on 30 January the situation had been transformed by an unguarded interview given by Baldwin on his return; the terms were now generally known, and it would be impossible to expect the American government to improve them. Most ministers were in any case ready to accept the US offer to fund the debt over sixty-two years, with only Bonar Law opposing, and he felt so strongly that better terms must be possible that he was prepared to resign. The cabinet adjourned without a decision, the Prime Minister threatening resignation if the terms were accepted, Baldwin, Derby and others determined to go if they were not. The following morning, the cabinet met without Law and with Cave in the chair; most agreed that the government could not stand Law's resignation and that the majority would therefore have to give way, but Derby remained unconvinced. Cave, Baldwin and Devonshire conveyed their views to Law, played heavily on his loyalty to the party by stressing the dire consequences that would follow his resignation, and asked him to give way. Under such a concerted attack on his emotional Achilles' heel, Law inevitably gave way, and on 31 January the cabinet agreed to accept the US offer.

On the merits of the case, it would appear that Law was justified in his views, for the basic level of Britain's trade was not affected by the settlement and other countries that held out longer got better terms. He relieved his feelings by writing to *The Times* as 'a Colonial' to denounce the terms that he was commending to the House of Commons. It was nothing new for Law to take his party's views more seriously than his own, and a similar crisis had produced a similar result in January 1913, but this time it soured things more seriously.[37] Law became even more pessimistic and even more ready to urge inaction, and his government never recovered its poise. The same lack of impetus was felt in the Commons, where the lack of a positive programme was causing disquiet among Unionist MPs. Attendance became less regular and cross-voting more common; the majority sank to twenty-two in February on a motion calling for universal old age pensions, and on 10 April the government was actually defeated by five votes in a snap vote on unemployment among ex-servicemen.[38]

The chief cause for concern within the government by this time was the health of the Prime Minister, and it was clear that his decision on 31 January had not saved him for the party for long. In March he was unable to speak in the Commons and had to take a long rest, only six months after returning to office. On 15 April the press hinted at a coming resignation and prophesied the return of Chamberlain and his friends, who had originated the reports themselves, but again party opinion made clear its opposition. At the end of April Law was sent on a long sea voyage by his doctor, but before his departure he attempted to bring Austen into the government as Lord Privy Seal and with a strong hint that if he accepted it he might hope to be Prime Minister in a few months. Chamberlain refused the offer and so was still outside the government when Law's health finally gave way in Paris a month later. A cancer of the throat was diagnosed and Law was not expected to live for more than a few months. He returned to London as a Prime Minister who must resign at once. The shock that this news caused was further testament to the party's real sense of loss.[39]

Over ten years as leader, Bonar Law always placed the interests of his party as high as anything in his priorities, and had provided a leadership in which the party rank and file could believe. If he was destined to become 'the Unknown Prime Minister', in Asquith's cruel phrase, then he was certainly not the unknown leader of the party. In the political style that he bequeathed to Stanley Baldwin, and in the strong party that exists to this day, Law's lasting contribution can be seen. If Asquith had paid more attention to the interests and opinions of the followers who had put him in office, he might have been as revered and admired in his party as Law was when he died in 1923. But Law's contribution to the party was an essentially negative one: he had pulled it back from the brink of total disintegration in 1911 by emphasizing its negative strengths; he had guided it through the shoals of coalition because he had always pulled up short of any decision that would damage it; by responding to its cry from the heart in 1922 he had articulated its wish to be rid of Lloyd George and given effect to that wish. He was a superb leader of opposition, and it was because he (like the party) treated coalition government as something that the party might in some senses oppose that he had been so successful under Lloyd George. But his talents could probably carry the party no further than it had gone by 1923, and had he lived longer his career would have disappointed his admirers greatly. What was needed now was a more positive and adventurous style of leadership if the party was to come to terms with the post-war world. But whatever else he had been he had certainly been (as he himself said at the Carlton Club) 'more of a party man than some people'.[40]

The party reacted to the crisis caused by Law's retirement with an unexpected firmness. As Austen Chamberlain was still outside he did not come into consideration for the leadership that had been his for the taking a month earlier. The only contenders were Curzon and Baldwin, and in this sense the real issue was settled before the contest for, different as they were on almost every question, they agreed in opposing Lloyd George and coalition; whoever won, the character of the government would not be substantially altered. There was indeed only a contest at all because Law did not choose between them for the succession; had he opted for either Curzon or Baldwin with the authority in the party that he possessed in 1923, then the party would surely have accepted his choice. Law was unwilling to recommend either of them to the King, partly because of his health but also because he had doubts about the suitability of both. He had had disputes with both of them in the past few months, with Baldwin over the US debts and with Curzon over the relations of Downing Street and the Foreign Office. These had left him with doubt about Baldwin's judgement and with an equal doubt about Curzon's arrogance. On personal grounds he certainly favoured Baldwin, but he found it difficult not to back such a faithful party servant as Curzon. Law was relieved to be told by Lord Crewe that he need not offer advice to the King if he chose not to do so; Lord Stamfordham, the King's secretary was told this and set out to take his advice elsewhere. Salisbury gave a guarded preference for Curzon but admitted the force of the counter-arguments, and Balfour plumped strongly for Baldwin. The King's own preference seems to have been for Baldwin, because it would be needlessly provocative to place the Prime Minister in the House of Lords where the Labour opposition was hardly represented at all.

One influence was probably a mysterious memorandum drawn up by J. C. C. Davidson (once Law's secretary and now a Unionist MP as well as the Prime Minister's PPS) and conveyed to Stamfordham in such a way as to give the impression that it contained Law's advice conveyed by his close friends. The memorandum may have formed part of a 'Baldwinite conspiracy' engineered by Davidson and Amery, who were certainly determined that Baldwin should be chosen and lobbied to help bring it about. But the memorandum itself merely underlined advice given by others and the views that the King already held: Baldwin should be chosen because he was in the Commons, because he was more in touch with the spirit of the Law government as it had been formed, and because Derby would serve under him but not under Curzon; most of all, Baldwin did not need Curzon but Curzon would certainly need Baldwin.[41] Baldwin was duly appointed Prime Minister on 22 May 1923; the least satisfactory part of the whole affair was the way in which Stamfordham treated Curzon, who expected until the very last moment that he was to be chosen. Once passed over, Curzon behaved very well indeed; he proposed Baldwin's election as leader and agreed to stay on at the Foreign Office where he remained a loyal colleague, but the disappointment was severe for, to Curzon, Baldwin was 'a man of the utmost insignificance'.

Few changes were made in the government, but those few did a little to strengthen it. Baldwin retained the Exchequer as well as the premiership but extracted a promise from McKenna that he would come in within a few months. Most other ministers remained in the same offices, but Lord Robert Cecil was made Lord Privy Seal, and both Hoare and Joynson-Hicks were promoted to the cabinet. Half-hearted efforts to bring in Austen Chamberlain were foredoomed to failure. Amery and other colleagues let it be known that they would not serve with Austen, and the whole party would have resisted the return of Birkenhead. A tactless approach to Austen therefore only gave further offence. Horne was more tempted by the offer of the Exchequer, but he eventually pleaded business commitments and refused to renege on his friends (an error that ended his ministerial career). The only one who fell for temptation was Worthington-Evans who went to the Post Office, hardly a large bait for a man who had held the War Office; for this decision he received opprobrium from his late friends (Austen Chamberlain said 'he will be a hound if he accepts') but little credit elsewhere, and the phrase 'worthy reasons' came to be used as a shorthand for dishonourable ambitions.[42] The refusal of the rest of the old coalitionists to serve when asked reduced their effectiveness as an opposition within the party, and the reconstruction created a more balanced team. The only change that took place later in the life of the government was the transfer of Neville Chamberlain to the Exchequer when McKenna finally refused to join in July; he was replaced at the Ministry of Health by Joynson-Hicks.

The reshuffle strengthened the government's debating power, and the emergence of Baldwin as an effective public speaker assisted its public communication, but none of this did much to meet the pressing external problems or the state of the economy. Germany's default over reparations payments led not only to the French occupation of the Ruhr in January 1923 but also to a state of tension between Britain and France that marked the virtual ending of the alliance that had existed since 1904. The impact of this tension was considered to be a reason for the continuing low level of trade. Some small advantage had been gained through the cessation of coal exports from the Ruhr, but by every measurement the British economy was still sluggish. Trade remained low, production revived only slowly, and unemployment remained near the one and a half million mark. The government derived some benefit from Baldwin's reduction of income tax from six shillings to five shillings in the pound, and it avoided the worst of its probable obloquy by abandoning the decontrol of rents after Mitcham. As worrying as anything was the high state of Labour morale in the Commons, where MacDonald had harnessed the high spirits of the new Clydeside MPs and fashioned them into a strong opposition. Demonstrations were staged against government measures to focus attention on unemployment; when Unionists protested about obstructionism, they were reminded of their own tactics ten years earlier. There was a much publicized debate on the principles of capitalism and socialism on 20 March, introduced by a motion put down by Philip Snowden; the government of course won the vote, but it was left to Sir Alfred Mond, a Liberal, to provide the best defence of capitalism,[43] and there was a strong impression that the Labour party was winning too many of the arguments.

All this made the government, and Baldwin in particular, receptive to the idea that it must find some bold new initiative if it was to hold on to power, for it had gained the reputation of being a do-nothing government in a time of deepening economic crisis. In the Lords, Birkenhead pointed out 'that there were dangers to meet, and that more was required of the Ministry than the mere affirmation that Conservative principles would be maintained'.[44] The final influence in this direction was the continuing agricultural depression – a depression that continued in fact for the rest of the inter-war years, with about 100,000 acres going out of cultivation every year until 1944. Demands increased for direct government intervention to help the farmers. Law had only reluctantly agreed to meet a farmers' deputation and a farmworkers' delegation in March, and when he met them had given no real hope of concessions; one result was a prolonged strike in Norfolk. When the cabinet considered detailed proposals in April there was disagreement over the reintroduction of wage boards; the National Farmers' Union lobbied strongly for either subsidies or full-scale agricultural protection. It was finally agreed to drop wage boards, but to reduce rates on agricultural land to a quarter, and this was included in Baldwin's budget. This policy was forced through the Commons against Liberal and Labour criticism, but it did not meet the farmers' demands and did little to halt the depression. A proposal to tax imports of malting barley ran into trouble when it was found to conflict with foreign treaty obligations, and the government put the whole matter off by setting up a committee to investigate it.[45]

A similar situation arose when the President of the Board of Trade, Lloyd-Greame, proposed a duty on imported silk early in August, and the matter was again deferred. In view of its past convictions, it is not surprising that the party should see both a way out of its tactical dilemma and a way of dealing with the industrial and agricultural depressions in the introduction of tariffs. The only way forward seemed to be to go back to the politics of tariff reform, the party's only positive contribution to political economy, its only real point of positive belief, and a policy that might have been made popular by years of depression. By the summer then, tariffs were back on the agenda, and the only thing that held the party back was the pledge given less than a year ago by Bonar Law that tariffs would not be introduced without an election.

Baldwin had not envisaged the need to review Law's pledge when he had become Prime Minister in May; he had waved aside objections to the choice of the protectionist McKenna as Chancellor on the ground that such views would not be relevant in 1923. In the next few months, though, the worsening economic and political situation changed his view and pushed him back to his previous commitment to tariffs. The final influence was the Imperial Economic Conference in October; colonial premiers asked for preference and as in 1902 this stirred Unionists into action. At about the same time a story broke that Lloyd George was about to embarrass the government by declaring for protection himself, so reinforcing his alliance with Austen Chamberlain. There is no evidence whatsoever that Lloyd George ever really entertained such intentions, but it is certainly true that Baldwin, Stanley Jackson (Party Chairman), and other ministers believed that he might do so. A Baldwin declaration for protection would thus serve two purposes; it would give the government a positive answer to the unemployment issue, and it would detach the coalition Unionists from Lloyd George.[46] Sanders, now Minister of Agriculture, negotiated with the NFU and the agricultural MPs, and got their agreement to a tariff scheme for industry, to be balanced by subsidies for agriculture.

On 23 October 1923 Baldwin told his cabinet that he had come to the conclusion that tariffs were necessary, and that he would announce this at the party conference. At this stage he envisaged an election only after about six months, and it was on these terms that the cabinet backed him. Surprisingly, Derby did not express strong opposition and Salisbury was quiet too; only Cecil opposed the whole idea, but Curzon deprecated any talk of an election. Baldwin thus announced his conversion to tariffs at Plymouth on 25 October, amid the cheers of his party; the main point of his argument was the need for tariffs as a weapon against unemployment:

> If I can fight it I am willing to fight it. I cannot fight it without weapons. I have for myself come to the conclusion that owing to the conditions which exist in the world today, having regard to economic environment, having regard to the situation of our country, if we go pottering along as we are we shall have grave unemployment with us to the end of time, and I have come to the conclusion that the only way of fighting this subject is by protecting the home market.

On the following morning, a debate on agriculture passed a resolution calling for subsidies with only five dissentients, the proposers claiming Baldwin's support for their views.[47] Speculation had taken place in the few days before the Plymouth speech, but it was nevertheless a political bombshell. Baldwin had been careful to make no reference to an election and had committed only himself to tariffs; but, as Curzon and Cave had both predicted, such niceties were lost in the furore, and an election atmosphere erupted from the morning of 26 October. Prime Ministers cannot announce strong personal convictions without committing their governments, and a vital policy that requires an election cannot be delayed merely to avoid one. In the next three weeks the cabinet searched vainly for a way out of the mess in which Baldwin had landed them, for none of them actually favoured the idea of a quick election. Robert Cecil and Salisbury wanted to delay a decision because they did not want either an election *or* the tariff; Amery wanted a delay precisely because he favoured tariffs and saw the need for a period of propaganda before putting them to the electoral test. But the logic of the situation carried all before it; by early November, some ministers had come to see that an election was inescapable and the Party Chairman was advising one (even though Central Office had no means of predicting the result). The idea of an immediate election was discussed in cabinet on 9 November, and by that stage most of the House of Commons ministers thought that it was unavoidable. The final decision was Baldwin's own; he had forced the pace throughout, and his own advisers and motives remain shadowy. Over the following weekend he decided to take the plunge, and announced on 13 November that parliament would be dissolved, with polling to take place after the minimum interval on 6 December.[48]

It was one thing to rush through the decision to hold an election, but it was wholly another to secure a united campaign. At first Baldwin's strategy seemed to have succeeded, for there were no resignations from the cabinet and only one junior minister left. Grumbling was rife, but mainly in private, for those who had opposed the election could now see that unity was the only way to rescue the party from it. Austen Chamberlain came out in favour of the cause of his father, and this prompted another attempt to bring him back into government. Once again the approach was bungled and Baldwin had to retract the offer, for other colleagues would not accept Birkenhead in the cabinet and Austen would not return without him. The reasons for distrusting Birkenhead were outlined by Salisbury to Baldwin:

> F.E. is disreputable and has been hitherto unfriendly to your government. I do not imagine he has got many political principles and most of what he has got are wrong. . . . Poor devil, he will probably drink himself to death. What however we have to consider is the effect the quasi-public reception of him may have amongst the leaders of thought in the democracy. They are panting after ideas which they are afraid may be slipping from them. They have no sympathy whatever with the hard-shelled defence of the Haves against the Have-nots. I think F.E. without ideals and with his crude attachment to the interests of wealth would lose us more than Austen would gain us.[49]

Derby, Salisbury and Amery would have resigned rather than serve with him, and so neither Austen nor Birkenhead returned. After a brief flurry of conspiracy with Churchill and Lloyd George, the old coalitionists had to come back to the party without inducements or rewards, while Lloyd George sought to reunite the Liberals to fight for free trade. By the middle of November, the election had at least succeeded in its secondary aim of reuniting the party leadership; the campaign showed that it had had an opposite effect on the party in the country.

Few MPs had favoured an election and the Chief Whip had advised against the holding of one; Joynson-Hicks told Baldwin that 'it would be most unpopular with our party in the House. They have all paid one thousand pounds to get there and their wives do not want to pay another thousand with the risk of being thrown out.'[50] But finance and the fear of their wives were not the main reasons for opposing an election; many saw how unpopular a tariff election would be at Christmas time, and some knew how embarrassed they would be by their own previous pledges. There was a time of confusion as MPs tried to sort out their relations with the local parties and other groups who had previously supported them. More than twenty Unionist MPs had been elected as out and out free traders in 1922, and several more who held equally strong views had not pledged themselves; most of these were in Lancashire, where the trouble now centred. The only resignation from the government had been by Colonel Albert Buckley, who was in an impossible position as a free trader at the Department of Overseas Trade; on 21 November his local party in the Waterloo division of Lancashire adopted another candidate. Similar disputes occasioned the withdrawal of sitting MPs at Southport, Croydon, Bolton, Tamworth and the Wrekin, all at the last moment. Other local parties were more tolerant, or were more free-trading in their own views, or were just too desperate to drop their candidates so late; at least twenty free-traders were adopted as official Unionists, against the party line.[51]

When campaigning began it soon became apparent that the free-trade MPs were only the tip of a large iceberg, and that many other candidates were not convinced either of the need for an election or of the case for tariffs. It was not easy to find out exactly what the tariff policy was, for the manifesto was vague in the extreme, and Central Office had no time to bring out educative leaflets. Both the Party Chairman and the Principal Agent were out of London fighting tough campaigns of their own, and Younger had to come out of retirement to take over Central Office, but this time without the help of either Sanders or Fraser. The keynotes of the campaign were therefore apology and confusion: apology was needed to justify an election at Christmas time, resented as a party trick; confusion was inevitable when every candidate was left to devise his own explanation of what the tariff policy would actually mean to his constituents. Apology and confusion were exploited by Liberals and Labour, sure at least of the negative case for free trade. No amount of positive leadership could remedy the confusion in the constituencies, and so, realizing that the tariff message was not getting across, the party almost abandoned it in the last week, concentrating instead on Baldwin's leadership and on scaremongering anti-socialism. All the advantages of the 1922 campaign were absent in 1923. The moderate Unionist press that opposed the election gave little support in the campaign; the

Beaverbrook and Rothermere papers were hostile for reasons that were to recur with greater significance later – they would only back a tariff policy that was positively imperial, as Baldwin's was not. In view of the nature of the campaign it is surprising that Central Office should have so badly misjudged the outcome, although this perhaps reflects its own lack of direction. Whatever the reason, Central Office predicted an outcome like that of 1922, which merely increased Baldwin's despondency when the results were announced.[52]

The Unionists had a net loss of 88 seats, Liberals a net gain of 42, Labour a net gain of 47, but this disguised a baffling variety of cross-currents. More than a quarter of the seats changed hands and there were even twenty Unionist gains to balance over a hundred losses. The net loss was entirely in England (the rest of the UK elected exactly as many Unionists as in 1922); the West Midlands remained faithful to the policy of Chamberlain, but in the rest of England the Unionists lost about a third of the seats they defended, mainly to Labour in London and the North, to the Liberals elsewhere. There was a net swing of about 5 per cent away from the Unionists where contests were the same in 1922 and 1923, and the Unionist showing was best in agricultural areas, worse in the middle-class urban areas. Many agricultural seats were lost because of local variations from this pattern, and because many of them were so marginal in the first place. Overall the Unionists held their share of the popular vote, but this disguises a real setback; fewer Unionist seats were uncontested and the Unionists fielded more candidates, so the 38 per cent of 1923 represented a full Unionist tally, whereas the 38 per cent of 1922 did not. Fear that tariffs would increase prices seems to have caused Unionists to abstain or to vote Liberal, but the offer of agricultural subsidies did something to stem the tide of defeat. In the longer term there were causes for optimism, for the party polled a million more votes than Labour or Liberals even on an unpopular policy and when many Unionists had not voted. At the next election, if tariffs were to be abandoned after defeat (as in 1910) the party would have much easy ground to make up. Many of the seats lost had turned over on very small majorities, especially to the Liberals, and so the return of Unionist abstentions would in itself bring back quite a lot of seats. In the meantime, the party had clearly lost the election, but no other party had won it; the Unionists remained the largest party and so could determine the course of politics in the new parliament.[53]

On the day after the election, Baldwin lapsed into a mood of dejection. Rejection, he said, was the fate of all honest men in politics, and he even compared his rejection to that of Christ. In this mood he decided to resign at once, a decision reinforced by early conversations with Lloyd-Greame, Worthington-Evans and Joynson-Hicks, all of whom wanted to clear the ground for a combination to keep Labour out of office. After the weekend, though, Baldwin decided that he would remain in office until defeated; he was encouraged in this decision by Davidson, Amery and Bridgeman, and also by the King. On Tuesday 11 December the cabinet decided with no dissentients that it would meet parliament before resignation. This swift change of course dictated the subsequent events that led on to a Labour government, although few realized it at the time. Over the weekend there had also been a vigorous little intrigue, set in motion by Birkenhead with the object of displacing Baldwin to create a Liberal and Unionist ministry under Balfour (Austen Chamberlain, Derby and Birkenhead himself had been alternative suggestions). Several ministers went along with this, partly through a horror of a Labour government, partly because Baldwin seemed likely to go of his own volition and they wanted to be in a position to influence the succession. Balfour knocked the whole idea on the head before the cabinet met by letting it be known that he would not participate: Baldwin had improved his standing during the election campaign, he was now an electoral asset to the party, and he should meet parliament.[54]

Many ministers and MPs had rallied to Baldwin against these plots, from a determination that nothing should be done to compromise the party's hard-won independence. Salisbury admired Baldwin's honesty and did not believe that he should be blamed for the defeat; others helped Baldwin to stay in office for the opposite reason that it would give more time to put together an anti-Labour combination. However, by its decision on 11 December, confirming Baldwin in office for another month, the cabinet effectively decided the whole crisis, for by then Baldwin had resolved that there must be a Labour government. For the next six weeks he retained the authority of Prime Minister and would countenance no approach to Lloyd George or Asquith to keep Labour out.

Baldwin had long entertained a more realistic view of the likely effects of a Labour government than had the majority of his colleagues, was more moderate in his attitude to Labour MPs, and saw the value that a term of office would have in strengthening the position of the Labour moderates against their own extremists. He therefore used his last weeks in office to make sure that MacDonald would succeed him, but that Asquith would have the apparent responsibility of installing him in office. Since the Unionists were to meet parliament in January, Baldwin pressed on with a King's Speech that would force the Liberals to bring him down. Liberals and Labour had combined to oppose his tariff policy at the election,and now they must take the responsibility of defeating it in parliament and form an alternative government. Asquith announced on 18 December that he would turn Baldwin out, but Baldwin had already left him no option; by then it was also known that Labour would accept office as a minority government after the Liberals had joined them to defeat Baldwin. Over the six weeks between the election and the meeting of parliament, the idea of a Labour government gradually became more generally acceptable, and the panic fears of early December subsided; if Labour were to be a force in parliament then they must have a share in government sooner or later and, as Asquith made abundantly clear,

Labour could do little harm as long as it was in a minority. The Liberals made a grave tactical error when they failed to extract terms from MacDonald before making him Prime Minister but it is unlikely that they would have been offered any. But the weakness of the Liberal position was created not by Asquith or Lloyd George, but by Baldwin. No alliance was ever offered to Asquith by any Unionist who could hope to deliver it; so as the leader of the third party he had no choice but to turn the largest party out and install the second party in office.[55]

On 17 January 1924 a Labour amendment to the Address was moved by Clynes, and when it came to the vote the Unionist government was defeated by 72 votes. Baldwin resigned on the following day and MacDonald became Prime Minister at once. After fifteen undistinguished months in office, the Unionist party had fewer MPs than in 1910; they had thrown away a good majority with four years to run; they were unhappy about the prospect of Labour in office, and some lacked confidence in Baldwin too. For all that, the party was really in a strong position: the tactical dilemmas of the past three years had at last been settled, and the party had opted to break the Liberal party rather than ally with it, and to adopt a friendly attitude to parliamentary Labour. The reaction in the constituencies, where there was a howl of rage at the creation of a Labour government – a howl directed at the Liberals – gave the prospects of good hunting in the future. The new government's weak parliamentary position made it likely that the next election would not be long delayed, and in the meantime the party could avoid responsibility for the deteriorating situation. Suggestions that this fortunate situation had been deliberately arranged by Baldwin can be safely dismissed; he had espoused protection in October partly to pull the party together, but he had certainly not intended then that he should lose an election or leave office. The cabinet had confirmed him in office, but they had neither envisaged nor intended that they should all be turned out as a result. It was, as Austen Chamberlain told Hoare, a good outlook, but not one for which much credit could be claimed: 'We have got (unexpectedly and by our blunders and Asquith's greater folly) a second chance. Have we got the wit to take it?'[56]

Notes and References

1 Cook, *Age of Alignment*, 49–87.
2 Chamberlain to Hoare, 28 Jan. 1924: Templewood MSS, 5/1.
3 For 'Hexter's Law' see Hexter, *Reappraisals in History*, 182–3.
4 Cowling, *Impact of Labour*, 123–4; Jones, *Whitehall Diary*, iii, 75–6.
5 Samuel Roberts, Autobiographical Memorandum.
6 National Union Conference minutes, Liverpool Conference, 17 Nov. 1921.
7 Sanders Diary, 2 July 1922.
8 Neville Chamberlain to Austen Chamberlain, and Sanders to Austen Chamberlain, 29 Nov. 1921, Fraser to Austen Chamberlain, 31 Dec. 1921: Austen Chamberlain MSS, 32/2/13, 32/2/16 and 32/4/1a.
9 'A short diary of a press campaign': Austen Chamberlain MSS, 32/4/15; Cowling, *Impact of Labour*, 136–7.
10 Younger to constituency chairmen, 9 Jan. 1921: Sanders MSS (also to be found in many constituency minute books, as at West Wolverhampton).
11 Cowling, *Impact of Labour*, 170–1.
12 Blake, *Unknown Prime Minister*, 447–8.
13 Sanders Diary, 25 June 1922.
14 Blake, *Unknown Prime Minister*, 443.
15 Baldwin to Austen Chamberlain, 10 Apr. 1922: Austen Chamberlain MSS, 24/4/2.
16 Griffith-Boscawen to Austen Chamberlain, 12 Oct. 1922: Austen Chamberlain MSS, 32/2/49.
17 Austen Chamberlain to Curzon, 20 May 1922: Austen Chamberlain MSS, 24 Feb. 1922.
18 'Notes on a conference with the Under-Secretaries', 20 July 1922: Austen Chamberlain MSS, 33/2/4; Sanders Diary, 21 July 1922.
19 Sanders Diary, 4 Aug. 1922.
20 Austen Chamberlain to Leslie Wilson, 12 Oct. 1922: Austen Chamberlain MSS, 33/2/43.
21 Younger to Austen Chamberlain, 18 Oct. 1922, Austen Chamberlain MSS, 33/2/85.
22 Balfour's notes on a conversation with Law, 22 Dec. 1922; Balfour MSS, Add. MSS 49693; Taylor, *Beaverbrook*, 198.
23 Cook and Ramsden, *By-elections*, 25–42.
24 Le May, *British Government*, 365–8; Austen Chamberlain to Wilson, 20 Nov. 1922, Austen Chamberlain MSS, 33/2/95.
25 Kinnear, *British Voter*, 104–5; Davidson, *Memoirs of a Conservative*, 129–33; McEwen, 'Conservative and Unionist M.P.s', Ch. 6.

26 National Union minutes, Executive Committee, 19 Oct. 1922.
27 Letter signed by Coalitionist Ministers, 19 Oct. 1922, and Report of House of Commons dinner, 30 Nov. 1922; Austen Chamberlain MSS, 33/2/93 and 33/2/148.
28 Selborne's 'Reminiscences', 1936: vol. i, Selborne MSS.
29 Wright, *Portraits and Criticisms*, 85–7.
30 Blake, *Unknown Prime Minister*, 475; Jones, *Whitehall Diary*, i, 217–18.
31 *British General Election Manifestos*, 12.
32 Blake, *Unknown Prime Minister*, 496–7.
33 Sanders Diary, 28 Jan. 1923.
34 National Union Conference minutes, London Conference, 15 Dec. 1922; *Home and Politics*, Dec. 1922.
35 Cowling, *Impact of Labour*, 246, 250.
36 *Gleanings and Memoranda*, 1928.
37 Sanders Diary, 4 Feb. 1923; Wrench, *Geoffrey Dawson and our Times*, 215.
38 Sanders Diary, 15 Apr. 1923.
39 Blake, *Unknown Prime Minister*, 508–9, 511–13.
40 Le May, *British Government*, 368.
41 Hazlehurst, 'The Baldwinite Conspiracy', 168–91.
42 Sanders Diary, 1 June 1923.
43 Beattie, *English Party Politics*, ii, 412–34.
44 Wright, *Portraits and Criticisms*, 87.
45 Sanders Diary, 21 June 1923.
46 Cook, *Age of Alignment*, 113.
47 National Union Conference minutes, Plymouth Conference, 25–26 Oct. 1923.
48 Sanders Diary, 11 Nov. 1923.
49 Salisbury to Baldwin, 26 Jan. 1924: Baldwin MSS, vol. 159.
50 Cook, *Age of Alignment*, 119.
51 *Ibid*, 137–9.
52 Jones, *Whitehall Diary*, i, 257.
53 Cook, *Age of Alignment*, 156–79.
54 Cowling, *Impact of Labour*, 331–8.
55 Cook, *Age of Alignment*, 183–93.
56 Austen Chamberlain to Hoare, 28 Jan. 1924: Templewood MSS, 5/1.

Part III

Baldwin's New Conservatism

'Our great enemies of the future are not going to be the Liberals, who are moribund, but Labour, which is very much alive. You are not going to beat Labour on a policy of tranquillity, negation or sitting still. There is a vitality in Labour at present in the country, and unless we can share a vitality of that kind we shall be unable to conquer.'
(Stanley Baldwin, speaking at the Hotel Cecil, 11 February 1924.)

'A strong Conservative Party with an overwhelming majority and a moderate and even progressive leadership is a combination which has never been tested before. It might well be the fulfilment of all that Dizzy and my father aimed at in their political work.'
(Winston Churchill to his wife, 8 March 1925.)

Chapter 9

The 'New Conservatism', 1924

The first priority after the resignation of the Baldwin government was to decide the status of the tariff policy after its decisive defeat; it would also be necessary to consider Baldwin's position as leader and future relations with Austen Chamberlain and his followers. The question of the tariff was taken out of Baldwin's hands, as out of Bonar Law's in 1912–13, by Derby's decision to force the pace in Lancashire.

In Lancashire the election had been chaotic, with Unionist candidates in adjacent constituencies campaigning as free-traders, safeguarders or wholehearted protectionists. Failure was inevitable and many seats were lost, five in Manchester and two in Liverpool all going to the Liberals.[1] In the aftermath of defeat, Derby joined the conspiracy against Baldwin but he was quick to abandon it when it seemed likely to fail. Nevertheless, he shared the conviction of his Lancashire followers that something must be done to mark the party's displeasure with Baldwin's recent actions. The obvious forum was the meeting of Lancashire Unionists due at Manchester on 9 February, at which Derby would take the chair. Colonel Buckley, who had lost his government post, his seat and his entire career as a result of Baldwin's policy, intended to move a resolution which would commit Lancashire against the tariff. Archibald Salvidge thought that Buckley was going too far, but he intended to move an amendment that was almost as damaging.[2]

On the day that Salvidge wrote to tell Derby of his plans, Derby also heard that the coalitionists had accepted Baldwin's leadership and that they were prepared even to come back into the party. Birkenhead could now see the impossibility of a centre party and entertained hopes of bringing Churchill back into the Unionist fold to be leader after a suitable interval. Austen Chamberlain was anxious that the party should not muff its new opportunity by Baldwin being deprived of good advice. Balfour was convinced of Baldwin's value as an electioneering asset and concerned above all not to have his reputation as the party's elder statesman ruined in 1924 as it had been in 1922. Baldwin was therefore able to bring the entire group back into line without making any real concessions; he was content to allow them a considerable freedom to influence policy if they would accept his lead and the continued independence of the party. A party meeting was called for Monday 11 February and a shadow cabinet for the previous Thursday, with the

Manchester meeting to take place between them. The protests of Salisbury at the inclusion of Birkenhead were brushed aside; the party was now aware of the need to use all its talent if its chance was not to be wasted.[3]

The meeting of the shadow cabinet was therefore determined in advance by its composition. Baldwin invited, as well as the ministers of his late government still in parliament, Austen Chamberlain, Birkenhead, Balfour and Lord Crawford. Amery, with tentative support from Bridgeman, urged retention of the full tariff policy, but he found no other backers. Baldwin remained silent and allowed Austen Chamberlain almost to chair the meeting. At the suggestion of Curzon and with the approval of the meeting it was decided to revert to Bonar Law's pledge of 1922 and to demand only the use of the existing Safeguarding of Industry Act to protect depressed areas.[4]

Two days later in Manchester the 'Lancashire Plot' fizzled out. Buckley's aggressive motion was quickly dropped in favour of Salvidge's amendment, and the only debate was on a counter-amendment proposed by Sir Joseph Nall MP. On the tariff issue Salvidge had urged no more than was now party policy anyway, but his motion also rapped Baldwin's knuckles for his failure to consult the party before calling the election. Nall asserted the need to leave matters of policy to the leader, but it was Salvidge's view that was approved. In an interview with the *Morning Post*, Derby emphasized

> the fact that before the Salvidge resolution was put to the meeting everybody understood, indeed it was so stated, that it should on no account be looked upon as a vote of censure on the leaders of the party. It was only meant to give advice as to the best way in the future of getting a proper combination between the leaders of the party, the Central Office, and local associations.[5]

Before the abandonment of the tariff policy and the reunion of the leadership, such a statement would have stood little chance of acceptance. The National Union tried to get on to the same bandwagon; at the Executive Committee meeting on 29 January, Sir Alexander Leith proposed that the National Union should be represented at the forthcoming party meeting, but he got little support for such a radical suggestion. At the Central Council meeting on 12 February there were stronger demands for a more democratic system in the running of the party. In reply the Party Chairman had to offer a reconsideration of the National Union's rules and the possibility of a liaison committee between the National Union and the leader.[6]

The substantive issue was formally settled by the ratification of Baldwin's leadership and the party's new policy at the Hotel Cecil on 11 February. Baldwin presided at the party meeting as its convenor and began proceedings with a declaration on future policy. He claimed that without an election in 1923, and with continuing unemployment, Labour would have come into power later with a majority and with unfettered freedom to do damage through its socialist policies. The electors had been misled by 'every sort of red herring' and by the skill of opponents in 'laying false tracks':

But, however that may be, I believe in facing facts, and I cannot resist this conclusion in my own mind, that, however mistaken on a long view of economic facts the electorate has been, the country as a whole did decide in a sense hostile to our main proposal . . . and in those circumstances I do not feel justified in advising the party again to submit the proposal for a general tariff to the country, except upon clear evidence that on this matter public opinion was disposed to reconsider its judgement of two months ago.[7]

The party would stick to safeguarding, which was a far easier policy to explain to the electorate than was a general tariff, and a new scheme would be devised to help agriculture The rest of his speech was devoted to an analysis of the political situation and a call for a new style of Conservatism to meet the fact that Labour was now the chief opponent:

The great source of strength of Labour in the country at present is that they have in their ranks a large number of men who believe in their policy. They have the type of man, and many of us who have mixed in the industrial world know him well, who will give the whole of his strength and the whole of his time to bring about, as he believes he can, a better condition for his fellow-men – with more equality of opportunity, and giving to them a better chance of enjoying more education and more of the good things of life – a perfectly genuine and altruistic feeling. It is that feeling which sends so many of the workers of the party to canvass, to do propaganda, and to conduct the business of elections without payment or reward. It is a spirit which can only be beaten by a similar spirit in our Party. (Hear, hear).

Secondly . . . the Labour party is looked to as the one organization through which the man with brains and energy in the lower order of society can hope to rise gradually through his municipal services and his political services into Parliament and into the Cabinet. Until we devise a similar avenue on our side, we are fighting with one hand tied behind our backs.[8]

This speech, one of Baldwin's greatest, set the keynote for what the press were soon calling the 'New Conservatism' and helped to establish what Lord Eustace Percy called Baldwin's 'moral authority' over his party. Balfour followed Baldwin with a fulsome tribute to the leader, with the assertion that Unionists could now place no reliance on the Liberals and must therefore 'rely upon ourselves and upon our own efforts'. He proposed a vote of confidence, which was seconded by Austen Chamberlain who made his by now traditional appeal for loyalty and urged that the past should be left to the historians. The resolution was carried unanimously and the party settled to the task of opposition greatly pleased with the easy resolution of its internal difficulties.

Clearing the air within a few weeks of leaving office certainly had a beneficial effect, for the next eight months saw very little discord. Reforms of the National Union were implemented to meet the criticisms voiced in February, but no more was heard of a liaison committee. Austen Chamberlain was a touchy colleague and on one occasion he was bitterly critical of a statement by Baldwin which the shadow cabinet had not approved, but these disagreements were kept out of the public eye. Birkenhead was shrewd enough to see how far his return had depended on Baldwin's magnanimity and he was as loyal a colleague as his adventurous disposition allowed. Only two disagreements surfaced, and one of these was probably a misunderstanding. In May Baldwin gave an interview to the *People* in which he was alleged to have talked about intrigues against him, with a clear hint that Birkenhead was behind them. The article was immediately refuted by Central Office, which pointed out that it had not been submitted to Baldwin for approval before publication. Perhaps Baldwin had intended a warning to Birkenhead, perhaps he assumed that he would not be quoted, perhaps he really had not said what was reported; in any event, Birkenhead did not hold it against him and wrote to tell him so.[9]

More serious was the effect of Churchill's intervention against the Unionist candidate in the Westminster Abbey by-election in March. Churchill had been moving to the right, but had been forced back to the Liberals in 1923 by the tariff question. Once he was again defeated and once the Liberals had installed Labour in power, he was anxious to join the Unionists on almost any terms. Baldwin was sympathetic but he was aware of hostility to Churchill in the party; some like Amery had detested Churchill since the Boer War, others had not forgiven him his desertion in 1904, and he was regarded (wrongly) as the architect of Gallipoli and the failed intervention in Russia. On the other hand he was a great anti-Socialist and a public figure whose adherence to the Unionist cause would be a major gain. Baldwin hoped to find Churchill a seat in due course, when his change of party would seem less opportunist, but Central Office certainly backed his ambitions at Abbey when the vacancy occurred. Churchill was not content to appear before a selection committee unless he was guaranteed success, and so he had to stand in the by-election as an independent against the official candidate, backed only by friends and by the Beaverbrook and Rothermere press. A roistering campaign followed, described by *The Times* as 'a daily variety show'. The most that could be hoped was that the shadow cabinet would remain neutral, although Birkenhead had persuaded Churchill to stand in the first place, but Baldwin had great difficulty in enforcing neutrality, as he told Davidson: 'This incursion of Churchill into Westminster has been a great worry. It is causing trouble in the Party just as I thought we were pulling together again. Leading the Party is like driving pigs to market.'[10] The contest was clearly going to be close, with the added worry that the Labour candidate might slip in on a divided vote, and under this strain unity cracked, as Baldwin recounted:

> Last Saturday I had a really worrying day. I got back tired and longing for bed soon after eleven on Friday night . . . I found a letter which, mercifully I opened. It contained a letter from Balfour to Winston wishing him success and a note saying he wouldn't send it if I objected. To leap into the car again and drive off to Carlton Gardens was the work of a moment. I stayed with [Balfour] till after midnight. He was leaving for Cannes in the morning. We had a long and intimate talk and he

consented without demur not to send the letter which I kept in my pocket . . .
  Next morning I opened my *Times* in bed as is my custom and to my horror saw a letter from Amery to Nicholson. I saw in a moment what that meant. By ten o'clock a letter came round from A.J.B. saying that Amery's letter had altered everything and that it wasn't fair etc., and his letter ought to go to Winston but he was leaving at once and left me to do as I thought right. About eleven, first communication from Austen: of course he was all over the place and if Balfour's letter was bottled up he would let fly![11]

The tension was considerable when a party crisis could be provoked by a letter from a shadow cabinet member in support of an official party candidate. Balfour's letter was released to balance Amery's and the division of the party made public. Churchill failed to win at Abbey by a narrow margin, but the victory of the official candidate helped to steady things. Central Office continued to press Churchill's claims but several constituencies turned him down. In May he appeared on a Unionist platform under the auspices of Salvidge, but he could not be selected for the imminent contest at West Toxteth because of his past attitude to Ulster. He was finally placed at Epping in September, where he would stand as a Constitutionalist but with the support of the local Unionists.[12] These alarums were, however, untypical of the mood of the party in 1924, the characteristic of which was harmony. Even the question of Churchill was finally settled in that spirit and the split of 1903 was at last laid to rest.

Meanwhile the months of opposition could be put to good use, and the irresponsibility of opposing a weak government could be enjoyment in itself. Younger had told Baldwin how well the party had fared in 1909 with only 140 MPs against a Liberal and Irish multitude; how much easier it would be with 260 MPs against a weak government and in bad economic times. In the 1924 parliament the Liberals usually split three ways on important votes, often with the largest group and the leaders absent. It was therefore comparatively easy for the Unionists to control the House, having the largest block of votes at their disposal. Enough Liberals could be relied on to defeat any socialist measures like the capital levy, in the unlikely event of MacDonald and Snowden proposing them, and other issues could be exploited to keep the Liberals divided. The only issues on which Unionist defeat was likely were the ones that derived from the recent election, the abolition of the McKenna duties and the repeal of the Safeguarding of Industry Act; Liberal and Labour MPs combined to re-establish free trade, but this may even have helped Unionists by emphasizing the one area of trade policy on which their policy had not changed. A Unionist introduced a motion against the capital levy in March and secured a large majority, with the Liberals badly split; a motion on sympathetic strikes was defeated in April but again the Liberals divided; the same tactics were used in debates on home rule for Scotland, proportional representation and safeguarding. Much capital was made out of the inability of the government to control its Rent Bill even with the Liberals dividing 53 to 22 in its favour.[13] The government's lack of control over its own backbenchers was also a means of exploiting its weakness in committee. Unionists demonstrated to the Clydesiders in 1924 that they had unrivalled experience of, and talent for, obstruction when they chose to make use of it, as one MP later recalled:

> I became a member of a small committee, known as the Procedure Committee, which was in fact an obstruction committee, and I took some part in the work of obstruction, both on the floor of the House and in Committee Rooms upstairs. During this short parliament, Kingsley Wood made his name. He could speak for half an hour on any subject.
>
> The Labour Government had introduced a Housing Bill, which was sent to Committee upstairs. This committee lasted fifteen days, and the first line of clause 1 was never completed. Major Barnet was the Chairman of Committee and I must admit allowed us too much rope. The proceedings always started with someone moving the adjournment . . . for a different reason. One day we moved the adjournment because the Attorney-General, Sir Patrick Hastings, had not been present for three meetings, and that we were entitled to the advice of the Government's legal representative. At the next meeting, Sir Patrick turned up, and we moved the adjournment because, after his long absence, he had no knowledge of the past debates.
>
> The main campaign of the obstruction consisted of a very long amendment to be inserted after the first word of clause 1. We then put on the paper a large number of amendments to the amendment, and then moved amendments to the amendment, till at last Major Barnet refused to accept what he called great-grandchildren amendments. He allowed an amendment to an amendment to an amendment, but would not let us go further.
>
> Another method of obstruction was for us to send two men into the Committee Room, and for the rest to sit in the passage, in the hope that in ten minutes from the start, there would be no quorum, when the sitting would be automatically adjourned until next day. If a quorum was formed, we all went in. The Labour Party adopted the correct antidote to obstruction and told their people to keep their mouths shut, but by putting either attractive or irritating flies across the room, we could nearly always get one of them to speak. This would give us the opportunity of making very long speeches in reply. After the fifteenth day the Government got tired of it and withdrew the bill.[14]

No wonder that Labour questioned whether anything would ever be achieved by a minority government. In the following year, when the Clydesiders attempted similar manoeuvres against a Conservative government with a solid majority, they found that it could not be done, and they ran up against the MP quoted above, now installed as a committee chairman: 'I had a great deal of disorder to deal with. . . . During one outbreak of pandemonium which lasted about a quarter of an hour, I got fifteen clauses of a bill passed. There was trouble about this, but nothing happened, and by the end of the session the Clyde was a calmer river.'

Obstruction in parliament raised the morale of MPs and no doubt contributed to the disillusion with which Labour laid down office after one gruelling and almost useless session, but by its nature it could not be made public. Criticism began to be heard after a few months that the Labour government was being given too easy a ride. There were allegations that the Unionists were keeping MacDonald in power by arranging for the absence of sufficient MPs to guarantee his safety from defeat. The Chief Whip took the charge seriously enough to issue a denial, and it was almost certainly untrue.[15] The government was regularly defeated on minor issues and only once did the number of Unionist MPs absent unpaired exceed the size of the government majority on a major issue. Nevertheless the Unionists were not really trying very hard to bring the government down: as early as the spring, the local parties had been told to expect an election in November, and in July there were forty-five Unionists absent unpaired when the government's majority was only fifty. It was necessary to find the right issue on which to bring Labour down and not to do it too soon; a defeat in the spring might have produced a minority Liberal government or minority Unionist government rather than a third election in three years. Labour was therefore allowed time to antagonize as many potential Unionist voters as possible and MacDonald was given enough rope to hang Asquith and Lloyd George too.

Outside parliament the months of opposition were used to promote Baldwin's standing and to prepare the Unionist programme. At the suggestion of the new Principal Agent, Herbert Blain, Baldwin undertook a lengthy series of public speeches all over the country that made him, by the summer, a strong trump card in the coming battle of personalities. His rapid rise in 1922 and 1923 had made him Prime Minister without his being known at all outside the House of Commons, and pressing problems of government had prevented him from repairing this omission before 1924. The story of his 1919 donation to the nation as 'FST' (Financial Secretary to the Treasury) became known and stories were circulated about the harmonious labour relations in his family firm, in all of which there was a considerable degree of truth. His speeches in the spring and summer of 1924 completed this process and established for him a moral authority in the country similar to that in the party.[16]

At least as important was the creation for the first time of a secretariat for the shadow cabinet and the adoption of professional methods in the making of policy. The system was described to the suspicious leaders of the National Union:

> In reply to a request for information as to what the Secretariat was, the Chairman explained that it was the staff serving a Department set up by the Leader of the Party for the purpose of dealing with the more important questions of policy. In reply to further questions, Sir Laming Worthington-Evans explained that the Leader has a Conference of Ex-Ministers, which was the Shadow Cabinet, composed of Members of both Houses of Parliament. In order to deal with current day to day business of the House of Commons, the Leader also had a Conference of Members of the House of Commons only, which met formally once a week, and whenever it was necessary. The Ex-Ministers placed in charge of the various Committees of the Party dealing with Policy also reported weekly to the Leader.[17]

For the first time since 1915 the party had the freedom to reconsider its policies, and for the first time it did not have access to the civil service. The secretariat was headed by Lancelot Storr, who had been Baldwin's secretary in Downing Street; his staff included a number of young Unionists including Geoffrey Lloyd and Robert Boothby, both of whom later became ministers. The secretariat shared accommodation with the leader's personal staff at Central Office, another aid to coordination.[18] Policy committees were made up of MPs and advisers, each under a shadow minister, and reported to Baldwin and Austen Chamberlain. When their work was completed, the findings were summarized by Neville Chamberlain in a pamphlet called *Looking Ahead; Unionist Principles and Aims*, which was published on 20 June. Baldwin introduced the main policy findings in a series of three speeches in June, and most of them went into the party's election manifesto in October. In the preparation of the manifesto, Central Office had the advice of Arthur Mann, editor of the *Yorkshire Post*, that quintessential provincial Tory newspaper which had the Party Chairman amongst its directors. At Mann's suggestion, the format was changed, the print was broken up with subheadings and italics to make the text more attractive, and a popular version was issued which summarized the party's proposals.[19] By the summer, then, the period of opposition had produced a new national leader and a new outline of policy ready to be put to the electorate.

Much attention was given to the party organization during 1924, for there was now a chance to renew the modernization interrupted in 1914. Many of these decisions were intended to bring the organization into closer conformity with Baldwin's concept of the party, and these are described in the next chapter, but some had an immediate impact. Whatever the future, it was clear that there would be another election in 1924 and that it would be of more than ordinary significance. Chris Cook has shown how the Liberals wasted the time available to them in 1924, but no such charge can be made against the Unionists.[20]

Organization could hardly be blamed for the defeat of 1923 and so there was no witch-hunt. The *Conservative Agents' Journal* wrote that 'of all elections we remember, it was the least blameworthy so far as organization was concerned', and the National Union executive passed Steel-Maitland's resolution 'that the work of the Central Office staff at the last election was extraordinarily good, and that the literature issued was the best ever known'. However, as Austen Chamberlain remarked at the party meeting on 11 February, there was always room for improvement in organization, and he may have known that a review was already going on. This began with a meeting over lunch of Worthington-Evans, Hoare, Wood and Joynson-Hicks, immediately after the election:

> We saw Baldwin and he appointed as a Committee Sam Hoare, Wood and myself. I drew a questionnaire to be sent to the country constituencies and some other selected ones, rather with the object of making the chairmen realize their

deficiencies and to stir up a desire to reorganize than as a means of getting information. Stanley Jackson was brought into consultation. . . . We again saw Baldwin and told him that he would have to take a decision as to the future of Central Office and that if he wanted us to take any further action he would have to say so and define our powers.[21]

By this stage, though, Baldwin was back in control of events and he decided to make no further use of Worthington-Evans and his friends. Ronald McNeill and John Buchan were used later in the year to consider literature production, but both of them were specialists in the field. With this exception, the reorganization of 1924 was conducted, unlike that of 1911, entirely from the inside.

The Chief Whip and Party Chairman, Eyres-Monsell and Stanley Jackson, were both popular in the party and apparently well suited for their jobs, so the only head to roll as a result of the 1923 defeat was that of the Principal Agent. Eyres-Monsell sat for a constituency bordering Baldwin's own and had been Baldwin's choice as Chief Whip in July 1923. He established good relations with Gervase Rentoul, chairman of the 1922 Committee, and that committee gradually developed during the 1924 parliament into its modern form as a sounding-board for the whole of the parliamentary party. At first it had been regarded as a trouble-making group, as all such committees had tended to be in the past, and Baldwin was not even keen to meet its representatives, but in 1924 it was accepted and a Whip was sent along to its weekly meetings to explain the business of the week and the reason for the attitudes the leaders proposed to take. In the long run the 1922 Committee has been a great strength to the leader, since it provided a respectable platform on which loyal backbenchers could give their views, an opportunity previously available only to rebels.[22]

Stanley Jackson had been Law's choice as Party Chairman when Younger was finally allowed to retire from office in March 1923; he was a fairly typical backbencher, although one with a national reputation since he had captained Yorkshire and England at cricket, and he went on to complete a typical career with minor office, a knighthood and the Governorship of Bengal. His appointment as Chairman had been a reward for loyalty and a guarantee of the party's continued independence, for Jackson had been a determined opponent of coalition. Sir Reginald Hall's appointment as Principal Agent at the same time had something of the same character, for Hall was a strong diehard and he was perhaps the only true diehard to be promoted by Law.[23] As Director of Naval Intelligence during the war, Admiral 'Blinker' Hall had played a major part in Britain's victory. He became an incorrigible anti-communist, incapable of seeing any real distinction between Russian Bolsheviks and British Labour, ready to find a red under every bed. He had been responsible for propaganda under the Lloyd George government and so he seemed to be a logical successor to Sir Malcolm Fraser. As Principal Agent he was a failure: he was the only MP ever to direct the professional side of the organization and found that he had insufficient time to give to the task; nor did he have the appropriate knowledge of electoral matters that made up the bulk of his subordinates' work. Ironically, Hall lost his seat at Liverpool in 1923 and so was now ready to devote himself full time to the work, but this was not sufficient to save him.

Hall was replaced by Herbert Blain in March 1924. Blain was a typical Baldwin choice, for he was a self-made man with considerable success in business, still a young man and a strong believer in conciliation. His career had begun in local government where he had been one of the founders of the National Association of Local Government Officers, and by 1924 he was General Manager of the London General Omnibus Company. He was the author of Pitman's handbook on office management, he was a Conservative by inclination but had not been politically active, and he had been responsible for the first road safety campaign. He was thus a relatively nonpolitical efficiency expert and his appointment as Principal Agent was intended to tighten up the party organization, first at Central Office and later in the constituencies.[24] As in 1912, the senior staff at Central Office were supplemented by other new appointments; Lord Linlithgow became Deputy Chairman and Joseph Ball was recruited from MI5 to look after propaganda – connections with the secret service that were to be useful before the year was out.

Within Central Office, literature services were expanded by Ball, although most of the improvement was probably due to the regularization of party politics. During 1924, excluding the election campaign, over eight million leaflets were produced and sold, more than four times the output of 1923; the same increase can be seen between the elections of 1923 and 1924, for this time the party programme and the probable date of the election were both known in advance.[25] The number of agents in the service of the party could not be rapidly expanded but the best agents could be and were moved to the important marginal constituencies, as table 9.1 shows. Local parties were urged to prepare for an election and do everything possible to be

Table 9.1   Appointments of Unionist agents, 1922–5[26]

Year	Retirements and new Agents transferred	agents appointed
1922	23	69
1923	33	117
1924	80	214
1925	28	102

ready with candidates, so that the last minute scramble of 1922 and 1923 would not be repeated. The rules of the National Union were changed to improve communications between constituencies and Executive Committee, and many local parties went through a similar process. The party was geared up at all levels so that it was as ready for an election in the autumn as it could ever have been after several years of quiescence. Local parties were more active and better financed than they had ever been; some credit for this is due to Central Office encouragement, but much more to the basic vitality of local Conservatism, at last fighting to win under a popular leader and, most important of all, jerked into action by the existence of a Labour government. Davidson's experience at Hemel Hempstead was typical; in defeat he discerned an opportunity, as he told Admiral Hall:

> Within the constituencies it is essential also to leave local associations to function. To do this, it is only a set-back such as I have suffered that enables the Conservative agent to reorganize everywhere. For instance at Wheathampstead, in spite of every endeavour, my agent has not been able to get either a men's or a women's association going. The local Squire has always assured us that 'on the day' he will poll 85 per cent for me. Owing to the rush tactics and the lying of the Liberal this was far from the case, and we have already set up committees of keen workers to win back the ground which was taken from us.[27]

This contains two important truths. Firstly, the assistance and help of Central Office was small when compared to what could be done when the local parties set about the task themselves; the underlying vitality of local Conservatism was exactly what distinguished it from Liberalism and goes far to explain the relative fortunes of the parties. Secondly, major changes in the Conservative party have always come after defeat; change is not popular in a conservative party and only the example of opponents in power makes it universally acceptable. The squire at Wheathampstead can stand for many whose objections to modern methods were swept away by the sight of Ramsay MacDonald in Downing Street.

Despite all these efforts, the party was not sure in the summer of 1924 that enough had been done to make success certain when the election should come. Writing on 'parties and prospects' in the *Evening News* on 30 July, Austen Chamberlain was not optimistic:

> It is then to the Unionist Party, if to any party, that we must look for sufficient strength to create a strong and independent Government. How has that Party fared since the disaster of last November? We may answer without hesitation that it has made good progress, but we must add, if we are ready to recognise facts, insufficient progress to secure a party majority. Undoubtedly we may expect that another election will do something to redress the ill-fortune of the last and restore a closer proportion between our voting strength in the country and our parliamentary representation, but it would be folly to pretend that there is such a marked reaction in our favour as would restore us to the position won by Mr Bonar Law in 1922.

So Austen had still not quite forgiven Baldwin for his rashness.

There had been few local elections since the 1923 general election and the pattern of by-elections had been confusing. There were only eight contests, which had produced two Unionist gains and one loss; both gains were untypical contests, for at Oxford the by-election had followed the unseating of the Liberal MP for corrupt practices and at Holland-with-Boston the vacancy was caused by the death of a Labour MP who had previously been the local Conservative chairman. The party had done well at Kelvingrove but badly at Toxteth and there was no obvious lesson at all from Burnley or Lewes.[28] The one cause for hope was the poor showing of the Liberals in all the contests, for the next election would certainly turn on the millions who had voted Liberal in 1923. The *English Review* saw how vital these voters were in a fervidly propagandist article:

> The basic fact of the whole situation is simply this: there is in this country no room for three parties. The disruptive forces which tear in Britain at the roots of civilization are represented by the Socialists and Communists, to oppose whom is the business of every decent Godfearing man and woman in the land. . . . In this fight not only is a third party not wanted, but its presence is fatal. . . . It confuses issues, it introduces an unreal factor into the sheer grapple between the powers of light and darkness. To get rid of the Liberal Party . . . is therefore of the first necessity.[29]

It was easy enough to agree that this *must* happen, but it was rather more difficult to be confident that it was actually doing so, as Austen Chamberlain noted:

> Whilst Labour gains a steady stream of recruits from the left wing of those who in other conditions and circumstances would have voted Liberal, there is at present no marked movement of moderate Liberalism to the Unionist side. To those who feel that the Liberal Party is without a future and will never again be in a position to form a Government, the great preoccupation must be how, in its gradual dissolution, we shall secure our share of its old supporters.[30]

Radical Liberals did seem to be more ready to desert to the left than were moderate Liberals to switch to the right; perhaps this was inevitable, for Liberals and Unionists had been opposed for as long as men could remember, while Liberals and Labour had been recent allies. Nevertheless, Churchill was a greater catch to the Unionists than any individual who left Liberalism for Labour, and there were many individuals who travelled in the same direction at a local level.[31] It was thus necessary not just to delay the election but also to make sure that it was fought on an issue that would smash the Liberal party once and for all.

In place of the orange card that the party might have played with success in 1915, Baldwin had available to him the red card of anti-socialism, calculated to maximize the Unionist vote and to divide the Liberals by exposing their fault line. In 1924 the Unionists were able to have it both ways to a quite remarkable extent: they had only allowed Labour into office because they recognized that Labour was moderate and would be powerless, but they then set about denouncing the same men as irresponsible and dangerous. In this they were assisted by circumstances without which the strategy would never have worked, as they were to find to their cost when they tried to repeat the exercise in 1929. Firstly, although the effective decision to put Labour in office was Baldwin's, it was left to Asquith to implement, and Asquith, believing that the experiment might be popular, took the credit and the subsequent blame. Secondly, although MacDonald's avowed aim was to use his time in office to show how moderate his party was, he persisted in a socialist rhetoric that lent credence to Unionist claims. Thirdly, other Labour politicians were far more outspoken than MacDonald in their speeches, giving Unionists the chance to claim that he would be cast aside as soon as the party gained a majority. Finally, Baldwin was able to trade on the reputation that he had built up over the year and to lend his authority to the attack.

Baldwin had carefully avoided unfair attacks on Labour in his tours around the country, but he had doubtless known that his supporters would show no such restraint when their turn came. From the start Unionist propagandists had concentrated on the aspects of Labour in office that were most likely to pay off. *Gleanings and Memoranda* published a monthly selection of press cuttings on 'Labour Politics', highlighting the close relations between social democrats and communists abroad, the undercover activities of the Comintern, the dissident views of Labour left-wingers, and the extravagant promises of Labour politicians in party meetings.[32] All this material was filed away by Unionist speakers for the coming election, but much of it was put to use at once. Zinoviev became a regular feature of anti-socialist speeches as Conservative politicians sought to awaken their audiences to the danger of international socialism. Long before the Zinoviev Letter, the name of Zinoviev would have been known to the readers of the Unionist press, certainly more familiar than either Trotsky or Stalin. Candidates in the by-elections of 1924 had discovered that the red card was extremely useful when played against a Labour government, that it brought out Unionists to vote and left the Liberal ranks in consternation.

A glorious opening was presented by the three problems that remained when parliament rose for its summer recess. The first was the terms of reference to be given to the Irish Boundary Commission, over which an agreement was eventually reached but which brought the orange card back into the pack. The other two were the treaties that the government had negotiated with the Soviet Union and the decisions first to prosecute and then not to prosecute the Communist editor of the *Workers' Weekly*, J. R. Campbell, for suborning mutiny in the armed forces. During the recess these came to the boil and presented the Unionists with the chance to vote Labour out of office on the most favourable ground. When parliament met in September it was clear that the Liberals would oppose the Russian treaties and criticize the handling of the Campbell Case, and that the government would treat both as issues of confidence, as much because of the sensitivity of MacDonald as for any merits in the actual cases. MacDonald finally decided to stake his survival on Campbell and was faced with a Unionist motion of no confidence and with a Liberal amendment calling for a select committee investigation. With an election staring them in the face, Liberal and Labour MPs now tried to devise procedural ways of beating a retreat. Once again they were beaten by Baldwin's superior footwork when he announced that the Unionists would vote for the Liberal amendment, so nailing Asquith's colours to the mast. Asquith had been made to appear as the creator of the Labour government and now he would appear as its destroyer too.[33]

On 8 October the Liberal amendment was carried by 364 votes to 199 and MacDonald declared that he must therefore face the electorate. After consultations with Baldwin and Asquith the King agreed to the dissolution of parliament, with polling to take place on 29 October. In the critical division two Unionist MPs had been so unsure about the future that they had joined fourteen Liberals and the Labour party in voting against their party. But these two were now well out of step with the mood of the party as a whole; at the National Union Conference in Newcastle in the previous week Baldwin had been given a hero's welcome for a speech which concentrated on 'the menace of communism'. The delegates dispersed certain that the coming contest was one that they could win.[34]

In the 1924 general election, Unionist candidates had to face none of the difficulties of 1923. They were already in the field in most places and this gave them a useful advantage over Liberals: where it was customary for only one anti-Labour candidate to stand, as in South Wales, it was important to have got in first, for this would place the onus for causing three-cornered contests entirely on the Liberals. The Liberals thus asked for a pact in West Scotland to protect Asquith's seat but had to make one very much on Unionist terms: there was only one anti-Labour candidate in each of the twenty-five constituencies covered by the pact, but this involved the withdrawal of nineteen Liberals and only two Unionists. Elsewhere there were a few formal pacts in towns where they had become traditional, and a few areas where Liberals and Unionists combined to support a Constitutionalist (usually a Liberal who was moving over like Churchill), but in most places there were no pacts because local Liberals had nothing to offer. When nominations closed, the number of Unionist candidates had risen to 552, Labour had risen substantially to 512, and Liberals had slumped to a mere 340. Labour was now bidding seriously for a majority and for the first time there was no possibility of the Liberals winning the election. Both these facts would be rammed home in the Unionist campaign.[35]

In the constituencies the pattern of candidatures gave even more help; Labour interventions in many seats which Unionists had lost to Liberals in 1923 would split the radical vote and so help the Unionist back in. Liberal withdrawals in another hundred seats would rally the anti-Labour vote to the Unionist. So in Sheffield there was no Liberal candidate in any constituency and the Liberal leader, Sir William Clegg, urged all Liberals to vote Unionist to defeat the Labour MPs who had treated his party so badly in the recent parliament. Similar advice was given all over the country, often by the Liberal candidates who had denied victory to the Unionists only a year earlier; the defection of the Liberal moderates which Austen Chamberlain had despaired of in July was all too evident in October. Nor were Unionists faced with the press hostility that they had met in 1923: the moderate Unionist papers were strongly for Baldwin, the Beaverbrook papers were on balance favourable, and the Rothermere papers beat the drum with no restraint whatsoever.[36]

The Unionist campaign had three main features, one devoted to each of the parties. There was a confident assertion of the Unionist programme worked out in the spring: industry should be safeguarded and agriculture assisted, both in order to counter unemployment; imperial unity, defence and an imperial foreign policy should be fostered, no doubt to cash in on the popularity of the Empire exhibition at Wembley; there was a long list of housing and social programmes, in contrast to the vague promises of 1922 and 1923. Baldwin made the greatest use of all this material, but there was something in the manifesto for every candidate, in any kind of seat and against any sort of opposition. The second leg of the Unionist campaign was the emphasis placed on the need to secure a stable and hence a lasting majority government. The belief in strong government was a traditional enough Unionist cry, but it had received new impetus from the chaos of the three-party system since 1918 and the experiment in minority government. This appeal was aimed above all at Liberal voters, especially where there was no Liberal candidate to vote for; now that the Liberals could not form a government, they could be held to be an irrelevancy that would merely prolong uncertainty. A government of real authority in 1924 could only be Labour or Unionist, and the effect of this point was not lost on the Liberal weekly the *Nation*:

> It is difficult to predict the final outcome of the three-party system. We feel certain that in its present form, with its concomitant of minority government, it is not destined to endure for long. . . . It has led to another result, which has impressed the public more than . . . the others – a third General Election within the space of two years. It is not surprising that the desire to put an end to this plague of annual elections should be uppermost in the minds of many voters.[37]

These two features of the campaign no doubt convinced many voters that the Unionists were the only party with a chance of winning and a moderate policy to carry out, but it was the third leg of the campaign that attracted the most attention.

From the start Unionist speakers devoted themselves to criticism of the Russian treaties and the Campbell Case; the treaties were denounced as sham agreements forced on MacDonald by his own left wing (a charge that was given countenance by the fact that the ILP had acted as mediators in the negotiations) and it was pointed out that money was being advanced without any certainty that previous loans would be repaid; Campbell showed that a Labour government would bend even the law to the dictates of party expediency. So far, this followed on from the debates in parliament, but in the heat of battle the Unionists threw caution to the winds and engaged in a red-baiting extravaganza, as Chris Cook has described:

> The Duke of Devonshire declared that the Labour Government was subject to marching orders from Moscow, whilst Curzon described MacDonald as the secret slave of the Communist Party. Birkenhead, Churchill and Joynson-Hicks all revelled in this kind of accusation, frequently mentioning MacDonald's pacifism in the war. . . . Again and again, Conservatives stressed that if the Socialists were returned, religion and family life would be destroyed. As the Peckham Conservative candidate observed, the destruction of all morality and religion was the first plank in the policy of the Communist Party, which was but the left wing of the Labour Party. . . . Even *The Times* added its own note of reason by observing of Labour's proposal to set up a national system of electricity generating stations that 'some such project was dear to Lenin'.[38]

Mond and Lloyd George on the Liberal side joined in the red scare with language as extravagant as that of the Unionists.

Baldwin was the pivot of the Unionist campaign, firstly because he was unopposed at Bewdley and so was able to tour the country without any need to worry about his own seat, and secondly because his image was vital to give the attack on Labour the stamp of moral authority. His stature was actually increased by tributes paid to him during the campaign by Labour opponents, who were anxious to denigrate the Liberals by comparison. MacDonald believed 'that Mr Baldwin and his friends honestly and sincerely think they are right'; Lunn described Baldwin as 'a straightforward and honourable Englishman' and Stewart declared that 'Mr Baldwin is an honest and admirable man'; Sir Henry Slesser thought Baldwin was 'an honest and decent man' and although he disagreed with 'the Conservatives on every point . . . he found them on the whole honourable men who at least stuck to their opinions'.[39] These tributes in mid-campaign were clear evidence of the extent to which Baldwin had already succeeded in raising the moral tone of Unionist politics. That success was used to denigrate the Labour party far more effectively than the unbridled rhetoric of Birkenhead. More in sorrow than in anger, Baldwin described the folly of the Russian treaties and called on Labour to rid itself of 'the extremist forces which appear to control it' and so become a 'patriotic and Constitutional Party'. At Southend on 20 October, Baldwin gave his comments in a similar vein on a recent speech by Zinoviev to the Comintern, using his usual mixture of studied moderation and gentle irony: 'It makes my blood boil to read of the way in which Monsieur Zinovieff is speaking of the Prime Minister of Great Britain today. At one time there went up a cry "Hands off Russia!" My word! I think it is time that someone said to Russia, "Hands off England!"'[40] The use of the word 'Monsieur' for Zinoviev, making him sound that much more alien than a mere 'Mister', the righteous indignation, and the appearance of defending MacDonald against his unruly allies were all hallmarks of the Baldwin speeches during the campaign. Five days after the Southend speech, though, it seemed to have a wholly different importance, when the *Daily Mail* published the famous Zinoviev Letter.

The letter published on 25 October, first by the *Daily Mail* with a front page spread of breathtaking impact and immediately by the rest of the press too, purported to be a letter of instruction from the Comintern to the British Communist Party. It ordered British Communists to create an agitation to force parliament to ratify the Russian treaties, and to step up their infiltration of the Labour Party and the armed forces.[41] It had been received at the Foreign Office on 10 October and the fortnight's delay had been due to the difficulty of contacting MacDonald on his election tour. MacDonald did not make it clear that the letter should not be made public without proof of its authenticity and, in his continued absence, the Foreign Office published the letter with a strong letter of protest to the Soviet government; these were both released to the press on 24 October.[42] The reaction was predictable, for the letter appeared to confirm everything that the Unionists had been saying all summer about the pressure that could be exerted against a Labour government from the left. In a long speech at Sheffield on 27 October Baldwin extracted the maximum advantage from the 'Red Letter' and from the long delay that had followed its appearance at the Foreign Office, still without departing from his tone of moderation:

I want to know why it is that the Prime Minister, as I am told he stated this afternoon, marked as a minute on that letter to the Foreign Office the word 'publicity' as long ago as October 16th, why we have had it held up till October 24th. Did he really mean that we should go through the election in ignorance of the letter?

I do not think that can be the case, and yet his Party have been urging us to vote for them on the ground of the Russian Treaty, and on the ground that by their action the Labour Party have introduced a fresh era of brotherliness between the Soviet Government and ourselves. They could hardly have desired that the English public should come to a conclusion on this matter without seeing that correspondence, which had been minuted nearly a fortnight ago with the word 'publicity'. Two days before he put that minute of 'publicity' on that paper he was telling the country that we were frightening old ladies with Bolshevik bogies.

There is still a very great mystery surrounding the conduct of the Government in this matter, but there is one quarter in which there is no mystery, and that is the attitude of the Russian Government. . . .[43]

It was masterly, creating the impression that MacDonald had lied without saying so. Only four days separated the publication of the letter from polling day, just enough time for charges to be made, but no time for the government to answer them satisfactorily. The last few days thus saw an intensification of the red scare, with Asquith and Simon joining in, and with Labour reduced to dumb apathy. Labour hinted that the letter was forged and Moscow denied all knowledge of it, but Lloyd George was able to recall a time when the Russian government had denied a similar 'transaction when I had positive proof in front of me'. On polling day, the electors had to believe that the letter was genuine and that it validated the whole Unionist case.[44]

We now know most of the truth about the Zinoviev Letter. It was forged in Poland by Russian emigrés in order to prevent the British government from giving aid to Soviet Russia. It then passed through the espionage network and was probably introduced into the Foreign Office through MI5, so that the Office could not tell how it had come into their hands. A copy of the letter found its way to the *Daily Mail* and it seems likely that the Foreign Office was stampeded into publication by broad hints in the press that it was about to come out anyway. In his first reactions in public, MacDonald remarked that it was 'a most suspicious circumstance that a certain newspaper and the headquarters of the Conservative Association seems to have had copies of the letter at the same time as the Foreign Office'. Central Office immediately denied that it had ever had a copy and the *Daily Mail* admitted that it had seen a copy before it was released, but only on 24 October. MacDonald did not return to the attack until 1927, but he apparently knew something of what had happened.[45]

It is now clear that Central Office did at least have knowledge of the letter's content, even if the letter itself had not been seen, and it seems likely that it was Central Office that put the *Daily Mail* in touch with the story. Baldwin's Southend speech, in which he brought the name of Zinoviev back into the campaign ten days after the letter reached the Foreign Office but five days before its publication, is too much to be explained away. Baldwin's staff were based at Central Office and Baldwin was returning to London between speaking engagements, so that any office rumour about the letter would be bound to reach him. There are several ways in which the letter could have got to Central Office: it could have been through the contacts of Reginald Hall or Joseph Ball in MI5; it could have been through Guy Kindersley, a friend of Donald im Thurn who had brought the letter to London, and a Unionist MP; or it could have been through Marjory Maxse, who was in charge of the women's side at Central Office and related to a member of the Foreign Office department which handled the letter. It does not really matter which it was, for with such a variety of contacts it is inconceivable that Central Office would not have known about the letter almost as soon as it reached London. But none of this suggests that Central Office, MI5 or the Foreign Office knew that the letter was forged. With a detailed knowledge of Comintern protocol, it was possible to detect errors, but nobody at Central Office had such knowledge; the letter was too great a bonus to be scrutinized carefully at Central Office, but the experts at the Foreign Office were equally convinced of its authenticity.

At all events, once they had the letter, Central Office moved with devastating effectiveness, through Philip Cambray. Cambray was a skilled manager of the press and he orchestrated the press and speaker campaign that followed publication of the letter. According to another Central Office staff member, 'that we won the last General Election by the margin we did was due in no small measure to the way he directed measures in connection with the Zinovieff Letter'. In Cambray's own view, this campaign was a textbook example of how such things should be done in 'the game of politics'.[46] The most that can be claimed is that Central Office saw a chance to exploit a letter which appeared to be genuine and that it used its chance to the utmost. The sequel of 1927, when Central Office paid £5,000 for Donald im Thurn's silence is far more suspicious. This cover up can be explained in two ways: by then it may have been known, or at least guessed, that the letter was forged, or it may just be that Central Office could not be sure that its role would be properly understood even if it had all been entirely innocent; in either case it was better to pay up and not to take the risk. So, in Conservative eyes at least, the Zinoviev Letter remained genuine until proved otherwise by the *Sunday Times* in 1967.[47]

When the polls closed on 29 October 1924 there was little doubt that the Unionists would win, but the scale of the triumph was entirely unexpected. 412 Unionists were returned, gaining 154 seats in all, and there were 151 Labour MPs and only 40 Liberals. Labour's vote had held up well, fortified by the example of Labour in power, but turnout had risen substantially to the advantage of the Unionists and many Liberals had clearly voted Unionist – not only where there was no Liberal candidate. The Unionists had more MPs than the Liberals in 1906 or Labour in 1945; it was the greatest *party* victory that modern Britain has ever seen. Unlike 1922, the victory was securely underpinned with a popular vote of 46.8 per cent for official candidates; if allowance is made for uncontested seats and Unionist votes for Constitution-alists, then the party's share would be over 50 per cent, and this on the highest turnout of the inter-war years. The electoral system had as usual magnified the triumph, but there had been a substantial increase in Unionist votes everywhere and every part of the country had returned more Unionists than in 1923.

After the results were announced, Labour made great play with the effects of the Red Letter and claimed that it had lost them the election,[48] a claim that has passed into Labour mythology along with the homes fit for heroes and the bankers' ramp. The evidence does not support this view for Labour increased its vote among its natural constituency, the working class, and could hardly have hoped for a much higher vote than it achieved in 1924. The letter may have helped to scare middle-class Liberals into the Unionist camp, but in doing so it only accelerated a trend. The experience of a Labour government and the abandonment of the tariff policy was going to push the Unionist vote over seven million in 1924 irrespective of the issues of the campaign. The pattern of the candidatures and issues like Campbell and the Russian treaties were quite enough to transform this into a substantial winning margin. The Zinoviev Letter no doubt increased the scale of victory, but it did not create it.

The Unionist victory was thus a positive one, the moment at which a new two-party balance was born. The final and most underestimated factor in the victory was Baldwin's attempt to lift his party on to a different plane. It remains to discuss Baldwin's Conservatism and to decide whether it deserves the name that the press gave to it in 1924. By the end of the year Baldwin had completed in all essentials his view of the party that he wished to lead; in the rest of the twenties he deepened the theme but did not substantially change it, and in the thirties he was trading on a reputation already made. What then *was* the New Conservatism?

Baldwin's contribution to Conservative thought was made neither in policy nor underlying philosophy. Like most refurbishings of Conservatism, Baldwin's was concerned with attitudes and responses rather than with either abstract theory or concrete policy. Such had been Peel's basic achievement in the 1830s and Disraeli's in the 1870s; such was to be the basis for success after 1945. New Conservatism, like Tory democracy and the property-owning democracy, contained much theorizing but was not theoretical in origin, and involved major implications for policy but was not conceived with them in mind. Like both it depended on the instincts of its creator, Baldwin himself.

Baldwin was a complex character who chose to masquerade as a simple one, perhaps the most difficult enigma for a historian to unravel. He had a good mind, but had been alienated from education at Harrow and Cambridge and had performed badly; in later life nothing gave him greater satisfaction than the promotion of Harrovians in his government and the honour that Cambridge did by electing him as Chancellor. He admired his father deeply and was convinced that the regime of harmony between management and employees which Alfred Baldwin had created was the example of how society itself would operate if given a chance. He succeeded his father as MP for Bewdley in 1908, already over forty, and made little impression on the Commons in his first ten years; in the turbulent world of Carson and Law there was little room for a backbencher who believed in peace and goodwill.[49] War had a profound effect on him and incidentally provided him with a political opportunity; he first entered the cabinet in 1921 and was Prime Minister two years later. In party terms, his opposition to coalition, his speech at the Carlton Club meeting, and his availability in May 1923 made him a possible leader, but he became a truly national leader for different reasons. The man who was so out of joint with the times before 1914 was perfectly placed to interpret them in 1924. In a remarkable way, he was able to sense the popular mood and to play on the popular mind, to identify public attitudes, and claim legitimately that he himself represented it – as few other politicians have ever done.[50] For fifteen years he seemed almost to have a direct personal line to the voice of public opinion and a readiness to heed it. So he told the victors of 1924 in the party's celebration rally:

> Can there be anything that stands before us more clearly or poignantly than the groups of our fellow-countrymen who listened in faith to what we had to say, who

trusted us and have given us their confidence, and who believe in their hearts that we have come to London to do what we can to right those things that are hard and difficult for them, and to help them in what is always a difficult struggle in life? Don't ever lose touch with your constituency; don't ever mistake the voice of the clubman and the voice of the Pressman in London for the voice of the country. It is the country which has returned you; it is the country which will judge you.[51]

At the end of his career, when he described the way in which MPs changed their views over the critical weekend in the Abdication Crisis, learning from their constituents what Baldwin had sensed all along, he mused 'I have always believed in the weekend. But how they do it I don't know. I suppose they talk to the stationmaster.'[52] How *he* did it is an even greater mystery, but an undeniable fact. Perhaps it was because in his own character he shared many of the national moods of the 1920s and 1930s. He was jolly in appearance, but his jollity hid a deep melancholy; he was certain in his faith, but very unsure about actual policies and well aware that honest men could honestly differ. Hence he spoke of the 'many-sidedness of truth' and once copied out the uncompromising motto: 'This is the most important lesson that a man can learn . . . that opinions are nothing but the mere results of change and temperament, that no party on the whole is better than any other, that no creed does more than shadow imperfectly some side of truth.'[53] This uncertainty led him into a conviction that faith was ultimately more important than works, and in an age when (as Salisbury wrote to him) 'the leaders of thought in the democracy' were 'panting after ideals which they are afraid may be slipping from them' Baldwin's identification with the nation was complete.[54]

The character of Baldwin's Conservatism may be analysed in five ways, for it was self-consciously ordinary, moral, unprovocative, English and professional. It was *ordinary* in the same sense as Bonar Law had been ordinary, in that it placed no emphasis on Leadership, but rather sought authority in the people; policies were validated not just by being right but also by being representative. As he himself said of Law, people heard that Lloyd George had said that he was 'honest to the point of simplicity' and had said to themselves, 'By God, that is what we are looking for'.[55] Baldwin made excellent use of the radio when it came into political use in 1924 and became a skilled exponent of the technique of the 'fireside chat'. In a technical sense it was no doubt good advice and the inability of MacDonald and Lloyd George to adjust to the new medium that made the impact of Baldwin's broadcasts so great, but he took to it so well because he spoke naturally, for all the world as if addressing the elector across his own fireside.[56]

In the party Baldwin went out of his way to identify with the rank and file, as no leader had ever done. So at the Victory Rally:

> Since the battle of Alma [surely he means Inkerman?] there has been no such rank and file victory as we have just achieved. . . . I am under no temptation to believe that that victory was the result of leadership. It was the result of hard, continuous,

genuine and self-sacrificing work on the part of countless men and women from one end of the kingdom to the other.[57]

This theme recurred over and over again in party meetings, but was perhaps best expressed at the conference of 1928:

> I have had forty years experience of politics, most of it in the rank and file. There is nothing I ask you to do that I have not done myself. I have marked off polling cards. I have addressed envelopes (laughter), and I have shepherded the last batch of voters from the public house (cheers, and laughter). I gained my experience in an old borough and there is nothing you can teach me.
>
> . . . I am proud to lead such a party with such a tradition. I sprang from the rank and file and they have supported me in good times and bad. They stood by me after the general election of 1923, when many stout hearts wavered. They have stood by me since. . . . They have trusted me. (Prolonged cheers.)[58]

It is hard to imagine Balfour or Austen Chamberlain or Churchill achieving this *rapport* with the constituency workers of their party, but then they had probably done none of the things that Baldwin described. Baldwin was in truth sprung from the ranks and he never forgot the fact (or allowed anyone else to forget it either).

His overriding concern was to involve as many people as possible in the political process, from an awareness of how thin was the crust of political society and how deep the wells of apathy and indifference. He constantly urged the party to draw in women and the young, both groups who had come to politics with the war, as he pointed out in February 1924:

> The new electorate called into being since the war comprises a vast proportion of women and young men. The sordid and miserable experience of those war years have left people peculiarly open to the presentation of ideals; and it is perfectly useless, in my view, to think that you can secure the support of a majority of the nation as it exists today and in the frame of mind in which it finds itself today, unless your appeal is not only to their head but to their heart.[59]

The party would therefore work for participatory representation and must do so if democracy was to survive; the corollary of this was increased respect for the electoral mandate. On the one hand this allowed Baldwin to drop protection in 1924 without charges of inconsistency, but on the other it involved him in severe difficulties when he could not detect a mandate for rearmament in the thirties. The assiduous cultivation of democracy was as relevant to the party as to the country, as he made clear in October 1924:

> Nothing has given me greater pleasure than to find that one of my ambitions is being realized, and that the working men of this country are coming to take their proper place in the ranks of our Party and that a ladder is being set up amongst us which may serve them no less effectively than the ladder that exists today in the Labour Party, by which a man, whatever his means or his origin, may hope, by the exercise of his natural ability, to render service to his country into whatsoever office he may be called. . . . Many today are now in the ranks of Labour who ought to be with us, for there are no more crusted Tories in England than many of those

who sit not only on the back but on the front bench of the Labour Ministry today.[60]

Respect for democracy, belief in mandates, and equality of opportunity all stopped well short of egalitarianism. Baldwin defined democracy as 'but the government of the people, by the people, through their freely-elected representatives', and the characteristic of his governments was paternalist. Indeed, in 1925 he met the egalitarian argument head on: 'Men are not born free. They are not born equal. They are not born fraternal, and I will ask any mother in the audience if she does not agree with me?'[61] Baldwin then sought to identify with the people and to base his authority on their support, but there was no commitment to the ideology of equality.

The New Conservatism was *moral* in direct imitation of Baldwin's own views. He believed that he had been chosen to lead the nation from the divisions in 1922 to a more harmonious order. He asserted duties rather than rights and tried to impart moral conviction into everything that the party set out to do; he argued in 1924 that 'the assertion of the people's rights has never yet provided the people with bread. The performance of their duties and that alone can lead to the successful issue of those experiments in Government that we have carried further than any other people in the world'.[62] An unsleeping moral purpose was vital to the party and the nation, as he told an audience of Cambridge undergraduates in 1924:

> You have got to make up your mind that as you come into the party and into politics you will never let the party sleep in these matters of social reform that affect the lives and conditions of our people, knowing that you are following the very traditions of Disraeli himself adapted to the present day. . . . It is all very well to talk about international brotherhood. The brotherhood at home comes first.[63]

Moral purpose was thus exhibited above all in the need for a humanitarian social policy, later in the evocation of the horrors of war and the measures that must be taken to avoid them. Conviction was necessary if politics were to have any real justification, as he told the victory rally:

> I want to see the spirit of service to the nation the birthright of every member of the Unionist party – Unionist in the sense that we stand for the Union of these two nations of which Disraeli spoke two generations ago; union among our own people to make one nation of our own people at home, which if secured nothing else matters in the world. I urge on you all as workers in the great Unionist party to render all the service you can to the common weal in the districts in which you live. There is always work and to spare for human betterment in every parish in the country. And to all those workers for the party and Members of Parliament I say this in conclusion: you cannot better serve your party, and through your party your country, than in dedicating your lives to that service.[64]

Baldwin explained the success of his appeal by asserting that the ordinary man and woman would respect genuine convictions even if they did not share them. More cynically put by Malcolm Muggeridge to Lord Linlithgow ten years later: 'To succeed pre-eminently in English public life it is necessary to conform either to the popular image of a bookie or of a clergyman; Churchill being a perfect example of the former, Halifax of the latter.'[65] On this analogy, the transition from Lloyd George to Bonar Law was the transition from the bookie to the clergyman, the transition from Law to Baldwin was merely a change from embattled Presbyterianism to evangelical Anglicanism. There may be something in this idea that the public like their politicians to be recognizably good or bad – but that being bad in this sense does not make them less likely to win votes – and in this distinction Baldwin was clearly on the side of the angels. It has been suggested by A. L. Rowse among other denigrators of Baldwin, that his moral convictions were no more than the assumptions of a clever politician. Such was far from the case; letters, diaries and the recollections of friends and opponents all make it abundantly clear that Baldwin's belief was real, that he was an honest and moral man. As he told Harold Nicolson in 1943, 'you will find in politics that you are much exposed to the attribution of false motives. Never complain and never explain.'[66]

The *unprovocative* nature of Baldwin's Conservatism followed naturally from its moral basis; it was this that most cut him off from Birkenhead and Churchill. His belief in conciliation and appeasement (in the strict sense, meaning the promotion of peace) meant that under his lead the party would be an emollient, would seek compromise rather than confrontation. This was reinforced by the need to appeal outside the old Unionist ranks for support, looking especially to ex-Liberals and to men and women of no party for a personal mandate. It was on this base that Baldwin's 'national' standing was based in 1924 and it was for this reason that Baldwin fitted so well into the national governments of the 1930s. The party must be reformist in outlook both because of the need to seem moderate to such non-Unionist supporters and because it followed also from his conviction of the need for betterment. This led on inevitably to the battles over India and the trade union question, and to his being called a 'semi-socialist' by at least one close supporter. So he proclaimed at Manchester in July that 'we have no sectional, or narrow, partisan, or class policy. Our duty is to the nation as a whole, and to the Empire as a whole, and on that broad basis we shall rejoice to have the cooperation of all who are animated by a similar spirit.'[67] In his speeches of 1924 he returned regularly to the theme that 'Socialism divided, Unionism unites'. To make this theme plausible in government, it would be necessary to jettison all the provocative material that the party had acquired in the recent past: hence he spoke increasingly of Conservatism rather than Unionism, or used Unionism in his own sense as quoted above, thus by-passing the issue that had most completely divided British parties in the past; so he disposed quietly of the party's proposals to restore the House of Lords, to emasculate the trade unions and to impose a general tariff; so he disposed of the country's imperial destiny. Most of the shifts were disguised, but each led ultimately to trouble in the party. In the end though, it was usually the unprovocative line that triumphed.

The unprovocative nature of Baldwin's thought was rooted in its *English*ness, as he told the victory rally of 1924:

> It was a victory above all for English sanity of outlook and sobriety of speech. For myself, I refrain, as I have always done, from displaying visions of a new heaven and a new earth emanating from Whitehall. I gave no pledges that we would introduce the millennium, nor did I prophesy universal peace. And yet we won.[68]

Baldwin contributed as much as anyone to the classic characterization of English history, the view that it has profited above all from a readiness to settle disputes by honest compromise. He raised this to a new level by subtly suggesting that the attitude was natural to the people, autochthonous compromise that sprang from the very soil and climate. Baldwin considered himself to be English and this self-identification is more valuable than any calculation of his parentage which shows a Celtic strand in his make up. Nor did he claim to be 'British' for it was the land of England that he spoke for; Zinoviev was warned 'Hands off England', his first book of speeches was called *On England* and his last *An Interpreter of England*, and he urged his supporters in 1924 'not to forget the character of the English people, in which and in love of that character pursue your work and help them'. The character of English history was evoked to justify the principle of concession, a tradition traced back to Peel and Disraeli – as if the character of Conservatism was shared with that of the nation:

> We all have that slight subconscious reluctance to take a long step forward – that perhaps makes us Conservatives. We do not do it for the fun of the thing, but, on the other hand, if we close our minds to arguments against ever taking a step forward, if Conservative leaders had always done that and allowed these subconscious instincts to dominate them, where would the Conservative Party have been in these days of universal manhood and womanhood suffrage?[69]

Nothing raised Baldwin's eloquence to greater heights than consideration of England, the English character and English history, for which he expressed a mystical reverence:

> To me England is the country, and the country is England. And when I ask myself what I mean by England, when I think of England when I am abroad, England comes to me through my various senses, through the ear, through the eyes, and through certain imperishable senses. I will tell you what they are, and there may be those among you who feel as I do.
>
> The sounds of England, the tinkle of the hammer on the anvil in the country smithy, the corncrake on a dewy morning, the sound of the scythe against the whetstone, and the sight of a plough team coming over the brow of a hill. . . . The wild anemones in the woods in April, the last load at night of hay being drawn down a lane as the twilight comes on, when you can scarcely distinguish the figures of the horses as they take it home to the farm, and above all, most subtle, most penetrating and most moving, the smell of wood smoke coming up in an autumn evening, or the smell of the scutch fires: the wood smoke that our ancestors, tens of thousands of years ago, must have caught on the air when they were coming home with the results of the day's forage. . . . These things strike down into the very

depths of our nature, and touch chords that go back to the beginning of time and the human race, but they are chords that with every year of our life sound a deeper note in our innermost being.

These are the things that make England, and I grieve for it that they are not the childish inheritance of the majority of people today in our country.[70]

These vivid images were backed by pictures of Baldwin himself, leaning over a stile to poke a pig or enjoying a glass of beer in a country pub. They give a powerful impression of the importance that rural English life played in his thoughts. 'Britain' was hardly mentioned and references to the Empire were dutifully tacked on to his 1924 speeches, more for the look of the thing than from any deep conviction. Indeed, Baldwin's concept of the Empire was of a family of Englishmen, separated but sharing the ties of kinship, many of whom would come home for their retirement. His view of the English countryside bears a striking resemblance to the impression of England seen by an imperialist abroad, very similar to the Sussex of Kipling's writings and the Worcestershire to which Elgar retreated when he tired of imperial triumphs in London. It was then the England of the returning imperialist, appropriately enough for a party that was itself retreating from the imperial role that Disraeli had carved out for it in the 1870s, retreating back to the more familiar role of English nationalism that Disraeli himself had celebrated thirty years earlier.

Finally, the New Conservatism was *professional* in the sense that it was a creed of the player not the gentleman. Kipling had taken far more interest in the working men of Empire than the plumed proconsuls, and his cousin shared this preference for workers over drones. In a rare speech of bitterness, Baldwin talked of the gentleman diehards 'who sit in the smoking rooms of clubs and never do a hands turn of work' and who thought that Conservatism was merely 'Coningsby and County Cricket'.[71] New Conservatism was businesslike and organized, tough not in its adherence to old ideas but in its pragmatic realism. This was emphasized in comparison with Labour's plans, which to Baldwin were impossible dreams even where the ends were desirable. He said at Edinburgh in March 1924, 'We cannot compete with the Socialists in promises of what can be done. . . . We cannot attempt to compete in promising free provision for all the ills that flesh is heir to. We do not believe it to be practicable.'[72] At Manchester in September he urged the need for a strong and businesslike government to deal with India, qualities that he did not detect in MacDonald's administration. It may be argued that Baldwin himself never lived up to this side of his thought, that he was lethargic in his own attitude to government. Such claims are true in part, but Baldwin was certainly not as 'lazy' as has been alleged; when trouble threatened, as over the General Strike, he spent so freely of his nervous energy as to leave himself in a state of collapse. Much of what Baldwin lacked in the execution of policy was in any case made up by the presence of Neville Chamberlain in his governments; Chamberlain had codified the policy side of the New

Conservatism in 1924 and in this sense he should perhaps be seen as its co-author. Baldwin did, though, continue to use the rhetoric of business sense, as when he reviewed the suggestion that the franchise for men and women should be equalized at twenty-five in 1927:

> I will just put this question to any provincial candidate the next election. You will be asked 'are you in favour of a man having the vote at 21 or not?' He will be a bold man who will stand up and say 'I am not'. He will find it politically, in my view, an impossible position to maintain. . . . To take away a franchise centuries old in a democratic country is a thing which, in my opinion, is not practical politics.[73]

As with tariffs after the election of 1923, there was no question of whether the policy was right or wrong, no question of whether the ends were desirable, only that it was not practical political business.

Baldwin of course denied that what he was propounding in his speeches was new, except in the sense that the First World War had made all things new. What he was concerned with were 'the very traditions of Disraeli himself adapted to the present day', and Disraeli figures quite prominently in the speeches. So he cited Disraeli to justify an advanced social programme for the party:

> If there is any party in the State which, by its traditions and its history, is entitled to put in the forefront of its work and its programme the betterment of the conditions of life of the working classes, it is our party. (Hear, hear.) We were fighting the battle of the factory hand long before he had a vote; and when the Liberals were tied up in the shackles of *laisser faire* we were speaking in favour of the combination of working men, long before the Liberals had thought of the subject. It is more than fifty years ago that Disraeli was calling the attention of the country to housing and health problems and they mocked him with a policy of sewage. The sanitation, or let me say the spiritual sanitation, of our people should have the first call on the historic Tory Party.[74]

This view of Tory history had just received powerful reinforcement from Maurice Woods's *History of the Tory Party* and it was shortly to have its classic exposition in the hands of R. L. Hill.[75] The name of Disraeli was a powerful charm to refute those who thought that Baldwin's policy was all too close to MacDonald's. In other words, Baldwin used both the classic methods whereby Conservative leaders can persuade their followers to accept change; by stressing that the First World War had been a great watershed, he convinced them that it was too late to stop it, and, by using the name of Disraeli, he argued that it had been party policy all along. As Harvey Glickman has observed, 'the development of the Conservative Party since the 19th Century is a history of persuading the Tories that the changes that must be accepted have indeed occurred'.[76]

For all his protestations, Baldwin was enunciating a Conservatism that was both new and highly personal. What cannot be disputed is the effect that this had on the future. A Baldwin legend grew up to reinforce the Disraeli myth about the inevitability of concession in the history of the Conservative Party.

Baldwin's impetus was felt through the radio, through the mass rallies at which he spoke (many of which attracted tens of thousands merely to hear him speak), and through the several volumes of his published speeches, some of which went into many editions.[77] By the 1930s there was a recognizably Baldwinian style of politician on the left of the party, a style that encompassed the very different talents of R. A. Butler and Harold Macmillan, more recently of the One Nation Group, of Robert Carr, Reginald Maudling and Edward Heath.

All this was far in the future in 1924, triumphant as Baldwin had been in the general election. It would now be seen whether the New Conservatism could be made to work in the party and in government.

Notes and references

1 Cook, *Age of Alignment*, 159.
2 Salvidge to Derby, 18 Jan. 1924: quoted in Churchill, *Derby*, 561–2.
3 Middlemas and Barnes, *Baldwin*, 252; Hyde, *Baldwin*, 201.
4 Cowling, *Impact of Labour*, 393.
5 *Morning Post*, 11 Feb. 1924.
6 National Union minutes, Executive Committee, 29 Jan. 1924, and Central Council, 12 Feb. 1924.
7 *Gleanings and Memoranda*, Mar. 1924.
8 *Ibid.*
9 Hyde, *Baldwin*, 209–217.
10 Cook and Ramsden, *By-Elections*, 56–8.
11 Baldwin to Joan Davidson, 20 Mar. 1924: quoted in Davidson, *Memoirs of a Conservative*, 194–5.
12 Gilbert, *Winston S. Churchill*, v, 41–8.
13 Cook, *Age of Alignment*, 242–4.
14 Samuel Roberts's Autobiographical Memorandum.
15 *Conservative Agents' Journal*, July 1924.
16 Hyde, *Baldwin*, 207; Wickham Steed, *The Real Stanley Baldwin*, 71; *Gleanings and Memoranda*, Jan. 1924. The F.S.T. story first appeared with Baldwin's name attached to it in the *Birmingham Post* on 29 Nov. 1923.
17 National Union minutes, Executive Committee, 11 Mar. 1924.
18 Middlemas and Barnes, *Baldwin*, 264; Jones, *Whitehall Diary*, i, 276.
19 Ramsden, 'Organisation' (thesis), 228–9.
20 Cook, *Age of Alignment*, 251–62.
21 Ramsden, 'Organisation', 292; Worthington-Evans's Memorandum on the events of Oct.–Nov. 1923: Worthington–Evans MSS.
22 Goodhart, *The 1922*, 20–7.
23 Cowling, *Impact of Labour*, 254.
24 *Conservative Agents' Journal*, Apr. 1924, *Gleanings and Memoranda*, June 1924.
25 Ramsden, 'Organisation', 226.
26 Calculated from announcements in the *Conservative Agents' Journal*.
27 Davidson to Hall, 19 Dec. 1923, Davidson MSS.
28 *Gleanings and Memoranda*, Sept. 1924; Cook and Ramsden, *By-elections*, 44–71.
29 Quoted in Beattie, *English Party Politics*, ii, 357.
30 *Evening News*, 30 July 1924.
31 Liberal switchers to Conservative at a local level were regularly reported in *Gleanings and Memoranda*: there were few in 1924, rather a lot in 1925–26.
32 For example *Gleanings and Memoranda*, July 1924.
33 Cook, *Age of Alignment*, 276.

34   National Union Conference minutes, Newcastle Conference, 2 Oct. 1924.
35   Cook, *Age of Alignment*, 288, 294.
36   *Ibid*, 304–5.
37   The *Nation*, 23 Oct. 1924, quoted in Beattie, *English Party Politics*, ii, 346.
38   Cook, *Age of Alignment*, 300–1.
39   *Yorkshire Post*, 17 Oct. 1924; *Glasgow Herald*, 25 Oct. 1924.
40   *The Times*, 21 Oct. 1924.
41   *Daily Mail*, 25 Oct. 1924.
42   Chester *et al.*, *Zinoviev Letter* 131–2.
43   *Sheffield Daily Telegraph*, 28 Oct. 1924.
44   *Daily Chronicle*, 28 Oct. 1924.
45   Chester *et al.*, *Zinoviev Letter*, 132–4.
46   Cambray, *The Game of Politics*, 83.
47   Chester *et al.*, *Zinoviev Letter*, was worked up from the *Sunday Times* articles of 1967, and has provided the basis for the foregoing account.
48   See for example Tom Jones's account of the last meeting of the Labour cabinet, in *Whitehall Diary*, i, 298–9.
49   Baldwin gratefully seized on hopes of peace in Ireland in 1914 when all the evidence pointed against it. See A. W. Baldwin, *My Father*, 78.
50   Keith Middlemas makes this point in van Thal, *The Prime Ministers*, ii, 268–9.
51   *The Times*, 5 Dec. 1924.
52   Young, *Baldwin*, 242.
53   Quoted in Glickman, 'Toryness of English Conservatism', 119–20.
54   Salisbury to Baldwin, 26 Jan. 1924: Baldwin MSS, vol. 159.
55   Quoted in Young, *Baldwin*, 43.
56   Middlemas and Barnes, *Baldwin*, 275.
57   *The Times*, 5 Dec. 1924.
58   National Union Conference minutes, Yarmouth Conference, 7 Oct. 1928.
59   *Gleanings and Memoranda*, Mar. 1924.
60   *Newcastle Journal*, 3 Oct. 1924.
61   Quoted in Glickman, 'Toryness of English Conservatism', 122.
62   *The Times*, 5 Dec. 1924.
63   *Cambridge Daily News*, 1 Mar. 1924.
64   *The Times*, 5 Dec. 1924.
65   Muggeridge, *The Green Stick*, 44.
66   Rowse, 'Reflections on Lord Baldwin' in *The End of an Epoch*; Nicolson, *Diaries and Letters*, ii, 307; did Baldwin know that he was once again quoting Kipling (from *Something of Myself*, 223)?
67   *Manchester Guardian*, 28 July 1924.
68   *The Times*, 5 Dec. 1924.
69   Quoted in Glickman, 'Toryness of English Conservatism', 141.
70   Baldwin, *On England*, 5.
71   Quoted in Baldwin, *My Father*, 172.
72   *Scotsman*, 25 Mar. 1924.
73   Quoted in Glickman, 'Toryness of English Conservatism', 140.
74   *Gleanings and Memoranda*, Mar. 1924.
75   Woods, *The History of the Tory Party*; Hill, *Toryism and the People*.
76   Glickman, 'Toryism of English Conservatism', 119.
77. A speech at Welbeck Abbey in 1927 was filmed for Pathe News with the caption 'over 72,000 listen to Mr Baldwin', *Pathe Gazette*, 1507.

Chapter 10

Organizing the New Conservatism

Party organization reflects not only the demands of a political situation but also the intentions of the party; it can even be said to mirror the party best of all, for in organizing itself a party is free to present itself to the outside world as it collectively chooses and to put forward the image by which it wishes to be known. So it was fitting that the penny-farthing organization of Derby's time should be run from the offices of a family solicitor and a West End club; it was equally fitting that Bonar Law's arrival should coincide with a more businesslike approach in the party. Similarly, the principles of the New Conservatism can be seen to have permeated every level of the party, through the agency of J. C. C. Davidson, a man who was as typical of Baldwin's regime as anyone.

Davidson was the son of a prominent surgeon, but by no means a wealthy man, and had served as political secretary to Loulou Harcourt and then to Bonar Law, before becoming Unionist MP for Hemel Hempstead in 1920. He became very close to Law and Baldwin when both worked at the Treasury from 1916 and 1918 and was PPS to Law when he was Prime Minister. He became even closer to Baldwin, and a warm personal and family friendship was developed, despite over twenty years difference in age.[1] Davidson was like a son to Baldwin and he represented in himself much of the new spirit that Baldwin was trying to instil into the party; he was young and active, fiercely moral in his attitude to politics, and well to the left of the party on social issues – but very much a realist. Like Baldwin, Davidson was convinced of the need to recruit from the left and from the young if the party were to survive in a democratic age; he was also determined to promote women at all levels of the party, perhaps made conscious of this great reservoir of potential Conservatism by his own wife, who was a zealous political activist, already a leader of the Conservatives of Hertfordshire and destined to succeed him as MP for Hemel Hempstead when he retired. Davidson was put forward for the Party Chairmanship by Younger in 1923 but was not considered by Law to be weighty enough for a key post. When Stanley Jackson was appointed Governor of Bengal in 1926 Davidson succeeded him as chairman; he was then thirty-seven and had had just two years of junior ministerial office. Baldwin was more sure about the appointment than Davidson himself, partly because the Chairmanship involved the sacrifice of income from government office, partly because he was aware that he had enemies who regarded him as no more than Baldwin's shadow. He finally accepted the post on Baldwin's insistence and was Chairman from 1926 to 1930.[2] The negative side of his character was perhaps less well known to Baldwin: he was a born intriguer, preferring to remain out of the limelight and to pull strings from behind the scenes, and he was intensely suspicious of the motives of others. These characteristics were to make him rather less successful at Central Office than he might have been, but there is no denying that he brought drive and enthusiasm to the task, or that he achieved a great deal.

The central pillar of organization was as always the provision of finance. Jackson's Chairmanship had not been a financial success; capital was spent to meet current costs and the system of management was not properly sorted out. The difficulties created by Lord Farquhar's refusal to part with the party funds in 1922 had been severe, but Farquhar had conveniently died early in 1923. Younger succeeded him as treasurer after he ceased to be Chairman and the party's capital was placed in three trusts, each with legally appointed trustees and provision for majority voting so that no individual could ever again hold the party to ransom. Income was channelled through a 'Chairman's account' and so, although most of it went on to the National Union account at Hoare's Bank for normal party purposes, there was a substantial fund available under the Chairman's own control. It was from this fund that Davidson paid off Donald im Thurn in 1927, and it was from this fund that discretionary payments were made to Conservative MPs in danger of bankruptcy or in other difficulties that might bring the party into disrepute.[3] This reorganization removed past difficulties but created a new one. Younger interpreted his new job narrowly and insisted that the party treasurer had no obligation to collect money for ordinary expenditure. This had some validity in past practice for Farquhar had done little fund-raising recently and Younger had had to do it as Chairman. Having at last escaped from the Chairmanship, he had no intention of carrying over part of its burdens to his new post; the most he would agree to do was to conduct an appeal when the next election should come. The raising of money thus reverted to the Party Chairman, although Davidson was able to secure the assistance of Albert Bennett MP as deputy treasurer in 1927. The final irony came when Younger died shortly before the 1929 election and so even the election appeal fell to Davidson.[4]

However, when Davidson and Bennett made a start on raising money in 1927, they were very successful indeed; Davidson's estimate was that he had raised over a million pounds in three years and although such large sums are not shown in the party accounts, he was probably broadly correct, for as well as the money that went directly to the party, more was spent from the

Chairman's account and appeals were raised for special purposes. The basic method was described to Neville Chamberlain:

> The City have already raised something like £150,000 and are continuing to raise further funds for the Party, for the simple reason that they are thoroughly frightened of a Socialist Government. The way the City was worked was that I went down to a private meeting, and told them that only big money was any good to me. The result was that at a lunch given in November by Hunsdon, £130,000 had already been raised in £5,000 subscriptions. Stanley made a speech on the dangers of Socialism to finance and credit, one of those inimitable little speeches so free from Party bias that you felt that the dangers seemed all the greater as no allowance had to be made for partisanship.[5]

After this auspicious beginning, about fifty industrialists worked for funds in centres outside London, to be encouraged by another dinner at which Baldwin would speak, this time with Londonderry in the chair. But this was poaching on the preserves of the local parties and Davidson had to reassure Neville Chamberlain that his method was for the best for the party as a whole, for 'it is a matter of common knowledge, however, that a man may be perfectly willing in the company of others similarly disposed to give £5,000 or £10,000 to a central fund who would think £500 an extravagance to his local association'.[6] The Londonderry dinner was finally held on 26 June 1929 for the general election appeal, but local criticisms were met by a rebate scheme, whereby a proportion of the money raised would be returned to the constituencies from whence it had come; this concession was more apparent than real, for only £1,484 in rebates was paid out of the £156,000 that was collected. Most of the money eventually went to the local parties to pay for their election campaigns, but it was dispensed by Davidson and not by the local parties themselves.[7]

The idea of getting businessmen together and then appealing to their capitalist solidarity, through the 'non-partisan' medium of Baldwin illustrates an assumption that could not have been made before 1914. In the 1920s, it could be assumed that owners of businesses were sufficiently committed to the Conservatives (or at least against Labour) to make such an appeal worthwhile. It was noted in 1927 that most of the businesses in Gravesend were now contributing to party funds and that several businessmen had been brought over by the Conservative–Liberal 'Municipal Committee' which had been set up to save the town from the Labour party. The Yorkshire coal-owners were equally unanimous in their support for the party by this time, although some of them had been Liberals right up to the General Strike.[8] Davidson's efforts made possible a great increase in the party's expenditure, from £180,000 in 1926 to £248,000 in 1928; expenditure on the 1929 general election was also very high at £297,000, twice the figure for 1922. This increase in expenditure is outlined in table 10.1.[9]

Table 10.1   Summary of expenditure, 1925–29

	1925	1926	1927	1928	1929
1. Central Office	£95,869	£85,399	£98,625	£106,591	£114,391
2. House of Commons Office	138	157	128	128	1,287
3. District agents	24,282	25,270	26,714	30,180	29,710
4. Special campaigns	14,354	18,782	21,682	17,661	12,459
5. Constituency grants	26,941	21,574	33,174	38,048	25,789
6. Grants to other organizations	675	1,024	657	1,639	922
7. London dept.	9,937	10,904	15,096	17,027	14,620
8. Junior Imperial League	3,335	3,547	6,658	7,950	5,460
9. Miscellaneous	11,255	13,541	12,734	19,199	30,231
	£186,791	£180,113	£216,675	£248,256	£234,875

Further appeals earmarked for specific purposes made possible other advances. When Davidson wished to entice Patrick Gower into the party service from the civil service, the negotiations had a frankly financial side; Gower pointed out that he would sacrifice a great deal by coming to Central Office: 'Now compensation for pension rights alone would cost close on £6,000. I know that I am asking a lot, but would it be possible to screw one of your rich friends up to putting down a lump sum of £10,000 in all?'[10] They compromised on £8,000, which Davidson raised from one 'rich friend' of the party, and Gower was thus acquired for the party for the rest of his working life. A similar method was used to launch a new party college at Ashridge, with the buildings paid for by one donor and an endowment fund of £200,000 raised from three others; Ashridge remained a party asset until the Second World War.

Davidson's success as a fund-raiser, like Steel-Maitland's, was based on personal appeals to the party's richest backers. The pattern naturally changed over the years; as the party became more closely associated with business, a change reflected in its personnel and its attitudes, business became a more important contributor. The next stage, whereby most business contributions became corporate rather than personal, recognized the changing character of business but did not reflect a change of support.

It remains to consider the question of honours and rewards, in view of J. C. C. Davidson's later assertion that he conducted a crusade against corrupt methods in high places.[11] Before 1914, Unionists criticized the Liberal government for corrupt practices and at the same time raised funds by awarding peerages in advance of their return to power. By the 1920s, Conservative attitudes had been affected by experiences under Lloyd George and they had to give at least the appearance of cleaning things. Conservatives indeed continued to disparage Lloyd George's methods even after his fall, drawing a rebuke from Augustine Birrell in 1927, who remarked that the Lloyd George Fund was 'one half – the other side has got the other half – of the Coalition swag, or booty, or loot'. Central Office was quick to claim that:

> the suggestion is without foundation and that as a matter of fact, there was no joint Coalition Fund. It is explained that the formation of the Coalition Government involved no changes in the financial arrangements of the Conservative Party. During the whole of the Coalition period, the finances of the Conservative wing were as separate as before from the funds of the Liberal wing of the Coalition. . . . Lord Younger . . . states that he has no knowledge of the origin of Mr. Lloyd George's Fund or the purpose for which it was subscribed, and at no time has he had any financial interest in it.[12]

With the exception of Farquhar's activities in his last months, this statement seems to be true. There never was a joint coalition fund and there was no joint selling of honours, but this disposes of only half of Birrell's charge: it was just as possible to sell honours independently of Lloyd George as to do so in collaboration with him, and this appears to be what was done. Younger's press release of 1927 was supplemented with a private letter to Baldwin, in which he explained exactly what he had done as Party Chairman:

> The Chairman . . . superintended the collection of annual subscriptions and the contributions occasionally made through the medium of the Honours List. I never, so to speak, sold an honour, nor did I ever make any bargains; but from time to time I did raise a substantial contribution and I agree with old Lord Salisbury that no great party can be run unless the Fund from time to time can be so strengthened. The charge against L.G. is not that he raised such subscriptions but that he used his position as P.M. to fill his own *political* coffers, while ours were placed in trust & solely used for the necessities of the Party to which the donor belonged.[13]

The distinction was a fine one, but no less vital for that; and the distinction was not between selling honours and raising contributions 'through the medium of the Honours List' but between trading honours with supporters and selling them on the open market. It was a distinction that Lloyd George could not grasp because it involved a view of the Conservative Party which he naturally did not share. Conservatives had always stressed their support for the great national institutions and many of them had come to see their own 'great party' as one of the institutions that must be preserved. It is only such an instinct that makes sense of the attitude of Younger and Bonar Law to Austen Chamberlain in 1922, and it was only a short step from there to a position where contributions to Conservative funds were regarded as a public service that could rank with donations to charity. The important criterion was thus the question of who received the honour and whether his subscription was a natural consequence of his views and his political position. The Lloyd George Fund was made up by selling honours to friends and enemies alike, as Lloyd George himself admitted,[14] so the theory could not be maintained that the honour could have come without the subscription or the subscription without the honour.

Evidence from the Unionist hierarchy during the coalition years supports this interpretation of what had been going on. From the start there was criticism of the disproportionate share of honours going to Lloyd George's nominees and of the indiscriminate methods of his agents. By 1920 George Younger was writing angrily to Bonar Law that the Coalition Liberals 'seem to be rolling in money and we certainly are not, and I mean to scan the Honours List very narrowly this year'.[15] On the day after the next list was published, Younger sent off a detailed analysis; after noting that the Coalition Liberals had got three peers out of four, ten baronets out of sixteen, and nineteen knights out of thirty-three, he went on to specific cases. Some of the men rewarded were most unsavoury types who would never have been rewarded on a Central Office list and, worst of all, the Coalition Liberals had actually sold an honour to the Conservative chairman in Ebbw Vale – 'poaching on our preserves with a vengeance'.[16] Nothing could more clearly illustrate the double standard inherent in Conservative attitudes to the Lloyd George Fund: for the Conservatives to sell honours to Conservatives was natural, but for the Liberals to sell honours to Conservatives was both undesirable and constitutionally dangerous. Moreover, Conservatives would exercise enough restraint to prevent the system from falling into abuse. Hence the outcry occasioned by Lloyd George's list of 1922 and the determination of Baldwin and Davidson to clean things up.

Davidson thus began a campaign against 'the blatant selling of honours for Party funds', but with the emphasis on the word 'blatant', for it is clear that Davidson shared Younger's double standard. He was certainly affronted by Lloyd George's methods, but he was more concerned to eradicate the abuses than to end the system itself. He thus directed his hostility towards Maundy Gregory and the other middlemen: 'Davidson regarded the elimination of Gregory and all that he stood for as a public duty.'[17] His tactics, apparently approved by Baldwin, were a good deal less straight than his motives: double agents were infiltrated into the Gregory network to destroy it from the inside by making sure that none of Gregory's nominees was ever honoured. A similar deviousness was detected by A. J. P. Taylor in Davidson's negotiations with Beaverbrook in 1929, in which Davidson promised an honour for Andrew Holt in return for cash, but did not deliver the goods. After the general election, Davidson returned the cheque to Beaverbrook with a virtuous letter denying that any bargain had been made, but in the meantime the Beaverbrook papers had been kept quiet during the election. Taylor concludes of this 'mysterious episode' that 'Holt did not receive a knighthood, and therefore no honour was sold', but 'money was paid. A knighthood was promised. Baldwin's claim to clean hands is hardly redeemed by the fact that the promise was not kept.'[18] A similar approach through T. P. O'Connor was treated with the same self-righteous disdain in 1927. No doubt Davidson believed that it was necessary to fight fire with fire when dealing with the middleman, but his own attitude was far less clear than his memoirs would suggest. The whole operation was rather less like the cleansing of an augean stable than the periodic clearing out of a rabbit hutch.

When Patrick Gower was brought over from the civil service in 1927, he demanded a knighthood as part of the transfer fee, and was duly knighted. Here an honour was sold for service if not for cash; and the 'rich friend' who put up the money to buy Gower out of the civil service was given a peerage. He is described only as 'a member of a famous tobacco-business family' in the Davidson memoirs, in an account that is far from complete; the Davidson papers make it clear that he was Sir Gilbert Wills, created Lord Dulverton in 1929.[19] There is the same ambivalence about the donations that funded the college at Ashridge. The Davidson memoirs make much of the fact that Davidson waited until Sir Edward Brotherton had been nominated for a peerage before asking him for money; this really makes little difference, for Brotherton got his peerage and the party got £100,000. Other donors for Ashridge were equally fortunate: Urban Broughton became Lord Fairhaven and Lord Inchcape became an earl.[20] The case of A. J. David, quoted anonymously in the Davidson memoirs, was as open an approach as many that were turned down with self-righteous indignation, as Davidson noted in a memorandum dictated after seeing David:

> SECRET. Mr. David called. He was very frank. He thinks that the great house which has done so much to build up the industrial prosperity of the British Empire in the East, both in India and China, should receive an honour and he wants a peerage. I think it might be a good thing if this were done not in the Party list but in the official list as a joint recommendation of the Secretary of State for the colonies and the Secretary of State for India. He wishes to become a subscriber to the Party, and would undertake to give £5,000 a year for twelve years.

Neither the India Office nor the Colonial Office would accept this scheme and so only the party list was left; the bundle of correspondence in Davidson's papers is marked simply 'Mr. David, Baronetcy; I.O., C.O., £30,000'.[21] It seems clear then that, apart from tidying up the worst excesses of the Lloyd George era, Davidson did not materially alter his party's attitude to honours. It is probably true that honours were never 'sold' and no explicit bargains were made, but then, if Younger is to be believed, the party had never done this. But subscribers received honours and quite a lot of honours went to the party's supporters, so the net result was not very different. Davidson's memoirs can be charitably explained as having been written much later, when the party's attitude really had changed.

The second pillar of organization was the provision of appropriate senior staff. Linlithgow was only Deputy Chairman for a short time and Lord Strathcona for only a few months in 1926, before Lord Stanley was appointed in 1927. Stanley was an MP, son of the Earl of Derby, and a young man who seemed destined for a brilliant political future; he was made Deputy

Chairman at Davidson's own request and given special responsibility for the Junior Imperial League and the Young Britons, the party's two youth movements. Over the next two years, relations remained good on the surface, but there was no personal warmth between Stanley and Davidson and a good deal of mutual suspicion. The chief bone of contention was the role of women in the party, about which Davidson cared deeply but to which Stanley was indifferent. The memorandum that Davidson dictated after they had met to discuss the matter in 1928 gives a good indication of their relationship and of how easily Davidson was made suspicious:

> I dined last night with Lord Stanley, and there was also present Mr. Topping. The impression I came away with after the discussion that followed dinner was that in spite of the fact that S[tanley], by combining the posts of Deputy Chairman of the Party and Chairman of the Junior Imperial League, placed the Junior Imperial League in a very favoured position, he was not prepared to admit the women to a similar position because it would interfere with his personal position. This was a very great disappointment to me because I had hoped that S[tanley] would have had enough vision to accept a proposal which was for the ultimate good of the Party, and would not have set himself up as a barrier, especially founded on self-interest. I have been too long in politics not to realise that 99% of the men in it adopt that attitude, but I had hoped that I had a lieutenant who shared in practice my own views on life. I fear however that the S[tanley] blood will out. I think I shall have to watch very carefully how the position develops during the next few months and how far the word loyalty in his vocabulary travels in the same direction as his father's. I noticed the use in the conversation of the word 'co-chairman' twice.[22]

This neurotic aide-memoire shows how completely relations had broken down by March 1928. In 1929 their letters barely concealed their mutual antipathy and Stanley publicly joined Davidson's critics after the general election defeat; in October 1929 Stanley proposed at the Executive of the National Union that the Party Chairman should no longer be *ex officio* chairman of that committee. Something at least was gained from Stanley's time at Central Office in the development of the idea of a deputy to the Chairman with defined responsibilities. When Stanley resigned, this was widened and Davidson at last got his way, for the new National Union rules of 1930 allowed for two Deputy Chairmen: Sir George Bowyer MP took over the responsibility for candidates that had been the Deputy Chairman's job ever since Sanders was appointed in 1918, and Lady Iveagh was given executive responsibility for the women's organization. This provided the Chairman with two authoritative assistants at the political level, with their duties sensibly divided, and this system remained until after the Second World War.[23]

Problems also arose over the Principal Agent and these involved equally difficult matters of ambition and protocol. The past seemed to show that things worked well when the head of the professional organization was himself a professional, the best example being Boraston between 1912 and

1920, but it was difficult to find a professional organizer who had the talents and authority for the highest office, as was shown when Boraston was replaced by William Jenkins in 1920. Jenkins had been a successful chief organization officer but he proved to be quite unfitted for command and had to be replaced after only a few months. The short-term problem was solved by appointing Sir Malcolm Fraser as principal agent, a man who had never engaged in constituency work but who had been at Central Office for ten years and earned the agents' respect by his skills as a publicist. Fraser's successor, Admiral Hall, had not been a success, and so he was again succeeded by a professional of sorts in Herbert Blain. Blain got on well with the agents and did a great deal for them, but his methods were not at all liked by the voluntary side of the party, some of whom resented the autocratic habits that he had brought with him from the world of business and the salary of £5,000 that had been necessary to get him to take the job.[24] Davidson was amongst those who did not get on with him, hardly surprising in view of their difference of approach, and according to his memoirs, his first task as party chairman was to remove the Principal Agent from office:

> If I erred, it may well have been because I pursued a policy of complete loyalty to the Leader who had appointed me. That was an unknown virtue to Sir Herbert Blain, and . . . at my first interview with him he behaved extraordinarily unwisely from his point of view; he made it quite clear that one of his main objects was to get rid of the Leader of the Party, whom he regarded as a semi-socialist, an attitude which showed he had no conception of the authority that Baldwin had after the victory of 1924. . . . I had a tremendous row with Blain on the first and only time that I saw him and talked to him, and dismissed him. He never came back to the office.[25]

This account, recorded over thirty years later by Davidson, makes a very good story but cannot have been very close to the truth. Blain was not sacked instantly and he was still working at Central Office until a week before the month's notice from his resignation expired. He had offered to resign in March 1926 but had been persuaded to stay on; by the end of the year when he left he had more or less completed the task for which he had been appointed. There may well have been a row between the two men, but it is unlikely that Blain had sufficient political interest to take such a strong line against Baldwin; more likely he was trying to impress on the new Chairman the feeling that was reported to him from the constituencies. Blain may have underestimated the authority in the nation that Baldwin had won in 1924, but Davidson was certainly underestimating the discontent in the party caused by Baldwin's actions in 1925 and 1926. Davidson expected doglike loyalty to Baldwin and was constantly disappointed to find that nobody else in the party seemed to feel it.

Whatever the reason for Blain's departure, the job was not easy to fill, for it raised again the question of whether or not to promote an agent from the ranks. The choice fell eventually on Leigh Maclachlan, an organizer of great experience who had begun as a Liberal Unionist agent and had been chief organizing agent since 1920. Maclachlan was near to retirement and was rapidly becoming deaf, so this could only be a temporary appointment, but it raised the agents' expectations and made the problem of his successor even more difficult. In one year of office, Maclachlan proved to be as unsuitable as Jenkins had been and yet could not be persuaded either to retire or to take a more active interest in the job. Davidson first suggested that Baldwin should demand reports from the principal agent on the work of the party in the hope that this would produce an improvement of what he called 'M's attitude' or a realization that he should give way to a younger man. In the end though Maclachlan had to be sacked, as Davidson told Stanley:

> As I look to the future I am convinced that a happy, cohesive team in the Central Office will have a great effect not only upon our colleagues in the House of Commons, but on the organisation in the country. I believe that Mac's methods make such a cohesive team an impossibility. He is unpopular with Members of Parliament, and he is regarded with disfavour by some and with ridicule by others of the Executive of the National Union and the leaders of the Party in the country. It was generally recognised that he was appointed as a stop-gap, and the date at which he vacates his post is entirely within my discretion to decide. That was one of the conditions of his appointment. I have come to the conclusion that his undoubted detailed knowledge of persons and practice of our Party organisation is counter-balanced and even outweighed by his lack of courage and initiative and his ineradicable love of intrigue.[26]

Davidson's choice for Maclachlan's successor was Robert Topping, the Central Office agent for the north-west and previously chief agent for Cardiff. Topping was recognized as one of the best of the professional agents, but the experiences of Jenkins and Maclachlan had created doubt about the wisdom of such an appointment. When Davidson wrote again to Stanley, he had to report that both Younger and Neville Chamberlain were opposed to Topping's promotion:

> Now, my dear Edward, what am I to do? Right throughout our organisation in the country and amongst our leading supporters in London and the Provinces, the post of Principal Agent is regarded first as a pivot appointment in the organisation of the Party, and second one which has not been held with the exception of Mac by any agent heretofore (*sic*). That is an attitude that only time can change. . . . Younger expressed the view quite unsolicited that the agents would welcome rather than resent the appointment of someone outside their own ranks. That is his view not mine.[27]

However, Davidson and Stanley stuck to their decision and Topping was appointed, but with reduced powers. In Stanley's words, 'there is no need for a superman as we have decided that in the future the P.A. is to be the head of a Dept. and not the "Managing Director" of the Party as he has been in the past'.[28] Davidson set out to forestall criticism by announcing the appointment at a dinner of the 1922 Committee, with Baldwin present to signify his support. Maclachlan wrote to Baldwin to resign, complaining rather pathetically that he had at least expected to be allowed to fight one election in charge, and Topping was offered the job 'in place of Sir Leigh Maclachlan who has resigned'. Concern for Topping's status was shown also by the promotion of Marjory Maxse to be deputy Principal Agent and by the purchase of Patrick Gower from the civil service. Topping, Gower and Miss Maxse, together with Joseph Ball, made up a strong team in command at Central Office, allowing the Party Chairman and his deputies to take on a more political role.[29]

Central Office had been much improved by Herbert Blain, both in its internal working and in its influence on the party. A new filing system and a comprehensive card-index of party activists and employees was set up in Blain's time and was still in use over forty years later. Blain was especially worried about the improvement that could be made in the 'derelict' constituencies and this could be undertaken only with a great deal of money, as Steel-Maitland had found. When money was not available, Blain wrote to Baldwin and threatened to resign:

> I would not have taken this step if I had been able to see a policy pursued in connection with the organisation which I regard as vitally essential, namely the establishment of Agents and an effective local organisation in the 50 or so derelict constituencies of England and Wales, a step which I have been urging practically ever since I undertook the work, and which you may remember I mentioned to you last November. These gaps in the official organisation may be the decisive factor in the next Election.[30]

Blain won his point and massive financial aid was given to the worst of the local parties. Early in 1928 there were twenty-seven trainees and sixteen acting agents all working in poor constituencies at the expense of Central Office.[31] Davidson expanded the programme as more money became available, but it originated with Blain. This all reveals an interesting attitude at Central Office, one that assumed that no constituency was unwinnable. The more sophisticated modern reason for fighting hopeless seats (to keep the enemy occupied at home) was not considered; it was only after the elections of 1929 and 1931 that Central Office recognized that the new two-party system had come to stay and so adopted a 'trench-warfare' view of elections, regarding some seats as safe, others as hopeless and a third group as the 'no-man's-land' that would decide the result. Hence it was in 1930 and after that the worst constituencies were grouped together for the first time, in East London, South Wales, Durham and South Yorkshire, so that a skeleton organization and a presence could be maintained without undue cost. In 1929 though the party put up 590 candidates, its largest number at any election between 1910 and 1945, and there was an agent and an organization in almost every constituency. The nature and scale of this improvement in Central Office activities is demonstrated in tables 10.2 and 10.3; such expansion of effort required more money and far more staff.[32]

Much of the improvement was carried out through the Central Office

Table 10.2   Summary of Central Office expenditure, 1926–1929

	1926	1927	1928	1929
Chairman's department	£414	£1,729	£1,049	£851
Organization department	9,150	7,467	7,234	7,357
Speakers' department	7,618	8,696	5,936	5,141
Publicity departments	22,269	29,586	49,599	49,786
Finance department and National Union Secretary	6,088	5,494	2,611	3,837
Women's department	7,547	8,664	11,853	11,161
Rent, rates etc.	9,422	11,090	12,568	15,219
General administration	22,887	25,874	24,759	21,740
	£85,399	£98,625	£106,591	£114,391

Table 10.3   Number of staff employed at Central Office

	1926	1927	1928	1929
Organization and administration	60	75	123	127
Publicity departments	43	65	54	50
Women's department	16	15	29	22
	144	185	228	218

agents, working as before as channels for organizational and financial aid. Major Thornton, Central Office agent for Yorkshire, made extravagant claims to Neville Chamberlain's investigating committee in 1930, but these claims were backed by Geoffrey Ellis, a member of the committee and chairman of the National Union in Yorkshire:

> The Constituency Organisation of the Party has undoubtedly improved out of all recognition during the last seven years, and this has been due to a large extent, in my opinion, to the influence that the Central Office Agents have been able to exercise in the constituencies. . . . I was able to get a large measure of control in the County. In fact, no Constituency meetings were held without an invitation being extended to me, and no Agents were appointed except in consultation with me.[33]

A similar influence was exerted in other parts of the country by the better Central Office agents, like T. W. Ainge in the south-west and Robert Topping in the north-west. Topping attended a meeting of the Darwen Conservative Association in 1924 and told them that 'previous to the War, the work of registration was considered all important, but since the termintion of the War, it has been fully recognised that Organisation and Propaganda are of equal, if not greater importance; and that such should be continuous rather than occasional'.[34] On Topping's advice the Darwen Conservatives sacked their agent as 'unsuitable . . . in . . . the altered conditions of the electorate', and Topping was also present at the next meeting to make sure that a suitable man was appointed to fill the vacancy. One piece of evidence to the Chamberlain Committee in 1930, seemingly from Maclachlan, regretted the new mood of interventionism in Central Office agents and suggested that it was unwelcome in the local parties. The Committee did not agree: 'The men's side seems to be a little afraid of what they term "interference with local autonomy" but from the evidence produced . . . we are satisfied that where the ground is covered and tact is employed, Central Office advice and assistance is, as rule, welcomed.'[35] This makes the essential point: advice was welcome if it came along with assistance, and aid could be given with strings attached. In the four years from 1926 over £136,000 passed from the party funds to the local parties through the Central Office agents, but 51 per cent of this was for the payment of professional speakers nominated by Central Office. A further 10 per cent was given in the form of literature, so only 39 per cent was given in cash; even much of this last proportion was earmarked for the payment of agents and would be given only if a suitably qualified man was appointed at the right salary. There were classes at the Central and district offices for amateur speakers; once again aid was given only on terms dictated by Central Office itself.[36]

The expansion of activities necessitated a reconsideration of the internal structure of Central Office. Davidson's aim was the separation of 'operations' from 'organization', so that new methods could be used without their coming under 'the dead hand of the agents'. Lord Stanley headed a small investigating committee and recommended a tripartite structure; this was implemented in 1928 and is outlined in table 10.4.[37]

Table 10.4   Internal structure of Central Office, 1928–30

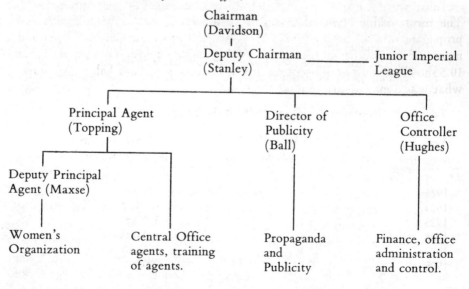

This new system enabled Davidson to get away with the promotion of Topping, for he would be no more than first among equals, but it was not very successful. Within two years another investigating committee under Neville Chamberlain found that it had led to confusion and to unnnecessary duplication and division. The system was again centralized in 1930 and Topping became 'General Director' – which is exactly what Davidson and Stanley had sought to avoid. Topping held this post until 1945 and did much to shape the direction of the party throughout this time.[38]

So the deliberations of the Stanley and Chamberlain Committees had illustrated a new problem that Central Office was beginning to pose to the Party Chairman as its activities increased in scope. It had become more effective but was now suffering from all the strains that are inherent in a large organization. The staff, which had been so tiny in 1910, had grown to over two hundred, and with another fifty or so scattered about the country in eleven district offices. It would be surprising if Central Office agents did not sometimes resist a plan of which they disapproved by pleading entrenched local opposition, or if departments in Central Office did not use their specialized knowledge for the same purpose. It had been necessary to sack Philip Cambray in 1927 for intriguing in the office behind the Chairman's back and this had been another reason for the removal of Maclachlan and Blain. It was becoming difficult to exert the authority of Central Office as a united force in the party because it had become too large to have a united view. By 1930 Central Office had become an entrenched bureaucratic force in the party, set against the social and political forces represented by the National Union and the parliamentary party.[39]

The most visible signs of organizational advance were in publicity and propaganda. In the production of literature, better staff at Central Office and increased availability of money led to a veritable explosion of output. Table 10.5 shows the output of literature for normal purposes and Table 10.6 shows what was done for the general election.[40]

Table 10.5   Production of literature, 1923–28 (excluding elections)

Year	Leaflets produced (millions)	Monthly circulation of party magazines
1923	1.5	46,000
1924	8.1	187,000
1925	5.3	360,000
1926	6.8	450,000
1927	19.4	500,000
1928	9.7	500,000

Table 10.6   Literature produced for general elections, 1910–29

Year	Leaflets (millions)	Posters
1910 (Jan.)	46	1.1
1910 (Dec.)	40	0.9
1918	5	n.a.
1922	18	0.3
1923	26	0.3
1924	36	0.5
1929	93	0.4

The peak in production in 1927 was the result of a special campaign in favour of the Trades Disputes Act of that year, a campaign which alone involved the circulation of nine million leaflets.[41] The reduced use of posters reflects the move towards new forms of visual aid and was more than compensated in any case by the number of leaflets; in 1929 Central Office actually sold to candidates more than four leaflets for each elector, and this in addition to election addresses and other literature that was produced locally. This outpouring can be contrasted with the situation since 1945: the highest output from Central Office since 1945 has been 19 million leaflets and 200,000 posters in 1945, and this had shrunk to a mere 6½ million leaflets and 31,000 posters by 1970.[42] The 1920s was the heyday of political literature and there was a large subsidy in the literature that the party produced; there was an annual loss of about £6,000 on literature services and the entire cost of the central administration of the scheme was paid for from party funds too. There were as always some complaints about the quality of the literature and its price, complaints somewhat belied by the quantity that the local parties and candidates actually bought.

Quality improved as well as quantity. The *Westminster Library* began to appear in 1925, cashing in on the new popularity of cheap paperbacks; these were detailed accounts of party policy and other political issues, much along the lines of what the Left Book Club were to produce in the 1930s. The party also pushed sales of Baldwin's speeches, both in pamphlet form and hardback reprints. *On England* went through many editions and eventually appeared as a paperback in the Penguin list too. Baldwin's name also helped to sell the most popular single publication, a reprint of his three speeches of 1925 on *Peace in Industry*. Leaflets were made more attractive in presentation through the advice of an advertising agency, S. H. Benson.[43]

The party magazines shared in this general upgrading in several forms: *Popular View* became *Man in the Street* in June 1924, and was also issued in different covers as *Home and Politics* (for sale to the women's organization) and as *The Imp* (for the Junior Imperial League). As a mass circulation monthly magazine it could draw on contributions from the most eminent men and women in the party; in 1925 the National Union asked for 'one or two good articles' in each issue and during the 1924–29 government twelve cabinet ministers and eight other ministers wrote articles about their work. At the same time the higher level of local activity produced more material on which to draw and a larger potential readership. They could therefore include nature notes, recipes, fashion items and social calendars, as well as political comment. An article by Neville Chamberlain on the plans of the Ministry of Health was thus sandwiched between anecdotes about canvassing practice and biographical notes on provincial party worthies. This was valuable because, although most copies of the magazines were sold in local editions, this was not usually made clear. *Man in the Street* was sold by the Banbury Conservatives as *The Popular View in North Oxfordshire*, with outside pages and a cover printed in Banbury; this made it appear that cabinet ministers were writing regularly for a local magazine and produced a far more impressive magazine than could ever have been produced by the local party on its own. By 1928, there were 144 local editions, all enjoying the same ambiguous status.[44]

Management of the press presented a different problem from that before 1914. It was no longer sufficient to keep the newspapers alive and in the hands of owners who were prepared to call themselves Conservatives. Central Office generally backed the Berry brothers in the battle that was taking place to buy up the provincial press, because they were less risk than either Beaverbrook or Rothermere. So in 1928 Davidson was concerned that Rothermere might get hold of the *Derby Express* and helped to persuade Sir William Berry to buy it instead. William Berry was also consulted by Davidson on matters of party strategy in the publicity field in the run-up to the 1929 election, and in return Berry suggested himself for a peerage. Davidson agreed that Berry's services merited reward but suggested that it might be better if it was delayed until the election was over. Berry became Lord Camrose in the resignation honours list. Even hostile newspapers, as the *Daily Express* had become, could still be managed by working through their editors rather than their proprietors: in 1927 Davidson not only suggested to R. D. Blumenfeld that the *Express* should send a reporter to Central Office from time to time but suggested one who would be acceptable. In reply Blumenfeld reminded Davidson that it was Central Office not the paper that had broken off relations, and agreed to resume them on the old amicable terms.[45] The most reliable paper was the *Morning Post*, in the 1920s glorying in the final triumph of its anti-coalitionism. The editor from 1911 until the paper merged with the *Daily Telegraph* in 1937 was H. A. Gwynne, a staunch Conservative and a strong party man, and the paper had been bought in 1924 by a group of Conservatives headed by the Duke of Northumberland. So close was the *Morning Post* to the party line that the National Union asked in 1927 if there was any direct connection: 'It was pointed out that the Party had no official connection with the paper, although its success was desired as it was the one staunch paper upon which reliance could be placed to put forward the programme of the Party.'[46] It is possible that party money was keeping the *Morning Post* going, but more likely that close relations with its editor and owners ensured a genuine identity of outlook.

The regional pattern of the Unionist press presented special problems for the party after the First World War; there had been a great reduction in the number of local papers and especially in the south-eastern third of England, where they were in direct competition with the national dailies from London. This area had only one local Unionist daily paper, in Brighton, and weekly papers were a poor substitute. Hence Davidson's plea to Gwynne for the active support of the *Morning Post* for the party in the London County Council elections of 1928. The local papers that survived and were kept out of the hands of the press lords were usually dependent on other sources, often local party leaders: so the *North Berkshire Herald* was only saved for Abingdon Conservatives 'through the generosity of our member', the MP for East Wolverhampton had to give money to keep the *Wolverhampton Evening Post* going, and the *Darwen Gazette* also depended on the local MP. One applicant for an honour in 1936 calculated that the *Norfolk Chronicle* had cost him over £14,000 in the past four years, and all this 'at the request of Central Office'. Samuel Roberts was given very little choice in the matter when he was MP for Hereford:

> The editor of the Hereford Times came to see me and told me that the owner of the paper had not been getting any income from it and wanted to sell it. He suggested – and here comes the blackmail – that the Cocoa Press would pay a large price in order to combine the [two local] papers, get rid of competition, and run the newspaper in the Radical interest. He also told me that he had been in touch with the Harmsworths, who at the recent by-election had supported my opponent.... In fact if either of these sales took place, the press in the County was bound to be hostile, but [he] would prefer to sell the paper to me, and asked for £25,000.[47]

Roberts was in fact very lucky: he was able to persuade his local party chairman to put up half of the capital required, he improved the running of the paper and so made both an income and a capital profit on it, and he was able to keep secret the fact that he owned it, so that he was able to write anonymous editorials in a newspaper in his own constituency. Few other MPs were so fortunate, but many others were as involved. When Stanley Jackson became a minister in 1922, he asked Bonar Law if he need resign as a director of the *Yorkshire Post*, 'a purely Conservative paper, and the shareholders are limited to people of our views'. Criticism of the local press at Harborough was quickly stilled when the association chairman announced that he was also chairman of the *Leicester Mail*. So, many local papers were kept alive, and in most towns where there had been two rival party newspapers before 1914, it was the Liberal paper that had gone by 1939; among other places this happened in Sheffield, Leeds, Cardiff, Liverpool and Bristol. Although the local press had shrunk considerably, Central Office was still supplying about

230 newspapers on the Conservative side in 1927.[48]

Publicity in the 1920s also involved the use of techniques that had not been available before the First World War; one reason for getting rid of Maclachlan was that he was 'ignorant of the possibilities of the new forms of propaganda'. Baldwin made expert use of the radio, and Amery believed that it was the middle-class ownership of radios and cars that made possible the defeat of the General Strike. The National Union too recognized the value of the radio during the strike and instructed the Chairman to 'convey verbally to Mr. Reith a message of the Committee's appreciation of the work of the B.B.C. during the General Strike'; it also saw that it would be better not to make its appreciation public. By 1929 elaborate and early preparations were being made for the use of radio during the election.

The same readiness to see new opportunities can be detected in the case of film, already a medium that could attract a far wider audience than public meetings or the written word. From 1923 Baldwin made shrewd use of the newsreels to put across the image of a calm and confident man; by the 1930s and the advent of sound he was a skilled performer who invariably appeared to good effect in comparison with opponents. Party propaganda films were pitched at any appropriate level, from a cartoon about Labour policy ('Red Tape Farm', a curious pre-echo of George Orwell) to Baldwin introducing George Arliss delivering four of Disraeli's greatest speeches. The commercial circuits were not open to overt propaganda and so the party had to devise its own methods for getting its films to the public. Davidson was especially keen on the use of mobile cinema vans that could be used in daylight; a free cinema was always certain of a large audience and in towns the vans could usually attract a daily audience of about two thousand. The party had only one van in 1927, but ten by the end of 1928 and twenty-two by the time of the 1931 election. Costs were high, over £13,000 in 1928, and a special Conservative and Unionist Films Association was formed to raise money in the London Clubs in 1931. In all these areas, as in the use of advertising consultants, the party was the least conservative of all in the adoption of new techniques.[49]

A minor sideshow in the propaganda battle concerned intelligence and political espionage. Forward planning could only be carried out with success if the party had advance knowledge of its leader's actions, but it would be better if it had advance knowledge of opponents' actions too. This Davidson set out to achieve:

> With Joseph Ball I ran a little intelligence service of our own, quite separate from the Party organization. We had agents in certain key centres and we also had agents actually in the Labour Party Party Headquarters, with the result that we got their reports on political feeling in the country as well as our own. We also got advance 'pulls' of their literature. This we arranged with Odhams Press, who did most of the Labour Party printing, with the result that we frequently received copies of their first leaflets and pamphlets before they reached Transport House. This was of enormous value to us because we were able to study Labour Party

policy in advance, and in the case of leaflets we could produce a reply to appear simultaneously with their production.[50]

This was all in keeping with the spirit that had exploited the Zinoviev Letter and the unofficial connections that remained between Central Office and MI5. The same spirit ensured that Central Office had at least a day's notice of the announcement of a general election from Baldwin when he was Prime Minister; in some places this enabled agents to lay on their meetings where they wanted and then to book so many halls that their opponents were forced out into the suburbs.

Davidson also placed great emphasis on the need for political education, aided by the existence of a party college and by services provided from Central Office. The Library and Information service employed thirty-two members of staff and its services were available to all members of the party for an annual subscription of a guinea. The Information Department issued skeleton speeches, background information on Labour and Liberal candidates, help in writing letters to the press, and even advice on National Insurance problems. The most expensive service was the library of press cuttings, occupying the time of sixteen members of staff servicing two million cuttings. All these resources were available to party members who had been trained as voluntary speakers, for an increasing emphasis was placed on them and the corps of professional speakers on the Central Office payroll was being run down. Speakers were trained at evening classes and on weekend courses at the college at Overstone, presented to the party by Sir Philip Stott in 1922. By 1927 the Stott College was being used by about a thousand students a year, each paying about £7 for a week or weekend course, many of them sent at the expense of their local party. By that stage it was already too small for the party's needs and so Davidson secured the new college at Ashridge, opening in the summer of 1929 as the Bonar Law Memorial College. In all these fields the stress was placed on helping the voluntary members of the party to become more active and more politically aware, an essential part of Baldwin's concern to use the party itself as a means of political education[51].

Under the aegis of Central Office, and especially of Herbert Blain, the professional party agents took a long step forward in the 1920s towards the achievement of a full professional status. Improvement had gone on ever since the change from lawyer-agents in the early years of the century, but it was the reshuffle of agents in 1924 and decisions taken in Blain's time that made the real difference. By the 1930s Conservative agents had professional standing in their own eyes, in the official eyes of the party and in the eyes of outsiders. This advance can be traced through several features common to the professions: a professional journal, pensions, a qualification and examination system, equality within the profession, and financial status.

The *Conservative Agents' Journal* was a useful symbol, and it was also an important influence towards professionalisation in its own right. After it resumed publication in 1910 under T. H. Packer, it gradually built up its subscriptions, open only to members of the National Society of Agents. By the First World War it was financially viable, and in 1919 it became a monthly, available to anyone in the party. The content of the *Journal* gives a good indication of the changing work and interests of the party agents, set down in table 10.7.[52] In the early years of the century, the *Journal* had been filled with technical accounts of hearings in registration courts; since it was based on voluntary contributions, the change in content reflects a genuine change in agents' interests. By the 1920s it was filled with reports of agents' meetings, notes on propaganda and fundraising methods, and social information from the profession.

Table 10.7   Content of the Conservative Agents' Journal

Year	Percentage of total copy devoted to registration
1902	33
1908	32
1913	16
1920	11
1924	7
1929	4

The *Journal* also played a key role in the evolution of a proper national body to represent the agents; it is no coincidence that both the major developments in this direction were taken when editors of the *Journal* were chairmen of the National Society of Agents, for this was the only way that an agent could build up a real national reputation when the profession was still run by separate regional groups. Packer brought the regions together into a national body in 1904 and Elton Halliley, the agent for Bury St Edmunds and editor of the *Journal* for over twenty years from 1920, played the same role in 1925. Before 1925 membership of the National Society was left for the provincial bodies to determine by their own rules, and these differed widely; an agent who qualified in Bristol might lose his qualification by accepting a job in Newcastle. Officers of the National Society were nominated by the provincial groups in rotation and held office for one year only, which militated against the selection of the best men and against any sort of continuity. Blain persuaded the National Society to elect Halliley as chairman in 1925, even though it was the turn of the Welsh agents to nominate, because he intended to use the National Society to raise the status and efficiency of the agents and needed a strong chairman to assist him. During his year of office, Halliley arranged for a complete revision of the rules; the absolute rotation of offices was abandoned, and a uniform national qualification for membership was agreed. Henceforth, the National Society was the recognized spokesman for all the agents and its officers were well-known party figures in their own right.[53]

A pension scheme is important for a professional body because so much of its status derives from the job rather than its remuneration. The first Benevolent Fund had been set up in 1892, but it was an uneasy compromise between a charity and a pension fund; in 1902 it had only seventy members and it was never financially self-supporting. A real pension scheme was promised to the agents by Acland-Hood in 1907, when he recognized the need to persuade the local parties to pay an employers' contribution into the fund. This was finally instituted by Steel-Maitland in 1913 and about 250 agents had joined, with the support of their local parties, when the war intervened. It then fell away again, so that by 1923 there were only 117 contributing members. Blain had just the right talents, for he had set up a local government pension scheme in his days with NALGO. Malcolm Fraser had collected £6,000 in 1923 to save the old Benevolent Fund from bankruptcy, and Blain now proposed to use this, together with the assets of the 1913 pension fund, to launch a proper superannuation scheme. Previously, the pension had been paid at a flat rate of £75 a year irrespective of years of service or of contributions; now there would be a sliding scale with pensions up to £225 a year. Central Office employed actuaries to work out a detailed proposal and it was accepted by the National Society in 1926, another fruit of the close relations of Blain and Halliley. Central Office then put a great deal of pressure on the local parties to enrol their agents, and one of Blain's last tasks at Central Office was to send out a directive to the recalcitrant constituencies, urging them to join the scheme. When Central Office gave financial assistance to constituencies for an agent, it was a condition of such assistance that the man employed should join the pension scheme.[54]

The creation of an examination system was more contentious. From the earliest days the National Society had issued certificates to its members, but these were not worth much when only the agents themselves recognized them. There was nothing to stop the local parties ignoring certificates altogether and letters to the *Journal* regularly complained about the appointment to plum jobs of ex-officers who could afford to take a lower salary because of their service pension. In 1924 the National Society set up an examination scheme and resolved to give certificates only to those who passed. Here Blain stepped in and persuaded them to accept a system that still exists today. A Committee on the Status and Efficiency of Agents discussed the matter and set up a new joint examining board, composed equally of the representatives of the National Union, the National Society and Central Office. The National Society's Council accepted the scheme by only twelve votes to seven, for many agents feared that they were losing control of their own profession, but the outcome was exactly the opposite: Central Office (made up mainly of ex-agents) and the agents made up two-thirds of the new examining board, and the lay members could take little part in the actual setting and marking of papers. At the same time the presence of the National Union, representing the agents' employers, compelled them to respect the certificates that the board awarded. Central Office integrated its training methods into the new scheme, so that the final examination could only be taken by agents who had passed a preliminary test and spent some time as a trainee with an experienced agent. The college at Ashridge was used for training courses for agents as well as for the rest of the party. Inevitably, the new system took a generation to have its full effect. In 1926 certificates were awarded without examination to any agent who had been in post for more than four years; the worst had already been weeded out in 1924, and it is not very likely that the senior agents in the National Society would have submitted themselves to an examination, so a compromise was reached for the present and the tough new rules instituted for the future. Pressure on local parties seems to have been effective, and almost all vacancies that were advertised after 1926 were for 'certificated agents'; by 1937 there were 352 certificated agents and 99 certificated women organizers in the 512 constituencies of England and Wales. The 1933 *Handbook on Constituency Organisation* stated optimistically that:

> It is now generally recognised that efficient Constituency Organizations can only be maintained by the employment of full-time qualified officials. There has been for some time a growing movement to establish the position of Agents and Women's Organisers on a professional basis, and to ensure that their positions should, as far as possible, be made permanent, with suitable remuneration and provision for pensions. Preliminary and Final Examinations are held for suitable applicants . . . and Constituency Associations are recommended only to employ those who have received the certificate of the Examining Board. The National Union . . . has decided that only those so qualified will in future be recognised as Constituency Agents or Women Organisers by the official Party Organisation.

As a statement of fact this was premature, but it was on the way towards attainment. In June 1947, nearly 90 per cent of the party's agents were men who held certificates, and by then most had their certificates through examination rather than seniority.[55]

Changes in attitudes towards professional equality were also a long process and for some a painful one. In 1913 a letter to the *Journal* from 'an old agent' reprimanded one of his junior colleagues for using the address 'Mr' on his printed letterhead, since it was argued that only men of experience should do so. Similarly, there was a lively correspondence in the 1920s about who exactly was entitled to the letters FNS, an ancient honour meaning Fellow of the National Society; the net effect seems to have been that the practice died out altogether, and the acceptance of uniform membership rules in 1925 gradually brought about the acceptance of equality within the profession. In 1930 there was some anxiety when an agent was refused permission to join his local rotary club, and it was argued that this refusal impugned the standing of the entire profession. The blow was softened somewhat when it was explained that the rules of rotary prevented more than one member of any one occupation from joining a branch and that they could not allow the agent of one party to join to the exclusion of others without appearing to take sides. In 1938 the rules were changed to admit a special category of 'agents, political', so that clubs could admit one agent from each party on the analogy of clergymen from different denominations. It is doubtful whether many agents of other parties ever availed themselves of this right, but the Conservative agents regarded it as a proper recognition of their status.[56]

Financial standing is the most difficult of all to assess, because of the wide range that existed; there was not even a recommended national pay scale until after the Second World War, and each local party was free to pay their agent as little as he would accept. In 1910 there were reports of over two hundred applicants for a job that paid £250 a year, which suggests that this was well above average. The average income was more like £150, although some were still paid £100 or less. In 1915 there were protests against the cutting of salaries in wartime because some agents in the north were said to be already on the poverty line. Inflation had its effect, so that the Central Office model constituency budget of 1919 allowed £350 for the agent's salary (though this was hardly realistic since it allowed also for an income of £1,000 to the association). Horror stories of badly paid agents continued to appear in the *Journal*, but the Committee on the Status and Efficiency of Agents in 1925 made some improvements, as did supply and demand; after 1926 the local parties were under pressure to appoint only certificated agents, and these were always in short supply. By 1930 the lowest advertised posts offered £300, three times the lowest level of 1910 although the cost of living had barely doubled. The typical salary of the 1930s was more like £400 and there were usually additional bonuses such as a car, clerical assistance (often paid for out of the agent's salary in 1910), free accommodation and incremental payments. Fees for acting as election agents had been much reduced in 1918, but these now always came to the constituency agent rather than to an outsider. The average real income in the 1930s may have been about £500 a year, very roughly three times the average weekly wage of the time. It is doubtful if agents have ever been so well off since.[57]

The process of professionalization has been described mainly from the agents' point of view because their attitudes were crucial to the whole process. Without a readiness to accept the transformation of their job, the change could not have been made, and all the efforts of Packer and Steel-Maitland, or Blain and Halliley, would have been wasted. From the centre the purpose was not entirely altruistic: Blain wanted to set up a pension scheme, improve agents' pay and conditions, and force them into a truly professional body because this would make them a more useful asset to the party. Professionalization inevitably brought some loss of freedom for the voluntary side of the party, but this was the price of efficiency.

In 1930 the agents won a contest with the National Union that demonstrated their new position for all to see. A new set of rules for attendance at the party conference and at Central Council were drawn up, and these did not allow specifically for the attendance of the agents. Previously every constituency could send its 'principal paid agent or secretary' in what was effectively an extra place on its delegation, but under the new provisions agents would have to compete for their places with other members; since agents usually attended at the local party's expense, while most other delegates paid for themselves, they could not even compete on equal terms. The problem was more serious than it might appear, because the party conference was the only meeting of the entire profession that took place in the normal party year; along with the other conference activities went the AGM of the National Society, an agents' dinner, meetings for the pension fund and other business meetings. About four hundred agents had attended in 1928 and 1929, although critics alleged that they had spent more of their time in the bars than in the conference hall. Official protests were lodged by the National Society and by individual agents to their local parties. In May 1930 the National Union proposed a compromise whereby agents would automatically qualify to attend, but without the right to vote. When the new rules came before a special conference in June, even the non-voting clause was dropped, and the agents won a complete victory.[58]

Developments in the professional organization under Blain and Davidson had made it a more businesslike and effective adjunct to the party, well within Baldwin's view of how the party should develop. Conversely, the advances made in the local parties stressed the moderate, participatory and unprovocative side of the New Conservatism.

Notes and References

1 Davidson, *Memoirs of a Conservative*, 83–4.
2 *Ibid*, 262–3, 462–7.
3 *Ibid*, 276–7; chequebook counterfoils are in the Davidson MSS.
4 *Ibid*, 264–5; Ramsden, 'Organisation' (thesis), 129.
5 Davidson to Neville Chamberlain, 8 Jan. 1929: Davidson MSS.
6 *Ibid*.
7 Party accounts for 1929: Davidson MSS.
8 *Conservative Agents' Journal*, Oct. 1923; Yorkshire Area Finance Committee minutes, 31 Aug. 1928.
9 Compiled from Party accounts for 1926–29 in the Davidson MSS.
10 Gower to Davidson, undated [1928], Davidson MSS: an exaggerated account of these negotiations is in Davidson, *Memoirs of a Conservative*, 271.
11 Davidson, *Memoirs of a Conservative*, 278–88.
12 *Gleanings and Memoranda*, Mar. 1927.
13 Younger to Baldwin, 27 Aug. 1927: Davidson MSS.
14 Davidson, *Memoirs of a Conservative*, 279.
15 Younger to Law, 24 Dec. 1920: Law MSS 99/8/17.
16 Younger to Law, 2 Jan. 1921: printed in full in Beaverbrook, *The Decline and Fall of Lloyd George*, 241–3.
17 Davidson, *Memoirs of a Conservative*, 280.
18 Taylor, *Beaverbrook*, 257–8.
19 Davidson, *Memoirs of a Conservative*, 271; the letter to Davidson sending the cheque is from 'Gilbert' at 26 Wilton Crescent, the home of Sir Gilbert Wills.
20 Ramsden, 'Organisation', 346–7.
21 'Note of Interview with A. J. David', 9 Oct. 1928: Davidson MSS.
22 Memorandum by Davidson, 13 Mar. 1928: Davidson MSS.
23 Ramsden, 'Organisation', 118.
24 Younger to Davidson, 5 Nov. 1926, Davidson MSS.
25 Davidson, *Memoirs of a Conservative*, 265–6.
26 Davidson to Stanley, 17 Jan. 1928: Davidson MSS.
27 Davidson to Stanley, 25 Jan. 1928: Davidson MSS.
28 Stanley to Davidson, 27 Jan. 1928: Davidson MSS.
29 Ramsden, 'Organisation', 125.
30 *Ibid*, 293; Blain to Baldwin, 25 Mar. 1926: Baldwin MSS, vol. 53, file 6.
31 List of Central Office Staff, 1927: Davidson MSS.
32 Compiled from party accounts and lists of staff: Davidson MSS.
33 Evidence to the Chamberlain Committee: Templewood MSS, box VI, file 3.
34 Darwen Conservative Association minutes, 8 May 1924.

35 Chamberlain Report, 1930: Baldwin MSS, vol. 53, file 4.
36 Party accounts: Davidson MSS.
37 Stanley Report, 1928: Baldwin MSS, vol. 53, file 4.
38 Blake, *Conservative Party*, 231–2.
39 See Pinto-Duschinsky, 'Central Office and "Power" in the Conservative Party'.
40 Reports to National Union Central Council, 1910–1929.
41 National Union minutes, Central Council, 28 June 1927.
42 Butler and Pinto-Duschinsky, *The British General Election of 1970*, 312.
43 Ramsden, 'Organisation', 227–8.
44 *Ibid*, 229–30.
45 *Ibid*, 236.
46 *Gleanings and Memoranda*, May 1924; National Union minutes, Executive Committee, 12 Apr. 1927.
47 Ramsden, 'Organisation', 240; Samuel Roberts's Autobiographical Memorandum.
48 Ramsden, 'Organisation', 241.
49 *Ibid*, 264–5; Beattie, Dilks and Pronay, *Neville Chamberlain*.
50 Davidson, *Memoirs of a Conservative*, 272.
51 Ramsden, 'Organisation', 258–9.
52 Compiled from the total contents of the *Conservative Agents' Journal* for the specified years, using normal methods of content analysis.
53 Fawcett, *Conservative Agent*, 33–4; Ramsden, 'Organisation', 315–16.
54 Ramsden, 'Organisation', 316–18.
55 *Ibid*, 319–21.
56 *Ibid*, 305, 321; the position of Rotary was clarified for the author in 1970 by the secretary of Rotary International, Mr J. H. Jackson.
57 *Ibid*, 321–3.
58 National Union minutes, National Society of Agents minutes, and *Conservative Agents' Journal*, Feb. to May 1930.

Chapter 11

Local Conservatism in the 1920s

Throughout their history, local Conservative parties have been jealous guardians of their independence, and although some concessions were made towards efficiency and uniformity in the 1920s independence remained the keynote. As always, the chief support of independence was financial. Central Office gave help to poor constituencies but never commanded sufficient resources to allow it to encroach on the majority; the total running costs of the local parties were about double the expenditure of Central Office, most of which was required in any case to pay for central administration. In finance at least, the local parties were usually left to their own devices.

The end of the First World War and the 1918 redistribution of seats provided a financial watershed as local organizers prepared their plans for a resumption of normal politics. Most drew up plans that were far more ambitious than those of 1914. The new association for Cirencester and Tewkesbury decided from the start that they would not ask their candidate for a subscription or to pay for his election expenses; they were only untypical in keeping to their decision. Most good intentions of 1918 and 1919 were shattered by the party difficulties of the coalition years, when the mood of party activists did not make possible great advances in fund-raising. All the same, most constituencies changed their financial priorities and increased their expenditure. Banbury budgeted for an annual expenditure of £800, about twice the pre-war level, and went on spending at that rate even when the association ran into debt.[1]

The direction of expenditure was changed above all by the new franchise of 1918 and the provisions that the state would take over registration and that qualification was greatly simplified. The local authority would now register Conservative electors free of charge, opposition electors could no longer be kept off the register by clever lawyers, and the actual number of registered electors became so large as to render the old methods practically useless. Some constituencies abandoned registration campaigns at once and the rest had recognized by 1921 that their efforts were a waste of money.[2] This cleared out the last of the lawyer-agents and completed the transition of the party to modern methods of political organization, whereby registration was replaced by propaganda and standing social organizations. These developments were expensive; by the end of the 1920s, the average local party had doubled its expenditure to about £800 a year.

The money still went mainly to pay staff, but in a way different from the pre-war pattern; as the agent's status rose, so his salary went up, and so he was more likely to need an assistant or a secretary. Most other expenditure was also used to service the agent, rather than to service annual registration campaigns. The agent now needed an office (with rates, light, heating, rent and telephone to pay for), full clerical equipment, and a car, if he was to do his job properly; this could easily run to another £250 a year on top of salaries. Administrative costs therefore amounted to about four-fifths of the local parties' outgoings. Increased costs were the result of increased demands on the organization, but they were also in some sense self-perpetuating: active propaganda needed an expert organizer who could only be retained at a high salary; salary and administrative costs required a higher income, which could only be kept up with the agent's professional skills. It became a circular process, with the agents scrambling to raise the money to pay their own salaries; but as a result the party was able to operate in a higher gear and the money-raising activities themselves brought the party into touch with the electorate more than registration had ever done.

Increased income was mainly derived from two sources, from far more small subscriptions and from a greater use of social events for fund-raising purposes. The detailed accounts for two neighbouring constituencies in Yorkshire illustrate the first trend. In Barkston Ash, the safe county seat which sent George Lane-Fox to parliament, there had been only 60 subscribers in 1922; this rose to 85 in 1926 and to 655 in 1928. In 1922 the number of subscribers of less than £2 was only 32 but by 1926 it was 579; these small subscriptions now made up over half of the association's income and the whole of the increase since the war.[3] A less spectacular change occurred in the very different constituency of York, where the number of subscribers doubled between 1921 and 1928, again with the emphasis on small sums. No local parties gave away free membership in the 1920s, quite consistent with Baldwin's emphasis on the duties of citizenship rather than its rights, and the sums that had been too small to collect before 1914 came in in large enough numbers to fund the increased expenditure.[4]

The drive for subscriptions was related not only to increased costs but also to the desire for independence, from candidates as well as from Central Office. Criticism of financial dependence was matched by obvious embarrassment when candidates actually exhibited their generosity. So in 1923 at the AGM of the West Woolwich association, there was a lively discussion of the effects of the generosity of Sir Kingsley Wood MP, initiated by the Treasurer:

> Mr. Cuff, speaking on the balance sheet, said he was not satisfied with the amount of subscriptions received. He considered it a sin that the Member should continually put his hand in his pocket to find the money to run the Association. He thought that proper efforts were not made to obtain the necessary funds. . . .

Sir Kingsley, in seconding, said that although he personally did not mind, he was glad of Mr. Cuff's remarks. It certainly showed he was looking to the future. If the Association continued in debt, it meant that when the time came for the selection of a candidate to fight a big election, it would not be in a position to select and that they would have to be content with whoever was placed before them, who might turn out to be detrimental to the Division and its Association. Mr. Campbell then stated that it had always been the same, at any rate as long as he had known the Association, and that the drawback was in having such good friends that it was left to them.

Successive meetings at Woolwich prompted similar discussions, but as long as Sir Kingsley Wood continued to be generous nobody was likely to make the considerable effort required to change things. Well into the 1930s then, West Woolwich remained in a chronic financial state, and Sir Kingsley went on picking up the bills. Other party leaders were not so complaisant and in 1924 the critics of this system were given the stamp of official approval by Baldwin; at the party meeting in February he argued that

if you must have a candidate who can water his constituency with £1,000 a year, you are going to have a choice of about half per cent of the population, and if you are going to fight a party that has the choice of the whole population, you will never beat them in this world and, more than that, you will never deserve to beat them.[6]

He went on to develop his argument at greater length at the AGM of his own constituency association a few months later:

An old tradition – and a very bad tradition it is today – still prevails in too many parts of the country. It is that the first thing a constituency has to do is to look for a member who will carry the association on his back, and who will subscribe to everything in the division; and, when they have got that, they do not much mind what else they have got. Now that was never a good thing; it is a particularly bad thing today. Since the war you may take it that, although there are some people who are richer than before the war, there is a very great majority of people – including myself – who are considerably poorer than they were before the war; and therefore the class from which you can hope in future to draw candidates who will be able to do all the finance for you is very limited. More than that, Parliament makes a far greater claim on the time of men than it did when I entered it sixteen years ago. Unless constituencies make up their minds that in return for the personal service that the member gives them nowadays they, in their turn, will do something to aid in organisation by subscriptions and by personal work, they will never get the best type of candidates and members.[7]

Four days later, Joynson-Hicks reinforced Baldwin's words, speaking in London: 'In my quarter of a century I have spent over £25,000 in politics, including the cost of seven contested elections. That is not right. We want today in the service of the State all the very best men, and not only those who are prepared to pay out of their own capital.'[8] Three elections in three years no doubt strained many a Member's pocket, and from 1924 there was a perceptible improvement. Persuasion was applied from Central Office, especially after Bowyer was appointed to look after the placing of candidates in 1930. By 1933, the party could state as a fact that money was no longer a criterion in selecting candidates: 'It is now generally appreciated that each association should be made self-supporting. . . . The day is past when the Member of Parliament, prospective Candidate, or a few supporters ought to provide all the necessary funds.' This was far from reality in 1933, but some improvement had taken place.

Baldwin was relieved of financial responsibility at Bewdley in 1928, Davidson given similar help at Hemel Hempstead and, when he received a peerage in 1937, Lady Davidson's election expenses as his successor in the seat were paid for her by the local association. Sowerby had begun collecting a fund to pay its candidate's election expenses by 1928, and Farnham had relieved its candidate of all obligations by 1929.[10]

A responsible attitude could not always be established without a struggle, as Worthington-Evans discovered. As MP for Colchester he had paid a large annual subscription, his election expenses, and the annual association deficit too; he calculated that he had paid out £1,650 in the four years to 1928, plus the cost of an election, while the whole association had raised only £1,425 in the same time. When he transferred to St George's, Westminster, in 1929, he was determined not to be treated in the same way; his correspondence with St George's provides a good case of the ethics of subscription-bargaining, for even a cabinet minister could be subjected to blackmail by his supporters. The association first demanded £300 a year, but he replied that 'I thought this procedure a survival of a vicious and pernicious tendency, too prevalent in the Conservative Party'. The association then pointed out that Walter Long had given £300 when he was their MP in 1921 and that MPs in neighbouring constituencies gave similar sums. However, their position was weakened by two considerations: firstly, they had been represented since 1921 by J. M. M. Erskine, who had originated as an independent, and who had not therefore owed or given them anything, and secondly because they did not begin the bargaining until after the election, by which time Worthington-Evans could call their bluff. Eventually they agreed on a subscription of £100 a year, but not before Worthington-Evans had given them another lecture. Having described his experiences in Colchester, he went on:

> But in St. George's the position is different. There is an actual surplus of revenue over expenditure. . . . A determined effort should be made throughout the country to rouse the supporters in the constituencies to make the constituency organizations self-supporting, and I would like them to go further, and themselves contribute to the election expenses of their Member. I believe that a strong movement of this sort is necessary for the salvation of the Conservative Party, and I will not, therefore, on principle, acquiesce in destroying this healthy position where it exists in St. George's.[11]

A few months later, he advised Duff Cooper to try for the nomination at Reigate, for 'Reigate Division is, from many points of view, very desirable. It must be self-supporting as regards funds, or at least it could be.' Cooper could not afford the luxury of a large subscription, and his previous candidature at Oldham had been financed by Lord Derby. In the end though he was helped by more than Worthington-Evans's advice, for he succeeded him as MP for St George's and so profited from his financial evangelism there.

It is difficult to judge the overall position from the evidence that remains, but it does seem clear that between a third and a quarter of local parties were self-supporting in the 1930s; the position was by no means as bad as Ian Harvey's allegations would suggest.[12] The irony was that it tended to be strong Conservative seats (Reigate, Bewdley, Hemel Hempstead, Westminster, Circencester and Tewkesbury and the like) that made the transition, and not the marginal seats of the Midlands and north. Even where constituencies continued to rely on their candidates, they did so with an increasing sense of guilt. There has thus been a tendency to underestimate the change that had taken place before the Maxwell-Fyfe reforms of 1949; in any case, it was only the continuous persuasion of the previous quarter-century that made the change of rules acceptable when it came. All that was done in 1949 was to universalize procedures that had been gaining ground for some time, and to enforce their acceptance on local parties which had recogized their desirability long ago.

Apart from persuasion, there were two reasons for the change of heart about financial relations with MPs. The one most quoted was that given by Baldwin in 1924, that to compete with Labour the party must attract the most talented men and must be seen to be open to talent, but the reason given by Sir Kingsley Wood in 1923 was equally influential. To rely on a single benefactor would place the local party at his mercy; if he should choose to economize then the local party would have to agree. This is exactly what happened in West Wolverhampton in 1929–30: when Sir Robert Bird lost the seat to Labour in 1929, he considered retirement, was pressed to stay on by the local party, and took a long time to make up his mind. For months the local party was paralysed while Bird thought the situation over, and a large overdraft accumulated; having little experience of raising money in good times, the local party had little chance of financial viability in a national financial crisis. Eventually Bird agreed to continue as candidate and resumed his subscription just in time to pull things together for the 1931 general election, but the local party had been warned by its experience and moved towards self-sufficiency in the 1930s.[13] This sort of thing had happened often enough before 1914, as *The Times* had pointed out in 1911, but with the new methods it was far more serious. An organization based on mass participation and active propaganda could not be placed on ice for a couple of years without a complete collapse – as the experience of the local parties in the Second World War demonstrated. Without a steady income, the agent would have to be sacked, the office would have to be closed and propaganda work stopped, with the result that the rest of the income would then dry up too. Relying on a rich benefactor was not only unsuitable in a democratic age, it was also fundamentally unreliable.

Despite increases in subscriptions, even the most successful local parties found themselves in occasional financial difficulty; when income was buoyant, there was a strong temptation to practice Parkinson's Second Law and spend all or more than was coming in; however large the income, there were always periodic deficits and overdrafts. The reaction which all local parties made sooner or later was to try a large fund-raising effort. If the special effort was an appeal for donations, then it might work once or twice, but with diminishing returns. Eventually every party came to see the value of social activities, originally once-for-all efforts but successful enough to become regular parts of the programme. Parties had always staged bazaars, fêtes and garden parties, but these had not been aimed primarily at raising money; a large outdoor event held every two or three years could raise as much as a year's annual income. As at Stockton, these were held to meet an occasional crisis and then became an indispensible part of the staple income. With an increased membership to aim at, social events were a rich vein to tap.[14]

Increased membership also necessitated changes to make the local parties more democratic; subscribers expected representation in return for their money. Abingdon's association became 'more democratic and representative' in 1919, and Waterloo adopted a 'better system of representation' in 1928. Every local party went through at least one improvement and some went through several. In 1909 Kincardine had been a textbook example of the unreformed system, as described in chapter 3; in 1923 the Kincardine and West Aberdeenshire Association adopted a minimum subscription of a shilling and a new set of rules. Henceforth the Executive Committee consisted only of the officers (not including Vice-Presidents), thirty delegates from branches, and ten members elected at the AGM. In 1906 the new rules at Newbury were claimed to be 'democratic' because they allowed the representation of ordinary members for the first time; in 1934 the association really became democratic, and henceforth there was a rotation of officers, officers were elected by ballot, and half of the Executive Committee were to be women.

The rotation of offices was particularly important in the advent of democracy. From 1910 the Executive Committee retired in rotation at Newark; from 1923, members at Banbury could serve on the Executive for only three years, with a third retiring each year; from 1920 the chairman at Epsom was to hold office for only two years. By the 1930s most local associations had a Central Council that included a large proportion of the active membership and an Executive Committee that represented the branches; in many cases the officers were elected by ballot and served for a specified time only. The ending of exclusiveness brought other changes in its train: in 1926 Camborne agreed that its Executive Committee would meet only on Saturdays, so that members who were 'wage earners' could attend. Thirsk and Malton rejected the suggestion of evening meetings for the same purpose in 1927, but had to agree to meet on Saturdays. Attitudes were changing as well as structures.[15]

The advent of local democracy was marked by a great influx of middle-class members and by a flourishing of the women's organizations. Local organizations for women had existed for half a century, with the Primrose League as the most successful in recruiting women to influence their husbands. All but one of the county constituencies of the Midlands had branches of the League or of the Women's Unionist and Tariff Reform Association in 1911; between them they had 216 branches in the thirty-two constituencies. But it was not until women received the vote in 1918 that they were really taken seriously by the party. The new National Union rules of 1918 reserved a third of the places on all its committees and delegations for women; one-third was equivalent to the position of women in the electorate, and this was raised to half when women received the vote on the same basis as men in 1928. In some places there were quick developments: in Abingdon, there were already thirty-seven women present at the meeting which adopted new rules to allow their presence; early in 1918 Barkston Ash already had a women's branch in every polling district.

There were difficulties with the Primrose League, which saw its old position threatened, but old branches of the WUTRA were integrated into the party with no friction, and there was considerable local variation. So in South Oxfordshire there were clashes with the Primrose League in some villages, but in others twenty-four habitations of the League were simply taken over by the party; there were disputes in Bradford but friendly cooperation in Banbury, Clapham and Aberdeenshire. Most of the women's branches had established a working relationship with the League by the middle 1920s, but an amicable relationship with the men's side of the party was more difficult to achieve.

The most favoured pattern was for separate branches of men and women in each polling district or ward, and for the parallel structures to be coordinated only at constituency level.[16] Rules could be changed easily enough, but there was still considerable suspicion. Sir James Oddy was frank when he introduced the new rules for Bradford in April 1918:

> The new Franchise Act will make it necessary to draw up a new party constitution, and the organisation should be placed on the most democratic lines. The women should be placed upon an equality with the men in the councils and the conducting of the affairs of the party. . . . We will have to be prepared to sacrifice some of the views held in the past.[17]

The days were past when party activity in the towns could consist of tours of the clubs and stag-night concerts in smoke-filled rooms, but it was hardly to be expected that the men would welcome the change. The National Society of Conservative Agents was slow to recognize the claims of professional women organizers and refused to admit them to membership. It was suggested in Ecclesall in 1929 that 'a lady agent' should be appointed instead of a man, 'but this suggestion was not entertained for a moment'.[18]

Mistrust was widespread, but actual clashes were rare, probably because most women's branches were not yet confident enough to assert their rights. In Bosworth the women seceded from the joint association in 1919 and set up their own organization, collecting their own subscriptions and employing their own organizer. Disputes followed about the allocation of joint resources and went on until the two bodies were re-amalgamated in 1925. The clash at Worcester dragged on for so long that Robert Topping, by then General Director of the Party Organization, had to go down to Worcester in order to settle it himself; a proposed amalgamation did not work here though and Lady Atkins refused the new compromise rule on behalf of the women's branches. The root of the problem was financial, for at Worcester as in many places the women were now raising the bulk of the party's income, but had little control over its spending. The dispute at Worcester was finally settled in the more prosperous times of the mid-1930s; with more money in the bank, it was possible to give the women more of what they wanted without depriving the men of what they already had. Cases like Worcester were certainly rare, but it shows the supreme importance of finance; the women's branches were already doing a great deal for the party, and were especially well-suited for the new approach to social fund-raising through parties, fêtes and whist-drives.[19] Hence the recognition that the women's contribution was vital was probably the factor that finally broke down antagonism, but right from the start the women began to influence the party as a whole. The support for temperance articulated by Lady Astor ran directly against the tradition of the party before 1914, and it is unlikely that party conferences in the 1920s would have spent so much of their time discussing family and social issues if it had not been for the large number of women delegates. Women did much to humanize the party, hence the important part that they played in the calculations of Baldwin and Davidson; in the 1930s, women from the party organizations played a major part in the National Council of Social Service and its attempts to combat the social consequences of the slump.[20]

The democratization of local parties and the advent of women was made possible only through the enhanced role of the party agents. The first leaders of the local women's branches were usually relatives of the MP or constituency chairman, as at Bosworth, Thirsk and Malton and Hemel Hempstead; the first national leaders of the women were all the wives of MPs, Lady Iveagh, Dame Caroline Bridgeman and Lady Elvedon. But the next generation of local leaders would not have experience of politics even at secondhand, and would almost certainly lack a business or professional training. Similarly the greater turnover of officers in the men's branches and in the associations as a whole greatly increased their dependence on professional advice; the agent was not only the sole trained servant of the associations, but he was also the element of continuity and the repository of experience.[21]

Democratic structures were more advanced in theory than in practice, for constituencies were small areas and local traditions did not break down quickly. County families and local landowners remained supreme in some county constituencies and businessmen took over the running of the party in the boroughs from the lawyers. It was no doubt thought to be desirable that association officers should be men of individual standing, but the rules no longer made this inevitable. Where exclusiveness remained, it was at least now an exclusiveness by election and so must have been acceptable to at least a large part of the active membership.

There remained one area in which democracy made no real progress, in the procedures for adopting parliamentary candidates. It was rare for any but a small selection committee to be involved, often quite unrepresentative even of the Executive Committee, and it was quite normal to leave such matters entirely to the chairman of the association; in Sheffield in the 1890s it was the chairman's task to 'find or grind' (that is to find a candidate or stand himself, and find the money too) and such traditions died hard. Exclusive informality was necessary as long as the association needed to be sure of a subscription as well as a candidate, for the frankly financial side of the transaction could hardly be conducted at a public meeting. The Executive Committee was rarely given more than two or three names from which to select, sometimes only one; Council and General Meetings were little more than rallies to present the man selected to the party faithful, and members at these meetings could only accept the choice or disown their leaders in front of the press. It must be said though that criticism was extremely rare, and when it did happen it was often traceable to disappointed ambition rather than to any discontent with the method of selection as such; demands for a candidate who was a local man were all too often set up by a local man who had ideas about standing himself.[22]

The resistance to democracy showed up even better in attitudes to the aspirations of working-class members. In November 1916 the Central Council discussed the composition of the Executive of the National Union after its recent election: 'Mr. Steel-Maitland in formally moving the adoption of the Report . . . added that Mr. Marston had expressed a desire to see more business men upon the Council and Executive Committee, and *he* would also be glad to see more responsible working men representatives.' It was decided to hold fresh elections, duly carried out at the next Central Council meeting in January 1917; the twenty-one men elected included nine MPs and four peers, together with respected National Union figures like Sir Alexander Leith, Sir Percy Woodhouse, Charles Marston, Sir Harry Foster and Sir Henry Imbert-Terry; half a dozen of the men elected could be called businessmen, but none were working men.[23] The same resistance was shown when it was decided to set up Unionist labour committees to promote the views of working men in the party in 1921. Barkston Ash had a committee in each polling district by 1921, but it was well in advance of most local parties, and Herbert Blain was still trying to get some local parties to join in the scheme in 1925. Banbury Conservatives decided that the scheme was 'impractical', but they agreed grudgingly to coopt four working men on to their ordinary executive committee. Thirsk and Malton was 'against the formation of anything in the nature of a sub-committee, but heartily supported the principle of good working-class supporters sitting on the Executive Committee', if they could get elected on their merits; Blain applied pressure and eventually it was agreed to set up an advisory committee 'at the urgent request of the London Central Office'. York agreed to set up an advisory committee too, but would go no further.[24]

The response varied widely between constituencies, but there was a clear regional pattern too. Lancashire was the keenest supporter of the Unionist labour committees, no doubt a testament to its long tradition of working-class Conservatism; in the four years from 1918, only £978 was raised by the National Union in Lancashire for ordinary purposes, but £5,425 was raised for the labour committees; Philip Stott of Oldham and William Bradford became national leaders of the movement, but neither of them were working men.[25] Conversely, Cheshire had no labour committee until 1925 and Yorkshire was always lukewarm. In 1921 the Yorkshire area was asked to allow the local labour committees representation on the area executive, and it was decided to admit representatives 'when progress justifies such a step'; in 1924 it refused to pay the expenses of working-class delegates to national meetings and in 1926 it rejected a proposal from Elland that it should hold its meetings outside working hours.[26] At the other extreme, the Eastern Area gave full support to the labour committees, urged its local parties to promote the interests of working men and spent a great deal on propaganda for that purpose. The distinction was probably that in Yorkshire and in Cheshire the county seats were very safe while the urban seats were for the most part hardly worth contesting; in Lancashire and in East Anglia there was a large number of marginal constituencies where working-class support would be vital.

A network of labour committees was eventually established throughout the country, but no power on earth could persuade the party actually to listen to their advice. There were three prerequisites for the further success of the labour committees in the party: firstly, they needed an overall party strategy that would allow no compromise with Labour, for their role depended on resisting claims that Labour represented the bulk of the working class; secondly, they needed the repeal of the 1913 Act in order to 'free' Conservative working men from the need to contract out of the political levy; and thirdly they needed an impressive looking band of working-class Conservative MPs. The first two aims were quite popular with the party as a whole in 1921–22, although even then they ran into the indifference of Bonar Law, who refused to give them his official backing, but with the party's change of direction in 1924 they ran directly contrary to Baldwin's political style. The ironic situation thus emerged whereby working-class Conservatives became the hard-liners and middle-class members the moderates; in 1925 a correspondent was writing to *Home and Politics* to deny that working-class members were in any way 'reactionary'.[27] Their influence in the party would of course have been much greater if they had succeeded in their third aim, and so established a beach-head in the parliamentary party. Here the proceedings of successive party conferences tell the tale.

In 1917 Bonar Law was reminded of the need for more working-class candidates; he replied 'I quite agree', but immediately pointed out that it was up to the constituency parties to select candidates.[28] In 1922 there was a long debate in an otherwise harmonious conference, and Gwylim Rowlands claimed to speak for 35,000 'anti-socialist trades unionists' in Glamorgan alone. In 1923 it was unanimously agreed to promote more working men to the Executive of the National Union. In 1924 a motion calling for more working-class candidates was carried with acclamation, one delegate remarking that 'our party has in the past made the mistake of putting money before brains'. The Party Chairman reported that Central Office was using all its influence but that the local parties were the only ones who could take the decisions. The same conference voted more propaganda among working men and for profit-sharing schemes, even though a working-class delegate explained that Conservative working men were not interested in such palliatives. In 1925 a debate on contracting-out produced an angry outburst: 'Gwylim Rowlands spoke of the difficulty of arousing enthusiasm on the subject among Conservative MPs sitting for safe agricultural constituencies. Unfortunately, the candidates who fought seats where this tyranny existed seldom arrived in the House of Commons.' Finally in 1926 a strong motion was passed against the advice of the platform and two further motions regretting the lack of action in the past were strongly supported: 'Councillor Wolston (Woolwich) urged the Conference . . . to tell the Government "we demand as delegates that these laws shall be altered and that the industrial worker shall have his freedom. Get on with it or get out." (Cheers.)' In 1928 there was yet another motion that called for more working-class candidates; this time it was Gwylim Rowlands, speaking from the platform, who replied that it was entirely up to the constituency parties.[29]

While the party refused to back the aspirations of its working-class members, it was taking in a great influx of members from the middle class. Membership rose in most areas in the 1920s, but this was concentrated in middle-class constituencies and middle-class wards. There had been about 7,000 Unionist members in the whole of Glasgow in 1913, but there were 20,000 in 1922 and 32,000 in 1929; only a tiny proportion of these were in the industrial constituencies, and the increase was overwhelmingly in the Central, Kelvingrove, Pollok, Hillhead and Cathcart divisions which comprised the bulk of the Glasgow middle class. In the West Midlands in 1929 there were high memberships in rural seats and small towns, and there was virtually no membership at all in mining and industrial seats like Stoke,

Walsall or West Bromwich. A membership drive raised the membership in South Kensington from 950 in 1928 to 3,500 in 1933. The membership of West Lewisham rose from 670 in 1922 to 3,035 in 1930, but almost the whole of the increase came in the middle-class ward of Sydenham. When branch quotas were fixed at Stretford in 1932, the three middle-class and commercial branches at Urmston, Stretford and Old Trafford were assesssed for £250, while the other six branches in working-class areas could be assessed only for a total of £100.[30]

The picture of local organization at the end of the 1920s is thus a mixed one; in some areas the party flourished as never before, in others it had almost died out. The grouping together of the worst constituencies in 1930 was not only due to an organizational rationalization, but also to the collapse of indigenous Conservatism that could support an organization on its own. These area groups in 1930 comprised about forty constituencies in all, and if the worst city centre seats and the other mining seats are added, it can be seen that the party had more or less ceased to maintain an active presence in some sixty-five constituencies, a tenth of the total. In the meantime, *Gleanings and Memoranda* went on celebrating the conversion of local Liberals, the tip of the iceberg of middle-class support, now moving over to a near unanimity, a process that had been much facilitated by the Liberal–Conservative pacts in local government.

The new mood in the party shows up in its preference for the interests of business and agriculture over those of labour and in the continuing refusal to select even a few working-class candidates. The north-western area received a resolution in 1928 suggesting the Conservative brewers should not give Labour party clubs the same preferential treatment that was given to Conservative clubs; the area executive refused to express an opinion and so the brewers went on as before, placing business before party. At Rotherham in 1918 there was a dispute over a candidate after the constituency had been allocated to the British Workers' League; when the association chairman revealed that he was also chairman of the selection committee of the Business Men's Party, 'explaining that his membership of the latter was solely on business grounds', his action was approved; so Rotherham ran a joint candidate with the Business Men's Party and the British Workers' League was ignored.[31] At Wolverhampton the same meeting which finally agreed to set up a labour committee in 1926 also opened negotiations with the Chamber of Commerce about joint candidates for the coming municipal elections; in Wolverhampton the number of working men in the Conservative group on the Borough Council actually fell during the 1920s.[32] In Woolwich there was a decision to allocate a number of wards to local businessmen who would run without a label, and associations in rural seats which would not consider working-class candidates were quite ready to collaborate with the National Farmers' Union, as at Newark.[33]

There was a commotion in the party in 1924 when the Labour government proposed to abolish the second votes of business proprietors, with the protests led by Salvidge. He calculated that the proposal would take away over 11,000 votes in the Exchange division of Liverpool, and 2,600 in the Castle Street ward alone – so much for Salvidge as the champion of the working-class Conservative. The Labour government could not carry its Bill in 1924, but in the following year the supporters of business went a step further; the 1925 party conference carried a resolution calling for votes not only for business owners, but also for directors and managers, an idea that would have added hundreds of thousands of Conservatives to the register for the second time.[34] The Baldwin government paid no attention to such ideas, but the business vote that already existed was worth quite a lot; it provided a few votes everywhere and a great many in a few city-centre constituencies; it may be that the second votes of businessmen and graduates deprived Labour of an overall majority in 1929, and it is certain that the abolition of second votes kept Labour in power in 1950.

The readiness to cooperate with businessmen and farmers contrasts with the deaf ear that was turned to working-class Conservatives, and it may be that the advent of middle-class control of the local associations actually made it more difficult to get working-class Conservatives selected. Despite resolutions at conference, the number of working-class Conservatives who ever achieved much was very small, as was evidenced by the publicity lavished on the few who did manage to break through. Gwylim Rowlands was the best known: he stood for parliament several times in Wales, always in hopeless seats, was a member of the National Union Executive and chairman of the National Union in 1929. Willie Templeton, MP for Banff from 1924 to 1929, has been considered to be the only working-class Conservative ever to sit for a Scottish seat.[35] Two others who won notable victories were Robert Gee, who beat Ramsay MacDonald at Woolwich in 1921, and James Kidd, who beat Emmanuel Shinwell at Linlithgow in 1924. Gee was a twenty-year serving soldier, but he had been commissioned in the First World War and had won the Victoria Cross, hence his attraction against a pacifist in a constituency that included munitions factories; after he lost at Woolwich in 1922, he went on to fight without hope at Consett, Bishop Auckland and East Newcastle, before emigrating to Australia. Kidd was claimed by the party as a moderate miner who could represent working-class opinion against Shinwell's extremism, but his experience as a manual worker had been much earlier; by 1924 he had become a solicitor. In his analysis of Conservative and Unionist MPs between the wars, Professor McEwen could find only one who deserved the label 'working man'.[36] The few working men who were promoted were far from typical; there was not a single real trade unionist amongst them, and no new generation of Mawdsleys to carry the party banner.

The failure to promote working men within the party was disguised by cosmetic means; after 1924 a few places on the National Union Executive were reserved for nominees of the leader, and Baldwin used these places to promote some working men. In 1928 he nominated Alderman William Bradford and Captain Matt Sheppard. Sheppard had fought hopelessly at Brightside in 1923 and 1924, had been a manual worker once, but had risen from the ranks during the war, won the MC and become a senior clerk at Vickers after 1918. He served on the executive for several years as Baldwin's nominee, was always treated with courtesy, but recalled later that he felt strangely out of place.[37] Expenses were paid for a small group of tame workers to sit on party committees and to fight industrial constituencies at elections; no more could be done as the local parties still refused to do individually what they all agreed to be necessary when meeting together.

Despite the limited concessions to its working-class members, the party went on attracting a large volume of working-class support. Political clubs still flourished as the main party approach to the working class, and many newly affluent local associations were glad to meet in the local Conservative club, as at Cannock and at Wakefield. Harold Macmillan was not the only MP to be impressed by the problems of his industrial constituency and his slim majority there; Robert Sanders noted in 1927 that Macmillan and his friends in the 'YMCA' were unable to support real Conservative policies because they might cost them their seats. The large Conservative majorities of 1924, 1931 and 1935 can only have increased this effect, for the most marginal seats were always the most working-class in composition; the moderation of Vyvyan Adams as MP for West Leeds in the 1930s is a good example. The influence of working-class interests was thus felt not through the labour committees and the party organization but through the upper- and middle-class MPs who had the bad luck to sit for working-class constituencies; the influence was therefore cast on the side of moderation rather than confrontation. However, what perhaps saved the working-class vote for the party was that the labour committees had probably misinterpreted its real nature. Recent studies have emphasized the extent to which working-class Toryism is now based as much on deference and tradition as on calculation or policy; it is unlikely that things were very different in the 1920s, and it was not therefore necessary for the party to outbid the Labour party, but rather that it had to maintain itself on the old line by combining a shrewd mixture of social betterment with a patriotic appeal. The promoters of the Primrose League, the organizers of the Hotel Cecil, and observers like Ostrogorski and Wallas had all appreciated the point. What had seemed doubtful was whether old-fashioned deference could go on in the twentieth century; could 'the deference due to a man of pedigree' be transferred to a self-made man of 'Bonar Law's dynasty' or to a 'man of the utmost insignificance' like Baldwin? Experience seemed to show that it could.[38]

The local parties were keenly involved between the wars in the debate within the party on the role that party politics should play in local government. Before 1914 the local parties had been free to intervene in local elections if they wished to do so, but Central Office had neither encouraged nor discouraged intervention.[39] The Unionist Organization Committee did not discuss local elections and seems to have taken no evidence on the subject. Central Office had no department dealing with local government and the National Union issued no literature for local elections. This non-policy can be explained both by the resistance of the local parties to interference in areas that they regarded as their own, and by the continuing reluctance of Conservatives as a whole to see local government politicized. County Councils had existed for only a single generation and most of them did not have Conservative members as such before the First World War. The cities had however already taken the plunge and results from local government elections there were printed in considerable detail in the *Conservative and Unionist* and later in *Our Flag*. Behind the scenes though the attitude was beginning to change. After its victory in the London County Council election of 1907, the London Municipal Society (LMS) resolved to make its services available to Conservatives outside London; a central municipal bureau was therefore set up by the LMS and used by other Conservatives who found themselves faced with a threat from Labour at the municipal level.[40] But it was all unofficial, and the most the Central Office could do was to publicize the existence of the LMS and circulate its literature.

After 1918 the pattern was confused by the numerous Conservative–Liberal pacts set up under various names to resist Labour, as in Bristol, Sheffield, Coventry, Crewe and Wolverhampton. Central Office encouraged intervention to support anti-Labour candidates, but was not able to produce a complete change of policy. Whenever a proposal was brought to the National Union for greater interventionism, it was supported as highly desirable but left to the local parties to judge its feasibility according to local circumstances. The LMS therefore broadened its base by accepting the affiliation of local ratepayers' organizations, provided that these were themselves approved of by local Conservatives. Until 1937 the London Municipal Society and National Union of Ratepayers' Associations (NURA) remained the only party body formally committed to politicizing local government and, as its name suggests, it was doing it in a very roundabout away. As Party Chairman, J. C. C. Davidson campaigned for party intervention, but had little success in breaking down the feeling that local government should remain non-political whenever this could be done.[41] Those who supported intervention did so because of the success of Labour locally, and there is no reason to doubt their reluctance. Central Office could only support the LMS with money and leave it to do the job that it would like to have done itself.

The process moved into a further phase in the 1930s with the failure of the LMS/NURA to fulfil its dual role effectively and with the climb back of Labour to municipal power after the defeat of 1931. Ratepayers' associations were as much concerned with economy in local government as with pure anti-socialism, and in the 1930s this sometimes conflicted with the plans of Conservative ministers to increase the burdens on local government. Hence the LMS and the NURA drifted apart and in 1938 they separated completely. By that time too the LMS had more than enough to do in London, where the London County Council had been lost to Labour in 1933 and not regained.[42] There was now no substitute for direct party intervention and demands at party conferences became more insistent. In 1937 the National Union considered setting up specialist committees on education, local government and local organization, hitherto regarded as the preserve of the local parties. Resistance prevented the scheme from being implemented in full, but from 1937 there was a Local Government Advisory Committee working under the Party Chairman and in collusion with Central Office. This became a force for greater intervention, all very much in keeping with the more partisan spirit of the National government under Neville Chamberlain.[43]

The Second World War halted this development towards a coordinated party attack on local government elections but it is unlikely that a complete change would have been achieved had there been municipal elections in 1939 and 1940. In many counties, Conservatives remained on councils in the guise of 'Independents' until the 1960s and 70s; in the 1950s the chairman of the Cleveland Conservative Association was regularly elected as an Independent member of the North Riding County Council, and there were many like him. Local Conservative parties often covertly supported these independents and throughout they retained their autonomy. The difference in attitudes remained much the same: to Central Office and the more determined organizers in the towns, local elections were means of building up strength for the greater fight for control of parliament; for many, especially in the counties, local elections were as important as national elections in their own right, and they would do nothing to hinder their independence or their autonomy. Only when faced with a direct threat from Labour, when Labour could be blamed for politicizing local government, would local Conservatives accept party intervention, whether urged by the LMS or by Central Office itself.

Another more trivial area that illustrated the same inability of the party to enforce uniformity on the local parties concerned party colours. There were of course different traditions of party colours in each county in the nineteenth century, and although a trend towards uniformity was already under way there was nothing that Central Office could do either to encourage or retard it. Conferences often debated motions for a single party colour, on the grounds that elections were now national events and that production of party literature and other propaganda would be assisted by the choice of one colour, but the most that could be agreed was that Central Office should conduct negotiations with local parties to see if agreement could be reached. If any negotiations were ever held, they were not very effective for a wide variety of party colours continued in use. In 1927 blue had become the favourite colour and was used by a little over half the constituencies. Nevertheless, about ninety of the local parties campaigned with red as their colour, mainly in the West Midlands, the north-east and in Middlesex, but including Baldwin's own constituency at Bewdley. Fifty constituencies sported patriotic colours of red, white and blue, especially in the port and garrison towns. Thirty-eight used purple and orange and about as many again used some similar combination; the pink of Norfolk and Cambridgeshire was the next most popular and the red, yellow and blue of Rutland the most exotic. It was not even possible to ensure local conformity; every constituency in Hampshire used a different combination of colours and, in the constituency of Galloway, blue was used for Kirkcudbright and red and white for Wigtown.[44]

As well as the constituency parties, which were established as the basic unit of the party organization by the 1920s, there were several intermediary levels between constituency and national level. The only one that flourished for any length of time was the provincial division of the National Union, which now coincided almost everywhere with the administrative areas used by Central Office. The reconstruction of this pattern after its abandonment in 1906 had been very slow. As early as 1907, it had been found to be impossible to run viable County Associations in East Anglia, and in that year an Eastern Division was reconstituted by Norfolk, Cambridgeshire and Huntingdonshire. Suffolk rejoined in 1914 (although Suffolk also insisted that the minutes should note that it was only 'at the initiation of Central Office'), Bedfordshire in 1922 and Hertfordshire only in 1930. Separation made little more sense in South Wales, where a provincial division was reconstituted in 1913, covering Brecon, Radnor, Carmarthen, Pembroke and Cardigan, but not Glamorgan or Monmouth. Where there was no advantage to be gained, progress was slower: Lancashire, Cheshire and Westmorland had been run together until 1906, but were then organized separately until 1925, and Cheshire then accepted amalgamation only when it had 'taken into account the strongly expressed view of Central Office'. By this time, few anomalies remained: Nottinghamshire was in the West Midlands for Central Office but the East Midlands for the National Union, and Middlesbrough hovered similarly between Yorkshire and the Northern Division. The pattern was finally tidied up in 1930 by a new set of National Union rules; henceforth each provincial division conformed to a Central Office area, and each was given a democratic structure that was a microcosm of the National Union.[45]

Within areas there were unavoidable tensions. Suffolk resented the role of Norfolk in the eastern area, and both combined to resent the lead taken by members from Hertfordshire after 1930, a lead that derived most of all from the fact that politics in Hertfordshire were more active and more partisan. The same tension existed between the political activists of Lancashire and the more quiescent Conservatives of Cheshire. In Yorkshire there was tension between the centre and the periphery, and resentment was expressed in Sheffield and Hull about the apparent domination of the area from Leeds, where the Central Office agent worked and where most meetings were inevitably held. By the 1920s, changes in the rules had anyway enlarged the role of the provincial divisions; the party conference became peripatetic, visiting each area in turn, and the host area was allowed to nominate the National Union President for the year. The conferences were also made more responsive to the party as a whole when Baldwin secured the attendance of front benchers on the platform; the leader did not attend the conferences, except to address a rally that was technically outside the conference programme, but his ministers had to listen to debates and to reply to them from 1925. This was all consistent with Baldwin's increased use of ministers in by-elections from 1927, in public meetings, and in party magazines.[46] Resolutions to the conferences could now be put only by constituency associations, which helped to reduce the absolute number and also made the conference a matter of interest to members who could not attend. The same sort of link was intended in the provision of 1925 whereby the Executive Committee of the National Union was to be elected for geographical areas. Previously the Executive had been elected by the Central Council, which placed it two removes away from the constituencies and even from areas; from 1925 the seats on the Executive were divided amongst each area according to its population, and representatives were to be elected by the area only on nomination from constituencies. In the National Union, as in the local parties, the rules were constantly changing to allow for a more accurate representation of constituency opinion.[47]

The increased emphasis placed on constituency parties and areas led to a reduction in the importance of the city parties. Most of the more centralized city parties had to devolve power and adopt a looser structure; Sheffield did so in 1920, and Birmingham two years later. The change in the mood of the party was reflected as much as anything by the changed position of Liverpool, which had been the model for all to emulate in 1911. Liverpool remained faithful to its old methods, did not enjoy the improvement that the other parties went through in the 1920s, and rarely even bothered to send delegates to conferences. In 1927 though even Salvidge came under attack, and his death in that year may well have saved him from overthrow, for MPs and constituency parties were no longer willing to play a subordinate role to a party boss.[48]

Much had been done to modernize and democratize the local parties and they were now Conservative in name as well as in effect, for the new National Union rules of 1925 finally relegated 'Unionist' to an additional form that was retained only for Scottish, Irish, and sentimental reasons. Local parties were on their way to take off, both social and financially, and it was perhaps only the lack of a serious Labour threat after 1931 that delayed further progress until Maxwell-Fyfe and Woolton set to work in 1945. But the process was in any case a gradual one, as Davidson found out when he proposed a new system of qualifications for attendance at the party conference in 1926.[49]

Previously attendance had been open to all honorary members of the National Union – these were direct subscribers under a more euphonious name – but only 140 of the over 2,000 such honorary members had actually attended in 1925. Davidson wanted to reduce the size of the conference and so he proposed to reduce the theoretical number by taking away the automatic claim of the honorary members. But he could not resist the temptation to say that 'the payment of one guinea is not exactly the kind of qualification that might be expected from a great democratic party like this'. He was swiftly answered by a delegate from Westminster who 'took exception to Mr. Davidson's mocking at the fifteen hundred honorary members who support the Association with their donations' and Davidson's plan was defeated on a show of hands. A great democratic party it might be in its structures, but it was not yet very democratic in its attitudes.

Notes and References

1 Ramsden, 'Organisation' (thesis), 357–8.
2 *Conservative Agents' Journal*, Sept. 1920, June and Sept. 1921.
3 Barkston Ash Conservative Association, Annual Reports.
4 Ramsden, 'Organisation', 360.
5 West Woolwich Conservative Association minutes, AGM, 4 July 1923.
6 Middlemas and Barnes, *Baldwin*, 267.
7 *Worcester Times*, 2 June 1924.
8 *The Times*, 4 June 1924.
9 *Handbook on Constituency Organisation*, 1933, 43.
10 Ramsden, 'Organisation', 362.
11 Worthington-Evans to General Cooper, 11 July 1929, Worthington-Evans MSS.
12 Ramsden, 'Organisation', 364; Ian Harvey's views on party finance are in Ross, *Parliamentary Representation*, 136–8.
13 West Wolverhampton Conservative Association minutes, 1929–30.
14 *Handbook on Constituency Organisation*, 1933, 45, 89–97; *Conservative Agents' Journal*, Mar. 1924 and Jan. 1925.
15 Ramsden, 'Organisation', 169–172.
16 *Ibid*, 172–3.
17 Bradford Conservative Association minutes, 27 Apr. 1918.
18 Sheffield Ecclesall Conservative Association minutes, 9 July 1929.
19 Bosworth Conservative Association minutes, 1918–1925; Worcester Conservative Association minutes, 1932–5.
20 Ramsden, 'Organisation', 174–5.
21 *Ibid*, 175–6.
22 *Ibid*, 176–7.
23 National Union minutes, Central Council, 16 Nov. 1916 and 18 Jan. 1917.
24 Ramsden, 'Organisation', 187.
25 Lancashire Area, Finance and Labour Committee minutes, 1918–1925.
26 Yorkshire Area, Executive Committee minutes, 12 Nov. 1921, 2 May 1924, 19 Nov. 1926.
27 *Home and Politics*, July 1925.
28 National Union Conference minutes, transcript of Special London Conference, 30 Nov. 1917.
29 *Ibid*, Conferences of 1922–28.
30 Ramsden, 'Organisation', 191–2.
31 North-West Area, Executive Committee minutes, 24 Mar. 1928; Rotherham Conservative Association minutes, 4 Oct. 1918.
32 West Wolverhampton Conservative Association minutes, 8 May 1926; Jones, *Borough Politics*, 370.

264 Baldwin's New Conservatism

33 Newark Conservative Association minutes, 19 Jan. 1921.

34 Conservative Agents' Journal, Apr. 1924; National Union Conference minutes, Brighton Conference, 8 Oct. 1925.

35 Urwin, 'The development of the Unionist Party in Scotland' (thesis), chapter 2.

36 Ramsden, 'Organisation', 195; McEwen, 'Conservative and Unionist M.P.s' (thesis), chapter 1.

37 Interview with Captain Matt Sheppard MC, Apr. 1970.

38 Ramsden, 'Organisation', 196–7; the idea of 'Bonar Law's dynasty' is discussed in Thornton, Habit of Authority, 292–347.

39 Conservative Agents' Journal, Aug. 1923.

40 Young, Local Politics, 104–8.

41 Ibid, 143–51.

42 Ibid, 162–9.

43 National Union minutes, Executive Committee, 16 June 1937.

44 National Union Conference minutes, London Conference, 16 Nov. 1911; Block, Sourcebook of Conservatism, 74–81; Central Office List of Certificated Agents, 1927.

45 Davidson to Baldwin, 15 Apr. 1930, Davidson MSS; Ramsden, 'Organisation', 201.

46 Correspondence on by-election speakers, Baldwin MSS, vols. 49–51.

47 National Union Rules, 1925.

48 Ramsden, 'Organisation', 208; Salvidge, Salvidge of Liverpool, 294–305.

49 National Union Conference minutes, Scarborough Conference, 7 Oct. 1928.

Chapter 12

The New Conservatism in action

The Conservative victory of 1924 marked a watershed in British politics, the end of a period of transition, as Baldwin himself recognized:

> For some time I felt things were shaping themselves towards the disappearance of the Liberal Party, but I did not think it would come so quickly. The next step must be the elimination of the Communists by Labour. Then we shall have two parties, the Party of the Right and the Party of the Left.[1]

The end of the years of political realignment meant that the new government had a rare opportunity to get on with its job and look to the future; there was no danger of another election and so the government could settle to a four-year term at least. The size of the majority provided an opening but it also brought its problems, as Baldwin and the Chamberlains all realized. In his first public appearance after the election, at the Guildhall on 10 November, Baldwin interpreted the result as

> the testimony of our fellow-countrymen in favour of ordered progress and not of stagnation; we know that it is a decisive vote against minority government; and we know that we have received support from many of those who at ordinary times might have given their support to other parties. But they have endeavoured to put in power a national government, and it is in the exercise of that trust that we shall endeavour to deserve their confidence.[2]

Austen Chamberlain told Baldwin that 'I am a little dazed. . . . So large a majority creates dangers of its own. I have one clear conviction which you will share. Reaction would be fatal.' Neville Chamberlain wrote to his sister that 'what alarms me now is the size of our majority, which is most dangerous. Unless we leave our mark as social reformers the country will take it out on us hereafter, but what we do will depend on how the Cabinet is made up. Poor S.B.'[3] There was a chance to create a powerful reforming administration that would bind up the nation's wounds – some of which the party's diehards had inflicted in the past few weeks.

The character of the government was created not by the cabinet-making of November 1924, but by the character of Baldwin himself; it was to reflect Baldwin's strengths in its moderation and determination, and it was to reflect his weaknesses in its caution and its ultimate uncertainty. The events of 1924 had affected Baldwin greatly, changing him from the unknown figure catapulted into a premiership that was too big for him into a confident leader in full control. It was not his way to dictate the terms of every argument or to run each department from Downing Street, but he showed within a few months that he was not afraid to stand against his cabinet when he believed that he was right, nor to rebuke the Palace when the King was in the wrong. Baldwin was fifty-six in 1924, at the height of his powers and giving his party an effective lead. He set its tone and its style, he determined the level at which debate would run, and he usually had the last word when he chose to try; it was little exaggeration to say that it was becoming a 'Baldwin Age'. His own view was that the government must avoid legislation that would provoke strong reaction in the country, whether it be action that might antagonize labour or social reforms for which the country was not yet ready. His belief in his personal calling had been strengthened by the election, and he was determined to continue in his attempts to raise the moral tone of British political life. At Stourport on 12 January 1925, he stated his political creed in a couple of sentences: 'There is only one thing which I feel is worth giving one's whole strength to, and that is the binding together of all classes of our people in an effort to make life in this country better in every sense of the word. That is the end and object of my life in politics.'[4] With Baldwin in control, government would not be reactionary but neither would it embark on social adventures. The essence of the man was caution but, given his willingness to leave ministers largely to their own devices, much would depend, as Neville Chamberlain had said, on the composition of the cabinet.

The task of making a cabinet contrasted sharply with Bonar Law's task in 1922 or Baldwin's in 1923; the problem now was not the lack of talent but the excess of it. Baldwin's first priority was to use the process of cabinet-making to settle finally the problems that lingered from the years of coalition. Hence, the first appointment was of Austen Chamberlain to the Foreign Office, a post of high enough status to satisfy an ex-leader and might-have-been Prime Minister; Austen was then flattered to be made deputy leader in the Commons as well. The cost of this appointment was the disappointment of Curzon, who regarded the Foreign Office as his private monopoly; but Curzon at the Foreign Office would endanger the close relations with France that MacDonald had built up, whereas Austen was a francophile. Moreover, Baldwin had surmised correctly that Curzon could be pressed into another honorific post as Lord President and leader in the Lords. Austen had originally suggested himself for a non-departmental office, but Baldwin was determined that all the ex-coalitionists should have their time fully occupied with a department and so be less tempted to engage in more damaging activities. For this reason, Birkenhead, Horne and Churchill presented difficulties. Birkenhead recognized the impossibility of throwing over Lord Cave in order to restore him to Woolsack, although it is doubtful if he even then realized that the party would not have accepted him in such a position, and asked instead to be made Lord Privy Seal. At the suggestion of Tom Jones of the Cabinet Office, Baldwin sent Birkenhead to the India Office. Robert Horne was more easily disposed of. Baldwin disliked Horne, who had refused to join him in 1923 after long consideration, and he wished to keep the Exchequer for Neville Chamberlain, but Austen pressed Horne's name forward. Horne was therefore offered the Ministry of Labour, without any indication that it would be a cabinet post, refused it, and was not considered again. As long as the Chamberlains, Churchill and Birkenhead were accommodated, Baldwin had no reason to fear Horne.[5]

Most of the other posts were filled without undue difficulty, except for the jobs that were to go to Churchill and Neville Chamberlain. Neville was marked down by almost everyone for the Exchequer but did not wish to go there. He had disliked the Treasury in 1923 and longed rather to return to the Ministry of Health, a longing reinforced by his conviction that the government would stand or fall on its social policy and by the realistic view that he was better fitted to conduct such a policy than anyone else; 'I ought to be a great Minister of Health, but am not likely to be more than a second-rate Chancellor.' Baldwin then put to him the idea that Churchill might have the Exchequer, an idea that Chamberlain regarded as 'worth further consideration'. A few minutes later Churchill was offered the post of Chancellor; Stanley Jackson was so surprised when he heard the news that he assumed that it must mean Chancellor of the Duchy of Lancaster. Churchill himself was duly grateful for such a senior post, as were Birkenhead and Austen Chamberlain, and Baldwin's generosity to them did much to hold the government together until 1929.

Churchill's appointment was very controversial; in favour, it would employ all his talents in the service of the party, and would keep him away from places like the Colonial Office where he might cause trouble by some high-spirited action; against it, he had only just returned after a twenty-year apostasy, he might try to dominate the cabinet from the Treasury, and his free-trade views might cause embarrassment. The first point meant that Baldwin had to face a party storm, but this he was ready to do; the second would just have to be faced, but Baldwin with his new confidence thought he could control Churchill; the third was dealt with by Churchill's promise to accept safeguarding as Baldwin had defined it in the election.[6]

Overall, the appointments were well received, criticism being aimed only at Churchill (who was predictably unpopular in the party) and Steel-Maitland at the Ministry of Labour (who was unpopular with everyone). Baldwin admired Steel-Maitland but doubted whether he would shine enough in the Commons. In any case he intended to keep industrial matters in his own hands, so it probably suited him to have a minister who owed his appointment entirely to the Prime Minister's patronage. Austen Chamberlain's considered view of the new cabinet is worth quoting:

> Setting aside the exclusion of Horne, which is not only a great grief but a great loss to me, and with the exception of Labour, I think all the Ministries adequate and

some of them exceptionally well-filled. Health, India, Exchequer and Agriculture [Edward Wood] are the ones I class as exceptionally well-filled. Hoare very good at Air, Bridgeman and Worthy adequate at Admiralty and War Office . . . Jack Gilmour obviously the right man for the Scottish Office and Jicks probably equal to the Home Office.[7]

It was a powerful team and one that was retained with little change until 1929, another Baldwin reaction to the Lloyd George days when offices had changed with bewildering rapidity. Changes were made only when Curzon, Cave and Birkenhead died or retired, when Cecil resigned, and when Wood became Viceroy of India. When Curzon died in 1925 he was replaced by Balfour, another elder statesman temporarily out of office, and when Birkenhead retured he was replaced by Peel who had been the previous Conservative Secretary of State for India. Twelve of the fourteen departments with ministers in the cabinet had the same chief for the full life of the government, and there was a similar continuity lower down.

It was a source of amazement to contemporaries (and to some ministers) that such a powerful team could operate under a man like Baldwin; as Lord Birkenhead put it, 'it is of course a tragedy that so great an army should have so uninspiring a Commander in Chief'. This missed the point, as he was to find within the year, for inspiration was exactly Baldwin's strong point. He practised as Prime Minister in the Bonar Law mould, leaving the substantive discussion and the departmental work to colleagues, striving to provide the atmosphere in which decisions could be taken by agreement. The youngest member of the cabinet, Lord Eustace Percy, believed that 'he alone, I think, could have held this mixed company together in good feeling for nearly five years, by his curious gift of unobtrusive moral authority'.[8]

Baldwin's unobtrusive control was demonstrated by two incidents in the first few months. Birkenhead had been criticized for writing articles in the press, which the King regarded as inconsistent with a post in his government, and which was contrary to a cabinet decision too. Birkenhead was not a rich man and was giving up a large legal income to hold office. Baldwin was aware of Birkenhead's difficulty, but firm in his insistence that the press work must stop; Birkenhead was given £10,000 from party funds to enable him to live in his accustomed style and his loyalty to Baldwin was further strengthened. In May 1925 a dispute between Churchill and Steel-Maitland was due to be considered in cabinet committee, as Tom Jones recorded:

At 4-15 the P.M. presided over the Unemployment Committee and did it in such good-tempered fashion that the conflict between the Chancellor and the Minister of Labour never emerged. For the first five or ten minutes the P.M. did nothing but work away at his pipe, scouring it out and filling it, lighting it and relighting it, meanwhile telling some quite amusing stories. We also had tea served, and by the time we came to business we were all in the friendliest mood. The upshot was to agree to a draft Bill being prepared, which Bill will go about half-way Winston wants to go.[9]

Baldwin's control took some time to establish and other incidents in the first year suggested that colleagues were only too ready to test their strength.

The cruiser crisis came about through a collision between Bridgeman and Churchill on the naval estimates for 1925–26. Churchill was determined to be true to his father and to leave the reputation of a Chancellor who had cut expenditure, especially military expenditure; in 1925 he reduced the income tax and committed himself to reducing expenditure by £10 million a year. But the Admiralty were still planning under the assumption of a naval threat from Japan, and their minimum demand was for six new cruisers, a demand supported by the threatened resignation of Bridgeman and most of his Board. *Punch* was not the only commentator which compared Churchill's retrenchment policy of 1925 with his demand for a stronger navy in 1913. Had they foreseen what would happen ten years later, they would have been even more surprised. Churchill was throwing himself wholeheartedly into the work of his department, without great regard for past attitudes or for consistency. He regarded the prospect of war with Japan as so remote as to be not worth the sacrifice of his financial policy; for once the Admiralty were thinking further ahead. Churchill threw himself into the debate with his accustomed enthusiasm and with a determination to win, so that the Cabinet became polarized. Bridgeman was supported by his advisers and also by Amery, the previous First Lord, and by Davidson (his junior minister), who proceeded to whip up support in the party. On the merits of the case the cabinet was mainly with Churchill, but Davidson was able to convince many in the party that the old gang of Churchill and Birkenhead were using the issue to impose their will on the cabinet prior to disposing of Baldwin. Davidson exaggerated the danger, but the Whips and the Party Chairman all made strong representations to Baldwin, and it took all Baldwin's skill to hold things together, as Davidson recalled:

> Birkenhead, Winston and Austen assembled with Bridgeman and myself in the Prime Minister's room in the House of Commons. Beatty and I flanked Bridgeman. As we assembled Chamberlain screwed his eye-glass in, shot his cuffs and, turning to Beatty, observed that this was a very vital meeting at which the Admiralty was going to have a little education in the art of government. Beatty was not in the least bit perturbed, and briskly retorted that he thought its purpose was to give the critics of the Admiralty a kindergarten lesson on the elements of strategy. Fortunately at that moment the Prime Minister entered . . .
>
> Once SB decided that Winston must accept the Admiralty's case, by patience and cunning he achieved that result, although with a majority against him he took an enormous risk.[10]

Davidson was again exaggerating, for Baldwin was in no danger, even if the unity of the government was, for the party would never have stood for the sacrifice of Bridgeman and the Board of Admiralty to Churchill in 1925. If there ever was a conspiracy, which is extremely doubtful, Baldwin had only to bring it into the open to destroy it; far more likely, Churchill had gathered all his force, his friends and supporters to pursue a policy in which he earnestly believed. The eventual compromise allowed Churchill to save some face, but there was no real doubt who had won; it was decided to build the six cruisers over eighteen months instead of a year. Baldwin owed his position as leader to his support in the party, while ministers owed their offices to his choice.

The steel debate never threatened to destroy the government but was equally important in its way. Back in 1923 Amery had urged Baldwin not to hold an election on tariffs but to introduce them gradually under the safeguarding system and then to seek approval afterwards; he had continued to press for this and it had not been ruled out by Baldwin's speeches in 1924 so the tariff reformers could still hope to see their policy brought in by the back door. In this they gravely misjudged Baldwin himself and the strength of Churchill; Baldwin intended to reintroduce the McKenna duties and the Safeguarding Act, but had no intention of going back on the narrow definition of safeguarding given during the election, which Churchill had accepted. The Cabinet therefore decided that safeguarding would only be extended to an industry after an inquiry, if the industry was a large one, if foreign competition was unfair, and if unemployment was being caused. These strict rules offended the tariff reformers but they were approved by parliament. The problem arose in May 1925 when the steel industry applied for safeguarding; steel was certainly a major and vital industry, but it was so central to the economy that a decision to safeguard steel would be followed by demands for protection of everything else. Steel could not be considered in isolation, so the cabinet found themselves debating again the whole issue of tariffs, with Churchill now present to threaten resignation. It was Churchill who suggested a means of escape by refering the question to the Committee of Economic Enquiry. In this contest Churchill in the end won, although Baldwin and some other ministers felt that the case for protection had been more than made out by the evidence given. Baldwin announced on 12 December 1925 that the application of the steel industry for protection would be refused.

It would be misleading to convey the impression that the government's early months were full of disagreements, for this was not the case. It was hardly to be expected that men who had been abusing each other only a few months before they met as a cabinet should settle down at once; but by the end of 1925 ministers had tested each others' strengths and weaknesses, Churchill had shown that he could win arguments of policy, and Baldwin that he could act as leader when needed. From this time on policy disagreements did not disrupt the working of the cabinet, and the only resignation, that of Lord Cecil in 1927, hardly caused a ripple in the party or the country. The rest of the work of the first years can be seen from two perspectives, the routine preparations for a full term of office, and the opening of new initiatives in peacemaking.

Cabinet routine worked well under Baldwin's influence; the King's Speech of 1924 offered little that had not been foreshadowed in the recent manifesto. In November 1924 Neville Chamberlain presented to the Cabinet a list of the reforms that he wished to implement in housing, health and local government. Baldwin gave full support to these plans, including extensions of national insurance and widows' pensions, and Chamberlain set to work to implement them; of the twenty-five proposals, twenty-one became law by 1929. Churchill's 1925 budget was well received and the return to gold at the pre-war parity was generally approved in the party; it was part of the restoration of the infrastructure of trade, as Baldwin's work on the US debts had been in 1923. In retrospect the return to gold has been seen to be a fatal mistake which overpriced British exports and so deepened the depression. At the time though, expert advice available to Churchill saw this as an unavoidable consequence that must be braved if the economy were ever to be set right. There were few in 1925 who were perceptive enough to see that there was a viable alternative to the dictates of classical economic theory.[11]

However, it was neither internal disagreements nor routine business which reflected the government's real purpose in 1925; Baldwin's attitude has been called 'the appeasement of England', and in a real sense the making of peace was the government's overriding aim.[12] In 1925 the government sought peace in Ireland, in Europe and in industrial relations. The Irish Question was not the least significant for British politics, and what remained to be settled was the boundary between North and South, for the boundary commission appointed under the treaty of 1921 completed its work in 1925. Ever since 1921 there had been disagreement about the commission's precise terms of reference: the Free State government believed that the commission would consider the border as a whole, and that it would be free to allocate large tracts of Northern Ireland to the South on grounds of its catholic and nationalist population, large enough tracts indeed to render the state of Northern Ireland both economically and politically unworkable. The Stormont government, the British government and the commission itself (including its Irish members) all interpreted the treaty as allowing only minor adjustments, and these in both directions. Hence the commission offered only small transfers from North to South (and also very small transfers from South to North, which the Free State government was bound to regard as a betrayal. It fell to Baldwin to secure acceptance of these proposals or to find some other means of avoiding a resumption of hostilities. Over the summer of 1925 he investigated the opinions of all concerned, but his hand was forced when the *Morning Post* published a map that purported to reveal the boundary commissioners' proposals; the map was misleading in detail but correct in outline, so the problem broke before the report was even published. Baldwin was made aware from the party that any pressure on Ulster to give away more than the boundary commission had offered would be much resented, and it is possible that the *Morning Post* had exactly this in mind when it published its map. He took the precaution of using Salisbury, Amery and

Joynson-Hicks in the subsequent negotiations as a sign to the party of his good faith. Tripartite talks took place at Chequers in late November and against all expectations an agreement was reached. Through Baldwin's mediation and with Churchill's active help, the two Irish governments agreed to retain the frontier as it stood rather than accept the boundary commissioners' report, and the bitter pill was sweetened for the Free State by the cancellation of £155 million of debts that it had taken over in 1921. Salisbury could not bring himself actually to sign the agreement, but Amery and Joynson-Hicks signed with Baldwin, Churchill and Birkenhead for the British government. Relative peace was established between the British and Irish governments and the Irish Question passed out of party politics at last; appropriately, it was in the same year that the party dropped the name 'Unionist' and reverted to 'Conservative'.[13]

The settlement of Europe was a matter that Baldwin was content to leave to Austen Chamberlain, although he supported him against the mild criticisms of Curzon. The government decided at an early stage not to ratify the Geneva Protocol negotiated by MacDonald, since it involved unacceptable commitments to the League of Nations. Later this came to be seen as a step in the downward path of the League, but it was by no means clear that MacDonald's government would have ratified the Protocol either. Chamberlain worked for an agreement by bilateral agreements outside the League and finally brought about a five-power meeting at Locarno; by the Locarno Pact, Britain, France, Germany, Belgium and Italy agreed to respect each others' frontiers and to back up their guarantees by force if needed. From the 1930s, Locarno seemed to be a hollow agreement, but it was hailed as a triumph in October 1925, as a new step in diplomacy, for the powers had renounced their right to change frontiers by force. The 'Locarno spirit' was expected to lead to a new understanding in Europe and for a few years these exaggerated hopes were realized. In the euphoria after the treaty was signed (what A. P. Herbert called 'Locarny-blarney') its implications were certainly overestimated, but it did achieve something for Britain. For the next few years, Britain's governments could give their full attention to problems at home and in the Empire without any fear that European entanglements might ruin their plans. Austen Chamberlain was given deserved credit and awarded the Garter at the King's suggestion; he himself was optimistic for the success of his policy of 'appeasement from strength'.[14]

Appeasement from strength would also be an apt description of what Baldwin was trying to achieve at home. His opportunity arose in March 1925 with the introduction of a private member's Bill on trade union law, introduction by a Scottish Conservative, F. A. Macquisten. The Bill was not really Macquisten's at all, but rather the Conservative party's Bill, and in deciding its attitude the government could not but be aware of the party's feeling.

The party had been officially opposed to the existing system of the political levy from which a trade unionist might 'contract out' ever since it had been introduced in the Trades Union Act of 1913. Conservatives felt that some trade unionists (they said many of them) remained under the political levy through fear or apathy and so supported the Labour party with their money although they voted Conservative or Liberal. Some no doubt were merely taking a good opportunity to weaken a political rival, knowing how far the Labour party depended on the political levy, but others believed in the need for a change with a passionate intensity (as did the members of the Conservative party's labour committees). Although it had been a party commitment, nothing was done by the Lloyd George government in wartime, not least because of the divisive effect that any action would have had. There was no mention of it in the coalition manifesto of 1918, but it was nevertheless a feature of the campaign of many a Unionist candidate, as it was again in 1922. Party meetings passed their resolutions on the subject and the National Union pressed for action, so that repeal of the Act of 1913 assumed almost equal significance with the House of Lords as a test of the Conservatism of the coalition.

The party was not content to sit and wait for its leaders to act when there was a Unionist majority in parliament; in 1922 Colonel Edward Meysey-Thompson introduced a Bill to reform the trade unions, including the abolition of the political levy, which was enthusiastically approved by the National Union and supported by resolutions from constituencies. A lively debate occurred when the Bill came up for its second reading, but in the complete absence of the government; Unionist backbenchers gave strong support, Labour MPs were equally strong opponents, but the advice of the government was not offered because Liberal ministers would not support the Bill and Unionists dare not oppose it. Meysey-Thompson's Bill was given a second reading, and Stanley Baldwin was one of the few ministers who voted – in favour of the Bill. But the government could at least agree on a policy of delay and so killed the Bill by refusing to make time available for further discussion. Other Bills in the next few years went through a similar course.[15]

Things might have been very different with a Unionist government in power in 1923, so the backbenchers tried again; this time Baldwin replied for the government and asked for time to take the advice of his ministers and from both sides of industry before coming to a decision. Admiral Hall wrote to Davidson, for Baldwin's attention, to suggest that

> if when the P.M. consults 'Labour' on the subject of the political levy, I venture to urge that he also consults our Conservative working men. The Labour Committees (Unionist) are very strong on this point and will undoubtedly feel that they have been let down if he doesn't! Verb. sap.![16]

There may have been consultations, but there was no action, for the government was soon embroiled with tariffs and the manifesto of 1923 again failed to mention the subject. In opposition pressure built up again and the policy committee that considered the matter opted for the policy that the diehards had wanted, as outlined in June 1924:

> POLITICAL LIBERTY: It is the right of every citizen to support the policy and the party in which he believes; to use an industrial organization in order to make him contribute out of his earnings to the funds of one political party, regardless of his private views, is an infringement of that right, and strikes directly at the political liberty which is one of the most treasured possessions of the British people.
>
> For this reason, the Unionist Party, whilst upholding Trade Unionism in all its legitimate objects, will endeavour to secure that every Trade Unionist shall be free to exercise his own unfettered discretion as to whether or not he should contribute to any political levy through his union.[17]

This was clear enough, and only nine months before Macquisten's Bill was introduced, but in the meantime the waters had again become clouded.

The positive commitment of June 1924 somehow disappeared when the manifesto was published in October, and Baldwin made no attempt to repeat the commitment in his speeches, no doubt because it would have clashed with his stance as a peacemaker. There was no mention of it in the King's Speech, so the backbenchers once again set out to force their leader's hand; Macquisten came out well in the ballot for private members' Bills and the honour fell to him. The National Union took no risk that their views would be unknown; in February 1925 Stanley Jackson reported that he and the Chief Whip had been coopted on to the cabinet committee considering the Bill (a most unusual procedure) so that the party's views would be taken into account. Under his control Central Office drafted a very strong resolution in favour of the Bill and sent it to each local party with the suggestion that they should pass one like it; hundreds of them did so and sent their resolutions to their MPs and to Baldwin. When the cabinet met to reach a decision, they could be in no doubt about the strength of party feeling; any weakness now would be regarded as a betrayal of the commitments made over years and renewed only a few months earlier. Not surprisingly, most of the cabinet saw no alternative but to take over the Bill as their own and so accede to what the party wanted.[18]

Baldwin resolved, though, to take on the party and stake his position on taming it, for this alone would give the New Conservatism a solid base in the one area of policy that really mattered. If the party was to use its majority for a policy that the labour movement would see as vindictive then it would destroy all that Baldwin hoped to achieve and make his stance in 1924 seem like a bogus prospectus. He was not alone in this view; a delegation of MPs from the left of the party urged him to caution on 25 February, a *Times* leader on 19 February advised the government to steer clear of the Bill, and discreet soundings in the cabinet revealed that some ministers had doubts even though the majority seemed to be against him.[19] At the critical cabinet meeting on 27 February Baldwin took the unusual course of asking for each minister's individual opinion, presumably because he needed to be sure of his ground before giving his own view; he then summed up in a way that astonished his colleagues. He intended to intervene in the debate at an early stage, before many MPs had been able to commit themselves either way, and although he would make it clear that the government supported the principle in the Bill, they would sacrifice their opinions to promote industrial peace. There would also be a warning that 'if this gesture did not meet with a favourable response from the Opposition, the Government would not hesitate to take action on their own responsibility'. The response to this announcement was graphically described by Edward Wood:

> When he finished, no one said anything, for everybody felt that they had just listened to something of a quite different order from what had gone before. Finally Birkenhead broke the silence to say that if the Prime Minister could say to the House . . . just what he had now said to the Cabinet, he thought that the speech would be made with the unanimous support of the Cabinet, and would carry conviction to the House.[20]

A pencilled note passed across to Baldwin from Birkenhead on an envelope added the encouraging words 'I think your action showed enormous courage and for that reason will succeed.'[21] The cabinet had had a sudden glimpse of Baldwin's moral authority – rather as if a clergyman had walked into a betting shop – and agreed unanimously to back his statement. Even Austen Chamberlain was moved to enthusiasm for Baldwin, impressed 'by the power that he showed in a Cabinet discussion on Friday on the political levy. Watch for this speech on the bill next Friday. I have bet Sam Hoare £5 that he will bring it off *triumphantly* – the Attorney-General to decide whether the adverb is justified.'[22] Austen won his bet, and the Attorney-General was not put to much trouble in adjudicating.

Baldwin prepared the ground with a speech which he was scheduled to make in Birmingham on 5 March, the evening before the second reading debate. He linked the government's search for peace and security in Europe with the need for harmony at home and pointed to the danger to that harmony posed by powerful trade unions:

> I plead for disarmament at home, and for the removal of that suspicion at home that tends to poison the relations of man and man, the removal which alone can lead us to stability for our struggling industry, and create the confidence in which our people may be able to go forward to better things. . . . I want a truce of God in this country, that we may compose our differences, that we may join all our strengths together to see if we cannot pull the country into a better and happier condition.[23]

All this had an obvious relevance to the programme of the following day, but no more direct reference was made. Baldwin was aiming at a wider audience than the House of Commons and he was also keeping his own position secret, with a sure sense of the impact that it would make when revealed. On the following day he moved an amendment to Macquisten's Bill, asserting the government's belief in the principle of the Bill but claiming that such contentious matters should be left to government legislation. His speech, probably the best of his career and one of the supreme parliamentary moments of the century, deserves to be quoted at length. Here was the New Conservatism in action, 'a truly Disraelian leap in the dark'.[24]

He began with an account of labour relations in his family firm, a heritage of cooperation that must not be allowed to die away in the new industrial world of large combines and powerful trade unions. It could be preserved only through direct collaboration between management and labour, a collaboration that might be aided by the government's ability to create the right general climate, but which must rely mainly on the spirit of partnership inside industry. He then linked these themes to the immediate situation:

> For two years past, in the face of great difficulties, perhaps greater than many were aware of, I have striven to consolidate, and to breathe a living force into my great Party. Friends of mine who have done me the honour to read my speeches during that time have seen clearly, however ill they have been expressed, the ideals at which I have been aiming. I spoke on that subject last night at Birmingham, and I shall continue to speak on it as long as I am where I am.
>
> We find ourselves, after these two years, in power, in possession of perhaps the greatest majority our Party has ever had, and with the general assent of the country. Now how did we get here? It was not by promising to bring this Bill in; it was because, rightly or wrongly, we succeeded in creating the impression throughout the country that we stood for stable Government and peace in the country between all classes of the Community. Those were the principles for which we fought; those were the principles on which we won; and our victory was not entirely by the votes of our own Party, splendidly as they fought. I should think that the number of Liberals who voted for us at the last Election ran into six figures, and I should think that we polled more labour votes than the other side.
>
> That being so, what should our course be at the beginning of a new Parliament? I have not myself the slightest doubt. Last year, the Leader of the Labour Party, when he was Prime Minister, suspended . . . further progress for the time being on the schemes of Singapore. He did it on the ground that it was a gesture for peace, and he hoped that it might be taken as such by all the countries of the world. He hoped that a gesture of that kind might play its part in leading to what we all want to see, that is, a reduction in the world's armaments.
>
> I want my Party today to make a gesture to the country of a similar nature, and to say to them: 'We have our majority; we believe in the justice of this Bill which has been brought in today, but we are going to withdraw our hand, and we are not going to push our political advantage home at a moment like this. Suspicion which has prevented stability in Europe is the one poison that is preventing stability at home, and we offer the country today this: We, at any rate are not going to fire the first shot. We stand for peace. We stand for the removal of suspicion in the country. We want to create an atmosphere, a new atmosphere in a new Parliament for a new age, in which the people can come together. We abandon what we have laid our hands to. We know we may be called cowards for doing it. We know we may be told that we have gone back on our principles. But we believe we know what at this moment the country wants, and we believe it is for us in our strength to do what no other Party can do at this moment, and to say that we at any rate stand for peace.'
>
> I know, I am as confident as I can be of anything, that that will be the feeling of

all those who sit behind me, and that they will accept the Amendment which I have put down in the spirit in which I have moved it. And I have equal confidence in my fellow-countrymen throughout the whole of Great Britain. Although I know that there are those who work for different ends from most of us in this House, yet there are many in all ranks and all parties who will re-echo my prayer: 'Give peace in our time, O Lord'[25]

The Prime Minister sat down to an ovation from all sides and the support for Macquisten's Bill collapsed instantly. Churchill acknowledged that

Baldwin achieved a most remarkable success on Friday. He made about the only speech which could have restored the situation, and made it in exactly the right way. I had no idea he could show such power. He has never done it before. The whole Conservative Party turned round and obeyed without one single mutineer. . . . As Sieyes said of Napoleon . . . after the eighteenth of Brumaire 'Nous avons un maitre'. I cease to be astonished at anything.[26]

Others were even more generous and Baldwin was deluged with tributes from colleagues, from opponents, from the press and from the public. In one tribute much later, the Clydesider David Kirkwood summed up such reactions:

In your speech, you made flesh the feeling of us all, that the antagonism, the bitterness, and class rivalry were unworthy, and that understanding and amity were possible. You would not accept it from me, if I said that the speech caused the change. I prefer to say that it expressed the inarticulate feeling for a change and so materialised an ideal thought into a living reality.[27]

The new initiative was completed by a third speech, at Leeds on 12 March. Here Baldwin linked his desire for peace with an attack on the militants who threatened to destroy national unity for narrow political ends. The decision to put Labour in power in 1924 had been vindicated when the moderates had established their complete control and expelled the Communists, but this had merely moved the battle into the trade unions. The new need was to strengthen the hands of the trade union moderates (whose position would have been destroyed by Macquisten's Bill) so that they would be able to win a similar victory over the Minority Movement.[28] These three speeches at Birmingham, Leeds and in the Commons made an enormous impact; as a separate pamphlet called *Peace in Industry* they sold half a million copies in three months.

Reaction in the party was rather different. Many MPs were furious at Baldwin's change of front and from this time on he was never trusted by either the diehard wing or by the labour committees. The National Union Executive narrowly escaped a savage debate on 10 March; a critical motion put by Sir Philip Stott on behalf of the labour committees was ruled out of order because it was submitted too late to be on the agenda.[29] By the next meeting, the positive reaction in the country made protest worthless, but local parties continued to complain. At the Party Conference in the autumn, there was uproar at the opening session when a delegate tried to refer back the annual report to express disapproval of government industrial policy – 'It has no industrial policy'. Order was restored after several minutes of interruptions and the report was finally adopted with only three dissentients, but the next day produced further disorder. A resolution calling the immediate abolition of the political levy received strong support. For the platform, Stanley Jackson had to reply that,

> the Leaders of the Party . . . knew the feeling of the country on the question as well as anyone, and he could assure the Conference that that feeling was conveyed to the leaders of the party and they knew it thoroughly. . . . [Our] noble effort was made more difficult by an appeal to a sense of fairness and justice by the other side, but it appeared to him that this question appealed to him not because of the party advantage that someone might get one way or the other but as a matter of justice (applause). And you will agree that we cannot possibly attempt to sacrifice justice on the altar of political expediency. (Applause.)[30]

Thus fortified by the advice of the Party Chairman, who seemed to be describing Baldwin and his cabinet as 'the other side', the Conference unanimously supported the resolution and thereby disowned Baldwin's policy and attitude. The Central Council confirmed this position in February 1926 with a similar resolution. By this time though, Baldwin had gone on from his position of the previous March to a decision that caused even greater offence to his party.

When Baldwin made his third speech in March, he was already aware that his initiative was being interpreted as weakness by the trade union militants, hence his attack on them. This led on through the spring of 1925 to a clash with the trade unions as a whole and to the government climb-down on 'Red Friday' in July. On the principle of intervention in industry, Baldwin occupied a middle position, accepting with the 'YMCA' that the Tory tradition allowed intervention, but also accepting with the 'industrials' that intervention must be minimal and be consistent with economic policy. Baldwin saw the duty of government as 'holding the ring' while industry worked out its own solutions, much the attitude that he had taken in the Irish negotiations. It was hoped that the moderation that he had called for in March would be the right atmosphere for industrial negotiations, but that was as far as he was prepared to go. He therefore turned down the suggestion of a general industrial conference in which the government would take the chair.[31] This was a tragic error, for when such talks did begin (even without the government and after the General Strike) they led to a considerable lowering of the industrial temperature, but neither Baldwin nor his party saw this as the government's proper role. Such a scheme had failed in 1919 and was in any case too reminiscent of the methods of Lloyd George to appeal to Conservatives in 1925.

The lost opportunity deepened into an urgent crisis in 1925 through the coal industry, where exports had fallen sharply after the return to gold and the evacuation of the Ruhr by France. Advice to the government pointed to the fall of prices since 1920 and the uneconomic price of British coal in the world market; wages would have to fall if the industry were to become competitive, but some reductions would be justified in any case by the fall in the cost of living since current wage rates had been agreed. By this theory government intervention would be positively harmful, since it would delay the restoration of equilibrium between prices, wages and exports; the industry would have to contract, and government intervention would only hinder the one development that could restore competitiveness. By economic theory as well as by inclination it was believed that the government should stand aside and allow wages to be forced down. But in the case of coal the government was already deeply involved by the subsidy paid from the Treasury, due to expire in 1925. Moreover there was clearly no spirit of compromise from either side of the industry, for years of confrontation had left a unique legacy of bitterness. In the first industry in which Baldwin's policy could be put to the test, there was no readiness to compromise and no room for manoeuvre. With the industry set on a collision course the government resolved to be true to its belief, to allow the subsidy to expire and brave the consequences. There is little doubt that the party backed this view, consistent even with Baldwin's position of March.

Opinions wavered when the shape of the likely conflict became clearer. The miners gained the support of the Triple Alliance and of other unions, so that what might occur was not a single dispute but something more like a general strike. This would produce serious strains for the entire nation and it would kill Baldwin's new initiative before it was even launched properly. An inquiry set up by the government to help the owners and miners to find a way out of their conflict merely highlighted the area of disagreement. On 30 July the subsidy would expire, new wage rates would be imposed, and the miners would begin their strike. Baldwin and his ministers engaged in prolonged negotiations through July in an effort to avoid a strike, but although Baldwin himself persuaded both sides to give some ground, there was too wide a difference between them to allow a negotiated settlement. So far no mention had been made of a possible prolongation of the subsidy for Baldwin wished both sides to see the gravity of the situation and had no wish to allow either side to use the government as a shield between themselves and economic reality. When the cabinet met to take its decision, on 30 July, reconciliation was impossible and most of the ministers believed in the inevitability of conflict. Supported by Churchill and Neville Chamberlain, Baldwin again stood out against the majority and persuaded the cabinet to accept the subsidy for a further nine months, during which there would be a national debate on the subject and a new inquiry.[32]

This swift change of front would take a great deal of explaining, and was accepted only for contradictory reasons. Baldwin hoped that a delay would provide a chance to resolve the dispute without a strike; others like Cunliffe-Lister accepted it only because they saw a better chance of winning an inevitable fight if it could be delayed. Late on 30 July Baldwin announced the subsidy and secured the calling off of the new wage rates and the strike. This retreat on 'Red Friday' was interpreted by trade unions and by many Conservatives as a major government defeat, another sign of Baldwin's weakness. Because of the events of 1926, Red Friday has come to be seen merely as a prelude to the General Strike, a breathing space gained by a government that knew in its heart that it must fight and wished only to find a better ground for the battle. This is seriously misleading, for Red Friday marks the end of a chapter not a beginning; it was the logical consequence of March 1925 and, whatever the views of their colleagues, Baldwin, Churchill and Neville Chamberlain were as genuine in their desire for peace (and their readiness to incur odium in the search for it) in July as four months earlier. In March Baldwin had forced his party against its will not to fire the first shot, and in July he intervened to stop the shooting in the coal industry when both sides were ready to open fire. He could scarcely believe that the moderate majority would embark on conflict when compromise could be reached, and he thought even in July that there need not be a fight. Without such a conviction, his whole position in 1924–25 becomes inexplicable, and it was an act of considerable political courage to drag his party so far along a road of which most of them profoundly disapproved.

There was, though, another aspect of Baldwin's attitude that alone made his policy acceptable. In March he had been quite emphatic that his government would not shirk a fight if the militants insisted on one in the end. In July he was well aware that a battle remained likely and that public support would be vital if it were to be won. A delay would not only give time for organizational preparations, as his colleagues insisted, but would also enable the government to put its case across to the public. So when he defended the subsidy in the Commons on 6 August, he spoke not only of the dreadful consequences of a strike but of the responsibility that would fall on those who might bring it about. If conflict now came, then it would be clear at least that the government had neither sought it nor welcomed it; in this sense Red Friday was the Munich stage of the 'appeasement of England'.[33] If conflict should come, then the government would make sure that the battle were won; 'we shall not fire the first shot' was still Baldwin's message in July, but it did not preclude the determination to fire the last one. Unfortunately for all concerned the burden of this message was missed, missed as much in his own party as by the militants. Both sides persisted in regarding Red Friday as a sign of weakness, and many Conservatives felt the full force of A. J. Cook's words to the miners: 'We have beaten the most powerful government of modern times': Hitler made much the same mistake in 1938–39.

Despite this, Baldwin's initiative of 1925 may have helped in its real purpose. At the Trades Union Congress at Scarborough the speeches were inflammatory, and not at all in keeping with the call for moderation, but nevertheless the moderates were regaining control. The left began to lose ground in the General Council, the ultra-moderate Citrine became General Secretary, and the Industrial Committee made no real preparations for an industrial confrontation.[34] These developments owed as much to the internal power struggle in the Labour movement as to anything outside, but they could scarcely have taken place if there had been a General Strike in the summer or if the government had moved to take away the legal rights of trade unions. A trend to the right began in the trade unions which culminated in the virtual eradication of Communist influence by the end of the decade, a process which owed much to Baldwin's influence.

The government itself hoped for the best but prepared for the worst. The Supply and Transport Committee was placed under Sir John Anderson of the Home Office and prepared detailed plans for the organization that would be needed in the event of a general strike. Local authorities were mobilized and volunteers were recruited in advance by a semi-official body called the Organization for the Maintenance of Supplies (OMS), led by Lord Hardinge of Penshurst, ex-Viceroy of India and ex-Permanent Secretary of the Foreign Office. The OMS remained independent but was integrated into government plans and encouraged by the Home Secretary. In all these preparations the party played no official part. All the Civil Commissioners were Conservative ministers with local connections in the area that they were to administer, acting under the Postmaster General, Mitchell-Thompson. The OMS was 'strictly non-party in character' but many of its Council were prominent Conservatives (such as Archer-Shee, Rennell-Rodd, Falkland and Scar-borough) and most of the others were retired officers whose views were well to the right. Party publications gave publicity to the OMS,[35] readers were advised how to join and that the Home Secretary had given his approval. It may be coincidence that the OMS was run from St Stephen's House, which had accommodated Conservative Central Office until 1918, but this seems unlikely. But there is no evidence of any overt cooperation; the National Union never discussed the OMS or the government's plans, there was no attempt to assist the preparations through Central Office, and few local parties took any official notice of what was going on. It is certain that large numbers of individual Conservatives joined the OMS and it may be that contacts made through the party facilitated its work, but if so no evidence has survived; Conservative involvement remained entirely individual and unofficial. The party was indeed too busy criticizing the weakness of Baldwin's position to see its underlying strength, and his speech at the Party Conference in October 1925 was entirely defensive. The first eighteen months of government therefore ended with considerable government success in avoiding or postponing conflicts in every field, but with a great loss of enthusiasm among its own supporters.

Any discussion of 1926 and the later years of the Baldwin government is dominated by the General Strike. For all Baldwin's optimism, it was the cabinet ministers who insisted on preparing for a fight who were justified by the outcome. In the early part of 1926 attitudes hardened but nothing more could be done until the report of Samuel's Royal Commission came in. From the publication of the Samuel report in mid-March until the expiry of the subsidy at the end of April there were six weeks of intensive talks; as in July 1925 the government tried to conjure up an agreement and again was suspected of weakness by its supporters. By this time, the negotiations were four-sided, with the TUC and the government both directly involved, but it was still impossible to square the circle. The government accepted the Samuel report if it were accepted in the industry but stopped short of forcing acceptance. It may be that here again an opportunity was lost, but by this time Baldwin was under considerable pressure from cabinet and party. From the end of April the miners' strike went ahead and negotiations centred on the position of the TUC and the government, but there was little chance that the TUC would abandon the miners without at least a show of fight and without this the Conservative cabinet would not have accepted any agreement reached. The General Strike finally began when the cabinet heard that compositors on the *Daily Mail* had refused to set the issue of 3 May because it contained material critical of the unions. It is often suggested that the cabinet was relieved to have an excuse to break off negotiations and treated the *Daily Mail* incident as a pretext. On returning to Downing Street for a last attempt at negotiation, the TUC were told that Baldwin had gone to bed. This view ignores the rising tension of the previous few days and the fact that the TUC had already sent out its strike notices on the day before. It is clear that the TUC leaders did not want a strike and were not prepared for one, as *Home and Politics* told its readers:

> We are all apt to forget that the great strike began as a great bluff. The TUC was not prepared for a strike. It had neither the money nor the organization to sustain a fight against the rest of the community. What it banked upon was the belief that the Government would cave in at the last moment as every previous Government had done.[36]

It was not a revolutionary threat but an example of brinkmanship that had gone wrong, a bluff that was called.

Nevertheless, once the General Strike had been called, it was a serious threat, for a government defeat *would* have changed the whole constitutional situation. The party rallied to the government and there were demands for retaliatory action, but there was also a recognition of the extremity of the situation and a desire not to make things worse. The supply machinery and the OMS worked smoothly enough in the short time that they were needed; it may be that they would have broken down in a strike of several weeks, but such speculation is wide of the mark, for the TUC had no intention of putting it to the test. Once the strike began and Baldwin could take his stand on the constitution as well as on his desire for peace, the TUC were only looking for a way out without losing face, and after a week they were prepared even to confess failure to the extent of unconditional surrender. Baldwin recognized that the strike had even simplified things, that there could be no further negotiation until it was called off, and that he should stand aside and await the resumption of talks. In his parliamentary speeches and in his broadcasts he asked to be allowed to continue his role as peacemaker and even enhanced his reputation in that direction. He had seen surely enough that the middle-class public would rally to the government that they had put in power and that the TUC would not take the risk of pressing the fight to a finish: he had only to wait.

The role of the party during the strike remains rather shadowy. Ministers remained in London or at their posts as Civil Commissioners, Churchill was shunted into a siding at the *British Gazette* and many MPs like Harold Macmillan went to their constituencies to explain the government's case; but again, except for individuals the party did nothing. No meeting of the National Union could be convened and hardly any local parties could meet; the few that did call emergency meetings (as in Oxford) were all in towns where the lack of transport did not prevent movement, but they could do little more than pass resolutions deploring the strike.[37] The official organization could do little more, as the example of Maidstone shows.

On 7 May a circular to agents was received from Herbert Blain, urging the local party to take steps through normal propaganda channels to get the government's case across. A dummy 'Evening Gazette' was enclosed to show how the local party could bring out local newspapers based on the *British Gazette* and the news from the BBC; the information included in the dummy was highly tendentious, suggesting that the North had rallied to the government and that strikers were returning to work everywhere. Agents were to encourage party members to volunteer for service, but were to allow public speeches only if these would not cause disturbance. By this time the agent at Maidstone was distributor for the *British Gazette* in the area; distribution was later carried out through town halls, but party agents provided cars and Maidstone acted as a centre for East Kent, with cars coming in from adjoining constituencies to collect their copies. Some local news-sheets were issued, containing only news favourable to the government, such as the condemnation of the strike by Cardinal Bourne and Sir John Simon. Finally on 13 May, a circular from Blain thanked the agents for their 'excellent service'. Since little of this local activity has been noticed in national or local accounts of the strike, although it was supposed to be going on everywhere, it can be assumed to have made little impact. At the most it helped to disseminate the *British Gazette*, but it is not likely that that had much effect either. On 14 May the agent at Dover asked 'How are things going in the Maidstone area? I take it that you have had plenty of fun.' The reply gives something of the feelings of the party: 'Everything worked smoothly in Maidstone, trains and buses all running, but thank goodness it's all over.'[38]

Once the strike ended, the party basked in its victory; almost every local party passed a resolution of commendation for Baldwin and the National Union was warm in its praise. There was also a more ominous reaction, for opinion on trade union reform had now hardened even further. Local parties discussed the matter in advance of the Party Conference in the autumn, and made it clear to delegates that they expected action. Conciliation had been tried and had failed; now the party should show that it would not take no for an answer. Baldwin tried to be conciliatory again, intervening to stop the worst cases of the victimization of returning strikers, but he had neither the chance nor the wish to be conciliatory on the larger question. The continuation of the miners' strike through the autumn strengthened the hand of the diehards and increased the demand for action. There were a few in the party, later including even the diehard Sir Alexander Leith, who warned about the increasing bitterness in the mining areas, but the majority were more interested in fighting the miners to the finish and then going on to change the law on trade unions to underline their victory.[39]

The question of legislation, postponed in March 1925, had first been considered by the cabinet during the General Strike; for a time the majority favoured a punitive reaction which would sweep away all the legal gains won by the unions since Taff Vale, but Baldwin had stopped such a Bill from being produced and continued to argue against any action until the dispute was actually over. The Party Conference administered a sharp reminder of the mood of Conservatives and there was a real fear that the diehard wing would cause serious damage if they did not get what they wanted. It was to say the least fortunate that Stanley Jackson was at this point sent off to govern Bengal and replaced in the Party Chairmanship with Davidson. It was at exactly this time, though, that Davidson is supposed to have heard Blain describing Baldwin as a 'semi-socialist', probably because he was reporting the views that he had heard in the party. Lord Younger, still a man with his ear close to the ground, told Davidson about the same discontent among 'many of our closest supporters, and . . . there is much grumbling about [the government's] weakness and their *Socialistic* tendencies'. The most recent meeting of the National Union Executive had discussed the resolutions passed at the Party Conference and had passed on the demand for a trade union Bill to Baldwin with the express support of the Executive and with a request for information as to the government's intentions. Younger could see threatening signs of a repetition of the events of 1920–21, with the National Union becoming a stronghold of the diehards and a refuge for rebels of every kind. The next few months confirmed these fears and more.[40]

In February 1927 Baldwin himself made a rare appearance at the Executive and was greeted with another debate on the trade union question and with a strong resolution urging him to consult the party on legislation. By the following month the mood was even more hostile, for still no Bill had appeared:

Colonel Gretton referred to the feeling which he said prevailed amongst members of the Council at the last meeting that the passing of these resolutions was useless as nothing seemed to come of them, and there was a general desire that something definite should be done. He further thought that if they were not going to be acted upon some reason should be given. The Chairman pointed out that the Resolutions were always forwarded to the Government Departments involved and that he thought, although there might be criticism of the Government's policy, it was not for the Committee to dictate the Policy of the Government.[41]

A Trades Disputes Bill was finally published on 27 March 1927, and the next meeting of the Executive duly passed a resolution of thanks, but the discontent in the National Union did not die away so quickly. Criticism continued to be voiced and Davidson continued to defend Baldwin from attack; the four years after 1926 were almost as stormy as those after 1918.

Delay had been occasioned not by doubt as to the principle of legislation but by uncertainty about its content. By the beginning of 1927 Baldwin recognized that party opinion could not be resisted any longer, and so gave his support to the preparation of legislation. But it was support based on political necessity rather than conviction or enthusiasm. In that sense the Baldwin government lost its way in 1926 because its leader lost the will to determine its course. He had suffered physically and emotionally from the events of 1926, and he was to need regular rests for recuperation for the rest of his career.[42] Although he continued to preach conciliation, he had lost the certainty that it was a practicable course to pursue and he was no longer optimistic; as he himself admitted in the midst of the General Strike: 'Everything I care for most is being smashed to bits.'[43] The cabinet reasserted its independence and he became the arbitrator between ministers rather than their dominating force.

There were a few ministers who hoped to make a constructive contribution to labour relations, especially Steel-Maitland, Neville Chamberlain and Lord Cecil, but they were worn down by the majority, who were more concerned with retribution and future safety than with reconciliation. Baldwin took little part in the debates, although he could surely have secured at least some of what the moderates wanted. The Bill produced was entirely negative, although not as drastic as the diehards had dreamed of; it reversed or amended all the legal immunities of trade unions won in or since 1913, but it did not go the whole way and restore Taff Vale. General and sympathetic strikes became illegal, contracting out was replaced by contracting in, and the law of picketing was tightened up. There was a howl from Labour, apparently unaware that legislation would not have been introduced if there had not been a General Strike, and a powerful Labour campaign was mounted in the country to portray the Bill as a piece of class legislation intended to secure an unfair party advantage. There was obstruction in parliament and Baldwin was subjected to personal abuse for the first time, but the government majority and the guillotine ensured a quick passage of the Bill into law. There was also a Conservative campaign in the country to explain the new Act, and the public took the whole issue somewhat pacifically. When it came into force a third of the trade union members of the Labour party decided not to 'contract in' to continued membership, which suggests that Conservatives had at least some justification for their criticism of the previous system. In a deeper sense though the Trades Disputes Act did considerable harm to the Conservative party, for it damaged irreparably the reputation of fairness and moderation that Baldwin had foisted on it against its will in 1924–25. Baldwin's own reputation survived, and he was able to add the General Strike to the legend of English history as his own contribution to the tradition of moderation and good sense. The 1927 Act also provided a spur to the opposition parties; Baldwin could now be portrayed as an honest man fallen amongst thieves, a man whose intentions were good but whose colleagues would prevent him from realizing them, and in this they could create a general impression of the Conservative party as a party of reaction.

Other issues in 1927 and 1928 helped to confirm the impression of a rising tide of reaction, especially Russia, Home Office affairs, and the House of Lords. The diehards had bitterly resented the resumption of relations with Soviet Russia in 1924 and had expected after the election of 1924 that relations would be broken off and Communists in Britain ruthlessly suppressed. They were thwarted by Baldwin's wish to avoid all inflammatory gestures, by the need to keep up trade wherever possible, and by the view of the Foreign Office that links should be kept open whenever possible. Attacks on Communists had been limited to the prosecution of the leaders of the party in 1925 as a precautionary preparation for the General Strike, but the party had continued its attacks on Russia, and especially on alleged Russian espionage in Britain. The diehards in the cabinet worked up their case over Soviet activities in China and India, but they too were more interested in Britain. In May 1927 the offices of the Soviet Trade Delegation and an associated company were searched by the police on the orders of the Home Secretary; enough incriminating material was found to establish that the offices were used for espionage and propaganda, and the diehards had no real difficulty in forcing the cabinet into a final breach with Russia. Trade relations continued, but diplomatic contacts were ended; the real venom of the diehards on this issue is shown in Birkenhead's reaction: 'We have got rid of the hypocrisy of pretending to have friendly relations with this gang of murderers, revolutionaries and thieves. I breathe quite differently now we have purged our capital of the unclean and treacherous elements.'[44]

It was appropriate that Joynson-Hicks had figured in the severing of relations with Russia, for he was becoming a chief opposition target, a diehard bogeyman at the Home Office. He banned *Pravda* in 1925 and made continuing efforts to flush out spies and other undesirable aliens. He also made considerable use of the unrepealed sections of the Defence of the Realm Act to clean up London in another sense too: the Home Office encouraged a police crusade against vice and immorality, through a series of raids and prosecutions that drew a great deal of publicity and took DORA right to her legal limits. Such a campaign ran against the prevailing mood of London in the 1920s and drew unfavourable responses, especially after the unsuccessful prosecution of Sir Leo Money for immorality in Hyde Park. It was in one sense a deserved reaction, for Joynson-Hicks was quite open about what he was trying to do, but in another sense it was somewhat unfair, for he was also a sensible Home Secretary who left a deserved reputation as a Borstal reformer.[45]

The question of the House of Lords was another sign of the recovery of the initiative by the diehards and of divisions in the party. Baldwin had refused to take on such an incubus in 1923 but in opposition he had had to renew his party's commitment to strengthen the Upper House and to reform its composition. *Looking Ahead* had contained a firm pledge to get on with reform and, although the 1924 manifesto was again silent on the subject, pressure had mounted after the election, just as over the trade unions. Once the Trades Disputes Bill was in parliament, the House of Lords was the diehards' next target. An unguarded statement by Birkenhead committed the government to bringing in a Bill, but this pitched it into the same minefield that Lloyd George had failed to cross in 1918 and 1922. Even with a party that broadly favoured the principle, it was impossible to find any scheme that met with enough approval to pass into law. But the government, once committed, had to go ahead or meet another chorus of party disapproval; again Baldwin gave way without conviction, but this time managed to extricate himself in the end.

The agreed scheme was attacked as readily from the left of the Conservative party as from outside. Harold Macmillan told his constituents at Stockton that the whole subject should be dropped since the party would never agree on a scheme and because it would get them a bad reputation for no useful gain, a view with which the Stockton Conservatives agreed. When the Bill was presented, it was opposed by over a hundred Conservative MPs, by now anxious at the turn that their party was taking. It was killed by John Buchan, newly elected a Conservative MP and making his maiden speech: he pointed to the Bill's contradictions, questioned its usefulness, and urged his party to trust the people, for 'there will be no constitutional revolution in Britain until the great bulk of the British people resolutely desire it, and if that desire is ever present, what statute can bar the way?' Baldwin was among those who congratulated Buchan, for he had rescued his leader from an impossible situation. The Bill perished and the diehards added it to their list of issues on which they had been let down, while the moderates realized how dangerous an impression had been given by its introduction in the first place.[46]

With such fertile ground to till it is not surprising that the opposition parties made headway. In the government's first two years the only problem had been from Labour, but this was concentrated in the urban seats that were

Labour's home ground; turnout in by-elections did not fall far from the peak of 1924 and Conservative votes held up. Baldwin remained guardedly optimistic, for losses to Labour in the towns would not matter very much if the rural seats remained secure. The problems changed in and after 1927, with a Liberal revival and a falling away of the Conservative vote, as table 12.1 shows.[47] The same pattern could be detected in the results of local government elections, with the government doing reasonably well until 1926 and then losing support steadily, to Labour in the towns and to the Liberals in the counties and suburbs. The electoral coalition that Baldwin had put together to win so handsomely in 1924 had disintegrated by 1928. In this way the chronological profile of the second Baldwin government ran counter to the normal pattern. Most governments begin with their most partisan legislation and reach their nadir in their third year, but Baldwin's administration began moderately and then became more partisan, so reserving its greatest unpopularity for the end. The other parties deserve much of the credit, for both had been able to recover their spirits and their confidence after their poor showing in 1924. The Labour campaign against the Trades Disputes Act at least revived its own morale and directed attention in the trade unions on the only forum where legal immunities could be restored, much as the Taff Vale case had done.[48] The Liberals had recovered their unity for a time after Asquith's death and mounted a successful land campaign under Lloyd George. But neither could have made much headway if the door had not been opened for them by the government. By 1928 Baldwin's New Conservatism seemed to be in ruins and his party seemed to have reverted to type.

Table 12.1   *By-elections in the parliament of 1924*

Year	Conservative seats lost to Labour	Conservative seats lost to Liberals	Swing from Conservative %
1925	Nil	Nil	4.0
1926	3	Nil	5.3
1927	1	2	5.2
1928	3	3	6.4
1929	3	2	9.2

And yet the Baldwin government had much to be proud of in the second half of its term, much that derived directly from the new departures of 1924–25. In the main area of its apparent failure, industrial relations, there was a long-term success. Talks between employers and trade unionists finally got under way in 1927; the government took no direct part, but Baldwin had always argued that cooperation should come within industry and that the government could only give background assistance. The Mond-Turner talks achieved little in themselves, except by aiding the final victory of the moderates in the TUC, but they were a useful pointer to the way the mood of the unions had changed: 1927 was the most peaceful year in industry since the First World War and ushered in a long period of harmony that almost took industrial relations out of politics altogether.

Much had also been done on the imperial front. Early cabinet disputes on imperial trade had led to the creation of the Empire Marketing Board, which helped to foster imperial development. The Empire Exhibition at Wembley was kept open for a second year, again reinforcing the ties of sentiment; Baldwin's tour of Canada had similar purpose and effect. Balfour was put in charge of the reconsideration of constitutional links between the Dominions, and his deliberations finally bore fruit in the 1931 Statute of Westminster and in the transition from 'Empire' to 'Commonwealth'.[49] The same bipartisan approach was used in relation to India, which Baldwin was already coming to see as one of his greatest responsibilities. Public disorder had continued after the Montagu-Chelmsford reforms and a firm but moderate Viceroy was needed in 1925 to continue the move towards internal self-government. Edward Wood was made Lord Irwin and installed as Viceroy amidst approval from all but the Tory diehards, and he was backed up by an all-party constitutional commission under the Liberal lawyer Sir John Simon. The tripartisan policy was underlined when Birkenhead intervened with Baldwin in 1927 to ensure that Simon should not be opposed if he should not have returned from India by the time of the coming election. Great efforts were needed to persuade the Spen Valley Conservatives to stand down, but these were ultimately successful and Simon had a free run in 1929.[50] This approach, by which the moderates combined to ensure a responsible policy in defiance of their more extreme colleagues may be seen as a dress rehearsal for the National government of the 1930s. India was also a rehearsal in another sense, for the men who engineered what may be fairly described as the appeasement of India in the decade after 1925 (Irwin/Halifax, Hoare, Simon, Baldwin and MacDonald) were the same men who dominated British foreign policy from 1931 until 1937, in both cases meeting strong opposition from the Labour left and the Conservative right.

At the Ministry of Health, Neville Chamberlain had been passing Bills in each session, but the crowning achievement was put off until the end, largely because of the problem of carrying a scheme even through the cabinet. This was the reform of local government to sweep away the Poor Law, wind up the boards of guardians and place their work under the ordinary local councils. Up to this point Chamberlain had enjoyed the enthusiastic backing of Churchill and the full support of the cabinet, but now he lacked both. Ministers shared the view of the party managers that a drastic reform of local government would antagonize local vested interests and that the dispossessed guardians would fight for their retention. Churchill had no wish to obstruct the reform itself, but wished to tack on to it a reform of local authority finance which would give greater influence to the Treasury. He was also anxious to leave some large scheme of reform as a memorial to the government and to give some relief to agriculture and industry. The need to link all these issues together postponed the plans into 1928 and so, although they were eventually pushed through with Baldwin's support, they only came into effect in 1929. On the longer view, both the structural and the financial reforms were improvements of great importance, but in the short run they were a disaster for the government. Industry and agriculture were allotted a smaller share of the financing of the new authorities, so allowing Labour to denounce this whole derating plan as a handout to farmers and industrialists. When the first rate assessments at the new level were delivered to householders the general election was only a few weeks away.[51]

There was much that the government had achieved, but little that could be unequivocally defended. Chamberlain's reforms had all created a little antagonism somewhere, the diehards were suspicious about the government's attitude to India, and any credit for industrial relations had to be left to industry itself. The same applied to the extension of the franchise in 1928, following commitments given by Baldwin in 1924 that the franchise for men and women would be equalized during the parliament. Few Conservatives actually wanted to extend the vote to young women but it was impossible to equalize the franchise at any age but twenty-one. In the teeth of the expressed opinion of the party agents, of Central Office and of the National Union, the government redeemed its pledge.[52] Credit could not be claimed without raking over disagreement. Disagreement continued too on the tariff issue, for continuing unemployment brought back the very case that Baldwin himself had made out in 1923. But there was no way of uniting the party on tariffs, of persuading Baldwin to evade his pledge of 1924, or of convincing Churchill; the party was still deprived of the only policy which the majority of its members deemed to be necessary.

It was thus an unhappy party that approached the general election, due by 1929. Much had been done, but little of which the party really approved and nothing that could be the centrepiece of an election campaign. So much had been done though that the government did not have much left to offer for the next parliament. After the victory in 1924 the policy secretariat that had done so much useful work was wound up and, from the party point of view, research stopped. Amery had seen the consequences of this at the time and had written to Baldwin to point them out:

The need for such a Secretariat is, in our view, even greater when the Party is in office than when it is in opposition. In opposition a party naturally tends to think of the next election, of framing programmes, of winning public support, and its leaders are naturally kept in touch with the party machinery. In Office a Government rapidly becomes so immersed in administration and in the administrative point of view as to lose sight both of the electoral aspect of its actions and of the need for continuous and effective propaganda. This, the greatest danger to any Party in Office, can only be overcome if there is the closest *liaison* and inter-communication. . . . It is no less essential that the Party should be preparing a programme for the future, not based on departmental ideas, but on political considerations. The idea that the Party in office can rely for its materials for preparing a political campaign upon departmental officials or upon the Cabinet Secretariat is, we think, wholly erroneous.[53]

It would be difficult to better this account of what went wrong with the government, and yet it was written in 1924. Communication with the party was neglected, not least because the Party Chairman did not attend the cabinet as he did the shadow cabinet. Davidson's appointment in 1926 was at least of a man with direct access to Baldwin, but he was insufficiently independent to act as an adequate intermediary. Demands for research were made at regular intervals. In 1926 Lancelot Storr circulated a memorandum that reiterated Amery's case from 1924 and urged action long before the next election. In 1928 John Buchan wrote to Baldwin, claiming the support of Neville Chamberlain for the creation of a 'Conservative Research Department' which would concentrate on social and economic policies, but no action was taken. A Political Education Department was set up at Central Office under Buchan, but it was very limited in scope and Buchan spent most of his time arguing with Joseph Ball as to who was in charge of it.[54]

When preparation for the next election finally began in 1928, it was done through the Cabinet Office rather than through the party. Baldwin's secretary wrote to each minister to ask for information and ideas that might be included in a manifesto; ministers were of course too busy for such work and so most of the replies came from civil servants. The same thing happened when the government considered its attitude to the Labour statement *Labour and the Nation*; again the only information available was from government departments.[55] It was hardly to be expected that the civil service would provide information for debating points suitable to be used in an election or for policies that would make up a coherent party appeal for an election. The manifesto finally produced in 1929 was twice as long as that of 1924, had far less real content, and was infinitely less well written. The only stance left open was defensive; the party must stand on its record, a record that was already characterized as reactionary and unadventurous.

At the end the government and party realized the weakness of their position, but too late to do anything about it. A reshuffle of ministers was considered in the hope of livening up the party's appearance, but this was shelved as being equally likely to lead to further discontent.[56] The *Conservative Agents' Journal* ran a competition a few weeks before the election to find a new slogan for the party, but it was all too late. When parliament was dissolved on 11 May 1929 there was no option but to fight a campaign under the banner of 'Safety First'.

After the election, 'Safety First' was widely criticized as a cause of defeat, and so it was in a sense. The slogan appeared on a poster with Baldwin's picture and the words 'The man you can Trust'; the idea was suggested by

Bensons, and was timed to coincide with a road safety campaign using the same slogan. As an electioneering stunt this was valid enough, and Davidson reacted angrily when the National Union asked who had been responsible; he pointed out that while Central Office had produced it, it was the candidates and local parties who had bought and displayed many thousands of copies. If it was a failure, it was a failure of the whole party and not just of Central Office.[57] Nevertheless, 'Safety First' *was* a failure, precisely because it showed up the party's real stance in the election; safety first and nothing second.

Most of the party campaign was devoted to attacks on Labour plans and Liberal promises, so forfeiting the advantage that should accrue to a government in office; there was not much else to say though, when the party record was apparently unpopular and party programme non-existent. For all this, 'Safety First' might have worked well enough if there was anything to be feared; most of the emphasis in 1924, 1931 and 1935 was on safety, but this appealed only when the electorate was really scared. A Red scare was very implausible after the expulsion of the Bolsheviks from London and the taming of the trade union militants; a cry of social danger was invalidated by the very success of the government in healing national divisions; the promise of conciliation was tarnished by the events since the General Strike. David Low cut very near the bone with a cartoon that showed Baldwin anxiously awaiting a letter from Zinoviev to rescue him.[58] Most important of all, a policy of relative inaction had failed to make an impression on the greatest current problem, that of unemployment. It is hardly surprising that the electorate were ready to try something more adventurous. In every way the party that had been so closely in touch with the national mood in 1924 was completely out of touch in 1929.

Baldwin expected to win the election, though without much of a majority, but was probably affected in his judgement by the favourable reception that he himself drew on his speaking tour. He took the precaution of speaking to MacDonald about India and other issues in case MacDonald should become Prime Minister. Other predictions were less optimistic and foretold that the Conservatives would lose their majority.[59] These gloomier forecasts were confirmed by the results; over a hundred seats were lost, many because of the intervention of Liberals where there had been a straight fight in 1924. The Liberal revival produced only fifty-nine MPs, but it put MacDonald back in office with the largest number of seats, 288. The Conservatives had 261, much the same as 1923, although they polled more votes than Labour; with a much increased electorate, the party's poll rose by half a million votes, but it was the worst Conservative performance of the inter-war years. The bold new initiative of 1924–25 had risen and receded like the tide, and it seemed that it all had to be done again.

Notes and References

1 Jones, *Whitehall Diary*, i, 301.
2 *The Times*, 11 Nov. 1924.
3 Hyde, *Baldwin*, 324.
4 Hyde, *Baldwin*, v.
5 *Ibid*, 227–30.
6 Gilbert, *Winston S. Churchill*, v, 58–60.
7 Austen to Hilda Chamberlain, 9 Nov. 1924: quoted in Hyde, *Baldwin*. 33.
8 Percy, *Some Memories*, 128.
9 Jones, *Whitehall Diary*, i, 316–7.
10 Davidson, *Memoirs of a Conservative*, 216.
11 Gilbert, *Winston S. Churchill*, v, 100.
12 Middlemas and Barnes, *Baldwin*, title of Chapter 10.
13 Hyde, *Baldwin*, 257–65.
14 Petrie, *Austen Chamberlain*, ii, 244–92; *Gleanings and Memoranda*, Dec. 1925.
15 *Hansard*, 5th series, cliv, 691–770.
16 Hall to Davidson, 23 Aug. 1923: Davidson MSS.
17 'Looking ahead', quoted in *Gleanings and Memoranda*, July 1924.
18 National Union minutes, Executive Committee, 13 Jan. and 10 Feb. 1925.
19 Middlemas and Barnes, *Baldwin*, 293.
20 Hyde, *Baldwin*, 242.
21 Young, *Baldwin*, 91.
22 Middlemas and Barnes, *Baldwin*, 294.
23 *Birmingham Post*, 6 Mar. 1925.
24 Middlemas and Barnes, *Baldwin*, 295.
25 *Hansard*, 5th series, clxxxi, 834–41.
26 Gilbert, *Winston S. Churchill*, v, 103–4.
27 Middlemas and Barnes, *Baldwin*, 298.
28 *Ibid*, 299.
29 National Union minutes, Executive Committee, 10 Mar. 1925.
30 National Union Conference minutes, Brighton Conference, 9 Oct. 1925.
31 Middlemas and Barnes, *Baldwin*, 378–88.
32 *Ibid*, 388.
33 *Ibid*, 389–90.
34 Martin, *Communism and the British Trade Unions*, 64–6
35 *Gleanings and Memoranda*, Nov. 1925.
36 *Home and Politics*, June 1926.
37 See for example the minutes of the Wolverhampton and Stretford Conservative Associations.

38 'General Strike Correspondence, 1926' of the Maidstone Conservative Association.
39 Hyde, *Baldwin*, 296.
40 Younger to Davidson, 27 Dec. 1926. Baldwin MSS, vol. 53, file 6.
41 National Union minutes, Executive Committee, 15 Mar. 1927.
42 He later suggested that the premiership would ruin the health of any man who held it, Middlemas and Barnes, *Baldwin*, 316.
43 *Ibid*, 411.
44 Hyde, *Baldwin*, 282–3.
45 Blythe, *The Age of Illusion*, 15–42.
46 Smith, *John Buchan*. 318–19.
47 Cook and Ramsden, *By-elections*, 72–4.
48 Austen Chamberlain had warned against anything like another Taff Vale, but this is exactly what the 1927 Act became.
49 Dugdale, *Balfour*, ii, 373–85.
50 Davidson to Birkenhead, 25 Oct. 1927: Davidson MSS.
51 Sanders Diary, 7 Feb. 1930.
52 Correspondence on 'Electoral reform': Baldwin MSS, vol. 52.
53 'Memorandum on the Policy Secretariat', 18 Nov. 1924: Baldwin MSS, vol. 48.
54 Ramsden, 'Organisation', 257–9.
55 Baldwin MSS, vol. 53, files 12 and 14.
56 Hyde, *Baldwin*, 297–8.
57 National Union minutes, Executive Committee, 18 June 1929.
58 Middlemas and Barnes, *Baldwin*, 525.
59 Tom Jones, *Whitehall Diary*, ii, 186.

Part IV

The Era of Neville Chamberlain

'Mr Baldwin . . . was wont to describe himself as an ordinary man. But though he is no plain, ordinary man, though he is a combination of poet, philosopher, sage and statesman, for which I think our political history finds no parallel, he has a singular and instinctive knowledge of how the plain man's mind works.'
(Neville Chamberlain, in the House of Commons, 31 May 1937.)

'Tory spokesmen are not talking sheer nonsense when they claim that the National Government has pulled Great Britain through the greatest depression in history. Of course, it was not mainly their doing. It was due mainly to Great Britain's, or rather British capitalism's extraordinary financial and economic strength. . . . But, if they had been muffs, they could have muffed things up; and, on the whole, except in foreign affairs (which will probably be their undoing yet), they have not.'
(G. D. H. Cole, in Fact, Feb. 1938).

Chapter 13

The last battle for the tariff, 1929–1932

Between 1902 and 1940 the party had five leaders: Balfour, Austen Chamberlain and Neville Chamberlain were all driven from office by the hostility of their supporters, while Bonar Law had come near to overthrow in 1913, 1916 and 1923, surviving only by bending to the convictions of others. Leading the party was certainly no bed of roses, but no leader had to face a more sustained assault on his position than Baldwin met after defeat in 1929. In October 1929 Neville Chamberlain could write, 'Heaven knows I don't want the job. It is a thankless one at any time and never more so than now when the party is all to pieces.'[1] For two years, the leader and his backers were subjected to ceaseless criticism in the press, in the lobbies and in the National Union, criticism that ranged over the whole area of policy and personality. Each time Baldwin struck back and re-established himself a new attack from another direction threatened all that had been achieved. Negotiations and policy statements followed each other in quick succession, the sequence punctuated by party meetings, at each of which the leader was completely but ineffectively vindicated. It is easy to set this down to the party's anger at the loss of office, pointing to parallels with 1880–85, 1906–11, and 1974–75, and to conclude that Conservatives naturally turn on their leaders in the hour of defeat, but this will not do as a sufficient explanation. The party crisis after defeat in 1929 was an inherent part of the course that had been followed since the retirement of Bonar Law, and both Baldwin's discomfiture and his eventual survival were an integral part of that process.

By 1929 Baldwin had made many enemies in his party, men whose anger already transcended the bounds of group loyalty. In the new initiative of 1924–25, he had dragged his supporters far away from their chosen path, by appealing over their heads directly to the national electorate. In the second half of his government they had made him pay for his apostasy by forcing on him policies of which he clearly disapproved, but they had only been half successful. Now that he was unable to enjoy the prerogatives of a Prime Minister, his opponents moved more on to the offensive, entrenched as they were in every area of the party. The range of opponents, each alienated by some policy or other pursued in the past five years, was a wide one. Most clearly, Baldwin had lost the support of the old imperialist wing, the group that had provided the backbone of continuous opposition to Lloyd George, was most powerful in the House of Lords, and which looked to the *Morning Post* as its prophet and spokesman. The Baldwin government's Indian policy made a parting of the ways inevitable. Hardly less serious was the increasing intransigence of the tariff reformers, who had resented the decision to drop tariffs in 1924, but who had then comforted themselves with the assurance that no Conservative government would actually keep such a pledge. They fully expected that protection would be gradually extended under the guise of safeguarding until it had become a general tariff in all but name; it would then be put to the electorate as a defensive measure of consolidation, a vote for the *status quo*. In this they misjudged both the strength of Churchill in cabinet and the determination of Baldwin to keep to his word. They therefore watched helplessly as the level of trade fell and as Britain failed to derive any real benefit from the general European prosperity of the mid-1920s. Other issues had created a more generalized discontent among the rank and file: the failure to grasp the nettle of the House of Lords of course offended the National Union, and in 1928 the Executive disclaimed all responsibility for a future 'constitutional catastrophe' since its warnings had been ignored; the extension of the franchise and the reform of the Poor Law, both carried in the teeth of party opposition and *after* consultations within the party, strengthened the opinions of those who saw Baldwin's Conservatism as half way to socialism.[2]

A combination of these causes had alienated the bulk of the Conservative press by the time of the election. Beaverbrook and Rothermere both felt that Baldwin had unfairly excluded them from an influence that proprietors of great newspapers had a right to exercise, and both felt for him the same personal antipathy that he felt for them. Once they had an open rift to exploit and an organized group of rebels to support, they would be a serious threat. The consolidation of the popular press in the 1920s and the circulation battles of the time had increased both the effective control of the press lords over their own medium and their determination to have their influence recognized. The *Daily Mail* and the *Daily Express* between them accounted for over three and a half million copies a day by 1930; if the Labour *Daily Herald* and the Liberal *Daily News* were added, then all four of the highest circulation dailies would be hostile to Baldwin, with a combined circulation of over six million, against a circulation of less than a million and a half for papers that would normally support him. It was an unusual position for a Conservative leader to find himself in, and it made the opposition to Baldwin considerably more dangerous to him.[3]

However, much of this opposition had been present in 1927–28 and Baldwin had been able to retain control then because of two assets that were lost to him after the election. As Prime Minister he had the grudging but continued support of his cabinet colleagues, and as a progressive leader he had the enthusiastic backing of a sizeable band of MPs on the left of the party. It was the support of these 'YMCA' MPs that had enabled Neville Chamberlain to push through his social policy, and it was the 150 or so younger members who had allowed John Buchan to kill the plan to restore the House of Lords. This wing of the party had been decimated at the election because so many of its members had sat for industrial seats in the north and Midlands; Macmillan, Loder, O'Connor and Duff Cooper all lost their seats, and Geoffrey Lloyd failed to get elected in Birmingham.[4] The diehard group suffered few losses because most of them were peers or sat for safe seats in the south, and they were strengthened by the return of George Lloyd from Egypt. The balance of the parliamentary party therefore shifted, more because of the loss of moderates than the increased number of diehards; the diehard groups, which had been about 60 out of over 400 in the parliament of 1924, could muster at least 50 out of 261 in 1929. Nor were the moderates as reliable in Baldwin's support as in the past; some wanted cooperation with Lloyd George to secure a more positive policy against employment, and the same motives led Macmillan, Boothby and Walter Elliot to flirt with the ideas of Oswald Mosley in 1930.[5]

Even so, it was the disintegration of the collective leadership that most damaged Baldwin's position. In office, cabinet critics had been able to convince themselves that they could restrain the party from the inside, but once power was lost they had no such cause for restraint. The projected reshuffle of 1928–29 did nothing to give the party a new impetus, but it was effective in keeping existing ministers in line. There had been antagonism even with ministers who accepted Baldwin's political stance. Churchill's dislike of his Indian policy was absorbed by his involvement at the Treasury, Amery's frustration on tariffs was mitigated by the hope of winning Baldwin over, the Chamberlains' discontent with the Prime Minister's unbusinesslike methods was suppressed in the interests of unity, and Salisbury's dislike of the whole trend of policy had not led him to resign. Once the election was lost, all these discontents burst into the open and all were directed at Baldwin.

Against these disruptive forces, Baldwin retained one advantage that was to bring him through the years of opposition, not unscathed but still leader: his critics had neither an agreed alternative policy nor a clear alternative leader who would fight for the post. Throughout 1930 and 1931 the critics rarely managed a united opposition, and when they seemed to have done so in March 1931 Baldwin briefly decided to resign. Churchill rapidly became more diehard than the diehards, but his past made him still unacceptable as leader and his doubts on fiscal policy separated him from other critics of Baldwin. Even opponents who were using the press lords as a lever were distrustful of their personal claims, and Beaverbrook and Rothermere did not even coordinate their own activities very effectively. For all their weight, the critics could not muster a majority for any of the changes they wished to impose, and Baldwin survived by defeating them severally. He was further aided by the incompetence that his critics displayed, an incompetence that allowed him to pose as the defender of democracy and moderation against dark forces that threatened both. This stance enabled him to beat off each attack as it developed, but it could never remove the real cause of the trouble.

The final factor in the crisis, not usually given sufficient weight, was the deficiencies of Baldwin himself. He had lost two elections out of three by 1929, and he no longer seemed such an electoral asset. This was certainly compounded by his poor showing in opposition; to say that he was not a good leader of opposition would be a great understatement, for he certainly contributed to his own misfortunes by the attitude that he took up. He was temperamentally unsuited for the role of critic, having neither the application to develop a reasoned attack on government policy in detail, nor the flexibility of mind to denounce in principle policies with which he agreed. Leading opposition requires not an orator or a conciliator, but a sharp-tongued debater, and this he neither was nor was able to become. Moreover he did not even seem to want to be an effective leader against the Labour government. He assured MacDonald that he would not indulge in factious and indiscriminate opposition, and he responded warmly when MacDonald suggested that parliament, having no overall majority, should regard itself as a Council of State sharing the responsibilities of the government.[6] He continued to support policies of which the bulk of his party disapproved, especially over India, and he refused to countenance the obstructive tactics that had done so much to raise morale in 1912 and 1924. All this emphasizes the basic honesty of the man, but it also does much to explain the frustration of serving under him. When the party looked for a fight, it was given instead an object lesson in fair play and passivity. Irwin, who was both a close friend and supporter of Baldwin's policies, recognized his deficiencies clearly enough.[7]

> I always suppose that the trouble with S.B. is that to him the task of opposition is constitutionally repugnant, and he will never throw much heart into it. I remember him saying . . . that what we were at present fighting was not a programme, but an atmosphere, which no amount of promulgation of counter-programmes would affect. This could only be done by the hard teaching of experience. There is of course truth in this, but I can well believe that his temperament leads him to push it over far into encouraging himself to sit in the front row of the stalls while the play is being performed.

Baldwin's sensitivity to atmosphere paid off in the end, but his failings gave him a hard two years in the meantime.

His attitude added to discontent among colleagues, for without the demands of government business, he relapsed more and more into lassitude and apathy. He was deeply wounded by attacks from his own side and so the sharp words that the party longed to hear hurled at the government were reserved instead for internal battles. When he seemed about to be forced out in 1931 he seemed relieved to be free of the terrible burden that leadership had become, and during the great crisis of August of that year he seemed more determined not to sacrifice his holiday than to secure a place in government. Some explanation of this may be found in the gradual dismemberment of the

Baldwinite group that had backed him for the premiership in 1923, sustained him through the winter of 1923–24, and supported him in the cruiser crisis of 1925. By 1929 Amery had moved into opposition, Neville Chamberlain had detached himself, and Joynson-Hicks had retired with a peerage. Only Bridgeman, now also semi-retired with a peerage, and the faithful Davidson, remained to screw up Baldwin's courage when danger loomed. At the crucial times they were sufficient to persuade him to make a fight for it, but they could not transform him into the sort of leader who might surmount the difficulties by his own efforts. As a result, the party drifted rudderless in 1930, as in Balfour's last years as leader, with the leader doing just enough to save his own position but doing little to inspire the party or to revive its belief in itself. What positive work was done in opposition owed more to Neville Chamberlain than to Baldwin, and by 1931 Chamberlain had become not just the general factotum, but the obvious heir to the leadership and the controller of every sphere of the party in which he chose to interest himself.

The party crisis was actually a series of different problems that overlapped and interconnected. First, there was the immediate reaction to defeat, an assault on Baldwin and Davidson that mounted in intensity until Davidson was thrown to the wolves in May 1930. There were the two policy arguments over India and tariffs, which together took up the whole of 1930. Finally, there was the consolidated attack in the spring of 1931. After this came the improbable sequel of the party joining a coalition government under MacDonald, gaining its biggest ever election victory, and going on to implement its tariff policy, the end of thirty years of struggle.

After the 1929 defeat Baldwin had a problem not unlike that of 1923, whether or not to resign, and what the effect of resignation would be. His own reaction was such disappointment as to wish to be free of office as quickly as possible. This inclination was reinforced by the fact that the Conservatives could only stay in office either at the sufferance of Lloyd George or in coalition with him. There were attempts to keep Labour out of office, but Baldwin was too quick for them.[8] He decided to resign at once and the government accordingly left office on 3 June, the third day after the results were announced. The significance of resignation was underlined when the Conservatives put down an amendment to the Labour King's Speech calling for more protection of British industry. This forced a separation between Lloyd George and his Conservative contacts as in 1923. As before, cooperation with Liberals would be welcome, but only if the Liberals would abjure their Liberalism first, and cooperation with Lloyd George would not be welcome to Baldwin on any terms at all. In the medium term this strategy paid off handsomely when it brought over the Simonite Liberal Nationals on Tory terms, but in the short term, it merely raised the blood pressure of the diehards with the prospect of MacDonald again in office.

Davidson's own account of the first stage of the party crisis has been generally accepted, concentrating as it does on the malice of his critics, their certainty that they were striking at Baldwin by proxy, and the manipulation of discontent by the arch-fiends of the Baldwinite demonology, Beaverbrook and Lloyd George.[9] But Davidson does not point out that he had done more than enough to deserve his unpopularity. As Party Chairman he had an impressive tally of achievements to his credit, but he had also managed to antagonize a number of party notables quite needlessly. One such case concerned the chairmanship of the National Union in 1927. This was a purely honorific position, and conventionally the chairman was the senior vice-chairman of the previous year who was elected unopposed, while a new vice-chairman was elected each year to become chairman three years later. In 1927 Sir Robert Sanders was elected chairman, passing over the claims of John Gretton MP, who was senior vice-chairman. Davidson told the meeting that Gretton did not wish to stand, which Gretton then denied, asserting that it had been intended to 'kick him out'. Gretton did not oppose Sanders's election, but insisted on standing again for vice-chairman, with the result that there were four nominations for three posts, none of which had any real significance at all. On a ballot, Gretton was re-elected, and a year later he took his rightful place as chairman. The position was certainly not worth the argument, and Gretton was notoriously easy to offend, and as a result of these proceedings, Gretton became Davidson's implacable foe.[10]

Davidson no doubt believed that it was worth a chance to relegate one of Baldwin's most persistent critics, but this shows exactly what his critics disliked. As Party Chairman, appointed by Baldwin, Davidson was also the chairman of the National Union Executive and so the National Union's chief representative to the leader. Unless its representative was independent of the leader, as Younger had been in 1921–22, then the National Union had no real independence itself. Many felt that Baldwin was taking their party away from them in terms of policy and through Davidson was taking an unfair advantage over the National Union too. Davidson's reaction to criticism did little to quieten such fears. During his last year as Chairman he was in dispute with Lady Londonderry, Sir Alexander Leith, Sir Charles Marston, and Lord Halsbury; in none of these disputes was Davidson the aggressor, but in all of them he reacted sharply enough to increase the antagonism, and showed these stalwarts of the National Union that he was Baldwin's man rather than their own.[11]

At the Central Council on 2 July 1929 a resolution of confidence in Baldwin was passed, but Davidson came under fire; it was decided to send a questionnaire to the constituencies to ask their views on the causes of defeat. A fortnight later the Executive set up a committee to investigate the relationship of Central Office, National Union and the leader. This sub-committee recommended that the Party Chairman should continue to chair the Executive, that the leader should attend the Executive more often, and that resolutions should be conveyed to the leader by delegations; Davidson was to retain office, but he was to be bypassed. This occasioned further argument at the Executive, when Lord Stanley proposed unsuccessfully that Davidson should vacate the chair. The proposals were then rejected by the party Conference in November, and further negotiations continued into 1930. In the general review of National Union rules of 1930 it was resolved that the direct connection of National Union and Central Office should cease, that the principal agent should not be honorary secretary of the National Union and that the Party Chairman should be only an ordinary member of the Executive. Henceforth, the Executive would elect its own chairman, who would also communicate its views to the leader or lead delegations to him. In October 1930 Sir Kingsley Wood was elected first chairman of the Executive Committee, and it was decided to leave the honorary secretaryship vacant. Wood was a close associate of Neville Chamberlain, by then Party Chairman, and so there was cooperation rather than friction between the two posts. When the dust had settled in 1932, Topping was restored to the post of honorary secretary from which he had been excluded in 1930, and the direct connection with Central Office was restored.[12] This puts the whole affair in perspective: the criticism was of Davidson and his relationship with Baldwin, not of the system itself.

In the first year of opposition, Davidson continued to attract fire that would otherwise have fallen on Baldwin. As controller of Central Office, he had to lay down the party line on tariffs when candidates required advice or discipline, and as controller of publicity he had to negotiate with Beaverbrook.[13] To that extent he was fighting Baldwin's battle for him and taking blame that was at the least jointly deserved. The final straw for Davidson may well have been an article in the *Week-End Review* in May 1930, a cutting of which he filed among his resignation papers when he threw in the sponge a few days later. The article was by a Conservative backbencher, and summed up much of the criticism that had been voiced over the past years:

> The position of the Party Chairman is, under modern conditions, of great and increasing importance . . . and further, when the party is in Opposition, his task becomes still more exacting. He must be the 'Organizer of Victory'. . . . The Chairman is appointed by the Leader of the Party. But, when appointed, he must, from his personal status and abilities, be in a position to exercise an independent judgement and to give independent advice to the Leader, for in consultation with him he must represent the party and do his utmost to gather and to voice its views. Distinguished personal ability, independent party status, high public reputation – these are indispensable qualifications of the Chairman of the Party. And today, while it is in Opposition, it must be taken as an axiom that, so far as its future fortunes are concerned, the Chairmanship is second only in importance to the Leadership itself.[14]

The author may well have known that Neville Chamberlain was being canvassed as Davidson's successor. In 1911 it had been decided that the Chairman should be 'of cabinet rank', which Davidson certainly was not; as in 1911 the existence of a leader who made a poor show of opposition meant that a Party Chairman would have to do the job himself. The lesson was rammed home when the author came to discuss Davidson himself:

> Through no fault of his own, the present Chairman does not possess what must be regarded as the bare essentials for the task. He has no claim to be amongst leading Conservatives; he has not had the political experience and career fitted to give him a high independent status in the party, and until he was appointed Chairman he was quite unknown. . . . He is now . . . a definite hindrance . . . not only to the party. For he is injuring too the position and prestige of his Leader who appointed him. It is perhaps because Mr. Baldwin may be conscious of this that, with characteristic chivalry, he utterly refuses to consider his replacement and has, it is understood, made it known that he will regard any formal demand for a new Chairman as a vote of no confidence in himself. It is impossible not to admire this loyalty to his late secretary, though to many it may seem an extreme case of 'Love me, love my dog.' The ultimate danger thus is that those who are never weary of intriguing against the Conservative Leader may find in the question of the Chairmanship a weapon with which to strike him down. There is only one way, compatible with the well-being of the party, out of this most unfortunate situation. The Chairman must take the necessary step himself.

The force of these arguments was reinforced for Davidson by the advice of friends – and just as effectively by Baldwin's silence. Neville Chamberlain urged him to stand down and offered to take on the job himself. Davidson therefore announced his resignation at the end of May and Chamberlain took over. From this point on, attacks on Baldwin could not be disguised. From this point too, the party chairmanship could again become a proper focus for party opinion and a proper centre of party communications.

The first policy dispute of opposition concerned India, where trouble had been brewing for many years, at least since the Montagu-Chelmsford reforms had been launched. In and after 1919 cloudy assurances had been given about future developments, satisfying neither diehards nor Indian nationalists, but there had been provision for a new constitutional investigation after ten years to determine subsequent policy. Baldwin sent out Irwin as Viceroy in 1926 at Birkenhead's suggestion. Irwin shared both Baldwin's profoundly religious approach to politics and his progressive attitude, so that Baldwin's only doubt was whether he could be spared from Westminster. He was also in no doubt about the fight that they would have to produce to carry the sort of Indian policy that both wanted; hence the desire to put policy on an all-party basis, and hence also the beginning of a propaganda campaign. In 1927 Davidson told Irwin in India about a new committee that had been set up 'for the purpose of educating the British public with regard to India'. The committee was to be 'non-partisan', but would be housed at Central Office, launched with £1,000 from party funds, and run by Dudley Myers MP, who was joint honorary secretary of the Conservative India Committee in the Commons.[15]

The diehards used the Indian Empire Society for a similar propaganda purpose. No subject moved the party's imperialists to anger more swiftly than a moderate policy applied to India, as the Dyer episode of 1920 had shown, and this was as much due to personal ties and traditions as to political convictions as such. Fifty-two of the Conservatives in the 1929 parliament had been professional officers in the military, civil or colonial services and there can have been few of these who had not served away from Britain, many in India; at one-fifth of the parliamentary party it constituted the largest proportion that the services group was ever to attain after the First World War. To this must be added at least as many again who had fathers, sons or brothers who had served or were serving in India. India was not just the jewel of the Empire in an abstract sense to men of such families; it was the pinnacle of ambition for the service classes of Great Britain, the guarantee of the survival of their life-style and their attitudes. Increasingly it was also a refuge, for the men who ruled India were themselves increasingly out of touch with a Britain that could elect a Labour government and with a Conservative party that conciliated trade unionists. The attitudes of the 1890s were preserved in Anglo-Indian families at home and abroad, reinforced by the *Morning Post*, a paper that printed a full page of Indian news each day, that referred to 'Indians' when it meant Anglo-Indians and 'natives' when it meant Indians, and that was in truth an opinion-reinforcer rather than an opinion-former. Such families were still numerically significant in the upper and upper-middle classes in Britain, and they were of course unanimously Conservative in their politics. Retired officers and colonial civil servants made up a large part of the party hierarchy in many constituency parties in the south. The next stage of India's transition to self-government would only be carried through in the teeth of their determined opposition.

Baldwin was aware of all of this, but was still resolved to push through a progressive policy, for two reasons. He was impressed by the effect that the party battle over Ireland had had on two generations of British history and determined that India should never be used by his party as Ireland had been used.[16] It would have been easy enough for the Conservatives to raise the banner of white supremacy as their imperial policy in the 1920s, and it might well have been an election winner, but it would certainly have destroyed any chance of a peaceful transition in India. India could also be seen as a test case of the party's readiness to accept the changes necessitated by the Great War. Baldwin was much impressed by the exposed position of the Empire in a world of potential enemies, and he wished to strengthen it by resting it more securely on consent. If the party could not be educated to see the realities of world power, then it would not survive and would not deserve to survive. All this fitted in well enough with the rest of Baldwin's political philosophy, but he set clear limits to the progress that might be achieved. He was no more ready than Churchill to hand over India to the Congress party, and he did not expect to see a truly self-governing India in his lifetime. He emphasized the need for a progressive approach rather than the need for safeguards because the diehards were themselves advancing the arguments for the other side, but his own position was far less clearcut than they assumed.

The occasion of dispute in 1929 was the work of the Simon Commission and Irwin's attempt to involve the Indian nationalists in the planning of India's future. Irwin believed that the parties would only agree to a conference if the British government stated in advance that their aim was Dominion status for India. With this both Baldwin and MacDonald agreed, and there was discussion through the autumn of 1929 about the wording and timing of that statement. Through the failure of the government Simon was not consulted until a late stage and the Commission would not then approve a declaration before they had completed their work. Irwin made the statement about Dominion status on 31 October 1929 and so plunged his leader into an immediate crisis. Baldwin criticized the government for its failure to consult Simon, but he would not disown the declaration itself and he went out of his way to support Irwin: 'If ever the day comes when the Party which I lead ceases to attract men of the calibre of Edward Wood, then I have finished with my Party.' Nevertheless his speech was heard in almost complete silence on his own side, and Samuel Hoare reported that 'of all our people I was the only supporter of Stanley's attitude'.[17] It could be pointed out that Irwin had only put a gloss on a policy that had been known since 1919, but the diehards replied that they at least had never understood the policy to mean this, and that it would have a wholly disproportionate effect on British prestige in India. The *Morning Post* launched a strong attack, and the *Daily Mail* made a vicious attack on Baldwin for not consulting his colleagues. Baldwin was rescued by his own skill and his opponents' lack of judgement. In the Commons on 7 November he made an excellent speech; most of it was quite irrelevant to the issue at hand, but it included a barbed reply to the *Daily Mail*, and a reminder to the diehards that Birkenhead had suggested Irwin back in 1926. The critics did the rest: Birkenhead damaged their case with an intemperate attack on Lord Parmoor in the House of Lords and the other diehards were out of sympathy with both Houses. A piece of tactical quick thinking by Baldwin allowed the Commons debate to end without a vote.[18]

Discontent over India rumbled on though, coming to a head in the winter of 1930–31 when the Round Table Conference seemed likely to reach a successful conclusion. The diehards had counted on the Indian princes to do their work for them by refusing agreement; if this had happened there could only have been local self-government under a strong British central government. This hope collapsed when the princes, anxious to safeguard their own future, agreed to cooperate. Churchill had already parted company with Baldwin on the tariff issue in October 1930, but the breach had remained private.[19] He now raised the standard of revolt with a violent speech to the Indian Empire Society on 12 December. The conflict escalated in the following January when it became known that the Congress leaders would be released from custody and the Conference suspended while all shades of

Indian opinion were consulted. Backed by Hoare, who had led the party delegation to the Conference and who was now the party's chief spokesman on India, Baldwin supported the government and urged his party to recognize that the world had changed since 'the second jubilee of Queen Victoria'. Wounded by Baldwin's words as well as by his policy, Churchill now resigned from the shadow cabinet. In 1924 Baldwin had welcomed Churchill back with the reflection that 'it would be up to him to be loyal, if he is capable of loyalty'; he now made little attempt to hold Churchill back and regretted only that the incident marked another resignation from a team that had held together so well.[20] At the shadow cabinet before the debate, Churchill had expressed his opinion and Neville Chamberlain had passed a note over to Monsell with the words 'Vex not his ghost. O let him pass.'[21] The battle over India also cost Baldwin the support of Salisbury, who left active politics rather than go into active opposition. The battle continued nevertheless and merged into the general assault on Baldwin's leadership in the spring of 1931. Baldwin's personal line on India was not to the liking of many in the party, as Lane-Fox told Irwin:

> He spoke for about half an hour – without any notes – and Providence and his own good sense alone were behind him. Good backing, but I think he would have been safer if he had secured the consent of others. For several have suggested to me that his line was a surprise to them, and emanated from himself alone.[22]

Tariffs were also a problem that had carried over from government into opposition. In preparing for the 1929 election Baldwin had refused to advance from his 1924 pledge, convinced still that safeguarding was the most that the electorate would take. A letter to the Chief Whip in 1928 laid this down as the view that must be accepted by all candidates who sought the help of Central Office. Once in opposition discord resumed. Amery demanded a more positive policy, Churchill stuck to his free trade guns, and Neville Chamberlain announced publicly that defeat had freed the party from Baldwin's pledge. The position was complicated by the press lords, who produced an acute tactical problem. Amery, Davidson and Neville Chamberlain all agreed (as Baldwin would not) that Beaverbrook had a sincere attachment to Conservatism and could be won over for the party. It was agreed that Rothermere was no use to the party in any guise, but there was continuing argument about Beaverbrook, whether to woo him with fair words or to damn him with Rothermere. It was clear enough that they could not be ignored, for Beaverbrook had formed an Empire Crusade to agitate for Empire Free Trade (a neat way of making the old idea of imperial preference look new and as if it was really a free trade policy), and Rothermere gradually moved over to a similar position.[23] Amery worked with Lord Melchett and others to propagate support for an Empire Economic Union, and the Empire Industries Association stepped up its pressure on Conservative MPs. The first stage of the debate ended in November 1929 with a party committee and the new Conservative Research Department investigating the question, and with good relations between Baldwin and Beaverbrook. The Party Conference went well and Baldwin had a friendly reception for a speech which added nothing to his known views on tariffs. But this was only a prelude; during 1930 three separate attacks were launched on the party's tariff policy, fought out in the constituencies as well as at Westminster and each time Baldwin won by forcing his critics out into the open at a party meeting. Nevertheless, he had to give ground on each occasion and ended 1930 committeed to a full policy of protection, so in that sense the movement for Empire Free Trade may be accounted a successful one.

The first attack began with a breach between Baldwin and Beaverbrook in January 1930. Rothermere hd decided to press ahead with his new party and in February the *Daily Express* switched over from qualified support for Baldwin to outright opposition. Beaverbrook was now run by his own papers as the only leader who could carry the Conservative party forward to a sensible imperial policy. Such amazingly unrealistic views had a way of looking dangerous when they were delivered each day to millions of Conservative households that had no other informed comment available to them. Churchill, later in the year, told Beaverbrook that 'no one that I know of has ever risen to the first rank of politics in so short a time'.[24] This time the dispute centred on the party organization for, as the price of his support, Beaverbrook demanded the right to run an independent campaign in the country, much as the Anti-Corn Law League had done, but he also demanded that his campaign should not be fettered in any way by Central Office.

A foretaste of what would happen had already been provided in August 1929 at Twickenham; the Conservative candidate, Sir John Ferguson, announced his conversion to Empire Free Trade and so forfeited the support of Central Office, with the result that he almost lost a safe seat. If Beaverbrook were to encourage similar campaigns in the future by the threat of rival candidates, then he would simply take over the party's appeal to the country. A suggestion from Churchill to challenge the press lords in a miniature general election, four by-elections in representative seats, was discarded as being too risky; it was quite likely that seats would be lost either to Labour or to Empire Free Trade, which would be equally disastrous.[25] Instead Baldwin resolved to move nearer to Beaverbrook on policy, so as to deprive him of any excuse for a split in the constituencies. After talks with Beaverbrook, both directly and through Horne, Baldwin accepted the idea of a referendum on tariffs and secured the grudging acceptance of the shadow cabinet. The new policy was announced to the party at the Hotel Cecil on 4 March and immediately divided the critics, for Beaverbrook accepted it while Rothermere did not.

The second attack began almost at once, for Beaverbrook did not wish to split the United Empire party (UEP) that he and Rothermere had formed, and he seized on the Central Office pamphlet which explained Baldwin's new policy as the occasion for a new breach; he objected to the fact that he had not been consulted before the pamphlet was issued – a remarkable claim against the independence of the party. He also made an issue out of the pending by-election in Central Nottingham because the Conservative candidate, Terence O'Connor, would not go beyond Baldwin's policy. Under continuous pressure the party now wilted visibly; a rally at the Crystal Palace, at which Baldwin was planned to speak, was cancelled by the local party leaders because they could not get Beaverbrook to take the chair and dared not go on without him.[26] A Conservative by-election gain at West Fulham was claimed by Beaverbrook as a victory for Empire Free Trade; the victorious candidate swiftly denied such claims, but his denials were not of course reported in the *Mail* or the *Express*. It was at this time that Baldwin had to accept the resignation of Davidson and his replacement by Chamberlain, after he had failed to persuade Bridgeman to take on the job. The tide turned when O'Connor was elected in Nottingham on 29 May, a victory that owed nothing to Beaverbrook; Baldwin consolidated this with a series of speeches in the north and Midlands, assuring his colleagues that it was only in the south that disaffection was serious. He was given his chance when Beaverbrook declared his complete separation from the party and its policy on 17 June, which prompted even the National Union to rally to the leader.[27] He struck back at a party meeting on 24 June with a direct reply to the press lords. The official policy was put forward by Horne and Inskip, and secured a vote of two to one in its favour, thus leaving Baldwin free to concentrate on the issue of the leadership:

> We are told that there is a crisis in the Party. . . . there will be a crisis if you cannot make up your minds what you are going to do. . . . Now Lord Beaverbrook has appealed today in the papers to avoid personalities. . . . When you think of his papers during the last seven years and up to a week ago, when you think that even members of the Carlton Club have written for payment and worked and done all they can to destroy my position and, with me, the Party, to talk about avoiding personalities will not deceive a soul.[28]

He demonstrated how Rothermere's attitude had shifted from month to month with no regard for consistency, and compared the challenge from the press lords to the threat that had been presented by the General Strike. Finally he read a letter from Rothermere to Sir Patrick Hannon, which astonishingly Rothermere had given him permission to make public:

> 'I cannot make it too abundantly clear that, under no circumstances whatsoever, will I support Mr. Baldwin unless I know exactly what his policy is going to be, unless I have complete guarantees that such policy will be carried out if his Party achieves office and unless I am acquainted with the names of at least eight, or ten of his most prominent colleagues in the next Ministry.' . . . Now those are the terms that your leader would have to accept and when sent for by the King, would have to say: 'Sire, these names are not necessarily my choice, but they have the support of Lord Rothermere.' A more preposterous and insolent demand was never made on

the leader of any political party. I repudiate it with contempt and I will fight that attempt at domination to the end.

In the meeting and in the Commons, Baldwin was given an ovation, but it was due more to the failings of his enemies than to the support of his friends. Even those who were keen to see Baldwin depart could see that a change could not be made at the dictation of Rothermere. Once again time had been gained.

The third attack was more open; after mediation by Neville Chamberlain had failed, Beaverbrook resumed his attack in the constituencies, urging Conservatives to send their subscriptions to him to finance candidates who would stand against the official party. Chamberlain then embarked on his own initiative, and in August he announced what he called his own 'unauthorized programme', calling for a free hand on tariffs. Baldwin replied by reminding his constituents at Bewdley that a free hand was hard to reconcile with the idea of a democratic mandate. Beaverbrook's efforts bore fruit quickly in the Bromley by-election on 2 September: intervention by the UEP almost handed the seat over to the Liberals and the UEP itself ran a strong third. With more time for preparation, Beaverbrook's candidates would win seats, and Central Office looked forward to contests with foreboding. Again Baldwin had to give ground on policy to ward off the attack on the party as an organization, but this time he could do so with a little more conviction. The economic blizzard that hit Britain in 1930 had caused many to change their views: a Liberal group was forming behind Sir John Simon, which was hostile not only to the idea of deals with Labour but also to the continuance of free trade; MacDonald and Thomas in the cabinet were increasingly doubtful about free trade and were only held in check by Snowden's unflinching orthodoxy; business organizations and the chambers of commerce were calling for tariffs with greater urgency than ever before, and even Churchill accepted the need for a general tariff before the end of 1930.

Amery and Neville Chamberlain urged Baldwin to seize the opportunity to put the party at the head of this rising tide of protectionism and he used the Imperial Conference to do so. He accepted the suggestion of R. B. Bennett, Prime Minister of Canada, for a ten per cent tariff on all goods from outside the Empire, and attacked the government for refusing the demands of the Empire.[29] The party had now dropped all half-measures and was asking for a mandate to implement tariffs without further notice.

Party troubles still pressed, for it was expected that Beaverbrook's man would actually win the by-election at South Paddington, and yet another party meeting was called, this time for the day of the election; did Baldwin remember the result of Austen Chamberlain's decision to test opinion *after* polling at Newport in 1922? The issues were now clearly set out and Baldwin challenged his party critics directly: the debate took place on their own resolution, they were given the opportunity to begin and end the discussion, and Beaverbrook, who had wished to remain silent, was forced to declare his views. With his usual sense of drama, Baldwin told the photographers outside the Caxton Hall: 'Photograph me now gentlemen. It may be the last time you will see me.' His speech was a resounding call for loyalty and received an ovation; after he retired to Research Department to await the outcome, his position was approved by about four to one.[30] The apparent improvement in his position since June was due to the inclusion in this meeting of the more moderate parliamentary candidates as well as the MPs. In truth, Baldwin had made no advance at all in 1930: he had been compelled to sacrifice Davidson, he had been forced back on the tariff issue, and now only the leadership remained in dispute. If he had any doubt that that issue remained open, then it must have been confirmed by the result from South Paddington, where Beaverbrook's candidate took the seat comfortably from the official Conservative. The critics certainly did not take the vote at the Caxton Hall as final, and after a pause they redoubled their efforts.

The finale is worth describing in rather more detail because it contains all the elements from the previous crises, now all coming together. Again responsibility must be laid at Baldwin's own door. Most of the accounts of the crisis have been written from Baldwin's point of view and he has thus emerged as the injured party, but such injuries would have been unnecessary if he had been a better leader to his party. In view of the part that he was to play in saving Baldwin's career, the opinion of Duff Cooper may be cited to justify this view:

> Stanley Baldwin was proving an unsatisfactory Leader of Opposition. He had none of the qualities that the task demands. Bolingbroke wrote of the House of Commons more than two hundred years ago: 'You know the nature of that assembly, they grow, like hounds, fond of the man who shows them game, and by whose halloo they are used to be encouraged.' The nature of the assembly has changed little in the centuries. Mr. Baldwin never showed game, and when he saw hounds hunting his first instinct was to call them off. His love of peace could easily be mistaken for indolence, and his desire to be fair to his political opponents could be represented as secret sympathy for their views.[31]

The crisis of February–March 1931 had three direct causes. The diehards' anger had been roused again by the Indian policy that had brought about Churchill's resignation in January; in this mood they were ready, as in 1922, to wreck the party rather than accept a policy and leader that they now detested. This led on to the second point: because Baldwin could defeat the diehards but never subdue them he gradually lost the support of the moderates too. The diehards were both irreconcilable and immovable, but Baldwin was only irreconcilable, and so harmony would be restored only by his departure. Thirdly, this pushed a number of colleagues over to the side of the critics too. Men like Cunliffe-Lister, Hoare and Hailsham would have been happy to see Baldwin continue in normal circumstances, but they now felt that that party would never achieve anything under his lead. It was also clear by 1931 that Neville Chamberlain was an obvious and available successor. The old guard had now disappeared: Birkenhead, Balfour, Cave, Curzon and Worthington-

Evans had all died, Churchill had resigned, Austen Chamberlain had been ill, and Hailsham's acceptance of a peerage to be Lord Chancellor in 1928 had reduced his claims; among the leaders in the Commons Neville was now the obvious choice. He had consolidated his position with a gradual accumulation of responsibilities, and by March 1931 he was already doing much work that would otherwise have fallen to Baldwin. He had become chairman of the Research Department in March 1930 in succession to Lord Eustace Percy (a man more in Baldwin's mould), noting that this would give him control of 'the springs of policy'; he had become Party Chairman by encouraging Davidson's resignation, and so had put himself in the position of intermediary between Baldwin, Beaverbrook and the party; his 'unauthorized programme' had helped to force Baldwin's hand on the tariff issue, and he was the party's foremost debater in the House of Commons, leading the attack on the government. In all this Chamberlain's motives remained rather ambiguous. He knew that he must be Baldwin's successor if he should resign, but he was far too loyal to do anything to bring this about. In October 1929 he wrote that 'S.B. is my friend as well as my leader and I would not on any account play L.G. to his Asquith'. The loyalty that Austen had shown to Lloyd George in 1921–22 was now shown by Neville to Baldwin in exactly the same circumstances, but it made his position a frustrating one. When in July 1930 he was urged to seize the leadership, he responded that 'the commonest loyalty makes it impossible to listen to such a suggestion and yet the tragedy is that – most reluctantly – I have come to the conclusion that if S.B. would go the whole party would heave a sigh of relief. . . . Yet it looks as if I might have to go down fighting for S.B.'[32] The frustration was perhaps a little easier to bear when it seemed that Neville would only have to bide his time to gain the leadership without a fight.

The chance for Chamberlain seemed to have come in February 1931 with renewed tension over India, further advice from friends about the need to get Baldwin to resign, and the general level of party discontent. The weapon was placed in his hand by Robert Topping, who presented Chamberlain on 26 February with a memorandum on the state of party opinion. He pointed out that the revival of Baldwin's popularity after the Caxton Hall meeting had not lasted, and that 'there has been a very definite feeling that the Leader is not strong enough to carry the Party to victory, and that feeling appears to have grown stronger every day. . . . From practically all quarters one hears the view that it would be in the interests of the Party that the Leader should reconsider his position.'[33] Chamberlain, conscious of the extreme delicacy of his position, consulted his brother, Hoare, Cunliffe-Lister, Hailsham, Bridgeman and Monsell. It was generally agreed that Topping's memorandum must be passed on to Baldwin, Hailsham suggesting that Chamberlain should wait until after Baldwin had delivered an impending speech in Devon, scheduled for 6 March. The plot was made, but the delay was to prove fatal. It was now that the press lords blundered in and divided Baldwin's foes once again. They had resolved after South Paddington that they would fight every suitable vacancy, and at East Islington on 19 February they had managed to push the official Conservative into third place. This was bad enough, but the vacancy in the St George's division of Westminster was likely to be much worse, following the death of Worthington-Evans on 14 February. St George's, including Mayfair and Belgravia, was probably the safest Conservative seat in England and was a stronghold of exactly the social groups who were most opposed to Baldwin; a contest here would not be complicated by a Labour or Liberal challenge, so that Conservatives would have a free choice between the Empire Crusade and the official party.

The situation rapidly slid into anarchy, for the local party at St George's could not find a candidate to take up Baldwin's cause; of the four men on the short-list, three withdrew rather than fight for Baldwin against Beaverbrook and the fourth would not support Baldwin even if selected as the official candidate. Meanwhile Beaverbrook had put forward Sir Ernest Petter as an Independent Conservative against Baldwin; so by 1 March, less than three weeks before polling day, the Empire Crusade was ready but the party was not. As a result of these events, the movement against Baldwin at the top would have to be postponed; as Chamberlain gloomily wrote, 'We cannot possibly sit down . . . or allow S.B. to resign at their bidding. Therefore, just at the moment when the train was laid and the match actually lighted, Max has once more blundered in and upset the applecart.' All the same, the situation at St George's now demanded that Baldwin should see the Topping memorandum at once. Cunliffe-Lister explained to Baldwin that it represented the views of his colleagues and Chamberlain confirmed that it was his view too when he saw Baldwin on the afternoon of 1 March. Baldwin recognized that he could not but defer to such a universal demand for his replacement, saying that he would announce his retirement to the shadow cabinet on the next day. Chamberlain noted at 4.30 that 'S.B. decided to go at once', and *The Times* set up a leader headed 'Mr Baldwin withdraws'.[34]

Baldwin's mind was changed on the same evening though by the only two real friends that he still had among his colleagues. Davidson set the ball rolling when he craftily refused to confirm or deny a rumour that Baldwin would resign his own seat to fight St George's, thus ensuring that the story reverberated around Fleet Street for the rest of the day. Bridgeman 'alone of his colleagues told him to pay no attention to the agitation. . . . By the next morning, Baldwin had determined not only to hold his ground, but to make a vigorous offensive.'[35] At the bidding of Bridgeman and Davidson, Baldwin resolved not to give way to 'the yellow press' and he decided that he would fight St George's, thus following the rumour rather than creating it. When Chamberlain returned on the morning of 2 March, he was told of the decision, as described by Baldwin's biographers:

> Chamberlain arrived punctually and asked what Baldwin wanted to see him about. 'I have decided to go down fighting,' Baldwin replied 'and I propose to be

adopted the official candidate for St. George's.' Chamberlain said quickly, 'S.B., you can't do that.' Baldwin answered, 'Why not?' and got the reply, 'Think of the effect on your successor.' Baldwin saw immediately that Chamberlain's attitude had not been entirely disinterested and he said curtly, 'I don't give a damn about my successor'. There the conversation ended.[36]

Baldwin was now moved to an anger that made him a formidable opponent, and this was reinforced when Davidson presented evidence from Sir Patrick Gower which showed that party opinion was not as one-sided as Topping had alleged. The plan to fight St George's was quickly dropped, but it had served its turn in bringing Baldwin to a determination to defend himself.

By this time there was little time left to snatch victory from defeat. Duff Cooper was summoned back from Sweden and persuaded to take on the contest at St George's, giving up the safe seat that he was nursing at Winchester; he at least thought that he was making no real sacrifice, for he never expected to lose. He was a good candidate for the constituency, for he had a distinguished war record, was on good terms with Beaverbrook, and had a far more impressive bearing and appearance than Petter.[37] A fierce little skirmish had to be fought out with the diehards in the party's India Committee. Baldwin told Tom Jones that 'No party is so divided as mine. I have done my utmost to keep it together, but it ranges from Imperialists of the Second Jubilee to young advanced Democrats who are all for Irwin's policy. I am for that policy myself, and mean to say so.'[38] He appeared to come off badly in the Committee, but he more than repaired the damage in the Commons with a superb speech on 12 March, again urging his party to recognize that the world had changed, and enlivening his words with quotations from Churchill's moderate speeches on India in 1920. The consensus was nevertheless that Baldwin had only delayed his overthrow, and Chamberlain still expected to succeed him.[39]

The decision was now in the hands of the electors of St George's, for a Petter victory would have destroyed Baldwin beyond recovery. Neville Chamberlain loyally gave Duff Cooper all the help that Central Office could muster, and Baldwin went to speak for him at the Queen's Hall. This speech crowned two years of resistance to the press lords, removed the last chance that Cooper might lose, and saved Baldwin's leadership, but it was a pretty poor performance. The evidence that he produced of a press campaign of personal vilification was woefully unconvincing, and he traded in personalities with as little restraint as the *Daily Express* had ever done. But the audience lapped it up and cheered him to the echo – it was after all something of a novelty to hear Baldwin in such a mood. The most effective part was the reply to the *Daily Mail*'s unsigned allegation that a man who had lost his own private fortune was not fitted to preside over the state:

> The paragraph itself could only have been written by a cad. I have consulted a very high legal authority and I am advised that an action for libel would lie. I shall not move in the matter, and for this reason: I should get an apology and heavy

damages. The first is of no value, and the second I would not touch with a barge
pole. What the proprietorship of these papers is aiming at is power, and power
without responsibility – the prerogative of the harlot through the ages.[40]

These last words, borrowed from Kipling, rang through the Hall and the
constituency, as is well known. (What is less well known is the reaction of the
Conservative agent who heard them and exclaimed in despair 'Bang goes the
harlot vote!') Once the campaign had been wrenched on to the ground of the
press against the people, Cooper's victory was assured, and he was duly
elected on 19 March with a majority of five thousand.

Baldwin had won a largely bogus victory. He had been persuaded by his
friends that the issue at stake was the role of the press, although even his
critics and his heir-apparent recognized that the party could not be seen to
bow to Beaverbrook. He had then concentrated on the one area where he
could be certain to win, ignoring dissent in the party and treating dissent in
the shadow cabinet as disloyalty which was doing Beaverbrook's work for
him. In 1930 he had concentrated each time on Rothermere, but the
perorations of his speeches always talked more widely of 'these papers'. In
March 1931 he went a step further and tarred all his critics as stooges of
Rothermere. Beaverbrook learnt a hard lesson in the realities of politics from
Baldwin in 1931 and never forgave him for it. Although Cooper was backed
by some socialists and Liberals, for whom he was at least preferable to Petter,
he polled a lower proportion of the electorate than any other Conservative in
the history of the constituency, despite all the sound and fury of the campaign,
and despite Baldwin's help. But bogus and unimpressive as it was, it was a
victory nonetheless; in the fight to a finish, Baldwin outlasted his critics – just.
'Society' rallied to Cooper in St George's and thereafter the diehards worked
to change the party's policy rather than its leader. Beaverbrook accepted
defeat and moved to patch up relations with the party through the mediation
of Chamberlain. The terms that were agreed, called the Stornoway Pact after
Beaverbrook's London home, were a triumph for the party, for this time it
was Beaverbrook who gave ground and the battle in the constituencies was
called off.

Things were not so easily settled in the shadow cabinet, for Baldwin still
harboured resentment at the attitude of Chamberlain and Hailsham. His
anger had been enhanced at the critical point of the St George's campaign
when Austen Chamberlain had demanded in shadow cabinet that his brother
should be released from Central Office; the demand was ostensibly to make
Neville available to strengthen the front-bench team in the Commons, but it
was an obvious attempt to detach him from Baldwin and open up the
succession. This was rather hard on Baldwin, who had not wanted
Chamberlain at Central Office in the first place and who now believed that he
had used his position there to work against his leader. This suspicion was itself
unfair to Neville, who had behaved with the utmost probity throughout, and
who had not been consulted by Austen before the demand was made. With St

George's duly out of the way, Chamberlain retreated from Central Office and the Party Chairmanship went instead to Lord Stonehaven. This was a very good choice, for Stonehaven had been a colleague of all the men in dispute in Baldwin's first government, but had been Governor-General of Australia since 1925 and so had taken no part in the recent controversies. Baldwin was reconciled to Neville Chamberlain after a straight-talking interview on 24 March and patched up relations with Amery on the next day. On 26 March he asked the general advice of his shadow cabinet, and was told by Austen Chamberlain that he must take more trouble over his leadership if he wanted to remove the real causes of criticism.[41]

The last months of opposition, in the spring and summer of 1931, were unexpectedly easy for the party, but they showed that Baldwin had learnt at least something from the recent battles. He pursued the government with unaccustomed severity, producing delight amongst his supporters and pained surprise from MacDonald. This change of tactics was less difficult than it may have seemed, for Baldwin shared his party's conviction that the Labour government was doing nothing in the way of economic policy while the situation deteriorated, and he was also concerned by MacDonald's flirtation with Lloyd George. By-elections were again greeted with hope rather than despair and the Conservative gain of Ashton-under-Lyne in April was especially sweet, in Beaverbrook's old seat and in a constituency that had been lost to Labour in the run up to the 1929 general election. Swings to the Conservatives mounted to an average of ten per cent in the contests of 1931 and the LCC elections confirmed the trend. MacDonald's government staggered from crisis to crisis without much hope of surviving beyond the autumn, when a general election would presumably return the Conservatives to power with a substantial majority.

The improbable sequel to the party battles of 1929–31 owed little to Baldwin except in one vital way, that he was still there. Had he been succeeded by Neville Chamberlain in March it is unlikely that there could have been a National government in August, for he was already so feared and disliked by the Labour party that Labour ministers would have been no more ready to place their careers and policies under his control in 1931 than they were in 1940. In some ways, Neville Chamberlain may be considered as the architect of the National government, but he probably could not have brought it about without Baldwin as his party's leader. Although Baldwin had always promised MacDonald a fair run in office, he always turned down suggestions that their relations should be put on a more formal basis. When MacDonald appealed for support from the opposition parties in June 1930 Lloyd George accepted but Baldwin turned him down. In the following December MacDonald floated the idea of an all-party government before Baldwin's eyes after a discussion on India, but Baldwin told him that protection would always make such a combination impossible. A formal approach to Lord Stonehaven in July 1931 was met only with a blunt refusal even to negotiate, and with a speech by Baldwin in which he reminded his party that he had broken up one coalition and had no wish to form another. Neville Chamberlain agreed with Baldwin that Labour must take the full consequences of its policies, but by the end of July 1931 he recognized that the state of the economy might make joint action unavoidable.[42] Baldwin saw the May Report on the economic situation before he left for his holiday at Aix; he left Chamberlain to look after the party's interests in London, feeling like everyone else that the crisis would not break for a couple of months.

However, the publication of the May report accelerated events and threatened the immediate collapse of the Labour government, which could neither agree to accept the May proposals nor on any other policy that would secure a foreign loan. Baldwin was called back to London on 11 August, and he met with MacDonald, Snowden, and Chamberlain at Downing Street. Chamberlain was by this time keen to get the necessary economies imposed by a Labour government, and both the Conservatives and Liberals agreed to support MacDonald if he could produce an adequate programme. Baldwin, still thinking more of his holiday and of the need to allow Labour's previous folly to be seen, returned to France, as Chamberlain related:

I think he would agree that crises of this kind are not his forte. He had apparently given no thought to the situation, asked no intelligent question, made no helpful suggestion and indeed was chiefly anxious to be gone before he was 'drawn into something'. He left a final message for me that he was most grateful to me for sparing him the necessity of returning and he would 'back me to the end!'.[43]

Chamberlain recruited Hoare to assist in the negotiations, presumably because of his banking connections, and these two represented the party over the next few crucial days. A political crisis in August was not without its inconvenience, as Hoare later recalled: 'Chamberlain, whose house was also shut, and I met in our bedrooms in the annexe of the Carlton Club. The main building of the club was closed for cleaning.' On 20 August the government explained that the most that it could agree on was cuts of £56 million, although the budget deficit was now expected to reach £170 million. Conservatives and Liberals both rejected this as insufficient and MacDonald replied by asking 'Well, are you prepared to join the Board of directors?'[44] Baldwin was again called back to London, arriving on 22 August, and by that time MacDonald was on the point of resignation.

The shadow ministers who could be consulted urged cooperation, but Baldwin still inclined to the view that, if MacDonald could not govern, he should resign and there should be a Conservative government and an election. By the accident that Baldwin could not be found by the summons of the King, the Liberal leader Samuel went to the Palace first; Samuel urged the creation of a National government under MacDonald, which fitted exactly with the King's inclinations.[45] When Baldwin saw the King he was therefore asked if he would serve under MacDonald, and he had little option but to agree to do so. This course of action was urged on MacDonald by the King, and a subsequent meeting of MacDonald, Samuel, Baldwin and Chamberlain took the decision from which the National government stemmed. Baldwin took little part in the discussion, and it was left to Chamberlain to persuade MacDonald to retain the premiership.[46] On the morning of 24 August it was finally agreed to set up a National government, as a temporary expedient, purely to pass the necessary legislation for economies and increased taxes; there would then be an election, in which the parties would resume their independence. It was for the party a very fortunate outcome indeed; four days earlier Walter Elliot had remarked that 'if God succeeds in making Ramsay do Baldwin's economy for him . . . I really shall believe in a personal Deity – with one motto "This is my beloved son Stanley".'[47]

The party had played no collective part in the formation of the new government; the leader had been dragged in unwillingly, the discussions had been conducted by colleagues that he still did not fully trust, and neither the shadow cabinet nor the parliamentary party met until after the decision was taken. But once committed, Baldwin moved quickly to ensure that the party would go along with the new departure. The shadow cabinet accepted it without a single voice raised in opposition, and a party meeting on 28 August gave its approval when Baldwin emphasized that an election would come soon, and that it would be 'a straight fight on tariffs and against the Socialist Party'. On the same day, Neville Chamberlain and Sir Kingsley Wood explained what had happened to an emergency meeting of the National Union Executive. When asked if propaganda would go on, Chamberlain replied that 'the answer was emphatically "Yes", but there would have to be some modification, as obviously no attacks could be made on the Prime Minister [MacDonald] or the Chancellor of the Exchequer [Snowden], and it was also difficult to attack the Liberals, but propaganda on the Party's Tariff policy would continue'.[48] A resolution supporting the new government was proposed by Derby and passed unanimously; such a state of party harmony was almost unknown, testament indeed to the very real fear of financial collapse. In a newsreel appeal issued on 7 September Baldwin recalled 'the lesson from Germany', where 'but a few years ago, notes of thousands and thousands of marks were sold in the streets for a copper – as a curiosity'; there is no doubt that he spoke for many in articulating such fears.[49]

There was rather less harmony in the distribution of offices in the new government, and here Baldwin was more positive. Four Labour ministers retained their posts, and two posts went to Liberals, so there were only four cabinet seats for Conservatives in the ten-man crisis cabinet. Baldwin was deaf to Chamberlain's pleas on behalf of Hailsham, who was in any case ruled out by MacDonald, and so the posts went to Baldwin, Chamberlain, Hoare and Cunliffe-Lister. Hailsham had no job at all, nor did Churchill and Amery, and Austen Chamberlain was bitterly disappointed to get only the non-cabinet post of First Lord of the Admiralty. The government's National character was reflected in the share-out; of the forty-six ministerial posts, only twenty-one went to Conservatives, although the party made up the overwhelming bulk of the government's votes in the Commons. This caused some disappointment among aspirants to office, not least when the names of Liberal ministers were announced. Walter Elliot was not really very amused by the appointment of Lord Crewe to the War Office: 'Crewe!! He was past his work in Asquith's day. Bracken lost £1 on a bet that he was dead and John Boyd declared he *is* dead and has been appointed as a measure of economy.' Nevertheless, the party that had been so opposed to coalition in 1921–22, knuckled under to a 'Coalition of Coalitions' in 1931 with remarkably little fuss. England does not love coalitions but, as Keith Feiling has pointed out, 'England does not object to coalitions if they avoid the name'.[50]

The terms on which the government had been formed, and accepted by its constituent parts, were swiftly overtaken by events. Further economic difficulties were encountered when the refusal of naval ratings to welcome cuts in their pay was misreported as a mutiny; another run on the pound began and forced the government to abandon the Gold Standard. The *value* of the pound had been assured (if it was really threatened) by the government's very existence, in the sense that the internal strength of the currency was now guaranteed, but it was not easy to explain this point, and it looked suspiciously as if the government had failed in its central aim. Political hostilities were opened by the Labour party rather than the government, for Labour was soon able to convince itself that it had been unfairly forced from office by 'a bankers' ramp' and by the betrayal of its leaders. This in turn increased MacDonald's indignation with his late colleagues and reduced his reluctance to work with his new ones.[51] The government had a small Commons majority, but one that was neither stable nor reliable, and certainly not a sure foundation for a government of national survival. Advice to the government suggested that foreign opinion would not be mollified until it had asked for and gained a mandate.[52]

Pressure built up in the Conservative party during September, for Conservatives were keen to teach Labour a lesson at the polls and to get a majority for tariffs. *The Times*, the 1922 Committee and the shadow cabinet all urged Baldwin to bring about a quick election, a course of action that was supported in cabinet by MacDonald and Snowden after they had been expelled from the Labour party, but opposed by the Liberals. The King again intervened to brace MacDonald's nerve, and the cabinet decided on an election on 5 October.[53] Each party would argue its own case in its own literature, and the government as a whole would ask for a 'doctor's mandate'; it would continue in office after the election, still under MacDonald, and would pursue whatever policies then seemed most suitable. This fitted the Conservative bill exactly, for it ensured the cooperation of MacDonald and the Liberals in winning a majority that would be almost entirely Conservative (as MacDonald clearly recognized), without binding the party to any concessions on policy. Baldwin apparently assured the Prime Minister that he would not stand for victimization of the Labour ministers, and he kept his word, but he gave no pledges on policy.[54] It was exactly the sort of scheme that had failed to convince the party when put forward by Austen Chamberlain in October 1922.

The general election of 1931 was no sort of serious contest at all, for although there was an unusually high level of noise and violence, the Labour party had no real stomach for the fight.[55] The tale was told well enough by the evidence of the nominations, for fifty-six Conservatives and five Liberals were returned unopposed. There were 523 Conservatives supporting the National government, together with 20 National Labour and 160 Liberals, in three separate groups; pacts between Conservatives and Simonite Liberal Nationals ensured that the right sort of Liberals were elected – from the Tory point of view. The Conservative campaign was reminiscent of 1924, except that this time there was no need to invoke Russian bogies, for the domestic crisis could be laid squarely at the door of the ministers who had run away from it. Baldwin's sole concern was that the obvious success of the government's candidates should not encourage its supporters to stay at home, and his later speeches argued that 'any man or woman who abstains from voting at this crisis in the nation's history is failing in his or her duty to the country'. The results too were reminiscent of 1924, though in an even more exaggerated form, as Tom Jones told a friend on 28 October:

> I sat in Downing Street until three this morning, watching the tape ticking the monotonous Conservative gains from North and South and East and West. Of course you and I are glad the National Cause has won. I voted Conservative for the first time in my life and so did Rene. We had to do it. 'Labour' had to be thrashed, but it cannot be destroyed. We could not trust them with the Bank of England – just yet.[56]

Another lifelong socialist on the National government side, MacDonald was equally disconsolate at the size of the victory: 'It has turned out all too well. How tragically the Labour Party has been let down. . . . The Conser: Head Office pretended to do what it never did & unfortunately the size of the victory has weakened me.'[57] By comparison with 1929 the Labour vote dropped by well over a million, while the Conservative vote rose by over three million. Allowing for the unopposed returns the turnout was the highest at any election between the wars, and probably about 60 per cent of the voters would have voted Conservative if they had had the chance to do so. In all, 473 Conservatives were returned; Sheffield and Manchester both elected full slates of Conservatives for the only time in their history, and the results elsewhere were equally extraordinary. The government as a whole had a majority of over 500 over a Labour remnant of 52 (almost all from mining seats) and Lloyd George's family group of 4. The explanation was clear, that Liberals and Conservatives polled in the largest possible numbers for the National candidates, who in most places were Conservatives;[58] many Labour voters simply stayed at home. It was the biggest victory of all time, and it provided the Conservatives at last with a parliamentary majority for tariffs.

The formation of the National government had not changed the party's economic policy in any way, as the evidence of one propaganda medium shows. In a newsreel interview in the spring, Baldwin had argued that:

> the time has come for us to look after ourselves, and as the foreigner protects himself, so we must put the interests of our own people first. We will ask the country also to enter into trade agreements with our own dominions, under which we will ask them to buy our manufactured goods, we taking in exchange foodstuffs and raw materials. . . . We will ask the electorate to give us powers to stimulate wheat-growing.

In a propaganda film for the election itself, Baldwin dismissed fears that the 'free hand' idea had diluted his policy:

> With a free hand, we have power to use tariffs, as a means to restore the trade balance. We have powers to enter into trade agreements with the dominions, in order that we may find new markets for our manufactures in the Empire. We have power to take effective action to rescue agriculture.

Cinema audiences had also seen Baldwin opening the National government's election campaign in Birmingham with the words: 'I cherish the hope that the National government will carry into fruition those things to which we were pledged.'[59]

In theory, the election left the government still uncommitted about its future policy, but in practice there could be no further doubt. Tom Jones predicted that 'the Tory wolves will howl for high tariffs and will give S.B. hell'. The overwhelming majority in parliament was in favour of tariffs, and Stonehaven summed up the election results as showing that 'we now have a National government with a mandate to carry out Tory policy'.[60] Baldwin restrained his followers from such open jubilation when he could do so, but he had no wish to disagree with them on the substantive issue of policy. It was necessary to approach the question carefully, because of the danger that the resignations of Snowden and the Samuelite Liberals would remove the government's National appearance within a few days of its election triumph. In the transition to a permanent government after the election, MacDonald took care not to offend his free-trade ministers or to give the impression that the issue was already settled. Thus, while Conservatives occupied eleven of the twenty posts in the new cabinet, they were mainly in the military and non-departmental areas. Simon became Foreign Secretary and Samuel stayed at the Home Office, so satisfying both Liberal factions, but this meant that a Conservative must take the other major post at the Exchequer. Baldwin prefered to stay in a non-departmental office as Lord President, although he appropriated the Chancellor's residence in Downing Street as a means of facilitating communication with the Prime Minister next door; Bonar Law had done the same between 1919 and 1921. Despite MacDonald's reluctance to send a committed protectionist to the Treasury, he was obliged to appoint Neville Chamberlain, but this was balanced by the appointment of the Liberal

Runciman to the Board of Trade. In the event, Runciman proved easy for Chamberlain to persuade, and the rest of the government bowed to Conservative pressure too.

The protectionists had an easy victory in the preparation of the Abnormal Importations Act, a temporary measure that would give tariff powers while a permanent policy was being worked out. Chamberlain worked on his colleagues so effectively that before the end of 1931 he and Runciman had the power to impose emergency tariffs on any goods they liked, and at any rate up to 100 per cent.[61] On the permanent question, a cabinet committee under Chamberlain was given an open brief to consider the imbalance of trade and to recommend any measures that they thought necessary. Of course ministers did not agree, but the majority reported on 21 January 1932 that there should be a general tariff of 10 per cent, and that it should be linked with preference for the Dominions, which would be discussed at an Imperial Economic Conference at Ottawa later in the year. After threats of resignation from the free-traders, and after Monsell (until recently Chief Whip) told his colleagues that if they did not act soon, 'the House of Commons would take matters into their own hands', the cabinet accepted its committee's majority recommendation.[62] At the suggestion of Chamberlain, collective responsibility was suspended, so that the free-traders could speak and vote against government policy without resigning. This 'agreement to differ' looked odd in a government of national unity, but it was an inescapable consequence of the decision to prolong the government's existence in October 1931. Conservatives, who could alone make a non-Labour government a viable proposition, were not prepared to forgo tariffs now that they had the chance to impose them.

The delegation to the Ottawa Conference in August 1932 was led by Baldwin, who made all the appropriate noises to encourage its progress, but the working manager of the team was undoubtedly Chamberlain, who was armed with briefs from the Conservative Research Department as well as from the Treasury. After much hard bargaining agreement was reached at Ottawa and presented to the cabinet at the end of September. This was the point of no return for the free-trade ministers, who agreed to go on giving general support to the government but resigned their posts. The tariff proposals were implemented without difficulty, and the Conservatives and Simonites increased their hold over the government; together they now had sixteen of the nineteen cabinet posts. As Baldwin had hoped, the whole tariff issue now dropped out of the realm of serious political debate, so ending a long chapter of party and national history, as Chamberlain reminded the House of Commons:

> There can have been few occasions in all our long political history when to the son of a man who counted for something in his day and generation has been vouchsafed the privilege of setting the seal on the work which the father began but had perforce to leave unfinished. . . . His work was not in vain. Time and the

misfortunes of the country have brought conviction to many who did not feel that they could agree with him then. I believe he would have found consolation for the bitterness of his disappointment if he could have foreseen that these proposals, which are the direct and legitimate descendants of his own conception, would be laid before the House of Commons, which he loved, in the presence of one and by the lips of the other of the two immediate successors to his name and blood.[63]

There were high hopes now that this policy of a lifetime had at last been implemented; R. B. Bennett of Canada exulted that 'it is a matter of great satisfaction that I contributed under Providence to the agreement. . . . In the days to come, millions of men and women . . . will appreciate as they have never done before the proud boast, the boast that "I am a British subject".' In the event though, the tariff did little of what had been hoped from it. It did not make a material impact on the level of British unemployment in the short term, it did not reduce the level of imports and may even have hampered exports, and it certainly did not reverse the centrifugal tendencies that were driving the Dominions towards separate destinies. But in party terms none of this mattered, for the battle had been so long and so contentious that to have won it was quite sufficient. Sir Charles Petrie later remembered 'criticising the Government in, I think 1933, to an old Tariff Reformer, and for a while he agreed with me; but suddenly he interrupted with a catch in his voice: "That's all very well, but don't forget they gave us the tariff." There was a generation of British history in the words.'[64]

Notes and References

1 Macleod, *Chamberlain*, 132.
2 National Union minutes, Executive Committee, 11 Dec. 1928.
3 Seymour-Ure in Cook and Peele, *Politics of Reappraisal*, 233–7.
4 Macmillan, *Winds of Change*, 247.
5 *Ibid*, 267; Coote, *Companion of Honour*, 116–18.
6 Marquand, *MacDonald*, 489.
7 Davidson, *Memoirs of a Conservative*, 306.
8 Gilbert, *Winston S. Churchill*, v, 328.
9 Davidson, *Memoirs of a Conservative*, 305–45.
10 National Union minutes, Central Council, 1 Mar. 1927; Sanders Diary, 20 Feb. 1927.
11 Davidson, *Memoirs of a Conservative*, 312–3.
12 National Union minutes, 1929–30, *passim*.
13 Davidson, *Memoirs of a Conservative*, 330–1.
14 *Week-End Review*, 17 May 1930, in the Davidson MSS.
15 Davidson to Irwin, 7 Nov. 1927: Davidson MSS.
16 Middlemas and Barnes, *Baldwin*, 584–5; for an excellent account of the whole issue, see Gillian Peele's essay in Cook and Peele, *Politics of Reappraisal*.
17 Gilbert, *Winston S. Churchill*, v, 355.
18 Middlemas and Barnes, *Baldwin*, 544
19 Gilbert, *Winston S. Churchill*, 372.
20 *Ibid*, 382.
21 David Dilks in Butler, *The Conservatives*, 329.
22 Gilbert, *Winston S. Churchill*, v, 383.
23 Taylor, *Beaverbrook*, 271.
24 Gilbert, *Winston S. Churchill*, v, 365.
25 *Ibid*, 360.
26 Topping to Davidson, 2 May 1930: Davidson MSS.
27 National Union minutes, Executive Committee, 17 June 1930.
28 Middlemas and Barnes, *Baldwin*, 573.
29 *Ibid*, 576.
30 *Ibid*, 578–9.
31 Cooper, *Old Men Forget*, 170.
32 Macleod, *Chamberlain*, 132, 136.
33 *Ibid*, 139.
34 Middlemas and Barnes, *Baldwin*, 589.
35 Templewood, *Nine Troubled Years*, 34.
36 Middlemas and Barnes, *Baldwin*, 590.

37   Cooper, *Old Men Forget*, 173; Gillian Peele, in Cook and Ramsden, *By-elections*, 94.
38   Jones, *Diary with Letters*, 5.
39   Macleod, *Chamberlain*, 142.
40   Roberts, *Stanley Baldwin, Man or Miracle?*, 205–10.
41   Middlemas and Barnes, *Baldwin*, 601.
42   Marquand, *MacDonald*, 546, 578; Macleod, *Chamberlain*, 147–8.
43   Macleod, *Chamberlain*, 149.
44   *Ibid*, 150; Templewood, *Nine Troubled Years*, 16–17.
45   Marquand, *Macdonald*, 630.
46   *Ibid*, 635.
47   Coote, *Companion of Honour*, 123.
48   National Union minutes, Executive Committee, 28 Aug. 1931.
49   'Mr Baldwin on the Crisis', *Pathe News* issue 31/72, 7 Sept. 1931; Macmillan, *Winds of Change*, 273.
50   Coote, *Companion of Honour*, 124; Macmillan, *Winds of Change* (quoting Feiling), 272.
51   Marquand, *MacDonald*, 654.
52   Jones, *Diary with Letters*, 13.
53   Marquand, *MacDonald*, 663.
54   *Ibid*, 665.
55   Macmillan, *Winds of Change*, 280.
56   Jones, *Diary with Letters*, 20.
57   Marquand, *MacDonald*, 671.
58   This is certainly what happened in Stockton, where the Conservative vote rose by 10,000; Macmillan, *Winds of Change*, 280.
59   'Mr Baldwin speaks to the Conservative Party', *Paramount News*, unissued material, Visnews Library, 494; 'Election film, 1931' (made by the Conservative and Unionist Films Association), National Film Archive; *Paramount News*, issue 65, 12 Oct. 1931.
60   Jones, *Diary with Letters*, 20; Marquand, *MacDonald*, 710.
61   Macleod, *Chamberlain*, 155.
62   Marquand, *Macdonald*, 712.
63   Macleod, *Chamberlain*, 156–7.
64   Petrie, *The Chamberlain Tradition*, 238–9.

Chapter 14

The Conservative Party and the National government

The National government is conventionally dismissed as a mere facade behind which the Conservatives governed Britain for the decade before the Second World War. The partners who joined the Conservatives are therefore regarded as traitors, knaves or dupes, men whose tenure of office relied on their political masters and who toed the Tory line in order to survive. Such a view is misleading and unhistorical: misleading because it does not square with the way in which the National government actually worked, and unhistorical because it fails to recognize the extent to which it changed over the years. The government was little more than a Conservative front by 1937, but it is by no means so clear that this was so in 1931 or 1933. We must therefore ask not only if the National government was really national, but also when? The task is not made any easier by the fact that the government as a whole still awaits serious investigation; there has been a great deal of research on foreign policy, especially in the later years of the decade, but very little investigation of the way in which the government actually worked.

The first point to be established is that the government was National in a real sense in its origin, and that because of this origin it continued to operate unlike a party government until at least 1934–35; for the same reason it continued to evoke a response in the country unlike a party government. Baldwin only came into the government reluctantly and Conservatives as a whole were conscious that in joining they were giving up the certainty of a Conservative government and the near-certainty of an independent Conservative majority. Cabinet-making in 1931 showed how far Conservatives were prepared to sacrifice their interests (or at the least each others' interests) in the pursuit of national unity. For four years thereafter Baldwin not only did not try to seize the premiership which must have been his for the taking, but he positively resisted MacDonald's own attempts to withdraw. When the Samuelites withdrew in 1932, there was discussion of the idea of bringing in 'National Independents' to replace them – much as Lloyd George and Churchill used ministers with independent reputations in their wartime administrations.[1] The experience of Harold Nicolson in 1934–35 illustrates another side of this same truth. He had been prepared to stand as a Conservative when putting his name forward for selection at Sevenoaks, but he ultimately stood as a 'National' candidate in West Leicester, where he replaced a Samuelite on the government ticket. Nicolson had no strong party affiliations and did not much care what label was attached to him, but he was exactly the sort of man who would not have backed a partisan Conservative government. For their part, the Leicester Conservatives remained unconvinced until he was able to persuade Duff Cooper to visit Leicester and speak in his support.[2] The discussions within the government in 1932–33 were not conducted on party lines, and on several issues there was no identifiable party division at all, as on the issue of unemployment.[3] The informal inner cabinet was a committee of six, consisting of Baldwin and Chamberlain, MacDonald and Thomas, and Simon and Runciman; again, it operated as a team of colleagues rather than a meeting of party representatives. As late as the autumn of 1935, the committee entrusted with the task of devising an election manifesto included only five Conservatives out of nine; again it did not work on party lines.[4]

The generous public response in 1931 demonstrates how dangerous the crisis was thought to have been and how far the government was thought to deserve national backing. It was this spirit that led the King to instruct members of his household to vote for the government candidates in the election of 1931, a most rare intervention, and it was the same spirit that led both the King and the Prince of Wales to sacrifice part of their income as a symbolic gesture of retrenchment in the national cause. The Conservative party made the same gesture by cancelling all social events connected with the party conference of 1931.[5] The national spirit also made Liberals like Gilbert Murray and socialists like Tom Jones vote Conservative for the first time in their lives, in both cases a severe sacrifice. Of course, not all felt the same impulse, and for many whose first loyalty was to the Labour movement there was a sharp conflict – which many solved by abstention. Nevertheless, almost all the middle-class and about half the working-class electors supported the National government, so giving it a greater claim to represent a national consensus than any other government has ever had. By comparison with this vast electoral coalition, Labour could only appear as a sectional interest, a comparison that did much to enhance the government's standing.

In the election of 1935 most of this contrast remained. The Labour vote recovered to almost exactly its level of 1929, but the government still managed to poll almost twelve million votes, well over half the voters and far more than the Conservatives had ever polled on their own. By-elections before and after 1935 went badly, and in some spectacular cases safe seats were lost, but these results demonstrate not the weak base of the government but its strength. A National government would not expect support whenever its individual policies were put to the test, but it was in no danger at general elections where its actual survival was in doubt.[6] The electoral balance of the inter-war years was such that there was never as much as 40 per cent of the voters prepared to support Labour in a situation that might produce a Labour government. So long as the anti-Labour vote was consolidated, as it was in

1918 and 1922 but much more effectively in 1924, 1931 and 1935, then the anti-Labour combination would win a substantial majority. In 1924 Baldwin had deliberately sought to make an appeal that was 'national' in the senses that it was aimed at all classes equally, that it was aimed especially at Liberal and non-party voters, and that it promised a non-partisan policy after the election. The years after 1926 had shown that Baldwin could not easily redeem such a pledge in a wholly Conservative government, and Liberal voters had taken it out on him in 1929 – but they had merely succeeded in producing a Labour government. After 1931 Baldwin was able to see the advantage of pursuing his style of Conservatism in a government that included non-Conservatives, and many Liberals were anxious to assist him.

The National government was thus the natural culmination of Baldwin's New Conservative phase of 1924–25; it was founded securely on the collaboration of Liberals and Conservatives at Westminster as well as in the constituencies, and this collaboration was enough to secure a majority for the government. Continuity from 1924 showed up too in the relations of the National government with the trade unions and with women. The trade unions worked closely with the government, despite their conviction that Labour had been badly treated in 1931, for they recognized the extent of the government's following in the country. These close relations were signalized by the conferment of honours on several trade union leaders for their services to the nation in 1935.[7] Women certainly backed the National government to a far greater extent than men, as they had been said to back Baldwin in 1924–25; in 1935 the government held 132 of the 134 constituencies where women voters made up more than 55 per cent of the electorate.[8] In all these senses the government continued to evoke a response that went beyond that which has ever been achieved by any party government.

From the start it was MacDonald and his associates who were most in doubt about the new experiment in government. The idea of a ministry of the talents under his own leadership certainly appealed to MacDonald, as did the idea that the nation needed him, but he saw clearly enough that he would be a hostage to the other parties. After the departure of the free-traders he told the King that 'a Prime Minister who does not belong to the Party in power will become more and more an anomaly, and, as policy develops, his position will become more and more degrading'.[9] Like Lloyd George, MacDonald was a prisoner because his own party had taken away his only line of retreat. National Labour was only the icing on the government cake, but it was still a decoration worth preserving; as Neville Chamberlain had pointed out in 1931, MacDonald's support among MPs was less important than his following in the country, and this was enhanced by his personal victory at Seaham. MacDonald's health did not give way as completely as was generally believed, and he was certainly more than a figurehead in 1933 and 1934. He remained the most influential minister in relation to foreign affairs until the spring of 1934, keeping relations with the United States under his personal control. He was able to keep Sankey on as Lord Chancellor long after the Conservatives wanted him out, he was prepared to threaten the dissolution of parliament when necessary to stop the government becoming a purely Conservative one, and he did not resign until he was good and ready.[10] When the government appointed special investigators for the depressed areas in 1934, the man sent to South Wales was MacDonald's personal choice and a man entirely unknown to Conservatives.[11] But although MacDonald continued to exercise real power, he remained to exercise it only because Baldwin chose to allow him to do so. In July 1932, Davidson told Baldwin that MacDonald would have to be reminded of the fragility of his position:

> If he were to be so foolish as to try a fall with our organization, Ll.G.'s fate would be mild in comparison. If he starts to stick pins in the horse that carried him to the victory and is maintaining him in front of the race, he may find that however patient a nag the Tory Party may be, if he does put its back up, it will kick him over the moon.[12]

To all such suggestions, Baldwin replied curtly that if MacDonald were pushed out then he would go too. National Labour therefore developed a rudimentary organization, continuing to operate as a separate group and publishing its own magazine.[13] The defeat of the two MacDonalds in 1935 removed even the pretence that National Labour was electorally independent, for both were subsequently returned at by-elections under Conservative auspices, but the determination to preserve a semblance of National government continued. Almost all the National Labour MPs were ministers and as such continued to exercise personal influence, even if their group influence was negligible. Harold Nicolson pointed out that 'a Party which has a meeting of all its members and can only fill a dinner-table with seven, six of whom have Government jobs, cannot be called an ill-used party'.[14]

The case of the Liberal Nationals (Simonites) was very different, for they made up a larger proportion of the government's parliamentary base, preserved at least a theoretical line of retreat, and had a more definite base in the country outside. From 1931 the old Liberal party gradually split into three distinct factions, two of which detached themselves from the government. The Lloyd George faction had never joined the National government, but had only four seats in parliament and counted for little outside Wales. The Samuelites followed a tortuous path before leaving the government in 1932, and it was not until the autumn of 1933 that they moved over to the opposition side in the Commons. In the parliament of 1931, however, it was the Simonite Liberals who made up the largest group, and they remained members of the government throughout. There was thus no moment at which 'the Liberal party' broke with the National government, no point at which its members and supporters were given a clear lead. Local Liberal parties in the 1930s were either in a state of understandable confusion or moribund to the point of non-existence, and in 1935 there were few contests between Liberal Nationals and 'Liberals', so that the electorate still had no clear idea of where the Liberal vote should go. The Liberal Nationals gradually became indistinguishable from Conservatives, but by no means as quickly as has been generally supposed, and the careers of individuals do not make interpretation any easier. Sir John Simon had been an orthodox Asquithian who had never collaborated with Conservatives after his resignation from Asquith's government in 1916, when he had been replaced by Sir Herbert Samuel; their roles were now reversed. Gwilym Lloyd George, who opposed the National government, ended his career as a Conservative cabinet minister, while Clement Davies, who supported the National government, ended as leader of the Liberal party and the saviour of its independence in the 1950s. It was all very confusing, and it is hardly surprising that the Liberal voters should not have followed those who were to be Liberals when the party re-emerged after the Second World War, for they were not gifted with second sight.

Simon's role in government was testament to the Liberals' continued importance, for he was successively Foreign Secretary, Home Secretary and Chancellor of the Exchequer, ending as Churchill's Lord Chancellor until 1945. Throughout this time he was disliked by a large number of Conservatives, who regarded him as quite unfitted for such preferment, and his survival was certainly due to his forensic debating skills and to his status as a party leader.[15] In 1935 the Liberal Nationals were still operating quite separately as a party in parliament; in the reshuffle of 1937 there was still considerable anxiety that the Liberals should be kept satisfied, hence the appointment of Hore-Belisha to the War Office; 'Chips' Channon, though, noted that the risk of his appointment was not all that great for 'if he is a failure, we can cart him, for he is not a Conservative'.[16] Contemporaries still did not regard Conservatives and Liberal Nationals as synonymous. Throughout the 1930s, these Liberal Nationals continued to occupy an anomalous position, drifting towards the Conservatives but virtually never opposed by other brands of Liberals in their constituencies. They did not establish formal relations with the Conservative Party until the Woolton–Cheviot agreement of 1948, and they continued to operate as a semi-independent group, with its own Whip until 1966. Like the Liberal Unionists, it took a generation before they were absorbed. In the 1930s, though, they always occupied half or more of the seats in parliament held by those who called themselves 'Liberals' and hence had at least as good a claim on Liberal votes as Samuel and Lloyd George. The result of the 1935 election suggests that even after 'the Liberal party' had abandoned the National government, the Liberal voters continued to support it overwhelmingly.

It was in this sense that the National government had to be more than a mere facade for Conservatism, for National Labour and Liberal Nationals constituted the government's assured margin of superiority over Labour. At the least, it had to be a particular sort of non-partisan Conservatism that was practised by the government, exactly the style of politics that Baldwin had proposed since 1924 as what the nation needed, an appeal to which both

MacDonald and Simon responded warmly.

Baldwin and Neville Chamberlain both played vital roles in the government, Baldwin as its chief communicator and Chamberlain as its executive arm. Baldwin was surprised by the extent to which the government was able to work together as a team in the national cause, and he was forced to revise his strong prejudice against coalitions; without Lloyd George coalition had become acceptable. It provided a chance to work out many of the ideas that he had always stood for, in the creation of harmony, moderate policies, and consistency along a middle course. It also enabled Baldwin to play the political role for which he was best fitted, oiling the wheels of party management rather than determining details of policy, explaining the government's grand strategy rather than expounding complicated Bills. It sheltered him from the loneliness of supreme command, which he had found extremely uncomfortable in 1930–31, without sacrificing the principles that were his prime political motivation. Tom Jones noted that 'this being second and not first suits him perfectly'.[17] The less spectacular side of this consisted in spending hours in the House of Commons and the smoking rooms, talking to MPs and listening to them, so keeping closely in touch with the mood of his followers and enabling him to guide the government as to what they would accept. Chips Channon noted that Baldwin was always to be seen around the House of Commons, and Baldwin himself told Tom Jones in 1934 that he had 'three Committees of two hours each this week. . . . Of course, Ramsay has the House off his shoulders. I sit there and though I don't say much, I'm there.' To Mrs Davidson, explaining his refusal of a dinner invitation in 1935, he wrote: 'Alas! I fear I *must* stay in the House tonight. It was in a curious and rather ugly mood all yesterday; the debate is being continued, and the division will take place about dinner time. The whole debate, and the succeeding one, will want watching closely. The P.M. is no use on these occasions.'[18] Party management could be more positive though, as in the speech that Baldwin gave to a dinner of the 1922 Committee in 1936, a speech described by the *Observer* as 'Mr Baldwin's best' and recounted by Baldwin himself to Tom Jones:

> I said there were some who doubted whether I was a dyed-in-the-wool Tory. I told them I wore Tory colours in my pram in the 1868 election. My father voted Whig then, but our cook was a Tory and she saw to my politics. For 94 years a Tory had represented Bewdley. . . . How when the war ended we were in a new world and how class conscious and revolutionary it was; how I felt that our Party was being destroyed and how I determined to do what I could to rescue it. I did not mention L.G. or Winston. Then in 1931 we conformed to the King's wish and all colleagues agreed with me in doing so. I then touched on German rearmament.[19]

This cheerful badinage and party folk history was exactly the stuff that Baldwin specialized in, and he delivered similar speeches at rallies around the country right up to his retirement.

Baldwin's appeal in his National government days followed on closely from that of 1924, except that the emphasis was now rather more negative. The optimism of his earlier appeals had got lost in the party battles and economic troubles since 1926, and he was now able to rest on his laurels and his established reputation. All his public speeches continued to have the same elevated moral appeal, and to concern themselves with eternal verities rather than political issues as such. So, when he became Prime Minister for the third time in 1935, he told a party rally at Himley Hall that

> more than any country in the world today we are the guardians and the trustees for democracy, for liberty, for freedom – for ordered liberty and ordered freedom. . . . With a firm faith in God and with an unshaken confidence in, and love for, our own people, I am accepting from the hands of His Majesty the weightiest burden that can be laid on the shoulders of an Englishman.[20]

In 1931 he had told the country that the economic crisis in Britain had posed 'the acid test for democracy' and after its successful resolution he continually referred back to it as an achievement that must not be betrayed. In a speech in 1936, he contrasted dictatorship, fear, suspicion and civil war in Europe with the calm and relative prosperity at home:

> I think that we must all be full of a sense of profound thankfulness that we are living in this country, under a system of National Government. . . . True to our traditions, we have avoided all extremes. We have steered clear of fascism, communism, dictatorship, and we have shown the world that democratic government, constitutional methods and ordered liberty are not inconsistent with progress and prosperity.[21]

Much as he chafed under Baldwin's leadership, Neville Chamberlain had to admit: 'I am bound to recognise that if I supply the policy and the drive, S.B. does also supply something that is perhaps even more valuable in retaining the floating vote.'[22]

In the Treasury, Chamberlain was said to be more in control of his department than any Chancellor had been since 'Black Michael' Hicks Beach. Within the government as a whole, Chamberlain was the mainspring of action, the supplier of ideas and policies to every other department: 'The amount of work you have to do largely depends on what you make for yourself. Unhappily it is part of my nature that I cannot contemplate any problem without trying to find a solution for it.' In 1932 he remarked that 'it amuses me to find a new policy for each of my colleagues in turn', but it was an attraction that did not last. By 1935, he was complaining that 'I am more and more carrying this government on my back.'[23]

The party as a whole accepted the continuation of National government, having rejected coalition ten years earlier. The government's existence removed any danger of Labour coming to power, and for that much could be forgiven. It also gave the party most of what it wanted in matters of policy, and some, like tariffs, that could not have been achieved in any other circumstances. Negatively but no less importantly, it never seemed to threaten the independence of the party, for MacDonald was a far more manageable ally than Lloyd George had ever been. The pact with the other parties and the surrender of a small number of offices to allies seemed a small price to pay for what was gained. The party was also involved in government to a greater extent than under Lloyd George and so was less tempted to indulge in factious opposition. Early in 1932 Baldwin met the newly elected MPs over a weekend at Ashridge, party committees for backbenchers became more active, and the easy parliamentary situation gave opportunities for backbenchers to influence policy without making any threat to the government. With the approach of another election in 1934, Chamberlain persuaded Baldwin to revive the meetings of Conservative ministers. These were held at Conservative Research Department and were linked with the work that the department was doing for the party; in the actual meetings, Chamberlain took the lead and became effective chairman.[24]

Although defence and foreign problems have dominated the historiography of the 1930s, it was India that weighed most heavily on Conservatives until 1935. The argument that had been gathering since the Irwin Declaration moved to a climax in 1933 and produced a contest for the control of party policy in 1934-35. The decision had been pre-empted to a large extent by the Labour government, but the new proposals made the transformation of the Empire clear and irreversible, as they had never been acknowledged to be before. The man chosen to implement this policy for the National government was Sir Samuel Hoare, a man whose sympathies were well to the left of the party on most questions; he was to become a liberal Home Secretary and was described by Chamberlain as one of the two real socialists in the government. (Chamberlain himself was the other.) Hoare assembled in London and in India a strong team of moderates, and pursued his course through four years of constant criticism and dispute. Throughout he had the support of Baldwin, who still regarded India as one of his chief missions in life; he could also rely on the backing of the minority parties in the government and on a majority of Conservative MPs, a position that he encouraged by direct approaches to the 1922 Committee.[25] There was opposition, though, from the diehards on the right, who believed that too much was being conceded, and from the Labour left, who argued that progress was too slow. The size of the government majority and the large number of Conservative moderates in the Commons enabled Hoare to push his proposals through in the end. His difficulties were enhanced by the length of the preparations that were necessary as the India Office consulted all strands of Indian opinion; he confessed in May 1932 he wrote that 'the nearer we get to a Bill the more apprehensive I am becoming about its possible fate'.[26] It was not until the spring of 1933 that the process begun in 1929 finally bore fruit with the announcement of a definite policy in a white paper. In order to reduce party opposition this was then referred to a Joint Select Committee of both Houses, a stage that occupied a further eighteen months, even though the Select Committee was packed by the government to make sure that it produced the right report in the end.[27] It was therefore not until 1935 that the government was able to introduce a Bill. The very length of the argument had an unsettling and distracting effect on the party, but the final Government of India Act became something of a triumph.

The campaign against the government's proposals was led by Winston Churchill, already a critic in 1930–31 but now deprived of all cause of restraint by his isolation from the party leaders in government. The India battles became a personal crusade for Churchill, to at least as great an extent as rearmament later on. On India he refused all cooperation, regularly voted against the government and tried to bring it down by any means at his disposal, while on rearmament he worked with the government behind the scenes, he did not even abstain until after Munich, and he did not try to use the issue to wreck the government. The language and rhetoric he used in the two campaigns was similar, and so it became difficult to take seriously warnings about Hitler that he had applied in equally blood-curdling terms to Gandhi. The only other men of cabinet rank among the diehards were Salisbury and Fitzalan, both of whom showed rather more discretion than Churchill. There was therefore a fault line among the government's opponents, a division between the Churchill group and the rest, which the government could exploit in order to rule.[28] The government had some difficulty launching its own propaganda campaign because of the difficulty of persuading eminent men with Indian experience to act as leaders of its Union of Britain and India (UBI), but these were eventually solved.[29] In 1933–34, a bitter war was waged between the diehard India Defence League (IDL) and the moderate UBI, with the diehards constantly complaining that the party organization was taking sides quite unfairly. So in July 1933 the Party Chairman had to deny that the UBI was financially supported by Central Office (which was only half true) and the party magazine *Home and Empire* had to accept a reply from the IDL to an article from the UBI. The moderates were still handicapped by the lack of press support, for the *Mail* and the *Morning Post* were still actively hostile. They were helped by the increasing backing that was given to them by *The Times*, so that they were able at least to hold their own, while the IDL never greatly expanded the area of support that it could rely on from the beginning. The Select Committee eventually reported at the end of 1934, backing the government's proposals by nineteen votes to nine, and with a majority of Conservatives in favour.

Churchill had pursued his campaign with his accustomed verve, and his accusation of bias against all but the most diehard of the Indian Civil Service and his violent language throughout only increased the disgust that many Conservatives felt for him. He completed his estrangement from the official party by allegations that Hoare and Derby had committed a breach of parliamentary privilege by tampering with evidence to the Select Committee; there was certainly some substance in his charges, but he attacked Hoare with disproportionate venom and only earned a stinging rebuff when the Committee of Privileges reported against him and the House supported its Committee after sarcastic attacks on Churchill's motives by Amery and Simon, among many others. Churchill was motivated throughout by a conviction that the government were pursuing an irresponsible policy by questionable means. Ministers were equally ungenerous about Churchill's own motives: Baldwin told Tom Jones that 'there are diehards who'll stop at nothing to bring the government down', and Amery told the Commons that Churchill was being true to his motto *Fiat justitia, ruat coelum*, which he translated as 'If I can trip up Sam, the Government is bust'.[30]

In the constituencies, there was a reluctance to indulge in damaging arguments, and most local parties were content to follow the line that their MP had decided on, whether to support the government (as at Stockton or Ecclesall) or to oppose it (as at Hampstead or Aylesbury). J. C. C. Davidson received warnings in 1933 that Hemel Hempstead Conservatives were hostile to the government policy, but when Page Croft attempted to persuade local Conservatives to support diehards at the party conference, he was repudiated by the local Conservatives in a public statement. If there were disagreements, then they were determined to keep them in the family; when Brigadier Clifton-Brown MP was almost unseated for his diehard views at Newbury, the whole affair was kept very quiet.[31]

Despite this, the determination of the diehards ensured that the final legislation would not be carried without a final fling of dissent. The Commons would certainly support the government and so the diehards had to take their case to the National Union. Churchill remarked that

> one deep-throated growl from the National Union of Conservative Associations would be enough to stop the rot – to save India from an ordeal as hideous as that of China, to save the British Imperial power from a disastrous eclipse, and to save the character and texture of Toryism from a deed to which it would long look back with shame and sorrow.[32]

Since the new rules of 1930, the Executive had become much more moderate, composed now of men who were local leaders rather than men with a national reputation for independent views. So in February 1932 the Executive received a motion from Cumberland which supported the government's Indian policy, endorsed it and passed it on to Baldwin with approval. At the same meeting, Hoare explained his ideas and Sir Kingsley Wood 'in the name of the Committee, congratulated him on the splendid start that he had made as Secretary of State'. A critical motion on India was not placed on the agenda of the next Council meeting, on technical grounds only, and over the next three years the Executive continued to work against the diehards with all its powers; critical motions were passed to Baldwin for information, but motions supporting the policy of the government were endorsed. The composition of the critical Council meeting of December 1934 was fixed in favour of the moderates by a ruling that only peers and MPs who had previously attended the Council should be allowed to attend, so excluding hundreds of peers who were diehard to a man.[33] All the same, entrenched hostility continued to be expressed in Central Council and in conferences; in 1933 the government line was supported only by 189 votes to 165 by the Central Council, but thereafter there was always a much larger margin of safety.

The last round of the contest began with the Party Conference of 1934, when a critical motion was proposed and an amendment only narrowly carried. Page Croft called on the party to demonstrate its independence of a handful of Labour and Liberal ministers, a strong ground on which to appeal to the National Union. A show of hands produced an indecisive result and a ballot showed that the government amendment had been passed by 543 votes to 520; the result was declared 'amidst intense excitement' and R. A. Butler wrote that 'the audience would have been a credit to the zoo or wild regions of the globe'.[34] A few weeks later the Select Committee reported and the National Union moved to express its views again; a special meeting of Central Council was convened, and despite the exclusion of many peers and MPs the attendance was the highest of the decade. Special debating rules were adopted to allow for longer speeches than usual, and papers were made ready for a ballot. The diehards prepared for their last chance and the Executive met twice to ensure that all should go off smoothly. On 12 December 1934 the Council considered a motion in the name of Leo Amery to approve the Select Committee Report, and an amendment in the name of Salisbury to reject the whole idea of responsible central government in India. Amery was supported by Lord Eustace Percy, Derby and Austen Chamberlain (all ex-cabinet ministers), by Linlithgow (ex-Deputy Chairman of the party, chairman of the Select Committee and soon to be Viceroy), and by Lady Bridgeman (a leading figure in the women's side of the party). The diehards could not produce so impressive a team, but Salisbury was supported by Page Croft, Fitzalan and Churchill. The debate resolved itself into a call for party unity and loyalty on one side and an evocation of Britain's imperial role on the other; the Council voted by 1,102 votes to 390 to back the government, and so settled the issue once and for all.[35] This is not to say that an opposite vote by the National Union would have stopped the government from proceeding further, merely that a refusal by the National Union to support the diehards removed the last serious threat.

The parliamentary session of 1935 was a gruelling one, and the diehards fought to the bitter end, but the outcome was no longer in doubt. On each vote the diehards could muster only about eighty votes, so that even if Labour abstained the government could expect a large majority. Baldwin excelled himself in his Second Reading speech, lifting the debate back on to a higher level, and at the same time poking fun at the divisions among the Bill's opponents. George Lansbury regretted that there were not three lobbies, so that he would not have to vote alongside Churchill.[36] By the time of the 1935 Party Conference, the Government of India Act was on the statute book, so that party criticism had become irrelevant. But the long party debate was not wholly insignificant. On the positive side, it disarmed the critics of the National government at a time when it was going through a very difficult patch, and it made certain that a moderate Indian policy could be carried out. On the negative side, it delayed the decision by at least two years, so making sure that the Act could not be implemented until after the Second World War, by which time it had lost its immediacy. The debates also completed the isolation of Churchill from all but the most extreme diehards, with desperately serious consequences for him, for the party and for the country. Without the Indian debates Churchill would probably have been in government during the years of rearmament; without them he would also have been unavailable as an alternative Prime Minister in 1940.[37] In the longer term the diehard failure over India destroyed the old imperial wing of the party for ever, for the party had now quite consciously turned its back on Britain's imperial role. One result of this was that the right of the party remained in disarray for a generation. The right did not make the strongly nationalistic call for defence against Germany that had been heard before 1914, and in the Munich debate of 1938 many diehards were to be found with Page Croft on Neville Chamberlain's side. The breaking of the confidence of the Tory right may in that sense have made a major contribution to the weakness of British policy in Europe.

India was not the only question that threatened to drive a wedge between the National government and the party during its first term of office. Social, financial, economic and defence problems all contributed to the same disagreements, but in each case the government came under fire from both flanks. As Clive Wigram told Lord Bledisloe in 1933, 'it is difficult to say whether George Lloyd or Lloyd George is the more mischievous opponent of the Government'. George Lloyd himself explained to Bledisloe what the diehards were trying to do:

> You asked me whether there was any truth in reports that I was trying to lead a diehard Tory Opposition to Baldwin's Government. Of course, there is no truth at all in that. I am not an admirer of Stanley as a Conservative Leader but I have never had either the temerity or the desire to take the field against him. Quite apart from any other reasons, I should have no chances of success. On the other hand, there has been, and still is, very deep-seated and widespread dissatisfaction in the ranks of the Conservative Party, not only in regard to Baldwin's India and Defence policies, but in regard to the general Socialist and Liberal principles with which he seems to seek to infest all Conservative thought and actions. A good many of us have noted with increasing alarm the general slide and swing to the left of 'Conservative' thought as directed by S.B. and we have been trying to do what we can to counter these tendencies by throwing out some strong anchors to the right. . . . Our opponents, of course, try to pretend that we are aiming at the formation of new parties. That is, of course, not true. It is clear to me, however, that unless some asylum is found for right wing thought amongst all the young and middle-aged men in the party, these will break away from Conservatism to Fascism, or

other such nostrums. Already Mosley has drawn away a good deal of the more enthusiastic youth, and, if he were not personally somewhat distrusted and unpopular as a personality, I am persuaded that thousands more would have joined him in despair of getting anything done on imperial and Conservative lines through the medium of the Conservative leaders. That in a nutshell is the problem.[38]

On the opposite wing, Harold Macmillan had declared virtual independence of the party line on economic and social questions, and was campaigning for a more active policy of interventionism. By 1935 he had moved on from his middle position of *Industry and the State* in 1927 to the policy of the 'Next Five Years' Group with its commitment to planning and non-party government. He was aided in this by a rather unusual relationship with his local party at Stockton. After defeat in 1929, he had moved to a safe seat in the south, but had then been enticed back to Stockton in 1931, so that he had been able to lay down his own conditions for coming back. He was to be free to promote his views and the Stockton Conservatives gave him their full backing when he resigned the Whip in 1936, and again when he opposed the Munich agreement in 1938. In 1935 he gave his adoption meeting a summary of the proposals contained in *The Next Five Years*, and it was on that basis that he was adopted as official Conservative candidate for Stockton.[39] In parliament Macmillan cooperated with Gerald Loder, Robert Boothby and Ronald Cartland, and with Walter Elliot in the government, all men who felt that the Conservative party must be given a more human face if it was to offer a continuing challenge to Labour and a relevant policy for the country. These then were the terms of the debate: the diehards saw Baldwin as an opponent and sought to keep him anchored to the right so that Mosley should not be able to outflank him, while the moderates regarded him as an ally who should be supported. Baldwin himself leaned strongly to the left, but was obliged to respect the views of both sides. Tom Jones noted that the best service that Baldwin could render to the country was 'to keep moving leftwards with his party, and taking the edge off the programmes of the extremists'. Baldwin himself told R. A. Butler in 1935 that leading the party consisted in steering a path between Harold Macmillan and Henry Page Croft.[40]

Criticism of the government on grounds of economy came to a head early and provided a rare example of the 1922 Committee trying to influence policy in a positive sense. Shortly after the 1931 election the Committee apparently received an invitation from Neville Chamberlain to suggest areas where economies could be made. Meetings took place through 1932, with five special sub-committees considering possible expenditure cuts in local government, defence, transport, debt services and social policy. Inevitably these investigations only attracted the keen interest of those who wished to see draconian cuts imposed; so the work on health was superintended by Herbert Williams, a dedicated campaigner for economy who was still pursuing the same line in the 1950s. When the sub-committees had completed their work, the question of publication arose. If the reports were to be published by the 1922 Committee they would seem to have the support of the majority in the Commons, but they would thereby commit many MPs who had taken no part in the investigations. After a brief skirmish the reports were published on 16 November 1932, recommending total cuts of about £100 million in a full year. The reaction was almost universally hostile, for this was an axe more swingeing that that of Geddes in 1921, and coming this time after substantial cuts in the previous year. Conservative MPs worried about the effect the cuts might have on their constituencies, newspapers pointed to the lack of an overall plan linking the five reports, and the 1922 Committee itself virtually disowned them. Within a month the Committee had elected a new chairman to replace Sir Gervase Rentoul who had held office since the Committee was first formed. These divisions destroyed any impact that the reports might have made and so left the government free to ignore them, which is exactly what it did. By 1935 government expenditure had recovered from the cuts that were imposed and in almost every area expenditure was higher than in any year since 1921.[41]

The lack of support for economies was certainly explained in part by the orthodox policy that Neville Chamberlain was pursuing at the Exchequer. Orthodoxy was indeed the chief touchstone by which Conservatives judged any financial policy; the permanent effects of the First World War on financial and taxation policy had strengthened this tendency, but the apparent danger of national bankruptcy in 1931 had turned it into an article of faith. The absence from government of Churchill and Amery no doubt reinforced the same point. The balancing of budgets was the test of a Chancellor's reliability and any refusal to accept these rules of the financial game came to be seen as a confession of irresponsibility. Few Conservatives accepted with Macmillan and Steel-Maitland that Britain could learn something from the United States; Baldwin himself regarded the New Deal as the height of folly and Roosevelt as a dangerous firebrand.[42] All such fears could be easily calmed by the presence of Chamberlain at the Exchequer, and in 1933 his budget speech met the advocates of unbalanced budgets head on, stating his continued faith in tried and trusted methods:

> Look around the world today and you will see that badly unbalanced Budgets are the rule rather than the exception. Everywhere there appear Budget deficits piling up; yet they do not produce the favourable results which it is claimed would happen to us. On the contrary I find that Budget deficits repeated year after year may be accompanied by a deepening depression and a constantly falling price level. Before we embark on so dangerous a course as that, let us reflect upon this indisputable fact. Of all the countries passing through these difficult times, the one that has stood the test with the greatest measure of success is the United Kingdom. Without underrating the hardships of our situation, the long tragedy of the unemployed, the grievous burden of taxation, the arduous and painful struggle of those engaged in trade and industry, at any rate we are free from that fear which besets so many less fortunately placed, the fear that things are going to get worse.

We owe our freedom from that fear largely to the fact that we have balanced our budget.[43]

There was much justification for this view, for neither theory, nor experience, nor opportunity would have justified any other economic strategy than the one that Chamberlain followed. Most academic economists and bankers were still firmly wedded to pre-Keynesian ideas, and the alternative economic model of Keynes was not even published as a complete system until 1936. Business and banking confidence, on which Keynes laid even greater stress than his predecessors, would hardly have been reassured by the adoption of policies that were neither proved nor widely understood. If the advice of Keynes had been followed in 1931 it might well have led to financial collapse, not because it was wrong but because it was *believed* to be wrong. Nor did the experience of limited experiments in deficit-financing provide much support for unorthodox views. Sweden and the United States experimented but still continued to experience higher levels of unemployment than Great Britain; Germany and Russia adopted more ambitious schemes of public works, but at a social cost that was scarcely acceptable in Britain. The Micawberish desire to spend within income still remained an important influence, but any alternative remained unproved and as long as Chancellors were free to pursue the policy they wanted to pursue they would stick to orthodoxy. Only when confronted with greater risks, in the shape of German aggression and then war, would Chancellors like Chamberlain and Simon go in for experiment. Under the same influence, Sir Kingsley Wood (Chamberlain's protégé) became Britain's first Keynesian Chancellor.

The party debate took place against these overriding assumptions, and so was concerned only with details of policy rather than strategy. Political expediency demanded a high level of expenditure and hence a high level of taxation, but this was subjected to continuous criticism from such men as Hely-Hutchinson, Williams and O'Connor. The same restraints were imposed on the government from outside the party, for the basic rules of the game were accepted by all the parties in much the same form. In 1933 Chamberlain emphasized the extent to which his budget continued along lines marked out by Snowden, and he made similar references in 1934 and 1935. In 1933, too, Attlee for the Labour party attacked the Chancellor's proposals because they did not really balance the budget, while Samuel for the Liberals gave his support because in his view they did. When Chamberlain resorted to loans to pay for capital expenditure on defence in 1936, he was rebuked by Sinclair for the Liberals, who concluded that 'the Government's present path leads us to the edge of financial disaster'. Such mild experiments as the transfer of £4 million from the Road Fund to general revenue exposed Chamberlain to charges that he was setting dangerous precedents and departing unwisely from established practice.[44] In such an atmosphere, it is difficult to see that the government could have done more.

Social policy occasioned a serious dispute in 1933–34. The misery of the unemployed and the unpopularity of the means test were well known to all Conservatives, but until 1934 they resolutely resisted pressure to restore the cut in dole payments instituted in 1931. Labour-controlled local councils were kept in line with government policy, even where this necessitated placing poor relief under Special Commissioners, as at Durham and Rotherham, but even the Conservative councillors of Manchester came into conflict with the government. Conservatives continued to insist on the retention of the cut for economic as well as financial reasons, arguing that unemployment assistance must remain below local wage rates if recovery were ever to be generated. But by 1934 the pressure was irresistible, for the Unemployment Fund was once again in credit, so that there was no financial argument for further delay. The cut was restored in April 1934 and increases were made in other allowances to return them to their real value of 1931.

It was the tidying up legislation associated with this return to normal that produced the real difficulty. The Minister of Labour was Sir Henry Betterton, a man dedicated to producing order from the tangle of benefits and payments that came under his control; he was also keen to reduce what he saw as local extravagance in the administration of transitional benefits and to eradicate local differences in the rates paid. The Unemployment Act of 1934 thus transferred responsibility for transitional benefits (for the long-term unemployed in the main) to a new authority, the Unemployment Assistance Board. This was justified as an administrative means of ending abuses, but the impression was given that conditions would be generally improved. When the Board began operations in January 1935, with Betterton himself as its first chairman, it transpired that equalizing payments in different areas would involve a levelling down to the least generous rates and the complete ending of payments to some families. The storm of protest that followed this included strikes, demonstrations and petitions, but came to a head in the Commons on 28 January. Liberal and Labour MPs were given unexpected support from the Conservative benches and Boothby was as outspoken as anyone.[45] Baldwin himself, too busy with defence matters to take any part in the legislation and convinced like others that the new system would improve conditions, was appalled. Neville Chamberlain was placed in charge of a special cabinet committee and the government changed course within a week; a new Bill was rushed through parliament in a week after that, all cuts in benefit were restored and past reductions refunded. Again the advocates of economy were routed.

Apart from India, though, it was defence that constituted the party's most pressing concern in the early 1930s. During 1932 and 1933 a new mood of despair arose among the British people that owed at least as much to the foreign situation as to the slump at home. The fear of war rather than moral conviction was the real basis of this wave of 'pacifism', but it was a tide of opinion that swept the government along with it, partly at least because ministers shared in the mood themselves. Hoare has described how the idea of disarmament came to dominate his mind among others after 1918: 'When the war ended, there was a universal belief that as the world would never again be so mad and bad, another Armageddon was impossible.' When the tide began to flow Baldwin contributed to it as much as any man through the pessimistic tone of his speeches, especially the notorious message of 1932 that 'the bomber will always get through'.

There was hardly anyone left at the head of British politics who had held high office in wartime and parties of both left and right sought refuge in escapist dreams about disarmament rather than face the real threat of war.[46] Conservatives called for rearmament from 1933 (and hence embarrassed the government) but had to fight against the overwhelming weight of mass opinion. The anti-war tide was strengthened by the League of Nations Union, the various peace societies and the churches. Conservatives found it an unusual experience to be in conflict with the established Church, an experience that increased their difficulties. When Duff Cooper drew attention to the German threat in 1934 he was rebuked by Dean Inge, who 'did not see why the world should be plunged into war in order to please Mr Duff Cooper'. Cooper was then attacked by a canon from Liverpool when he suggested international occupation of the Rhineland. Cooper suggested that 'in view of the widespread pacifism in the Church of England the leaders of the Church should tell the public plainly where the church stood. ... I thereby incurred an undesired and undeserved reputation as a baiter of Bishops and an enemy of the Church.'[47] The connections between the churches and the LNU were very close, as Samuel Hoare noted:

> The meetings held by the League of Nations Union and the other organisations that supported disarmament became semi-religious services. I attended many of them. They began and ended with prayers and hymns, and were throughout inspired by a spirit of emotional revivalism. ... The combination of all these forces, moral, political and religious, created so strong a volume of opinion in favour of disarmament that no government, right, left or centre, could resist it.[48]

A few MPs like Cooper tried to make headway against the tide, but many more submitted like Samuel Roberts:

> In Hereford this Union had thousands of members, was supported by all the churches and all the women's organisations, and although I knew in my heart of hearts that the League was futile, I paid lip service to their principles and spoke on their platforms. I fear this was because their votes were many.[49]

In their hearts many Conservatives disagreed with the whole approach of the pacifists and the LNU, as they demonstrated clearly enough when they had the chance. It was the Conservatives in cabinet who pressed for early rearmament and continued to press for it, without much support from their allies. At the Party Conference of 1933 a diehard motion calling for greater expenditure on defence was proposed; although this was a clear reprimand to the government, no platform speaker rose to oppose or amend it and it passed unanimously. Similarly in 1935, the Conference expressed its views on defence forcibly. Leaving the conference hall, Chamberlain told reporters that 'there could be no doubt in the minds of any members of His Majesty's Government who were present, of the determination of the great audience to see the gaps in our defences filled at the earliest possible moment. Nor could we doubt either that they had fully counted the cost and were prepared to face it.' Chamberlain had told the delegates that he was quite prepared to give them a faster programme of rearmament if they were prepared to pay for it.[50]

In gatherings of Conservatives, support for rearmament could be openly expressed but in other gatherings they were sadly muted. Baldwin felt the same restraint and, although working actively on plans for armaments in 1933–34, he felt helpless in the face of such large demonstrations of public opinion as were manifested by the by-elections of 1933 or by the Peace Ballot of 1935. So neither Baldwin nor his party ever really took up the challenge of pacifism on the hustings or attempted to draw the electorate away from their worship of false idols. When the Peace Ballot was proposed, the Executive of the National Union discussed it in detail, but concluded that little could be expected from questions so loosely worded.[51] This was certainly a tenable point of view, but it was not publicly expressed, and the party took up no attitude at all while the Ballot was being conducted, making no effort to influence the result.

The dilemma for Conservatives was serious in 1933–34, not because they underestimated the danger from Germany but precisely because they saw how real that threat could be. If, as Baldwin himself subsequently argued and went on believing for the rest of his life, the party had gone on to the offensive and campaigned for quick and large-scale rearmament in 1933, the most likely result would have been the advent of a Labour government committed to *dis*armament and hence to the actual weakening of Britain's position.[52] This dilemma explains much of the party's passivity in the face of Hitler, but it was also based on the assumption that the public mood would change. In time the public would see the real danger and would then support rearmament, which is exactly what did happen in and after 1935, but by then it was too late. The evidence of aggression by Hitler and Mussolini in 1935–36 changed the attitudes of many in Britain, but by then Britain could only begin the armaments race in second place. The old policy of appeasement from strength was no longer an option that was available.

The depression in the party's fortunes in 1933–34 was very severe. Although the size of the 1931 victory had made some by-election defeats inevitable and although Baldwin had tried to prepare his party for some losses, there was shock and dissatisfaction when they actually occurred. The defeats of 1933 seemed so bad because they were measured against the party's best ever electoral performance in 1931, and East Fulham had an unsettling effect both on the government and on Baldwin's political confidence. In fact, only nine seats were lost out of the forty-eight that the government defended during the parliament, and there was no extended period in which the swing to Labour was large enough to suggest an overall Labour majority at a general election. Local elections went badly too, with Labour coming back strongly from its defeat in 1931; the London County Council fell to Labour in 1933 and remained under Labour control until it was wound up in 1965. So the party was reduced to a state of panic by 1934 and Central Office 'looked on no seat as safe'.[53]

Embarrassment was increased early in 1935 when Randolph Churchill, Winston's son, challenged the government's Indian policy by standing against the official Conservative at a by-election at Liverpool Wavertree. His intervention handed the seat to Labour and added still more to his father's unpopularity even though his father did not support his decision to stand. *The Times* concluded that 'the Wavertree election shows nothing more clearly than the fact that those who, in obedience to short-sighted or personal views seek to destroy the system of National Government, may indeed achieve success, but only the success of suicide'. Despite Wavertree, things improved during 1935, and the lessons of disunity had not been lost.[54] Serious consideration was given to bringing Lloyd George back into the government, a plan that was swiftly vetoed by Neville Chamberlain, and there was exaggerated alarm in the government when L.G. launched his last campaign for power through the Council for Action for Peace and Reconstruction, a combination with which some Conservatives were initially connected. And the Peace Ballot, ending in June 1935, showed the continuing public doubts about rearmament.

However, despite its depression in the winter of 1934–35, the party remained as jealous of its independence as ever, and the way forward lay in restoring the electoral coalition of 1931 rather than in bringing in either Lloyd George or Churchill. In 1934 Stonehaven had flatly rejected the idea of fusion between the government parties, and the same mood persisted. When the government began its propaganda preparations for another election in 1935, the party scented new schemes of fusion in plans for joint publicity, and the Party Chairman had to allay fears that the party was being bounced into a new coalition. Baldwin attended the next meeting of the Executive and was careful to explain what was intended; no fusion was contemplated, he would consult the party before committing it to any other party for the future, and he would make known the government's policy before asking for the party's support.[55] These fears were further eased when Baldwin took over as Prime Minister in May 1935, removing also the criticism of MacDonald's declining powers. The government was given a new look by the promotion of younger men – Eden, Stanley and Brown; it remained a mainly Conservative administration, with sixteen Tories now in a cabinet of twenty-two. Baldwin was able to use the Party Conference in October to tie the party and government together again; Tom Jones noted that he had, 'denounced the isolationists, reconciled the Party to the League by supporting rearmament, and reconciled the pacifists to rearmament by supporting the Covenant. Spoke strongly in favour of trade unions. All with an eye to the election.'[56] The party thus went into the election campaign in November united in its support for the National government; critics like Winston Churchill had to come into line when the alternatives were narrowed down to the continuation of National government or Attlee as Labour Prime Minister; Randolph Churchill actually stood as an official candidate. Observers in the House of Commons saw that Churchill and Baldwin were meeting again as friends.

The party was not well prepared for the election, for its date was not chosen until relatively late, and economies in party organization had reduced its effectiveness since 1931. Very little party propaganda had been undertaken prior to the campaign, and less than a million and a half leaflets had been produced. The Central Office estimate of the likely result in the summer was that the government would secure a majority of about a hundred, but this was qualified by the provisos that everything would depend on how Liberals voted and on the results in fifty marginal constituencies. Gower at Central Office told Baldwin that,

> even if the Socialist party did not obtain the support of a largely increased section of the electorate we could still lose the next election or at any rate arrive at a stalemate position if the bulk of the Liberal vote went over to them. From that point of view the Liberal vote is vital and no political issue is likely to influence them more than the question of peace and war and the future of the League of Nations.[57]

Conservatives were therefore delighted when Baldwin seemed to have found a means (and a good moment) to reconcile support for the League of Nations with support for rearmament, using Abyssinia as an example to demonstrate the need for arms, and they rallied enthusiastically to his policy. The party was able to pursue a middle course, arguing for armaments without meeting the tide of public opinion head on: 84 per cent of Conservative candidates called for rearmament and 82 per cent expressed support for the League in their election addresses. The only other issues to be mentioned even by half of the candidates or more were general anti-socialism, recollections of the 1931 crisis and the record of the National government.[58] There is thus no doubt that the Conservative party as a whole fought the election with a commitment to both rearmament and the League, and that those issues predominated over all other positive issues in the party's thinking at the outset. There was, though, something of a shift of emphasis as the campaign went on, with the leaders stressing their commitment to peace rather than their call for arms, and coming in the last week to a negative anti-socialism much like that of 1924 or 1931. Having put the case for arms to the electorate, the party was content to leave it on the table and to concentrate on more popular issues.

Baldwin's radio broadcasts and film appearances were thought to have had a significant impact, but these public appearances also contributed to the shift in emphasis of the campaign. Of his public speeches, the one that made the greatest impact was certainly an address to the Peace Society in which he gave a pledge not to introduce 'great armaments'. On film his main political speech balanced government achievements against the need for stable government, and concluded that

> We desire to go on working to maintain world peace, and to strengthen the League of Nations, and I give you my word – and I think you can trust me by now – our defence programme will be no more than is sufficient to make our country safe and enable us to fulfil our obligations. That much we must have.[59]

The extract from the speech shown on *Paramount News* included only this last part, so giving the impression that the speech was another pledge against great armaments. *British Gaumont News* showed a much longer version of the speech before the election; after the election, when commenting on the results they re-showed the clip containing the words quoted above.[60] Whatever Baldwin's intentions, the effect of his campaign was certainly to stress the limitations on rearmament rather than the need for arms, and this no doubt contributed to the government's victory.

There was only a feeble Liberal campaign; only 161 Liberal candidates were put forward, only one of these against a Liberal National (at Denbigh, where the Liberal National held the seat), and a large number of Liberal votes stayed with the National government. Conservatives held 386 seats and their allies 45, giving the government a majority of more than 200. Labour recovered to 154 seats, but the Liberals lost even some of the seats held in 1931 and were reduced to 21 MPs, two of whom promptly went over to the government after the election. In the aftermath of victory, relations with the other government parties were regularized by the National Union. There had been criticism by diehards of the refusal of Central Office to help a Conservative candidate against the government at Accrington, but the National Union Executive endorsed the actions of Central Office and thus formally, if belatedly, endorsed the electoral pact. They went further when they approved the fusion of anti-socialist groups in Barrow into one local association, and they allowed the new body to affiliate to the National Union; powers were delegated to the areas to make similar arrangements wherever appropriate; the way was thus opened for the local consolidation of the government majority and the perpetuation of the National government.[61]

George Lloyd's fear that Baldwin's moderation would drive the right wing of the party into the arms of Sir Oswald Mosley constitutes one of the most important non-events of the decade. Almost alone in Western Europe, Britain failed to throw up a fascist party that could mount a serious attack on democracy, and this was largely because the British Union of Fascists was never able to make inroads into the solid Conservative and Labour vote. It is easy to delineate the features that assisted European fascism and which were not present in Britain (economic collapse, national humiliation through defeat, street violence, polarization into two armed camps, a charismatic leader) but it is worth pausing to consider how many of these factors owed their absence from the British scene to the work of the National government. The saving of the currency in 1931 had removed middle-class fears for their savings, and since then salaried people had done rather well in a time of rising expectations and falling prices; the housing boom of the 1930s was bringing home-ownership to groups of lower-middle-class people for the first time, exactly the group that turned to fascism abroad. There had been no national defeat, but the government derived some support for its 'National' character, and patriotic pride was no doubt enhanced by Baldwin's reminders of what Britain had achieved since 1931. The relative lack of violence in Britain fitted in well with Baldwin's view of the nature of England and the English; there was actually more violence in Britain than has often been supposed, but its effect was reduced by the fact that the organizers of disorder were content to stop short of causing real trouble. This was as true of the hunger-marchers as of the fascists; the fascists tamely acceded when the government told them to take off their uniforms and go home. It might be argued that the fascists were too British to be successful fascists, and at the same time too fascist to be successful in Britain. The failure of Mosley's leadership was in part a personal failure, but it was also true to the tradition of political leadership that Baldwin and MacDonald had built up over the previous decade, the absolute antithesis of the *Fuehrerprinzip*. In a contest for public popularity with Baldwin, Mosley did not stand a chance.

The final reason for the failure of fascism is more subtle: the symbiotic relationship of fascism and communism in those countries where democracy was threatened. It is easy enough to see what might have happened in Britain: if there had been a powerful communist party which the government had been unable to suppress or control, then many Conservatives would have turned to extreme counter-measures, thus reinforcing the appeal of communism to the Labour party and escalating the polarization to extremes. But so long as the National government could easily keep the communists in check, there was no reason for its supporters to feel threatened. Between them, the government, the Labour party and the trade unions occupied the whole of the practicable political and industrial spectrum, and so prevented either communists or fascists from breaking through. At root, the millions who might have turned to fascism in other circumstances found themselves protected and well enough looked after by the Conservative ministers who governed Britain after 1931.

The Conservative party's official attitude to the British Union of Fascists is difficult to detect, because the BUF was rarely a serious enough force to merit more than passing interest. In June 1934 the Olympia meeting forced the party to take up an attitude, and the House of Commons was 'up in arms' demanding action against Mosley; Baldwin, more shrewdly, dismissed the subject with the reflection that 'Mosley won't come to any good, and we need not bother about him'.[62] Naturally enough, there was more interest in fascism on the left than the right, just as there were more worries about communism on the right. Mosley himself was distrusted by Conservatives as a renegade who had been a particularly virulent opponent since his desertion of the Conservative cause, and he never succeeded in persuading any party Conservative of stature to back him. He attracted intermittent assistance from such right-wing figures as Lords Nuffield and Rothermere, but neither of these had been orthodox Conservatives, and neither stayed with Mosley for long. When Mosley did make any perceptible headway, Conservatives were as ready as anyone to denounce him. After Olympia Conservatives who had been present at the meeting led the protests about the way in which it had been run, as a book that is far from favourable to the party makes clear:

> Many eminent and respectable eye-witnesses were outraged at what they had seen. Among the most forcible were three Conservative M.P.s – Geoffrey Lloyd: 'I came to the conclusion that Mosley was a political maniac, and that all decent English people must combine to kill his movement.' T. J. O'Connor: 'In the end we got up to go because we felt that we were being placed in the position either of being manhandled or of being cowardly cads for not interfering.' W. J. Anstruther-Gray: 'I had not been at the meeting for more than a few minutes before all my sympathies were with the men who were being handled with such gross brutality.'[63]

These three were representative of the party, and Lloyd had been Baldwin's PPS. The same party reaction was to be seen in 1936 after the fascist campaign of anti-semitism in East London culminated in the Battle of Cable Street. Conservative MPs gave full support to the Public Order Bill which banned political uniforms and allowed the police to ban any political demonstration likely to threaten disorder; their support allowed the Bill to be passed through parliament in a few weeks and to become law before the end of 1936. From the Conservative viewpoint the Public Order Act was aimed as much at the militant left as at the fascists, both being a threat to public order, and so the Act was used not only to ban fascist activities, but also to preserve the government's neutrality between the extremists of both sides. Labour was left to carry on the active campaign against Mosley, partly because Mosley was by then concentrating on areas where the Conservative party was almost non-existent, but also because Conservatives saw no reason to strengthen his appeal by siding with his militant opponents. By 1937 the BUF was no longer a serious threat either to the Conservative party or to the country; in Samuel Hoare's words, 'a troublesome nuisance rather than a political danger'.[64]

The international aspect of the ideological battle could not be so easily avoided. Most Conservatives still denied the need to align themselves either with international communism or with the dictators but, when forced to make the unpalatable choice (as over the Spanish Civil War) they were more likely to choose the right than the left.[65] However, there were some MPs who rejected this analysis and went out of their way to identify themselves with the fascist dictators, just as some on the Labour side made a similar identification with Stalin's Russia, and it is in this context that their activities must be seen. As the 1930s wore on the great debate increasingly divided the political nation on ideological lines, with some Labour leaders making comments on Russia that were uncritical to the point of hagiography, and some Conservatives making equally silly remarks about Germany and Italy. These stalwarts of the Tory right were duly exposed by the left-wing press and by the Left Book Club. So Simon Haxey's *Tory M.P.*, published in 1939, listed all the MPs who had made statements of support for Hitler or Mussolini and who were members of such bodies as the Link or the Anglo–German Fellowship. This analysis was as unfair as all such polemics, relying on taking statements out of context, on putting remarks of 1934 alongside events of 1938, and assuming that support for appeasement denoted support for Hitler. Even by these methods, Simon Haxey's list of fascist sympathizers came to only thirty, some of whom were Liberals (such as Clement Davies, leader of the Liberal party from 1945) and some of whom were certainly mis-represented. It may certainly be taken as a maximum list, and we may assume that the real number of hard-core fascist sympathizers was rather less.[66] The same book drew attention to about twenty MPs who could be called 'anti-fascist' because they had opposed either Hitler's Germany or government policy towards Germany. This is only a partial list and does not include either Geoffrey Lloyd or Terence O'Connor.

It seems likely on the evidence of Simon Haxey (as unfavourable a source as could be found) that the parliamentary Conservative party contained two opposed groups of approximately equal strength, supporting and opposing fascism in its European context. This leaves more than 80 per cent of the party unaccounted for, men who did not commit themselves either way, who saw no necessary contradiction in support for government policy without support for Hitler. The inside story of the making of foreign policy makes it quite clear that neither the pro-fascists nor the anti-appeasers ever exercised a discernible influence. Policy was made at government level, according to the constraints of diplomacy, armaments and the views of the ministers and their advisers; this policy was assured of the general support of the vast majority of Conservative MPs who remained firmly anchored to the middle. The final reason for the failure of British fascism, contrary to the fears of George Lloyd, is explained in *Tory M.P.* too. It was just those men from the Tory right, the old imperial right, who made up the anti-fascist group in the party; they were no longer as numerous or as influential as before, but rather than going over to fascism, they were to be found with Lloyd himself, alongside Winston Churchill.[67]

The recovery of the party's fortunes in 1935 was shortlived, and in the last year of his leadership, Baldwin plunged to the nadir of his unpopularity and then unexpectedly rose to the position of a national hero. In neither event did the party play any clear part, but so much did British Conservatism now depend on its leader that his fall and rise took the party with him. By 1936

Baldwin, clearly showing his age, was becoming increasingly deaf, and remained in office only because of the gravity of the international situation and the death of the King. But though he stayed in office, he delegated more and more of the business of leadership to Neville Chamberlain. In August 1936 Baldwin was told that he must take three months off and Chamberlain was left to act 'as if I were in fact PM'.[68] In October Baldwin missed the Party Conference for the only time in his leadership, and Neville Chamberlain, taking his place, was given a warm reception, the acclamation before his coming coronation.

Although international affairs provided a pretext for Baldwin's continuance in office after the 1935 election, he exercised only a watching brief over them and did not involve himself in them as much as a Prime Minister should have done. This produced the catastrophe of the Hoare–Laval meeting in Paris in December 1935 and the agreement to try to settle the Abyssinian conflict to the advantage of Mussolini. Vansittart and the Foreign Office were committed to the idea of separating Mussolini from Hitler, and the long hostilities in Abyssinia seemed to risk driving the two dictators closer together, but they had greatly underestimated the public reaction to terms such as Hoare and Laval agreed. On the most favourable reading of events, Baldwin was to blame for allowing Hoare to go to Paris without a clear brief and in a very tired condition, and for not calling him back to London as soon as the crisis broke. On the worst reading, the cabinet was more implicated in the scheme than they chose to admit, and they threw over Hoare to save themselves. The storm of public outrage shocked the government and Hoare was given the choice of making a full recantation or resigning. He chose to resign and defended his policy in the Commons, but this left Baldwin free to apologize on behalf of his government and to abandon Hoare's policy.

The volume of outside criticism helped to rally the party in support of its leaders, although many Conservative MPs were as critical in their hearts as were the opposition in public. Other methods had to be employed too, and Austen Chamberlain was kept quiet by something that looked suspiciously like the offer of the Foreign Office, a promise that was not redeemed when the crisis had blown over. Austen was now the most respected figure on the Conservative back benches, as critical of government policy as Churchill but less antagonistic to the party leadership. Most of the other party critics at this stage were on the left of the party, men who were concerned about the damage that the Hoare–Laval pact had done to Britain's standing and the position of the League. Robert Boothby thought that it was the opposition of such men from the rank and file that had forced the change in policy, but lobby opinion tended to the view that it was Austen who had been crucial.[69] The appointment of Anthony Eden to the Foreign Office was a guarantee of the government's good intentions towards the League, but Baldwin's stock had slumped, for it seemed that he had fought the recent election on a false prospectus, and he now seemed likely to retire in disgrace.

Hoare had been assured that he would not remain out of office for long and it was generally known that he would be back soon. He was mentioned for the post of Minister for the Co-ordination of Defence when it was decided to create the post in March 1936. Churchill was also strongly supported for the post by many Conservatives, but it eventually went to Sir Thomas Inskip. Hoare returned as First Lord of the Admiralty in June, but Churchill remained in isolation.[70] Satisfying Hoare removed one possible critic from the back benches, but criticism of the government's foreign and defence policies continued to grow in the Conservative party throughout 1936. In July Baldwin was forced to meet a powerful delegation of party critics, including Churchill, Austen Chamberlain, Salisbury, Amery, Horne, Lloyd, and Hugh O'Neill (chairman of the 1922 Committee) and to listen to their advice in two days of talks. His replies did little to satisfy them, but the meeting helped to calm things down. There was further embarrassment when Neville Chamberlain's remarks at a private meeting that the continuation of sanctions against Italy were the 'very midsummer of madness' were published in the press. Chips Channon noted that 'any sane man would agree, but his indiscretion has caused a tempest. It is of course an indication that all is not well in the Cabinet.'[71] Uncertainty continued until the government braved another storm of abuse by abandoning sanctions. All in all, 1936 was not at all a good year for the government on the foreign policy front, an especially serious situation because from the winter of 1935–6 foreign policy had become *the* issue.[72]

In 1936 though, Baldwin's main concern was with the problems raised by the new King and his wish to marry Mrs Simpson, and here the Prime Minister's control of the situation was complete, his footwork and timing superb. He kept the issue off the boil for as long as possible, not through any lack of concern, but in the hope that time would obviate the terrible decision that would have to be made if the King were forced to make a choice. By the autumn, revelations in the foreign press and the Simpson divorce case at Ipswich made it too urgent to allow further delay, and from that time he acted with the utmost firmness. The official party was with him throughout the crisis: Hoare and Duff Cooper, consulted by the King as personal friends, supported Baldwin's advice, and the correspondence that flowed into Downing Street was as overwhelmingly favourable as the similar avalanche after the Hoare–Laval talks had been hostile. Only once did opinion seem to waver, when it seemed that the King might make a fight of his demand for a morganatic marriage by rejecting the advice of his ministers and rallying support through Churchill and Beaverbrook. In the Commons on 4 December 1936 Churchill was supported by a large minority of Conservatives when he urged that no irrevocable decision should be taken without time for further consideration. Both Beaverbrook and Churchill were sincere in their wish to help the King and avoid an abdication, but it was widely believed that they were merely seizing on another issue with which to wreck the government.

Chips Channon could 'think of nothing else but the changes and terrors ahead, the Conservative party divided, the country divided, mental civil war going on, and schism in the Royal Family', and he found that society was dividing into 'Roundheads' and 'Cavaliers'.[73]

When parliament reassembled on 7 December Baldwin's control had been re-established, for the King had decided to give up without a fight and the feelings expressed to Conservative MPs over the intervening weekend had left them in no doubt of the opinions of their supporters. Churchill could not even get a hearing in the Commons, and the danger of a 'King's party' in the Tory ranks melted away. Throughout his negotiations with the King, Baldwin had insisted that he could predict how 'the public' would react to the idea of the King marrying a divorcee, and that weekend seems to vindicate spectacularly his claim to be 'an interpreter of England'. The public who made their views known was no doubt a very select group, representative at most of the Conservative rank and file, but it was sufficient. Other evidence suggests in any case that opinion against the King was more widespread. Walter Citrine, on behalf of the trade unions, was of the opinion that the King should go, and many others on the left had been antagonized by King Edward's apparently pro-German opinions. Robert Bruce-Lockhart found that most people he met were in favour of an abdication, Harold Nicolson was surprised to find that a church meeting in Islington refused to sing the National Anthem, and when the crisis was ended there was a boom on the stock exchange.[74] The ease with which the crisis was resolved may obscure the very real dangers that existed in December 1936, dangers that the monarchy itself might have been brought down and the Conservative party deeply divided, perhaps shattered, over an issue that was in truth peripheral to the country's real problems at the time. Baldwin became a national hero again, and received special praise for his Commons speech in which he told the story of the whole crisis. In the lobby afterwards, when congratulated on his speech, Baldwin replied, 'Yes, it was a success. I know it. It was almost wholly unprepared. I had a success, my dear Nicolson, at the moment I most needed it. *Now is the time to go.*'[75]

Baldwin waited only for the coronation of George VI, announced his impending resignation on 11 April 1937, and laid down his office at the end of May. He was again deluged with tributes; the Executive of the National Union passed a fulsome resolution of thanks for his services to the party and presented him with a bound volume that contained similar resolutions from 554 constituency parties. Nor were these tributes excessive, for as a party leader Baldwin has had few equals. He had enabled the Conservative party to take important strategic decisions in the 1920s that had kept it alive as an independent and vital political force. Under his leadership, the party had accommodated itself to the modern world to an extent that would have seemed inconceivable in 1923, an accommodation that had not been easy, as the successive attacks on his own position had shown. Under his immediate successors much of the impetus was lost, not through a change of policy but because foreign policy and then war took up all their time and their imagination, but the impetus was regained after 1945 by men who were truly Baldwin's successors in kind, so that his work finally bore fruit in the flourishing of the party in the 1950s. It is in that context, the very survival of the Conservatives as a governing party, that Baldwin must be judged.

Notes and References

1 Jones, *Diary with Letters*, 55–6, 124.
2 Bruce-Lockhart, *Diaries*, 323; Nicolson, *Diaries and Letters*, i, 215, 222.
3 Jones, *Diary with Letters*, 88.
4 Marquand, *Ramsay MacDonald*, 737; Harding, 'Conservative Party' (thesis), 12.
5 National Union minutes, Executive Committee, 15 Sept. 1931.
6 Cook and Ramsden, *By-elections*, 109–14.
7 Macmillan, *Winds of Change*, 375; Bruce-Lockhart, *Diaries*, 244, 318.
8 Harding, 'Conservative Party', 8; This is also larger than the usual preference of women voters for Conservatives, as noted in post-war surveys.
9 Nicolson, *King George V*, 498.
10 Marquand, *Ramsay MacDonald*, 736, 765–76.
11 Jones, *Diary with Letters*, 128.
12 Davidson, *Memoirs of a Conservative*, 379–80.
13 Marquand, *Ramsay MacDonald*, 677.
14 Nicolson, *Diaries and Letters*, i, 241–6.
15 Cooper, *Old Men Forget*, 179; Templewood, *Nine Troubled Years*, 98.
16 Channon, *Diaries*, 129.
17 Jones, *Diary with Letters*, 93.
18 Davidson, *Memoirs of a Conservative*, 406.
19 Channon, *Diaries*, 116; Jones, *Diary with Letters*, 128, 204.
20 'New Premier's first talk', *Paramount*, no. 448, 13 June 1935.
21 'Premier takes stock, finds Britain best', *Gaumont British*, no. 303, 23 Nov. 1935.
22 Macleod, *Chamberlain*, 185.
23 *Ibid*, 164–5.
24 Jones, *Diary with Letters*, 28; Macmillan, *Winds of Change*, 310; Macleod, *Chamberlain*, 163.
25 Butler, *Art of the Possible*, 63.
26 *Ibid*, 44.
27 Davidson, *Memoirs of a Conservative*, 395.
28 *Ibid*, 384.
29 Butler, *Art of the Possible*, 51.
30 Gilbert, *Winston S. Churchill*, v, 511–48; Jones, *Diary with Letters*, 126.
31 Newbury Conservative Association minutes, 20 Dec. 1934; Davidson, *Memoirs of a Conservative*, 395–6.
32 Gilbert, *Winston S. Churchill*, v, 465.
33 National Union minutes, Executive Committee, 23 Feb. 1932, 14 Nov. 1934.
34 Butler, *Art of the Possible*, 53.
35 National Union minutes, Central Council, 4 Dec. 1934.

36   Butler, *Art of the Possible*, 55–8; Gilbert, *Winston S. Churchill*, v, 588.
37   Templewood, *Nine Troubled Years*, 102–3.
38   Wigram to Bledisloe, 7 Nov. 1933 and Lloyd to Bledisloe, 9 July 1934; Bledisloe MSS.
39   Stockton Conservative Association minutes, 25 Oct. 1935.
40   Jones, *Diary with Letters*, 108; Butler, *Art of the Possible*, 30.
41   Goodhart, *The 1922 Committee*, 47–62.
42   Jones, *Diary with Letters*, 115.
43   Sabine, *British Budgets in Peace and War*, 16.
44   *Ibid*, 61, 81–4.
45   Branson and Heinemann, *Britain in the Nineteen-Thirties*, 34–6.
46   Templewood, *Nine Troubled Years*, 111; Cooper, *Old Men Forget*, 182–3, 193–4.
47   Cooper, *Old Men Forget*, 183, 197.
48   Templewood, *Nine Troubled Years*, 113.
49   Samuel Roberts's Autobiographical memorandum.
50   Petrie, *The Chamberlain Tradition*, 239; 'Mr Baldwin and Mr Neville Chamberlain at the Conservative Party Conference', *Gaumont British*, no. 185, 7 Oct. 1935.
51   National Union minutes, Executive Committee, 18 July 1934.
52   Channon, *Diaries*, 79; Macleod, *Chamberlain*, 183.
53   Cook and Ramsden, *By-elections*, 113.
54   Gilbert, *Winston S. Churchill*, v, 601.
55   National Union minutes, Executive Committee, 13 Feb. and 10 Apr. 1935.
56   Jones, *Diary with Letters*, 155.
57   Cowling, *Impact of Hitler*, 93.
58   Harding, 'Conservative Party', 26.
59   *Paramount*, no. 4710, 31 Oct. 1935.
60   *British Gaumont*, issues nos. 192 and 197, 31 Oct. and 18 Nov. 1935.
61   National Union minutes, Executive Committee, 20 May 1936.
62   Nicolson, *Diaries and Letters*, i, 174; Jones, *Diary with Letters*, 130.
63   Branson and Heinemann, *Britain in the Nineteen-Thirties*, 284.
64   Templewood, *Nine Troubled Years*, 242.
65   Channon, *Diaries*, 73.
66   Simon Haxey, *Tory M.P.*, 207–8.
67   *Ibid*, 228–230.
68   Macleod, *Chamberlain*, 195; Davidson, *Memoirs of a Conservative*, 412.
69   Bruce-Lockhart, *Diaries*, 335.
70   Templewood, *Nine Troubled Years*, 199; Macleod, *Chamberlain*, 193.
71   Channon, *Diaries*, 68.
72   Cowling, *Impact of Hitler*, 4–5.
73   Channon, *Diaries*, 84, 92–4.
74   Bruce-Lockhart, *Diaries*, 357, 360–1; Cooper, *Old Men Forget*, 202; Nicolson, *Diaries and Letters*, i, 280–2.
75   Nicolson, *Diaries and Letters*, i, 284.

Chapter 15

Neville Chamberlain's party

When Baldwin retired in May 1937 there was no doubt about his successor as leader. Neville Chamberlain had been heir-apparent since 1930 and had been an increasingly restive crown prince ever since. He had done more than enough to justify the succession: he had been a pillar of strength in every Conservative and National government since 1922 and Party Chairman in the critical year 1930–31; he had interested himself in every field of party organization and administration and had become one of the party's champions in debate, with a considerable personal following in the party in the country. For Chamberlain himself the long wait had not been easy, and he had occasionally wondered whether he would actually outlive Baldwin in political life. When acting as Prime Minister during Baldwin's illness in 1936, he remembered how near his father and brother had come to the highest office and asked himself 'whether Fate has some dark secret in store to carry out her ironies to the end'.[1] Such fears were not justified for Baldwin was determined that Chamberlain should have his turn, and he stage-managed his retirement in such a way as to ease the transition. There was a month between the time when Baldwin's time of departure was generally known and Chamberlain's actual succession, so he had plenty of time to make his dispositions in advance. Chamberlain was offering places in the new cabinet by 14 May, a fortnight before Baldwin resigned. When he at last kissed hands as Prime Minister on 28 May he was able to send the Palace a list of his ministers 'down to the last button' on the same afternoon, and to swear in his ministers on the same evening.[2] Having at last got his hand on the reins, Chamberlain did not intend to hang about. It was only three days later that he was elected to the leadership of the party, proposed by Derby and Churchill, and accepted with enthusiasm. It was the easiest succession since Balfour in 1902, an ominous comparison that entirely escaped comment at the time.

The first thing to note about the new Prime Minister is that he was not a Conservative. This is more than a merely semantic distinction, for he did not call himself a Conservative even when leading the party, and he did not hold views that can be regarded as falling within the mainstream of Conservatism. In background he had been a Liberal and then a Liberal Unionist, but for men whose political careers had begun before 1912 the distinction had not melted away with the fusing of organizations in that year, or with the change of party name in 1925. The party reverted to 'Conservative' in a national sense in 1925, but local organizations were still free to adopt any title that they wished. In Birmingham official candidates of the Conservative party were selected and backed by the Birmingham Unionist Association until after the Second World War, and so Neville Chamberlain was never actually elected to parliament as a Conservative MP as such. The family tradition of independence ensured that this still had real meaning to him, and he privately welcomed the advent of the National government in 1931 because it provided a chance 'that we may presently develop into a National Party and get rid of that odious title of Conservative which has kept so many from joining us in the past'.[3] Neville was thus just as attracted to the idea of an open-ended party of anti-socialists under a national label as Austen had been; he was more tactful in presenting his case to Conservatives, perhaps drawing the correct moral from Austen's fate in 1922. Nor could Neville Chamberlain be called a Conservative in his opinions, for he had little time for the preservation of old and tried methods where new ones seemed likely to be more effective, and even less time for the preservation of privilege merely because it was inherited. He had described himself to Samuel Hoare as a socialist, and he was certainly nearer to Fabian socialists than to the bulk of Conservatives in his views of domestic policy; with the Fabians he shared an optimism about social progress, a near obsession with administrative methods, and a contempt for the blimpish opponents of progress.

The significance of Chamberlain's relationship with Conservatism was pointed out clearly by the new Prime Minister himself in his acceptance speech, lest MPs should have doubt about what they had committed the party to:

> I recall that I myself was not born a little Conservative. I was brought up as a Liberal and afterwards as a Liberal Unionist. The fact that I am here, accepted by you Conservatives as your Leader, is to my mind a demonstration of the catholicity of the Conservative Party, of that readiness to cover the widest possible field which has made it this great force in the country, and has justified the saying of Disraeli that the Conservative Party was nothing if it was not a National Party. But today the Conservative Party is only an element, although it is the largest and strongest element in a National Government, and like Mr Baldwin I am convinced that the best interests of the country will be served by a continuation of the national character of the government.[4]

The words were chosen carefully, but they gave fair warning to 'you Conservatives' that they had committed themselves to a man who was not one of themselves. He was quick to point out that like Baldwin he regarded it 'as of the first importance to preserve the unity of the Conservative Party, today the most powerful political instrument in the country'; he adhered faithfully to this promise for the whole time of his leadership, but he used the powerful instrument of Conservative unity for national rather than party purposes. In May 1937 the party began a period of eighteen years in which its leaders were to be *in* it, but never quite *of* it in the way that Bonar Law and Baldwin had been.

The national status of the government was thus still a reality so far as the Prime Minister was concerned, but it looked much less real to an objective outsider. The new administration included fifteen Conservatives out of twenty-one cabinet ministers, and fifty-three out of sixty-four in the government as a whole. If the basis were merely head-counting, then the National government was by 1937 merely a façade for Conservative rule. It would also be difficult to maintain that the National government pursued under Chamberlain any policy that could not have been pursued by a party government, but this would be to miss the real point of the argument, for there is a world of difference between could and would. The National government pursued policies not unlike those that would have been pursued by a left-wing, moderate (or in Baldwin's sense 'national') Conservative administration. As long as it was called National there remained a clear guarantee that it would seek to be broader than a partisan government even when made up mainly of Conservatives, that it would govern in what was seen to be the national rather than the party interest. On this basis it appealed to Chamberlain, and on this basis it continued to enjoy wider support than a Conservative government would have been likely to get.

Despite Chamberlain's wish to avoid narrow party approaches to government, his accession to the premiership marked a raising of the temperature of the party battle, a matter both of instinct and of calculation. By 1937 Chamberlain exuded confidence as Baldwin had never done at any stage of his career, and he was not afraid to meet opponents head on when he was convinced that they were wrong. His personality and his knowledge of the detail of policy ensured that he won most of the argument, in cabinet and in the Commons, but they also created an increasing lack of tolerance for the views of others. He had never suffered fools gladly, but by this time he was wont to regard most opponents as fools and hence not to brook opposition lightly. The result was that he himself was hated by the Labour party with a quite remarkable degree of venom. He had never enjoyed good relations with Labour MPs, and he had been warned by Baldwin not to show that he looked on them 'as dirt'; the warning had not been effective, and relations continued to deteriorate. He joked about the subject in 1939, when discussing a recent article about his speeches:

> In this review it said that since I have been Prime Minister I have been subjected to more bitter hostility than any Prime Minister since the War. I am inclined to fancy that is true, although I cannot understand why, because I am the most reasonable of men and I never object to opposition so long as I can have my own way. But whether this hostility was justified or not, I have never allowed it to disturb my peace of mind, for I am convinced that, broadly speaking, whatever my opponents may say, the country as a whole approves the policy that I have been trying to follow.[5]

This dismissal of opposition, 'whether justified or not', the personalization of the debate, and the appeal to the nation were all keynotes of his style as Prime Minister. The same withering contempt was turned on opponents in the government and party, and the Prime Minister was all too ready to lump 'my opponents' together as beyond reason and beyond persuasion. Churchill had foreseen something of this in 1937: in seconding Chamberlain's election as Leader, he expressed the hope that he would not regard leadership in any 'narrow' or 'despotic' light, and that he would recognize like Baldwin that others were entitled to hold opinions differing from his own.[6] The experience of the next three years showed that such hopes were in vain. So in place of Baldwin's acceptance of differences and his readiness to let issues develop under their own momentum, Chamberlain was a leader who would exert a strong pull from the front and go to meet political issues; in footballing terms, he was a striker, where Baldwin had been a sweeper.[7] In foreign policy this change produced the shift from the Baldwin–Eden policy of cautious non-commitment to a positive drive for peace through a new European settlement. In domestic policy it produced a series of major triumphs, over housing, social policy and criminal law. In relations between the parties it added more bitterness than had been known since 1914. All this fitted in with Chamberlain's political instincts, but it fitted in with his calculations too. Like Austen, he believed in the principle of strong leadership and in the value of giving his supporters a banner around which to group themselves. The consequence of this belief was that every policy had to be expounded with absolute assurance, even when Chamberlain himself was tortured by doubts; if the leader were to be trusted implicitly, then he must at least seem to be fully in control.

For these reasons, the government of 1937 was Chamberlain's government in a sense that no government had ever been Baldwin's. He set the tone of the government, dominated its policy in any field in which he chose to interest himself, and he had no difficulty in getting his views accepted. He manipulated cabinet procedure when it suited him to do so and he was not challenged. He could be friendly and helpful to subordinates who had real doubts about his policy, as when Crookshank and Bernays criticized a speech on the League of Nations in February 1938, but he could also act with decisiveness when a minister stepped out of line in public. He sent a stinging reprimand to Duff Cooper in December and elicited a promise from the First Lord of the Admiralty that he would be more careful in his speeches in future.[8] The same treatment was handed out to Alan Lennox-Boyd and to Oliver Stanley. There was no doubt as to who was in control.

The party response to this new style of leadership was very favourable, partly because Baldwin's last year as leader had been characterized by a tendency to let matters drift even more than before. The new leader would seize the initiative and the party would be duly grateful; as Churchill put it, 'we have to combat the wolf of Socialism, and we shall be able to do it far more effectively as a pack of hounds than as a flock of sheep'. Chamberlain himself described his method of leadership as

> to try and make up my own mind first as to the proper course and then try and put others through the same course of reasoning as I have followed myself. As for the House of Commons, there can be no question that I have got the confidence of our people as S.B. never had it. They show it in lots of ways; by the tremendous reception they give me whenever I speak, by letters and by stopping me in the lobbies to tell me of their wholehearted support.[9]

The new vitality of the party's supreme command was exhilarating, and the party went along with it absolutely. Baldwin remarked on 24 June 1937 that 'at this moment there is more unity in our party than has ever been the case before'; in the following October, a *Times* leader talked of the 'remarkable harmony' in the party and of the 'contented conference' that had just ended. The advent of Chamberlain was welcomed throughout the party, and especially when he came under attack from the other side; when the BBC allowed Labour to broadcast criticism of the Prime Minister in March 1938 the National Union demanded an apology.[10] The welcome for Chamberlain came from many who were to be his opponents later, and Churchill was not the only critic of government policy who continued to speak of the Prime Minister in the warmest terms. Leo Amery, for example, spoke of Chamberlain in extravagant terms in July 1937: 'Mr Neville Chamberlain takes office at a time of great difficulty . . . but also I believe of great promise for the future. I believe the storm clouds in Europe will lighten, and I believe at home and in the Empire under his leadership we will go progressively from strength to strength.'[11] Amery had revised his view by the autumn of 1938, but most of the party continued in enthusiastic support for Chamberlain.

The new mood in the party was exemplified by the tightening up of party organization, a move that owed as much to pressure from the constituencies as to initiatives from the centre. Central Office worked hard to gear up the party for the election that was expected in 1939. Sir Malcolm Fraser was called back as Vice-Chairman to investigate the party's youth organizations; his report, shelved because of the war, provided the basis for the Young Conservative organization after 1945. Central Office announced in 1937 the extension of its scheme for training agents, and by the outbreak of war there were 392 qualified agents in the 520 constituencies of England and Wales. Speakers' classes were run at area offices, to equip party members for voluntary electioneering work, and a canvassing corps was set up for the same purpose. Finally, in 1938, a weekend course was run at Ashridge so that ministers and party managers could instruct prospective candidates on government policy and party tactics, an unprecedented step, but one that was much imitated later. From the constituencies came demands for reforms of organization in London, of party finance, and of the problem of candidates' financial contributions. Investigating committees were set up by Chamberlain in all these fields, and reforms were implemented. On the last, the tone of the National Union discussions suggests that when the war intervened the party was well on the way to adopting something like the Maxwell-Fyfe reforms of 1947.[12]

The party that Chamberlain led may be usefully compared to Bonar Law's party of 1914, with reference to the same sources used in Chapter 5.[13] The geographical distribution of Conservative MPs had not changed much over the years: in 1939 Conservatives held over three-quarters of the seats in the Home Counties, the south, west and east of England, over half in London, the Midlands, Scotland and the north-west, and under half in Yorkshire, northern England and Wales. The marginal areas where power was won and lost between the wars were still London, Lancashire and Scotland. The MPs in parliament in 1939 were overwhelmingly made up of the men who had been elected in 1931 and re-elected in 1935; seats had not been gained since 1931 and so there had been few recruits. A clear pattern had been established by inter-war elections, whereby the safest seats were mainly held by the MPs with the most privileged background and the marginal seats by Conservatives less likely to be connected with old families, to have had a traditional upper-class education, and more likely to be businessmen. Even so, an important change had occurred in the overall balance, as table 15.1 demonstrates.[14] There was a considerable reduction in the preponderance of landowners and officers, going even further than the figures suggest. Fewer landowning MPs now sat for their own counties, and only about half of the county members even lived in their constituencies. The number of MPs related to peers had fallen from 27 per cent of the party in 1914 to 19 per cent in 1939, and those from old landed families had fallen from 28 per cent to under 12 per cent. Of the officers, a much higher proportion were now professional serving officers trained at Sandhurst and Dartmouth, and less were scions of the old families appearing in disguise. The professions had more or less held their own, but there had been an increase in the proportion of MPs with interests in journalism and publishing. The main increase had come in commerce and industry, which had claimed two-fifths of Conservative MPs ever since 1918. The proportion fell slightly when seats were lost in 1923 and 1929 and rose slightly when seats were regained in 1924 and 1931, but it was never far from 40 per cent of the total. By the 1930s, this business sector was easily the largest single 'interest' in the party, but still well short of half the total. As a result of the increased number of business MPs, the average age had risen slightly and the average age of first election was higher too. There was an equivalent change in the educational background of MPs with the proportion coming from public schools falling from 68 per cent in 1914 to 59 per cent in 1939, almost all the fall coming at the highest end of the market, for the proportion from Eton, Harrow, Rugby and Winchester fell from 47 per cent to 39 per cent. The proportion with a university education had hardly changed at all, but this conceals a dramatic fall in 1918 (when only a third of new Conservative MPs had been to universities) and a gradual recovery later. In any case, the doubling of the number of university places between 1901 and 1925 meant that a university education no longer indicated quite such as privileged a background in the MPs of 1939 as it had done for the previous generation.

Table 15.1   *Occupations of Conservative MPs in 1914 and 1939*

	1914	1939
Land		
Large landowners	32	7
Small landowners	19	16
Heirs to estates	16	14
	67 (23%)	37 (10%)
Official services		
Armed Forces	55	58
Colonial and Diplomatic	10	16
	65 (22%)	74 (19%)
Professions		
Barristers	79	70
Solicitors	12	9
Printers and Publishers	2	11
Authors and Journalists	7	14
Teachers and lecturers	3	8
Others (mainly doctors)	–	11
	103 (36%)	123 (32%)
Commerce		
Merchants	14	25
Stockbrokers	6	11
Bankers	7	4
Insurance	1	6
Accountants	3	5
Others	9	36
	40 (14%)	87 (23%)
Industry		
Manufacturing	7	15
Shipping	2	8
Textiles	2	11
Iron and coal	7	4
Engineering	3	21
Building	–	4
Brewing	9	6
	30 (10%)	69 (18%)

The overall change should not be exaggerated, but there had been a shift from an old land-based ruling class to a wider ruling elite that was more dependent on industry and commerce. There were no more working men on the Conservative benches in the Commons in 1939 than there had been in 1914 and there was no likelihood that there would be in the near future. The second and third generations of Conservative businessmen had bought and married their way into Society and their sons had been educated into the elite through the public schools and universities, through the political clubs and the wider social world of Westminster. Nevertheless, a change really had taken place, albeit a slow and gradual one. Critics of the party like Simon Haxey, who concentrated on how many MPs were related to the Duke of Buccleuch, missed the point that the proportion would probably have been higher in any previous generation; the same numbers game was played with equally misleading effect by Anthony Sampson twenty years later.[15] In a conservative party, the element of social change can only be usefully measured against an expectation of continuity, and in this context, quite a substantial difference had emerged by 1939. The party in parliament was accommodating itself gradually to the social groups that supported it in the country.

Accounts of the first two years of Neville Chamberlain's government have all concentrated like the Prime Minister on the threat from Germany and on Britain's response, but this was by no means the government's only concern. Chamberlain himself recognized in June 1939 that his policy had been

> mostly concerned with foreign affairs. I wish it was not so. My object in going into politics over twenty years ago was concerned with home affairs. I went in because I wanted to do something to make things a bit better for the people – to get them better wages arising out of prosperity in industry and agriculture, to get them better housing and better life and more leisure to enjoy themselves as life was meant to be enjoyed. I think I can claim I have been able to make some contribution to those objects.[16]

Notwithstanding the threat from Hitler, no Chamberlain government would ever be concerned solely with foreign problems, and domestic policy produced some notable successes.

The clearest success for government policy was in housing, where the previous policy of the National government was carried on and intensified. One and three-quarter million houses were built in the five years before the war, easily the biggest sustained building programme of the century, and the total national housing stock increased by more than two million between 1931 and 1939. Under Chamberlain more of the impetus went into local authority building with subsidies; a campaign of slum clearance begun in 1933 was greatly speeded up by Sir Kingsley Wood in 1938, reaching about 25,000 dwellings a month, and a new Housing Act was passed to codify all the grants and regulations involved with housebuilding. This policy success no doubt helped to maintain the government's national popularity, but it occasioned some disquiet in the party. The National Union gave only grudging support to slum clearance, and in July 1938 the Central Council demanded a revision of compensation rates to protect the owners of property.[17] Housing policy was certainly conceived on a wider basis than satisfying the wishes of the Conservative party, and the same can be said of other reforms.

A Factory Act passed early in 1937 was implemented by the Chamberlain government as the first full-scale review of factory law since 1901. Describing it in *Politics in Review*, Geoffrey Lloyd of the Home Office linked it directly with the Conservative tradition of concern for the interests of factory workers, going back to Sadler, Shaftesbury and Disraeli. The Act raised minimum standards of health and safety provisions for about seven million workers, and brought another four million within the factory code for the first time. It was a piece of legislation welcomed with great enthusiasm by the TUC and rather more guardedly by the employers. There was also a government drive to extend the practice of holidays with pay in industry; a campaign of persuasion over the eighteen months to October 1938 extended the principle to cover 45 per cent of the work force, and a Bill was then introduced to extend it to the rest.[18] In other areas too, the government's social policy was extremely progressive, and the party accepted in the spring of 1939 the need for increases in old age pensions, urging the government to bring them in as soon as possible. The cost of rearmament did not prevent the government from spending more on pensions, education and roads. Under the National government, the number of cars on the road rose by over a third and the number of houses with telephones almost doubled. The 1930s were in many ways a time of great increases in standards of living; these were certainly concentrated in a fortunate half of the population, but it is still a fact that is far too often forgotten, and it alone explains the continuing popularity of the government.

But for the war the crown of the government's domestic programme would have been the Penal Reform Bill introduced by Sir Samuel Hoare, who had been transferred by Chamberlain to the Home Office. Hoare wished to leave a reputation as a liberal Home Secretary, conscious of his ancestors, who included both Elizabeth Fry and a founder of the Howard League. He was also no doubt anxious to keep himself at the centre of the political arena by promoting a major piece of legislation. The Bill was introduced at the end of 1938 and received an unusually wide measure of approval for its provisions on prison administration and criminal law. Clynes and Cripps both supported the Bill from the Labour benches, and the *Daily Herald* told its readers that 'this is no trifling piece of legislation. It is a great reforming measure.' The Warden of Toynbee Hall, J. J. Mallon, told the *Observer* that 'the new provisions . . . should be sufficient to produce a revolution in our criminal code'. It was however a very large Bill, and its detailed provisions were not so universally approved when they came to committee stage in the Commons. The Bill could not take precedence over war preparations, and so it was eventually abandoned, but it lingered on to form the basis of the Criminal Justice Act of 1948.[19]

In other areas, the government was much less successful, most of all in agriculture and in dealing with unemployment. The plight of farming was as desperate as ever; over a million acres went out of cultivation in the 1930s and countless thousands of farmers went out of business, so that in some parts of the country farms were let free of rent in order to keep up the capital value of land and buildings for the future. As in 1922, this had direct repercussions for the party, and the Agricultural Committee of MPs again became a hotbed of discontent. In November 1938 the Committee began a strong campaign for more active protection for the farmers, and W. S. Morrison, Minister of Agriculture, had to promise a stronger policy against dumping of foreign produce. The issue began to affect the local parties too. On 29 December the Skipton Conservatives considered co-opting a local farmer on to its advisory committee, on the grounds that the party was becoming dangerously out of touch with farming opinion. In January 1939 the issue came out into the open in the East Norfolk by-election; the government was represented by a Liberal National candidate, who was opposed by an independent Conservative supported by the NFU and by a number of local Conservatives. Chamberlain sent the usual letter of support to the government candidate, who held the seat, but only after he had promised to press for much stronger measures in future.[20] Unemployment too was a problem that refused to go away with the general return to prosperity, and even the rapid rearmament programme of 1938–39 made little impression on the numbers unemployed. In the summer of 1939 there were still over a million and a quarter people out of work, and by this time the party was beginning to call for drastic measures; in June 1939 the National Union Central Council called for a large programme of public works in order to create work.[21]

But neither unemployment nor the depression in agriculture could be dealt with unless the government had been prepared to change its entire economic strategy – which seemed to have worked well enough in other sectors of the economy. Chamberlain and Simon were prepared to countenance measures of financial unorthodoxy to pay for arms (although the failure to get the party to agree to the National Defence Contribution in 1937 showed that there were limits here too), but this seemed to them to strengthen the need for orthodoxy in other fields. The approach of war made it seem even more vital that resources should be husbanded and credit stored up to meet the danger. The pace of rearmament made it certain that Britain would not win a short war with Germany, and so it would be necessary to preserve Britain's staying-power by building up her sinews of war in the economic and financial sphere.

For all this, it was foreign and defence policies that occupied most of the party's attention and imagination. Here above all, the advent of a new Prime Minister seemed to provide new hope, for Chamberlain was clearly determined to halt the drift towards a war. For this reason, Chamberlain was welcomed by many like Robert Vansittart who were to find themselves out of sympathy with his policy as it developed.[22] Chamberlain at least guaranteed that problems would be thought through systematically and tackled with courage. He himself shared the general view that Britain must pursue a more positive policy towards the dictators than the one that Baldwin and Eden had followed since the beginning of 1936. In February 1938 he noted in his diary the objectives of his policy and the difficulties that it had already encountered:

> From the start I have been trying to improve relations with the 2 storm centres, Berlin and Rome. It seemed to me that we were drifting into worse and worse positions with both, with the prospect of having ultimately to face 2 enemies at once. France though very deeply attached to her understanding with us has been in a terribly weak condition, being continually subject to attacks on the franc and flights of capital together with industrial troubles and discontent which seriously affects her production of all kinds and particularly of arms and equipment. The U.S.A. has drawn closer to us, but the isolationists there are so strong and so vocal that she cannot be depended on for help if we should get into trouble. Again, our own armament programme continued to grow and to pile up our financial commitments to a truly alarming extent. The 1500 millions which we contemplated was evidently not the limit of what we should have to spend, while the annual cost of maintenance after we had finished rearmament seemed likely to be more than we could find without heavily increased taxation for an indefinite period. I therefore very early took the opportunity of making friendly references to Germany in my speeches, but though these seemed to be appreciated they elicited no corresponding response.[23]

His policy was then a dual one, rearmament to strengthen the bargaining position of British foreign policy and the search for a lowering of tension by a general European settlement. Although there was an element of inconsistency in pursuing these two aims at once, it was the policy that Chamberlain followed with characteristic singlemindedness until the actual outbreak of war. There was indeed little real choice for Britain by the time Chamberlain took over, for by that time Britain had fallen so far behind in the arms race that she could not contemplate war without a serious risk of defeat. Advice from the Chiefs of Staff went so far as to predict probable defeat for Britain in any war with Germany before the beginning of 1939. Until that time the British government was obliged to follow some sort of policy of appeasement, for it would have been highly irresponsible to have done anything else, and they were also forced to avoid any bluff that might be called. Chamberlain explained this to Daladier in April 1938 in justification of his reluctance to give full assurances of support to Czechoslovakia; he could not make such a declaration, 'even if the chances against war after such a declaration might be 100–1'.[24] With the benefit of hindsight such a policy may seem unduly timid, but it would have been a rash Prime Minister who would have risked what he was advised would be national defeat, so long as there was any possible alternative. It was this that led on to the weakness of the British response to the *Anschluss* and the German moves against Czechoslovakia; at the least it was a policy that bought vital time.

This is not the place to review the whole of Chamberlain's policy towards Germany, but some points about it must be made in the context of party. Firstly, because it was so clearly a personal line of policy, the party played virtually no part in its evolution. The cabinet gave full support, but they were set aside in September 1938, when Chamberlain worked with only an inner group of Halifax, Simon and Hoare.[25] The personal nature of the policy is also confusing in the context of Chamberlain's style of leadership, for it prevents us from knowing exactly what he himself really thought its chances of success to be. Since his leadership depended on a show of assurance, the outward show of confidence in 'Peace in our Time' certainly does not represent the whole truth, but it is impossible to know what the Prime Minister himself really thought. In the aftermath of Munich, he told his PPS, Lord Dunglass, that Hitler's signature would be useful if he kept his word, but would be equally useful if he broke it, for that would show the Americans 'what sort of a man he is'. Only a little later, he was telling the cheering crowds in Downing Street that he had brought back peace, and telling Lord Swinton that the Munich settlement should not be regarded merely as a respite for rearmament.[26] This ambivalence at the heart of his position was hidden throughout by the appearance of confidence, and the party rallied to him with equal assurance.

When Eden resigned in February 1938 there were none of the serious consequences that were feared. Chamberlain noted that 'some members of the cabinet were very much alarmed at the disastrous effect which his resignation would have. Elliott, always a weak brother in a crisis, talked of its meaning "the end of the Government".'[27] In the event, Eden was replaced as Foreign Secretary by Halifax, who had a higher party status, and the resignation caused scarcely a ripple. Years later Churchill recalled in his memoirs that Eden's resignation had caused him to despair, but at the time he acted very differently; when a round-robin was circulated on the back benches, expressing continued support for Chamberlain and his policy, Churchill was the fourth Conservative to sign it. When the House of Commons debated Eden's resignation, Eden kept the issue of his dispute with Chamberlain within narrow bounds and did not mount a general attack on the government. No Conservative MP voted against the government, and only a handful abstained. The mood of the House was one of confidence in Chamberlain rather than Eden, and Joseph Ball of Conservative Research Department set to work to ensure that the party in the country would take the same view.[28] There is no doubt that it did so, and went on doing so for another two years. In the aftermath of Munich Conservative Associations all over the country passed resolutions thanking Chamberlain for his efforts and assuring him of their continued support. Every area of the National Union passed similar resolutions, sending them to the National Union Executive, which passed them on with their own approval, and this went on well into 1939. Scores of constituency parties and areas were still expressing unabated confidence in Chamberlain in April, May and June of 1939, and not one local Conservative organization signified its disapproval.[29]

The attitude of the party was demonstrated equally by the way in which

Chamberlain's few Conservative critics were treated. Vyvyan Adams was carpeted by his local party in Leeds after his abstention over Eden's resignation, and he was warned that his continuation as candidate would depend on his future conduct. The Duchess of Atholl was dropped by her constituency association at Kinross and West Perthshire, and defeated when she resigned her seat to fight the issue out at a by-election. Ronald Cartland, Duff Cooper and Lord Cranborne all came under pressure from their local supporters, and Duncan Sandys was charged under the Official Secrets Act for disclosing figures to the House about the pace of rearmament, only to be rescued by the Committee of Privileges. Harold Macmillan had more difficulty at Stockton than he had experienced when following an equally independent line earlier in the decade, and even Winston Churchill was almost ousted from the candidature at Epping by local Conservatives who expected their MP to be more loyal to the Prime Minister. Brigadier Clifton-Brown was dropped as candidate by the local party at Newbury after he had disregarded warnings about his behaviour in parliament. In moving the resolution to accept Clifton-Brown's 'resignation', the Association President, Sir Arthur Griffith-Boscawen, explained that the first criterion in finding a new candidate was that he must be 'a loyal supporter of the Prime Minister's Foreign Policy'.[30] With Chamberlain's approval, Central Office was certainly trying to make life as uncomfortable as possible for the 'anti-appeasers' but there is no reason to think that the local parties needed any encouragement. The vast majority of Conservatives, inside parliament and in the constituency parties, were supporters of Chamberlain and his policy, and they expected that other Conservatives would support him too.

Chamberlain's position was further eased by the fact that his party critics were opposing him with one hand behind their backs, not only in the sense that their local supporters were keeping it there, but because they themselves had genuine doubts about what they should do. The myth that a staunch band of Conservatives opposed appeasement throughout the 1930s has been exploded, but it is not recognized that the anti-appeasers, like Chamberlain were pursuing a strategy of inconsistent objectives.[31] On the one hand, they were ambitious men, anxious for preferment and for the chance to influence their country's policy at a critical time, but on the other hand they felt bound to criticize the actions of the only man who could give them office and influence. Despite his harsh words in debate, Leo Amery assured Chamberlain of his continued support. Duff Cooper tried to take back his resignation in September 1938 when he discovered that no other minister was resigning with him, but Chamberlain did not see the need to take him back. Thereafter Cooper tried to avoid widening the breach and he wrote to Chamberlain at the end of the year to give his assurance of continued support – an obvious, clumsy and entirely ineffective bid for recall to office. A small group of anti-appeasers formed around Eden during 1938, but they never numbered more than twenty, they sought always to avoid embarrassing the government, and they kept well clear of Churchill lest they should incur the charge of disloyalty by association.[32]

Churchill himself was less outspoken in his opposition to government policy than his memoirs might suggest. His greatest point of criticism had been over the failure of the Baldwin government to keep its pledge of air parity with Germany, but by 1937 the failure had been admitted and the rearmament programme speeded up. Churchill was therefore less critical at the time that Chamberlain became Prime Minister, and he did not return to outright opposition until after Munich. He spoke in support of a resolution approving the government's foreign policy at the Party Conference in October 1937, and he lent his support more directly by appearing on the platform when Chamberlain addressed the delegates on his policy. In March 1938, when rumours of an intrigue in favour of Eden were circulating on the back-benches, Churchill was quick to see the Chief Whip and to assure him of his continued support for Chamberlain.[33] Munich changed Churchill's attitude, and he expressed his dissent for the first time by withholding his vote, but a single abstention does not amount to trenchant criticism of a policy, and even after Munich Churchill's voice was somewhat muted. The combination of his troubles at Epping, his own inherent loyalty, and his continuing wish for office helped to disarm him as a critic. Hence, the few convinced Conservative critics of Chamberlain's policy had little influence in the party and were at no time a threat to the course that Chamberlain wished to pursue. In comparison with the assurance with which Chamberlain expounded his aims, the hesitations of his critics were unlikely to make much headway. The only way in which they *might* have forced a change in policy was to meet the Prime Minister head on, and to risk the loss of their seats and their future prospects in a struggle for control of the party; it seems quite inconceivable that they would have succeeded.

In the autumn of 1938, Chamberlain was riding as high as ever, and he was advised by Halifax to dissolve parliament and secure a new majority on the strength of the popularity of the Munich agreement; he refused to do so because of the effect that an election campaign might have on national unity in a time of crisis, a decision with serious consequences.[34] From this point, a gradual drift of opinion began, so that although the Prime Minister kept the support of his party for the rest of his active career, the foundations of his authority were eroded. One sign was the increasing suggestions that the national crisis demanded a government on a wider basis, an idea that attracted even the Party Chairman by the end of 1938.[35] Another symptom was the increased public standing of Churchill, who directed his speeches after Munich at a national rather than a party audience. More and more politicians and newspapers began to indicate that Churchill's inclusion in the government would be a sign to Hitler of the government's intentions. In March 1939 these hopes were dashed, but a further bandwagon for Churchill began to roll in July. Lord Camrose made a rare venture into independent political action, and the *Daily Telegraph* urged Chamberlain not to ignore the current of Conservative opinion that was calling for Churchill in office. But there remained an equally vocal current of opinion that was still against Churchill, as Lady Davidson told the Prime Minister:

> John and I . . . have both been greatly worried in the last few days by the outrageous propaganda in practically all the newspapers on behalf of Mr. Churchill. This kind of thing has happened before, frequently in fact, when Mr. Churchill is wanting office, but the attacks on you because you have not already put him into the Cabinet seem so particularly bad at the moment, and I feel I must write as a very ordinary backbencher to say how much I hope you will *not* put him in the Cabinet.[36]

Fortified by such assurances that Churchill still carried little weight in the party, Chamberlain kept him out. Only when the invasion of Poland demonstrated the complete failure of his policy did Chamberlain offer office to Churchill. Nevertheless these last events of peacetime did provide a portent as to how things would develop; the press support for Churchill came from many politicians and papers that had not supported him before, and Chamberlain failed to respond.

Despite the failure of its policy and the accumulating opposition, the position of the government remained strong throughout the summer of 1939. Paul Addison considered that 'the most salient political fact of the last year of peace was the continuing strength and self-confidence of the Chamberlain Government. They feared the power of Germany in Europe, but not the power of the opposition in domestic politics.'[37] This strength was still based on Chamberlain's personal hold over his party; as long as he was backed by the Conservative majority in the Commons he need have no fear of Labour, and as long as he had the freedom to have whom he chose in his government he remained absolutely in control of policy. Conservative critics still hovered uneasily between the aims of joining the government and attacking it, and the government team still enjoyed the confidence of the party. This strong position was further reinforced by the likelihood of an election in the near future, an election that most observers expected to produce a renewed government majority. By-elections did not suggest that Labour would defeat the government on its own at a general election, and the Labour advocates of a popular front were motivated by the belief that there was no other way to bring Chamberlain down; in January 1939 Cripps argued that Labour could not expect more than 266 seats at any election held in the next eighteen months, so conceding a government majority of at least a hundred. Samuel Hoare believed that the bitterness of the Prime Minister's critics in 1939 stemmed from the frustrated conviction that they could not beat him either in the Commons or at the polls.[38]

The strength of this position was immediately undermined by the outbreak of war in September 1939, by the fact of war and by the way in which it was actually declared. War represented a clearer failure of the government's policy than anything that had happened before, as Chamberlain admitted quite openly, and it discredited retrospectively the judgement of ministers who had presided over the months of peace. The inner circle of the cabinet, especially Simon and Hoare, never recovered from this blow to their reputations, and the standing of the government was lowered correspondingly. The hesitation of the government in sending an ultimatum to Germany after the invasion of Poland created the first real disunity in the cabinet, and a bad impression outside. Chamberlain's reasons for delay were his difficulty in getting the French government to agree to a joint ultimatum and his wish to allow time for Hitler to pull back from the brink. He had no intention of dishonouring obligations to Poland, but the fact of delay seemed to suggest otherwise, even to cabinet colleagues.

Chamberlain's reputation was lowered still further by the measures he took to place his government on a war footing. He had originally intended to appoint a small war cabinet of non-departmental ministers like that of 1916, and to include Churchill in it, but by the time that war came the war cabinet had risen to nine members, almost all of whom would have a department. Other changes were kept to a minimum: Churchill and Eden joined the government, but only two ministers were dropped, and twenty-four of the thirty-one ministers from peacetime kept their offices.[39] The effect was that Chamberlain was soon being criticized as too unadventurous and too inflexible to organize the nation for war. At the same time the inclusion of Churchill and Eden changed the internal balance of the government, and not in Chamberlain's favour. For the first time he had ministers who did not owe their appointments to his favour, and in Churchill he had a subordinate of at least his own political stature. Churchill behaved towards Chamberlain with scrupulous loyalty over the next eight months, but there was an unavoidable tendency to see him as an alternative Prime Minister and to compare his claims with those of the incumbent. From September 1939 Chamberlain was no longer master in his own house, for Churchill's resignation would have brought down the government at any time. Nor did Chamberlain's political style or his remaining team accord with the demands of wartime. Men like Hoare and Simon had been capable men with a high party standing in peacetime, but they soon proved unequal to the new circumstances; when Chamberlain refused to remove them, their unpopularity was transferred to the Prime Minister. Chamberlain's habit of personalizing political issues and loyalties also laid him open to attack from the start. In his broadcast announcing the outbreak of war he acknowledged 'what a disappointment it is to *me*, that all my long struggle for peace has failed', and he was immediately attacked for placing his personal feelings at so high a premium at such a moment. All the bases of Chamberlain's power in the party began to crumble when the country went to war.

The erosion went on throughout the winter of 1939–40, for much the same reasons. He gave way to criticism sufficiently to sack Hore-Belisha from the

War Office in December, but refused to remove Simon at the same time, apparently on the ground that he could not ditch the two most senior Liberal Nationals at once. He made some minor changes in the government in the spring of 1940, such as giving Churchill wider powers over defence matters, but the changes were never sufficient to meet the charges against his team. Conversely, Churchill went from strength to strength in public esteem. As First Lord of the Admiralty he headed the only department that could shine in the early months of the war, but he won good press reports for his parliamentary performances and was careful to keep back items of good news for inclusion in his speeches and broadcasts.[40] By the spring of 1940 Churchill's few months in office had made him once again a strong contender for the premiership, now backed enthusiastically by the old anti-appeasers and by such unlikely papers as the *Daily Mirror*. All the same, the shift should not be exaggerated, for the overwhelming majority of Conservative MPs still supported the Prime Minister, even while urging changes of policy and personnel on him, and public opinion surveys showed that he remained popular with the general public too.

The change that was occurring was behind the scenes at Westminster, where support was slipping away so gradually that the Whips barely noticed the process. An all-party committee of MPs began to meet to harry the government, under the leadership of Clement Davies who had resigned the government whip in January. The 'Eden group' continued to meet under Amery when Eden joined the government, and it opened communications with Davies and with Labour, with a view to joint action. The final pressure group was far more dangerous for the Prime Minister; in April 1940 Salisbury formed a Watching Committee of elder statesmen, including nine former cabinet ministers, and intended not to embarrass the government but to press for changes in policy. In rejecting Salisbury's advice, just as he rejected the advice of other establishment figures like Beveridge, Salter and *The Times*, Chamberlain was sealing his fate.[41]

The gist of the advice to Chamberlain was remarkably consistent, and like the advice to Asquith in 1916 it concerned machinery as much as men. It was widely felt by April 1940 that the government and economy must be turned over wholly on to a war footing, and that many survivors from the pre-war government must go. For his failure to respond Chamberlain, like Asquith, was overthrown. The issue had to come to a head in the spring of 1940, for the trade unions were unlikely to accept a wider degree of labour mobilization without encouragement from the Labour party, and Labour would not serve under Chamberlain, but the failure of the campaign in Norway provided the critics with an opportunity too good to miss. It was only at this late stage that the Whips realized how dangerous the position had become, with all the opposition groups likely to combine to embarrass the government. The reaction of the Whips, and of Chamberlain himself, only increased their difficulties. The Whips tried to prop up the prestige of the Prime Minister by an attack on his rival through a whispering campaign; Churchill, it was said in the lobbies, was too old, too unfit, and too lacking in judgement. Chamberlain's PPS, Lord Dunglass, let it be known to Conservative MPs that if they would only remain loyal to the government Simon and Hoare would be dropped. Chamberlain treated criticisms over Norway as a personal issue of confidence, and called on his 'friends' to support him, once again personalizing a national issue. Boothby wrote at once to appeal for the help of Lloyd George:

> It is a direct challenge now. The P.M. has appealed to his 'friends' – as against the direct interests of the country. And there is to be another Maurice division. I think we may get as many as 40 Conservatives into our lobby. In any case he is done; because any kind of national unity under his leadership is now impossible.[42]

Persuaded by Conservative critics of the Prime Minister, the Labour party decided to press on to a vote, and the Eden group decided to vote against the government. The government won the vote on 8 May 1940 by 281 votes to 200, but this represented a resounding setback, for it had a normal majority of over 200. Thirty-three Conservatives and six other supporters of the government voted with the opposition, and twice as many abstained; the government failed to get the support of a quarter of its supporters on a vote of confidence, and the rebellion was actually greater among Conservative than among National Labour and Liberal National MPs The group most to be found among the rebels were the Conservative MPs serving in the army, many of whom had seen the deficiencies of rearmament at first hand and who had experienced the pull of service loyalties against those of party.[43]

Chamberlain negotiated with Labour in order to try to widen his government's base, and clutched at the German invasion of the Low Countries on 10 May as a reason for delaying a change of government, but he probably realized from the start that the vote of 8 May should be taken as notice to quit. He had to be seen to offer a coalition to Labour so that they could be seen to reject it, for this would make it easier for him to take a united Conservative party into a Halifax or Churchill government. His own preference was for Halifax, but opinion in parliament was very evenly divided: Conservatives may have marginally preferred Halifax, but if so it was a very narrow preference, and the Chief Whip did not make a positive recommendation. In the Labour party, despite their recent support for Churchill as a means of bringing Chamberlain down, there were as many who remembered Churchill's past career against him as there were those who saw him as a hope for the future. Churchill became Prime Minister in May 1940 because at the crucial time he pressed for the job harder than Halifax; Halifax offered to serve under Churchill, while Churchill remained discreetly silent, so that he had to be appointed.[44] Once the choice was made, Conservative MPs gave him loyal support for the duration of his government. One reason for this was Churchill's wish, compounded equally of natural magnanimity and the wish not to antagonize his supporters, to let bygones be bygones. As an historian,

Churchill was to wreak his vengeance on his old opponents in full measure, but as Prime Minister he treated them with generosity.

The new government of May 1940 was a great disappointment to those who had done most to bring it about. Hoare was dropped and soon afterwards sent to Spain as Ambassador, but Simon remained in the government as Lord Chancellor and Sir Kingsley Wood, Chamberlain's chief acolyte, replaced him at the Treasury. Halifax retained the Foreign Office and considerable freedom to follow his own policy. Chamberlain remained leader of the party at Churchill's request (though it is not clear that Churchill had any choice in the matter) and was made Lord President of the Council, taking up residence at Number Eleven Downing Street. Churchill had little more freedom in choosing his war cabinet, for it was generally agreed that it should contain only five ministers; apart from the Prime Minister, these must be two Conservatives (who would have to be Chamberlain and Halifax) and two Labour men (Attlee and Greenwood). Only four anti-appeasers were given ministerial posts and together with the Labour men they made up only a third of the total. The government was an alliance of Labour and orthodox Conservatives, with Churchill holding the balance, 'a clear triumvirate of forces'. Churchill told Chamberlain that 'to a very large extent I am in your hands – and I feel no fear of that'.[45] Chamberlain himself shared the general view that the new government might not last long and continued to entertain hopes that he might be Prime Minister again after the war. This balance remained then until the autumn of 1940, for Churchill had neither the opportunity nor the wish to remove more of the old Conservatives from office, though he was quite prepared to use the increasing public criticism of the old ministers to establish a greater personal authority in the government.

Chamberlain remained a force because he refused to bow out gracefully, and because even on 8 May he had retained the support of three-quarters of Conservative MPs. If there was any doubt about this, it was quickly removed by his reception when he first entered the Commons after the change of government, as Chips Channon noted:

> when . . . Neville entered with his usual shy retiring little manner, M.P.s lost their heads; they shouted; they cheered; they waved their Order Papers, and his reception was a regular ovation. The new P.M. spoke well, even dramatically, in support of the new All-Party Government, but he was not well received. And all the speeches that followed were mediocre. Only references to Neville raised enthusiasm.[46]

Over the next few months, it was the Labour MPs who provided the cheers for Churchill, unless they were specially drummed up for the occasion by the Conservative Whips. Within the government Chamberlain continued to exercise a major influence. He chaired the Lord President's Committee, which ran the war on the home front, and he was given other special tasks of importance by Churchill, as in the delicate negotiations with the Irish Republic and the setting up of the Special Operations Executive. Cabinet meetings were chaired by Chamberlain, when Churchill was not present, and Churchill does not seem to have made great efforts to attend.[47] Even when Churchill was there, Chamberlain played a major part in the discussions and his command of the detail of policy and administration enabled him as always to influence the decisions.

In the more political arena, Chamberlain was hurt by the increasing virulence of attacks on his pre-war government, but he was restrained by the need for national unity. In the privacy of the National Union Executive, he cast off restraint, though, and made it clear that he at least was unrepentant:

> He said that as far as he personally was concerned, he did not care a brass farthing, but as Leader of the Conservative Party his reputation did matter. It does not do to have the Leader of the Party discredited, and therefore, he wanted to say one or two words. The fact that the suggestion of our not having more tanks, aircraft and guns, and other equipment, was the responsibility of the present Leader of the Conservative Party, was not true. Everybody must share the responsibility for this state of affairs.[48]

He reinforced his case with some telling quotations from the Labour party manifesto of 1935 and from other Labour statements on armaments, and then moved on to 1938:

> After the Munich agreement, the Labour Party were relieved that we had escaped war. They now want to know why we did not call Hitler's bluff. If we get through this war successfully, then it will be to Munich that we shall owe it. In the condition our armaments were at that time, if we had called Hitler's bluff and he had called ours, I do not think we could have survived a week.

In the same speech, he urged the party to keep up its defences for the coming renewal of the party fight; meetings should be kept going at the constituency and branch level, funds should be raised, and agents should be kept in employment, by grouping constituencies if necessary.

In the government Chamberlain continued to play the strong party line, blocking the offer of office to Lloyd George with the threat of his own resignation on 28 May. At the Foreign Office Halifax and Butler went on with a policy for which Churchill had little sympathy but even less redress; when Butler was criticized for keeping open contacts with Germany through Sweden in June, Churchill had to guarantee to retain him at the Foreign Office for at least another year. Butler himself had no doubt of the strength of their position: 'If intrigue or attacks on the Government grow to any extent, all we have to do is to pull the string of the toy dog of the 1922 Committee and make it bark. After a few staccato utterances it becomes clear that the Government depends on the Tory squires for its majority.'[49] The force of this argument was demonstrated when the old anti-appeasers tried to bring about the removal from office of their old foes. This 'Under-Secretaries plot', brought to Chamberlain's notice by Ernest Bevin, was reported to Churchill who told Chamberlain that 'if there is any more of this nonsense they will go. We must have discipline in the government. He said he would see Amery tonight.'⁵⁰ When the All-Party Committee of Clement Davies tried to carry on its activities, its meetings were swamped by loyal Conservatives; on 3 July 180 Conservatives attended its meeting and passed a resolution of confidence in the government. Nevertheless Chamberlain and his supporters did lose ground outside parliament in the summer of 1940, for public opinion turned strongly against the pre-war ministers after Dunkirk, prompted by such publications as *Guilty Men* and by campaigns in the left-wing press. Chamberlain was able to get Churchill to call off the worst of these campaigns, with the help of Attlee, but only at the price of accepting the offer of a place to Lloyd George. But the position of the pre-war ministers was most of all weakened by Chamberlain's illness, for they had nobody to replace his determined leadership. Even with Chamberlain incapacitated, Churchill did not dare to move Halifax from the Foreign Office.

Chamberlain gave up government business at the end of July in order to undergo a series of serious operations, but he was urged by Churchill not to resign. He returned to work in September, a very sick man, but soon found it impossible to continue. By the end of September a decision on the future could not be delayed, and so when Chamberlain again offered his resignation it was accepted. His letter of resignation, in which he acceded to the Prime Minister's wish that he should retire, proved to be embarrassing to the government, and Margesson had to be sent down to help him redraft it; the revised version begged permission to be allowed to retire because of illness, for Churchill could still take no chances on the loyalties of Conservatives.⁵¹

Churchill's national standing after the summer of 1940 ensured that he would succeed Chamberlain as leader without difficulty, but the party was not ready to submit unconditionally. Chamberlain recommended Churchill and Halifax proposed his election, but both Halifax and Margesson went to the meeting determined to quash any suggestion of Eden becoming deputy leader. Churchill's age seemed to preclude a long tenure of office, and the party would thus keep its options open in the longer term. The meeting to elect Churchill as leader, on 9 October 1940, was opened to members of the National Union Executive as well as MPs, peers and candidates, a clear attempt to mobilize the widest possible party support for Churchill.⁵² In accepting his election, Churchill explained the need to bring the head of the government and leader of the party into the hands of the same man and went on to meet the fears of those who doubted his credentials:

> Am I by temperament and conviction able sincerely to identify myself with the main historical conceptions of Toryism, and can I do justice to them and give expression to them, spontaneously in speech and action? My life, such as it has been, has been lived for 45 years in the public eye, and very varying opinions are entertained about it (laughter) and about particular phases in it. I shall attempt no justification; but this I will venture most humbly to submit and also to declare, because it springs most deeply from the convictions of my heart, that at all times according to my lights and throughout the changing scenes through which we are

all hurried, I have always faithfully served two public causes which I think stand supreme – the maintenance of the enduring greatness of Britain and her Empire and the historical continuity of our island life. (Applause.)[53]

It was a statement much like that made by Chamberlain in May 1937; both men accepted that they were not in the orthodox Conservative mould, but they dealt with the point in opposite ways. Chamberlain showed that he recognized the importance of party loyalty while not saying much about principles or policy. Churchill talked about historic Toryism but did not have much to say about the ties of party. The consequences were profound, for it left the party for the next fifteen years under a leader who regarded himself as above mere matters of party, a fact that would bring troubles in its wake, and some advantages too.

In 1940, though, there was little reason to fear, for the party truce was preserving the party's position, and the war had enhanced the standing of men of longer vision and greater flexibility. The party's election of Churchill did have its ironic side, for there have been few politicians who have emulated Lazarus so successfully. Churchill had begun to drift away from Conservatism when Balfour became leader and denied him office in 1902. In the 1920s he had served with Balfour under Baldwin, and now, after a second apostasy, he had succeeded to Balfour's and Baldwin's place. *The Times* noted that 'time weaves "eternal artistries in circumstance"', but from the political history of recent years, no more unlikely pattern of events could have been predicted than that Mr Churchill, whose unorthodoxy has so often brought him into conflict with his party, should now be destined to be its leader'.[54]

Notes and References

1   Macleod, *Chamberlain*, 195.
2   Neville Chamberlain diary, 14 and 27 May 1937.
3   Macleod, *Chamberlain*, 162.
4   *The Times*, 1 June 1937.
5   *Ibid*, 10 June 1939.
6   Gilbert, *Winston S. Churchill*, v, 859.
7   The analogy was suggested by Alan Beattie, to whom I am grateful for giving me much insight into Chamberlain as leader.
8   Chamberlain to Duff Cooper, 17 Dec. 1937: Neville Chamberlain MSS, NC 7/11/30/39.
9   Quoted by David Dilks in Butler, *The Conservatives*, 252.
10 *Politics in Review*, Apr.-June 1938.
11 *The Times*, 3 July 1937.
12 *Ibid*, 7 Dec. 1937, 7 and 12 July 1938, 5 and 6 Jan. 1939.
13 I am again indebted to the work of Professor McEwen for the evidence on which this section is based.
14 McEwen, 'Conservative and Unionist M.P.s' (thesis), Ch. 13.
15 Haxey, *Tory M.P.*; Sampson, *Anatomy of Britain*.
16 *The Times,* 10 June 1939.
17 *Politics in Review*, Jan.-Mar. 1938 and *passim*.
18 *Ibid*., Jan.-Mar. 1937 and Oct.-Dec. 1938.
19 *Daily Herald*, 17 Nov. 1938; *Observer*, 20 Nov. 1938.
20 *The Times*, 10 and 17 Nov. 1938, and 5 Jan. 1939; Minutes of Skipton Conservative Association, 29 Dec. 1938.
21 National Union minutes, Central Council, 29 June 1939.
22 Colvin, *Vansittart in Office*, 139-40.
23 Neville Chamberlain diary, 19 Feb. 1938.
24 Colvin, *The Chamberlain Cabinet*, 266.
25 *Ibid*. 146-67.
26 Colvin, *Vansittart in Office*, 276.
27 Neville Chamberlain diary, 19 Feb. 1938.
28 Ball to Chamberlain, 21 Feb. 1938: Neville Chamberlain MSS 7/11/31/10.
29 National Union minutes, Executive Committee, 1938-9.
30 Newbury Conservative Association minutes, 12 Nov. 1938; West Leeds Conservative Association minutes, 28 Feb. 1938; Thompson, *Anti-Appeasers*, 193; Gilbert, *Winston S. Churchill*, v, 1014-15.
31 Powers, 'Winston Churchill's parliamentary commentary on British foreign policy, 1935-8'.

32 Thompson, *Anti-Appeasers*, 154–5.
33 Margesson to Chamberlain, 17 Mar. 1938: Neville Chamberlain MSS 17/11/31/188.
34 Mowat, *Britain between the Wars*, 635.
35 Addison, *Road to 1945*, 55.
36 Lady Davidson to Chamberlain, 5 July 1939: Neville Chamberlain MSS 7/11/32/61.
37 Addison, 'Political change' (thesis), 1.
38 *Ibid.* 2–3.
39 *Ibid.* 347.
40 Addison, *Road to 1945*, 78–9.
41 *Ibid.*, 67.
42 *Ibid.*, 97.
43 *The Times*, 10 May 1940.
44 Addison, *Road to 1945*, 100.
45 Addison, 'Political change', 472.
46 Channon, *Diaries*, 252.
47 Neville Chamberlain diary, 18 and 29 June 1940.
48 Report of National Union Executive Committee meeting (in this curious tense), 27 June 1940: Neville Chamberlain MSS 4/4/1.
49 Quoted in Addison, 'Political change' Ch. 5.
50 Neville Chamberlain diary, 18 June 1940.
51 *Ibid.,* 30 Sept. and 2 Oct. 1940.
52 *The Times*, 5 Oct. 1940.
53 *Ibid.*, 10 Oct. 1940.
54 *Ibid.*, 5 Oct. 1940.

Bibliography

Manuscript sources

Baldwin MSS (University of Cambridge Library)
Balfour MSS (British Museum)
Bledisloe MSS (in possession of the family)
Blumenfeld MSS (House of Lords Record Office)
Bull MSS (Hammersmith Borough Library)
Cecil of Chelwood MSS (British Museum)
Carson MSS (Ulster Record Office)
Austen Chamberlain MSS (Birmingham University Library)
Neville Chamberlain MSS and Diary (Birmingham University Library)
Davidson MSS (House of Lords Record Office)
Hewins MSS (Sheffield University Library)
Bonar Law MSS (House of Lords Record Office)
Milner MSS (Bodleian Library)
Roberts MSS (In possession of the family)
Salvidge MSS (in possession of the family)
Sanders MSS and Diary (in possession of the family, but available for consultation at
    the Conservative Research Department)
Selborne MSS (Bodleian Library)
Steel-Maitland MSS (Scottish Record Office)
Templewood MSS (University of Cambridge Library)
Wargrave MSS (House of Lords Record Office)
Willoughby de Broke MSS (House of Lords Record Office)
Worthington-Evans MSS (Bodleian Library)

Party records – national

(a) National Union Records (Minutes of Central Council and Executive Committee
    Meetings, National Union Rules, Annual Reports, and Reports of Party
    Conferences)
(b) Central Office Records (Reports of Party Organization Committees, Minutes of
    the 1922 Committee, lists of Conservative agents and organizers, and
    memoranda on organization)
(c) National Society of Conservative Agents Minute Books (now at the City of
    Westminster Central Reference Library)
(d) Primrose League Records (Minutes of Grand Council and Committees)

Party records – regional and city parties

Cornwall Division (in Truro Conservative Association offices)
Eastern Provincial Division (in Eastern Area Office)
West Midlands Provincial Division (in West Midlands Area Office)
North Western Provincial Division (in North West Area Office)
Yorkshire Area (in Yorkshire Area Office)
Wales Provincial Division (in Welsh Central Office)
Scottish Divisional Councils (in Glasgow Conservative Association Office)
Birmingham (in Birmingham Conservative Association Office)
Bradford (in Bradford Central Library)
Bristol (in Bristol Conservative Association Office)
Glasgow (in Glasgow Conservative Association Office)
Leeds (in Leeds City Library)
Sheffield (in Sheffield City Conservative Association Office)

Party records – constituency parties

[*The following Association records, mainly minute books, annual reports, accounts, and press cuttings, were consulted in the Association Office, except where stated otherwise*]
Abingdon; Accrington (Manchester University Library); Ashford; Banbury; Barkston Ash; Bewdley (Worcestershire Record Office); Birmingham Handsworth (Birmingham Conservative Association Office); Birmingham West (Sandwell Borough Library); Bolton and Westhoughton; Bosworth (Leicestershire Record Office); Bradford Central, Bradford South, Bradford West, Bradford North, Bradford East (all in Bradford Central Library); Brecon and Radnor; Bristol West; Mid-Bucks; Camborne; Cannock; Chelmsford; Cirencester and Tewkesbury; Clapham (in the London School of Economics Library); Darlington; Darwen; Denbighshire (in the Clwyd Record Office); Derbyshire West; East Grinstead; Epsom; Flintshire (in the Clwyd Record Office); Hammersmith (in the Hammersmith Borough Library); Hampstead; Harborough (in the Leicestershire Record Office); Hastings (in the Hastings Museum); Hertford (in the Hertfordshire Record Office); Huddersfield; Ipswich; Kensington South; Kincardine and Aberdeenshire West (in Aberdeen University Library); Knutsford; Lancaster; Leeds West (in Leeds City Library); Lewisham West; Lincoln; Maidstone (in the Kent Record Office); Middlesbrough; Middleton and Prestwich (in the Lancashire Record Office); Monmouth; Newark; Newbury; Northampton (in the Northamptonshire Record Office); Oswestry; Oxford; Oxfordshire South; Penryn and Falmouth; Rotherham; Rother Valley (in Rotherham Conservative Association Office); Rothwell (in Wakefield Conservative Association Office); Rushcliffe; Sheffield Brightside and Sheffield Central (in Sheffield Conservative Association Office); Sheffield Ecclesall (in Sheffield Heeley Conservative Association Office); Sheffield Park; Skipton; Sowerby; Stockton; Stretford; Thirsk and Malton; Truro; Wakefield; Waterloo (in Crosby Conservative Association Office); Wolverhampton West; Woolwich West; Worcester; York

Party publications

Constitutional Year Book
Gleanings and Memoranda, which later became *Politics in Review*
The Conservative, later *The Conservative and Unionist*, and then *Our Flag*
Home and Politics, also published as *Popular View, Man in the Street,* and *The Imp*
Conservative Agents' Journal
Primrose League Gazette
Conservative Clubs' Gazette
National Union *Leaflets and Pamphlets* series
Handbook on Constituency Organisation, 1933
Primrose League Election Guide, 1914
The Ratepayer

Books and articles – studies of the Conservative Party

BANKS, R. M. *The Conservative Outlook*, London 1929
BIRCH, N. *The Conservative Party*, London 1949
BLAKE, R. N. W. *The Conservative Party from Peel to Churchill*, London 1970
BLAKE, R. N. W. *The National Union, 1867–1967*, London 1967
BLOCK, G. D. M. *A Sourcebook of Conservatism*, London 1964
BLONDEL, J. 'The Conservative Association and the Labour Party in Reading', *Political Studies*, 1958
BRYANT, A. *The Spirit of Conservatism*, London 1929
BUTLER, LORD, ed. *The Conservatives*, London 1977
BUTLER, SIR G. *The Tory Tradition*, London 1914
CAVENDISH-BENTINCK, LORD H. *Tory Democracy*, London 1918
CECIL, LORD H. *Conservatism*, London 1912
CLOSE, D. H. 'Conservatives and coalition after World War One', *JMH*, 1973
COLVIN, IAN. *The Chamberlain Cabinet*, London 1971
COOPER, A. D. *The Conservative Point of View*, London 1926
CORNFORD, J. P. 'The parliamentary foundations of the Hotel Cecil', in *Ideas and Institutions of Victorian England, Essays presented to G. Kitson Clark*, ed. R. Robson, London 1967
CORNFORD, J. P. 'The transformation of Conservatism in the late nineteenth century', *Victorian Studies*, 1963–64
ELLIOTT, W. *Toryism and the Twentieth Century*, London 1927
FAWCETT, A. *Conservative Agent*, London 1967
FEILING, K. *What is Conservatism?*, London 1930
FEILING, K. *Toryism, a Political Dialogue*, London 1913
FEUCHTWANGER, E. J. *Disraeli, Democracy and the Tory Party*, Oxford 1968
FRASER, P. 'Unionism and tariff reform', *Hist. J.*, 1962
GLICKMAN, H. 'The toryness of British conservatism' *J. Brit. Stud.* 1961
GOLLIN, A. M. *Balfour's Burden*, London 1965
GOODHART, P. *The 1922 Committee*, London 1973
HARRIS, N. *Competition and the Corporate Society*, London 1972
HAXEY, S. *Tory M.P.*, London 1939
HAZLEHURST, C. 'The Baldwinite conspiracy', *Political Studies (Australia and New Zealand)*, 1974–5,
HEARNSHAW, F. J. C. *Conservatism in England*, London 1933

HILL, R. L. *Toryism and the People, 1832–1846*, London 1929
HOFFMAN, J. T. *The Conservative Party in Opposition, 1945–1951*, London 1964
JONES, R. B. 'Balfour's reform of party organisation', *Bulletin of the Institute of Historical Research*, 1965
LINDSAY, T. F. and HARRINGTON, M. *The Conservative Party 1918–1970*, London 1974
LOFTUS, P. *The Creed of a Tory*, London 1926
LUDOVICI, A. M. *A Defence of Conservatism*, London 1927
McDOWELL, R. B. *British Conservatism, 1832–1914*, London 1959
McKENZIE, R. T. and SILVER, A. *Angels in Marble*, London 1967
MALMESBURY, 5th EARL OF, ed. *The New Order*, London 1908
NORDLINGER, E. *The Working-class Tories*, London 1967
PETRIE, SIR C. *The Carlton Club*, London 1955
PINTO-DUSCHINSKY, M. 'Central Office and "power" in the Conservative Party', *Political Studies*, 1972
REMPEL, R. *Unionists Divided*, Newton Abbot 1972
ROBB, J. H. *The Primrose League*, New York 1942
RUBINSTEIN, W. D. 'Henry Page Croft and the National Party', *Journal of Contemporary History*, 1974
SCALLY, R. *The Origins of the Lloyd George Coalition*, Princeton 1975
SMITH, P. *Disraelian Conservatism and Social Reform*, London 1967
SOUTHGATE, D., ed. *The Conservative Leadership, 1832–1932*, London 1974
STEWART, R. *History of the Conservative Party*, vol. i, London 1978
WHITE, R. J., ed. *The Conservative Tradition*, London 1930
WOODS, M. *The History of the Tory Party*, London 1924

Books and articles – biographical (in alphabetical order)

AMERY, L. S. *My Political Life*, 3 vols., London 1953
(BALDWIN), BALDWIN, A. W. *My Father; the True Story*, London 1955
  BALDWIN, S. *On England; Our Inheritance; This Torch of Freedom; Service of our Lives; An Interpreter of England*, London 1926–39
  GREEN, J. *Mr Baldwin*, London 1933
  HYDE, M. *Baldwin*, London 1973
  MIDDLEMAS, K. and BARNES, A. J. L. *Baldwin, a Biography*, London 1969
  ROBERTS, B. *Stanley Baldwin: Man or Miracle?*, London 1936
  STEED, W. *The Real Stanley Baldwin*, London 1930
  YOUNG, G. M. *Stanley Baldwin*, London 1953
(BALFOUR), BALFOUR, A. J. *Opinions and Arguments*, London 1927
  DUGDALE, B. E. C. *Arthur James Balfour*, 2 vols, London 1936
  MALCOLM, I. *Lord Balfour, a Memory*, London 1930
  YOUNG, K. *Arthur James Balfour*, London 1963
(BEAVERBROOK), TAYLOR, A. J. P. *Beaverbrook*, London 1972
BIRKENHEAD: *see* SMITH, F. E.
(BOTTOMLEY), SYMONS, J. *Horatio Bottomley*, London 1955
BRUCE-LOCKHART, R. B. *Diaries, 1915–1938*, ed. K. Young, London 1973
(BUCHAN), SMITH, J. A. *John Buchan*, London 1965
BUTLER, LORD *The Art of the Possible*, London 1971
(CARSON), COLVIN, I. *The Life of Lord Carson*, 3 vols, London 1932–6

CECIL OF CHELWOOD, 1st Viscount, *All the Way,* London 1949

(CHAMBERLAIN), PETRIE, SIR C. *The Chamberlain Tradition,* London 1939

(CHAMBERLAIN, AUSTEN), CHAMBERLAIN, SIR J. A. *Politics from the Inside,* London 1936
    PETRIE, SIR C. *The Life and Letters of Sir Austen Chamberlain,* 2 vols, London 1939

(CHAMBERLAIN, JOSEPH), AMERY, J. E. *The Life of Joseph Chamberlain,* vols 4–6, London 1951–69
    FRASER, P. *Joseph Chamberlain,* London 1966
    JAY, R. *Joseph Chamberlain,* forthcoming

(CHAMBERLAIN, NEVILLE), BEATTIE, A., DILKS, D. and PRONAY, N. *Neville Chamberlain,* Inter-University History Film Consortium, Archive Series, No. 1, Leeds 1974
    FEILING, K. *The Life of Neville Chamberlain,* London 1946
    MACLEOD, I. *Neville Chamberlain*

CHANNON, H. *Diaries,* ed. R. Rhodes James, London 1967

CHILSTON, 3rd Viscount. *Chief Whip,* London 1961

(CHURCHILL, WINSTON S.), CHURCHILL, R. S. and GILBERT, M. *Winston S. Churchill,* vols 2–5, London 1967–76
    PELLING, H. M. *Winston Churchill,* London 1974
    POWERS, R. H. 'Winston Churchill's parliamentary commentary on British foreign policy, 1935–8', *Journal of Modern History,* 1954
    RHODES JAMES, R. *Churchill, a Study in Failure,* London 1970

COOPER, A. D. *Old Men Forget,* London 1953

DAVIDSON, J. C. C. *Memoirs of a Conservative: J. C. C. Davidson's Letters and Papers,* ed. R. Rhodes James, London 1969

(DAWSON) WRENCH, E. *Geoffrey Dawson and Our Times,* London 1955

(DERBY), CHURCHILL, R. S. *Lord Derby, King of Lancashire,* London 1959

(DEVONSHIRE), HOLLAND, B. *Life of Spencer Compton, Eighth Duke of Devonshire,* London 1911

(ELLIOTT), COOTE, C. *A Companion of Honour, the story of Walter Elliott,* London 1965

(GARVIN), GOLLIN, A. M., *The Observer and J. L. Garvin,* London 1960

(GEORGE V), NICOLSON, H. *King George V,* London 1952

(HALIFAX), BIRKENHEAD, 2nd Earl of. *Halifax,* London 1965

HEMINGFORD, 1st Lord. *Backbencher and Chairman,* London 1946

HEWINS, W. A. S. *Apologia of an Imperialist,* 2 vols, London 1929

HUME-WILLIAMS, SIR E. *The World, the House and the Bar,* London 1930

JONES, T. *Whitehall Diary,* ed. K. Middlemas, 3 vols, London 1969

JONES, T. *A Diary with Letters 1931–1950,* London 1964

(JOYNSON-HICKS), TAYLOR, H. A. *'Jix', Viscount Brentford,* London 1933

KILMUIR, 1st Earl of. *Political Adventure,* London 1964

KIPLING, RUDYARD. *Something of Myself,* London 1937

(LANSDOWNE), NEWTON, Lord. *Lord Lansdown,* London 1929

(LAW), BLAKE, R. N. W. *The Unknown Prime Minister. The life and times of Andrew Bonar Law,* London 1955

(LLOYD GEORGE), GILBERT, M. *Lloyd George,* New Jersey 1968
    TAYLOR, A. J. P., ed. *Lloyd George, Twelve Essays,* London 1971

LONG OF WRAXALL, 1st Viscount. *Memories,* London 1923

(MACDONALD), MARQUAND, D. *Ramsay MacDonald,* London 1977

MACMILLAN, H. *Winds of Change,* London 1966

MIDLETON, 1st Earl of. *Records and Reactions, 1856–1939,* London 1939

(MILNER), GOLLIN, A. M. *Proconsul in Politics, a study of Lord Milner,* London 1964

MOSLEY, SIR O. *My Life,* London 1968

NICOLSON, H. *Diaries and Letters,* ed. N. Nicolson, vol. 1, London 1966

PERCY OF NEWCASTLE, Lord. *Some Memories*, London 1958
SALVIDGE, S. *Salvidge of Liverpool*, Liverpool 1934
(SMITH), BIRKENHEAD, 2nd Earl of. *Frederick Edwin, Earl of Birkenhead*, London 1933
  BIRKENHEAD, 2nd Earl of. *F.E., the Life of F. E. Smith*, London 1959
  SMITH, F. E. *Speeches, 1906–09*, Liverpool 1910
TEMPLEWOOD, 1st Viscount. *Nine Troubled Years*, London 1954
(VANSITTART, LORD), COLVIN, I. *Vansittart in Office*, London 1965
WILLOUGHBY DE BROKE, 19th Lord. *The Passing Years*, London 1924
WRIGHT, P. *Portraits and Criticisms*, London 1925

Other books and articles used

ABRAMS, M. 'The failure of Social Reform 1918–20', *Past and Present*, 1963
ADDISON, P. *The Road to 1945*, London 1975
BAGEHOT, W. *The English Constitution*, with introduction by A. J. Balfour, Oxford 1928
BEALEY, F., BLONDEL, J. and McCANN, W. P. *Constituency Politics*, London 1965
BEATTIE, A. *English Party Politics*, 2 vols, London 1970
BEAVERBROOK, 1st Lord. *Politicians and the War, 1914–1916*, 2 vols, London 1928–32
BEAVERBROOK, 1st Lord. *Men and Power, 1917–1918*, London 1956
BEAVERBROOK, 1st Lord. *The Decline and Fall of Lloyd George*, London 1963
BIRCH, A. H. *Small Town Politics*, Oxford 1959
BLEWETT, N. *The Peers, the Parties and the People: the General Elections of 1910*, London 1972
BLEWETT, N. 'The franchise in the U.K., 1885–1918', *Past and Present*, 1965
BLYTHE, R. *The Age of Illusion*, London 1963
BRANSON, N. and HEINEMANN, M. *Britain in the Nineteen Thirties*, London 1971
BROWN, K. D., ed. *Essays in Anti-Labour History*, London 1974
BULMER-THOMAS, I. *The Growth of the British Party System*, 2nd edn, London 1967
BUTLER, D. E. *The Electoral System in Britain since 1918*, Oxford 1963
BUTLER, D. E. and FREEMAN, J. *British Political Facts*, London 1968
BUTLER, D. E. and PINTO-DUSCHINSKY, M. *The British General Election of 1970*, London 1971
BUTLER, D. E. and STOKES, D. *Political Change in Britain*, London 1969
CAMBRAY, P. G. *The Game of Politics*, London 1932
CHESTER, L., YOUNG, H., and FAY, S. *The Zinoviev Letter*, London 1967
CLARKE, P. F. *Lancashire and the New Liberalism*, Cambridge 1971
COMFORT, G. O. *Professional Politicians: a study of the British Party Agents*, Washington 1958
COOK, C. P. *The Age of Alignment*, London 1975
COOK, C. P. and PEELE G. R., eds. *The Politics of Reappraisal*, London 1975
COOK, C. P. and RAMSDEN, J. A., eds. *By-elections in British Politics*, London 1973
COOK, C. P. and SKED, A., eds. *Crisis and Controversy*, London 1976
COWLING, M. *The Impact of Labour, 1920–1924*, Cambridge 1971
COWLING, M. *The Impact of Hitler*, Cambridge 1975
CRAIG, F. W. S. *British General Election Manifestos*, Chichester 1970
DANGERFIELD, G. *The Strange Death of Liberal England*, London 1935
DONALDSON, F. *The Marconi Scandal*, London 1962
DOUGLAS, R. 'The N.D.P. and the B.W.L.', *Historical Journal*, 1972
DUNBABIN, J. P. D. 'British elections, 1868–1900, a psephological note', *EHR*, 1966
DUVERGER, M. *Political Parties*, trans. B. R. North, 3rd edn, London 1964
ENSOR, R. C. K. *England, 1870–1914*, Oxford 1936
FAIRLIE, H. *The Life of Politics*, London 1968

GILBERT, B. B. *British Social Policy, 1914–1939*, London 1970

GUTTSMAN, W. L. *The British Political Elite*, London 1963

GUTTSMAN, W. L. *The English Ruling Class*, London 1969

GWYN, W. B. *Democracy and the Cost of Politics*, London 1962

HANHAM, H. J. 'The sale of honours in late Victorian England', *Victorian Studies*, 1960

HANHAM, H. J. *The Nineteenth-Century Construction*, Cambridge 1969.

HAZELHURST, G. C. L. *Politicians at War*, London 1971

HELMORE, L. M. *Corrupt and Illegal Practices*, London 1967

INGLIS, B. *Abdication*, London 1966

JENKINS, R. *Mr. Balfour's Poodle*, London 1954

JOHNSON, P. B. *A Land Fit for Heroes*, Chicago 1968

JONES, G. W. *Borough Politics*, London 1969

KINNEAR, M. *The British Voter*, London 1968

KINNEAR, M. *The Fall of Lloyd George*, London 1973

KIPLING, R. *Rudyard Kipling's Verse*, London 1940

LE MAY, G. H. *British Government 1914–1963*, London 1964

McKENZIE, R. T. *British Political Parties*, 2nd edn, London 1963

McKIBBIN, R., MATTHEW, C. and KAY, J. 'The franchise factor', *EHR*, 1976

MANSERGH, N. *The Irish Question, 1840–1921*, 2nd edn, London 1965

MARTIN, R. *Communism and the British Trade Unions, 1924–33*, Oxford 1960

MARWICK, A. *The Deluge, British Society and the First World War*, London 1965

MORGAN, K. O. *The Age of Lloyd George*, London 1971

MORRIS, A. J. ed. *Edwardian Radicalism*, London 1974

MORRIS, M. *The General Strike*, London 1976

MOWAT, C. L. *Britain Between the Wars*, London 1955

MUGGERIDGE, M. *The Green Stick*, London 1975

MURRAY, B. K. 'The politics of the People's Budget', *Historical Journal*, 1973

O'LEARY, C. *The Elimination of Corrupt Practices from British Elections*, London 1967

OSTROGORSKI, M. I. *Democracy and the Organisation of Political Parties*, trans. F. Clarke, 2 vols, London 1902

PELLING, H. M. *The Social Geography of British Elections, 1885–1910*, London 1967

PELLING, H. M. *Popular Politics and Society and Later Victorian Britain*, London 1968

PETRIE SIR C. *The Powers behind the Prime Ministers*, London 1959

POLLOCK, J. K. *Money and Politics Abroad*, New York 1932

PUMPHREY, R. E. 'The introduction of industrialists into the British peerage', *American Historical Review*, 1959

RAE, J. *Conscience and Politics*, London 1970

RAYMOND, J. ed. *The Baldwin Age*, London 1960

ROSS, J. F. S. *Parliamentary Representation*, London 1943

ROSS, J. F. S. *Elections and Electors*, London 1955

ROWLAND, P. *The Last Liberal Governments*, 2 vols, London 1968–71

ROWSE, A. L. 'Reflections on Lord Baldwin', in his *The End of an Epoch*, London 1947

RUNCIMAN, W. G. *Relative Deprivation and Social Justice*, London 1966

RUSSELL, A. K. *Liberal Landslide, The General Election of 1906*, Newton Abbott 1973

SABINE, H. E. V. *British Budgets in Peace and War, 1932–1945*, London 1970

SAMPSON, A. *The Anatomy of Britain*, London 1960

SANDERSON, F. B. 'The swing of the pendulum', *Political Studies*, 1966

SEARLE, G. R. *The Quest for National Efficiency, 1900–1914*, Oxford 1971

SEYMOUR, C. *Electoral Reform in England and Wales*, Yale 1915

SHANNON, R. *The Crisis of Imperialism 1816–1915*, London 1974

STACEY, M. *Tradition and Change, a study of Banbury*, Oxford 1960
STEWART, A. T. Q. *The Ulster Crisis*, London 1967
STUBBS, J. 'Lord Milner and patriotic Labour', *EHR*, 1972
TAYLOR, A. J. P. *English History 1914–1945*, Oxford 1965
THOMAS, J. A. *The House of Commons, 1832–1900*, Cardiff 1939
THOMAS, J. A. *The House of Commons, 1906–1910*, Cardiff 1958
THOMPSON, N. *The Anti-Appeasers*, Oxford 1971
THOMPSON, P. *Socialists, Liberals and Labour: the struggle for London*, London 1967
THORNTON, A. P. *The Habit of Authority*, London 1966
VAN THAL, H. ed. *The Prime Ministers*, 2 vols, London 1975
WALLAS, G. *Human Nature in Politics*, London 1908
WELLS, H. G. *An Experiment in Autobiography*, London 1934
WINTERTON, LORD. *Orders of the Day*, London 1953
YOUNG, H., CHESTER, L. and FAY, S. *The Zinoviev Letter*, London 1967
YOUNG, K. *Local Politics and the Rise of Party*, Leicester 1975

Unpublished theses

ADDISON, P. 'Political change in Britain, 1939–1940', D.Phil. thesis, University of Oxford, 1970
BLEWETT, N. 'The British general elections of 1910', D.Phil. thesis, University of Oxford, 1967
COOK, C. P. 'The general elections of 1923 and 1924', D.Phil. thesis, University of Oxford, 1974
HARDING, A. 'The Conservative Party and the general election of 1935', M.A. thesis, Queen Mary College, University of London, 1976
JONES, G. 'National and local issues in politics: a study of East Sussex and the Lancashire spinning towns, 1906–1910', Ph.D. thesis, University of Sussex, 1965
JONES, R. B. 'The Conservative Party, 1906–1910', B.Litt. thesis, University of Oxford, 1960
McEWEN, J. M. 'Conservative and Unionist M.P.s, 1914–1939', Ph.D. thesis, University of London, 1959
RAMSDEN, J. A. 'The organisation of the Conservative and Unionist Party in Britain, 1910–1930', D.Phil. thesis, University of Oxford, 1974
URWIN, D. 'Politics and the development of the Unionist Party in Scotland', M.A. thesis, University of Manchester, 1963

Illustrations

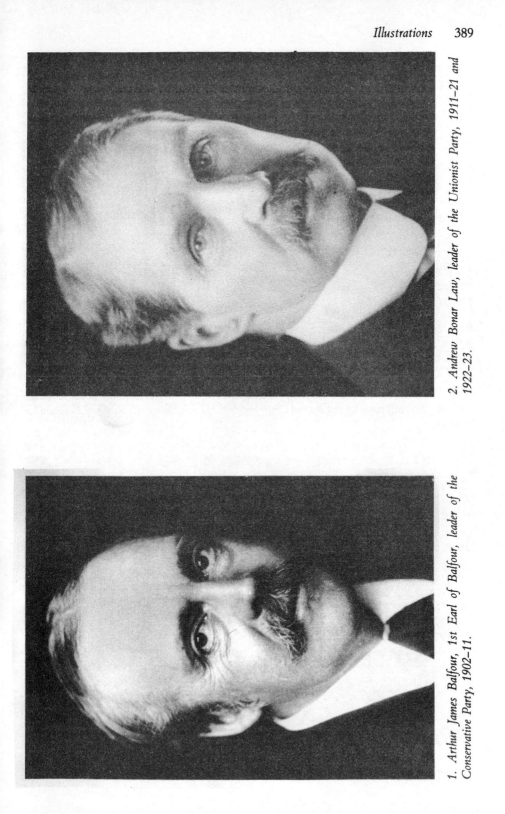

2. *Andrew Bonar Law, leader of the Unionist Party, 1911–21 and 1922–23.*

1. *Arthur James Balfour, 1st Earl of Balfour, leader of the Conservative Party, 1902–11.*

THE DORMOUSE WAKES UP.

A SEQUEL TO THE MAD TEA PARTY.

3. A Westminster Gazette *cartoon of December 1903, showing Devonshire as the dormouse upsetting the tariff party for Balfour and Chamberlain through his intervention in the Lewisham by-election.*

4. Joseph Chamberlain receiving a civic presentation during his seventieth birthday celebrations in Birmingham, the day before a stroke incapacitated him in July 1906.

6. *Walter Long, 1st Viscount Long of Wraxall.*

5. *Sir Austen Chamberlain, leader of the Unionist Party 1921–22.*

7. *Bonar Law addressing his first meeting as Party leader, at the National Union Conference in Leeds Town Hall, 16 November 1911.*

8. *The party leaders assembled to hear Lansdowne repudiate the idea of a referendum on tariffs at the Albert Hall, 14 November 1912. The platform party includes (left to right) Carson, Austen Chamberlain, Sir William Crump (National Union chairman), Bonar Law, Farquhar, Lansdowne, Steel-Maitland, Long, and Curzon.*

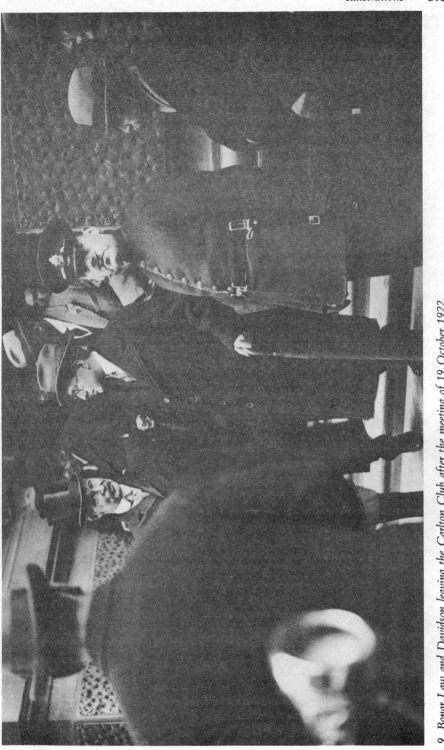

9. *Bonar Law and Davidson leaving the Carlton Club after the meeting of 19 October 1922.*

10. Sir George Younger, 1st Viscount Younger of Leckie, Party Chairman, 1916–23.

11. Sir Herbert Blain, Principal Agent, 1924–26.

12. J. C. C. Davidson, 1st Viscount Davidson, Party Chairman, 1926–30.

13. Sir Leigh Maclachlan, Principal Agent, 1927–28.

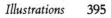

14. *Baldwin addressing a rally at Welbeck Abbey in July 1927, from a Pathe Gazette newsreel, showing the film van on the right in the picture.*

15. *The first Central Office daylight cinema van, touring the country for publicity purposes, 1926.*

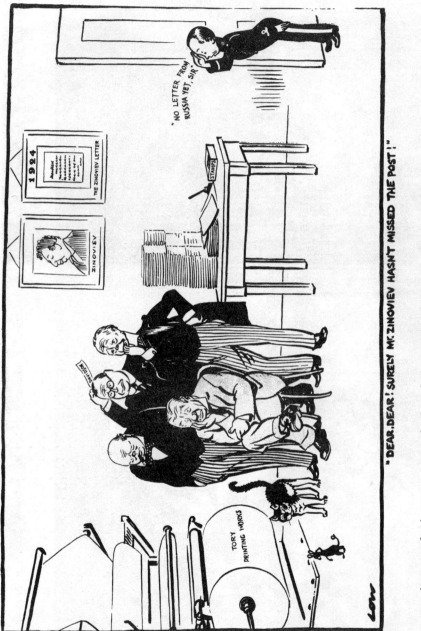

16. Low's cartoon for the Evening Standard, perfectly capturing the sense that something vital was missing from the Conservatives' 1929 election campaign.

17. *Baldwin speaking at a party meeting at the London Coliseum, 5 February 1930, after attacks on his leadership. The platform party includes almost the whole of the shadow cabinet, including Hoare, Bridgeman, and Irwin (left of picture) and Austen Chamberlain and Churchill (extreme right).*

18. *Stanley Baldwin, 1st Earl Baldwin of Bewdley, leader of the Conservative Party, 1923–37. This famous portrait by Vandyke was used widely in party publicity material, but most of all in this poster of 1929.*

19. *Neville Chamberlain, leader of the Conservative Party, 1937–40, leaving Downing Street during the Munich crisis, September 1938.*

Index